Developments in Marketing Proceedings of the Academy of Marketing Science

Founded in 1971, the Academy of Marketing Science is an international organization dedicated to promoting timely explorations of phenomena related to the science of marketing in theory, research, and practice. Among its services to members and the community at large, the Academy offers conferences, congresses and symposia that attract delegates from around the world. Presentations from these events are published in this proceedings series, which offers a comprehensive archive of volumes reflecting the evolution of the field. From 2014 on, new volumes will continue to deliver cutting-edge research and insights, complementing the Academy's flagship journals, *Journal of the Academy of Marketing Science* (JAMS) and *AMS Review*. Volumes are edited by leading scholars and practitioners across a wide range of subject areas in marketing science.

This book series is indexed in Scopus.

More information about this series at https://link.springer.com/bookseries/13409

Juliann Allen • Bruna Jochims • Shuang Wu
Editors

Celebrating the Past and Future of Marketing and Discovery with Social Impact

2021 AMS Virtual Annual Conference and World Marketing Congress

Springer

Editors
Juliann Allen
College of Business Administration
Nicholls State University
Thibodaux, LA, USA

Bruna Jochims
MINT Research Center
SKEMA Business School
Lille, France

Shuang Wu
Rohrer College of Business
Rowan University
Glassboro, NJ, USA

ISSN 2363-6165 ISSN 2363-6173 (electronic)
Developments in Marketing Science: Proceedings of the Academy of Marketing Science
ISBN 978-3-030-95348-5 ISBN 978-3-030-95346-1 (eBook)
https://doi.org/10.1007/978-3-030-95346-1

This Springer imprint is published by the registered company Springer Nature Switzerland AG
The registered company address is: Gewerbestrasse 11, 6330 Cham, Switzerland

2021 Academy of Marketing Science® Conference – Annual and World Marketing Congress

Celebrating the Past and Future of Marketing
&
Discovery with Social Impact
June 1–4, 2021
Virtual

AMS Officers (2020–2022)

AMS Board of Governors

2021 AMS Annual Conference

Co-chairs

Lauren Beitelspacher, Babson College, USA
Marko Sarstedt, Otto-von-Guericke University, Germany
Joseph F. Hair, Jr., University of South Alabama, USA

2021 AMS Annual Conference

Tracks and Track Chairs

Advertising and IMC
Hyunju Shin, Georgia Southern University, USA
Yuan Li, Georgia Southern University, USA

Artificial Intelligence and Augmented Reality
Nina Krey, Rowan University, USA
Graeme McLean, University of Strathclyde, UK
Jennifer Brannon Barhorst, College of Charleston, USA

Big Data, Marketing Analytics, and Research Methods
Haya Ajjan, Elon University, USA
Dana Harrison, East Tennessee State University, USA

Branding and Brand Management
Kevin Shanahan, Mississippi State University, USA
Michael Breazeale, Mississippi State University, USA

Consumer Behavior
Steffen Jahn, University of Oregon, USA
Marcel Lichters, Otto-von-Guericke University Magdeburg, Germany

Consumers in the Age of The Internet
Nicole Hess, Ludwig-Maximilians University, Germany
Sebastian Schubach, University of Passau, Germany

Digital Marketing
Kirk Plangger, King's College London, UK
Matteo Montecchi, King's College London, UK

Diversity and Inclusion
McDowell Porter III, California State University Fresno, USA
Aberdeen Leila Borders, Kennesaw State University, USA

International Marketing
Aliakbar Jafari, University of Strathclyde, UK
Lacramioara Radomir, Babes-Bolyai University, Romania

Marketing Pedagogy and Education
Adam Mills, Loyola University, USA
Narongsak (Tek) Thongpapanl, Brock University, Canada

Marketing Strategy
Sascha Raithel, Freie Universität Berlin, Germany
Manfred Schwaiger, Ludwig-Maximilians University, Germany

Innovation and New Product Development
Nicholas Zacharias, Martin-Luther University Halle-Wittenberg, Germany
Ad de Jong, Copenhagen Business School, Denmark

Personal Selling and Sales Management
Willy Bolander, Florida State University, USA
Corrine Novell, Pepperdine University, USA

Pricing
Dhruv Grewal, Babson College, USA
Abhijit Guha, University of South Carolina, USA

Retailing and Omni-Channel
Carol Esmark Jones, University of Alabama, USA
Stacey Robinson, University of Alabama, USA

Services Marketing
Sabine Benoit, University of Surrey, UK
Tobias Schäfers, Copenhagen Business School, Denmark

Social Media Marketing
Gerrit Cziehso, University of Münster, Germany
Ann-Christin Kupfer, University of Münster, Germany

Public Policy, Sustainability and Social Responsibility
Jeremy Kees, Villanova University, USA
Scot Burton, University of Arkansas, USA
Craig Andrews, Marquette University, USA

Special Sessions Submissions
Lauren Beitelspacher, Babson College, USA
Marko Sarstedt, Otto-von-Guericke University Magdeburg, Germany
Joseph F. Hair, Jr., University of South Alabama, USA

Doctoral Colloquium
Altaf Merchant, University of Washington Tacoma, USA
Mathieu Kacha, University of Lorraine, France

Mary Kay Inc. Doctoral Dissertation Competition
Rajshekar Agnihotri, Iowa State University, USA
Ritesh Saini, University of Texas Arlington, USA

Proceedings Editors
Juliann Allen, Nicholls State University, USA
Bruna Jochims, SKEMA Business School, France
Shuang Wu, Rowan University, USA

Special 50th Anniversary Sessions:

The Future of Marketing (Forecasting Marketing Trends)
Leyland Pitt, Simon Fraser University, Canada
Martin Key, University of Colorado, Colorado Springs, USA

Celebrating Marketing's History (Significant Contributions to Marketing)
Greg Marshall, Rollins College, USA
O.C. Ferrell, Auburn University, USA

2021 AMS Annual Conference Reviewers

Thank you to all the people who reviewed for the 2021 AMS Annual Conference. They include:

Mahdi Abouei
Susanne Adler
Raj Agnihotri
Billur Akdeniz
Khalid Al-Nabhani
Alexis Allen
Jacob Almaguer
Anupama Ambika
Suwakitti Amornpan
Jiyoon An
Demetra Andrews
Bahar Ashnai
Stephen Atlas
Barry J. Babin
Vishag Badrinarayanan
Tom Baker
M S Balaji
Aaron Barnes
Christian Barney
Barb Barney-McNamara
Michelle Barnhart
Robert Barnwell
Debra Basil
Brittney C. Bauer
Carlos Bauer
Ronny Behrens
Paul Bengart
Harriette Bettis-Outland
Tyler Hancock
Haley Hardman
Kendra Harris
Dana Harrison
Kristina Harrison
Barbara Hartl
Nate Hartmann
Ashley Hass
Simon Hazée
Jonas Heller
Monica Hernandez
Nicole Hess
Bryan Hochstein
Stefan Hock
Katharina Maria Hofer
Brandon Holle
Sandrine Hollet-Haudebert
Michael Houston
Sylvia Hristakeva
Shih-Hui Hsiao
Lei Huang
Yu-Shan (Sandy) Huang
Kenneth Hädecke
Omar Itani
Steffen Jahn
Kevin James
Narayan Janakiraman
Seongsoo Jang
Anita Pansari
Alec Pappas
Heejung Park
Janna Parker
Kiran Pedada
Lou Pelton
Valeria Penttinen
Beatriz Pereira
Vanessa Perry
Rob Peterson
Marcus Phipps
Doreen Pick
Mandy Pick
Karine Picot-Coupey
Nadine Pieper
Valentina Pitardi
Robert Pitts
Kirk Plangger
Chris Plouffe
Bastian Popp
Lea Postel
Harrison Pugh
Bora Qesja
Zhilei Qiao
Lacramioara Radomir
Omid Rafieian
Sascha Raithel
Sekar Raju

Nora Bezaz
Abhi Bhattacharya
Enrique Bigné
Nicola Bilstein
James Blair
Valerie Blanchard-McGehee
Julia Blose
Benjamin Boeuf
Natalie Bolen
Raghu Bommaraju
Yvette Bonaparte
Francesca Bonetti
Aberdeen Borders
Fatiha Boukouyen
Dan Bradbury
Corinna Braun
Erik Braun
Monique Breaz
Michael Breazeale
Florian Brodschelm
Tom Brown
Maximilian Bruder
Katja Brunk
Daniel Bruns
Isabella Bunosso
Rebecca Burcham
Bidisha Burman
Nawar Chaker
Eugene Chan
Victor Chernetsky
Yoon-Na Cho
Yeon Jae Choi
Christopher Conlon
Eilidh Cook
Kelley Cours Anderson
Ryan Cruz
Annie Cui
Carolyn Curasi
Gerrit Cziehso
Dan-Cristian Dabija
Steven Dahlquist
Svenja Damberg
Eileen Dauti
Lenita Davis
Ad de Jong
Svetlana De Vos
Subhash Jha
Zhenyu Jin
Soyoung Joo
David Jütte
Bernadette Kamleitner
Begum Kaplan
Mustafa Karatas
Mihalis Kavaratzis
Astrid Keel
Jeremy Kees
Adwait Khare
Rushana Khusainova
Achim Kiessig
Stephen Kim
Salman Kimiagari
Janina Kleine
Sreya Kolay
Sören Köcher
Tabea Krah
Alexandra Krallman
Nina Krey
Ann Kronrod
Riley Krotz
Michael Krush
Yunmei Kuang
Marc Kuhn
Frauke Kühn
Christina Kühnl
Russ Laczniak
Myles Landers
Lindsay Larson
Isabel Sophie Lazarovici
Marina Leban
Joel LeBon
Cong Li
Jin Li
Ruoou Li
Yiyi Li
Marcel Lichters
Tana Licsandru
Marc Linder
Kris Lindsey Hall
Tyrha Lindsey-Warren
Liu Liu
Jennifer Locander
Gautier Lombard
Deva Rangarajan
Adam Rapp
Jen Riley
Katharina Ritt
Stacey Robinson
Andreea Ioana Romonţi-Maniu
José Rosa
Spencer Ross
Maria Rouziou
Fabienne Ruoss
Jose Saavedra Torres
Verena Sablotny
Ritesh Saini
Roberto Saldivar
Manoshi Samaraweera
Swapnil Saravade
Ricarda Schauerte
Tobias Schäfers
Gustavo Schneider
Sebastian Schubach
Carsten D. Schultz
Manfred Schwaiger
Martina Schöniger
Andrei Mircea Scridon
Barbara Seegebarth
Samuel Sekar
Sarah Selinka
Marcos Severo
Sphurti Sewak
Esta Shah
Himani Sharma
Jagdip Singh
Priyanka Singh
Rakesh Singh
Sunil Singh
Alena Soboleva
Alma Softic
Sandrine Spahn
Jennifer Stephens
Jennifer Stevens
Kristin Stewart
Katharina Stolley
Keith Story
Stella Tavallaei
Ashely Thomas
John Thøgersen

Stephanie Dellande
Svenja Diegelmann
Larissa Diekmann
Rebecca Dingus
Amela Dizdarevic
David Duncombe
Khalid El-Shamandi Ahmed
Ahmed Gamal Elkattan
Ossama Elshiewy
Gözde Erdogan
Fuat Erol
Natasha Evers
Reto Felix
Hui Feng
Alexander Flaig
Martin Fritze
Martin-Paul Fritze
Pia Furchheim
Jia Gai
Inigo Gallo
Edith Galy
Lily-Xuehui Gao
Sylvia Gao
Janina Garbas
Mark Gleim
Gabe Gonzalez
Ashley Goreczny
Indranil Goswami
Louisa Gropengießer-Arlt
Jana Grothaus
Alina Grüner
Daniel Guhl
Monica Guillory
Deirdre Guion
Bingxuan Guo
Hugo Guyader
Jonne Guyt
Pascal Güntürkün
Johannes Habel
Mona Hagebölling
Abdullah Hamadi
Ye Han
Renaud Lunardo
Bruno Lussier
Benjamin Maas
Alexander Mafael
Amro Maher
Devdeep Maity
Ashish Malik
Ashwin Malshe
Stephanie Mangus
Sudha Mani
Kerry Manis
Kai Manke
Rebecca Mardon
Hannah Marriott
Sunil Mathew
Anil Mathur
Paul-Vincent Mayr
Colleen McClure
Sean McGrath
Katrin Merfeld
Melisa Mete
Adam Mills
Sitao Min
Emmanuel Mogaji
Haytham Mohamed
Jihad Mohammad
Ovidiu Ioan Moisescu
Matteo Montecchi
Stéphanie Montmasson
Lexi Moore
Ryan Mullins
Tichakunda Rodney Mwenje
Jana Möller
Steffen Müller
Lubna Nafees
Amin Nazifi
Vanessa O'Neill
Efua Obeng
Nele Oldenburg
Friederike Paetz
Stefanie Paluch
Nikolaos Panagopoulos
Monica Maria Tomşa
Kevin Trainor
Sambit Tripathi
Broderick Turner
Sebastian Ullrich
Olga Untilov
Rebecca Vanmeter
Swati Verma
Valter Vieira
Anne Volkmann
Stacie Waites
Sijun Wang
Shuqin Wei
Welf Weiger
Henri Weijo
Davina Weintz
Li Weixun
Jutong Wen
Pola Weryszko
Karen Wesely
Jörg Westphal
Mike Whittmann
Christian Winter
David Woisetschläger
Tobias Wolf
Jeremy Wolter
Andy Wood
Ruomeng Wu
Shuang Wu
Long Xia
Shuai Yan
Merve Yanar Gurce
Xisi Yang
Zhiyong Yang
Chebli Youness
Ruya Yuksel
Nicolas Zacharias
Mustafeed Zaman
Wenkai Zhou
Alexander Ziegler
Johanna Zimmermann
Fatma Zeynep Özata

2021 Academy of Marketing Science® World Marketing Congress

Discovery with Social Impact
June 1 – 4, 2021
Virtual

2021 AMS World Marketing Congress

Co-chairs

Jay Weerawardena, University of Queensland, Australia
Alastair Tombs, University of Queensland, Australia

2021 AMS World Marketing Congress

Tracks and Track Chairs

Marketing Communications and IMC
Anand Kumar, University of South Florida, USA
Jaafar El-Murad, University of Westminster, UK

Brand Management
Ravi Pappu, University of Queensland, Australia
Mark Brown, University of Queensland, Australia

Digital Branding/Marketing
Paul Harrigan, University of Western Australia, Australia
Claudia Gonzalez, University of Queensland, Australia

Consumer Behavior
Nick Pontes, University of Queensland, Australia
Ben Low, University of Kent, UK
Mark Arnold, Saint Louis University, USA

Consumer Culture
Alison Joubert, University of Queensland, Australia
Daiane Scaraboto, Catholic University of Chile / University of Melbourne, Chile

Cross-cultural/Multicultural Marketing
Monica Hernandez, St. Edward's University, USA
Wesley Pollitte, St. Edward's University, USA

Fashion and Luxury Marketing
Patsy Perry, University of Manchester, UK
Victoria-Sophie Osburg, Montpellier Business School, France

Wine and Tourism Marketing
Ulrich Paschen, Luleå University of Technology, Sweden
Gabby Walters, University of Queensland, Australia

Sports Marketing
Monica Chien, University of Queensland, Australia
Sarah Kelly, University of Queensland, Australia

Retail (Online/Offline)
Paul Ballantine, University of Canterbury, New Zealand
Kishore Gopalakrishna Pillai, University of East Anglia, UK

Business-to-Business Marketing
Margaret Matanda, University of Sydney, Australia
Rohan De Pallant, University of Queensland, Australia

Food Marketing and Consumption
Mary Brennan, University of Edinburgh, UK
Mary McCarthy, University College Cork, Ireland

Marketing Education
Ann Wallin, University of Queensland, Australia
Cassandra France, University of Queensland, Australia

Service Marketing and Consumer Experience
Usha Pappu, University of Queensland, Australia
Dahlia El-Manstrly, University of Edinburgh, UK

Technology Infused Services (AI, Robotics, VR, AR, Apps)
Nicole Hartely, University of Queensland, Australia
Alex Henkel, Open University, The Netherlands

Social Marketing and Prosocial Behavior Change
Josephine Previte, University of Queensland, Australia
Christine Domegan, NUI Galway, Ireland

Non-profit Marketing, Macromarketing and Bottom of the Pyramid (BOP) Markets
Gillian Sullivan-Mort, La Trobe University, Australia
Lily Cheung, University of Queensland, Australia

Research Methods, Big Data and Analytics
Clinton Weeks, Queensland University of Technology, Australia
Annie Pei-I Yu, National Chung Cheng University, Taiwan

Strategic Marketing
Leyland Pitt, Simon Fraser University, Canada
Vida Morkunas, Luleå University of Technology, Sweden

Relationship Marketing
Park Thaichon, Griffith University, Australia
Scott Weaven, Griffith University, Australia

Entrepreneurship, New Product Development, Innovation
Tek Thongpapanl, Brock University, Canada
Adam Mills, Loyola University, USA

Personal Selling and Sales Management
Rakesh Ranjan, University of Queensland, Australia
Wen Mao, University of Queensland, Australia

Special Sessions Submissions
Jay Weerawardena, University of Queensland, Australia
Alastair Tombs, University of Queensland, Australia
Barry J. Babin, University of Mississippi, USA

Proceedings Editors
Juliann Allen, Nicholls State University, USA
Bruna Jochims, SKEMA Business School, France
Shuang Wu, Rowan University, USA

2021 AMS World Marketing Congress Reviewers

Thank you to all people who reviewed for the 2021 AMS World Marketing Congress. These people include:

Aman Abid
Tanvir Ahmed
Frank Alpert
Amani Alsalem
Thomas Anning-Dorson
Tetsuya Aoki
Mark Arnold
Jaylan Azer
Hajer Bachouche
Paul Ballantine
Brittney Bauer
Stacey Baxter
Alex Belli
Daniela Berg
Gargi Bhaduri
Christo Bisschoff
Ellen Bloxsome
Silke Boenigk
Linda Brennan
Mary Brennan
Katja Brunk
Yi Bu
Zakari Bukari
Jacqueline Burgess
Mario Campana
Benedetta Cappellini
Marylyn Carrigan
Chiayang Chang
Jeffrey Hoyle
Lu Hsiao
Tsuen-Ho Hsu
Aimee Huff
Euejung Hwang
Severina Iankova
Jasmina Ilicic
Pramod Iyer
Nicolas Jankuhn
Byoungho Jin
Clark Johnson
Alison Joubert
Muhammad Junaid
Sertan Kabadayi
Kathy Knox
Harpreet Kaur
Sarah Kelly
Katie Kelting
Aileen Kennedy
Ann-Marie Kennedy
Huda Khan
Russel Kingshott
Jon Kirchoff
Sam Kirshner
Ahmet Koksal
Paul Koku
Ioannis Krasonikolakis
Aaron Kreimer
Christine Pitt
Elaine Plant
Liam Pomfret
Jerry Ponialou
Nicolas Pontes
Peter Popkowski-Leszczyc
Jo Previte
Josephine Previte
Sara Quach
Ananya Rajagopal
Rahul Ramachandran
Arilova Randrianasolo
Kumar Ranjan
Rakesh Ranjan
Sally Rao Hill
Mignon Reyneke
Deborah Roberts
Jeandri Robertson
Karen Robson
Claire Roederer
Sudeep Rohit
Imam Salehudin
Sridhar Samu
Deepak Sangroya
Bridget Satinover-Nichols
Daiane Scaraboto
Sharon Schembri
Valentina Schmitt

Cassandra Chapman
Lily Cheung
Arthur Chiang
Lanlung Luke Chiang
Monica Chien
Kerry Chipp
En-Yi Chou
Jiun Sheng Chris Lin
Chih-Ying Chu
Laurel Cook
Lauren Copeland
Diego Costa Pinto
Adam Craig
Oliver Cruz Milan
Charles Cui
Nurdilek Dalziel
Iain Davies
Anouk de Regt
Svetlana De-Vos
Pinar Demir
Maria Dharmesti
Christine Domegan
Katherine Duffy
Sherese Duncan
Steven Dunn
Sujay Dutta
Abhishek Dwivedi
Toni Eagar
Dhouha El Amri
A. Banu Elmadağ Baş
Tess Eriksson
John Fahy
Jessica Felix
Cai Feng
Caitlin Ferreira
Joerg Finsterwalder
Felix Flores
Leisa Flynn
Jamye Foster
Anne Fota
Cassandra France
Pao Franco
Marie-Louise Fry
Alexandria Gain
Andrew Gallan
Edith Galy
Alicia Kulczynski
Anand Kumar
Minu Kumar
Kyriakos Kyriakopoulos
Joey Lam
Ryan Langan
Felicia Lassk
Linda Lee
Kevin Lehnert
Alexander Leischnig
Kate Letheren
Chih-Chin Liang
Chen-Yu Lin
Cheng-Yu Lin
Joerg Lindenmeier
Luke Liska
Hongfei Liu
Matthew Liu
Steven Liu
Gajendra Liyanaarachchi
Sarah Lordferguson
Ben Lowe
Nadina Luca
Matthew Lunde
Eddie Luo
Katja Lurie-Stoyanov
Marian Makkar
Wen Mao
Rebecca Mardon
Adam Marquardt
Brett Martin
Christine Mathies
Frank Mathmann
David Matthews
Mieszko Mazur
Mary McCarthy
Bob McDonald
Peter McGoldrick
Kanika Meshram
Adam Mills
Mayoor Mohan
Lisa Monahan
Ejindu Iwelu Morah
Vida Morkunas
Beth Morris
Dann Moudrý
Christopher Schumacher
Jürgen Schwill
Abhishek Sharma
Nazuk Sharma
Piyush Sharma
Da Shin
Hamid Shirdastian
Susan Sieloff
Flavia Silveira Cardoso
Woojong Sim
Sonika Singh
Aishwarya Singhal
Louise Spry
Gillian Sullivan-Mort
Katarzyna Szczepańska-Woszczyna
Lisa Tam
Jia-Wei Tang
Ngan Tang
Arry Tanusondjaja
James Tarbit
Serdar Temiz
Park Thaichon
Mrugank Thakor
Sabrina Thornton
Alastair Tombs
Ting-Hsiang Tseng
Sven Tuzovic
Ramaprasad Unni
Barbara Valenzuela
Sajeev Varki
Ekant Veer
Rohan Venkatraman
Nanda Viswanathan
Peter Vitartas
Katja Wagner
Kathryn Waite
Ann Wallin
Gabby Walters
Di Wang
Fatima Wang
Ying Wang
Yong Wang
Henri Weijo
Stan Westjohn
Hume Winzar
Sabrina Wong

Maher Georges Elmashhara
Claudia Gonzalez
Kishore Gopalakrishna Pillai
Ahir Gopaldas
Saheli Goswami
Charles Graham
Guido Grunwald
Lauren Gurrieri
Hugo Guyader
Felicity Hardley
Paul Harrigan
Nicole Hartley
Anna Hartman
Rajibul Hasan
Vuesal Hasanzade
Kamel Hedhli
Monica Hernandez
Eric Holdack
Heiko Holz
Mona Mrad
Laurent Muzellec
Anne-Maree O'Rourke
Obinna Obilo
Victoria-Sophie Osburg
Adesegun Oyedele
Ravi Pappu
Usha Pappu
Ulrich Paschen
Pablo Paul
Patsy Perry
Dan Petrovici
Ngoc Pham
Nhat Tram Phan-Le
Megan Phillips
Christopher Pich
Rico Piehler
Diego Pinto
R Mohan Pisharodi
Steve Wood
Chi-Cheng Wu
Chung-Ping Wu
Henry Xie
Takako Yamashita
Natalia Yannopoulou
Gallayanee Yaoyuneyong
Nick Yip
Vignesh Yoganathan
Annie Yu
Qionglei Yu
Yunzhijun Yu
Maria Carolina Zanette
Srdan Zdravkovic
Tingting Zhang
Yu Zhihao
Joyce Zhou

Preface

The Academy of Marketing Science was founded in 1971, held its first Annual Conference in 1977, and has grown and prospered ever since. The relevancy of the Academy's mission and activities to our chosen target market of the marketing professoriate has been a key factor in attracting the discipline's best and brightest from all over the world.

The revised Articles of Association of the Academy, approved by the Board of Governors in the spring of 1984 and by the general membership in the fall of that year, define the mission of the Academy as follows:

1. Provide leadership in exploring the normative boundaries of marketing, while simultaneously seeking new ways of bringing theory and practice into practicable conjunction.
2. Further the science of marketing throughout the world by promoting the conduct of research and the dissemination of research results.
3. Provide a forum for the study and improvement of marketing as an economic, ethical, social, and political force and process.
4. Furnish, as appropriate and available, material and other resources for the solution of marketing problems, which confront particular firms and industries, on the one hand, and society at large on the other.
5. Provide publishing media and facilities for fellows of the Academy and reviewer assistance on the fellows' scholarly activities.
6. Sponsor one or more annual conferences to enable the fellows of the Academy to present research results; to learn by listening to other presentations and through interaction with other fellows and guests; to avail themselves of the placements process; to conduct discussion with book editors; and to exchange other relevant information.
7. Assist fellows in the better utilization of their professional marketing talents through redirection, reassignment, and relocation.
8. Provide educator fellows with insights and resources as may be available to aid them in the development of improved teaching methods, materials, devices, and directions.

9. Seek means for establishing student scholarships and professional university chairs in the field of marketing.
10. Offer fellows of the Academy status to business and institutional executives and organizations.
11. Modify the Academy's purpose and direction as the influence of time and appropriate constructive forces may dictate.

Thibodaux, LA, USA Juliann Allen
Lille, France Bruna Jochims
Glassboro, NJ, USA Shuang Wu

Acknowledgments

This book contains the full proceedings of the 2021 Academy of Marketing Science (AMS) Conference – Annual and World Marketing Congress. This year's conference presented a pioneering and special format for AMS. For the first time, the conference combined the Annual Conference and the World Marketing Congress (WMC) in one virtual experience. Appreciation and gratitude are extended to the organization committee for completing and handling the various tasks associated with merging two conferences into one coherent event of this scale.

As part of the 2021 AMS Annual Conference, this conference celebrates the history of marketing and explores its future for the 50th Anniversary of the Academy of Marketing Science under the theme "Celebrating the Past and Future of Marketing." This volume explores the influence of marketing innovations leveraged by the rising influence of artificial intelligence, virtual reality, a proliferation of data, changing economic power concentration, and a myriad of other factors. This includes research on possible new theory discoveries and findings that could lead to more efficient and impactful responses by marketers to the current multi-faceted global challenge array.

The Academy of Marketing Science would like to acknowledge the individuals who have made the conference a success. Special recognition goes to the Annual Conference co-chairs, Lauren Beitelspacher, Marko Sarstedt, and Joseph F. Hair, Jr. An incredible commitment is necessary to coordinate and organize a conference of this measure, especially under the uncertainties and challenges of a first-ever virtual conference. Further, track chairs were essential in encouraging submissions, managing the review process, and organizing session details.

This volume also includes the work of authors originally scheduled to present at the 2020 World Marketing Congress with the theme of "Discovery with Social Impact" in Australia. While the WMC was postponed and integrated into the 2021 AMS Conference, the Academy of Marketing Science would still like to thank the 2020 WMC co-chairs, Jay Weerawardena and Alastair Tombs, for their resilience and efforts to ensure the accommodation of these authors. And of course, the work and help of all the WMC track chairs and reviewers has not been forgotten.

Lastly, the Academy of Marketing Science extends sincere appreciation to all authors who submitted and presented their research and contributed as reviewers and session chairs. In addition, the success of the virtual meeting depended on tireless volunteers including the AMS officers and directors. Gratitude is also extended to the AMS home office who diligently worked behind the scenes to ensure the success of the event. Thank you to all attendees from around the world who made this conference another special AMS event. The 2021 Academy of Marketing Science Conference – Annual and World Marketing Congress would not have been possible without the support of all of these individuals.

Juliann Allen
Bruna Jochims
Shuang Wu

Contents

Special Session: Super Sonic Logos: The Power of Audio Branding: An Abstract

David Allan

Abstract Audio branding is not new. Neither are audio logos. What is new is an appreciation of sound. Not surprising sound is riding the wave of smart speakers. Houses are becoming more voice-activated every day turning lights and sound. We are telling Alexa and Google daily to not only play our favorite music and podcasts but to buy our groceries and clothes. By the end of 2021, 23.5 million people will have made a purchase using a smart speaker (eMarketer 2020). Voice shopping is also expected to jump to $40 billion in 2022 (OC&C 2018). The father of "atmospherics" Philip Kotler (1973), believes that today's atmospherics (sound) must be designed for devices as well as spaces (Minsky and Fahey 2017). Sound has always been and continues to be a powerful atmospheric for not just marketing but movies, television, media, sports, etc. It is clearly the time for brands to really focus on audio branding because "brands without an audio presence will have no presence" (Ciccarelli 2019).

Audio branding is defined as "the approach of using unique, proprietary sound and music to convey a brand's essence and values. Just as visual branding defines a brand using color and shape, audio branding defines a brand through sound and music" (American Marketing Association 2019). Sonic branding serves two primary functions: "the essence of sonic branding is twofold: the creation of brand expressions in sound and the consistent, strategic usage of these properties across touchpoints" (Jackson 2003). A sonic logo can be considered a brand's musical nickname. "The audio logo represents the acoustic identifier of a brand and it is often combined with an (animated) visual logo. It should be distinct/unique, recognizable, flexible, memorable and fit the brand by reflecting brand attributes" (Bronner 2009). It has "a powerful sonic mnemonic function" (Renard 2017). It is "a vessel for associations" (Jackson 2003).

D. Allan (✉)
Saint Joseph's University, Philadelphia, PA, USA
e-mail: dallan@sju.edu

J. Allen et al. (eds.), *Celebrating the Past and Future of Marketing and Discovery with Social Impact*, Developments in Marketing Science: Proceedings of the Academy of Marketing Science, https://doi.org/10.1007/978-3-030-95346-1_1

Whether you consider them to be music to your ears or earworms, this special session celebrates the twelve most noteworthy sonic logos of all time, and the people who gave them the notes. So open your computer and meet Water Werzowa (Intel) and Brian Eno (Windows 95). Turn on your favorite television show or movie and say hello to Mike Post (Law and Order), Dr. James "Andy" Moore (THX), and John Williams (Jaws) and don't forget to hum those NBC chimes. Keep your phone on in case you get a ring from Lance Massey (T-Mobile) and Joel Beckerman (AT&T). And if you get hungry, there's always Coca-Cola (Joe and Umut) and McDonald's (Bill Lamar). And you can charge it on your Mastercard (Raja Rajmannar).

Keywords Audio · Sonic · Branding · Logos

An Apology Is More Than Just Saying "Sorry": Framing Effects in Online Service Recoveries: An Abstract

Wolfgang J. Weitzl, Robert Zniva, Gerald Petz, and Charlotte Pichler

Abstract The current research draws scholars' attention to the need to further investigate framing effects in the context of online complaining. While much research has been conducted on the topic of service recoveries via social media (e.g., Weitzl et al. 2018), little is known about consumers' reactions to corporate responses which apply either (positive/negative) attribute or goal framing. This research is one of the first to shed light on the special case of individuals (i.e., complaint observers) who witness a dissatisfied customer's public online complaint and the framed response by the company involved in a product/service failure.

We know that many consumers source product information from fellow shoppers online (i.e., electronic word-of-mouth (eWOM)) before making a purchase and that the way companies react to overt online criticism (i.e., negative eWOM) is critical for the observers' ultimate purchasing decision. Research suggests that framing these corporate responses in a certain way can strongly influence observers' attitude towards the company (e.g., Her and Seo 2017; Tran et al. 2020). However, some of the existing conclusions have to be revised in the light of the present study: First, in contrast to the assumingly *very robust* valence-consistent influences for attribute framing (i.e., positive framing – such as "We give you a voucher, with which you will safe 90% of the total amount at your next visit." – is more favored than negative framing – such as "We will give you a voucher, with which you will only 10% of the total amount at your next visit."), this research shows that also negative framing can have similar effects. Second, we further show that for goal framing, a positive valence conveyed in the recovery message is more effective than a negatively framed information. This means that in the current research context (i.e., low involvement

---

W. J. Weitzl (✉) · G. Petz
University of Applied Sciences Upper Austria, Steyr, Austria
e-mail: wolfgang.weitzl@fh-steyr.at; gerald.petz@fh-steyr.at

R. Zniva
Salzburg University of Applied Sciences, Puch, Austria
e-mail: robert.zniva@fh-salzburg.ac.at

C. Pichler
Seeburg Castle University, Seekirchen am Wallersee, Austria

J. Allen et al. (eds.), *Celebrating the Past and Future of Marketing and Discovery with Social Impact*, Developments in Marketing Science: Proceedings of the Academy of Marketing Science, https://doi.org/10.1007/978-3-030-95346-1_2

consumer decisions) a 'positivity bias', where the positively framed goal is perceived as a sincere apology, is more likely than the regularly assumed 'negativity bias'. These insights suggest that in terms of framing effects, scholars should consider the specific boundary conditions given in the context of online complaining.

Keywords Service recovery · Online complaints · Framing · Cognitive bias

Differences in CSR Authenticity Evaluation Between Cultures: Lessons Learned from Korean and US Consumers: An Abstract

Soyoung Joo

Abstract Authenticity and consumers' quest for authenticity have been viewed as a new business imperative in contemporary marketing (Gilmore and Pine 2007). While it has been proposed that various attributes (e.g., congruency, transparency) influence stakeholders' perceptions of CSR authenticity (Beckman et al. 2009), there has been little understanding in regard to what components contribute to consumer evaluations of CSR authenticity in different cultures.

As such, drawing on the CSR and authenticity literature, the current research aims to explore some CSR evaluation differences between Korean and US consumers as a means of understanding how different cultures evaluate CSR authenticity. Using focus groups and semi-structured interviews with Korean and US consumers, the current research proposes CSR authenticity as a powerful, theoretical construct capable of understanding different consumers' CSR evaluations across cultures—advancing knowledge of how consumers' CSR authenticity evaluations vary across cultures.

The findings showed that various attributes influenced Korean and US respondents differently in their CSR authenticity evaluations. While congruence and transparency positively influenced Korean respondents' CSR authenticity evaluations, these attributes did not have a favorable impact on US respondents, primarily due to the lack of transparency of the US sport entity and the perceived manipulation of its CSR programs. The findings also showed that personal connection to a social cause had a positive impact on US respondents' CSR evaluations however, this was not observed among Korean respondents. The current research between Korean and US respondents adds empirical evidence of the cultural differences regarding consumers' CSR authenticity evaluations in different cultures. In doing so, the current research fills the knowledge gap in CSR authenticity literature and helps organizations to adequately respond to consumers' pursuit of authenticity and also maximize

S. Joo (✉)
Siena College, Louedonville, NY, USA
e-mail: sjoo@siena.edu

J. Allen et al. (eds.), *Celebrating the Past and Future of Marketing and Discovery with Social Impact*, Developments in Marketing Science: Proceedings of the Academy of Marketing Science, https://doi.org/10.1007/978-3-030-95346-1_3

their CSR endeavors to increase the well-being of consumers and their long-run benefit to society in different locations.

Keywords Corporate social responsibility (CSR) · Authenticity · CSR authenticity · Well-being

Differentiating the Destination Branding Methods of Emerging Markets: A Systematic Review: An Abstract

Serwaa Karikari and Omar J. Khan

Abstract Destination branding is a phenomenon gaining widespread interest due to increased global competition for tourists (Matiza and Slabbert 2020). Described as an offshoot of place branding, destination branding tends to be focused mainly on achieving tourism objectives (Braun 2012). One key antecedent of the increased global competition for tourists is the opening of emerging markets. Emerging markets have been positioned as the "growth engines of the world" (Sinha and Sheth 2018, p. 217). Despite this, there is a notable dearth of research on the destination branding of emerging markets (cf. Martinez 2016).

To gauge the progress of this stream of research and inform future research, it is necessary to conduct a review of refereed journal articles (Williams and Plouffe 2007). This review aims to answer the following questions, (i) what are the trends in terms of journals, themes, emerging markets studied, and methodology?, and (ii) what branding methods have been used and which ones are more effective? This paper will provide a systematic review of the research on destination branding in emerging markets, something that has not been done to date. Although Dinnie (2004) and Vuignier (2017) review the literature, their reviews neither focus on destination branding nor on emerging markets.

In line with the systematic search procedures e.g., Hao and Paul (2019), we searched for articles published in peer-reviewed journals on electronic databases and by scrutinizing the reference lists of related reviews. Overall, the search yielded 31 articles published in 13 journals spanning the years 2008–2019. The findings show that the majority of the articles were published in the Place Branding & Public Diplomacy journal. Additionally, emerging markets in East Asia (e.g., China) and the Middle East and North Africa (e.g., United Arab Emirates) were the most studied, while the Eastern European and South American emerging markets were not as widely studied. Moreover, the most widely-studied theme was destination/place image. With regard to the methodology, an overwhelming majority of papers used exploratory

S. Karikari (✉) · O. J. Khan
Morgan State University, Baltimore, MD, USA
e-mail: sekar1@morgan.edu; omar.khan@morgan.edu

J. Allen et al. (eds.), *Celebrating the Past and Future of Marketing and Discovery with Social Impact*, Developments in Marketing Science: Proceedings of the Academy of Marketing Science, https://doi.org/10.1007/978-3-030-95346-1_4

methods such. Our analysis of offline versus online branding efforts revealed that both are important; however, a combination of both is the most effective.

In sum, this study developed a novel approach to analyzing destination branding. Research implications include the need for more confirmatory methods to enhance generalizability of findings. This study's major limitation was having to make inferences due to the limited branding information. Thus, future research should incorporate more in-depth examinations of branding. For practitioners employing online techniques such as influencer marketing, it is best to use influencers who are natives of the destination to enhance credibility.

Keywords Destination branding · Place branding · Emerging markets · Online branding · Offline branding · Social media · Social media influencers

Consumer Reactions to Dynamic Pricing as a Norm-Breaking Practice with Increasing Levels of Company Clarifications: An Abstract

Silke Bambauer-Sachse and Ashley Young

Abstract Companies that use pricing tactics such as dynamic pricing risk being considered norm-violating particularly by customers who pay higher prices than others. Price-disadvantaged customers are likely to develop lower fairness perceptions and to engage in retaliatory behavior. As few companies disclose information about the pricing criteria, customers are often left feeling confused, which can result in higher perceptions of price complexity. Therefore, to better understand price-disadvantaged consumers' perceptions of price fairness and price complexity, complaint and purchase intentions in the context of dynamic pricing, we examine and compare four pricing scenarios. Uniform pricing represents the non-norm-violating pricing practice, and dynamic pricing is present in the three remaining situations, with various degrees of explanations (none, a short description of dynamic pricing, and a complete explanation of the differentiation criteria). There is currently no research on how service providers' explanations of dynamic pricing influence consumers' perceptions and behaviors, particularly of the price-disadvantaged customers. This study will lead to a better understanding of whether companies can use dynamic pricing strategies without forming negative perceptions by customers, and if service providers' attempts to mitigate any negative customer responses through explanations are effective.

We tested four pricing tactics (uniform pricing, dynamic pricing without an explanation, a short, or a complete explanation) applied to a touristic flight. In the scenarios with dynamic pricing, the customer was always in a disadvantaged price position. We measured price fairness and complexity perceptions, as well as purchase and complaint intentions.

The study results show that marketers who use dynamic pricing can increase customers' fairness perceptions by explaining the criteria used to set the varying prices. Interestingly, both complete and short explanations can bring fairness per-

S. Bambauer-Sachse (✉) · A. Young
University of Fribourg, Fribourg, Switzerland
e-mail: silke.bambauer-sachse@unifr.ch; ashley.young@unifr.ch

J. Allen et al. (eds.), *Celebrating the Past and Future of Marketing and Discovery with Social Impact*, Developments in Marketing Science: Proceedings of the Academy of Marketing Science, https://doi.org/10.1007/978-3-030-95346-1_5

ceptions up to the same level of fairness, as in the case of uniform pricing. Furthermore, perceptions of complexity decrease with the amount of additional information provided on dynamic pricing. However, even a complete explanation of the criteria leading to the varying prices cannot bring down perceived complexity to the level that is measured for uniform pricing. Therefore, additional explanations on pricing criteria can fully restore consumers' fairness perceptions but at the same time do not fully eliminate complexity perceptions. The results for purchase and complaint intentions, which represent consequences of immediate fairness or complexity perceptions indicate that a complete explanation of the criteria used for dynamic pricing helps to establish intentions similar to those in the case of uniform prices.

Keywords Dynamic pricing · Norm-breaking practice · Fairness perceptions · Complexity perceptions

"Point-and-Click" – B2B-Customer Loyalty in the Internet: An Empirical Study on Potential Antecedents Exemplified at German Company "WERU"

Alina Heinold, Marc Kuhn, and Meike Grimme

Abstract The Internet is an indispensable platform for the provision of products and services of a company and for the communication with customers. A significant increase in the number of e-commerce interfaces in the Business-to-Business (B2B) environment has already been noticed for several years. One of the biggest challenges facing small and medium-sized enterprises (SMEs) in the construction industry is the complex issue of retaining customers in B2B-relationships. Especially in an internet-based, constantly changing context, this is an uncertain and ambitious challenge. In our study, we investigate the antecedents of customer loyalty of B2B-customers using the internet. Based on the findings of Janita et al., we developed a conceptual model containing the constructs potentially influencing loyalty of B2B-customers in the internet. Conducting an online survey with the B2B-customers of WERU, a German industrial component manufacturer in the building sector, our final data set contains 187 observations. Results show a direct, highly significant effect of customer satisfaction and trust and a highly significant total effect of image via customer satisfaction on customer loyalty.

Keywords Customer loyalty · B2B · SME · Internet · E-commerce · SEM

A. Heinold · M. Kuhn (✉) · M. Grimme
Baden-Wuerttemberg Cooperative State University, Stuttgart, Germany
e-mail: aheinold@lehre.dhbw-stuttgart.de; marc.kuhn@dhbw-stuttgart.de; meike.grimme@dhbw-stuttgart.de

J. Allen et al. (eds.), *Celebrating the Past and Future of Marketing and Discovery with Social Impact*, Developments in Marketing Science: Proceedings of the Academy of Marketing Science, https://doi.org/10.1007/978-3-030-95346-1_6

Introduction

Due to changes in the general economic environment and competition, the important position of managing a customer relationship, especially customer loyalty, was recognized over 40 years ago (Hoffmann 2008). In 1975, Bagozzi began to study the exchange process between supplier and consumer, through which a stronger connection can be established (Bagozzi 1975). Relationship marketing (Berry et al. 1983), which replaced the outdated individual transaction between two organizations is characterized by a long-term customer relationship (Hoffmann 2008). Through technological advancement, companies have the opportunity to develop customer loyalty activities in the form of virtual communities, websites, customer clubs, web stores or electronic services on the internet (Keuper et al. 2002; Schwartz 2017). Neither scientifically nor practically has the topic of customer loyalty lost any of its importance nowadays, but it is becoming increasingly important for companies (Barsch 2019; Kunze 2000).

In contrast to B2C-markets, B2B-marketing is especially focused on long-term relationships with the related customer organization (Fredebeul-Krein 2012). By cultivating that relationship, the loyalty of the B2B-customer and derived future business is estimated to be strengthened (Ramaseshan et al. 2013). Furthermore, the number of current and potential customers in a B2B-market is much smaller than in a B2C-market (Barsch 2019). Therefore, the product is more closely tailored to the customer, which results in a higher degree of individualization (Fredebeul-Krein 2012). Especially in the construction industry, the service and quality of products are very important. On the basis of these factors, it becomes apparent that the driving variables of customer loyalty in B2B are considered to be different from B2C (Forooz Pishgar et al. 2013). However, studies in that present research context only exist in very small numbers. Most studies regarding customer loyalty in the internet are concerned with the B2C-market (Dowling 2002; I. Eid 2011; Srinivasan et al. 2002). Even if the internet doesn't seem to change the fundamental idea of customer loyalty and its structure, it extends additional types of possible interactions with B2B-customers (Strauss 2011). That raises the question about specific internet related antecedents of B2B-customer loyalty.

As a consequence, we see a research gap regarding to the influencing factors of customer loyalty in the Internet for SEM in the B2B-sector. Accordingly, we define the following research questions:

RQ1: Which factors influence B2B-customer loyalty in the internet?
RQ2: What related actions should industrial SMEs take in the B2B-sector?

To answer these questions, this paper is structured as follows: Firstly, we offer a structured overview of studies that investigate customer loyalty in B2B. Secondly, we derive our conceptual model and address our research hypotheses. Thirdly, we present our results after having performed a structural equation model analysis. Finally, we discuss the effects of our results on the theory; we also give practical recommendations for WERU. Future research areas on the topic and limitations of the study are addressed as well.

Theoretical Background and Research Approach

On the basis of the economic and behavioral theories, we analyzed four models with respect to their suitability in the context of this study.

The European Performance Satisfaction Index (EPSI) model (González Menorca et al. 2016) was introduced in 1999 for a European country comparison of customer satisfaction. The quality and significance of the index has already been confirmed in several studies (Bruhn 2008). The study came to the conclusion that expectations affect the image and that the product quality perceived by the customer is dependent on the customer expectations regarding the product. The expectations as well as the perceived quality positively influence the perceived value and the customer satisfaction as well as the image positively influence loyalty. However, the connection between perceived value and customer satisfaction is not very high (González Menorca et al. 2016). The EPSI model offers valuable approaches for customer retention on the internet. Moreover, the importance of all variables of the model has been repeatedly confirmed by the theories. The application for industrial SMEs in the B2B-context is possible due to the robustness against changes in the company, the sector, and the geographical area. However, the model cannot be used completely without restrictions for the present study, since specific influencing factors regarding the Internet are not part of it.

The Theoretical Framework of Customer Loyalty (Cheng et al. 2008) was developed to identify the driving indicators regarding customer loyalty of a Chinese internet provider. The results of this study showed that especially customer satisfaction and service quality have a significant impact on customer loyalty (Cheng et al. 2008). Focusing on services, the approach of Cheng et al. might not be completely transferred to industrial manufacturing companies, as internet provider offer a smaller range of services. Nevertheless, potential with regard to service quality and switching costs has been seen for the expansion of the future investigation model. The switching costs in the B2B-sector can be closely related to the economic switching costs, as the theories have shown several times before.

The development of the Modified Technology Acceptance Model (I. Eid 2011) was based on the previously limited research in the field of e-commerce in Saudi Arabia. The aim was to gain initial knowledge of the factors influencing customer satisfaction, trust and loyalty of e-commerce customers. In this model, customer satisfaction is identified as a significantly influencing variable of customer loyalty and serves as a mediator between the individual constructs. The quality of the user interface and the information quality of e-commerce websites represent an indirect influence variable of loyalty (I. Eid 2011). Regarding the context of our study, it can be stated that customer loyalty on the internet of the B2B-environment has hardly been researched. Although the model was developed for the B2C-sector, it seems to be transferable to B2B-relationships. There are no limitations regarding the company size or industry. However, the application of this model can lead to differentiated results in a cross-national comparison. In addition, predominantly male respondents were interviewed, which is also expected in the context of this study.

The Model of Antecedents of Client Loyalty (Janita et al. 2013) deals with B2B electronic marketplaces in Spain, especially in the construction industry. Image, perceived quality, perceived value, and customer satisfaction have proven to be important factors influencing customer loyalty. In contrast to some B2C studies, this study has shown, that there is no correlation between the perceived quality of service and customer satisfaction (Janita et al. 2013). In view of these variables, the model can be applied to our present research context, since it was also applied to the B2B-sector with regard to electronic marketplaces. Additionally, the industry sector corresponds to the context of this study and there are no limitations regarding the size of the company.

Taking into account the model assessment, we used an extended version of the Model of Antecedents of Client Loyalty by Janita et al. (2013). Nevertheless, it should be noted that a modification of the selected model will be made. First of all, the expectations as a construct are neglected in the investigation model. This is due to the fact that several studies have already come to the conclusion that the effects of expectations on customer loyalty either do not exist at all or are very small (Gronholdt et al. 2000). In addition, the construct commitment is also excluded. The commitment was hardly considered in the theories presented and the models examined. This is possibly due to the fact that commitment contains similar aspects of loyalty (Janita et al. 2013). Furthermore, the switching costs are recorded as a construct of the switching barriers. The social influences will not be considered. This is based on the assumption that in B2B-relationships the influence of the social environment is not taken into account when deciding to switch the manufacturer (Jones et al. 2000). The attractiveness of competitors is to be integrated as a single construct because of the large number of competitors in the market. The perceived risk is included as an additional construct for the research model, by reason that every purchase decision is associated with a certain risk. The construct trust is also included in the research model, as this has proven to be an important predictor for successful cooperation with customers in the B2B-environment (Gounaris 2005). With the digital age, trust is gaining importance, as interaction with customers is becoming much easier as an important influence on future partnerships (Schmitt 2019).

This model provides a basis for answering our research questions (Fig. 1). The following assumptions are expected based on the model and theory analysis (Table 1):

Methodology

We conducted a standardized online survey in Germany with approximately 1030 specialized retailers of the industrial company WERU. WERU is one of the leading manufacturers of windows and doors in the European market. WERU bought the company Unilux in 2014, creating the WERU Group, which can operate as a full-range supplier in the market. A total of 1150 employees are employed which puts WERU in the SME segment. The retailers of WERU were asked to participate in the online survey. The participants were asked to rate each question on a 5-point Likert scale (1 = do not agree at all, 5 = agree completely). The items and their associated constructs are shown in Table A1. The total sample size was 187.

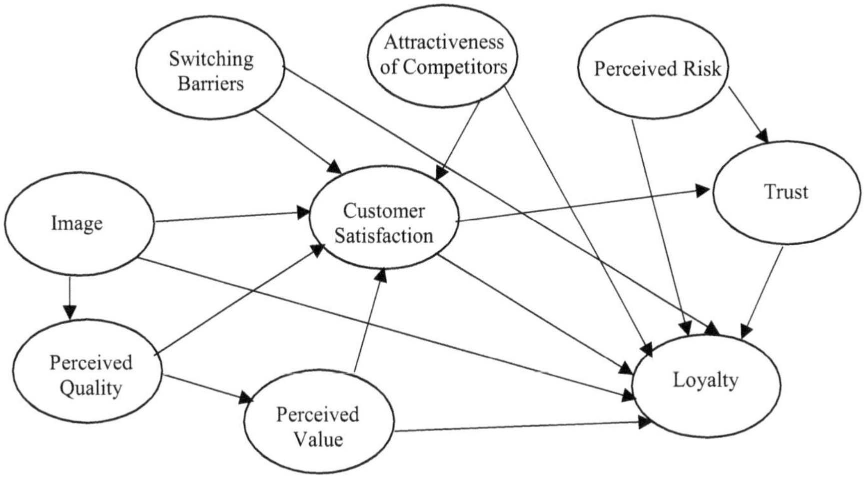

Fig. 1 Conceptual model

Table 1 Overview of expected influences regarding the constructs

	Hypotheses
H1:	The better the image, the higher the customer satisfaction.
H2:	The better the image, the higher the perceived quality.
H3:	The higher the trust, the higher the loyalty.
H4:	The higher the perceived barriers to switching, the lower the customer satisfaction.
H5:	The higher the satisfaction, the higher the trust.
H6:	The higher the satisfaction, the higher the loyalty.
H7:	The higher the perceived quality, the higher the perceived value.
H8:	The higher the perceived quality, the higher the customer satisfaction.

Data Analysis and Results

Our data analysis draws on partial least squares structural equation modeling (PLS-SEM) using SmartPLS 3.3.0. For the significance tests, we perform the bootstrapping procedure with 5000 subsamples and apply the option without sign change (Hair et al. 2017). The constructs attractiveness of competitors (ATCO), image (IMG), switching barriers (SB), perceived risk (PR) and loyalty (LOY) were measured reflectively. The evaluation of the construct reliability leads to the exclusion of the construct from the initial measurement model. The analysis reveals acceptable results for the rest of the constructs (min. Cronbach's $\alpha > 0.82$, min. $\rho A > 0.83$, min. $\rho C > 0.82$) (see Table A2 for fully reported results of internal consistency) (Hair et al. 2014). We also tested the convergence validity. For this purpose, the indicator loadings were evaluated. The indicator loadings should correspond to a value of 0.7, in the best case 0.708, which all indicator loadings have achieved. A second criterion for convergent validity is the extracted average variance (AVE).

The AVE scores are above the minimum threshold of 0.5 for all constructs, indicating that on average, all reflectively measured constructs account for more than 50% of the variance of their indicators. To evaluate discriminant validity, we first consider the Fornell-Larcker criterion, which states that a latent variable should share more variance with its items than with any other latent construct (Hair et al. 2017). This condition is met since all AVE measures are greater than the inter-construct correlations. Second, we evaluate the discriminant validity using the heterotrait-monotrait ratio of the correlations (HTMT). The HTMT values in both groups are well below the threshold of 1, whereas the 95% bias-corrected confidence intervals do not include the value of 1, which means that the measurement models fulfil the recommended rule of thumb (Hair et al. 2017). Furthermore, the indicator loadings are larger in both groups than the cross loadings. Taking these three criteria, we can conclude that discriminatory validity is achieved, thus indicating a satisfactory extent to which the five factors differ from each other. The constructs perceived quality (PQ), perceived value (PV), customer satisfaction (CS) and trust (TRU) were measured formatively. Therefore, the first criterion is multicollinearity. This expresses the linear dependence of manifest variables on other manifest variables (Walter 2009). None of the values exceeds the threshold value of 5, so that there is no multicollinearity. The next step is to check the external weights of the formative indicators. It is noticeable here that not all indicators are significant. PV1 with $p = 0.45$ and PV3 with $p = 0.99$ have not proven to be significant. Hair et al. (2017) justify this by stating a higher number of indicators for measuring a construct increases the probability that indicators are not significant. Nevertheless, this is unexpected, since the construct was made measurable by empirically proven items. Besides the p values, we had to consider the 95% bias-corrected confidence intervals of the indicators. The limits here are 2.5% and 97.5% and were fulfilled. Furthermore, a value of 0 should not be present (Hair et al. 2017). This can be confirmed in Table 2.

Finally, looking at the structural model, we need to evaluate multicollinearity by considering the value of variance inflation factor (VIF). The first run showed that some values far exceeded the maximum target value of 5 (Hair et al. 2014). For this reason, the elimination of different constructs and their effects were tested. In view of this, it was recognized that the link between image and loyalty and the link between perceived value and loyalty generated outliers to a high degree, so that no basis for further testing was provided. Accordingly, the decision was made to remove these two links from the model. The test procedure has finally shown that the results are no longer distorted. The obtained VIFs for the modified model are well below the number of 5, which means that there is no serious collinearity problem among the predictor variables (Hair et al. 2014). Path coefficients as well as their significance are summarized in Table 2.

Finally, this table addresses our first research question and gives an overview of the factors which strongly influence customer loyalty on the internet and which influence it less.

Table 2 Path coefficients and significance

	Path Coefficient	*p value*	Sig.	95% bias corrected confidence intervals
CS → LOY	0.37	0.00	***	[−0.07;0.42]
CS → TRU	0.79	0.00	***	[0.13;0.91]
IMG → CS	0.32	0.00	***	[0.17;0.50]
IMG → PQ	0.77	0.00	***	[0.65;0.85]
IMG → TRU	0.18	0.00	***	[−0.47;0.35]
PQ → CS	0.36	0.00	***	[0.20;0.50]
PQ → PV	0.73	0.00	***	[0.62;0.80]
PR → LOY	−0.10	0.00	***	[−0.90;0.26]
PR → TRU	−0.03	0.00	***	[−0.64;0.17]
PV → CS	0.30	0.00	***	[0.16;0.43]
SB → CS	0.07	0.15	ns	[−0.03;0.31]
SB → LOY	0.26	0.00	***	[0.01;0.36]
TRU → LOY	0.34	0.00	***	[−0.55;0.45]

Note: ***$p \leq 0.001$; **$p \leq 0.01$; *$p \leq 0.05$; *ns* not significant

Conclusion, Discussion and Future Research

Our results could also empirically confirm the strong theoretical role of customer satisfaction as a precursor of loyalty. These findings are clearly similar to those of previous research on both online B2C and online B2B e-commerce which report strong evidence for such a relationship (Chumpitaz et al. 2004; Pin Luarn et al. 2003; Ding et al. 2011). However, satisfaction was not only a pioneering factor for loyalty, but also a direct, very strong influencing factor in our study. Therefore, we can also underline the theoretical assumption (Selnes 1998). In turn, trust has been cited in most studies and theories as a significant factor influencing customer loyalty, especially on the internet. Our results also determine a significant correlation within this path (Brunner et al. 2008).

It is clearly recognizable that image is the most important influence for perceived quality. In this context, the established hypothesis H2 can be confirmed, as there is a strong, highly significant correlation. For this reason, it is advisable for SME in this industry to provide sufficient information to customers through an active communication policy via the internet. This can be made for example via e-newsletters or social media channels (Kreutzer et al. 2020). In the course of this survey, it was found that Instagram and Facebook are the main channels which are used. In this case, the focus should be on WERU's competence and know-how as the analysis showed. However, the reputation of producing high quality products should not be neglected either as the image has a very strong impact on the perceived quality by the customers. The perceived quality has also proven to be a influencing factor of loyalty via the perceived value and the customer satisfaction. For this reason H7 can also be confirmed. On the basis of the survey and the analysis, it was found that the image is important for customer satisfaction. H1 can be divided on the basis of the moderate, highly significant correlation. Moreover, the provision of e-learning tools or community platforms via internet can also provide a way to counteract

B2B-customer concerns (Kreutzer et al. 2020). Besides, the study has shown that a simple and convenient ordering process in the form of a web store for ordering doors and windows via online stores on the internet is required, as competitors and online providers already offer (Fensterversand.com 2021; Veluxshop.de 2021). As a premium manufacturer, the perceived product quality and value for the customers is also significant in this case. Therefore, the early involvement of customers in the development process of products could be useful to increase long term customer loyalty. To identify customer requirements via the internet, the creation of user groups might be helpful. These groups could enable particularly innovative customers, sales staff and internal employees to collaborate. In those groups, people can work together on new product introductions, further developments and elimination of products, independently of location and time, due to the internet (Kreutzer et al. 2020). Excluding the total effects, satisfaction has the strongest direct effect on customer loyalty. According to the theory, we confirm H6. Consequently, special attention should be paid to this construct. Satisfaction is an alignment of the expectations with the actual achievement, so that the communication measures are particularly important. In this case, a company should only communicate what it can actually implement. This must be ensured, especially for social media, as contributions can be distributed very quickly (Buchberger 2016). WERU is advised to carry out a continuous learning process through regular online satisfaction survey analyses. Due to the important role of the service, assessment possibilities should be provided in the internet, in the form of automated mails, feedback possibilities by means of follow-up processes or social media applications. If WERU decides to implement a survey, it is important to the customers that the measures and suggestions are actually considered and implemented (Kreutzer et al. 2020). Our investigation model exhibits a further effect path of the satisfaction on the loyalty. The connection of satisfaction and trust has proven to be the strongest relationship in the entire research model which confirms H5. The basis of trust seems to address the online communication between WERU and its customers. The customers emphasized open and honest communication as highly important. Accordingly, any changes in the future affecting the customers should be communicated online. Due to Covid-19, WERU for example has produced a short online video, showing B2B-customers who measured WERU during the Covid-19 pandemic. This activity could be applied permanently via the internet for customers in order to openly provide them with information even in crises and thereby strengthen their trust in WERU.

The survey shows that the perceived risks is a minor factor influencing trust. A significantly stronger effect on trust was expected due to the high average age of the customers and the unfamiliarity with this topic. However, when introducing a web shop, it should be ensured, that customers are given a sense of reliability beforehand and that concerns about the possible consequential risks of such an ordering process are dispelled. For example, extended guarantees or the existence of service hotlines can be communicated via internet (Huber 2013). Overall, it can be stated that trust has the greatest influence on loyalty after customer satisfaction. This significant connection can also be determined with H3. A fundamentally uniform, constant and professional customer-communication in the internet can create a radiating effect. This concerns the strategic orientation of the company, the customer orientation and the related philosophy, the product offers and services as well as the positioning and identity of the brand (Huber 2013). In summary, communication measures on the Internet can generate a multitude of opportunities in terms of customer loyalty. This study provides relevant insights to possible factors determining the increase of customer loyalty. The consideration of this study is practice-oriented with very significant values compared to the existing literature.

Nevertheless, there are some limitations and also starting points for further research, which are discussed in the following. The selection of the constructs for the investigation model is based on empirical research and theories, but it can be assumed that, in addition to the constructs examined, a large number of other factors can influence customer loyalty. In this respect, a more intensive analysis could be achieved by integrating further constructs. In addition, the indicators of the constructs were determined based on the context of the investigation. Therefore, comparability with other research in the field of customer loyalty is not given. Thus, a uniform, standardized definition of constructs, which have been confirmed by repeated studies, could counteract this. It should be mentioned that due to the limited scope of the investigation, restrictions were accepted regarding the detailed operationalization of the items. The study was carried out exclusively in the German market, so that an unrestricted transferability into other cultures is difficult and could lead to different results. In view of the high dynamic nature of changes on the internet, it should be noted that the importance of the various drivers may change over time. This could mainly be due to changing customer requirements and experience attitudes on the internet and the development of competition.

Appendix

Table A1 Item summary – questionnaire for the retailers of WERU

Measurement model	Scale/item
Image	*5-point Likert scale (1 = fully disagree, 5 = fully agree)*
IMG1	In my opinion, WERU has a good reputation.
IMG2	WERU has a reputation for producing high quality products.
IMG3	WERU has a reputation for providing good services.
IMG4	In my opinion, WERU has a better image than its competitors.
Perceived quality	*5-point Likert scale (1 = fully disagree, 5 = fully agree)*
PQ1	WERU provides a high quality of product.
PQ2	In my opinion WERU is reliable.
PQ3	WERU handles my complaints immediately.
PQ4	The employees of WERU are competent.
PQ5	For me, the order process at WERU is simple and comfortable.
Perceived value	*5-point Likert scale (1 = fully disagree, 5 = fully agree)*
PV1	For me, the price-performance ratio of WERU is good compared to the competition.

(continued)

Table A1 (continued)

Measurement model	Scale/item
PV2	For me, the product quality is high.
PV3	For me, the price level is appropriate.
PV4	The service quality I receive from WERU is worth my time.
Customer satisfaction	*5-point Likert scale (1 = fully disagree, 5 = fully agree)*
CS1	Overall, I am satisfied with WERU.
CS2	I am satisfied with the products I receive from WERU.
CS3	In general terms, I am satisfied with the way of ordering.
CS4	I am satisfied with the service I receive from WERU.
Loyalty	*5-point Likert scale (1 = fully disagree, 5 = fully agree)*
LOY1	I intend to continue to do business with WERU.
LOY2	I would post positive messages about WERU on some internet message board.
LOY3	The probability that I will recommend WERU first to my customers is high.
Switching barriers	*5-point Likert scale (1 = fully disagree, 5 = fully agree)*
SB1	To change to another company involves the sacrifice of existing benefits accumulated with WERU.
SB2	To change to another company involves investing time in searching for information about other companies.
SB3	For me, the cost of switching to another manufacturer seems high.
Attractiveness of competitors	*5-point Likert scale (1 = fully disagree, 5 = fully agree)*
ATCO1*	Compared to WERU, there are other manufacturers with which I would probably be equally or more satisfied.
ATCO2	In comparison to other manufacturers, WERU offers a wider range of products.
Trust	*5-point Likert scale (1 = fully disagree, 5 = fully agree)*
TRU1	In my opinion, WERU is generally trustworthy.
TRU2	WERU communicates always honest with us.
TRU3	We trust that WERU keeps our best interests in mind.
TRU4	We trust that WERU is competent at what they are doing.
Perceived risk	*5-point Likert scale (1 = fully disagree, 5 = fully agree)*
PR1	For me, the decision to transact via webshop involves a significant amount of risk.
PR2	The purchase of products on the internet that does not meet expectations may result in a waste of my time.
PR3	For me, buying WERU products via webshop seems unreliable.
PR4	The purchase of the product demands a great amount of information.

Note: Items marked with an asterisk * are removed from the entire data set due to high share of missing values

Table A2 Criteria for assessing convergent validity and reliability for reflective constructs as well as multicollinearity and significance for formative constructs

Reflective						Formative				
Construct	Items	Outer loadings	AVE	Cronbach's α	Dijkstra-Henseler's ρ_A	Composite reliability ρ_C	Outer loadings	VIF	p-value	95% bias-corrected confidence intervals
Image	IMG1	0.847	0.615	0.863	0.871	0.864				
	IMG2	0.681								
	IMG3	0.850								
	IMG4	0.747								
Loyalty	LOY1	0.875	0.661	0.847	0.873	0.852				
	LOY2	0.663								
	LOY3	0.902								
Perceived risk	PR1	0.836	0.538	0.824	0.839	0.820				
	PR2	0.683								
	PR3	0.767								
	PR4	0.770								
Switching barriers	SB1	1.0	0.626	0.816	0.915	0.824				
	SB2	0.640								
	SB3	0.778								
Perceived quality	PQ1						0.713	1.80	0.01	[0.05;0.37]
	PQ2						0.894	2.71	0.00	[0.20;0.53]
	PQ3						0.832	2.30	0.00	[0.11;0.43]
	PQ4						0.666	1.76	0.01	[0.05;0.23]
	PQ5						0.724	1.37	0.00	[0.20;0.50]
Perceived value	PV1						0.565	2.20	0.45	[−0.12;0.25]
	PV2						0.829	1.51	0.00	[0.30;0.60]
	PV3						0.624	2.51	0.99	[−0.23;0.21]
	PV4						0.915	1.72	0.00	[0.46;0.79]

Customer satisfaction	CS1						0.862	2.34	0.00	[0.22;0.47]
	CS2						0.816	2.06	0.00	[0.16;0.40]
	CS3						0.702	1.56	0.00	[0.11;0.36]
	CS4						0.864	2.11	0.00	[0.25;0.49]
Trust	TRU1						0.877	1.97	0.00	[0.27;0.57]
	TRU2						0.892	2.70	0.00	[0.13;0.52]
	TRU3						0.861	3.06	0.01	[0.09;0.52]
	TRU4						0.748	2.19	0.01	[0.06;0.36]

Note: Outer loadings and AVE refer to convergent validity. Cronbach's α, Dijkstra-Henseler's ρ_A and Composite Reliability ρ_C refer to reliability. VIF refer to multicollinearity. *P* value and confidence intervals refer to significance

References

Bagozzi, R. (1975). Marketing as Exchange. *Journal of Marketing, 39(4)*, 32–39.

Barsch, T. (2019). Stand der Digitalisierung im B2B-Neukundenvertrieb. Entwicklung von Beurteilungskriterien und Erstellung eines Reifegradmodells [State of Digitalization in B2B New Customer Sales. Development of Assessment Criteria and Creation of a Maturity Model]. Wiesbaden: Springer VS.

Berry, L.L., Shostack, G.L., & Upah G.D. (1983). Emerging perspectives on services marketing. *American Marketing Association Proceedings Series,* Chicago, IL.

Bruhn, M. (2008). Qualitätsmanagement für Dienstleistungen. Grundlagen, Konzepte, Methoden [Quality management for services. Basics, concepts, methods]. 7th edition. Wiesbaden: Springer VS.

Brunner, T.A., Stöcklin, M., & Opwis, K. (2008). Satisfaction, image and loyalty: new versus experienced customers. *European Journal of Marketing, 42(9/10)*, 1095–1105.

Buchberger, P. (2016). Maßnahmen zur Steigerung der Kundenzufriedenheit. Managementansätze zur Prozessoptimierung [Measures to increase customer satisfaction. Management approaches for process optimization]. Wiesbaden: Gabler.

Cheng, T.C.E., Lai, L.C.F., & Yeung, A.C.L. (2008). The Driving Forces of Customer Loyalty. *International Journal of E-Business Research, 4(4)*, 26–42.

Chumpitaz, R. & Paparoidamis, N.G. (2004). Service quality and marketing performance in business-to-business markets: exploring the mediating role of client satisfaction. *Managing Service Quality, 14(2/3)*, 235–248.

Ding, D.X., Hu, P.J.H., & Sheng, O.R.L. (2011). e-SELFQUAL: A scale for measuring online self-service quality. *Journal of Business Research, 64(5)*, 508–515.

Dowling, G. (2002). Customer Relationship Management: In B2C Markets, Often Less is More. *California Management Review, 44(3)*, 87–104.

Eid, M. (2011). Determinants of E-Commerce Customer Satisfaction, Trust, and Loyalty in Saudi Arabia. *Journal of Electronic Commerce Research, 12(1)*, 78–93.

Fensterversand.com (2021). Homepage Fensterversand [Window webshop]. Online available at https://www.fensterversand.com/, 22.05.2021.

Forooz P., Samira D., Farzaneh G., Nazanin S., & Mahboobeh A. (2013). The Impact of Product Innovation on Customer Satisfaction and Customer Loyalty. *Arabian Journal of Business and Management Review, 2(5)*, 135–142.

Fredebeul-Krein, T. (2012). Koordinierter Einsatz von Direktmarketing und Verkaufsaußendienst im B2B-Kontext [Coordinated use of direct marketing and field sales in a B2B-context]. Wiesbaden: Gabler.

González Menorca, L., Fernández-Ortiz, R., Fuentes Lombardo, G., & Clavel San Emeterio, M. (2016). The EPSI model as the main factor for identifying customer satisfaction: empirical research. *Total Quality Management & Business Excellence, 27(3-4)*, 447–463.

Gounaris, S. P. (2005). Trust and commitment influences on customer retention: insights from business-to-business services. *Journal of Business Research, 58(2)*, 126–140.

Gronholdt, L., Martensen, A., & Kristensen, K. (2000). The relationship between customer satisfaction and loyalty: Cross-industry differences. *Total Quality Management, 11(4-6)*, 509–514.

Hair, J.F., Babin, B.J., Anderson, R.E., & Black, W.C. (2014). Multivariate data analysis. 7th edition. Harlow, Essex: Pearson.

Hair, J.F., Hult, G.T.M., Ringle, C.M., Sarstedt, M., Richter, N. F., & Hauff, S. (2017). Partial Least Squares Strukturgleichungsmodellierung: Eine anwendungsorientierte Einführung [Structural Equation Modeling: An application-oriented introduction]. München: Vahlen.

Hoffmann, A. (2008). Die Akzeptanz kartenbasierter Kundenbindungsprogramme aus Konsumentensicht. Determinanten und Erfolgswirkungen [The acceptance of card-based loyalty programs from a consumer perspective. Determinants and effects on success]. Wiesbaden: Gabler.

Huber, S. (2013). Social Media in der Organisationskommunikation. Empirische Befunde und Branchenanalysen [Social media in organizational communication. Empirical findings and industry analyses]. Wiesbaden: Springer VS.

Janita, M.S. & Miranda, F.J. (2013). The antecedents of client loyalty in business-to-business (B2B) electronic marketplaces. *Industrial Marketing Management* 42(5), 814–823.

Jones, M.A., Mothersbaugh, D.L., & Beatty, S.E. (2000). Switching barriers and repurchase intentions in services. *Journal of Retailing, 76(2)*, 259–274.

Keuper, R. (2002). Electronic Business und Mobile Business. Ansätze, Konzepte und Geschäftsmodelle [Electronic Business and Mobile Business. Approaches, concepts and business models]. Wiesbaden: Gabler.

Kreutzer, R.T., Rumler, A., & Wille-Baumkauff, B. (2020). B2B-Online-Marketing und Social Media. Handlungsempfehlungen und Best Practices [B2B online marketing and social media. Recommendations for action and best practices]. 2nd edition. Wiesbaden: Gabler.

Kunze, K. (2000). Kundenbindungsmanagement in verschiedenen Marktphasen [Customer loyalty management in different market phases]. Wiesbaden: Gabler.

Pin, L. & Hsin-Hui, L. (2003). A Customer Loyalty Model for E-Service Context. *Journal of Electronic Commerce Research, 4(4)*, 156-167.

Ramaseshan, B., Rabbanee, F.K., & Tan Hsin Hui, L. (2013). Effects of customer equity drivers on customer loyalty in B2B context. *Journal of Bus & Indus Marketing, 28(4)*, 335–346.

Schmitt, M.C. (2019). Quick Guide digitale B2B-Kommunikation. Content, Influencer, Blogs & Co: wie Sie Ihre Kunden an allen digitalen Touchpoints erreichen [Quick Guide digital B2B communication. Content, influencers, blogs & co: how to reach your customers at all digital touchpoints]. Wiesbaden: Gabler.

Schwartz, M. (2017). KfW: E-Commerce steckt im Mittelstand noch in den Kinderschuhen [E-commerce is still in its infancy in SMEs]. Online available at: https://www.kfw.de/PDF/Download-Center/Konzernthemen/Research/PDF-Dokumente-Fokus-Volkswirtschaft/Fokus-2017/Fokus-Nr.-161-Februar-2017-E-Commerce.pdf, 22.05.2021.

Selnes, F. (1998). Antecedents and consequences of trust and satisfaction in buyer-seller relationships. *European Journal of Marketing, 32(3/4)*, 305–322.

Srinivasan, S.S., Anderson, R., & Ponnavolu, K. (2002). Customer loyalty in e-commerce: an exploration of its antecedents and consequences. *Journal of Retailing, 78(1)*, 41–50.

Strauss, S.C. (2011). Neukundengewinnung und Kundenbindung im Internethandel unter Berücksichtigung rechtlicher Aspekte [New customer acquisition and customer retention in Internet commerce, taking legal aspects into account]. Hamburg: Diplomica.

Veluxshop.de (2021). Homepage VELUX [Window webshop]. Online available at https://www.veluxshop.de/?gclid=EAIaIQobChMIn6bQyanb6wIV2evtCh3c4QC6EAAYASAAEgJ2CvD_BwE&gclsrc=aw.ds, 22.06.2021.

Walter, A. (2009). Methodik der empirischen Forschung [Methodology of empirical research]. 3rd edition. Wiesbaden: Gabler.

Value Co-creation and the Media Market Segment: A Multiple Case Studies Analyzed under the Approach of Service Dominant Logic of Marketing: An Abstract

Flávio Régio Brambilla, Ana Flávia Hantt, and Bruno Morgado Ferreira

Abstract The consumption of information on multimedia platforms and the widespread use of social networks have had a direct impact on the management of print media. Value co-creation and service-centered marketing from the perspective of the Service Dominant Logic (SDL) of Marketing are pointed out as mechanisms of interaction between newspaper companies and their advertising clients, in which both work together to create new products and maximizing results. In order to understand how printed communication vehicles develop co-creative solutions for their clients, this research makes use of a multiple case study strategy. We seek to analyze, from the perspective of co-creation, business models that have been adopted by print media, pointing out ways that can be adopted in the search for a new business model.

In Vargo and Lusch (2004, 2006, 2008, 2011, 2016) SDL, all actors (workers, managers, suppliers, consumers and other stakeholders) are seen as co-creators, and this experience adds value for processes. The SDL implies interactivity and unity among beneficiaries, suggesting a focus on working together to integrate resources to create mutual value. From the crossing references related to business model of the printed communication vehicles, and also SDL, it is understood that co-creation of B2B value in a printed communication vehicle occurs when the vehicle (actor A) integrates their knowledge of content production and qualified receiving public; and when the advertising company (actor B) integrates its specialized knowledge in a

F. R. Brambilla (✉) · A. F. Hantt
Universidade de Santa Cruz do Sul, Santa Cruz do Sul, Brazil
e-mail: flaviobr@unisc.br; ppga@unisc.br

B. M. Ferreira
Polythecnic Institute of Viseu, Viseu, Portugal
e-mail: morgado.ferreira@estgv.ipv.pt

J. Allen et al. (eds.), *Celebrating the Past and Future of Marketing and Discovery with Social Impact*, Developments in Marketing Science: Proceedings of the Academy of Marketing Science, https://doi.org/10.1007/978-3-030-95346-1_7

market segment, and also the provision of service (resources) to generate benefits for itself and for the other.

A qualitative and exploratory approach was applied. We decided to adopt a multiple case studies strategy (Yin 2015), choosing three cases involving communication vehicles and partner companies from different areas. For data collection, in-depth interviews were used in semi-open format. We also analyzed physical artifacts. Data was analyzed by data triangulation technique.

The three cases showed that the partnership of printed media with advertising companies, are business models that favor a co-creation environment. Four key points are highlighted: (1) printed media seek out partner companies that share the same institutions; (2) integration of resources in service ecosystem seeks to highlight the expertise of each actor; (3); involvement of all stakeholders, especially media professionals, is essential for value co-creation; (4) learning.

Keywords Printed media communication · Service marketing · Service Dominant Logic (SDL) · Value co-creation · Multiple case studies

Examining the Role of Implicit Self-Theories in Celebrity Meaning Transfer toward eSports: An Abstract

Se Jin Kim

Abstract Electronic sports (eSports) have enjoyed a giant leap in the entertainment industry. However, eSports have faced negative images after the effort to become categorized under sport. Currently, they do not have a fixed identity due to a marginal appeal as a sport product. This study aims to explore if an athlete celebrity can transfer meaning to a sport organization (eSports) in which the brand personality is less established and examine if the debate of eSport being a sport can be eased by using traditional sport spokesperson's expertise. To do this, we will conduct an in-depth review of the literature and an experiment to identify if potential factors (i.e., implicit self-theory and celebrity meaning transfer) affect the meaning transfer. Furthermore, how these transferred meanings influence consumer behaviors (attendance intent, merchandise purchase intent, perceived athleticism, brand attitude, and brand image) will be examined.

Based on the literature review and proposed hypotheses, we expected a more substantial meaning transfer from the celebrity condition than a non-celebrity condition. Also, we anticipated the moderating effect of an individual's implicit self-theory. Participants who were manipulated to be an entity theorist will be more affected by the celebrities, compared to the incremental theorists, due to their urge to signal their positive attributes (Dweck and Leggett 1988; Elliott and Dweck 1988). This is due to the assumption that individuals have an urge to enhance self and consume positive brands to construct self-perceptions by identifying and attaching oneself to the brand. In this study, we have hypothesized that human brands with desirable personalities can also be used as a brand to attach oneself to, and entity theorists will see celebrities as a chance to signal their positive qualities, acting more favorably to celebrities (Carlson and Donovan 2013; McCracken 1989; Thomson 2006).

This study will add to the meaning transfer model (McCracken 1989) by identifying which meanings transfer to organizations depending on the celebrity meanings. We anticipate that our findings will extend knowledge in the celebrity

S. J. Kim (✉)
University of Massachusetts Amherst, Amherst, MA, USA
e-mail: sejinkim@umass.edu

J. Allen et al. (eds.), *Celebrating the Past and Future of Marketing and Discovery with Social Impact*, Developments in Marketing Science: Proceedings of the Academy of Marketing Science, https://doi.org/10.1007/978-3-030-95346-1_8

endorsement literature and the meaning transfer model. Also, this study will extend the literature in celebrity endorsement to sport settings, specifically in eSports. Further, practitioners will benefit from the findings from the moderating effects of implicit self-theories.

The current study creates a new line of sponsorship and celebrity research in eSports. As eSports are in a developing phase, celebrity endorsements and sponsorship studies have not been widely discussed (Reitman et al. 2019). However, this study will be able to provide evidence of the importance of sponsorship opportunities in eSports.

Keywords Celebrity endorsement · eSports · Implicit self theory · Meaning transfer model

Tactical Churn of Contractual Services: An Analysis of the Phenomenon and the Determinants: An Abstract

Mona Hagebölling, Barbara Seegebarth, and David Woisetschläger

Abstract Due to the target group-specific pricing policies of service providers, different prices exist for the same service across customer groups like new or reacquired customers compared to existing customers. Current customers may notice these offers but do not receive any benefits for their loyalty. Consequently, they may react with a 'tactical churn' to the target group-specific pricing policy of companies without having a clear intention to switch their providers. A 'tactical churn' comprises two aspects: (1) the cancellation of an existing contract with the objective of obtaining better contractual conditions and (2) the intention to remain with the current provider. Thus, this study examines the phenomenon of tactical churn and its determinants by conducting 19 qualitative interviews. The findings give first evidence for the phenomenon of 'tactical churn' as new type of customer churn behavior. The majority of the interviewees was familiar with the phenomenon and had already tactically cancelled their service contracts in different industries. The study shows that especially the price comparisons of existing customers with up to four reference groups are decisive for tactical churn. These are (a) new customers of the current provider, (b) other existing customers of the current provider, (c) customers of other providers, and (d) the price/value-change in the case of automatic renewal of the contract. If the comparison is not in favor for existing customers, this has a negative effect on the perceived price fairness and appreciation. This results in the pronouncement of a cancellation of the service contract without the clear intention to switch providers, but with the intention to get a better deal. Further, moral obligation and subjective norms of tactical churn behavior have also been identified as possible determinants of tactical churn. With regard to the question why customers remain in the relationship, the findings indicate that their decision depends on both affective and calculative commitment.

Keywords Customer loyalty · Targeting · Fairness · Contractual services

---

M. Hagebölling (✉) · B. Seegebarth · D. Woisetschläger
Technical University of Braunschweig, Braunschweig, Germany
e-mail: m.hageboelling@tu-braunschweig.de; b.seegebarth@tu-braunschweig.de; d.woisetschlaeger@tu-braunschweig.de

J. Allen et al. (eds.), *Celebrating the Past and Future of Marketing and Discovery with Social Impact*, Developments in Marketing Science: Proceedings of the Academy of Marketing Science, https://doi.org/10.1007/978-3-030-95346-1_9

Digital Voice Assistants in Service Encounters: An Abstract

Carsten D. Schultz

Abstract Digital voice assistants are becoming a pervasive technology with the potential to change entire business processes and models. These voice assistants are at the forefront of organizational frontlines, service encounters, and customer experience. In the wake of digitalization and artificial intelligence, companies embrace such technologies by rule-based automating business processes. One area of application for digital voice assistants is service encounters in call centers. Research on call centers identifies service expertise, interaction competence, and linguistic qualities of human agents as key determinants of consumers' satisfaction and loyalty (e.g., Cheong et al. 2008; Dean 2004; Gerpott/Paukert 2012). This study investigates acceptance of digital voice assistants as call center agents. If consumers accept the technology in such service encounters, it questions whether digital voice assistants can either reduce workload or replace human call center agents.

The empirical results present a general willingness of consumers to engage with digital voice assistants in such service encounters. Consumers expect such service encounters to be free of effort and that the technical system is readily available, flexible, and reliable. Male consumers particularly emphasize technical usability. Even though the empirical results do not statistically support the effect of linguistic qualities, this finding can be attributed to the preexisting experience with voice systems in smartphones and smart speakers. Consumers consequently assume that digital voice assistants perform in service encounters at least as good as their personal devices. In contrast, consumers do not attribute much interaction competence to digital voice assistants. Consumers seem to be predominantly interested in the solving capabilities of digital voice assistants in the service encounter.

As a result, service expertise is perceived as more important than emotional value. Digital voice assistants need to primarily fulfill their perceived intended purpose if they are to assume the role of call center agents and resolve corresponding service tasks. Emotional value also positively affects consumers' perceived usefulness. Regarding the engagement with digital voice assistants, consumers value a

C. D. Schultz (✉)
University of Hagen, Hagen, Germany
e-mail: carsten.schultz@fernuni-hagen.de

J. Allen et al. (eds.), *Celebrating the Past and Future of Marketing and Discovery with Social Impact*, Developments in Marketing Science: Proceedings of the Academy of Marketing Science, https://doi.org/10.1007/978-3-030-95346-1_10

positive, enjoyable, and relaxed atmosphere. These aspects are in particular relevant for female consumers in the present service encounter setting.

Digital voice assistants should not only provide requested information but also process and resolve consumers' concerns. As a result, digital voice assistants should facilitate problem-solving in a professional service fashion. Based on their accessibility and usefulness, consumers anticipate digital voice assistants being informative, useful, and positive in service encounters. Consumers thus form favorable attitudes towards engaging with these digital assistants and are intending to use these assistants in the foreseeable future.

Keywords Artificial intelligence · Call center · Digital voice assistant · Emotional value · Interaction competence · Linguistic quality · Service encounter · Service expertise

Consumer Switching Behavior in Omnichannel Retailing Context: An Abstract

Anh Thi Van Nguyen, Robert McClelland, and Nguyen Hoang Thuan

Abstract Different from traditional shopping journey, omnichannel customers can move freely between channels in an omnichannel journey. They can start their customer journey in one channel and close deal at another channel and as there is no barrier between channels, the customers enjoy complete and seamless shopping experience. This behavior is also regarded as channel switching behavior, which is closely related to the "free-riding behavior". Since 2014, researchers observed two typical switching behaviors, namely, showrooming and webrooming. Showrooming is the behavior when the customers search for information about the product offline but purchase online (Basak et al. 2017; Bell et al. 2014; Rapp et al. 2015; Verhoef et al. 2015). Whereas, webrooming is the practice of researching a product online or on a mobile device but purchasing it offline (Kramer 2014).

In recent years, there has been growing research interest in customer showrooming and webrooming behavior in the omnichannel retailing context. Most of the research focused on how firms deploy strategies to retain customers during the whole shopping journey (Verhoef et al. 2015). In previous studies of the reasons behind channel switching, Verhoef, Neslin and Vroomen (2007) employed the theory of reasoned action to explain three reasons for channel switching in multichannel context which are low channel lock-in, cross-channel synergy, and channel attributes. Evidence for the attributes reasons have been mixed. Furthermore, there has been no detailed investigation of the determinants for the behavior in omnichannel context. The paper looks at these reasons from an interpretive perspective to propose a framework for omnichannel switching behaviors. Qualitative in-depth interviews were conduct with eighteen omnichannel customers of electronic goods retailers in Vietnam. The findings reinforced the three reasons for channel switching in the research shopper model by Verhoef, Neslin and Vroomen (2007). The synthesized qualitative result strengthened the previous argument on the influence of perceived channel attributes on switching behavior. Two other reasons for channel

A. T. Van Nguyen (✉) · R. McClelland · N. H. Thuan
RMIT University, Ho Chi Minh City, Vietnam
e-mail: anh.nguyenthivan3@rmit.edu.vn; robert.mcclelland@rmit.edu.vn; thuan.nguyenhoang@rmit.edu.vn

J. Allen et al. (eds.), *Celebrating the Past and Future of Marketing and Discovery with Social Impact*, Developments in Marketing Science: Proceedings of the Academy of Marketing Science, https://doi.org/10.1007/978-3-030-95346-1_11

switching were observed from respondents which are social influence, customer self-confidence in the behavior.

This study contributes a deeper understanding of the customer switching behavior to both academics and practitioners. It is the first study to undertake a qualitative study on the determinants of omnichannel switching behavior. However, it is beyond the scope of this study to examine the journey of customers during switching. The research is also unable to encompass the entire populations of customers as different groups of customers might have different switching preferences. This raises interest for future research in customer segmentation, channel choice and usage, and customer experience during channel switching in the omnichannel context.

Keywords Switching behavior · Omnichannel · Customer behavior · In-depth interviews

Transhumanist Technologies for the Transhumanist Consumer: An Abstract

Vitor Lima and Russell Belk

Abstract Over the last few years, tech companies, like Samsung, have been developing implantable healthcare devices to diagnose diseases and treat the human body from the inside (Lee et al. 2020). Although sounding likc a speculative fiction storyline, this high-tech scenario is at the heart of the Transhumanism movement. Transhumanists envision the creation of "more-than-humans" by the integration of cybernetic devices and biochemical solutions with the human body (Deretić and Sorgner 2016). Recently, scholars have begun to call for studies exploring the thus far undertheorized combination of emerging and speculative technologies and their relationships with consumer behavior and social implications (Schmitt 2019). To begin responding to these pleas, this conceptual work presents an overview of the Transhumanism movement, two of its technological domains, and psychosocial and ethical issues regarding consumers' acceptance of such technologies.

The *Dryware* transhuman domain encompasses machines that are attached to or implanted into the human body to enhance its biological condition. As an example, the North Sense is a miniaturized circuit board that allows for sensing Earth's magnetic field. It works as a compass and is attached to the sternum bone. Within this transhumanist context, a number of social and ethical issues arise. For instance, would those who undergo a surgical procedure to have a North Sense installed feel stigma, harassment, and even physical aggression from others lacking such enhancements? The second technological domain to be considered here is *Wetware*, which comprises biochemical technologies. As an example, in the case of genetic engineering, it is theoretically possible to select the sex, colors for eyes and hair, improved athletic abilities, cognitive skills, and so on. As of 2021, such a procedure can easily cost around US$ 25,000 per attempt at fertilization. Additionally, for some, bioengineering human life leads to the objectification and the instrumentalization of their lives (Habermas 2003).

The issues are numerous and much more complex than the pragmatic and technophilic view of human-technology interactions often considered in marketing and

V. Lima (✉) · R. Belk
York University, Toronto, ON, Canada
e-mail: lmv2607@yorku.ca; rbelk@schulich.yorku.ca

J. Allen et al. (eds.), *Celebrating the Past and Future of Marketing and Discovery with Social Impact*, Developments in Marketing Science: Proceedings of the Academy of Marketing Science, https://doi.org/10.1007/978-3-030-95346-1_12

consumer research (Kaliyamurthy and Schau 2019). If consumers are already implanting cybernetic body parts, editing genes, or trying to live forever, then we, as a society, must tackle the issues outlined here. Due to the nature of Transhumanism and the space required to elaborate on it, we have briefly noted only a few possibilities of related consumption practices and issues. Acknowledging that several areas remained untouched in this conceptual study, we suggest that future work explore not only market for additional transhumanist technologies but also their philosophical implications.

Keywords Transhumanism · Cyborgs · Dryware · Wetware · Technology · Human enhancement technology

Deserving Pleasure through Pain: An Abstract

Haley Hardman, Christian Barney, and Myles Landers

Abstract Approaching pleasure and avoiding pain is a central mechanism for survival (Leknes and Tracey 2008). Approaching pleasurable experiences is associated with positive outcomes (Arnold and Reynolds 2012), while pain is generally negative (Eccleston and Crombez 1999). It is a common notion that consumers actively avoid pain (Crowe and Higgins 1997; Higgins 1997), which is "an unpleasant sensory and emotional experience…" (International Associations for the Study of Pain 1994, p. 210). Although pain has negative connotations, there has been recent research that suggests consumers may actually approach pain in some instances (Keinan and Kivetz 2011; Scott, Cayla, and Cova 2017).

The current study examines the positive outcomes derived from pain. This study finds that undergoing certain activities, such as a wellness regime, may lead to perceptions of pain. Wellness regimes, in the form of a strict diet and exercise program, are often associated with pain (Liu, Mattila, and Bolton 2018). In fact, researchers studying fitness have found that pain is a fundamental component of exercise (O'Connor and Cook 1999). In addition to exercise, diets bring about bodily discomfort as well (Fuhrman et al. 2010). Undergoing pain results in a feeling of deservingness, which are the outcomes that are congruent with the actions taken by an individual (Cavanaugh 2014; Feather 1999, 2003). Seeing as deservingness is predicated on actions, a positive action should produce a positive outcome. Those who undergo pain in order to reach a goal are more deserving than those who do not (Toyama 2019). It was found that a sense of deservingness leads consumers to be more likely to treat themselves. If consumers partake in effortful, positive behavior, then their outcomes should be reflective of such effort and positivity (Feather 1999).

H. Hardman (✉) · M. Landers
Mississippi State University, Starkville, MS, USA
e-mail: heh189@msstate.edu; vlanders@business.msstate.edu

C. Barney
Georgia Southern University, Statesboro, GA, USA
e-mail: cb3496@msstate.edu

J. Allen et al. (eds.), *Celebrating the Past and Future of Marketing and Discovery with Social Impact*, Developments in Marketing Science: Proceedings of the Academy of Marketing Science, https://doi.org/10.1007/978-3-030-95346-1_13

The following study offers numerous implications. First, pain is analyzed in a way that examines positive outcomes rather than the typical negative consequences found in the literature. This showcases that pain is multifaceted and consumers may pursue it intentionally. By approaching this study from a wellness regime perspective, an extension is made into the health services and the exercise industry. Many gyms offer products in addition to their services (ex. smoothie bar, workout clothing) and by leveraging a deservingness appeal they may be able to enhance their sales. One of the major implications offered by this study is that practitioners may wish to find a way to instill a sense of deservingness in consumers. When consumers feel that they are deserving, it can lead to the purchase of a product to reward themselves for positive actions. Overall, this shows that pain can bring about positive outcomes as it increases one's sense of deservingness.

Keywords Pain · Deservingness · Wellness regime · Treat

From Birthdays to Anniversaries: The Rituals of Celebrating a Brand's Age Insights and Research Agenda: An Abstract

Nada Maaninou and Fabien Pecot

Abstract Many companies celebrate their brands' anniversary with various audiences and claims. Such celebrations are key opportunities for brands to showcase their identity, history, achievements, and future perspectives. While there is a clear interest from managers, brand anniversaries as a managerial practice lacks theoretical foundations.

Anthropologists and sociologists study people's birthday celebrations as (social) rituals. Management studies have developed research on organizational rituals, marketing researchers consider the role of rituals in the internal implementation of corporate heritage but to the best of our knowledge, no research has explored how the celebration of anniversaries of abstract objects (i.e., brands) are ritualized when projected to external audiences (i.e., consumers). In addition, the operationalization of temporality in specific ritualized events (i.e., brand anniversaries) is neglected. Building on three streams of literature (birthdays as rituals, organizational rituals, and corporate brand heritage), this research aims to extend theory on brand management by answering the following research objectives: (a) to understand the ritual associated with brand anniversaries celebrations; (b) to relate the brand anniversaries celebrations' ritual to brand temporality.

An exploratory methodological design mobilizes the qualitative analysis of 52 cases of brand anniversary celebrations (various locations, industries and age celebrated). Findings inform that such celebrations involve five key dimensions and seven symbolic meanings associated with specific temporal orientations, and with three major intended outcomes. The latter are consistent with an existing typology

N. Maaninou (✉)
EM Strasbourg Business School, Strasbourg, France
e-mail: nada.maaninou@em-strasbourg.eu

F. Pecot
TBS Business School, Barcelona, Spain
e-mail: f.pecot@tbs-education.es

J. Allen et al. (eds.), *Celebrating the Past and Future of Marketing and Discovery with Social Impact*, Developments in Marketing Science: Proceedings of the Academy of Marketing Science, https://doi.org/10.1007/978-3-030-95346-1_14

and functions of corporate rites. From these results, a research agenda presents three research proposals for further research on brand management.

Keywords Brand anniversary · Temporal perspective · Corporate rituals · Brand heritage · Corporate heritage · Brand management

What Are You Looking At? Using Gaze Following to Understand Web Browsing on E-commerce Sites: Insights from Eye-Tracking: An Abstract

Anil Mathur

Abstract Although website designers consider aesthetic appcal and usability in designing web pages, it is important to understand which areas of website or design elements are more appealing and informative to visitors than other design elements. Visitors will most likely be more inclined to spend more time looking at more appealing design elements than others. In turn, these appealing design elements will have greater influence on the purchase behavior of site visitors than other elements on the site. Two underlying processes might play a role in directing visitors to pay more attention to certain areas of the site as opposed to other areas: inward bias and eye gaze following.

The objective of this research is to examine the effect of inward bias and eye gaze following on the web surfing behavior of individuals on e-commerce sites. Essentially, inward bias means that in framed images people prefer those images in which figures/people face inwards as opposed to outward, particularly when these figures/people are located away from the center of the framed image toward the periphery (e.g., Chen and Scholl 2014; Minton, Sperber, and Hernik 2020; Palmer and Langlois 2017; Palmer, Gardner and Wickens 2008). The space in front of the person in the image is inherently more interesting than the space behind the person in the image because it represents the area where future action will take place.

Gaze following can be defined as "the act of following another person's line of regard" (Brooks and Meltzoff 2014, p. 171). Also, called deictic gaze, it "indicates spatial attention, suggests future actions, and defines the target of facial signals" (Shepherd 2010, p. 1). It serves as the basis of joint attention. The direction in which a person is looking indicates the objects he or she may be paying attention to, his or her interests, and possible intentions with respect to that object (Bock, Dicke, and Thier 2008).

A. Mathur (✉)
Hofstra University, Hempstead, NY, USA
e-mail: anil.mathur@hofstra.edu

J. Allen et al. (eds.), *Celebrating the Past and Future of Marketing and Discovery with Social Impact*, Developments in Marketing Science: Proceedings of the Academy of Marketing Science, https://doi.org/10.1007/978-3-030-95346-1_15

In an experimental study (female participants, $n = 66$) using eye tracking technology (Tobii screen-based eye tracking hardware, X3-120, and Tobii studio software) this study found evidence of inward bias among users of e-commerce sites. Also, although evidence was found that supported operation of eye gaze following, it was not conclusive. These findings have implications for designers of e-commerce sites in terms of how models and other elements of the page could be oriented to make them more appealing to shoppers and potentially produce more positive results.

Keywords Eye tracking · Inward bias · Gaze following · E-commerce sites

Facebook as a Source of Information about Presidential Candidates: An Abstract

Shawn T. Thelen and Boonghee Yoo

Abstract Social media has become a powerful tool for influencing opinions citizens have about politics, political candidates, and social issues. The social media environment today is characterized by a myriad of sources providing innumerable amounts of information, expressed as opinion or fact, about every imaginable subject in a public forum. There is some evidence that social media users do not exhibit different levels of trust in articles published by fictional versus a known news source (Sterrett et al. 2019). This counters prior research that found source cues important (Lee and Sundar 2013; The Media Project 2017) and information posted by trusted figures are far more credible than posted by non-trusted figures (Sterrett et al. 2019). The lack of clarity in results indicates research explaining people's view about the credibility of information presented in social media outlets is nascent and a fertile subject area for further research.

Prior research has examined models to explain message (Appelman and Sundar 2016) and medium credibility (Fadl Elhadidi 2019; Ognyanova and Ball-Rokeach 2015) as individual constructs as well as contributing to information credibility (Li and Suh 2015). Because of the desire to improve the understanding how the credibility of information is perceived on social media, specifically Facebook – the second most popular online platform and most popular social media source for news (Gramlich 2019) – we are employing the elaboration likelihood model (Li and Suh 2015) for application to Presidential candidates. Information Credibility is expected to be positively related to media dependency, interactivity, medium transparency, argument strength, information quality, and personal expertise. Understanding what influences information credibility on Facebook allows political marketers to understand how to best put forward information about Presidential candidates that will be accepted by voters.

In addition to assessing the ELM model, we ask voters which sources of information, e.g., friends, family, celebrities, news media, community leaders, are trustworthy enough to influence for which Presidential candidate they would cast their

S. T. Thelen (✉) · B. Yoo
Hofstra University, Hempstead, NY, USA
e-mail: shawn.t.thelen@hofstra.edu; boonghee.yoo@hofstra.edu

J. Allen et al. (eds.), *Celebrating the Past and Future of Marketing and Discovery with Social Impact*, Developments in Marketing Science: Proceedings of the Academy of Marketing Science, https://doi.org/10.1007/978-3-030-95346-1_16

vote. A ranking of most trusted sources about Presidential candidates on Facebook provides insight to political marketers which sources have the greatest impact on voters' decision-making process.

Keywords Facebook · Social media · Political marketing · Elaboration Likelihood Model (ELM) · Persuasion theory

Self-Augmentation and Consumer Experiences: An Exploratory Study: An Abstract

Anupama Ambika, Varsha Jain, and Russell Belk

Abstract Today, digital content is dominated by interactive and immersive technologies (Mckinesy 2019). Brands are rapidly adopting technologies such as Augmented Reality (AR) for virtual product experiences (Pantano 2015). AR refers to the superimposing of the digital content on consumers' real-world contexts, thereby bridging the gap between physical and virtual purchase situations (Mealy 2018). Two popular AR-based applications are Ikea place (furniture) and Youcam Makeup (cosmetics). At present, AR is on a growth trajectory, as immersive technology growth (pre-COVID-19) was pegged to exceed $55 billion by the year 2021(Research and Markets 2019). Existing research on AR focuses on user experiences, customer engagement, brand attitudes, and purchase intentions (Hilken et al. 2017; Kim and Hall 2019; Park and Yoo 2020; Scholz and Smith 2016). As technology increasingly intertwines with consumers' lives and decisions, it is essential to continue expanding the research into the lived experience of AR-mediated shopping (Chylinski et al. 2020). Hence this paper focuses on the self-augmentation experiences through the virtual product try-on apps. The virtual try-on apps let consumers try out virtual replicas of actual products (cosmetics, apparel, jewelry, etc.) on their real-time images, captured via tablet or smartphone-based selfie cameras. The context of the study is AR virtual try-on apps in the cosmetics industry, owing to their popularity and adoption by consumers. Based on the concepts of extended self, consumption experiences, self-referencing theory, and mental imagery (Belk 1988; Holbrook and Hirschman 1982; Lutz and Lutz 1978; Rogers et al. 1977), this study follows an exploratory approach using netnography and in-depth interviews. The initial findings suggest that using AR try-on tools helps consumers choose the products that enable them to craft unique self-expression rather than conforming to

A. Ambika · V. Jain (✉)
MICA, Ahmedabad, India
e-mail: anupama_fpm18@micamail.in; varsha.jain@micamail.in

R. Belk
York University, Toronto, ON, Canada
e-mail: rbelk@schulich.yorku.ca

J. Allen et al. (eds.), *Celebrating the Past and Future of Marketing and Discovery with Social Impact*, Developments in Marketing Science: Proceedings of the Academy of Marketing Science, https://doi.org/10.1007/978-3-030-95346-1_17

societal stereotypes. Further, AR facilitates experimentation with new consumption patterns, irrespective of age and gender, giving opportunities for consumers to embrace their unique interests. Consumers save their self-augmented images to share among connections via social media, indicating digital expression before actual purchase and use. Thus AR provides an opportunity for brands to be a part of consumers' virtual selves before actual consumption through digital expression. The study's findings open up new avenues for brands to be a meaningful part of consumer extended selves and the role of AR in enabling consumers to express their "true selves" which may be seen as more of an aspirational self given enhancements of face shape and eye size commonly employed in these apps.

Keywords AR · Self · Experience · Consumption · Virtual try-on

To Protect and Serve? The Impact of Retailers' Customer Policing Policies on Frontline Employees: An Abstract

Patrick B. Fennell, Melanie Lorenz, and James Mick Andzulis

Abstract Consumers are not always honest, nor do they always follow the rules. Research on deviant behaviors exhibited by consumers covers topics ranging from showrooming to shoplifting. Shoplifting can be a tremendous burden on retailers' bottom lines. While FLEs have traditionally served customers, the role of these employees has evolved and expanded to include monitoring and enforcement of customers' deviant behaviors. Thus, the role of FLEs has evolved into not only serving customers, but also to policing customer compliance. While academic studies have proposed the use of FLEs to help reduce deviant behavior, and despite acknowledgement of academia's limited insights on the relationship between employee guardianship and organizational commitment (Potdar, Garry, Guthrie, and Gnoth 2019, p 77), little is known about the impact of using FLEs in a guardianship capacity. Thus, the current work seeks to better understand the mechanisms and outcomes of expecting FLEs to act as guardians against consumers' deviant behaviors, in our case shoplifting.

The present study draws on appraisal theory of emotions and equity theory to investigate the impact of retailers' customer deviant behavior policies on FLEs. Three experiments shed light on the phenomenon. *Study 1* demonstrates that the addition of guardianship responsibilities to FLE duties incites anger and reduces perceptions of employee policy fairness. *Study 2* expands on these findings and explores how guardianship policy elements, such as permitting vs. requiring FLEs to confront shoplifters, affect employee perceptions of the policy. Specifically, study

P. B. Fennell (✉)
Salisbury University, Salisbury, MD, USA
e-mail: pbfennell@salisbury.edu

M. Lorenz
Florida Atlantic University, Boca Raton, FL, USA
e-mail: lorenzm@fau.edu

J. M. Andzulis
Ohio University, Athens, OH, USA
e-mail: drmick@ohio.edu

J. Allen et al. (eds.), *Celebrating the Past and Future of Marketing and Discovery with Social Impact*, Developments in Marketing Science: Proceedings of the Academy of Marketing Science, https://doi.org/10.1007/978-3-030-95346-1_18

2 examines the role of empowerment in explaining feelings of anger and policy fairness perceptions and introduces social implications of customer (bystander) relationships. The results demonstrate the adverse effects of requiring FLEs to engage shoplifters are exacerbated in the presence of loyal (vs. transactional) customers. *Study 3* explores additional policy elements such as prohibiting FLEs from approaching suspected shoplifters. This study demonstrates that as FLEs' job role anxiety increases, policy fairness perceptions become less favorable. Additionally, Study 3 expands on the previous studies by extending the phenomenon to include more managerially relevant employee responses in the form of turnover intentions.

Across three experiments and multiple settings, we generally establish the negative effect of guardianship behavior, in our case the shoplifting policies on FLEs attitudes and job behaviors. We also identify how and when deviant behavior policy requirements can affect outcomes such as perceptions of policy fairness and employee turnover intentions.

Keywords Frontline employees · Deviant behavior · Policy fairness · Turnover intentions

Brand Personality of Presidential Candidates: An Abstract

Shawn T. Thelen and Boonghee Yoo

Abstract Political marketing has become a separate discipline of its own as a result of the union between political science and marketing. Political branding has become a distinct sub-discipline within the political marketing field (Scammel 2015). Politicians running for office increasingly use branding strategies and techniques to the point that they are labeled "*brandidates*". Political professionals construct and present a politician's persona as a brand personality, similar to when products present a brand personality, which is eventually "bought" by voters. Academics studying political marketing and political operatives running campaigns continue to investigate how politicians' brand personalities connect with voters.

This research responds to the call for examining political branding utilizing a "*theoretical lens [concepts, theories, and frameworks] from other disciplines across marketing, psychology, and social sciences*" (Pich and Newman 2020, p.11). The purpose of this research is to determine which independent variables, societal priorities (post-materialism) for the country (Inglehart 1977, 1981), political orientation (Nail et al. 2009), and comparative life satisfaction (Meadow et al. 1992) explain voter preference for different political brand personalities in Presidential candidates.

In order to select which brand personality traits would be adopted, a review of literature addressing brand personality (Aaker 1997; Verable et al. 2005), political brand personality (Caprara et al. 2002; Guzman and Sierra 2009; Smith 2009), leadership traits important to voters (Pew Research 2015) was performed. The identified traits were employed on a bi-polar scale anchored by Biden and Trump to determine which trait was most associated with each of the Presidential candidates.

The Inglehart Index, utilized for decades in national and global research projects, was adopted to determine societal values most important to voters. Nail et al. (2009) initially developed the political orientation scale, equally balanced between conser-

S. T. Thelen (✉) · B. Yoo
Hofstra University, Hempstead, NY, USA
e-mail: shawn.t.thelen@hofstra.edu; boonghee.yoo@hofstra.edu

J. Allen et al. (eds.), *Celebrating the Past and Future of Marketing and Discovery with Social Impact*, Developments in Marketing Science: Proceedings of the Academy of Marketing Science, https://doi.org/10.1007/978-3-030-95346-1_19

vative and liberal issues, for researching political orientation and social cognition. Meadow et al. (1992) introduced the congruity life satisfaction scale (CLS) to assess a person's level of satisfaction is based on social and aspirational comparison to evoked standards.

Examining the relationship among political orientation, societal values, and life satisfaction with candidates perceived brand personality helps establish a theoretical foundation for understanding how voters select, support, and eventually vote for candidates. A greater understanding of traits, i.e., brand personality, voters seek in a President and factors contributing to these preferences, will result in deeper theoretical insight and understanding of their application in political campaigns. This research will aid politicians to be more adaptable to their target audiences.

Keywords Political marketing · Candidates · Brandidates · Branding · Political branding · Elections

The Effects of Response Strategies Used in Product-Harm Crisis on the Evaluation of the Product and Re-purchase Intention in Different Cultures: An Abstract

Fuat Erol and F. Zeynep Özata

Abstract Product-harm crises are becoming more widespread with each passing day, and these crises may cause many negative effects both on the firm/brand and stakeholders of the firm. Thus, managing a product-harm crisis is a challenging period, especially for the firms operating in different countries, since culture plays a vital role as a perceptual lens to shape and interpret information and other factors. As a matter of fact, cultural characteristics, namely uncertainty avoidance and individualism/collectivism, could determine various aspects such as how individuals will evaluate firm strategies (proactive vs passive), whether they will attribute blame to the firm, how they will process information (functional or emotional) in their evaluations for the product and how their expectations differ according to the firms' corporate reputation levels (high vs low). Therefore, two different studies with a 2 × 2 between-subjects factorial design were conducted. Study 1 was performed using the data obtained from Turkey selected as a collectivist structure with a high level of uncertainty avoidance country. It was concluded that blame attribution and negative emotions were serially mediated the effect of crisis response strategies on repurchase intention. Study 2 was conducted with the data obtained from the USA, which has an individualist structure and a low level of uncertainty avoidance; the functional evaluation was found to mediate the relevant process. Also, it was

This research has derived from the doctoral dissertation conducted under the supervision of Assoc. Prof. Dr. F. Zeynep Özata and accepted by Anadolu University Graduate School of Social Sciences. This research was supported by the Anadolu University Scientific Research Projects Commission under Grant [1908E140].

F. Erol (✉)
Karamanoğlu Mehmetbey University, Karaman, Turkey
e-mail: ferol@kmu.edu.tr

F. Z. Özata
Anadolu University, Eskişehir, Turkey
e-mail: fzozata@anadolu.edu.tr

J. Allen et al. (eds.), *Celebrating the Past and Future of Marketing and Discovery with Social Impact*, Developments in Marketing Science: Proceedings of the Academy of Marketing Science, https://doi.org/10.1007/978-3-030-95346-1_20

observed that corporate reputation had a moderating role on the indirect effect of firm strategies in both studies, where these effects also showed differences between studies depending on the culture. While proactive efforts of the firm with the high reputation level appreciated more in the collectivist and high level of uncertainty avoidance country, proactive efforts of the firm with the low reputation level provided better results in individualist and low level of uncertainty avoidance country. Theoretically, culture causes differentiation of individuals' information processing, blame attribution, and perceptions of corporate reputation. Thus, practitioners are advised to understand the cultural characteristics of the market they serve for taking appropriate steps in the face of product-harm crisis, especially for creating the correct message content or offering satisfactory compensation.

Keywords Product-harm crisis · Product recall · Corporate reputation · Attributed blame · Uncertainty avoidance · Collectivism/individualism

Taking the Conversation Offline?: The Impact of Response Strategies on Potential Hotel Guests: An Abstract

Pia Furchheim, Anja Collenberg, and Steffen Müller

Abstract Online reviews have proliferated in recent years – especially in the tourism sector. For potential customers, they present a fast and convenient way to compare and evaluate service providers (Sparks, So, and Bradley 2016). Accordingly, the consequences and effects of online reviews on future clients have sparked interest in the research community for a while (e.g., Cheung, Lee, and Rabjohn 2008; Kwok and Xie 2016; Mauri and Minazzi 2013). While a vast body of research has investigated the effects of online reviews for consumers, this paper studies the effect of different response strategies and its impact on potential customers' evaluations such as trust and subsequently booking intention.

In study 1 (n = 399), we test four different response strategies that hotels and restaurants can use to reply to negative online in an experimental setting. We assigned participants to one of four conditions (hotel response: explanation, sending a private message, explanation and sending a private message, no reply). We incorporated the hotel response directly under the review to create the illusion of a real online review. The control group only saw the online review with no reply. We find that that an extensive response strategy has the strongest influence on trust. Sending a private message only might be beneficial in dealing with the immediate service recovery (i.e., the customer who wrote the review) but it does not lead to trust inferences for third party stakeholder (i.e., online review readers). Moreover, in line with existing literature, no reply did not produce any favorable inferences.

In study 2 (n = 801), we additionally manipulate the severity of the service failure described in the online review and show that this is an important boundary condition. We applied a 2 (severity: medium; severe) × 4 (Hotel response: explanation, private message, explanation and private message, no reply) between-subject design. We used the same stimulus material from study 1 for the medium case. Additionally, we altered the hotel review for the severe case. Study 2 corroborates the findings of study 1. All three reply strategies increased the trust towards the hotel. Trust in turn, positively affected booking intention. The combined approach

P. Furchheim (✉) · A. Collenberg · S. Müller
ZHAW School of Management and Law, Winterthur, Switzerland
e-mail: furc@zhaw.ch; cole@zhaw.ch; muef@zhaw.ch

J. Allen et al. (eds.), *Celebrating the Past and Future of Marketing and Discovery with Social Impact*, Developments in Marketing Science: Proceedings of the Academy of Marketing Science, https://doi.org/10.1007/978-3-030-95346-1_21

(explanation and private message) had the strongest effect on trust in general. However, results of the moderated mediation indicate that this type of recovery strategy is particularly favorable in case of a medium service failure while its effect is buffered in case of a severe service failure. The findings of study 2 therefore suggest the effect of recovery efforts (i.e., replying to online reviews) are more fruitful and pronounced for cases that are not severe whereas the effect diminishes in case of severe service failures.

Keywords Online reviews · Service recovery · Response strategies · Service failure

Consumers' Environmental Sustainability Perceptions on Their Attitude: The Moderating Effect of Price: An Abstract

Gözde Erdogan, Joan Llonch Andreu, and Maria del Carmen Alarcon del Amo

Abstract In the present, brands are seeking new ways to engage with customers (Ind et al. 2013). They listen to their brand communities and ask questions to customers to test their offerings (Füller et al. 2008; Gouillart 2014) since consumers are increasingly seeking solutions to their concerns to create a better world. Likewise, they make their purchase decisions guiding by their moral values (Hollenbeck and Zinkhan 2010). Hence, they push companies to carry out corporate social responsibility (CSR) practices (Iglesias et al. 2018). On the other hand, some studies also showed that consumers demonstrate closeness to brands that care about well-being, security, equality, and respect (i.e., Shaw et al. 2005). In other words, consumers' choices may depend on their higher-order needs for social, economic, and environmental justice (Kotler et al. 2010). Environmental sustainability is one of the ethical actions that companies should perform and many firms noticed the importance of it and give importance to their CSR activities to get a competitive position by helping to preserve natural resources, minimize waste, and reduce emissions (Krause et al. 2009).

This paper focuses on the relationship between environmental sustainability perception and different consumer behaviors such as consumer loyalty, satisfaction, and purchase intention: it considers this relationship in the light of moderating effect of price. Environmental sustainability actions can positively encourage consumers' attitudes. However, sustainability practices can increase the cost of opera-

G. Erdogan (✉)
Universidad de Deusto, San Sebastian, Spain
e-mail: gozdeerdogan@deusto.es

J. L. Andreu
Universitat Autonoma de Barcelona, Barcelona, Spain
e-mail: joan.llonch@uab.cat

Maria del Carmen Alarcon del Amo
Universidad de Murcia, Murcia, Spain
e-mail: mcarmenalarcon@um.es

J. Allen et al. (eds.), *Celebrating the Past and Future of Marketing and Discovery with Social Impact*, Developments in Marketing Science: Proceedings of the Academy of Marketing Science, https://doi.org/10.1007/978-3-030-95346-1_22

tions, and it may lead organizations to charge a higher price for their goods and services. Therefore, the price may have a moderating effect between these different consumer attitudes and environmental sustainability actions of the companies. In this research, the Social & Exchange Theory was implemented. This theory provides to measure the cause-and-effect relationship between sustainability practices and different consumer attitudes. On the other hand, a quantitative research technique was conducted to test the relationship between these variables through an online survey. The survey methodology was conducted to test the hypotheses and it was distributed to 454 random participants regardless of their functions, ages, and genders to make a heterogonous composition from Istanbul, Turkey. The findings confirmed the positive relationship between environmental sustainability actions and consumer attitudes. Besides, it also confirmed that price has a moderating effect between these actions of the companies and consumer attitudes. This research shows that consumers care about environmental issues as long as the price is reasonable. Likewise, firms need to consider the optimal price level by conducting environmental sustainability practices to get a competitive position in the market.

Keywords Environmental sustainability · Consumer loyalty · Consumer satisfaction · Consumer purchase intention · The price effect

Brand Disengagement on Social Media Platforms: An Abstract

Björn Kruse and Carsten D. Schultz

Abstract After the initial course of user-driven dissemination, organizational use of social media has taken hold in recent years. Even though Facebook still maintains the largest user base, the landscape of social media platforms has become more diverse. Consequently, brands are adjusting their social media strategies and allocate their budgets accordingly. Even though a broad body of literature exists that discusses strategies of brand engagement in social media and the subsequent benefits of extending relevant activities, there is another side to the story. Several new social media platforms have emerged serving different purposes, thus creating challenges for brands to target the right customer base. This dynamic environment challenges brands to continuously adjust their social media strategies. In particular, brands can no longer rely on one or two social media platforms alone, as more niche platforms increase in significance.

Based on Facebook, our study investigates 23 brands of four industries (Banking, Automotive, Retailing, Apparel) and demonstrates different types of organizational exit strategies from established social media communities. Besides outright abandoning their online communities, brands can reduce either output quality or lower the frequency of their activities, thereby upsetting their communities and potentially harming activities on other social media platforms. Overall, we identify four exit strategy archetypes based on brands' general efforts to pursue an exit (long posting intervals, less activity, and less own content) and the speed at which the disengagement takes place. In consequence, current research tends to over-emphasize the importance of expanding the use of social media, while largely ignoring reverse activities taking place on these platforms. Practice already deals with the phenom-

B. Kruse (✉)
South Westphalia University, Meschede, Germany
e-mail: kruse.bjoern@fh-swf.de

C. D. Schultz
University of Hagen, Hagen, Germany
e-mail: carsten.schultz@fernuni-hagen.de

J. Allen et al. (eds.), *Celebrating the Past and Future of Marketing and Discovery with Social Impact*, Developments in Marketing Science: Proceedings of the Academy of Marketing Science, https://doi.org/10.1007/978-3-030-95346-1_23

enon, using different ways of disengagement that range from slowly decreasing activity to abandoning communities entirely.

The social media landscape will continue to grow in the foreseeable future. For instance, Facebook is still expected to be an integral part of social media brand activities, but not maintaining its (prior) monopoly. Our study is only a first (explorative) step to shed light on the adverse side effects of having to manage a growing social media portfolio and operating on a budget that may not be growing as exponentially as the social media landscape. Social media research has to provide guidance on how to handle different approaches of disengagement and provide suitable methods to re-adjust the social media strategies. We hope that our initial results provide an avenue for future research on different aspects of brands' disengagement in social media.

Keywords Abandoning · Disengagement · Exit strategy · Organizational archetypes · Post frequency · Post interval · Post length · Post number · Social media

Understanding Omnichannel Customer Experience through Brand Trust and Its Impact on Shopping Intention: An Abstract

Francisco Jesús Guzmán Martínez, Ana Valeria Calvo Castro, and Lizet Marina González Salgado

Abstract An omnichannel experience occurs when a customer orders from multiple platforms (omnichannel retailing) and this order is filled from any location using inventory and other fulfillment assets flexible across channels (Taylor 2019). Previous literature indicates there are five omnichannel experience dimensions; connectivity, integration, consistency, flexibility, and personalization (Shi et al. 2020). Even though there are several industries impacted by the development of the omnichannel experience in the market, studies related with this topic mainly focus on retailers whose main activity is the sale of goods (Alexander and Blazquez 2020; Shi et al. 2020; Shin and Oh 2017), not services.

Hence, this is particularly important to investigate considering that the omnichannel experience in the service industry is growing; specially, the entertainment and arts industry reflects a growing trend of 15% accumulated value from 2015 to 2019, representing 1.5B USD (Euromonitor 2019). Moreover, the cinema category represents one of the key drivers of this growth, reaching 58.9 million USD (Euromonitor 2019).

The results revealed that three omnichannel dimensions labeled as connectivity, consistency and flexibility, were good predictors associated with brand trust, which further impact customer shopping intention. In contrast, integration and personalization were not significantly associated. Hence, this study offers insights regarding customer experience in the service industry that build on previous omnichannel experience literature (Grewal 2009; Shi 2020); particularly on customer shopping experience and how the different dimensions influence the customer behavior towards brand trust and how they impact customers shopping intention.

For retail practitioners, our findings suggest that brand trust is a significant determinant when discussing a customer's shopping intention. For the service industry,

F. J. G. Martínez (✉) · A. V. C. Castro · L. M. G. Salgado
EGADE Business School, Mexico City, Mexico
e-mail: paco.guzman@tec.mx; avaleria.calvo@tec.mx; a01093049@itesm.mx

J. Allen et al. (eds.), *Celebrating the Past and Future of Marketing and Discovery with Social Impact*, Developments in Marketing Science: Proceedings of the Academy of Marketing Science, https://doi.org/10.1007/978-3-030-95346-1_24

the results of this study suggest that managers must focus on three dimensions. First, connectivity, that relies on a seamless unification of brick-and-mortar and online channel features, like commodities information and continuous and connected reading content across channels. Second, consistency, across channels; evenness of intangibles, like service level, performance and responsiveness. Third, flexibility; provide flexible options from one channel to the other and continuity when migrating tasks.

Keywords Omnichannel customer experience · Consistency · Flexibility · Connectivity · Brand trust · Shopping intention

Effects of Distribution Channel Types and Determinants Influencing the Market Share of National Brands and Private Labels: An Abstract

Philipp Brüggemann, Rainer Olbrich, and Carsten D. Schultz

Abstract The competition between national brands (NBs) and private labels (PLs) as well as the regulatory framework for competition have led to a noticeable decline in NBs' market share in the retail sector (Olbrich et al. 2016; Quelch and Harding 1996). In recent decades, this development has been attributed to intense – sometimes ruinous – price competition, resulting in increased concentration in the retail sector and the proliferation of PLs (Hyman et al. 2010; Olbrich et al. 2016). Manufacturers therefore need to develop strategies to maintain competitive advantages (Cuneo et al. 2019; Verhoef et al. 2002). Knowledge about determinants of NBs' market share and the impact of distribution channels supports manufacturers and retailers by developing and executing effective marketing strategies. This study consequently analyzes determinants of the NBs' market share and unravels differences and similarities regarding different types of distribution channels based on 7.211.154 purchases from 98.326 households. The household data refers to the three distribution channels: discounters, supermarkets, and hypermarkets.

An increase in regular price of PLs, the share of NB price promotions, and the share of NB variety positively affect the market share of NBs across distribution channels. The share of PL price promotions has surprisingly no significant impact on the market share of NBs. Retailers do not need to use changes in share of PL price promotions, as they can control the market share by changes in the share of NB price promotions. Regarding the types of distribution channels, an increase in the regular price of PLs exerts the strongest positive effect on the market share of NBs in supermarkets. An increase in the share of NB price promotions, on the other hand, only has a weak positive effect on the market share of NBs in supermarkets. Our findings are in particular beneficial for retailers evaluating the effect of price changes and shares of promotional prices. Due to the prohibition of retail price

P. Brüggemann (✉) · R. Olbrich · C. D. Schultz
University of Hagen, Hagen, Germany
e-mail: philipp.brueggemann@fernuni-hagen.de; lehrstuhl.marketing@fernuni-hagen.de; carsten.schultz@fernuni-hagen.de

J. Allen et al. (eds.), *Celebrating the Past and Future of Marketing and Discovery with Social Impact*, Developments in Marketing Science: Proceedings of the Academy of Marketing Science, https://doi.org/10.1007/978-3-030-95346-1_25

maintenance, manufacturers can only exert a limited influence. For the branded goods industry, the change in the share of NB variety is especially relevant, because an increase in the share of NB variety has the strongest positive effect on the market share of NBs in supermarkets, discounters, and hypermarkets. Further, the market share of NBs in supermarkets increases as brand preference intensifies. This is particularly relevant for the branded goods industry, since both share of NBs variety and brand preference of households can be influenced by the manufacturer brand industry by, for example, product innovations and advertising campaigns.

Keywords Brand management · Distribution channels · FMCG · Household panel · Market share · National brand · Private label · Retailing · Sales

Something Good Comes out of Crises: An Empirical Study on Responding Strategies to Business Misdeeds: An Abstract

Lei Huang

Abstract While no firm wants a corporate misdeed scandal, firms pay a high price immediately in order to repair the damages. The current study aims to address the following research questions: (1) how consumers react to three major crisis management approaches: the prompt acknowledgement of the misdeed, the response plan to address the misdeed, and the correction plan for the misdeed; and (2) how these approaches impact on current and potential consumers. Particularly, this research examines the influences of these approaches on different types of misdeeds: either product/service performance related (PPR) or business ethics related (BER).

The results from 440 participants suggest that a promptness apology is important for current consumers but not for potential consumers. More importantly, the response plan has less impact on the current consumers when a misdeed is business ethics related than product performance related while the correction plan is more important when a misdeed is product performance related compared with business ethics related misdeeds; for the potential consumer, on the contrary, the response plan has less impact when a misdeed is product performance related than business ethics related.

This research provides a framework for brand managers to craft just-right, just-in-time responses and remedy strategies. It offers brand managers a systematic way to gauge what they should say and do during that hard time. As various response strategies have their own advantages and disadvantages, the findings in the current study suggests that the relative efficacy of remedy strategies depends on the type of

L. Huang (✉)
State University of New York (SUNY) at Fredonia, Fredonia, NY, USA
e-mail: huang@fredonia.edu

J. Allen et al. (eds.), *Celebrating the Past and Future of Marketing and Discovery with Social Impact*, Developments in Marketing Science: Proceedings of the Academy of Marketing Science, https://doi.org/10.1007/978-3-030-95346-1_26

business misdeed as well as the status of the consumers in the market. Managers should evaluate the situation to determine which remedy action(s) is the most effective for the situation and then tailor their responses according to the crisis situation.

Keywords Business ethics · Product performance · Misdeed · Scandal · Crisis management

Using Celebrities' Voices for Social Causes: An Investigation into how Attachment to Celebrities Impacts Consumers' Behaviors toward Social Causes: An Abstract

Gina A. Tran and Taehoon Park

Abstract Celebrities have a wide and captive audience, which may be used to effectively raise awareness, impact donations and influence people to volunteer for causes. Celebrities as human brands have the power to impact change in a potentially positive way. The present study is the first to investigate the role of brand attachment in the celebrity as a human brand and social cause context.

An essential goal of charities is to encourage the public to participate in philanthropic activities through both financial donations and volunteer efforts. The massive success of "The Ice Bucket Challenge" in 2014 indicates the importance of celebrities as the message source, with various public figures such as entrepreneurs, athletes, actors, actresses, and singers sharing the message to get engaged and involved in the social cause. This research examined the role of celebrity message sources in philanthropic activity communication. Specifically, this study suggests a model explaining when and why consumers comply with a celebrity's philanthropic message based on self-verification, self-enhancement, and attachment theories. This study tested a model where an individual's actual and ideal self-congruities with a celebrity positively affect attachment to the celebrity human brand, which leads to receptivity towards the celebrity-endorsed message and willingness to donate money and time to the cause. This study used cross-sectional data to test the hypotheses. Structural equations modeling (AMOS 26) was used to analyze the responses. Questionnaire items were adopted and adapted from previously-validated scales.

The findings indicated that an individual's attachment to the celebrity human brand is positively related to their receptivity towards the endorser's message and willingness to donate money and time. This research integrated identity and brand attachment theories to explain processes through which celebrities influence individuals' behaviors regarding social causes. The results contribute to the existing

G. A. Tran (✉) · T. Park
Florida Gulf Coast University, Fort Myers, FL, USA
e-mail: gtran@fgcu.edu; tpark@fgcu.edu

J. Allen et al. (eds.), *Celebrating the Past and Future of Marketing and Discovery with Social Impact*, Developments in Marketing Science: Proceedings of the Academy of Marketing Science, https://doi.org/10.1007/978-3-030-95346-1_27

bodies of knowledge on celebrity endorsement and cause marketing. Clearly, an individual's attachment to a celebrity influences receptivity towards social cause messages from the human brand, which positively affects willingness to donate money and time. The results contribute to the existing bodies of knowledge on celebrity endorsement and cause marketing with empirical support for the effect of celebrity endorsement in philanthropic communication.

Keywords Human brand · Social cause · Willingness to donate · Attachment · Receptivity towards message

Consumer Motivations in Emerging Markets: Risk, Uncertainty, and Emotions: An Abstract

Gregory Kivenzor

Abstract Consumer culture theory developed for and tested in more stable Western economies insufficiently explains the dynamics of consumption preferences in emerging markets (EMs) (Nielsen et al. 2018). EM consumers remain under emotional stress stemming from steep political and socio-economic transformations. COVID-19 crisis exacerbates already acute concerns, disrupts many established consumption practices, and amplifies the feeling of uncertainty for the future.

The main research question of the present conceptual study attempts to address: which compulsory and hedonic drivers motivate a substantial increase of luxury consumption in EMs? Addressing this question, our study examines a critical role played by social group subcultures as dominant factors affecting the purchasing decision-making process of EM consumers. We also discuss the antecedents and consequences of consumption choice in social environments affected by cultural transformation. First, we analyze the effect of emotional stress induced by the social transition on consumer value orientation. Second, we review the process of social migration in EMs and the dynamics of intrapersonal psychology in light of the prevailing cultural norms in desired social groups. Third, we examine cultural transformation in EMs at the societal and group level as a factor motivating hedonic consumption. Fourth, we suggest the probabilistic model explaining the phenomenon of burgeoning luxury consumption in EMs resulting from the consumer volitional and compulsory choices. Finally, we discuss the managerial implications and directions of future research.

In Ems, upward-moving 'social migrants' have a strong desire to join higher-status social groups but lack information about the cultural and consumption norms of those groups. We theorize that the uncertainty of choice torments them, affects their self-concept, and motivates consumers to overspend on luxuries to ascertain social acceptance. In other words, the desire to join a particular group at a higher social level serves as a compulsory factor making aspirants allocate an excessive share of their income for the public consumption of luxury in an attempt to signal

G. Kivenzor (✉)
University of Connecticut, Stamford, CT, USA
e-mail: gregory.kivenzor@uconn.edu

J. Allen et al. (eds.), *Celebrating the Past and Future of Marketing and Discovery with Social Impact*, Developments in Marketing Science: Proceedings of the Academy of Marketing Science, https://doi.org/10.1007/978-3-030-95346-1_28

their perceived congruity with a target social group. Middle-class consumers have to resolve the major discord between the perceived risk of non-acceptance by the target group – if they spend too little – and acute financial loss of over-spending – if they spend too much.

The suggested conceptual framework recognizes the emotional stress of middle-class consumers caused by political and socio-economic uncertainties in EM societies and provides a different perspective on the "pattern-level dynamics of the social world" (Brewer 2016). Deriving from the analysis above, we outline a shift of cultural norms and extensive social migration as the primary antecedents of luxury consumption, while hedonic motivation becomes a secondary factor coming into play mostly upon acceptance by the desired social group.

Keywords Emerging markets · Cultural transition · Middle-class · Consumer motivations · Social group

How Technology Influences Customer Experience in Complex Service Settings: An Abstract

Maarten Bosma and Laurence Dessart

Abstract The holistic and contingent construct of customer experience is widely researched in contemporary marketing. While we know that technology may strongly impact and change customer experience for businesses and consumers, little is known about how technology may create motivations, or conversely barriers for customers in interacting with businesses providing complex services (Kranzbühler et al. 2018). The aim of this paper is to identify the impact that technology adoption has on customer experience in complex service settings. A specific onlook at complex service settings is taken as an extreme case of customer experience, where technology may be particularly helpful or challenging in a B-to-B-to-C setting.

This research is done based on an analysis of the literature on customer experience and technology adoption. In particular, the insurance industry is taken as an industry focus, because it epitomizes the uniqueness of complex service settings (e.g. Mikolon et al. 2015).

The exhaustive review of the literature allows developing a conceptual model whereby technology has the potential to positively or negatively influence customer experience, due to the motivation and barriers it generates for customers. Specific technology related barriers and motivations are thus put forward as impacting customer experience. The impact of these motivations and barriers is shown to be further enhanced by industry-specific and contextual factors present in complex service settings.

A conceptual model is proposed, evidencing technology-related motivations and barriers, moderated by context-specific industry factors, influence customer experience. The research contributes to the growing field of customer experience and its relationship with technology (e.g. Singh and Söderland 2019; Vakulenko et al. 2019), by stressing the particularly vivid challenges encountered in complex service settings. This conceptual model helps businesses operating in complex services

M. Bosma (✉) · L. Dessart
University of Liège, Liège, Belgium
e-mail: m.bosma@uliege.be; laurence.dessart@uliege.be

J. Allen et al. (eds.), *Celebrating the Past and Future of Marketing and Discovery with Social Impact*, Developments in Marketing Science: Proceedings of the Academy of Marketing Science, https://doi.org/10.1007/978-3-030-95346-1_29

directing their resources toward customer experience optimization, and opens a new agenda to research interactions between different constructs and antecedents.

Keywords Customer experience · Technology · Complex services · Insurances · Technology acceptance · Technology adoption · Customer journey

Secondary Market and New Release: An Abstract

Yeon Ju Baik

Abstract Durable goods are frequently traded in the used market or secondary market after a certain period of use. Due to the possibility of disposal in the secondary market, new buyers' willingness to pay in the primary market depends on thc salvage value of the used product. On the other hand, the used product can also substitute new products in the primary market, lowering the willingness to pay. Therefore, the demand changes in the primary market induced by the secondary market transaction can affect the frequency of new releases (launch) and the technology advancement of durable goods. This paper investigates the monopolistic manufacturer's new release and investment decisions when used product is traded in the secondary market. A theoretical model that can capture consumers' choice and the manufacturer's dynamic decision is built, and the equilibrium effect is analyzed. I simulated the impact of the quality difference between the new and used on the probability of new release and the size of used goods demand. The effect of the level of friction in the secondary market, measured by the additional cost of selling used goods, on the secondary market and release choices is also analyzed. I find the product with the larger quality gap between the new and used is likely to have a longer wait time before the new launch and higher used goods demand. Product with better quality is expected to increase the demand for used products because of the substitution induced by the higher price. Additionally, the simulation shows how external factors can affect the primary and secondary market equilibrium. I find empirical evidence from smartphone industry which support theoretical result. First, the product with higher specs, such as better CPU, higher resolution, is likely to have a longer wait time before the new launches. Second, the increase in the used product demand occurring with the new launches of high-end products is likely to be larger than the mid-low range product market changes. Last, the effect of external changes in the primary market is verified by the increase in used product transactions after enacting the policy, which restricts the subsidy on the new mobile phones. The study explains why the manufacturers are diversifying their product portfolio and

Y. J. Baik (✉)
University of Wisconsin-Madison, Madison, WI, USA
e-mail: ybaik2@wisc.edu

J. Allen et al. (eds.), *Celebrating the Past and Future of Marketing and Discovery with Social Impact*, Developments in Marketing Science: Proceedings of the Academy of Marketing Science, https://doi.org/10.1007/978-3-030-95346-1_30

increasing the friction in the secondary market. The manufacturer may need to consider the potential cannibalization effect, which may be differed by the quality when they make a pricing, new launching decision.

Keywords Used goods · Durable goods · Secondary market · New launch

The Interplay of Marketing and Creativity Capabilities in International Marketing: Effectuation-Prediction Perspective: An Abstract

Yoel Asseraf and Kalanit Efrat

Abstract The purpose of this study is to advance our understanding of the effectuation (EF) and predictive (PR) logics interplay and its consequences on international performance. EF's proponents emphasize unplanned creative entrepreneurial thinking and embrace creativity capabilities. In contrast, PR's proponents highlight the need for analytical, planned managerial thinking and build on marketing capabilities. Specifically, this study examines the role of tolerance for failure as an antecedent of EF-PR logics and investigate their interplay on international performance through the lens of their reflected capabilities: organizational creativity and marketing capabilities. A survey-based quantitative study was used.

The findings reveal that tolerance for failure impacts international performance only indirectly through creativity and marketing capabilities. The findings of our model provide support to the view that tolerance for failure does indeed have a positive impact on organizations, as it had a positive influence on organizational creativity and marketing capabilities. The strong impact of tolerance for failure on organizational creativity was expected and is in line with the recent notion of Pisano (2019) that tolerance for failure is an important characteristic of innovative thinking. In contrast to previous EF-PR studies, PR logic in the form of marketing capabilities was found to be more beneficial to international performance then EF logic in the form of organizational creativity.

However, while under international circumstances, the trophy is awarded to PR logic, the interaction effect of both capabilities on international performance was found negative. To enhance international performance, managers would do well (a) to encourage a tolerance-for-failure culture in their organizations, as it will facilitate promoting creativity and marketing capabilities, (b) to slough off the entrepreneur's skeptical approach of market research, and (c) to embrace a combined 'predictable effectuation' logic but to exercise caution in placing excessive reliance on creativity.

Y. Asseraf (✉) · K. Efrat
Ruppin Academic Center, Kfar Monash, Israel
e-mail: yoela@ruppin.ac.il; kalanite@ruppin.ac.il

J. Allen et al. (eds.), *Celebrating the Past and Future of Marketing and Discovery with Social Impact*, Developments in Marketing Science: Proceedings of the Academy of Marketing Science, https://doi.org/10.1007/978-3-030-95346-1_31

The research on the EF-PR tension in the field of international marketing is still in its infancy, comprising mostly qualitative studies focusing solely on the benefits of EF logic. This quantitative study deepens our understanding of the joint roles of EF and PR logics on international performance.

Keywords Marketing capabilities · Creativity capabilities · International performance · Tolerance for failure

Analyzing the Downstream Consequences of a Politician's Snarky Attack on Opponents: An Abstract

Sphurti Sewak

Abstract With the advent of social media, politicians have found a new avenue to connect to their supporters and reach out to many others who could be potential supporters. This is evident from growing money spent by politicians on digital advertising, with a Statista report stating that about 1.8 billion USD were spent on the 2018 midterm elections and this amount increased to 2.8 billion dollars during the 2020 presidential elections (Statista 2021). Our research takes a look at these social media posts by politicians and their persuasiveness, measured as the attitude towards the candidate. Grounded in Persuasion Knowledge Model (PKM), our theorizing is based on accessibility to persuasion motives, which in this case would be garnering votes by the politician.

A large body of research has explored how individuals respond to political marketing efforts. However, little is known about how the content of a politician's posts on social media can influence the voter's decision. This is an issue of significant theoretical and practical relevance since research has recognized that Twitter has been extensively utilized by effectively communicating with existing supporters and engaging new ones (Bode and Dalrymple 2016). Political persuasion is an interesting amalgamation of political and marketplace activities and studying persuasiveness in a political context can be applied to other consumption contexts (Kim, Rao, and Lee 2009).

This research makes several important contributions. Prior research has recognized that the impact of social media on civic and political participation has increased dramatically over the last twenty years (Boulianne 2020). However, no research has established a link between a politician's posts and resultant attitude formed towards the candidate, improving our understanding in this regard. Further, this research makes a theoretical contribution to the stream of political marketing, persuasion, and social media literature. This research also has practical implications for managers as many times, organizations openly support political candidates, which could potentially gain more customers or lose customers. A politician's posts

S. Sewak (✉)
Florida International University, Miami, FL, USA
e-mail: ssewak@fiu.edu

J. Allen et al. (eds.), *Celebrating the Past and Future of Marketing and Discovery with Social Impact*, Developments in Marketing Science: Proceedings of the Academy of Marketing Science, https://doi.org/10.1007/978-3-030-95346-1_32

predictive of attitude that will be formed by individuals could greatly impact the organization's plan to support (or not) a certain candidate.

Keywords Social media · Twitter · Political marketing · Persuasion knowledge model

As if the Product is Already Mine: Testing the Effectiveness of Product Presentation via Augmented Reality versus Website and Real World: An Abstract

Thomas Alt, Franz-Rudolf Esch, and Franziska Krause

Abstract Since customer journeys take increasingly more place in the online sphere, the optimization of the digital product presentation becomes focal for scholars and practitioners alike. In terms of sensory richness, the reality offers the best potentials for an effective brand experience (Petit et al. 2019). For that reason, the reality-based product presentation should be considered as the benchmark for evaluating digital types of product presentation (Porter and Heppelmann 2017). However, multi-sensory brand experiences are difficult to evoke online (e.g., Beck and Crié 2018; Pantano et al. 2017; Yoo and Kim 2014).

Against this background, we investigate Augmented Reality's (AR) effectiveness on consumers' decision confidence and purchase intention. For this purpose, we develop a conceptual model identifying psychological ownership and customer inspiration as mediators. We apply the conceptual model in a series of two confirmatory studies using lab experiments. The model shows strong explanatory power and provides evidence for AR's superiority over the website-based product presentation. We also find evidence for the AR-based product presentation to be similarly effective as the reality-based product presentation. By determining the effectiveness of the AR-based product presentation compared to alternatives, we answered the call for comparative studies investigating AR's performance differential (e.g., Dacko 2017; Yaoyuneyong et al. 2016). The work of Dacko (2017) and Yaoyuneyong et al. (2016) suggested future research to conduct comparative studies in the field of AR. We are first in investigating the effectiveness of the AR-based product presentation compared to the website-based and reality-based alternatives.

T. Alt · F. Krause (✉)
EBS University of Business and Law, Oestrich-Winkel, Germany
e-mail: thomas.alt@henkel.com; franziska.krause@ebs.edu

F.-R. Esch
Esch Brand Consultants, Saarlouis, Germany
e-mail: f.-r.esch@esch-brand.com

J. Allen et al. (eds.), *Celebrating the Past and Future of Marketing and Discovery with Social Impact*, Developments in Marketing Science: Proceedings of the Academy of Marketing Science, https://doi.org/10.1007/978-3-030-95346-1_33

By means of a longitudinal study, we are able to show that AR-effects are stable over time and not affected by a novelty effect. Our study did not provide any evidence for the presence of a shiny new object syndrome promoting a short-lived overvaluation of AR which other scholars theoretically assumed (e.g., Bulearca and Tamarjan 2010; Hilken et al. 2017; Owyang 2010). In contrast, we found support for the classification of AR's components as not being novel for consumers anymore. Hence, we conclude that the reality-like effectiveness of the AR-based product presentation is of a durable nature.

Keywords Augmented reality · Digital product presentation · Psychological ownership · Customer inspiration

The Sporty Framing Effect: How Framing an Activity as Sporty Affects Consumer Engagement through Competitive Mindset and Social Value: An Abstract

Reynald Brion, Renaud Lunardo, and Jean-François Trinquecoste

Abstract Given the increasing popularity of sport related activities, such as esports – that is competitive video gaming –, this research builds on sport, experiential and consumer behaviour literatures to propose that consumers favour activities when they are framed as a sport. Because sports are socially valued, people would exhibit a more competitive mindset, then leading to more anticipated social value from the activity framed as sporty. Such social value would then be a driver of consumer engagement intention into the activity.

To test these predictions, Study 1 presented participants (N = 197) with "Kendama" (a Japanese activity) either framed as a sport or as a hobby. As hypothesized, results yielded a serial mediation whereby framing the activity as sporty indirectly increases engagement through the mediating effects of competitive mindset and social value.

We then considered narcissism as a moderator of this serial mediation. Indeed, narcissistic people tend to avoid shame in relation to others and to protect themselves with self-protection strategies. Therefore, we expected narcissistic people not to show the competitive mindset needed to engage in activities framed as sports.

Study 2 (N = 281) thus exposed participants to an activity called "Diabolo", a juggle game, framed as either a sport, or not. Study 2 replicated previous results, with a significant serial mediation emerging that linked the sporty framing, competitive mindset, social value and engagement intention. We also found a significant direct effect of the sporty framing of the activity on the willingness to engage in the activity. Interestingly, results also yielded narcissism as the moderator of this serial

R. Brion (✉) · R. Lunardo
KEDGE Business School, Talence, France
e-mail: reynald.brion02@kedgebs.com; renaud.lunardo@kedgebs.com

J.-F. Trinquecoste
Université de Bordeaux, Bordeaux, France
e-mail: jean-francois.trinquecoste@u-bordeaux.fr

J. Allen et al. (eds.), *Celebrating the Past and Future of Marketing and Discovery with Social Impact*, Developments in Marketing Science: Proceedings of the Academy of Marketing Science, https://doi.org/10.1007/978-3-030-95346-1_34

mediation, with narcissism moderating the relation between sporty framing and competitive mindset.

With this research, we provide evidence for the sporty framing effect, and show that merely framing an activity as a sport increases consumer engagement through the mediating role of competitive mindset and anticipated social value. Further, we have provided evidence for the notion that the sporty framing effect is observed only for people who are low in narcissism. For practitioners, this research thus highlights the potentials of framing an activity as sporty, with non-narcissistic people being identified as the main target for such a positioning of the activities framed as sporty.

Keywords Engagement · Sport · Narcissism · Competitive mindset · Social value · Experience

Opportunities and Challenges Facing AI Voice-Based Assistants: Consumer Perceptions and Technology Realities: An Abstract

Hannah R. Marriott and Valentina Pitardi

Abstract Where AI has become especially pivotal for users' interactions is in the case of voice-based assistants (VAs), such as Apple's Siri and Amazon's Alexa. From what is initially perceived as being a tool to play music, read out news reports and set timers, VAs have developed considerably in recent years and their functionality goes way beyond initial perceptions. For example, Amazon Alexa will be able to give out health advice to users in the United Kingdom as health-related questions will be automatically searched for using the official NHS website (MIT Technology Review, 2020). Some reports go as far to discuss how Amazon has plans to be able to run someone's entire life from the Alexa on the basis that the systems are getting so sophisticated and the data being collected is so vast that the Alexa will be capable of predicting needs (Hao, 2019). Nevertheless, users still appear to be resistant to use VAs, with some even reluctant to engage with this technology entirely (PwC, 2018). Most of these constraints to VA adoption primarily relate to lack of trust, perceived data privacy and security concerns and lack of knowledge or understanding.

Despite the benefits and opportunities of AI software, it is inherently limited by capabilities surrounding planning, reasoning, knowledge, natural language processing, ability to move and to empathise. It is this lack of emotional connection that is a fundamental component of users being less trusting towards AI voice-based assistants. This research investigates the role of emerging capabilities, privacy concerns and trust towards VAs using a mixed-methodology design. Results from the qualitative element of the study reveal that it is more about trusting the capabilities and functionalities than being scared over personal data. This theme will subsequently

H. R. Marriott (✉)
Cardiff Metropolitan University, Cardiff, UK
e-mail: hmarriott@cardiffmet.ac.uk

V. Pitardi
University of Portsmouth, Portsmouth, UK
e-mail: valentina.pitardi@port.ac.uk

J. Allen et al. (eds.), *Celebrating the Past and Future of Marketing and Discovery with Social Impact*, Developments in Marketing Science: Proceedings of the Academy of Marketing Science, https://doi.org/10.1007/978-3-030-95346-1_35

be examined further in a follow-up experimental study to examine the role of context towards these perceptions. The focus of the experimental design will subsequently consider the direct relationship between perceived behavioural control and intention to continue to use VAs with consideration into the indirect effects of privacy concerns and trust and the moderating role of perceived capabilities.

The findings, thus far, show how VAs, as new technologies and leaders of machine learning capabilities, can enhance customer experiences, improve customer relationships and add value to firms. As privacy concerns are often dismissed, if customers benefit from the sharing of their information, yet their capabilities being under-appreciated, firms can focus attention to the high-quality functions of these devices to encourage their more frequent use.

Keywords Artificial intelligence · Voice based assistants · Privacy · Trust

Effects of Temperature and Social Density on Consumer Choices with Multiple Options

Martina Katharina Schöniger and Susanne Jana Adler

Abstract Environmental contexts, like temperature and social density, can influence consumers' decision making considerably. Although previous research established a bidirectional link between temperature and social proximity, it examined temperature and social density's downstream consequences in isolation, neglecting possible interaction effects. Moreover, the research produced conflicting results (e.g., on preferences for premium products), suggesting fit effects and compensatory effects. We address this research gap in a preregistered experiment with an orthogonal design on temperature and social density, and expand research on temperature and social density's downstream consequences by measuring preferences for products with different premium, innovativeness, safety, scarcity, or uniqueness levels. Building on previous research, we hypothesize that temperature and social density have similar effects, but find they have distinct effects. Specifically, the interaction effect for safety and premium products indicates that under cold or neutral temperature conditions high tier choices increase when social density is high, but not under warm conditions—suggesting that warmth has an attenuating effect. Furthermore, choices for high tier innovative products profit from cold and low social density primes, whereas the results for scarce and unique products are inconclusive. These findings suggest that temperature and social density have complex product-category-specific consequences and require follow-up research.

Keywords Social density · Crowding · Temperature · Consumer choice · Innovativeness · Premium · Safety · Scarcity · Uniqueness

---

M. K. Schöniger (✉)
Chemnitz University of Technology, Chemnitz, Germany
e-mail: martina.schoeniger@wirtschaft.tu-chemnitz.de

S. J. Adler
Otto-von-Guericke-University, Magdeburg, Germany
e-mail: susanne.adler@ovgu.de

J. Allen et al. (eds.), *Celebrating the Past and Future of Marketing and Discovery with Social Impact*, Developments in Marketing Science: Proceedings of the Academy of Marketing Science, https://doi.org/10.1007/978-3-030-95346-1_36

Introduction

Context is an essential factor in consumer decision making (Meiselman 2019; Roschk et al. 2017). For example, temperature and social density (which refers to the number of people in a fixed space, Blut and Iyer 2020) are important influencing factors in terms of consumer product evaluation and decision making (Levav and Zhu 2009; O'Guinn et al. 2015; Park and Hadi 2019).

Researchers investigating temperature or social density effects mainly draw on the temperature-density link, that is, the semantic link between warm (vs. cold) conditions and physical or social proximity (Ijzerman and Semin 2009, 2010). Nevertheless, researchers hitherto examined the effects of temperature or social density predominantly in isolation, neglecting possible interaction effects. For example, research on consumer preferences (e.g., for premium products) reveals distinct effects for temperature and social density. On the one hand, there is congruity (fit effect) between premium products and cold conditions (Park and Hadi 2019), as well as between premium products and less socially dense stores (O'Guinn et al. 2015). On the other hand, further research (Madzharov et al. 2015) suggests that consumers consider premium products to compensate for negatively perceived warm or dense environments (compensatory effect). These distinct effects highlight the temperature-density link's complex consequences for decision making. Due to the predominantly isolated examination of temperature and social density, the abovementioned research neglects the possibility that temperature and social density do not always correlate (e.g., a dense, cold environment or a less dense, warm environment).

We aim to address this research gap by adopting an orthogonal design for temperature and social density. Building on the temperature-density link, we hypothesize that high social density and warm conditions have similar effects, but find they have distinct effects. Our results, therefore, indicate that a noteworthy boundary condition is present and suggest a new research agenda.

Theoretical Background

Research on temperature and social density's effects on consumers' product evaluations and decision making has experienced a surge over the last years. The semantic relationship between temperature and social proximity, that is, the "perceived distance between self and other," was the basic premise of prior research (Ijzerman and Semin 2009, p. 1215). Recent research has shown that warm (vs. cold) conditions lead to lower psychological distances and higher relational foci; vice versa, social proximity leads to warmer perceived temperature (Ijzerman and Semin 2010, 2009). Affirmatively, research has revealed relationships between physical and social warmth (Williams and Bargh 2008), between coldness and social exclusion (Zhong and Leonardelli 2008) and has established a link between body temperature and feelings of social connection (Inagaki and Human 2019). Furthermore, Zwebner et al. (2014) linked temperature to the perceived spatial distance between consumers and products.

The aforementioned effects point to a positive and bidirectional link between temperature and social density. In addition, several researchers have examined the effects of (i) temperature and (ii) social density on consumer product evaluation and decision making:

(i) Cold (vs. warm) temperature conditions increase product perceptions in terms of their status and luxury, resulting in enhanced overall evaluations (Park and Hadi 2019); furthermore, cold conditions also increase preferences for innovative products (Cheema and Patrick 2012). Zwebner et al. (2014), however, showed enhanced product evaluations in warm vs. cold temperature conditions and find that the elicitation of emotional warmth and the subsequent positive reactions mediate this temperature premium effect. In addition, Baek et al. (2018) showed that this temperature premium effect is especially prevalent in respect of people with high relational needs, although this effect is mitigated in respect of luxury brands.

(ii) Furthermore, low social density is linked to higher status inferences (e.g., income), which entails higher product valuations (O'Guinn et al. 2015). Basically, due to personal space violations, higher social density is perceived as aversive, resulting in reduced feelings of control over the environment (Blut and Iyer 2020). These feelings could trigger an avoidance reaction affecting consumption decisions. Higher density also entails more varied and unique choices (Levav and Zhu 2009), higher preferences for innovative products (Xu et al. 2019), and it enhances safety-oriented and prevention-oriented choices (Maeng et al. 2013).

The literature streams (i and ii) highlight the various effects of temperature and social density on consumer evaluations and preferences. With the exception of Madzharov et al.'s (2015) study on the effects of ambient scent's perceived warmth, researchers have predominantly examined temperature and social density in isolation. To connect temperature and social density, we refer to Madzharov et al. (2015) who primed the cold vs. warm temperature concept by using a corresponding cool vs. warm scent. Based on the semantic link between temperature and social proximity, Madzharov et al. (2015) argue that warm scents—eliciting a subjective feeling of warmth—increase perceived social density and decrease consumers' perceived control over the environment, thereby engendering a power restoration motivation, leading to an increased preference for premium products. Consequently, consumers may compensate for negatively perceived warmth or dense environments by preferring premium products (compensatory effect).

Recent research can be challenged if both temperature and social density are allowed to vary as in real-life scenarios. Although it might be possible to regulate the temperature accordingly in a real-life scenario, it is only possible to influence the social density level to a very limited extent. Consequently, we address these concerns and extend prior research by using an orthogonal design for temperature and social density.

Following Madzharov et al. (2015), we assume that temperature and social density entail a compensatory effect. This effect builds on aversion to warm or dense environments and motivates consumers to achieve goals such as distinguishing or protecting themselves from others. Premium products serve these goals by signaling status and power (Madzharov et al. 2015; O'Guinn et al. 2015), which effectively increases their purchasers' perceived distance from other people (Magee and Smith 2013). These goals can also be related to products that target different levels of innovativeness, safety, scarcity, or uniqueness: Unique products might have a similar effect due to their ability to distinguish those who purchase them from non-purchasers (Levav and Zhu 2009), which also applies to innovative products (Xu et al. 2019). High social density also stimulates a motivation to protect own resources against others; a motivation that manifests in elevated preferences for safety-related products (Maeng et al. 2013). Similarly, a depleted inventory leads to elevated quality inferences and, subsequently, to a bandwagon effect, that is, an increased preference for a depleted (scarce) option (van Herpen et al. 2009). Therefore, we propose that consumers in warm or dense environments faced with choice sets of multiple products will choose the product option that is the most innovative, has the highest premium, is the safest, is the scarcest, or is the most unique (high tier option). Consequently, we hypothesize:

H_1: Cold/warm temperature leads to less/more purchasing of (a) innovative, (b) premium, (c) safe, (d) scarce, or (e) unique products.

H_2: Low/high social density leads to less/more purchasing of (a) innovative, (b) premium, (c) safe, (d) scarce, or (e) unique products.

Design and Methodology

To test our hypotheses, we employed an online study with a 3 (temperature conditions: cold, neutral, warm) x 3 (social density conditions: low, middle, high) between-subject design (see Fig. 1) and measured product choice within-subject (see Fig. 2) to test our hypotheses.

For manipulation, we used a video of approximately one-minute duration showing a shopping trip and providing visual and verbal information about the temperature and social density. We pretested the video to ensure that the manipulations of the temperature (cold, neutral, warm) and the different social density levels (low, middle, high) were perceived as intended, and that the shopping trip scenario was accurately conveyed and relevant. Similar to Park and Hadi (2019), we visually manipulated the temperature conditions by using a winter vs. summer scenario and blueish vs. orange-reddish color hues to induce coldness or warmth (see also Sester et al. 2013). We induced no specific season in the neutral condition by using achromatic, grayish colors (see Maier et al. 2008). We manipulated the social density by

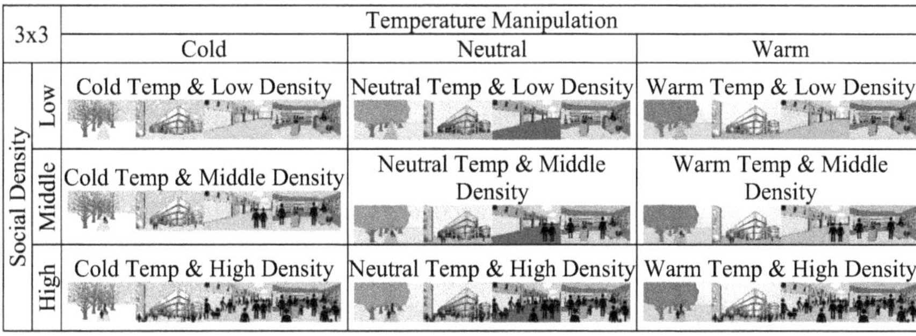

3x3
Temperature Manipulation
Cold
Neutral
Warm
Social Density
Low
Middle
High
Cold Temp & Low Density
Neutral Temp & Low Density
Warm Temp & Low Density
Cold Temp & Middle Density
Neutral Temp & Middle Density
Warm Temp & Middle Density
Cold Temp & High Density
Neutral Temp & High Density
Warm Temp & High Density

Fig. 1 Experimental design of the context conditions and visual manipulation. (Note. Screenshots of each video scene (tree avenue, pedestrian zone, shopping center, shop); Temp = Temperature)

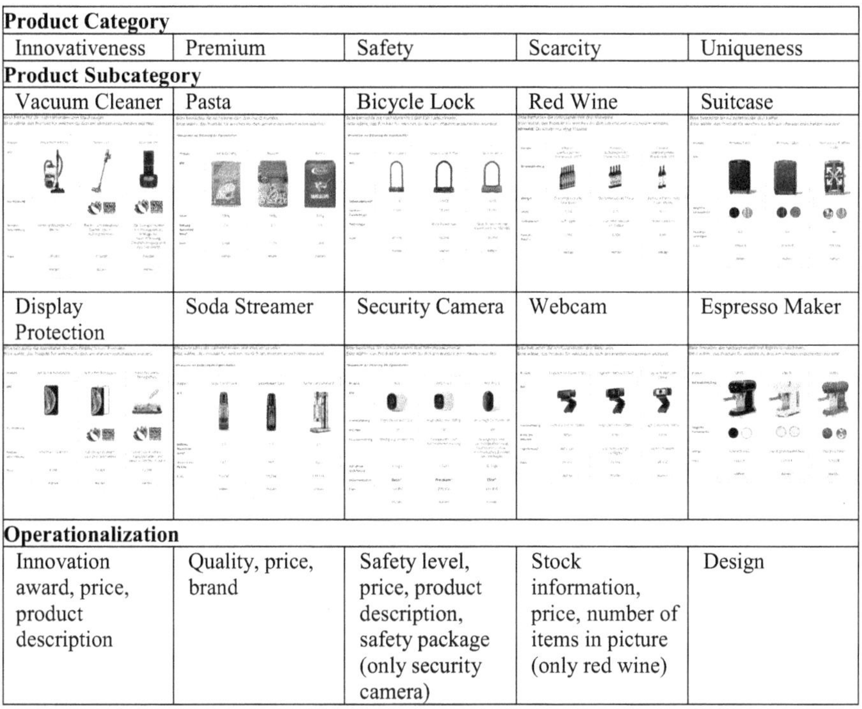

Product Category
Innovativeness
Premium
Safety
Scarcity
Uniqueness
Product Subcategory
Vacuum Cleaner
Pasta
Bicycle Lock
Red Wine
Suitcase
Display Protection
Soda Streamer
Security Camera
Webcam
Espresso Maker
Operationalization
Innovation award, price, product description
Quality, price, brand
Safety level, price, product description, safety package (only security camera)
Stock information, price, number of items in picture (only red wine)
Design

Fig. 2 Product choice sets

including a small (one person), middle (15 people), or high (65+ people) number of other people in the scenes. People were represented as silhouettes to avoid confounding social inferences (O'Guinn et al. 2015). Throughout the video, the verbal information that described the scenario was altered by using various wordings, and further supported by different background sounds.

We measured the product choice by presenting the participants with choice sets, each comprising three products with different levels of the respective targeted characteristic (premium, innovative, safety, scarce, or unique). We designed two choice sets per product category, resulting in a 5 (product categories: innovativeness, premium, safety, scarcity, and uniqueness) x 2 (product subcategories: e.g., different types of pasta and soda streamers in the premium product category) choice set design (see Fig. 2). Each choice set included a low, middle, and high tier option. For example, in the premium category, we had a choice set with three different pasta products. The first pasta product (low option) represented an inexpensive, no-name branded, low-quality-rated pasta. By contrast, the third pasta option represented an expensive, premium-branded, high-quality-rated pasta product (high tier option), with the second pasta product (middle option) falling in between. The same principle was applied to create the other choice sets. Consequently, the high tier option was the most premium, innovative, safe, scarce, or unique product option in the respective choice set.

The participants were randomly assigned to one of the nine conditions. The online survey started with several personality scales, after which the participants watched the manipulation video and were shown the ten product choice sets (see Fig. 2) in random order. We assessed the perceived social density by asking the participants to estimate the number of people in the video, how they perceived the location's spaciousness (items adapted from Madzharov et al. 2015), and how they perceived the crowding (scale adapted from Bateson and Hui 1992; Grewal et al. 2003). They subsequently evaluated the ambient temperature of the scenario in the video and indicated how cold or warm they felt (adapted from Sester et al. 2013). Thereafter, the participants answered the transportation scale (Appel et al. 2015) that we had modified to capture the degree to which the participants empathized with the described situation. Lastly, the participants answered questions on their demographics, their color vision ability, the ongoing SARS-CoV-2 pandemic, and the effort they put into completing the survey. Prior to data collection, we preregistered the study at the Open Science Framework (OSF) of the Center for Open Science. The preregistration and further supplementary data and material associated with this article can be found at https://osf.io/xry4p and https://osf.io/gc3f2/.

Results

Sample Description

A total of 407 participants completed the online survey. We excluded those under the age of 16, as well as those who failed the attention check, who indicated that they had paid very little effort when completing the survey, who had responded comparatively very fast or slowly (the 2.5% fastest and slowest respondents), and who had a relevant visual impairment (e.g., red-green blindness in the warm condition). This yielded a dataset with 341 cases (i.e., slightly below our planned sample size, n = 343) with 30 to 47 participants per group.[1] The sample comprised 55.1% females (44.9% male, no diverse) with no significant differences between the nine groups ($\chi^2(8) = 4.36$, $p = .82$). Their age ranged from 17 to 82 years with M = 31 years (SD = 12.66, median = 26). Again, there were no significant differences between the groups ($F(8, 332) = .87$, $p = .54$).

Manipulation Checks

Temperature The manipulation check confirms that the participants evaluated the video's warm condition as reflecting the highest temperature (M = 5.11, SD = 1.69) and the cold condition as reflecting the lowest temperature (M = 2.81, SD = 1.83), with the neutral condition falling between the aforesaid conditions (M = 3.98, SD = 1.42). An ANOVA indicates that all the group comparisons are significant ($F(2, 338) = 53.52$, $p < .001$, $\eta^2 = .24$, all Tukey's post hoc tests: $t \geq 4.99$, $p < .001$). Furthermore, the temperature manipulation affected how warm or cold the participants felt ($F(2, 338) = 7.94$, $p < .001$, $\eta^2 = .045$). They felt warmer after watching a video with a warm temperature manipulation (M = 4.61, SD = 1.33) than after watching a video showing a neutral (M = 4.19, SD = 1.15, $t(338) = 2.38$, $p = .047$) or a cold temperature manipulation (M = 3.91, SD = 1.39, $t(338) = 3.98$, $p < .001$, difference between neutral and cold temperature condition: $t(338) = 1.65$, $p = .226$). We found no group differences in the perceived ambient temperature ($M_{warm\ temp} = 4.95$, $SD_{warm\ temp} = 1.27$; $M_{neutral\ temp} = 4.99$, $SD_{neutral\ temp} = 1.16$; $M_{cold\ temp} = 4.88$, $SD_{cold\ temp} = 1.23$; $F(2,338) = .26$, $p = .768$, $\eta^2 = .002$).

Social Density We tested (social) density perception in the video by means of an average crowding score ($\alpha = .93$). An ANOVA revealed significant differences between all three groups ($F(2, 338) = 229.00$, $p < .001$, $\eta^2 = .575$; and all Tukey's post hoc tests $t(338) \geq 5.83$, $p < .001$), indicating that the participants perceived the high density condition as most crowded (M = 5.46, SD = 1.11), followed by the middle (M = 3.30, SD = 1.00) and low density condition (M = 2.45, SD = 1.16). We obtained similar results regarding whether the video was full of people ($F(2, 338) = 360.3$, $p < .001$, $\eta^2 = .681$; all Tukey's post hoc tests: $t(338) \geq 8.28$, $p < .001$ with $M_{high\ density} = 5.85$, $SD_{high\ density} = 1.38$, $M_{middle\ density} = 2.88$, $SD_{middle\ density} = 1.28$, $M_{low\ density} = 1.50$, $SD_{low\ density} = 1.08$). The same applied to whether the mall and shop in the video (average score of two variables, $r = .41$) were perceived as 'spacious' ($F(2, 338) = 20.32$, $p < .001$, $\eta^2 = .107$; all Tukey's post hoc tests: $t(338) \geq 2.43$,

[1] More precisely: $n_{warm\ temp,\ high\ density} = 32$, $n_{neutral\ temp,\ high\ density} = 36$, $n_{cold\ temp,\ high\ density} = 47$, $n_{warm\ temp,\ middle\ density} = 37$, $n_{neutral\ temp,\ middle\ density} = 42$, $n_{cold\ temp,\ middle\ density} = 34$, $n_{warm\ temp,\ low\ density} = 30$, $n_{neutral\ temp,\ low\ density} = 40$, $n_{cold\ temp,\ low\ density} = 43$.

$p \leq .041$ with $M_{high\ density} = 3.42$, $SD_{high\ density} = 1.17$, $M_{middle\ density} = 3.80$, $SD_{middle\ density} = 1.11$, $M_{low\ density} = 4.40$, $SD_{low\ density} = 1.25$).[2]

Hypotheses Tests

We dichotomized each of the product choices to 1 = choice of target (high tier option) and 0 = other options (middle or low). We submitted our data to generalized linear mixed models (GLMM) per product category with the target choice as the dependent variable. We used the temperature and density conditions as fixed effect variables, and the product as a random intercept variable. We calculated the hierarchical models by starting with the main effects and adding the interaction effects in the next step. See Fig. 3 for a graphical representation of target choice shares and Table 1 for the model results.

Innovativeness In terms of innovative product choices, the model comparison favors the full model ($\chi^2(4) = 10.10$, $p = .039$). This model indicates that—contrary to H_{1a} and H_{2a}—participants favor the high tier option less in warm (vs. cold) temperature conditions ($z = -1.95$, $p = .051$, $OR = .43$) and in high (vs. low) density conditions ($z = -2.09$, $p = .037$, $OR = .46$). The model also shows an interaction effect, indicating an opposite trend for neutral temperature manipulation, especially through comparatively higher target choices under high density ($z = 1.93$, $p = .053$, $OR = 2.67$, see the according panel in Fig. 3).

Premium The main effects model does not indicate meaningful differences between the groups regarding premium product choices (H_{1b}, H_{2b}; all $|z| \leq 1.36$, all $p \geq .175$, $.85 \leq OR \leq 1.30$). The full GLMM indicates interaction effects based on the warm temperature, high density (vs. cold temperature, low density) condition ($z = -1.87$, $p = .061$, $OR = .40$) and warm temperature, middle density (vs. cold temperature, low density) condition ($z = -1.78$, $p = .076$, $OR = .40$), indicating a decrease in high tier choices in the relevant conditions when compared to the other conditions (all of the other effects: $|z| \leq 1.27$, all $p \geq .203$, $.99 \leq OR \leq 1.56$).

[2] We asked the participants to estimate the number of people in the video ($M_{high\ density} = 63.82$, $SD_{high\ density} = 48.09$, $M_{middle\ density} = 15.24$, $SD_{middle\ density} = 9.81$, $M_{low\ density} = 3.12$, $SD_{low\ density} = 3.91$) and the number of people that are currently around them ($M_{high\ density} = 1.31$, $SD_{high\ density} = 2.13$, $M_{middle\ density} = 1.03$, $SD_{middle\ density} = 1.23$, $M_{low\ density} = 1.82$, $SD_{low\ density} = 4.84$). We found significant differences between all the groups in respect of the number of people in the video ($F(2,338) = 144.3$, $p < .001$, $\eta^2 = .461$, all Tukey's post hoc tests: $t(338) \geq 3.19$, $p \leq .0045$; Using log-values, we also found significant differences between all the groups with $F(2,338) = 642.3$, $p < .001$, $\eta^2 = .792$, and all Tukey's post hoc tests: $t(338) \geq 15.51$, $p \leq .001$). However, we found no significant differences in the participants' estimation of the number of people around them ($F(2,338) = 1.88$, $p = .154$, $\eta^2 = .011$, all Tukey's post hoc tests: $t(338) \leq 1.92$, all $p \geq .136$), which is probably due to a high number of participants who completed the survey being either alone or, at most, having just one other person in their vicinity ($n = 239$; 70%).

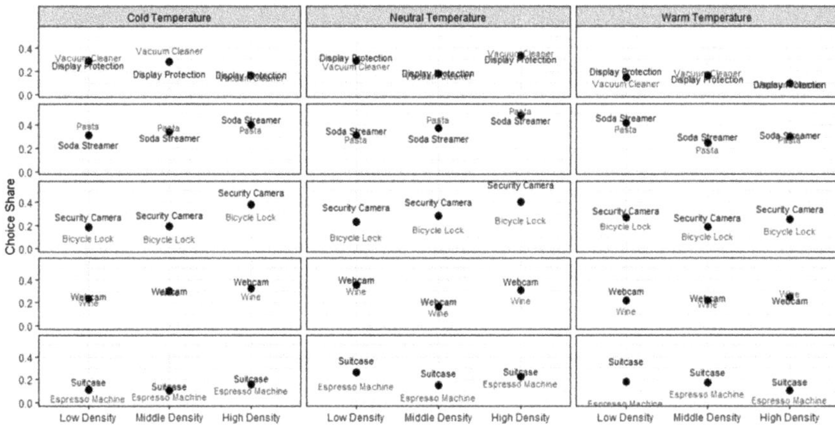

Fig. 3 Choice shares of target choice option. (*Note.* Choice shares of the high tier option per condition, product subcategory (labels), and product categories (dots))

Specifically, the relevant panels in Fig. 3 show an increase in high tier choices (mainly pasta) in high density (vs. low and middle density) conditions in the neutral temperature, and (mainly soda streamers) in the cold temperature. As indicated by the interaction, warmth attenuates this effect. However, despite these trends, the full model's fit does not exceed—in a convincing manner—the main effects model's fit ($\chi^2(4) = 7.75$, $p = .101$).

Safety Regarding choices for safety products, we observe—consistent with H_{2c}—a positive trend related to the density conditions, indicating that participants in high density conditions choose the high tier option more often than participants in a low density condition (main effects model: $z = 3.2$, $p = .001$, $OR = 2.01$, full model: $z = 3.0$, $p = .003$, $OR = 2.89$, respectively). Nonetheless, warmth attenuates this effect, as indicated graphically and by means of a significant interaction effect ($z = -2.1$, $p = .038$, $OR = .32$). However, adding the interaction terms does not improve the model fit significantly ($\chi^2(4) = 5.50$, $p = .24$). Contrary to our H_{1c}, the temperature condition only has small and insignificant effects on the target choice (main effects model: $|z| \leq 1.3$, $p \geq .205$, $.87 \leq OR \leq 1.31$, full model: $|z| \leq 1.2$, $p \geq .236$, $1.32 \leq OR \leq 1.63$).

Scarcity In respect of scarcity choices (H_{1d}, H_{2d}), the main effects model indicates that there is no relationship between the choice of a high tier option and the conditions (main effects model: $|z| \leq 1.23$, $p \geq .219$, $.76 \leq OR \leq 1.14$). However, we do observe an interaction effect from neutral temperature and middle density condition (vs. cold low density, $z = -2.54$, $p = .011$, $OR = .26$), which indicated a decrease in the high tier choices in this condition, and an amplified effect in the neutral temperature condition (vs. cold, $z = 1.66$, $p = .096$, $OR = 1.78$, all other effects: $|z| \leq 1.35$, $p \geq .18$, $.52 \leq OR \leq 1.57$).

Table 1 Hierarchical regression models per product category

	Innovativeness	Premium	Safety	Scarcity	Uniqueness
Model 1: Main effects	b (SE)	b (SE)	b (SE)	b (SE)	b (SE)
Intercept	−0.98 (0.19)[a]	−0.68 (0.17)[a]	−1.40 (0.45)[b]	−0.92 (0.22)[a]	−1.94 (0.54)[a]
Neutral temp	0.13 (0.21)	0.16 (0.19)	0.27 (0.21)	−0.04 (0.21)	0.65 (0.26)[c]
Warm temp	−0.68 (0.26)[b]	−0.16 (0.20)	−0.13 (0.23)	−0.27 (0.22)	0.26 (0.28)
High density	−0.32 (0.23)	0.26 (0.19)	0.70 (0.22)[b]	0.14 (0.21)	−0.13 (0.25)
Middle density	−0.25 (0.23)	−0.09 (0.20)	0.02 (0.23)	−0.24 (0.22)	−0.33 (0.26)
Model 2: Main and interaction effects (full model)					
Intercept	−0.89 (0.24)[a]	−0.78 (0.23)[a]	−1.58 (0.50)[b]	−1.20 (0.28)[a]	−2.20 (0.59)[a]
Neutral temp	−0.02 (0.34)	−0.01 (0.33)	0.28 (0.39)	0.58 (0.35)[d]	1.06 (0.43)[c]
Warm temp	−0.84 (0.43)[d]	0.45 (0.35)	0.49 (0.41)	−0.09 (0.40)	0.56 (0.48)
High density	−0.77 (0.37)[c]	0.39 (0.31)	1.06 (0.36)[b]	0.45 (0.34)	0.38 (0.45)
Middle density	−0.06 (0.36)	0.11 (0.35)	0.04 (0.42)	0.34 (0.37)	−0.14 (0.53)
Interaction: Neutral temp, high density	0.98 (0.51)†	0.34 (0.46)	−0.19 (0.52)	−0.66 (0.49)	−0.62 (0.60)
Interaction: Warm temp, high density	0.24 (0.67)	−0.92 (0.49)†	−1.15 (0.55)*	−0.27 (0.55)	−1.02 (0.70)
Interaction: Neutral temp, middle density	−0.56 (0.52)	0.14 (0.48)	0.28 (0.56)	−1.34 (0.53)*	−0.57 (0.67)
Interaction: Warm temp, middle density	0.15 (0.60)	−0.91 (0.51)†	−0.50 (0.60)	−0.35 (0.56)	0.09 (0.71)
Model comparison					
Deviance (model 1)	699.49	879.85	742.06	777.33	573.71
Deviance (model 2)	689.39	872.10	736.56	770.25	569.03
	$\chi^2(4) = 10.10$*	$\chi^2(4) = 7.75$	$\chi^2(4) = 5.50$	$\chi^2(4) = 7.08$	$\chi^2(4) = 4.68$

Note. Temp = Temperature; [a]p < .001, [b]p < .01, [c]p < .05, [d]p < .1

Uniqueness Lastly, we find no support for H_{1e} and H_{2e}. However, a high tier choice from unique products is amplified in the neutral (vs. cold) temperature condition (main effects model: z = 2.54, p = .011, OR = 1.91; full model: z = 2.44, p = .015, OR = 2.87). All the other effects are insignificant (main effects model: $|z| \leq 1.27$, $p \geq .204$, $.72 \leq OR \leq 1.30$; full model: $|z| \leq 1.46$, $p \geq .143$, $.36 \leq OR \leq 1.75$).

Overall, the hierarchical GLMM showed that the inclusion of interaction effects only improves innovativeness's model fit ($\chi^2(4) = 10.10$, p = .039, all other: $\chi^2(4) \leq 7.75$, $p \geq .101$). Summarizing, we did not find evidence of generally enhanced high tier choices in high density and warm temperature conditions. Furthermore, our results provide preliminary support for our notion that temperature and density conditions have distinct effects on consumer choices.

Discussion and Conclusions

Following previous literature on the relationship between social density, temperature, and their consequences (Madzharov et al. 2015; Maeng et al. 2013; Ijzerman and Semin 2010, 2009), we conducted a study to assess temperature and social density's main and interaction effects on consumer choices. We argued that high social density is perceived as aversive due to consumers feeling that they lack control over the environment. To compensate for their lack of control (Madzharov et al. 2015), consumers favor the product option that promises to distinguish or protect themselves most from the group, that is, the most premium, innovative, safe, scarce, or unique product (high tier) option. In light of the bidirectional link between social proximity and temperature (Ijzerman and Semin 2010, 2009), we expected the same pattern of results regarding warm temperature conditions.

However, our results indicate a more complex choice behavior, suggesting that temperature and social density conditions have distinct effects. Furthermore, these effects differ between product categories. The choice of high tier premium and safety products increased in highly dense conditions when the temperature prime was either cold or neutral. Warm conditions attenuate this effect. Consequently, we suggest that warm conditions restrict the aversion engendered by high social density conditions. A possible explanation, calling for further research in this context, might be that warmth entails a lower psychological distance and a stronger relational focus (Ijzerman and Semin 2009). Accordingly, people in warm environments are more concerned about the people around them and focus more on their interconnectedness. This could render high social density less aversive and reduce the need to distinguish and protect oneself from the group, which is manifested in fewer premium and safe product choices. Since our results, at present, are unable to test the aforementioned mechanism behind the identified effects, they call for further research.

Concerning the other product categories, innovative products seem to profit from cold temperature (Cheema and Patrick 2012) and, partially, from lower social density. The latter may be related to innovative products' risky nature, which renders them inappropriate to distinguish or protect oneself from the group. A replication and a more in-depth analysis of this effect could be a valuable path for further research. Our scarce and unique products' results remain inconclusive, which could be due to our choice set design. The manipulation of scarce products might have been too weak. Specifically, the participants could have considered the low stock level irrelevant, as they still had the option to choose the product. In addition, we did not explicitly address whether the scarcity was due to a supply restriction or excess demand (van Herpen et al. 2009). Regarding the unique product choice sets, we chose unusual color designs to indicate the uniqueness of high tier options, which might elicit a polarizing effect.

In summary, our data suggest that despite the temperature-density link, temperature and social density do not have similar effects on product choices in an orthogonal design. Since temperature and social density can vary independently in real-life scenarios, this represents an important boundary condition. This is especially relevant for practitioners who cannot always control such environmental contexts. Nevertheless, retailers could accordingly alter, for example, their store design, element placement, or in-store promotions. Advertisers could benefit from promoting specific product categories in certain environments, for example, safety or premium products in dense and cold areas.

References

Appel, M., Gnambs, T., Richter, T., & Green, M. C. (2015). The transportation scale – short form (TS–SF). *Media Psychology, 18*(2), 243–266. doi:https://doi.org/10.1080/15213269.2014.987400.

Baek, E., Choo, H. J., & Lee, S. H. (2018). Using warmth as the visual design of a store: Intimacy, relational needs, and approach intentions. *Journal of Business Research, 88*, 91–101. doi:https://doi.org/10.1016/j.jbusres.2018.03.013.

Bateson, J. E. G., & Hui, M. K. (1992). The ecological validity of photographic slides and videotapes in simulating the service setting. *Journal of Consumer Research, 19*(2), 271–281. doi:https://doi.org/10.1086/209301.

Blut, M., & Iyer, G. R. (2020). Consequences of perceived crowding: A meta-analytical perspective. *Journal of Retailing*(3), *96*, 362–382. doi:https://doi.org/10.1016/j.jretai.2019.11.007.

Cheema, A., & Patrick, V. M. (2012). Influence of warm versus cool temperatures on consumer choice: A resource depletion account. *Journal of Marketing Research, 49*(6), 984–995. doi:https://doi.org/10.1509/jmr.08.0205.

Grewal, D., Baker, J., Levy, M., & Voss, G. B. (2003). The effects of wait expectations and store atmosphere evaluations on patronage intentions in service-intensive retail stores. *Journal of Retailing, 79*(4), 259–268. doi:https://doi.org/10.1016/j.jretai.2003.09.006.

Ijzerman, H., & Semin, G. R. (2009). The thermometer of social relations: Mapping social proximity on temperature. *Psychological Science, 20*(10), 1214–1220. doi:https://doi.org/10.1111/j.1467-9280.2009.02434.x.

Ijzerman, H., & Semin, G. R. (2010). Temperature perceptions as a ground for social proximity. *Journal of Experimental Social Psychology, 46*(6), 867–873. doi:https://doi.org/10.1016/j.jesp.2010.07.015.

Inagaki, T. K., & Human, L. J. (2019). Physical and social warmth: Warmer daily body temperature is associated with greater feelings of social connection. *Emotion. 20(6)*, 1093–1097. doi:https://doi.org/10.1037/emo0000618.

Levav, J., & Zhu, R. (2009). Seeking freedom through variety. *Journal of Consumer Research, 36*(4), 600–610. doi:https://doi.org/10.1086/599556.

Madzharov, A. V., Block, L. G., & Morrin, M. (2015). The cool scent of power: Effects of ambient scent on consumer preferences and choice behavior. *Journal of Marketing, 79*(1), 83–96. doi:https://doi.org/10.1509/jm.13.0263.

Maeng, A., Tanner, R. J., & Soman, D. (2013). Conservative when crowded: Social crowding and consumer choice. *Journal of Marketing Research, 50*(6), 739–752. doi:https://doi.org/10.1509/jmr.12.0118.

Magee, J. C., & Smith, P. K. (2013). The social distance theory of power. *Personality and Social Psychology Review, 17*(2), 158–186. doi:https://doi.org/10.1177/1088868312472732.

Maier, M. A., Elliot, A. J., & Lichtenfeld, S. (2008). Mediation of the negative effect of red on intellectual performance. *Personality and Social Psychology Bulletin, 34*(11), 1530–1540. doi:https://doi.org/10.1177/0146167208323104.

Meiselman, H. L. (2019). *Context: The effects of environment on product design and evaluation.* Cambridge: Woodhead Publishing.

O'Guinn, T. C., Tanner, R. J., & Maeng, A. (2015). Turning to space: Social density, social class, and the value of things in stores. *Journal of Consumer Research, 42*(2), 196–213. doi:https://doi.org/10.1093/jcr/ucv010.

Park, J., & Hadi, R. (2019). Shivering for status: When cold temperatures increase product evaluation. *Journal of Consumer Psychology, 30*(2), 314–328. doi:https://doi.org/10.1002/jcpy.1133.

Roschk, H., Loureiro, S. M. C., & Breitsohl, J. (2017). Calibrating 30 years of experimental research: A meta-analysis of the atmospheric effects of music, scent, and color. *Journal of Retailing, 93*(2), 228–240. doi:https://doi.org/10.1016/j.jretai.2016.10.001.

Sester, C., Deroy, O., Sutan, A., Galia, F., Desmarchelier, J.-F., Valentin, D., & Dacremont, C. (2013). "Having a drink in a bar": An immersive approach to explore the effects of context on drink choice. *Food Quality and Preference, 28*(1), 23–31. doi:https://doi.org/10.1016/j.foodqual.2012.07.006.

van Herpen, E., Pieters, R., & Zeelenberg, M. (2009). When demand accelerates demand: Trailing the bandwagon. *Journal of Consumer Psychology, 19*(3), 302–312. doi:https://doi.org/10.1016/j.jcps.2009.01.001.

Williams, L. E., & Bargh, J. A. (2008). Experiencing physical warmth promotes interpersonal warmth. *Science, 322*(5901), 606–607. doi:https://doi.org/10.1126/science.1162548.

Xu, L., Mehta, R., & Herd, K. B. (2019). Look at me! Or don't… : How mere social presence impacts innovation adoption. *Journal of the Association for Consumer Research, 4*(3), 269–279. doi:https://doi.org/10.1086/703565.

Zhong, C.-B., & Leonardelli, G. J. (2008). Cold and lonely: Does social exclusion literally feel cold? *Psychological Science, 19*(9), 838–842. doi:https://doi.org/10.1111/j.1467-9280.2008.02165.x.

Zwebner, Y., Lee, L., & Goldenberg, J. (2014). The temperature premium: Warm temperatures increase product valuation. *Journal of Consumer Psychology, 24*(2), 251–259. doi:https://doi.org/10.1016/j.jcps.2013.11.003.

Let's Get Social: The Influence of Consumer Factors on Online Consumer Engagement: An Abstract

Brian A. Vander Schee, James W. Peltier, and Andrew J. Dahl

Abstract Social media usage has become commonplace with over 3 billion users worldwide (von Abrams 2019). Prior research demonstrates that consumers are willing to interact with brands online (Laroche et al. 2012). However, little is known about the characteristics of consumers who choose to engage with brands via social media. The objective of this research is to contribute to the literature by extending the understanding of consumer factors that lead to online consumer engagement. Consumer factors are considered as social media dispositions (i.e., social media information sharing and social media trust) and social media goals (i.e., social media information seeking and social media experience).

Consumers are motivated to purposely seek out, connect with, and utilize social media to meet their specific needs. As such, uses and gratifications theory posits that consumers are active participants and not just passive recipients of media exposure (Dolan et al. 2016). It is proposed in this study that consumer engagement satisfies social media dispositions and goals to address utilitarian as well as hedonic and social motivations. Drawing on the work by Barger et al. (2016), van Doorn et al. (2010), and Hollebeek et al. (2014), consumer engagement in social media in this study is defined as, "a consumer's cognitive, affective, and behavioral social media connection displayed by contributing and creating digital content."

Scales were adapted from the extant literature. Information sharing survey items were adapted from an opinion leader status scale (Risselada et al. 2016). Survey items for social media trust were adapted from scales measuring trust and social recommendations (Dahl et al. 2019; Turcotte et al. 2015). The items measuring the social media information seeking construct were adapted from a scale on information interest by Chahal and Rani (2017) and a scale on information seeking by Shao

B. A. Vander Schee (✉)
Indiana University, Indianapolis, IN, USA
e-mail: vandersb@iu.edu

J. W. Peltier · A. J. Dahl
University of Wisconsin – Whitewater, Whitewater, WI, USA
e-mail: peltierj@uww.edu; dahlaj18@uww.edu

J. Allen et al. (eds.), *Celebrating the Past and Future of Marketing and Discovery with Social Impact*, Developments in Marketing Science: Proceedings of the Academy of Marketing Science, https://doi.org/10.1007/978-3-030-95346-1_37

and Ross (2015). Social media experience was measured with survey items adapted from a popularity scale (Zywica and Danowski 2008). The measures for consumer engagement were adapted from Muntinga et al. (2011) and recommended by Barger et al. (2016).

Survey items were measured on a 5-point Likert-type scale ranging from strongly disagree to strongly agree. The survey was pretested with business faculty to assess clarity and face validity. The revised survey was then completed by a convenience sample of college students enrolled at a Midwestern public university. Regression analysis and structural equation models (SEM) were used to analyze the data from the completed surveys. The results showed that social media experience mediates the relationship between social media dispositions and consumer engagement. Firms can more efficiently spend on social media marketing by providing mechanisms to enhance the social and self-promotion aspects of the social media experience.

Keywords Social media dispositions · Social media goals · Consumer engagement · Digital marketing

The Effect of Fear and Social Distancing on Chatbot Service Usage during a Pandemic: An Abstract

Yu-Shan Sandy Huang and Wei-Kang Kao

Abstract Social distancing is an important non-pharmaceutical intervention that policymakers rely heavily on to stop the spread of COVID-19. In spite of its benefits, the practice of social distancing has been associated with negative consequences, such as the loss of motivation (Williams et al. 2020) and increased levels of anxiety (Tuzovic and Kabadayi 2020). Given the mixed views on the practice, in this research, we seek to examine what factor would influence customers' evaluations of the practice and how the evaluations affect their behavior of using service technologies (e.g., chatbot technologies), which can help organizations limit human-to-human contact during service encounters (Gursoy and Chi 2020; Shin and Kang 2020).

To answer these research questions, we propose a theoretical model by drawing upon the theory of reasoned action (Ajzen and Fishbein 1980; Fishbein and Ajzen 1975) and the feeling-as-information literature (Schwarz 2012). To examine the hypothesized model, we conducted an experimental study and recruited 200 U.S. consumers to participate in the study. The results show general support for our hypothesized relationships such that in a utilitarian (hedonic) service situation, customers' fear of being contaminated affects their usage of chatbot services via their positive attitudes (subjective norms) toward social distancing and then their perceived usefulness of chatbots in practicing social distancing.

We seek to provide meaningful theoretical contributions and practical implications through this research. First, as the theory of reasoned action has largely overlooked the influence of situational and emotional factors, we extend this theory by examining the moderating influence of service situations and by suggesting fear as a possible antecedent to subjective norms and attitudes. Second, our research

Y.-S. S. Huang (✉)
Texas A&M University-Corpus Christi, Bryan, TX, USA
e-mail: sandy.huang@tamucc.edu

W.-K. Kao
Harrisburg University of Science and Technology, Harrisburg, PA, USA
e-mail: wkao@harrisburgu.edu

J. Allen et al. (eds.), *Celebrating the Past and Future of Marketing and Discovery with Social Impact*, Developments in Marketing Science: Proceedings of the Academy of Marketing Science, https://doi.org/10.1007/978-3-030-95346-1_38

contributes to the literature on chatbot services by proposing that, in addition to the perceptions toward chatbots, the perceptions toward a social interaction practice can also influence customers' willingness to interact with chatbot service agents. Third, we broaden the growing body of social distancing literature by answering Ali et al.'s (2021) call to examine how social distancing can influence customers' behavior during service encounters. Finally, we offer practical implications for managing frontline encounters during a pandemic.

Keywords Fear · Social distancing · Perceived usefulness · Chatbot services · Theory of reasoned action

Marketing-Sales Alignment and Business Practices: An Abstract

Nora Bezaz, Thierry Himber, and Sébastien Soulez

Abstract Coordination between marketing and sales departments is a recurrent managerial problem and represents a major performance issue for companies (Homburg and Jensen 2007; Inyang and Jaramillo 2020; Pal 2019). Difficulties encountered in coordinating the two services are long-standing (Malshe et al. 2017; Pal 2019). Moreover, digital transformation has also redefined the sales perimeter and the sales profession, has generated new objectives for the teams such as mass lead generation for marketers versus customer conversion at the best conditions and expectations of qualified prospects for salespeople (Pöyry et al. 2017; Sabnis et al. 2013).

In this context, the objective of this research, conducted in a French context, is to understand the development and implementation of alignment between the marketing strategy and the sales department, and to identify the solutions put into practice by managers to solve the coordination problems encountered. A content analysis conducted with three types of respondents of French firms (marketing managers, sales managers and consulting firm managers) identified various critical practices such as the absence of regular meetings involving the heads of the departments, the absence of internal procedures determining the respective objectives or the absence of collaborative projects.

These results lead to the recommendation of coordination mechanisms and modalities to be mobilized and to identify those to be avoided to maximize the chances of success. The digitalization of companies impacts the relationship between marketing and sales departments and creates new constraints in their coordination, new tensions, a restructuring of their missions and new needs (in terms of

N. Bezaz (✉) · T. Himber
University of Lorraine, Epinal, France
e-mail: nora.bezaz@univ-loraine.fr; thierry.himber@univ-loraine.fr

S. Soulez
University of Lumière Lyon 2, Lyon, France
e-mail: sebastien.soulez@univ-lyon2.fr

J. Allen et al. (eds.), *Celebrating the Past and Future of Marketing and Discovery with Social Impact*, Developments in Marketing Science: Proceedings of the Academy of Marketing Science, https://doi.org/10.1007/978-3-030-95346-1_39

data, digital tools, training or recruitment). Therefore, critical practices are identified such as the lack of regular meetings involving department managers, the absence of internal procedures determining respective objectives or the absence of collaborative projects. Managers, and in particular sales managers, must use pedagogy and communication skills to explain, reassure and legitimize strategic choices, and finally get their teams to accept these changes. Therefore, from the outset, sales managers must also be aware of the issues and be convinced of the strategic choices they make, and to do so, their involvement must be worked on.

The results show the importance of formalizing communication, creating trust between services (Malshe et al. 2017) through the valorization of successes, co-construction of value. It is essential for managers to push sales and marketing teams towards common and shared customer-oriented objectives.

Keywords Marketing practices · Business practices · Marketing and sales alignment · Performance · Digital management

Optimizing Established Company - Startup Cooperation Taking a Startup Perspective: An Abstract

Nele Oldenburg and Nicolas Zacharias

Abstract Inter-organizational cooperation is considered highly important for company success (e.g., Borys and Jemison 1989; Rindfleisch and Moorman 2001), which is why it has been a ubiquitous phenomenon for decades (e.g., Hagedoorn 2002; Kale and Singh 2009). While the concept of inter-organizational cooperation itself is well-established, the great potential of cooperation specifically with startups emerged within the last few years (Homfeldt, Rese, and Simon 2019; Weiblen and Chesbrough 2015). Interestingly, the overall results emerging from this kind of cooperation between established companies and startups often do not live up to the expectations of their initiators. Researchers state that many of today's startup cooperation activities seem to be "new and shiny innovation initiative[s]" (Kohler 2016, p. 348) without a clear definition of objectives (Kruft, Gamber, and Kock 2018). Considering the lack of profound understanding of established company – startup cooperation, we strive to answer the question: *How can established companies develop a generic approach to manage startup cooperation effectively and efficiently?*

In a first step as part of a broader research endeavor, this study examines the difficulties lying in this kind of cooperation from the startup perspective. The insights from this perspective help to identify the issues established companies need to solve in order to interact with startups in a productive way. Within this empirical study, the examination of first contact initiatives shows, that only a minority of cooperation ties forms after established companies reach out to startups. For established companies, this implies plenty of unused potential, which could be used by strengthening outreaching activities. Another distinct result of the study is the lack of goal alignment within the cooperation in many cases. Practitioners within established companies should therefore ensure a clear definition of goals within the cooperation with their startup partners. Also, the results of the study show that even though a broad variety of different cooperation forms is used, the satisfaction with those coopera-

---

N. Oldenburg (✉) · N. Zacharias
Martin Luther University Halle-Wittenberg, Halle, Germany
e-mail: nele.oldenburg@wiwi.uni-halle.de; nicolas.zacharias@wiwi.uni-halle.de

J. Allen et al. (eds.), *Celebrating the Past and Future of Marketing and Discovery with Social Impact*, Developments in Marketing Science: Proceedings of the Academy of Marketing Science, https://doi.org/10.1007/978-3-030-95346-1_40

tion forms seems to be rather low. We therefore suggest practicioners to carefully consider, which cooperation form is fitting in respect to the cooperation goals.

In order to shed some more light on the topic of efficient and effective cooperation between established companies and startups, we used this initial study as a profound base for an extensive follow-up study and gathered a large quantitative data set investigating the established company perspective, i.e., the "other side" of the cooperation. Based on the analysis of this large-scale data in a next step, the results will offer guidance for strategic decisions on startup cooperation initiatives and consequently enhance the chances of realizing the high expectations associated with startup cooperation.

Keywords Innovation management · Inter-organizational cooperation · Cooperation management · Startup cooperation

Touchy Issues in Adaptive Choice-Based Conjoint Analysis: An Abstract

Frauke Kühn, Marcel Lichters, and Verena Sablotny-Wackershauser

Abstract The advancement of smart mobile technology has changed the way market research works. Importantly, an increasing number of consumers use direct touch (e.g., touchscreens) instead of indirect touch (e.g., mouse/keyboard combo) interfaces. However, the touch interface type's role in market research methods' performance has been largely neglected.

Choice-based conjoint analysis (CBC) is one of the most widely applied market research methods to elicit consumer preferences (Schlereth and Skiera 2017). Recent research, however, finds deficiencies in CBC. Therefore, its results may have only limited managerial relevance (Schlereth and Skiera 2017). Consequently, research on machine learning has introduced an upgraded version, namely adaptive choice-based conjoint analysis (ACBC) (Johnson and Orme 2007; Wackershauser et al. 2017).

During an ACBC analysis, respondents undergo three mandatory stages: a Build-Your-Own (BYO) stage, a Screening stage, and a Choice Tournament stage. All three stages are interrelated and allow for learning efficiently about consumers' preferences (Orme 2014, p. 132). The BYO stage is of pivotal importance as its results set the stage for the remainder of the ACBC study. Within the BYO stage, consumers configure their ideal product by selecting specific product features at varying feature prices.

In this research, we argue that the type of touch interface a consumer uses in ACBC influences the BYO stage's outcomes. This is because research in other contexts, such as car configurators, suggests that consumers accept higher-priced options when configuring products using a direct vs. an indirect touch interface (Hildebrand and Levav 2017). We first meta-analyze 12 ACBC data sets provided by market research agencies and academics to address this concern. In line with our

F. Kühn (✉) · V. Sablotny-Wackershauser
Otto-von-Guericke University, Magdeburg, Saxony-Anhalt, Germany
e-mail: frauke.kuehn@ovgu.de; verena.sablotny-wackershauser@ovgu.de

M. Lichters
Chemnitz University of Technology, Chemnitz, Saxony, Germany
e-mail: marcel.lichters@wiwi.tu-chemnitz.de

J. Allen et al. (eds.), *Celebrating the Past and Future of Marketing and Discovery with Social Impact*, Developments in Marketing Science: Proceedings of the Academy of Marketing Science, https://doi.org/10.1007/978-3-030-95346-1_41

concerns, the majority of ACBC studies indicated that the configured BYO products of the direct (vs. indirect) touch interface users had a higher price.

We subsequently conducted two studies (one online ACBC and one lab experiment) to analyze the interface type's effects. We highlight its consequences for the ACBC's results in terms of the estimated utility functions, relative price importance, willingness to pay, and predicted market demand. The lab study additionally provides an explanation of the interface type's impact. Especially consumers with a high autotelic need for touch (Peck and Childers 2003) experience higher study enjoyment when using a direct (vs. indirect) touch interface during an ACBC. We extract highly relevant managerial implications. Researchers should control for respondents' interface type in order to adjust the interface type used in ACBC studies with the one future customers will use when purchasing the focal product and services.

Keywords Adaptive choice-based conjoint · Need for touch · Sensory marketing · Touch interface

Game and Punishment Criminal Justice Lens on Commission Structure Ethics: An Abstract

Kristina Harrison and Aaron D. Arndt

Abstract Gaming behaviors may cause salespeople to bend or break agreements with customers, reducing customer trust (Román and Ruiz 2005) and increasing supply chain costs to business customers. The salesperson's firm is also directly harmed by gaming behaviors. The opportunity to engage in gaming behaviors increases as the complexity of the commission structures increases (Larkin 2014; Owan, Tsuru, and Uehara 2015; Oyer 1998, Tzioumis and Gee 2013). Tiered commission structures, also known as nonlinear compensation plans, may be particularly prone to gaming behaviors because salespeople can earn greater commission rates as they reach certain levels of sales performance during a commission period (Freeman et al. 2019; Larkin 2014; Owan et al. 2015).

Commission structures are often complex. In tiered commission structures, the percentage of variable pay changes at different levels of sales performance. Salesperson behaviors may change just prior to commission deadlines, depending on goal achievement. According to the deterrence doctrine, people weight temptation versus consequences before engaging in unethical behaviors. When the difference between tiers is large, it creates a larger temptation. Furthermore, salespeople should frame sales revenue differently depending on whether it leads to a new commission tier. Salespeople are likely to justify and downplay the consequences of gaming behavior that avoids rewards framed as a "loss" compared to gaming behavior intended to achieve a "gain." Using a sample of professional salespeople participating in an experiment, this research shows that salespeople are more likely to engage in gaming behavior to avoid a loss, particularly when rewards stakes are high and their visibility within the organization is low. These findings demonstrate that commission plan structure has an impact on salesperson behaviors above and beyond the extant paradigm of variable versus fixed compensation.

K. Harrison
University of Southern Mississippi, Hattiesburg, MS, USA
e-mail: kristina.m.harrison@usm.edu

A. D. Arndt (✉)
Old Dominion University, Norfolk, VA, USA
e-mail: aarndt@odu.edu

J. Allen et al. (eds.), *Celebrating the Past and Future of Marketing and Discovery with Social Impact*, Developments in Marketing Science: Proceedings of the Academy of Marketing Science, https://doi.org/10.1007/978-3-030-95346-1_42

Keywords Sales ethics · Sales commission structure · Compensation · Salesperson behavior · Unethical behavior · Sales management

When Authenticity Backfires: Genuine CSR Intent Could Cause More Harm than Good: An Abstract

Kristina Harrison and Lei Huang

Abstract There are numerous reasons firms engage in CSR activities; however, many firms will at some point, or another experience a publicly known fraud or wrongdoing, which may complicate how individuals perceive firms that have been using CSR. This research questions how individuals will view firms that engage in different types of CSR with various expected benefits when fraud has come to light. When CSR motivations are seen by consumers as profit driven, attitudes are more negative towards the firm, but when motivations appear socially motivated, firm attitudes are more favorable (Becker-Olsen et al. 2006). Additionally, CSR motivations influence consumer perceptions of a firm –firms with low salient benefits from CSR appeared more sincere and had higher evaluations than firms with higher salient CSR benefits. (Yoon, Gürhan-Canli, and Schwarz 2006).

The results suggest that the expected CSR payoffs moderate the moderation of the indirect effect of CSR fraud perceptions on the purchase intention through ethical CSR beliefs by the type of CSR activities. When firms use CSR that is positioned to aid stakeholders outside of the firm coupled with low expected financial benefits, individuals will judge firms more harshly with fraud than if the firm had high expected financial benefits and CSR positioned to benefit those inside or close to the firm. These findings imply that when there is congruence between CSR ethical values and a firm's CSR motivations, consumers may feel deceived, resulting in a backlash effect. Therefore, firms should be truthful about the real intent of CSR behavior, and subsequently, consumers will not judge those firms as harshly, even if CSR motivations are purely financially driven.

K. Harrison (✉)
University of Southern Mississippi, Hattiesburg, MS, USA
e-mail: kristina.m.harrison@usm.edu

L. Huang
State University of New York at Fredonia, Fredonia, NY, USA
e-mail: lei.huang@fredonia.edu

J. Allen et al. (eds.), *Celebrating the Past and Future of Marketing and Discovery with Social Impact*, Developments in Marketing Science: Proceedings of the Academy of Marketing Science, https://doi.org/10.1007/978-3-030-95346-1_43

Keywords Corporate social responsibility · CSR · Ethics · Fraud · Corporate hypocrisy · CSR motivation

Do Not Buy our Product: Consumers' Responses towards Green-Demarketing Ad Messages: An Abstract

Catalina Wache, Jana Möller, Alexander Mafael, Viktoria Daumke, Brenda Fetahi, and Nora Melcher

Abstract In response to the negative impact of consumption on ecological sustainability, green marketing (GM) messages have become increasingly common. In GM ad messages, brands encourage purchases of products that respect the environment and the limited capacity of resources aiming to drive the share of sustainable products in consumers' baskets (White et al. 2019). However, reducing consumption overall is more effective at reducing environmental pollution and saving natural resources (Benton 2015). Through claims like "Buy Less, Demand More" (Patagonia 2021) brands have begun to practice green demarketing (GDM). GDM is an extension of demarketing that discourages demand for products for the sake of the environment. GDM thus contradicts brand activities that aim to increase sales (Bruce et al. 2012). Compared to GM, GDM is a more radical approach in the sense that companies no longer promote their green products, but rather promote a general reduction of consumption. Due to the unconventional character of GDM ad messages, it is important to investigate consumer's responses and the underlying mechanisms of GDM ad processing. Also, engaging in GDM is likely to become increasingly interesting for brands that target environmentally conscious consumers. The present study adds to existing research (e.g., Armstrong et al. 2015, Reich et al. 2016) by examining the impact of GDM messages on attitudes toward the ad. Moreover, we shed light on the processing of GMD messages. We propose two opposing mechanisms that affect consumer's attitudes towards a GDM ad message. Since social and environmental business practices have the potential to entail positive consumer responses (e.g., Reich et al. 2016; Luo and Bhattacharya 2006; Olsen et al. 2014), we suggest that due to their focus on sustainability, attitudes toward

C. Wache (✉) · J. Möller · V. Daumke · B. Fetahi · N. Melcher
Freie Universität Berlin, Berlin, Germany
e-mail: catalina.wache@fu-berlin.de; jana.moeller@fu-berlin.de; vic0611@zedat.fu-berlin.de; fetab97@zedat.fu-berlin.de; melchen96@zedat.fu-berlin.de

A. Mafael
Stockholm School of Economics, Stockholm, Sweden
e-mail: alexander.mafael@hhs.se

J. Allen et al. (eds.), *Celebrating the Past and Future of Marketing and Discovery with Social Impact*, Developments in Marketing Science: Proceedings of the Academy of Marketing Science, https://doi.org/10.1007/978-3-030-95346-1_44

GDM ad messages are more positive compared to traditional marketing (TM) ad messages, but not different from GM ad messages. While GDM ad messages might profit from their sustainability focus, attitudes toward GDM ad messages are likely to be compromised by low processing fluency and increased skepticism. As GDM ad messages are considered to be unconventional, they are likely to be processed less fluently than TM and GM ad messages, evoking higher levels of consumer skepticism and thus results in lower levels of attitudes towards the ad. Results showed that attitudes toward sustainable ad messages were significantly higher than attitudes toward the non-sustainable ad message. Additionally, results revealed a positive and significant direct effect of GDM ad message on attitudes toward the ad and a negative significant indirect effect mediated serially by processing fluency and skepticism on attitudes toward the ad.

Keywords Demarketing · Green marketing · Sustainability · Processing fluency

Why Brands Should Use Female Influencers to Endorse Male Fashion: An Abstract

Walter von Mettenheim and Klaus-Peter Wiedmann

Abstract The physical attractiveness of influencers is considered as one of their major success factors. However, in previous literature, attractiveness was considered as a unidimensional requirement, without regarding (potential) contingencies. This has left some research gaps and open questions: According to the attractiveness dimension of the famous Cialdini (2011) principle on Likeability, high attractiveness of a communicator is a universal advantage. However, if the receiver her/himself is of low attractiveness, this statement clashes with another dimension of the Likeability principle: Similarity. As receivers tend to like communicators being similar to them, and attractiveness-related similarity is a relevant subdimension of similarity (Bekk et al. 2017), a conflict is looming. To make matters more complicated, the advantageousness of attractiveness may also depend on the gender of the endorser and receiver: According to the theory on the anti-attractiveness bias, individuals may disadvantage highly attractive individuals of the same gender (Agthe et al. 2010). Finally, gender might also play a role, detached from attractiveness. According to the similarity dimension of the Cialdini (2011) principle on likeability, similarity can also occur on the level of gender. Most fashion endorsers stay in compliance with this principle as they merely endorse fashion for receivers of their gender. However, it also happens that an influencer endorses fashion for consumers of the opposite gender: Is such an endorsement completely absurd? Or is it, after all, worth to know what a member of the opposite gender thinks looks good on you?

In this study, the effects of influencers' and receivers' attractiveness and gender on influencer likeability, credibility and brand purchase intention are investigated. To this aim, an experiment including 374 observations was carried out and analyzed by means of structural equation modeling in SmartPls. Two models, on female (F) and male (M) receivers were designed and statistically compared by means of multigroup analysis. The results reveal that in most of the cases, a highly attractive influencer is more advantageous than one of low attractiveness, even if the receiver is of low attractiveness. In this case the "high attractiveness dimension" of the

W. von Mettenheim (✉) · K.-P. Wiedmann
Leibniz University of Hanover, Hanover, Germany
e-mail: vonmettenheim@m2.uni-hannover.de; wiedmann@m2.uni-hannover.de

J. Allen et al. (eds.), *Celebrating the Past and Future of Marketing and Discovery with Social Impact*, Developments in Marketing Science: Proceedings of the Academy of Marketing Science, https://doi.org/10.1007/978-3-030-95346-1_45

Liking Principle seems to beat the (attractiveness based) similarity dimension. More surprisingly, for male fashion, a female influencer appears to be more advantageous. Counter-intuitively, an anti-attractiveness bias was not found to occur among females, but among males.

Practitioners can gain important insights from this. (1) Selecting physically attractive influencers is more advantageous, no matter how attractive the targeted consumers are. (2) It is certainly possible to endorse fashion for male by a female, however the opposite is not advisable. (3) Males may have negative feelings towards highly attractive male endorsers.

Keywords Influencer marketing · Attractiveness · Gender · Fashion

Mobilizing the Inner Forces: Salesperson Political Skill, Co-Worker Relationship Satisfaction and Salesperson Internal Support

Achim Kießig and Cornelia Zanger

Abstract A considerable body of research stresses the importance for salespersons to gain access to internal resources and obtain internal cooperation from co-workers to be effective in today's complex selling environments. Research in this area has therefore started to explore the precursors and consequences of salesperson's internal relationships and social networks. However, to date no study investigates the skills that help salespersons to foster obtainment of internal support from co-workers. In light of this, this study examines the role of salesperson political skill for salesperson internal support from co-workers and identifies co-worker relationship satisfaction as an important intermediate link in this relationship. Dyadic survey data from 43 salespeople and 92 of their co-workers employed at a provider and distributor for telecommunication solutions is used to test the hypothesized relationships. The results provide evidence for the positive impact of political skill on co-worker relationship satisfaction, which subsequently enhances internal support for salespersons. This study contributes to sales theory and practice by underlining the role of political skill for salespersons to be effective at obtaining internal support.

Keywords Salesperson · Co-worker · Internal support · Political skill · Relationship satisfaction

Introduction

Aiming at building strong and long-lasting customer relationships the sales function has changed from being isolated to be an integrated function that bridges boundaries to other departments to fulfil demanding customer needs (Storbacka et al. 2009;

A. Kießig (✉) · C. Zanger
Chemnitz University of Technology, Chemnitz, Germany
e-mail: achim.kiessig@wirtschaft.tu-chemnitz.de; cornelia.zanger@wirtschaft.tu-chemnitz.de

J. Allen et al. (eds.), *Celebrating the Past and Future of Marketing and Discovery with Social Impact*, Developments in Marketing Science: Proceedings of the Academy of Marketing Science, https://doi.org/10.1007/978-3-030-95346-1_46

Bradford et al. 2010). Against this background, the sales literature's interest in exploring the so called 'intra-organizational dimension' of sales has been growing rapidly in recent years (Plouffe 2018). In course of this, sales researchers have broadened their perspective beyond the salesperson-customer interface to investigate salesperson's internal interactions and relationship ties (e.g. Steward et al. 2010; Bolander et al. 2015; Plouffe et al. 2016) that are important for salespersons to foster support from co-workers (skills, knowledge, time or information), which in turn is necessary to fulfil day-to-day sales duties to eventually enhance individual sales performance (Bradford et al. 2010; Plouffe 2018; Bradford et al. 2019).

Although literature has pointed out the importance for salespersons to secure valuable internal resources and achieve co-worker's cooperation (e.g. Plouffe and Barclay 2007; Bradford et al. 2010), research on this issue is scarce. To date, the limited literature suggests that salespersons effectiveness at garnering valuable internal resources depends on salesperson's internal ties (i.e. relationship diversity and internal tie strength) (Steward et al. 2010), personal traits (i.e. salesperson allocentrism) (Bradford et al. 2019) and behaviors (i.e. salesperson exploratory navigation) (Plouffe and Barclay 2007; Plouffe and Grégoire 2011; Bradford et al. 2019). Even though, these works undoubtedly provide an important foundation to understand the origins of internal support for salespersons, the existing studies, however, have not fully investigated the skills that help salespeople to successfully mobilize internal support. However, there is a rich research tradition on the role of salespersons skills at the interface between salespersons and their customers (e.g. Verbeke et al. 2011). Against the backdrop of the growing importance of salesperson internal interactions, it is promising for sales theory and practice alike to further expand this line of research to the salesperson-co-worker level. To move research in this area forward, it is important to open this 'black box' by developing a deepened understanding of the skills and interpersonal mechanisms that result in enhanced levels of internal support gained by salespersons.

The current research contributes to close this research gap by identifying political skill as an important interpersonal competency for salespersons to secure internal support from co-workers. Applying Social Exchange Theory (Blau 1964), we develop a model that suggests co-worker relationship satisfaction to be an interpersonal mechanism that links salesperson political skill to salesperson's effectiveness at garnering internal support. To test our hypothesis, we use matched data from 43 salespersons and 92 of their co-workers. The current research is, to our knowledge, the first work that tackles the issue of salesperson internal support from a dyadic perspective.

Theoretical Foundations and Hypothesis

Salesperson Internal Support and Salesperson Political Skill

In demanding business environments individual salespersons are often not equipped with all knowledge and competencies that are necessary to independently serve customers (Yang et al. 2011). Thus, individual sales success is not only a function of salesperson's ability to sense and satisfy customer needs, but is also highly dependent on the salesperson's internal interactions and relationships (Bolander and Richards 2018). The mobilization and coordination of internal resources have therefore become integral demands of the sales role (Bradford et al. 2010; Plouffe and Barclay 2007). This reasoning is complemented by empirical studies that highlight the positive impact of salesperson's resource access and internal support on sales outcomes, such as overall sales performance (Li et al. 2017; Bradford et al. 2019; Plouffe and Grégoire 2011; Steward et al. 2010), customer satisfaction (Susskind et al. 2003) and customer relationship quality (Bradford et al. 2019). Hence, the issue of internal support becomes increasingly important for sales research. Despite the relevance of salespersons' individual support at an interpersonal level, to date, the majority of sales research has mainly investigated internal cooperation between sales and other functions from an inter-departmental perspective (e. g. Ernst et al. 2010; Rangarajan et al. 2018; Johnson et al. 2019). Moreover, the little research that has been done at the salesperson's individual level does not provide a uniform concept of salesperson internal support. Instead, past studies on salesperson's obtainment of support put forth a variety of related concepts, such as 'coordination of expertise' (Steward et al. 2010), 'customer coordination' (Plouffe and Grégoire 2011), or 'effectiveness in getting internal support' (Bradford et al. 2019). The different concepts highlight different aspects of internal support. Coordination of expertise and customer coordination underscore salesperson's effectiveness in synchronizing the organizational inputs necessary to close pending sales transactions. Effectiveness in getting internal support, on the other hand, puts salesperson's success at leveraging internal resources at the core of the concept. Even though the support concepts are – to some extend – different, all concepts have one clear overlap: They all pay attention to salesperson's effectiveness at mobilizing internal resources that are linked to co-workers, to satisfy customer needs. To provide a unifying conceptual foundation of salesperson internal support for the current work, we turn to the general field of organizational research. Even though, organizational research has also suggested a variety of concepts related to interpersonal support at work (Bolino and Grant 2016), research in this area distinguishes two basic types of interpersonal support: socioemotional support and instrumental support (Mathieu et al. 2019). Our concept of salesperson internal support is equal to the latter one, whereby we define salesperson internal support as the co-worker's willingness and actual efforts to provide a salesperson with assistance and supportive resources (i.e. skills, knowledge, time and information) in pending sales transactions (Susskind et al. 2003).

To explore the skills that help salespersons to achieve internal support, we look at political skill, which is a multifaceted social competency that refers to the ability to a) understand and interpret social environments, and b) to apply this knowledge to accomplish personal and/or organizational objectives in work related contexts (Ferris et al. 2005). The political skill construct thereby comprises four facets that reflect a person's sensitiveness for understanding social environments and interactions (social astuteness), the ability to exert interpersonal influence in a flexible manner (interpersonal influence), the competence to build strong relationships and networks (networking ability) and the talent to appear as honest and sincere (apparent sincerity) (Ferris et al. 2007). The focus of this research is on political skill because politically skilled people are especially apt at exerting influence on others to achieve organizational or personal goals (Ferris et al. 2007). As salespeople success at garnering internal resources is dependent on his or her ability to exert influence on co-workers (Plouffe et al. 2016), we expect political skill to be highly relevant for salesperson internal support. Past research supports this intuitive link to some degree, as political skill has already shown to positively impact salesperson social capital (Bolander et al. 2015) and salesperson resource access (Li et al. 2017). However, the link between salesperson political skill and salesperson internal support and its underlying mechanisms are still underdeveloped.

The Link Between Salesperson Political Skill and Salesperson Internal Support: Co-Worker Relationship Satisfaction

To understand the linkage between salesperson political skill and salesperson internal support in more detail, we draw on social exchange theory (Blau 1964; Cropanzano and Mitchell 2005). Social exchange theory (SET) understands interpersonal relationships as a series of resource exchanges that result in obligations between interaction partners (Emerson 1976). This sense of obligation arises from a person's feelings of being treated favourably by an interaction partner and the resulting desire to repay the favourable treatment to ultimately maintain the relationship. The quality of the relationship between the interacting partners thereby alters the nature of the exchange process in such a way that high quality relationships reinforce reciprocal behaviors (Cropanzano and Mitchell 2005). Thus, SET considers relationship quality as a catalyst of ongoing interpersonal resource exchanges. Applying SET to our research, we construe salesperson internal support as co-worker's reciprocal behaviors toward a salesperson and expect co-worker's perceptions of relationship quality with a salesperson to enhance co-worker's willingness to maintain the relationship through acting for the benefit of the relationship partner (i.e. salesperson). This SET guided reasoning is also supported by research that highlights the relevance of high-quality relationships at work, as they support positive organizational and individual outcomes (Dutton and Heaphy 2003). The literature that focuses co-worker relationships further shows that co-workers can indeed develop high-quality relationships at work (Ferris et al. 2009). High-quality relationships in turn positively influence interpersonal processes and outcomes such as interpersonal or peer citizenship behavior, that comprises behaviors such as helping and assisting others at work (Setton and Mossholder 2002). Declining relationship quality, in contrast, hinders co-worker's cooperation (Golden and Veiga 2018). In short, research has revealed the obtainment of instrumental support (i.e. task assistance) to be a key function of good relationships at work (Colbert et al. 2016). Though a considerable body of research deals with relationship quality, there is yet no univocal concept of relationship quality (Ragins and Dutton 2007) and research brought up various dimensions that can be employed to characterize high quality relationships (e.g. Ferris et al. 2009). In this research, relationship quality is defined in terms of a general affective assessment of a relationship. We therefore draw on past sales research and adapt the concept of customer relationship satisfaction (Rapp et al. 2006; Agnihotri et al. 2017) to our study's context. More specifically, in the current study co-worker relationship satisfaction is defined as the co-worker's overall satisfaction in a salesperson-co-worker relationship, whereas feelings of satisfaction stem from the assessment of the effort and evaluation of the inputs a salesperson devotes to a salesperson-co-worker relationship.

To understand how salespersons may enhance co-worker's perceptions of relationship satisfaction in the first place, it is important to consider the reciprocal nature of work relationships. Because SET posits that cycles of resource exchanges between two exchange partners are fundamental to the development of strong relationships, it is not only important for salespeople to receive co-worker's resources, but also very relevant to provide meaningful resources to their co-workers. It is further important to note that the exchanged resources need to be valuable and relevant to the exchange partners to result in strong relationships and enduring reciprocation (Blau 1964; Cropanzano and Mitchell 2005). If a salesperson, for instance, is equipped with the competence to sense, which resources are valued by a particular co-worker and the behavioral flexibility to deliver these relationship inputs in an appropriate manner, this salesperson should be able to generate higher levels of relationship satisfaction with co-workers that should eventually result in enhanced levels of salesperson internal support. Politically skilled employees are generally good at building friendships and leveraging resources which are under their co-worker's control (Ferris et al. 2007; Bolander et al. 2015). Due to their ability to develop social ties, politically skilled salespeople should be especially apt to easily develop connections to co-workers and cultivate norms of reciprocity (Fang et al. 2015; Bradford et al. 2019). Once a politically skilled salesperson gets close to co-workers, this person understands what behaviors fit a given situation to reach personal objectives in a social context by conveying believability, trust and confidence (Ahearn et al. 2004). Through this behavioral flexibility in combination with his or her sensing skills a politically skilled salesperson is in the position to accurately address co-workers' needs. A politically skilled salesperson understands co-worker's motivations and knows what socio-emotional or instrumental resources a particular co-worker values. This helps salespeople to engage in behaviors that co-worker's wish to 'repay' (Frieder et al. 2019). Moreover, through their talent to exert influence in adaptive ways and their sincere appearance (Ferris et al. 2007) politically skilled salespeople possess the ability to deal with the varying requirements when interacting with different co-workers and the competence to exchange resources in an appropriate manner. Frieder and Basik (2017) furthermore found that political skill enhances others perceptions of behavioral integrity. Applied to salesperson-co-worker relationships we can therefore assume that co-workers should perceive high levels of salesperson's word-deed alignment when interacting with a politically skilled salesperson. This presumably induces feelings of consistency between the behavior of the salesperson and relationship expectations from the co-worker's point of view, which should result in heightened levels of co-worker relationship satisfaction.

Building on the core assumptions of SET, and the general belief of political skill to be a driver of relationship development (Ferris et al. 2009; Ferris et al. 2012; DeRue et al. 2011), we propose:

H1: Salesperson political skill positively affects co-worker relationship satisfaction.
H2: Co-worker relationship satisfaction positively affects salesperson internal support.

Methods

Sample and Measures

To test our hypothesis, we collected data in cooperation with a medium sized (1000+ employees) German solution provider and distributor for information and telecommunication hard- and software. Before data collection, we interviewed the companies (sales)managers to make sure that there is sufficient task interdependence between the sales force and other departments that requires salespeople to mobilize internal support to successfully fulfil day-to-day sales duties. After we obtained permission to collect data, we provided the sales managers with survey packages that were distributed to the sales force of the company (total of 70 salespeople). As desired by the company's managers, data collection was conducted via a paper-pen questionnaire to enhance the internal acceptance and engagement for the study. Each salesperson received an envelope containing one questionnaire for themselves and four further envelopes (closed) containing questionnaires for co-workers. Salespeople were required to pass on the closed envelopes to four different co-workers that they regularly ask for support to successfully fulfil their day-to-day sales tasks. Moreover, salespeople were asked to select co-workers from other departments than the sales department. To ensure high anonymity and to make sure that we could match the questionnaires afterwards, salespersons were instructed to mark their questionnaires and all of the four envelopes with a self-selected code of five numbers. Co-workers were asked to transfer this number to their questionnaire after opening the envelope that they had received from the salesperson. Through the paper-pen strategy and the vital engagement of the company's management, we collected complete data from 43 salespeople (53.5% female) and 92 of their co-workers (59,8% female). Salespersons organizational tenure was 9.1 years on average. Co-workers organizational tenure, on average, was 11.3 years. For each salesperson, on average, 3.3 co-workers reported on their perception of the relationship they have with a salesperson. In turn, each co-worker, on average, reported on 1.5 salesperson-co-worker relationships. This resulted in 142 dyads and a cross classified data structure, where collected data is nested in a cross classification between co-workers and salespersons.

Existing scales from the literature were used to measure the constructs and were adapted where necessary. For all measures, respondents reported on 7-point Likert-type scales, with *1 = strongly disagree* and *7 = strongly agree* as anchors. To assess salesperson political skill, salespersons reported to the 18-PSI (Ferris et al. 2005). In accordance with prior studies (e.g. Li et al. 2017), we employed a composite scale of political skill which showed good internal consistency ($\alpha = .85$). To assess co-worker relationship satisfaction, we adapted the three-item relationship satisfaction sub-scale of the relationship quality scale developed by De Wulf et al. (2001) to the interpersonal context of our study. Items used in the current study are: "I have a very good work relationship with this salesperson", "I am happy with the efforts this salesperson is making towards maintaining a good work relationship with me", "I am satisfied with the work relationship I have with this salesperson" ($\alpha = .72$). To assess salesperson internal support, co-workers reported to an adapted version of the co-worker support scale taken from Susskind et al. (2003), which was complemented by an adapted item taken from Plouffe and Grégoire (2011) ("I always provide this salesperson with the required support that she or he needs when coordinating the details of transactions"). We added this item as it touches the very core of our concept of salesperson internal support. Although we adapted items for this scale from validated existing scales, the internal consistency of the salesperson internal support scale was not ideal ($\alpha = .63$). However, this cronbach's alpha value is above .60, and still tolerable, especially because only few items were used (i.e. 4 items) to assess salesperson internal support (Hair et al. 2006).

Given the research that links organization tenure to salesperson's success at network building (Bolander et al. 2015), we controlled for salesperson's and co-worker's 'shared' organization tenure that reflects the shared period of time a specific salesperson and a responding co-worker worked for the company expressed in years. That allowed us to control for the possibility that the shared organization tenure of a salesperson and a co-worker might influence salesperson-co-worker relationship satisfaction. We furthermore controlled for co-worker's equity sensitivity, as more benevolent co-workers might provide more support in spite of their relationship satisfaction. We assessed co-worker's equity sensitivity with the equity sensitivity instrument (King and Miles 1994) and calculated co-worker's benevolence value according to the procedure outlined by King and Miles (1994).

Analysis and Results

Taking account of the cross classified data structure, where responses are nested within co-workers and salespersons, a multi-level strategy for data analysis is the appropriate approach in this study. In fact, the intra class correlation values for co-worker relationship satisfaction ($ICC_{Salesperson} = .115$; $ICC_{Co\text{-}worker} = .083$) and salesperson internal support ($ICC_{Salesperson} = .012$; $ICC_{Co\text{-}worker} = .688$) indicate a notable amount of variance between salespersons and between co-workers. With respect to the non-hierarchical nested data and to avoid the risk of biased parameter estimates,

Table 1 Correlations and Descriptive Statistics

Salesperson variables	1	2	3	4	5
1. Salesperson political skill	–				
Co-worker variables					
2. Co-worker relationship satisfaction	.259[a]	–	.272[a]	.099	
3. Salesperson internal support	−.037		–	.084	
4. Co-worker benevolence	−.056			–	
'Shared'variables					
5. Shared organizational tenure	−.035	.039	−.045	.070	–
Mean	5.59	6.43	6.54	31.00	6.44
Standard deviation	.60	.52	.43	6.50	5.36

Correlations between salespersons' political skill, co-worker variables and shared variables were computed by disaggregating salesperson' political skill (below diagonal); correlations between co-worker variables were computed at the co-worker level (above the diagonal)
[a]p < .01

when ignoring multi-level data structures (Hox et al. 2018, p. 244), we used the $2^{(A)}$-1–1 multi-level framework suggested by Luo (2017) to test our hypothesis. We decided to implement this framework as it was developed for testing hypothesis where one of the crossed factors is associated with the initial predictor at Level 2 (i.e. salesperson political skill) (Luo 2017, p. 675). Controlling for co-worker random effects, this approach allows to test if salesperson political skill affects co-worker relationship satisfaction and if co-worker relationship satisfaction subsequently enhances salesperson internal support. To test the hypothesis, a two-step approach would have been desirable where, first, the measurement model was evaluated, and then, the structural model was tested. However, our small sample size of 43 units on the higher-level led to an inappropriate sample to parameter ratio which rules out this procedure. To examine our model, we therefore used the composite scores of the constructs as single indicators in the structural model (see Vermeeren 2014). Table 1 provides descriptive statistics and correlations of the constructs.

The hypothesized relationships were examined in Mplus Version 8.4 (Muthén and Muthén 2017). Mplus was selected because it provides the necessary procedures to examine the complex structure of our cross classified data set by employing a bayesian estimation method which is especially suitable for small sample sizes (Muthén and Asparouhov 2012). The estimated model showed good model fit ($PP_p = .45$).[1]

Hypothesis 1 posits that salesperson political skill positively affects co-worker relationship satisfaction in the salesperson-co-worker relationship. The results provide support for this hypothesis as the bayesian 95% credibility interval (CI) does not include zero (β = .24, CI-95%: 0.079–0.404). Hypothesis 2 suggested a positive relationship between co-worker relationship satisfaction and salesperson internal

[1]The posterior predictive p-value (PPP), which is the proportion of chi-square values replicated in the simulated data that exceeds the chi-square values of the observed data, indicates good model fit.

support. The results of the analysis indicate that co-worker relationship satisfaction positively affect salesperson internal support at the within-level of analysis (β = .20, CI-95%: 0.069–0.339). However, a positive effect of co-worker relationship satisfaction on salesperson internal support on the between-salesperson-level is not supported by the data (β = .18, CI-95%: −2.138-2.871). Thus, hypothesis 2 does find support on the within-, but not on the between-level of analysis. In a further step we added the control variables to our model. Incorporating salesperson's/co-worker's shared organization tenure and co-workers' benevolence in our model does not substantially change the results. We still find support for the positive relationship between salesperson political skill and co-worker relationship satisfaction (β = .27, CI-95%: 0.096–0.421) and for the positive relationship between co-worker relationship satisfaction and salesperson internal support in the within-level of analysis (β = .20, CI-95%: 0.074–0.338).

Discussion and Implications

This study builds a conceptual and empirical link between salesperson political skill and salesperson internal support through co-worker's perceptions of relationship satisfaction. However, our analysis produced somewhat inconsistent findings. Thus, the study's results provide support for a positive impact of relationship satisfaction on salesperson internal support at the within-, but not at the between-level of analysis. This finding may be caused by the implemented multi-level approach to analyse the collected data. By aggregating co-worker data to the higher-level (salesperson-level) variance in co-worker relationship satisfaction at the lower-level (co-worker-level) of analysis gets lost. However, individual co-workers presumably differ in their perceptions of relationship satisfaction with a salesperson and subsequently vary in their supportive behaviors for a salesperson. These inter-individual variations are masked at the higher-level of analysis, which possibly explains the inconsistent results at different levels of the analysis. Notwithstanding, the current research underlines the importance of relationship satisfaction for internal support in sales environments.

Even though, existing sales research suggests internal networks and relationships to be beneficial for gaining access to internal resources and support, to date, research remains largely silent on how internal support for salespeople arises at an interpersonal level of analysis and what interpersonal dynamics between salespersons and their co-workers result in different levels of salesperson internal support. Social capital theory-based research deliberatively neglects interpersonal dynamics at the micro level for the sake of exploring the role of the structure of social networks (Steward et al. 2010, Gonzalez et al. 2014; Bolander et al. 2015). Hence, this stream of research focuses on the configurations and quantity of social ties and does therefore not allow a deep exploration of the significance of the micro level mechanisms of salesperson-co-worker relationships and interactions for the acquisition of internal support. The little research that applies a social exchange lens on the other hand, does not investigate the role of salesperson skills, does not explicitly capture co-worker perceptions of relationship quality, and does not assess the level of support salespeople receive from the co-worker's perspective (Bradford et al. 2019; Murphy and Coughlan 2018). This study contributes to this line of research by investigating how a specific salesperson skill enhances internal cooperation through heightened levels of relationship quality. More precisely, we tested the role of salesperson pollical skill as an individual difference in this context. Contributing to the body of research that suggests salesperson political skill to be important for network development, this study's results provide support that this competency positively affects co-worker relationship satisfaction and subsequently salesperson internal support. Beyond this, the study's design allowed us to empirically examine this issue from both sides of the salesperson-co-worker dyad by assessing political skill at the salesperson level and using co-worker responses to measure co-worker relationship satisfaction and salesperson internal support. From a theoretical point of view, this study contributes to research on the skills and interpersonal dynamics that lead to salesperson internal support, and thereby expands sales theory related to salesperson internal interactions. Moreover, the current research tests a key tenet of SET in a sales context and contributes to answering the call for more research on the role of political skill for relationship quality assessments in work relationships (e.g. Munyon et al. 2015, p. 172). From a managerial perspective it is important to recognize the role of high-quality relationships between salespersons and their co-workers. As a result of this research, we suggest that enhancing the sales force's level of political skill can be understood as a worthwhile approach to achieve internal relationship satisfaction. Past research has suggested that political skill development can be supported through training programs (see Munyon et al. 2015). Complementing sales trainings by a 'political skill component' and/or using political skill as a personnel assessment criterion (Ferris et al. 2012) can help to improve the sales force's relationship building skills and salesperson internal support, which in turn is likely to influence individual sales performance (Bradford et al. 2019).

Limitations and Future Research

This research is not without limitations. Firstly, though we deliberately collected data in cooperation with a single company to reduce the risk of unintended influences of organizational-level variables on the hypothesized relationships, this procedure also mitigates the generalizability of the study's results. Therefore, further studies are needed to explore if these findings hold up in multiple companies and industries. For instance, a company's hierarchy and culture possibly affect the relationships investigated in this study. Secondly, the reliability of the salesperson internal support scale was not ideal. Future research that focuses on the refinement of the scale that captures the amount of support a salesperson receives from his or her co-workers would be promising to move empirical research forward. Thirdly, past research has called for more work on the different mechanisms through which the four political skill dimensions affect important outcomes (Ferris et al. 2012). Additionally, work on positive co-worker relationships points to the fact that relationship quality comprises different facets (Ferris et al. 2009). This study focuses on relationship satisfaction. It would be interesting to broaden the scope of our research by conducting dimensional analysis in the relationship between salesperson political skill and co-workers' perceptions of different facets of salesperson-co-worker relationship quality. This would contribute to a deeper understanding on the modes of operation of salesperson political skill in salesperson-co-worker relationships. In this context, longitudinal studies could also broaden our understanding on the relevance of different political skill dimensions in various relationship development stages. For example, it would be plausible to assume that the apparent sincerity dimension of political skill is especially important in the relationship formation stage to build a sense of trustworthiness which should promote the initiation of resource exchanges. Finally, the relevance of this research is based on the premise that internal support eventually drives sales performance. Hence, future studies should assess the impact of salesperson internal support on sales performance and explore boundary conditions that strengthen or attenuate this relationship.

References

Agnihotri, R., Gabler, C., Itani, O., Jaramillo, F., & Krush, M. (2017). Salesperson ambidexterity and customer satisfaction: examining the role of customer demandingness, adaptive selling, and role conflict. *Journal of Personal Selling & Sales Management, 37*(1), 27-41.

Ahearn, K. K., Ferris, G. R., Hochwarter, W. A., Douglas, C., & Ammeter, A. P. (2004). Leader political skill and team performance. *Journal of Management, 30*(3), 309–327.

Blau, P. M. (1964). *Exchange and power in social life.* New York, John Wiley.

Bolander, W., & Richards, K. A. (2018). Why study intraorganizational issues in selling and sales management? *Journal of Personal Selling & Sales Management, 38*(2), 169-171.

Bolander, W., Satornino, C. B., Hughes, D. E., & Ferris, G. R. (2015). Social Networks within Sales Organizations: Their Development and Importance for Salesperson Performance. *Journal of Marketing, 79*(6), 1-16.

Bolino, M. C., & Grant, A. M. (2016). The Bright Side of Being Prosocial at Work, and the Dark Side, Too: A Review and Agenda for Research on Other-Oriented Motives, Behavior, and Impact in Organizations. *The Academy of Management Annals, 10(1)*, 599-670.

Bradford, K. D., Brown, S., Ganesan, S., Hunter, G., Onyemah, V., Palmatier, R., Rouziès, D., Spiro, R., Sujan, H., & Weitz, B. (2010). The embedded sales force: Connecting buying and selling organizations. *Marketing Letters, 21*(3), 239-253.

Bradford, K. D., Liu, Y., Shi, Y., Weitz, B. A., & Xu, J. (2019). Harnessing Internal Support to Enhance Customer Relationships: The Role of Networking, Helping, and Allocentrism. *Journal of Marketing Theory and Practice, 27*(2), 140-158.

Colbert, A. E., Bono, J. E., & Purvanova, R. K. (2016). Flourishing via workplace relationships: Moving beyond instrumental support. *Academy of Management Journal, 59*(4), 1199-1223.

Cropanzano, R., & Mitchell, M. S. (2005). Social Exchange Theory: An Interdisciplinary Review. *Journal of Management, 31*(6), 874-900.

DeRue, D. S., Nahrgang, J. D., Wellman, N., & Humphrey, S. E. (2011). Trait and behavioral theories of leadership: An integration and meta-analytic test of their relative validity. *Personnel Psychology, 64*(1), 7-52.

De Wulf, K., Odekerken-Schröder, G., & Iacobucci, D. (2001). Investments in Consumer Relationships: A Cross-Country and Cross-Industry Exploration. *Journal of Marketing*, *65*(4), 33-50.

Dutton, J. E., & Heaphy, E. (2003). The power of high-quality connections. In K. S. Cameron, J. E. Dutton & R. E. Quinn (Eds.), *Positive organizational scholarship: Foundations of a new discipline*: 263-278. San Francisco, CA: Berrett-Koehler.

Emerson, R. M. (1976). Social Exchange Theory. *Annual Review of Sociology, 2*, 335-362.

Ernst, H., Hoyer, W. D., & Rübsaamen, C. (2010). Sales, Marketing, and Research-and-Development Cooperation Across New Product Development Stages: Implications for Success. *Journal of Marketing, 74(5)*, 80-92.

Fang, R., Chi, L., Chen, M., & Baron, R. A. (2015). Bringing Political Skill into Social Networks: Findings from a Field Study of Entrepreneurs. *Journal of Management Studies, 52*(2), 175-212.

Ferris, G. R., Liden, R. C., Munyon, T. P., Summers, J. K., Basik, K. J., & Buckley, M. R. (2009). Relationships at work: Toward a multidimensional conceptualization of dyadic work relationships. *Journal of Management, 35*(6), 1379-1403.

Ferris, G. R., Treadway, D. C., Brouer, R. L., & Munyon, T. P. (2012). Political Skill in the Organizational Science. In G. R. Ferris & D.C. Treadway (Eds.), *Politics in Organizations. Theory and Research Considerations*: 487-528. New York, Routledge.

Ferris, G. R., Treadway, D. C., Kolodinsky, R. W., Hochwarter, W. A., Kacmar, C. J., Douglas, C., & Frink, D. D. (2005). Development and Validation of the Political Skill Inventory. *Journal of Management, 31*(1), 126-152.

Ferris, G. R., Treadway, D. C., Perrewé, P. L., Brouer, R. L., Douglas, C., & Lux, S. (2007). Political Skill in Organizations. *Journal of Management, 33*(3), 290-320.

Frieder, R. E., & Basik, K. J. (2017). Political skill, behavioral integrity, and work outcomes: Test of a multistage model. *Journal of Leadership & Organizational Studies, 24*(1), 65-82.

Frieder, R. E., Ferris, G. R., Perrewé, P. L., Wihler, A., & Brooks, C. D. (2019). Extending the metatheoretical framework of social/political influence to leadership: Political skill effects on situational appraisals, responses, and evaluations by others. *Personnel Psychology, 72*(4), 543-569.

Golden, T. D., & Veiga, J. F. (2018). Self-Estrangement's Toll on Job Performance: The Pivotal Role of Social Exchange Relationships with Coworkers. *Journal of Management, 44*(4), 1573-1597.

Gonzalez, G. R., Claro, D. P., & Palmatier, R. W. (2014). Synergistic Effects of Relationship Managers' Social Networks on Sales Performance. *Journal of Marketing, 78*(1), 76-94.

Hair, J. F., Black, W. C., Babin, B. J., Anderson, R. E., & Tatham, R. L. (2006). *Multivariate data analysis*. (Vol. 6), Upper Saddle River, NJ: Pearson Prentice Hall.

Hox, J. Moerbeek, M., & van de Schoot, R. (2018). *Multilevel Analysis*. New York, Routledge.

Johnson, J. S., Matthes, J. M., & Friend, S. B. (2019). Interfacing and customer-facing: Sales and marketing selling centers. *Industrial Marketing Management, 77*, 41-56.

King Jr. W. C., & Miles, E. W. (1994). The measurement of equity sensitivity. *Journal of Occupational & Organizational Psychology, 67*(2), 133-142.

Li, J., Sun, G., & Cheng, Z. (2017). The Influence of Political Skill on Salespersons' Work Outcomes: A Resource Perspective. *Journal of Business Ethics, 141*, 551-562.

Luo, W. (2017). Testing mediation effects in cross-classified multilevel data. *Behavior Research Methods, 49*(2), 674-684.

Mathieu, M., Eschleman, K. J., & Cheng, D. (2019). Meta-analytic and multiwave comparison of emotional support and instrumental support in the workplace. *Journal of Occupational Health Psychology, 24*(3), 387-409.

Munyon, T. P., Summers, J. K., Thompson, K. M., & Ferris, G. R. (2015). Political Skill and Work Outcomes: A Theoretical Extension, Meta-Analytic Investigation, and Agenda for the Future. *Personnel Psychology, 68*(1), 143-184.

Murphy, L. E., & Coughlan, J. P. (2018). Does it pay to be proactive? Testing proactiveness and the joint effect of internal and external collaboration on key account manager performance. *Journal of Personal Selling & Sales Management, 38*(2), 205-219.

Muthén, B. O., & Asparouhov, T. (2012). Bayesian SEM: A more flexible representation of substantive theory. *Psychological Methods, 17*(3), 313-335.

Muthén, L. K., & Muthén, B. O. (2017). *Mplus: Statistical Analysis with Latent Variables: User's Guide*. Version 8, Los Angeles, CA.

Plouffe, C. R. (2018). Is it navigation, networking, coordination … or what? A multidisciplinary review of influences on the intraorganizational dimension of the sales role and performance. *Journal of Personal Selling & Sales Management, 38*(2), 241-264.

Plouffe, C. R., & Barclay, D. W. (2007). Salesperson navigation: The intraorganizational dimension of the sales role. *Industrial Marketing Management, 36*(4), 528-539.

Plouffe, C. R., Bolander, W., Cote, J. A., & Hochstein, B. (2016). Does the customer matter most? Exploring strategic frontline employees' influence of customers, the internal business team, and external business partners. *Journal of Marketing, 80*(1), 106-123.

Plouffe, C. R., & Grégoire, Y. (2011). Intraorganizational employee navigation and socially derived outcomes: Conceptualization, validation, and effects on overall performance. *Personnel Psychology, 64*(3), 693-738.

Ragins, B. R., & Dutton, J. E. (2007). Positive Relationships at Work: An Introduction and Invitation. In J. E. Dutton & B. R. Ragins (Eds.), *LEA's organization and management series. Exploring positive relationships at work: Building a theoretical and research foundation:* 3-25. Lawrence Erlbaum Associates Publishers.

Rangarajan, D., Sharma, A., Paesbrugghe, B., & Boute R. (2018). Aligning sales and operations management: an agenda for inquiry. *Journal of Personal Selling & Sales Management, 28(2),* 220-240.

Rapp, A., Ahearne, M., Mathieu, J., & Schillewaert, J. (2006). The impact of knowledge and empowerment on working smart and working hard: The moderating role of experience. *International Journal of Research in Marketing, 23(3),* 279-293.

Setton, R. P., & Mossholder, K. W. (2002). Relationship quality and relationship context as antecedents of person- and task-focused interpersonal citizenship behavior. *Journal of Applied Psychology, 87*(2), 255-267.

Steward, M. D., Walker, B. A., Hutt, M. D., & Kumar, A. (2010). The coordination strategies of high-performing salespeople: internal working relationships that drive success. *Journal of the Academy of Marketing Science, 38 (5),* 550-566.

Storbacka, K., Ryals, L., Davies, I., & Nenonen, S. (2009). The changing role of sales: viewing sales as a strategic, cross-functional process. *European Journal of Marketing, 43*(8), 890-906.

Susskind, A. M., Kacmar, K. M., & Borchgrevink, C. P. (2003). Customer service providers' attitudes relating to customer service and customer satisfaction in the customer-server exchange. *Journal of Applied Psychology, 88*(1), 179-187.

Verbeke, W., Dietz, B., & Verwaal, E. (2011). Drivers of sales performance: a contemporary meta-analysis. Have salespeople become knowledge brokers? *Journal of the Academy of Marketing Science, 39(3),* 407-428.

Vermeeren, B. (2014). Variability in HRM implementation among line managers and its effect on performance: A 2-1-2 mediational multilevel approach. *The International Journal of Human Resource Management, 25*(22), 3039-3059.

Yang, J., Brashear Alejandro, T. G., & Boles, J. S. (2011). The role of social capital and knowledge transfer in selling center performance. *Journal of Business and Industrial Marketing, 26(3),* 152–161.

Is Ethical Consumption Intuitive? A Comparative Study on Food, Cosmetic and Clothes Markets

Stéphanie Montmasson, Sandrine Hollet-Haudebert, and Brigitte Muller

Abstract For decades, marketing research in ethical consumption has been facing the gap between attitude and behavior of the ethical consumer. This topic has been explored mainly through a rational and cognitive approach. We intend to develop a new approach with the socio-intuitionist psychological model on three different markets: food, cosmetics and clothes. These three markets are interesting from a sociological and marketing view. Based on an online panel composed of 1080 consumers, structural equation modeling is used to analyze intuitive judgments and ethical concerns. Our results indicate that inferential intuition significantly predicts the ethical reasoning, which in turn significantly influence the purchase and the attention paid to the ecological and social commitments of the chosen products of ethical consumption behavior. The effects are however different according the three markets we analyzed, suggesting that marketing managers should focus on non-rational influences such as inferential and emotional intuition to effectively promote ethical consumption.

Keywords Ethical consumption · Moral intuitions and reasoning · Food · Cosmetics · Clothes

Introduction

If European consumers were considered in 2019 as actors of "better consuming", French consumers are even more demanding in terms of "less consuming" and "doing things differently". Indeed, 57% of French consumers believe that we need to "completely review our economic system and get out of the myth of infinite

S. Montmasson (✉) · S. Hollet-Haudebert · B. Muller
Université de Toulon, Toulon, France
e-mail: stephanie-montmasson@etud.univ-tln.fr; sandrine.hollet-haudebert@univ-tln.fr; brigitte.muller@univ-tln.fr

J. Allen et al. (eds.), *Celebrating the Past and Future of Marketing and Discovery with Social Impact*, Developments in Marketing Science: Proceedings of the Academy of Marketing Science, https://doi.org/10.1007/978-3-030-95346-1_47

growth".[1] They are aware that the consumption of sustainable products is no longer enough, but that they should rather eliminate superfluous items and reduce their consumption in general. This phenomenon is already emerging in their purchasing habits: for example, in the cosmetic and hygiene products sector, more than two thirds of consumers say they are buying fewer products. In the clothing sector, 44% of French people declared they would voluntarily buy less clothing in 2018.[2] Finally, in the food sector, reducing food waste is a major priority for 2020.[3] At the same time, the French are increasingly turning to local and socially responsible offerings. The COVID-19 pandemic has confirmed this tendency, almost half of the consumers have stated that they prefer choosing brands committed to reduce their impact on the environment and inclined to help local communities.[4] These elements correspond to the definition of ethical consumption proposed by Low and Davenport (2007, p:341) as "human, animal and environmental concerns" which is not so easy to implement in the daily life.

The traditionally rationalist and cognitive literature is confronted with this gap between the attitudes of ethical consumers and their actual consumption intention and behavior, leaving many questions unsolved. Marketing researches are becoming aware that the predominant rational view of ethical decision-making does not take into account sufficiently cognitive elements such as values, virtues, ethical ideology and beliefs (Vitell 2015) that underlie the ethical identity and intuitive response of the consumer (John and Caldwell James 2013). A part of the literature on ethical consumption has turned to intuitionist perspectives and in particular to the socio-intuitionist model (Haidt and Graham 2007), thus recognizing the coexistence of two psychological systems (Epstein 1999) and the importance of moral intuition in ethical consumption behavior.

We therefore chose to investigate the role of intuitions in ethical consumer behavior in order to determine what role they can play in ethical consumer decision-making. We intend to determine whether they have the same influence on the food, cosmetics and ready-to-wear markets. We conducted a quantitative study on a representative sample of 1080 French consumers question on three different market (food, cosmetics and ready-to-wear). Our results highlight the role of intuitions and in particular the influence of affective intuitions, which do not play the same role in each of the markets, thus we continue the research of Zollo et al. (2018). We propose innovative recommendations for marketing managers.

---

[1] Etude Greenflex 2019, https://www.greenflex.com/communique-de-presse/barometre-consommation-responsable-2019-sortons-mythe-croissance-infinie/

[2] IFM 2018, https://www.modeintextile.fr/marche-francais-textile-habillement-se-transforme-linfluence-consommateurs/

[3] https://www.agro-media.fr/analyse/tendances-alimentaires-2020-lannee-de-tous-les-possibles-pour-lagroalimentaire-38134.html

[4] https://comarketing-news.fr/consommation-le-mythe-dun-monde-dapres/

Theoretical Background

Ethics and Consumption

From the philosophical point of view, ethics can be defined as an element of foundation of the human person, in its roots, which allows the good living, the good doing for the well-being of others. In the academic literature, the concept of ethics encompasses the notions of sustainability and responsibility. The notion of relationship to others in a present and future temporal vision is fundamental for each of the three concepts. Ethical consumption serves as a means of ethical and moral action based on subjective moral judgments applied to individual products and brands throughout the cycle of production, consumption and disposal (Brunk 2012). However, what is ethical summarizes different expressions, concerns and issues for each person. Cooper-Martin et al. (1993) define the ethics of consumer behavior as "decision making, purchasing and other consumer experiences that are affected by the ethical concerns of the consumer". In contrast to typical consumer decision making, which focuses on maximizing immediate benefits to the individual, sustainable choices involve long-term benefits to others and nature (White et al. 2019).

The Ethical Decision-Making Process and the Attitude-Behavior Gap

Researchers traditionally use rational cognitive models in which ethical decision-making is fully conscious, intentional and individually controlled (Rest 1986). Research on ethical consumption has highlighted the prevalent presence of dissonant or inconsistent behaviors (Mc Eachern 2010). Consumers claim that their behavior is influenced by values and attitudes that do not necessarily translate into actual behavior. This is called the attitude-behavior gap (Chatzidakis et al. 2007). Consumers are not always willing to disclose their true attitudes towards ethical products. Indeed, attitude measurements are self-reported and lead to socially desirable responses (Pelsmacker et al. 2005). White et al. (2019) put forward five categories of factors influencing sustainable behavior, including feelings and cognition, which are addressed jointly, as consumers generally take one of two options: affect or cognition (Fedorikhin 1999). This approach is consistent with the theories suggesting that an intuitive and affective or more deliberative and cognitive pathway may dominate decision making. However, the authors recognize that rationalist approaches that identify, encourage and evaluate sustainable behaviors do not provide a complete psychological framework (White et al. 2019). Thus, we believe that research on the role of intuition in ethical consumer behavior may be relevant to investigate the antecedents of moral consciousness and the psychological micro-mechanisms that lead to ethically acting decisions.

In the Moral Field, the Socio-Intuitionist Approach Is a Necessary Complement

In philosophy, intuitionism refers to the idea that moral truths exist. When people grasp these truths, they do so not through a process of ratification and reflection but rather through a process closer to perception, in which one "simply sees, without argument, that they [truths] are and must be true" (Harrison 1967, p: 72). Jung (1933) described intuition as a primary mode of perception that works unconsciously. Intuitive people prefer to react by imagining possibilities and patterns of detection, which contrasts with the other types of perception that prefer concrete details. The debate between rationalism and intuitionism is old (Haidt 2001). Both currents agree that individuals have emotions and intuitions, engage in reasoning. Both intuitions and reasoning are influenced by each other. It is therefore a question of clarifying how these processes are articulated. Rationalist models focus on reasoning and then discuss other processes such as emotions, environments and social interactions in terms of their effects on reasoning. The central claim of the socio-intuitionist model (see Fig. 1) is that moral judgment is caused by rapid moral intuition (system 1) and is followed (if necessary) by slow, post facto moral reasoning (system 2). System 1 is automatic, impulsive, unconscious, fast, instinctive and reflexive, innately programmed in human cognition (Haidt 2001). According to Epstein (2010), the intuitive system is resistant to change and remains context-specific. System 2 is slow, controlled, logical, deliberative, reflective and conscious, thinking is hypothetical (Kahneman 2003). Associated with the intuitionist model, the system model reveals that moral intuition is the a priori cognitive process embedded in system 1; moral reasoning is the post hoc rational cognitive process within system 2 (Zollo et al. 2018).

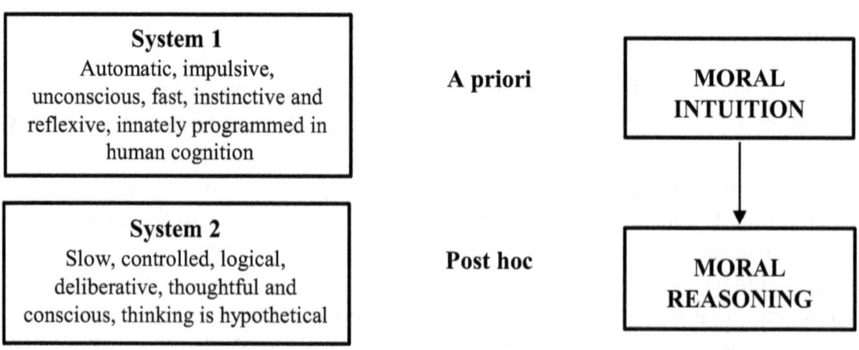

Fig. 1 Social-intuitionist model in ethical decision making. (Zollo et al. 2018)

Socio-Intuitionism, A New Light on Ethical Consumer Behavior

In the ethical consumption context, implicit moral attitudes are introspective evaluations that suddenly appear unconsciously (Marquardt and Hoeger 2009), influencing ethical decision-making at a subconscious level, just like moral intuition forms intuitive moral judgments (Haidt 2001; Haidt and Graham 2007). Marketing theorists are becoming aware that the rational view of ethical decision-making does not take into account cognitive elements such as values, virtues, ethical ideology and beliefs (Vitell 2015) that underlie the ethical identity and intuitive response of the consumer (John and Caldwell James 2013). Consequently, a few studies (Tenbrunsel et al. 2008) referred to the socio-intuitionist model recognize "the importance of moral intuition, without any awareness of having gone through a process of rcsearch, evaluation of evidence or conclusion" (Haidt 2001, p:818). Thus, intuitive and unconscious processing of information provides a priori answers to ethical dilemmas, while moral reasoning plays a deliberative and post hoc justification role. Explicit moral attitudes combine individual considerations, evaluations, and concerns about particular sustainable, environmental, or ethical behaviors, thus recalling the moral awareness, judgment, and intent inherent in moral reasoning (Carlson et al. 2009).

Research Framework and Definition of Hypotheses

In line with recent literature (Zollo et al. 2018), we propose an integrated framework that considers both moral intuition and moral reasoning as important cognitive processes in ethical decision-making. More specifically, we wish to empirically verify whether moral intuition a priori affects moral reasoning and then influences the ethical consumption behavior of food, cosmetic and apparel products. Studying these three different markets is interesting for several reasons. First, they all three occupy a strategic place in the French economy. Secondly, from a sociological point of view, the food, clothes and cosmetics markets offer consumers numerous opportunities to express their personality, to assert themselves and to distinguish themselves as autonomous individuals free to make their own choices given their great diversity. Thirdly, from a marketing point of view, these three mature markets are marked by decrease of consumption, return to natural and "less is more" trends. They are experiencing significant growth on the organic and local or fair-trade product segments which are important in food, less important in cosmetics and still marginal in clothing.

Our research question is: *What role do intuitions play in ethical consumer decision making in the food, cosmetics and clothes market and how do they interrelate?*

First, we wish to determine the influence of the three types of intuitions: affective, inferential and holistic. Holistic intuitions have been distinguished into "big picture" holistic intuitions, which emphasize global rather than detailed perspectives, and "abstract" holistic intuitions, which tend to privilege theoretical knowledge over concrete facts. Zollo et al.'s (2018) research has demonstrated only the influence of inferential intuitions on moral reasoning and on general ethical consumption. In this research, we wish to investigate the links that might exist between different types of intuition, especially affective intuitions and their influence on moral reasoning on defined markets.

H1: *Moral intuition is positively correlated to moral reasoning (EMCB) of the (i) Food, (ii) Cosmetic and (iii) Clothes market.*
H1a: Emotional Intuition (INTEMO) is a positive antecedent of Holistic Big Picture Intuition (INTHI).
H1b: Holistic Big Picture Intuition (INTHI) is a positive antecedent of Holistic Abstract Intuition (INTHA).
H1c: Holistic Abstract Intuition (INTHA) is a positive antecedent of Inferential Intuition (INTINF).
H1d: Inferential Intuition (INTINF) is a positive antecedent of moral reasoning (EMCB).

In order to measure moral reasoning, we consider that the EMCB scale (Ethically Minded Consumer Behavior) (Sudbury-Riley and Kohlbacher 2016) reflects moral reasoning (Haidt 2001) and that it reveals explicit values of moral attitudes (Marquardt and Hoeger 2009) by identifying specific, ethically conscious moral attitudes towards the beliefs and values that precede ethical behavior (Roberts and Bacon 1997). Based on the ethical marketing literature, we measure ethical consumption behavior in the food, cosmetic and fashion markets through a dozen ethical consumption behavior topics which are common to the three markets. First the purchase itself: buying locally manufactured products or organic or labeled products. Second the propensity to pay more for ecologically and socially responsible products and a seeking information on the brand's commitments. These topics remain fairly general in order to make as objective comparisons as possible between the three markets.

H2: *Moral reasoning (EMCB) influences positively the (i) Food, (ii) Cosmetic and (iii) Clothes Ethical consumption.*
H2a: EMCB influences positively pro-environmental and pro-social (i) Food, (ii) Cosmetic and (iii) Fashion product attention (ATT).
H2b: EMCB influences positively pro-environmental and pro-social (i) Food, (ii) Cosmetic and (iii) Fashion product purchase (RESP).

Based on the review of the literature and the hypotheses developed, the social-intuitionist framework is conceptualized in Fig. 2.

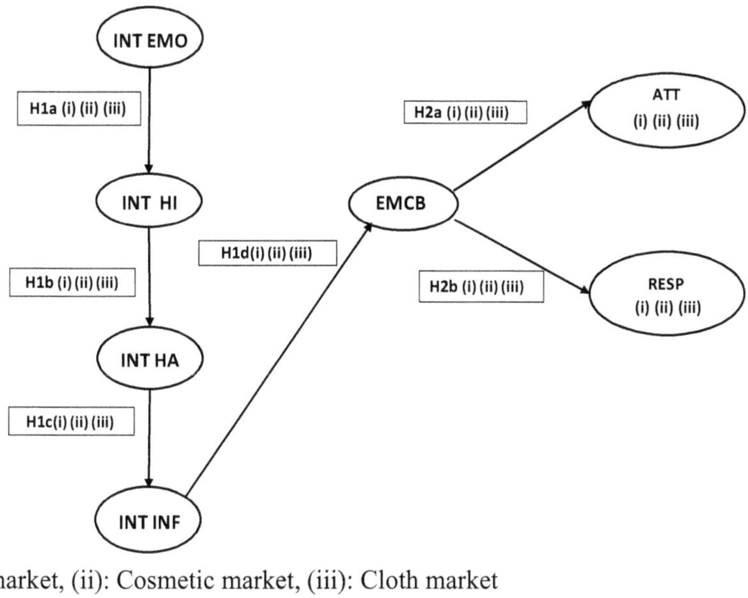

Fig. 2 Hypothesized model. (i): Food market, (ii): Cosmetic market, (iii): Cloth market

Methodology

Sample and Measurements

This study was administered via the Internet in January 2020 to a representative sample of the French population of 1080 people in terms of gender (male: 49.7%, female: 50.3%) and age (mean: 41.9, standard deviation: 13.53). In order to avoid a phenomenon of fatigue caused by the length of the questionnaire, respondents were randomly questioned only for two of the three markets, thus obtaining: 720 respondents for food products, 720 for cosmetic products and 720 for clothing.

We measured the four different kinds of intuitions: holistic-big picture, holistic-abstract, inferential, and affective using the 29 items of the TInTS (Types of Intuition Scale (Pretz et al. 2014). We treated the four subdimensions of intuition as separate constructs because "these scales measure distinct and independent types of intuition" (Pretz et al. 2014, p. 461). In order to measure moral reasoning, we used the 10 items of EMCB scale (Sudbury-Riley and al. 2016) that conceptualizes the variety of consumer choices related to environmental issues and corporate social responsibility. We also used 10 items in order to measure ethical consumption behavior on food, cosmetic and fashion market (Fletcher 2008). All measurement scales were rated on a five-point Likert scale (from strongly disagree to strongly agree.)

Results

In order to check the reliability of our measurement scales, we undertook Explanatory Factor Analysis. Results are presented below in Table 1. In order to get a good reliability, we reduced number of items on TInTS scale (Pretz 2014). Regarding emotional intuitions, the final number of measured items was three: "*I generally don't depend on my feelings to help me make decisions*", "*I prefer to follow my head rather than my heart*", "*It is foolish to base important decisions on feelings*" leading to acceptable Cronbach-alpha (see Table 1). We kept three items (out of eight) regarding inferential intuitions: "*When making a quick decision in my area of expertise, I can justify the decision logically*", "*If I have to, I can usually give reasons for my intuition*", "*When making a quick decision in my area of expertise, I can justify the decision logically*". The new scale showed good reliability index. Holistic big picture intuitions could be measured by two items for which scale reliability is also good: "*I try to keep in mind the big picture when working on a complex problem*", "*I am a "big picture" person*". The holistic abstract intuition scale wasn't reliable, so we were not able to measure this kind of intuitions.

The EMCB scale (Sudbury Riley et al. 2016) presented a good reliability with 8 items, for example: "*When there is a choice, I always choose the product that contributes to the least amount of environmental damage*", (FOOD, $\alpha = 0.898$, COSM, $\alpha = 0.904$, FASHION $\alpha = 0.836$).

In order to measure the ethical consumption of the three markets we proposed questions that allowed us to compare ethical consumption behavior. We first measured the "RESPONSABILITY" with 4 items (FOOD, $\alpha = 0.834$, COSM, $\alpha = 0.757$, FASHION $\alpha = 0.757$), and "ATTENTION" with 3 items (FOOD, $\alpha = 0.734$, COSM, $\alpha = 0.858$, FASHION $\alpha = 0.894$) (see Appendix).

We used Structural Equation Modeling (SEM) to empirically test the proposed hypotheses (see Fig. 2) and to simultaneously assess the causal relationships among our manifest and latent variables (Bagozzi and Yi 1988; Bentler 1990). Results indicate a fairly good fit with the data for the three structural models, as inferred from the goodness of model fit indices (see Table 2 below).

The examination of the coefficients on the 3 markets validated the hypotheses formulated with the exception of H1b and H1c. The models did not allow to demonstrate the influence of emotional intuition on abstract holistic intuition and the influence of abstract holistic intuition on big picture holistic intuition on the ethical consumption of food, cosmetics and clothes.

All other hypotheses were validated (see Table 3) and thus indicated that intuitions influence ethical consumption. In relation to the literature, we wanted to examine the existence of links between the types of intuition. Thus, we first confirm the direct link highlighted by Zollo et al. (2017) between inferential intuition and moral reasoning on ethical consumption in general, by using the EMCB on each of the 3 markets with slightly higher values (see Table 3) ($\beta = 0.29$, 0.33 and 0.24) than on the study of Zollo et al. (2017) ($\beta = 0.16$).

Table 1 Correlation matrix factors on food/cosmetic/fashion market

Food

FACTOR	MEAN	SD	EMCB (α = 0.898)	FOODRESP (α = 0.898)	INT INF (α = 0.898)	INT EMO (α = 0.898)	FOODATT (α = 0.898)	INTHI (α = 0.898)
EMCB	27.16	6.43	1.000					
FOODRESP	13.07	3.09	0.686	1.000				
INTINF	11.3	1.89	0.156	0.247	1.000			
INTEMO	9.76	2.25	0.115	0.199	0.289	1.000		
FOODATT	10.36	2.61	0.617	0.615	0.117	0.033	1.000	
INTHI	7.6	1.39	0.343	0.408	0.511	0.407	0.240	1.000

Cosmetics

FACTOR	MEAN	SD	EMCB (α = 0.904)	COSMRESP (α = 0.757)	INT INF (α = 0.746)	INT EMO (α = 0.898)	COSMATT (α = 0.858)
EMCB	27.30	6.04	1.000				
COSMRESP	5.89	1.87	0.677	1.000			
COSMINF	11.41	1.78	0.200	0.166	1.000		
INTEMO	9.79	2.27	0.139	0.122	0.270	1.000	
COSMATT	9.25	3.12	0.678	0.671	0.165	0.013	1.000

Clothes

FACTOR	MEAN	SD	EMCB (α = 0.894)	INTINF (α = 0.757)	FASHRESP (α = 0.851)	FASHATT (α = 0.836)	INTEMO (α = 0.696)
EMCB	27.30	6.28	1.000				
INTINF	11.33	1.86	0.201	1.000			
FASHRESP	5.92	1.64	0.440	0.092	1.000		
FASHATT	8.56	2.91	0.692	0.146	0.514	1.000	
INTEMO	8.27	2.200	−0.132	−0.292	−0.151	−0.53	1.000

Table 2 Model fit

	CHI^2	DF	p	Cmin/DF	GFI	AGFI	TLI	CFI	RMSEA	SRMR
FOOD	629.269	213	p < 0.001	2.954	0.927	0.906	0.941	0.95	0.052	0.048
COSM	647.666	217	p < 0.001	2.985	0.924	0.903	0.940	0.949	0.053	0.048
FASHION	515.562	181	p < 0.001	2.848	0.936	0.919	0.942	0.95	0.051	0.044

Table 3 Confirmatory factor analysis results

	FOOD		COSMETICS		FASHION	
	β	R^2	β	R^2	β	R^2
TOTAL EFFECTS						
EMO → HI	0.69[a]	0.23	0.39[a]	0.59	−0.44[a′]	0.19
HI → INF	0.83[a]	0.48	0.77[a]	0.15	0.77[a]	0.6
INF → EMCB	0.29[a]	0.08	0.33[a]	0.07	0.24[a]	0.06
EMCB →_ATT	1.02[a]	1.03	0.95[a]	0.90	0.87[a]	0.75
EMCB →_RESP	0.90[a]	0.81	0.78[a]	0.61	0.50[a]	0.25
INDIRECT EFFECTS						
EMO →_ATT	0.12[a]		0.08[a]		−0.05[a′]	
EMO →_RESP	0.10[a]		0.06[a]		−0.1[a′]	
INF →_ATT	0.26[a]		0.26[a]		0.19[a]	
INF →_RESP	0.29[a]		0.21[a]		0.36[a]	
HI →_ATT	0.24[a]		0.26[a]		0.14[a]	
HI →_RESP	0.22[a]		0.16[a]		0.25[a]	

[a]$p < 0.001$

Our results highlight the links between emotional and holistic big picture intuitions and then inferential intuitions. The consumption of clothing stands out, on this point, from food and cosmetic consumption. Indeed, emotional intuitions have positive influences on holistic big picture intuition in the food and cosmetics market (β = 0.69 and 0.39), but negative in the clothes market (β = −0.44). The influences of the different variables tested show positive effects on the three markets with relatively close coefficients, except for the clothing market, where the influence of moral reasoning on RESPONSABILITY shows lower coefficients than in the other two markets (β = 0.50 versus 0.90 for food and 0.78 for cosmetics). On ATTENTION the variables are significantly close (β = 1.02, 1.03 and 0.87).

To test whether the effects of intuitions on ethical consumption were mediated by moral reasoning (EMCB), bootstrapping in AMOS 22.0 was conducted. The bootstrapping approach enabled the examination of confidence intervals for indirect effects that Emotional, Inferential and Holistic Big Picture intuitions might have on purchase and attention on the three markets.

The indirect effect of the three kinds of intuitions was significant on the three markets (see Table 3). These results confirmed that intuitions influence ethical consumption indirectly through reasoning and directly also, in a less important way (p-value >0.001, coefficients are lower, see Table 3).

General Discussion

To study the antecedents of ethical consumption, we relied on the socio-intuitionist model (Haidt 2001). As Zollo et al. (2017), we hypothesized that moral intuition influences moral reasoning. More specifically, we confirm that the only significant antecedent of consumers' positive attitudes towards ethical food, cosmetic and clothes consumption is inferential intuition, based on analytical and logical information from previous decision-making experiences (Pretz and Folse 2011; Pretz et al. 2014) and consumption experiences also. Inferential intuition is influenced by holistic big picture intuition that emphasizes global rather than detailed perspectives. Emotional intuition which is derived from feelings and emotional reactions (Pretz and Totz, 2007; Pretz et al. 2014) is an antecedent of holistic big picture intuition. Consistent with the marketing literature (John and Caldwell James 2013; Sekerka and Bagozzi 2007), we argue that consumers use both unconscious and conscious criteria to guide their pro-environmental pro-social decisions and actions. Researchers argue that consumers' ethical values, beliefs, and identities shape their intuitive and impulsive ethical behavior (Cherry and Caldwell 2013; Sekerka et al. Bagozzi 2007; Sekerka and Bagozzi 2014). We find that consumers behave ethically according to the automatic inferential information processing of system 1 (Kahneman 2003; Stanovich and Ouest 2000) which is itself influenced by affective intuitions and holistic big picture intuitions. These findings are consistent with previous research (Sekerka and Bagozzi 2007; Sekerka et al. 2014) that showed emotional reactions were considered as antecedents of ethical decision-making.

Our results also show that emotional intuitions do not have the same influence depending on the studied market. Indeed, emotional intuitions have a positive influence on the holistic big picture intuitions on the food ($\beta = 0.69$) and cosmetic markets ($\beta = 0.39$) but negative on the clothes market ($\beta = -0.47$). This confirms the role of affect as a determinant of ethical consumption in the three markets studied. As with other green consumption decisions, the decision to engage in responsible clothing consumption behaviors requires trade-offs between conflicting goals (e.g. style vs. ethics) and can be more difficult depending on personality traits and personal values (Niinimäki 2010; Moisander 2007). This complexity can be attributed to the unique nature of clothing, which goes beyond a utilitarian role satisfying an individual's need for identity formation, social acceptance and distinction (Joy et al. 2012). Our study thus highlights the negative influence of emotional intuitions on other types of moral intuition (inferential and holistic big picture), moral reasoning and ethical consumption. Our study shows that people who have already experienced moral intuition derived from repeated and repetitive behavior is the most likely antecedent of ethical behavior as shown by the link between inferential intuitions and moral reasoning (Food: $\beta = 0.29$, Cosmetics: $\beta = 0.33$, Fashion $\beta = 0.24$), which implies that ethical attitudes are instinctively predetermined (Zollo et al. 2017). Instead, effects-based intuitions (Pretz and Totz 2007; Pretz et al. 2014) may be temporary, transitory, and do not predict future ethical decisions. Hence, values, traits and virtues can generate unconscious and cognitive first-order ethical desires "stimulating actions" (Sekerka and Bagozzi 2007) and "automatic self-regulation" in the processing of inferential information (Sekerka et al. 2014, p. 16). Extending this argument, we demonstrate empirically that unconsciousness influences post hoc rational decisions to behave ethically according to one's moral intuition (Pretz et al. 2014).

In undertaking this study, we intended to apply the intuitionist model (Haidt 2001) to the ethical consumption literature to show how non-rational elements such as intuition may influence consumers when they form ethical attitudes and make ethical decisions regarding pro-environmental and pro-social consumption behavior on food, cosmetic and fashion market. Analysis of the data indicated that inferential intuition was a significant antecedent motivating moral reasoning, which, in turn, highly influenced pro-environmental and pro-social dimensions of the food, cosmetics and clothes consumer. But the inferential intuitions are influenced first by emotional intuitions and second by holistic big picture intuitions.

These results are important from a managerial point of view. Indeed, ethical communication must be based on inferential elements: the whole consumer experience (purchase, use and disposal) must be solicited and improved in order to create new consumer habits in the food, cosmetics and clothes markets. Holistic big picture intuitions have an important influence on inferential intuitions. Thus, there is a need to broaden the consequences of product choices more widely than the consumption of the products itself. Showing its impact on the environment, human kind and animals is a key point. Finally, if food and cosmetic brands can rely on affect and emotions as shown by our results, they appear to play a negative role in the ethical consumption of clothing, it is therefore a question of proposing a less emotional communication but more based on concrete and rational elements regarding fashion.

Some limits and avenues for further research have to be underlined. The TInTS measurement scale (Pretz 2014) doesn't seem to be very suitable in a French context. Indeed, we had to delete several items in order to improve scale reliability, reducing the initial scale to 8 items (instead of 29). Second, our research was conducted in three specific markets, analyzing moral intuitions and moral reasoning. Although this approach is highly original, the questionnaire was very long and didn't allow us to get precise details on the overall consumption of these markets. Focusing on one dedicated market should allow researchers to inquire more deeply about intuitions and consumer personal values regarding ethical consumption in its entirety.

Appendix: CFA Results

	FOOD			COSMETICS			FASHION		
	γ	CR	AVE	γ	CR	AVE	γ	CR	AVE
REASONING (EMCB)		**0.885**	**0.492**		**0.796**	**0.520**		**0.892**	**0.713**
When there is a choice, I always choose the product that contributes to the least amount of environmental damage	0.746			0.738			0.738		

(Continued)

	FOOD			COSMETICS			FASHION		
	γ	CR	AVE	γ	CR	AVE	γ	CR	AVE
I have switched products for environmental reasons	0.752			0.768			0.741		
I do not buy household products that harm the environment	0.671			0.716			0.724		
If I understand the potential damage to the environment that some products can cause, I do not purchase those products	0.620			0.671			0.631		
I do not buy products from companies that I know use sweatshop labor, child labor, or other poor working conditions	0.610			0.643			0.664		
I do not buy products from companies that I know use sweatshop labor, child labor, or other poor working conditions	0.815			0.793			0.793		
I have paid more for environmentally friendly products when there is a cheaper alternative	0.704			0.705			0.674		
I have paid more for socially responsible products when there is a cheaper alternative	0.669			0.726			0.723		
EMOTIONAL INTUITIONS		**0.721**	**0.464**		**0.725**	**0.468**			
I generally don't depend on my feelings to help me make decisions (R)	0.646								
I prefer to follow my head rather than my heart (R)	0.716								
It is foolish to base important decisions on feelings (R)	0.805								
INFERENTAL INTUITION		**0.787**	**0.554**		**0.749**	**0.500**		**0.760**	**0.516**
When making a quick decision in my area of expertise, I can justify the decision logically	0.776			0.651			0.648		
If I have to, I can usually give reasons for my intuition	0.791			0.700			0.707		
When making a quick decision in my area of expertise, I can justify the decision logically	0.659			0.759			0.792		

(Continued)

	FOOD			COSMETICS			FASHION		
	γ	CR	AVE	γ	CR	AVE	γ	CR	AVE
HOLLISTIC BIG PICTURE INTUITION		**0.72**	**0.563**		**0.667**	**0.500**		**0.667**	**0.502**
I try to keep in mind the big picture when working On a complex problem	0.737			0.730			0.763		
I am a "big picture" person	0.563			0.884			0.650		
RESPONSABILITY		**0.825**	**0.445**		**0.868**	**0.621**		**0.852**	**0.742**
I buy organic food /cosmetic/ apparel products	0.767			0.813					
I buy food /cosmetic/ apparel products with labels	0.671			0.771			0.834		
I buy locally made food / cosmetic/ apparel products	0.665			0.728			0.888		
I buy fair-trade food /cosmetic/ apparel products	0.834			0.837					
ATTENTION		**0.805**	**0.580**		**0.821**	**0.605**		**0.813**	**0.593**
I find out about the ethical commitments of the food/ Cosmetic/apparel brand I buy	0.745			0.771			0.709		
I am willing to pay more for food/cosmetics/apparel products That contribute less to environmental damage	0.815			0.806			0.837		
I am willing to pay more for cosmetic/apparel food products That pay for the work of the producers in a decent way	0.721			0.756			0.759		

References

Brunk, K. H. (2012). Un/ethical Company and Brand Perceptions: Conceptualizing and Operationalizing Consumer Meanings. *Journal of Business Ethics*, *111*(4), 551–565.

Carlson, D. S., Kacmar, K. M., & Wadsworth, L. L. (2009). The Impact of Moral Intensity Dimensions on Ethical Decision-making: Assessing the Relevance of Orientation 1, *XX* (4), 534–551.

Chatzidakis, A., Hibbert, S., & Smith, A. P. (2007). Why People Don't Take their Concerns about Fair Trade to the Supermarket: The Role of Neutralization, 89–100.

Epstein, S. (2010). Demystifying intuition: What it is, what it does, and how it does it. *Psychological Inquiry*, *21*(4), 295–312. https://doi.org/https://doi.org/10.1080/1047840X.2010.523875

Etude Greenflex 2019, https://www.greenflex.com/communique-de-presse/barometre-consommation-responsable-2019-sortons-mythe-croissance-infinie/

Haidt, J. (2001). The Emotional Dog and Its Rational Tail: A Social Intuitionist Approach to Moral Judgment. *Psychological Review*, *108*(4), 814–834. https://doi.org/https://doi.org/10.1037/0033-295X

Haidt, J., & Graham, J. (2007). When morality opposes justice: Conservatives have moral intuitions that liberals may not recognize. *Social Justice Research*, *20*(1), 98–116.

Harrison, J. (1967). Ethical objectivism. In P. Edwards (Ed.), The encyclopedia of philosophy (Vols. 3-4, pp. 71-75). New York: Macmillan.

Joy, A., Sherry, Jr., J.F., Venkatesh, A., Wang, J., Chan, R. (2012). Fast fashion, sustainability, and the ethical appeal of luxury brands. Fashion Theory 16 (3), 273–295.

Jung, C. G. (1933). (First published in 1921.) Psychological Types. New York: Harcourt, Brace, and Company. Kaempf, G. L., Klein, G., Thordsen, M. L., & Wolf, S. 1996

Kahneman, D. (2003). A perspective on judgment and choice. American Psychologist, 58.

Low W., Davenport E. (2007). To boldly go...exploring ethical spaces to re-politicize ethical consumption and fair trade. Journal of Consumer Behavior, 6:336-348.

Marquardt, N., & Hoeger, R. (2009). The Effect of Implicit Moral Attitudes on Managerial Decision-Making: An Implicit Social Cognition Approach, 157–171.

Pelsmacker, P. D. E., Driesen, L., & Rayp, G. (2005). Do Consumers Care about Ethics? Willingness to Pay for Fair-Trade Coffee, *39*(2), 363–385.

Pretz, J. E., Brookings, J. B., Carlson, L. A., Humbert, T. K., Roy, M., Jones, M., & Memmert, D. (2014). Development and Validation of a New Measure of Intuition: The Types of Intuition Scale †, *467*(May), 454–467. https://doi.org/https://doi.org/10.1002/bdm.1820

Roberts, J. A., & Bacon, D. R. (1997). Exploring the Subtle Relationships between Environmental Concern and Ecologically Conscious Consumer Behavior. *Journal of Business Research*, *40*(1), 79–89. https://doi.org/https://doi.org/10.1016/S0148-2963(96)00280-9

Sekerka, L. E., & Bagozzi, R. P. (2014). Self-Regulation: The Moral Muscle in Online Ethical Consumerism Self-Regulation : The Moral Muscle in Online Ethical Consumerism Menlo College Deborah Brown McCabe Menlo College, *8*(January), 9–20.

Sudbury-Riley, L., & Kohlbacher, F. (2016). Ethically minded consumer behavior: Scale review, development, and validation. *Journal of Business Research*, *69*(8), 2697–2710. https://doi.org/https://doi.org/10.1016/j.jbusres.2015.11.005

Tenbrunsel A. E., Smith-Crowe K. (2008): 13 Ethical Decision Making: Where We've Been and Where We're Going. *ANNALS,* **2**, 545–607, https://doi.org/https://doi.org/10.5465/19416520802211677

Vitell, S. J. (2015). A Case for Consumer Social Responsibility (CnSR): Including a Selected Review of Consumer Ethics / Social Responsibility, 767–774.

White, K., Habib, R., & Hardisty, D. J. (2019). How to SHIFT consumer behaviors to be more sustainable: A literature review and guiding framework. *Journal of Marketing*, *83*(3), 22–49.

Zollo, L., Yoon, S., Rialti, R., & Ciappei, C. (2018). Ethical consumption and consumers' decision making: the role of moral intuition. *Management Decision*, *56*(3), 692–710.

The Making of the "Instaworthy": Social Media Influencers as Interpreters of Commercial Messages: An Abstract

Heini Vanninen and Eveliina Kantamaa

Abstract Social media influencers are an integral element of firms' social media marketing strategies. Despite growing academic interest, only a few articles address managing influencer marketing from a firm's perspective. In addition, there is scant knowledge of how influencers interpret organizations' guidelines and produce the content associated with their commercial collaborations with brands. This omission is critical as influencers are in control of the message conveyed to the social media audiences and require managing in order to avoid image incongruity between the firms's own and influencers' communications. Drawing on a multi-method study including semi-structured interviews with destination marketing organizations and influencers, ethnographic observation and semiotic analysis of social media content, the findings contribute to two-step flow communication theory by showing how the "second step", the influencer, decodes and transmits the commercial messages to his/her followers in the context of destination marketing. Destination marketing serves as an appropriate context for studying influencer marketing dynamics due to its complexity. In addition to more tangible elements, there are various intangible and immaterial characteristics of tourism offerings. Social reality – the destinations, milieus, places and businesses to be visited – and the campaign objectives are all entangled in the content narrative and interpreted by the influencer and her knowledge of her audience into what they could mean and become in the social media environments' semiotic and symbolic landscapes. Influencer's perception is embedded into the materiality of the social media environment. We argue that the interpretation and contextualization of the message occurs via two mediating layers: influencer's creative process and the chosen technological platform's materiality. While more tangible elements can be communicated easily to the target audience, more intangible elements require influencers' interpretation. Influencers' own interpretation and understanding of the intangible objectives and influencers' perception of the social media audience's understanding of the certain intangible element are

H. Vanninen (✉) · E. Kantamaa
LUT University, Lappeenranta, Finland
e-mail: heini.vanninen@lut.fi; eveliina@bazarkustannus.fi

J. Allen et al. (eds.), *Celebrating the Past and Future of Marketing and Discovery with Social Impact*, Developments in Marketing Science: Proceedings of the Academy of Marketing Science, https://doi.org/10.1007/978-3-030-95346-1_48

determinative in the interpretation and contextualization of marketing messages of the campaign's commercial stakeholders.

Keywords Influencer marketing · Social media · Opinion leadership · Social media influencers

Exploring the Role of Human and Digital Interactions in Online Customer Support: An Abstract

Aleksandra Petelina-Walsh

Abstract The main goal of this study is to explore how human and digital interactions online can enhance customer-organisation relationships through driving a change in customers' cognitive and affective evaluations and behaviours. Process of digitalisation has changed consumers' behaviours considerably through integration of digital technology in nearly every aspect of consumers' life (Zeithaml et al. 2006). Hence, organisations have recognised the importance of delivering high-quality and efficient interactions as a distinguishing factor to achieve competitive advantage and build relationships with consumers (Lemon and Verhoef 2016). Accordingly, throughout the literature, there have been a number of conceptual papers debating the role of digital technologies and human employees (Bowen 2016; Larivière et al. 2017; Robinson et al. 2019; De Keyser et al. 2019). For instance, Shankar (2018) argues that service employees will work in tandem with digital technologies, whereas Huang and Rust (2020) debate that once technology develops empathy, service jobs will disappear.

Throughout literature, it can be seen that the research in a field of technology, social presence, service employees, and consumer behaviour is fragmented. There is no unified framework that would explain how digital and human interactions affect a change in cognitive and affective evaluations and behaviours. Following technology adoption framework and theory of social presence, there is little evidence on whenever social presence conveyed through human and digital characteristics' influence a change in consumers' cognitive and affective evaluations and behaviours (Short et al. 1976; Hassanein and Head 2007; McLean et al. 2020). Thus, building upon TAM and behavioural theories, this research aims to make a novel contribution and develop a framework that would explain how interactions with human and digital during service encounters affect behavioural responses towards a firm.

Hereafter, this research addresses the theoretical knowledge gap by investigating how interactions with digital technology, particularly virtual agent (artificial intel-

A. Petelina-Walsh (✉)
University of Reading, Reading, UK
e-mail: a.petelina@pgr.reading.ac.uk

J. Allen et al. (eds.), *Celebrating the Past and Future of Marketing and Discovery with Social Impact*, Developments in Marketing Science: Proceedings of the Academy of Marketing Science, https://doi.org/10.1007/978-3-030-95346-1_49

ligence), and service employee impact consumer behaviour. Hence, it is suggested to conduct an experiment under two motivational conditions and manipulate level of empathy and responsiveness of customer service agents. This will help to determine how human and digital characteristics can enhance social presence which in turn will affect customers' cognitive, affective and behavioural responses towards a firm. By closing this gap, it will add to existing knowledge on technology adoption and social presence theory and will help to understand how organisations can achieve competitive advantage and build relationships with consumers through balancing digital and human interactions within service encounters (Bolton et al. 2018; Verhoef et al. 2019).

Keywords Human and digital interactions · Chatbots · Service employees · Customer service journey · Cognitive · Affective and behavioural engagements

Social Attachment Theory and the Relationship between Satisfaction, Luxury Brand Attachment, and Influencer Attachment: A Focus on Young Chinese Online Consumers under Quarantine: An Abstract

Siyuan Yu and Virginie de Barnier

Abstract The rapid development of social media and influencer marketing has tremendously changed the way in which consumers collect information, make purchase decisions, and communicate with brands (Lou and Yuan 2019; Neal 2017; Scott 2015). Marketing practitioners, especially those from luxury brands, are explosively increasing their budget on influencer marketing more than ever for its payoff in sales performance (Lou and Yuan 2019). During the worldwide quarantine and social distancing due to the breakout of COVID-19 pandemic, influencer marketing has become one of the most prevailing marketing approaches.

Researchers have revealed a variety of impacts of influencer marketing on both consumer behaviors and branding performance (Blackwell et al. 2017; Hollebeek et al. 2016; Schivinski et al. 2016; Vanmeter and Grisaffe 2015). However, there is a lack of evidence to answer whether consumers develop emotional attachment and to what extent towards the influencer and the brand involved in the brand-influencer collaboration. This research, founded on social attachment theory (Mawson 2005), adopts a mixed methodology approach to investigate the relationship between consumer satisfaction derived from influencer promoted purchases, influencer attachment, and luxury band attachment.

In the context of influencer marketing, our research reveals positive relationships between consumer satisfaction, influencer attachment and luxury brand attachment respectively; furthermore, the positive impact of consumer satisfaction on influencer attachment is stronger than on luxury brand attachment. This research also identifies a positive moderating role of brand sponsorship on the relationship between consumer satisfaction and luxury brand attachment. Although the

S. Yu (✉) · V. de Barnier
Aix-Marseille University, Aix-en-Provence, France
e-mail: siyuan.yu@iae-aix.com; virginie.de-barnier@univ-amu.fr

J. Allen et al. (eds.), *Celebrating the Past and Future of Marketing and Discovery with Social Impact*, Developments in Marketing Science: Proceedings of the Academy of Marketing Science, https://doi.org/10.1007/978-3-030-95346-1_50

COVID-19 crisis has caused severe social and business isolation, it brings some exceptional opportunities for brands to bond with their target consumers through social media and influencer marketing. Our results show that consumers more autonomously engage in behaviors that enhance the development of attachment due to the social isolation under quarantine. This finding qualifies social attachment theory (Mawson 2005) to explain the occurrence of affiliation in the context of influencer marketing and identifies influencers as attachment figures to their online communities.

Keywords Influencer marketing · Attachment theory · Satisfaction · Luxury · Online · Brands

What It Takes to Be Loved? An Empirical Examination of Human Brand Authenticity: An Abstract

María Lucila Osorio, Edgar Centeno, and Jesús Cambra-Fierro

Abstract Empowered by traditional and social media, human brands enjoy a prominent position in contemporary societies and benefit from the establishment of strong consumer-brand relationships. However, as current times are marked with uncertainty and fakeness, authenticity has become a critical element for the development of these relationships, especially for human brands. We propose and test a model that depicts the relationship between human brand authenticity, understood as "being true to one-self", and brand love. A stratified random sample of 748 non-student respondents was obtained from a web-based survey distributed through social media. OLS regression analysis was employed to test the proposed model. Results show that human brand authenticity has a positive and significant effect on brand love. Moreover, differences by human brand contexts are analyzed, offering some insights into how celebrity authenticity is processed across human brand types. Our study revealed that the effect of authenticity is stronger for politicians, CEOs, bloggers, religious leaders and television hosts, for whom showing consistency in behaviors and being true to themselves is critical for the attainment of brand love. In addition, a negative moderation by consumer's age was identified, signaling to the decreasing importance of authenticity as a driver of brand love as consumers mature. No moderations were found by consumer's gender. We conclude with important managerial implications suggesting that investments in fostering human brand authenticity will pay off through the establishment of long-lasting, loving and loyal relationships, which are crucial for building brand equity, especially in the contexts where human brand authenticity yielded higher effects on

M. L. Osorio (✉)
Tecnológico de Monterrey, Monterrey, Mexico
e-mail: lucilaosorio@tec.mx

E. Centeno
Tecnológico de Monterrey, Mexico City, Mexico
e-mail: ecenteno@tec.mx

J. Cambra-Fierro
Universidad Pablo de Olavide, Sevilla, Spain
e-mail: jjcamfie@upo.es

J. Allen et al. (eds.), *Celebrating the Past and Future of Marketing and Discovery with Social Impact*, Developments in Marketing Science: Proceedings of the Academy of Marketing Science, https://doi.org/10.1007/978-3-030-95346-1_51

brand love. Instead of aiming for perfection, human brands and their managers must carefully design brand positioning strategies anchored in authenticity. Maintaining similar behaviors over time allows for the stability, continuity and consistency necessary for attaining perceptions of authenticity. In conclusion, human brands may trade in their authenticity for being liked, but to be loved, they must be authentic.

Keywords Human brands · Brand love · Brand authenticity · Consumer-brand relationships

Psychosocial Elements that Connect the Digital Influencers to their Followers

Igor de Jesus Lobato Pompeu Gammarano and Emilio José Montero Arruda Filho

Abstract This theoretical article aims to analyze the psychosocial elements as meanings, attitudes, subjective behaviors and intentions that emotionally connect the digital influencers to their followers. Four psychosocial elements have been identified in the literature that allow this connection to be established, characterized as: Expertise, Number of Followers, Life stream and Storytelling. The combinations of these elements also generated factors that influence the motivation of the followers for keeping up with the routines of activities communicated in the virtual environment by their digital influencers. The factors identified from these combinations were: social status, popularity, strategic reconstruction of the digital self and the reputation of digital influencers. The managerial implications of this study are related to the identification of the characteristics of the digital influencers that contribute to increase their capacity of persuasion and thus lead the virtual users to become their followers and future consumers.

Keywords Digital influencer · Digital narratives · Digital lifestyle · Number of followers · Expertise

Introduction

For decades, marketing has used public figures and socially distinguished people as high-credibility communication sources, as a strategy to promote brands and products (Martensen et al. 2018; Sternthal et al. 1978). The intention is to influence consumer decisions through traditional communication channels such as TV, radio and outdoor advertising. With the growing popularity and use of digital technologies, the rise Web 2.0, and the global reach of networked social media, companies

Igor de Jesus Lobato Pompeu Gammarano (✉) · Emilio José Montero Arruda Filho
University of Amazon – UNAMA, Belém, PA, Brazil
e-mail: emilio.arruda@unama.br

J. Allen et al. (eds.), *Celebrating the Past and Future of Marketing and Discovery with Social Impact*, Developments in Marketing Science: Proceedings of the Academy of Marketing Science, https://doi.org/10.1007/978-3-030-95346-1_52

have adapted their marketing strategies to this new and constantly changing digital technological context.

The digital revolution democratized the access to the internet, giving voice to many people. The set of influencers continues to broaden. People with unique styles, personalities and messages are able to use virtual channels to propagate their opinions, tastes, lifestyles, and other aspects of their daily lives – again, as a way to accumulate followers and influence them (Sanchez-Cartas and Leon 2018). Thus, virtual communication channels – such as websites, blogs, fotologs, e-commerce, portals, among others – are often used as tools for communication across brands, connecting social influencers and their followers (Dholakia and Reyes 2013).

According to Katz and Lazarsfeld's (1955) two-step flow theory, certain individuals are recognized as opinion leaders and process incoming information so they can then pass it to others, increasing their degree of influence. In the diffusion model of innovation Rogers (2010), opinion leaders are the first to adopt products, services and innovations (early adopters). Tomaszeski (2006) also states that opinion leaders are more informed and more willing to consume media content.

It is observed that most of the studies related to opinion leaders are related to face-to-face contact and personal interaction in the offline environment (Uzunoğlu and Kip 2014). However, technological development allowed personal interaction to be transferred to online communities and the digital environment. Thus, opinion leaders moved to these virtual spaces in order to influence people in an active and collaborative way, then being called digital influencers (DI) (Uzunoğlu and Kip 2014).

From the social interaction provided by social media, consumers can create and distribute their own content (Casaló et al. 2018). Therefore, in this virtual context, the nature of DI as common consumers is modified, since these individuals can get "Likes" and earn a follower audience in a short time, besides of developing continuous communication in which their contents are shared authentically, organically, and consistently with their followers (Martensen et al. 2018). DI can also achieve fame based on their social activities, having similar characteristics to celebrities with consequent growing persuasion (Martensen et al. 2018).

By doing so, the companies attempt to reach ever-larger segments of the public with the hope of converting some of them into consumers of their products and services. This process gives an additional digital voice to brands, allowing them to be closer to their customers, with the DI acting as intermediaries connecting the brands to their networks of followers (Sanchez-Cartas and Leon 2018). Brands increasingly seek to operate through DI who are aligned with the goals, values and the personality of the brands and their corporate parents. The naturalistic behavior and everyday communication style of DI – about the types of products these influencers consume and approve — results in authentic and creative content that could lead to newer forms of source credibility and persuasion.

In natural and authentic ways, DI foster behaviors and create new consumption patterns, dialoguing directly with their followers and enhancing brand desirability in a subtle and less invasive ways. Depending on the degree of engagement of the followers, these digital influence patterns can produce real results for companies and their brands, ranging from greater diffusion and consumption of these brands by those who follow the DI.

Most followers receive the recommendations of DI in non-evaluative ways. They observe the communications from DI as good news or a beneficial novelty brought by someone close, a person who they can trust, someone who will assist them in solving a particular need or will present them with something good. Some of these followers could be fans who wish to have experiences similar to the experiences that the influencers have had. Therefore, these individuals end up consuming the endorsed products, being inspired by the tastes and preferences communicated by their influencers.

Thus, based on the phenomena related to the impact of DI on consumer behavior through social and emotional persuasion and influence, this study seeks to answer the following questions: What psychosocial elements connect and relate the DI to their followers?

The literature indicates some characteristics expressed by DI that emotionally envelop their network of followers, stimulating trust and engagement. Therefore, this study aims to present the attributes described by the DI that allow to accumulate more followers and influence them.

The article is divided as: after this introduction exposing the objectives of the study, the second section presents the psychosocial characteristics characterized as meanings, attitudes, subjective behaviors and intentions that emotionally connect DI to followers. Next, we present the combinations of psychosocial elements that deepen the relationship between DI and their followers. Finally, the theoretical partial considerations are addressed, with the empirical proposition that must be developed in the future for this research.

Psychosocial Elements that Emotionally Connect the Digital Influencers to their Network of Followers

Expertise

The expertise is tied to an individual's specialization or ability to perform a specific or difficult task (Martensen et al. 2018) and an individual's ability to make valid statements such as financial analysis, healthy diet suggestions, tips on fashion, foreign language proficiency, ability to play musical instruments, and skills to harmonize makeup colors. Those DI that present knowledge, experiences and skills in specific contexts (Martensen et al. 2018) in their social networks are observed by followers as references in the areas in which they are currently proposed.

However, being qualified in a specific area and passing on knowledge about a particular subject is not enough to be recognized as someone who is an expertise. Such expertise must be legitimized. According to Schaefer (2012), social proof is responsible for legitimizing an individual as an expert in the virtual environment.

Therefore, social proof is defined as small clues that can convey authority and trust, such as the number of followers, the amount of "likes" and positive comments in the posts, the amount of sharing of these posts, among other elements that may contribute for persuasion (Martensen et al. 2018).

In addition, the expertise (Martensen et al. 2018) also bestows prestige (Henrich and Gil-White 2001), recognition, "know-how" and respect (Cheng et al. 2013), as the public recognizes the skill that DI present based on the experience and qualification they have in their field. This particular knowledge grants social status to the DI (Henrich and Gil-White 2001; Martensen et al. 2018), as the network of people accompanying their activities perceive them as differentiated and reliable people who have an exclusive knowledge and end up becoming reliable references to be followed (Martensen et al. 2018).

The depth in which DI discuss topics, analyze products and make suggestions of use and consumption can give them authority, as they demonstrate extensive experience in their fields of work (Lin et al. 2018; Martensen et al. 2018). Figures of authority and influence as celebrities established in the offline context can shift this influence to the digital environment (Lin et al. 2018; Ramdarshan Bold 2018). However, this context is also occupied by an emerging class of DI, such as emerging authors and celebrities who gain visibility and recognition at particular times and in specific domains (Lin et al. 2018; Ramdarshan Bold 2018).

The authority that DI presents, make followers to trust in their arguments and the brands they indicate (Lin et al. 2018; Martensen et al. 2018). The information provided in the online environment about certain products, as well as DI opinions on quality, perceived utility and product experience, are used as reference source for followers who seek for reliable information to make decisions (Martensen et al. 2018) in pre-purchase scenarios. The information provided by DI is persuasive and more reliable than other methods developed by companies to promote their brand (Lin et al. 2018; Martensen et al. 2018).

In this way, the clothes they use, the places they attend, the people they interact, among other elements, can serve as a benchmark and impact the consumption decision spontaneously. Thus, the self-identification of followers associated with the authority of DI feed trust (Martensen et al. 2018; Ramdarshan Bold 2018) and inclines followers to adopt products and brands inspired by DI communication.

In this scenario, the expertise and legitimacy presented by the DI give them leadership and knowledge that contributes to characterize them as authorities in their fields, influencing the confidence of those who follow them in order to have information about a specific niche and products that interest them (Lin et al. 2018; Ramdarshan Bold 2018).

Number of Followers

Brands and potential followers perceive the number of individuals who follow a DI as a metric of credibility, related to their published profile and content (De Veirman et al. 2017). The number of followers of a DI works in this case as a reference volume that grants popularity and inclines potential followers to follow the daily routine of DI, their contents, besides being easily seduced by the consumption suggestions undertaken by these individuals (De Veirman et al. 2017). In addition, the greater the number of followers presented by an DI, the greater the possibilities of the brands that endorse these individuals, promoting their products and services (De Veirman et al. 2017; Martensen et al. 2018).

Some studies indicate that the number of followers (low × high) of an DI directly impacts perceived legitimacy, social status, credibility, popularity and on the motivation of followers to interact (De Veirman et al. 2017). The number of followers also impacts on popularity (De Veirman et al. 2017), on the prestige (Henrich and Gil-White 2001) and online status of the DI (Uzunoğlu and Kip 2014). In this way, the brands, by chosen a DI to represent them, seek to focus primarily on the number of followers and the similarity between the profile of the DI and the profiles presented by those who follow them, since the similarity between profiles will favor the deepening of affinity and confidence (De Veirman et al. 2017; Martensen et al. 2018), converting followers into consumers.

Thus, DI seek to create organic, fast and natural links with their followers in order to create humanized links that enable more followers to join their social networks. Due to these factors, the companies adapted their digital marketing strategies with the objective of obtaining a greater participation with the public, based on the indications that the DI perform in their social media. In addition, DI have been used as a more viable option for companies that wish to communicate more directly with their target audience.

Therefore, if an DI has a high number of followers and a deep engagement of them, it is possible that content in text, photo or video of a few seconds, containing indications about a particular product or that shows the DI himself using the item, bring expressive consumption results to the brand of the product, due to the number of connected followers. This improves the interaction between DI his followers and establishes a deep bond of trust and credibility (De Veirman et al. 2017).

Digital Narratives (Storytelling)

Some followers look for inspiration and security in the achievements the DI communicate in the virtual environment. Thus, realizations and digital narratives (also known as storytelling) (Ben Youssef et al. 2018; Larkey et al. 2018; Romney and Johnson 2018) involving DI generate a sense of closeness and involves emotionally followers, making them follow the daily lives of their followers with greater effectiveness.

Another element that is analyzed by brands and that encourages potential followers to make the decision to follow and strengthen the link between DI and their network of followers is the reputation presented by these individuals (Casaló et al. 2018). According to Leal et al. (2014), the reputation of a DI in a virtual community is a determining factor for it to be legitimized through social proof (Schaefer 2012), making him a reference in a particular subject or niche of performance.

The prestige of DI (Henrich and Gil-White 2001) makes their followers recognize them as individuals who have more knowledge and experience on specific subjects (Martensen et al. 2018). In this way, the accumulation of this know-how, the performance trajectory and the shared experiences, will help in the formation of a consistent reputation, attracting the attention of the followers to the accomplishments of the DI.

This flow of personal content (Larkey et al. 2018) shared by DI establishes a detailed history of the personal and daily information of these individuals (Martensen et al. 2018). This fact allows the followers to feel close and connected, being able to access all the life experiences communicated by their DI in their social media and in their communication channels, simulating a real and aspirational relationship (Martensen et al. 2018). This established attachment deepens even further when a relationship of trust is established and the sense of similarity, since this feeling of similarity fosters the identification of the follower to the DI profile, which in turn enhances their capacity for persuasion along with his network of followers (Martensen et al. 2018).

In this way, the contents created by the DI related to the products or brands, allow the creation of stories (Storytelling), since the creation of visual and textual elements allows the insertion of the brand in the plot, making DI as characters in a film (Martensen et al. 2018). These types of digital narratives generate comments and 'likes' but can also provoke emotional responses that contribute to the persuasion of followers (Martensen et al. 2018).

In this way, it is perceived that the quality of the narrative affects the reputation of the DI, because it is through the description of their life trajectory that the potential followers can identify themselves or not with the contents shared (Larkey et al. 2018). This identification impacts on the trust of the followers, facing the opinions and suggestions of their DI, thus generating a deep connection through the feeling of satisfaction and emotional involvement (Larkey et al. 2018), affective and cognitive (Ben Youssef et al. 2018), maintaining a loyalty relationship between followers and their influencer (Ben Youssef et al. 2018).

These digital narratives are powerful because they catch the attention of the audience, making the audience think about the brands, which in turn impacts the followers' buying intentions (Romney and Johnson 2018). In addition, Romney and Johnson (2018) indicate that digital narratives are effective tools to convey ideas and engage the public. Therefore, the engagement of individuals is directly related to a particular psychological state of affective and emotional connections and/or performed actions (Martensen et al. 2018). Such actions elevate the level of motivation to interact and cooperate in a community of members, whether commenting, clicking, reacting, posting, making check in, sharing, giving "likes" or even adhering to a suggestion given by an DI in the virtual context (Wongkitrungrueng and Assarut 2018).

Digital Lifestyle (Lifestream)

The use of mobile technologies, such as personal computers, tablets and especially smartphones, amplified the process of extending Self to the digital environment (Belk 2013, 2014). This was done through the insertion of information about identity characteristics of the users in their Timelines and through the publication of photos and daily activities in their Stories (Ferreira et al. 2018; Romney and Johnson 2018; Sheth and Solomon 2014).

These asynchronous communications work as digital footprints left on social media (Muhammad et al. 2018), which enable faster transmission of messages and stimulate intimacy and closeness between DI and their followers. Through these digital resources, DI can strategically manage the content they want to publish, reshaping their Self in the digital environment (Baym 2010, p. 8) in order to expose what individuals would like or desire to be, rather than what they really are (Jain 2018).

In this way, it has become easy to redefine the Selfie digitally, because with digital tools, you can edit the information, reshape the aesthetics of the contents produced to make it more attractive to the audience, and perfect features that in the offline environment could not to happen. Therefore, these digital environments grant greater security to the DI, since the version of themselves, represented there, can be edited and calculated, due to the flexibility of time that these individuals have for the interaction happen, thus reinforcing a great result (Ferreira et al. 2018; Romney and Johnson 2018), in order to make the image of the DI socially accepted and popular (De Veirman et al. 2017).

Therefore, DI seek to communicate that they are individuals with a digital lifestyle (Sheth and Solomon 2014), with high levels of self-construction of the image and their Self, in order to persuade their followers and express positively the conception of the Self together the collectivity (Sheth and Solomon 2014). Therefore, the main objective is self-promotion and self-affirmation, since to show to your followers their daily lives, the belongings and people who have value to them, the brands they use, their professional skills and the places they attend, is an effective way of add value to their sense of self and generate popularity (De Veirman et al. 2017), to convince their followers to adopt their consumption suggestions. This fact allows the followers to perceive them as a differentiated person who has social status, credibility and popularity (De Veirman et al. 2017) in the digital environment, thus creating a digital lifestyle "lifestream" (also called "social footprints" and "digital life"), which is reflected in the off-line environment (Sheth and Solomon 2014).

However, when the DI confess that it is being paid to make postings on demand for a particular brand, its followers identify this act as advertising (Evans et al. 2017). This may have a negative impact on the sharing of this type of content, probably because the credibility of DI is diminished when the characteristics of trust and authenticity are also absent (Casaló et al. 2018; Evans et al. 2017). In addition, features such as the Instagram Stories allow followers to have a sense of closer proximity to DI, because the content is shared almost instantaneously (Ferreira et al. 2018; Romney and Johnson 2018). However, it is possible to manage the presentation of the DI before publish the content.

Before the DI carry out their publications, it is possible that the produced content will be revised and edited by using filters and visual effects (Ferreira et al. 2018; Romney and Johnson 2018), as a dog face, a king crown, among other options, that digitally modify the essence of the publication, adding hedonic elements that make them visually attractive. It is not enough just to post a photo, it is necessary constantly to look for something new to modify them in order to generate interesting contents to the public follower. Thus, fluency is generated in the communicated content and provides to the DI an anchor point to increase the relative stability of their extended self in the digital environment by relating to their followers (Ferreira et al. 2018; Romney and Johnson 2018).

Therefore, it is possible to observe that the memories distributed in the virtual environment through the extension of the self of the DI impact on the interpersonal trust of the followers (Domenicucci 2018). This way, it is perceived that this online involvement caused by the self-identification of followers with their DI and by the construction of the symbolic value involved in this interaction, enables the formation of the trust of the followers, resulting in their commitment (Wongkitrungrueng and Assarut 2018).

Borders and Intersetions that Involve the Psychosocial Elements Identified

Some of the psychosocial characteristics indicated in the literature that attract individuals' interest in following, trusting, engaging and adhering to DI consumption suggestions could be described, evaluating meanings, attitudes, subjective behaviors and intentions that connect followers to their DI.

Thus, we observe four (4) elements that motivate followers to choose to follow DI. The expertise, which is linked to the specific skills, competences and activities that characterizes the DI as an expert of the subjects in which he proposes to expose in the digital environment (Martensen et al. 2018). The number of followers that accompany the activities of a DI also serves as a social proof (Schaefer 2012) and an indicator of social status, credibility, and popularity (De Veirman et al. 2017).

Storytelling describes the experiences of DI through the creation of stories, transmitted in visual and textual formats (Ben Youssef et al. 2018; Larkey et al. 2018), which generate a strong emotional involvement between DI and their followers. This fact occurs due to the approach that the routine of posting and the monitoring of activities of the DI generate in the followers. And the digital lifestyle (Lifestream), which is characterized by strategically edited content (Baym 2010, p. 8; Belk 2013, 2014; Sheth and Solomon 2014), so DI can engage followers and achieve a satisfactory result about the performance that these individuals wish to obtain (Ferreira et al. 2018; Romney and Johnson 2018).

The boundaries established between the psychosocial elements identified can be established by observing the symbolic meaning of each element and the influence they exert on each other. The expertise related to the specific knowledge of DI is applied in order to attract a large number of followers interested in disseminated content. However, the DI will only be legitimized as an expert on the subject if it presents social proofs (Schaefer 2012) that their skills and experiences are truly qualified. Therefore, a DI is only considered an expert if it obtains an expressive Number of Followers that can confirm its condition of expert in the subject.

A DI can also raise its number of followers by showing their digital lifestyle (Sheth and Solomon 2014). Therefore, experiences that can impart social status motivate people to follow certain DI for the desire to live the lifestyle and the experiences of high social standard that these individuals transmit in their social media.

This digital lifestyle is communicated through storytelling with specific content, exposed through visual and textual elements, posted with a certain frequency, and serves to connect emotions and feelings in a subjective way (Stubb 2018), inspiring followers and motivating them to be close to their DI.

These digital narratives, in addition to carrying elements that communicate the DI digital lifestyle, can also communicate the expertise of DI that have specific abilities. Thus the achievements, life trajectories, and unique deeds that these individuals have performed are transmitted and available so that their followers can connect emotionally, perceiving these DI as differentiated individuals in whom followers can be inspired (Martensen et al. 2018).

However, the intersection between these elements also generates behaviors and encourages the advent of several factors that influence the followers' decision to follow their DI (Fig. 1). In this way, it is noticed that when a DI presents expertise on a certain subject and has a high number of followers, it is possible to obtain social status (Henrich and Gil-White 2001; Martensen et al. 2018). This is due to the prestige (Henrich and Gil-White 2001), know-how, recognition and respect (Cheng et al. 2013) that DI obtain by demonstrating their specialties to a large network of followers.

When the intersection between the number of followers and the digital lifestyle is observed, it is found that the strategically produced content, directed to a large number of followers, generates Popularity (De Veirman et al. 2017). This popularity is due to the constant monitoring of DI routines by a great number of followers as a way to inspire the ideal of shared life through content produced by DI.

Regarding the intersection between digital lifestyle and digital narratives, it is perceived that DI seek to redefine their self-sense in the digital environment (Belk 2013, 2014). When DI produce content aiming to manage their images in a positive way, the type of content, frequency and quantity of the posts (Leal et al. 2014) will cause digital narratives to be established, fostering redefinition of the selfs with the intention of transforming the self-image of the DI in reference to their followers (Belk 2013, 2014). This fact is established through the creation of strategically modified contents that describe the experiences of DI in an idealized and platonic way (Leal et al. 2014).

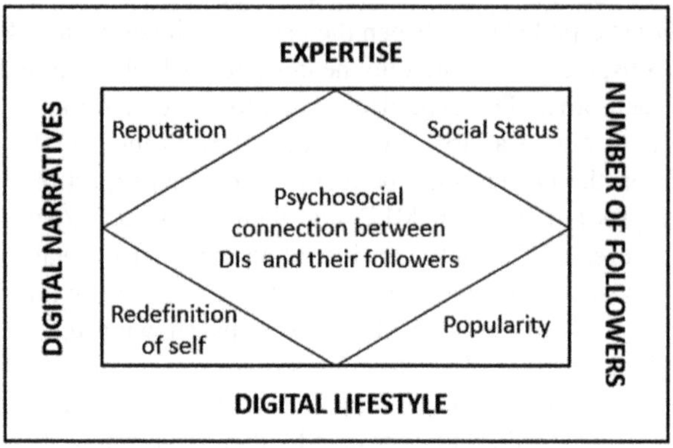

Fig. 1 Psychosocial elements and its combinations that connect the DI to their followers. (*Source*: Adapted from Kozinets (2007))

Finally, we observe the intersection between Expertise and Digital Narratives, which is established when DI describe their activities and achievements, giving them a strong reputation (Casaló et al. 2018). In this way, when the life trajectory of these individuals is communicated through tools such as Stories and Timelines in a constant way, their followers end up perceiving them as references in the subjects they seek to deal with.

General Discussion

The present study aimed to analyze the psychosocial elements that emotionally connect the followers to their DI. Therefore, four elements were identified in the literature that allow this connection to be established, characterized as: Expertise, Number of Followers, Lifestream and Storytelling.

The intersections between the identified elements also generated factors that influence the motivation of the followers to keep themselves connected to the routines and activities of their DI. Social Status was shown to be the result of the intersection between Expertise and Number of Followers, while Popularity was presented as the consequence of the combination of the Number of Followers and the Digital Lifestyle. The result of the intersection between the Digital Lifestyle and the Digital Narratives was the Redefinition of the Digital Self of the DI, while the intersection between Digital Narratives and Expertise promotes Reputation.

In this way, it is aimed with a exploratory qualitative study to understand the factors that stimulate followers to become consumers of brands, products and services used and disseminated by DI, based on the elements identified in the literature and factors from their boundaries, and intersections to empirically analyze psychosocial elements as meanings, attitudes, subjective behaviors, and intentions that emotionally connect DI to their followers.

In this context, managerial implications related to the results of empirical studies may provide a basis for understanding the factors that lead individuals to follow and subsequently become consumers. With this more focused reflection on the relationship between the influencers and their followers, companies can increase their market outcomes by promoting their brands, products and services through DI that have specific psychosocial characteristics and provide a more efficient model for influencers to impact and retain their networks of followers, through social attitudes and values expressed in the virtual environment.

References

Baym, N. (2010). Personal Connections in the Digital Age. Malden: Polity Press.

Belk, R. (2014). Digital consumption and the extended self. *Journal of Marketing Management*, *30*(11-12), 1101-1118.

Belk, R. W. (2013). Extended self in a digital world. *Journal of Consumer Research*, *40*(3), 477-500.

Ben Youssef, K., Leicht, T., & Marongiu, L. (2018). Storytelling in the context of destination marketing: an analysis of conceptualisations and impact measurement. *Journal of Strategic Marketing*, 27(8), 696-713.

Casaló, L. V., Flavián, C., & Ibáñez-Sánchez, S. (2018). Influencers on Instagram: Antecedents and consequences of opinion leadership. *Journal of Business Research*, 117, 510-519

Cheng, J. T., Tracy, J. L., Foulsham, T., Kingstone, A., & Henrich, J. (2013). Two ways to the top: Evidence that dominance and prestige are distinct yet viable avenues to social rank and influence. *Journal of personality and social psychology*, *104*(1), 103.

De Veirman, M., Cauberghe, V., & Hudders, L. (2017). Marketing through Instagram influencers: the impact of number of followers and product divergence on brand attitude. *International Journal of Advertising*, *36*(5), 798-828.

Dholakia, N., & Reyes, I. (2013). Virtuality as place and process. *Journal of Marketing Management*, *29*(13-14), 1580-1591.

Domenicucci, J. (2018). Trust, Extended Memories and Social Media. In *Towards a Philosophy of Digital Media* (pp. 119-142). Palgrave Macmillan, Cham.

Evans, N. J., Phua, J., Lim, J., & Jun, H. (2017). Disclosing Instagram influencer advertising: The effects of disclosure language on advertising recognition, attitudes, and Behavioral Intent. Journal of Interactive Advertising, 17(2), 1–12.

Ferreira, E., Costantino, F. A., & Lima, J. S. (2018). Cotidiano e Instagram: efemeridade e narrativas de si no recurso Stories. *Esferas*, *1*(11).

Henrich, J., & Gil-White, F. J. (2001). The evolution of prestige: Freely conferred deference as a mechanism for enhancing the benefits of cultural transmission. *Evolution and human behavior*, *22*(3), 165-196.

Jain, V. (2018). Luxury: Not for Consumption but Developing Extended Digital Self. *Journal of Human Values*, *24*(1), 25-38.

Katz, E. and Lazarsfeld, P. (1955), Personal Influence, The Free Press, New York, NY.

Kozinets, R. V. (2007). Technology/ideology: How ideological fields influence consumers' technology narratives. *Journal of consumer research*, *34*(6), 865-881.

Larkey, L., Del Toro-Mejías, L., DiFulvio, G., & Gubrium, A. (2018). Narrative Influences on "Desire to Act in My Community" in Digital Storytelling Workshops for Latina Teens. *International quarterly of community health education*, *38*(3), 163-167.

Leal, G. P. A., Hor-Meyll, L. F., & de Paula Pessôa, L. A. G. (2014). Influence of virtual communities in purchasing decisions: The participants' perspective. *Journal of Business Research*, *67*(5), 882-890.

Lin, H. C., Bruning, P. F., & Swarna, H. (2018). Using online opinion leaders to promote the hedonic and utilitarian value of products and services. *Business Horizons*, *61*(3), 431-442.

Martensen, A., Brockenhuus-Schack, S., & Zahid, A. L. (2018). How citizen influencers persuade their followers *Journal of Fashion Marketing and Management: An International Journal*, 22(3), 19

Muhammad, S. S., Dey, B. L., & Weerakkody, V. (2018). Analysis of factors that influence customers' willingness to leave big data digital footprints on social media: A systematic review of literature. *Information Systems Frontiers*, *20*(3), 559-576.

Ramdarshan Bold, M. (2018). The return of the social author: Negotiating authority and influence on Wattpad. *Convergence*, *24*(2), 117-136.

Rogers, E. M. (2010). *Diffusion of innovations*. Simon and Schuster.

Romney, M., & Johnson, R. G. (2018). Show me a story: narrative, image, and audience engagement on sports network Instagram accounts. *Information, Communication & Society*, 23(1), 94-109.

Sanchez-Cartas, J. M., & Leon, G. (2018). On "Influencers" and Their Impact on the Diffusion of Digital Platforms. In *International Conference on Practical Applications of Agents and Multi-Agent Systems* (pp. 210-222). Springer, Cham. Schaefer

Schaefer, M. (2012), Return on Influence: The Revolutionary Power of Klout, Social Scoring, and Influence Marketing, McGraw-Hill, New York, NY.

Sheth, J. N., & Solomon, M. R. (2014). Extending the extended self in a digital world. *Journal of Marketing Theory and Practice*, *22*(2), 123-132.

Sternthal, B., Dholakia, R., & Leavitt, C. (1978). The persuasive effect of source credibility: Tests of cognitive response. *Journal of Consumer research*, *4*(4), 252-260.

Stubb, C. (2018). Story versus info: Tracking blog readers' online viewing time of sponsored blog posts based on content-specific elements. *Computers in Human Behavior*, *82*, 54-62.

Tomaszeski, M. S. (2006). A baseline examination of political bloggers: Who they are, their views on the blogosphere and their influence in agenda-setting via the twostep flow hypothesis (Electronic Theses, Treatises and Dissertations. Paper 1282). Retrieved from. http://diginole.lib.fsu.edu/etd/1282.

Uzunoğlu, E., & Kip, S. M. (2014). Brand communication through digital influencers: Leveraging blogger engagement. *International Journal of Information Management*, *34*(5), 592-602.

Wongkitrungrueng, A., & Assarut, N. (2018). The role of live streaming in building consumer trust and engagement with social commerce sellers. *Journal of Business Research*, *117*, 543-556.

Enabling Creative Small Business Innovation in a Crisis: An Abstract

Ashley Hass, Kelley Cours Anderson, and Corky Mitchell

Abstract The COVID-19 pandemic has impacted many businesses but has especially impacted small businesses (Dua et al. 2020, Eggers 2020). In the early months of the pandemic, many small business owners did not have thc financial ability to sustain their services due to lacking funds during the shut-down (Bartik et al. 2020). This has significant long-term effects on the global economy as small-to-medium size businesses comprise 90% of all global businesses and 55% of GDP (Salesforce 2019). The demise of small businesses could have incomprehensible long term impacts on the global economy. As a result, it is not surprising that many scholars are calling for more research to understand how businesses can continue their services during the global pandemic (e.g., Batat 2020; Heinonen and Strandvik 2020; Sajtos et al. 2020).

Although past research has investigated crisis management from a marketing perspective, little research has explored how small businesses are able to continue services in a crisis of this extent. Past research recognizes that business model innovation can offer new profitable opportunities and/or provide a shield against dynamic environmental changes (McDonald et al. 2019; Teece 2018), but less work has explored how small businesses can attain business innovation models in the challenge of a significant crisis, such as the COVID-19 pandemic. As such, we explore the following research question: *What can enable small businesses' business model innovation during a crisis?*

To investigate this research question, we take an inductive, qualitative approach. Using qualitative interviews with 10 industry-diverse small business owners and 5 small business resource providers, the data reveals there are multiple paths to pursuing their interests in sustaining business. Specifically, we identify that through a cocreative process, small businesses rely on technology and intermediary organizations to foster new forms of pursuing business, specifically engaging in business model innovation (BMI). This research answers calls for research inquiring how

---

A. Hass (✉) · K. C. Anderson · C. Mitchell
Texas Tech University, Lubbock, TX, USA
e-mail: ashley.hass@ttu.edu; kelley.anderson@ttu.edu; corky.mitchell@ttu.edu

J. Allen et al. (eds.), *Celebrating the Past and Future of Marketing and Discovery with Social Impact*, Developments in Marketing Science: Proceedings of the Academy of Marketing Science, https://doi.org/10.1007/978-3-030-95346-1_53

businesses, and specifically small businesses, are able to help others cope with the crisis and support the economy (Pantano et al. 2020).

Keywords SBOs · Cocreation · Innovation · Crisis · Qualitative

Special Session: The University of Google? A Panel Discussion about the Disruptive Changes in Marketing Education and What Programs May Look Like in the Not-So-Distant Future: An Abstract

Amy Watson, Holly Syrdal, John Osborn, Rita McGrath, Al Ringleb, Tanya Botten, Sara Leoni, and Matthew Waller

Abstract Amid skyrocketing costs and student debt, much has been written about the increasing skepticism of whether a traditional four-year degree is "worth it." The general consensus among outlets such as Forbes, The WSJ, and CNBC (each citing

A. Watson (✉)
Valdosta State University, Valdosta, GA, USA
e-mail: amywatson@valdosta.edu

H. Syrdal
Texas State University, San Marcos, TX, USA
e-mail: hollysyrdal@txstate.edu

J. Osborn
CEO at OMD USA, New York, NY, USA
e-mail: john.osborn@omd.com

R. McGrath
Rita McGrath Group/Columbia Business School, New York, NY, USA
e-mail: maria@ritamcgrath.com

A. Ringleb
CIMBA, Paderno del Grappa, TV, Italy
e-mail: ringleb@cimba.it

T. Botten
Beckman Coulter Diagnostics, San Diego, CA, USA

S. Leoni
CEO at GreenFig, San Mateo, CA, USA
e-mail: sara.leoni@greenfig.com

M. Waller
Dean at Walton College of Business, University of Arkansas, Fayetteville, AR, USA
e-mail: mwaller@walton.uark.edu

J. Allen et al. (eds.), *Celebrating the Past and Future of Marketing and Discovery with Social Impact*, Developments in Marketing Science: Proceedings of the Academy of Marketing Science, https://doi.org/10.1007/978-3-030-95346-1_54

recent polls) is that families' attitudes toward higher education is changing, due to sharply rising costs. This change does not favor traditional college degree programs. In the midst of this transformation, branded digital marketing certificates have presented themselves as a more economical alternative. Perhaps the most worrisome of which are the recently announced "Google Career Certificates," which are six-month programs geared to prepare workers for the digital economy. Google leadership states these new certificates are meant to be the equivalent of a four-year degree given that "college degrees are out of reach for many Americans, and you shouldn't need a college diploma to have economic security." The purpose of this panel session is to discuss what the traditional marketing degree program response should be to the changing perceptions of value and increased competition.

The potential consequences of Google entering higher education have been further exacerbated by impacts of the COVID-19 pandemic. Disruption that many thought leaders have been talking about for years was accelerated in the span of a few months. The result was a wave of student questions and criticism of the value of online education directed against even the most renowned institutions. While pandemic-related impacts to teaching modality may not be long-term, it will likely take much longer for student sentiment to recover. Evidenced by over seventy lawsuits currently pending against colleges and universities, this confluence of factors should not be ignored. Rather, we need to view this as an opportunity for existential reflection on the most basic of marketing principles as they apply to higher education as a marketable service. As such, in this panel session, the following questions will be addressed by a diverse group of stakeholders: Will industry and prospective students/families accept these certificates as a substitute to a traditional degree? How should traditional marketing degree programs adapt or change program offerings to be more competitive/appealing? What is academia's value proposition? How do we communicate this effectively with prospective students and their families? How do we train students on technologies many professors have never themselves used? Are there opportunities for public/private collaboration that provide technical skills, produce job-ready graduates, and lower costs? What could these look like? Student, industry, and academic representatives will discuss these questions and engage the audience in a lively conversation about the future of marketing education and the changing role of marketing academics.

Keywords Marketing education · Disruption · Google · Certificate programs · Digital · Marketing · Alternative · Innovation

How CEOs Twitter with Customers: Key Insights and Future Research Directions: An Abstract

Tong Wu, Jonathan Reynolds, Jintao Wu, and Bodo B. Schlegelmilch

Abstract In recent years, social media has emerged as a popular communication channel for senior management, especially for chief executive officers (CEOs). Twitter is one of the most popular social media platforms because of its ease in reaching out to customers, employees, media, and the general public (Weber Shandwick 2017). Some of the current and former CEOs on Twitter include Richard Branson (Virgin Group), Tim Cook (Apple), John Legere (T-Mobile), Aaron Levie (Box), and Michael Dell (Dell).

This study analyzes how CEOs communicate with their customers via Twitter. The aim is to help develop guidelines that leverage Twitter in leadership communications with customers. Based on a large-scale content analysis, we propose a model that categorizes differences in CEO Twitter use according to four dimensions: content professionalism, language professionalism, interactional effort, and information cues. We also develop coding schemes and measurement scales to map the relative position of each CEO account onto the four dimensions.

Our study makes five specific contributions. First, it draws theoretical and managerial attention to the important role of corporate leaders on social media, which is lacking in prior research. Second, it presents the first comprehensive content analysis of the tweeting CEO phenomenon. Third, the study offers a useful tool for research on CEOs' practice on Twitter. The four-dimensional model provides

The research is funded by National Natural Science Foundation of China (No.71802201 and No.71672200).

T. Wu · J. Wu (✉)
Sun Yat-sen University, Guangzhou, China
e-mail: wutong39@mail.sysu.edu.cn; lnswjt@mail.sysu.edu.cn

J. Reynolds
University of Oxford, Oxford, UK
e-mail: jonathan.reynolds@sbs.ox.ac.uk

B. B. Schlegelmilch
WU Vienna University of Economics and Business, Vienna, Austria
e-mail: bodo.schlegelmilch@wu.ac.at

J. Allen et al. (eds.), *Celebrating the Past and Future of Marketing and Discovery with Social Impact*, Developments in Marketing Science: Proceedings of the Academy of Marketing Science, https://doi.org/10.1007/978-3-030-95346-1_55

researchers with a useful instrument to examine and categorize Twitter practices. Fourth, we developed a coding matrix and measurement scales for all four dimensions. This matrix should be useful in guiding practitioners on measuring, comparing, and monitoring Twitter usage of corporate executives. Fifth, our study presents four maps that capture the over 300 CEO Twitter accounts' position relative to one another on each dimension. Our scores and maps of tweeting CEOs provide scholars and managers with useful knowledge on CEOs' practice on Twitter.

Keywords Twitter · Social media · CEO · Leadership communication · Content analysis

When Chatbots Fail: Exploring Customer Responsibility Attributions of Co-Created Service Failures: An Abstract

Daniela Castillo, Ana Canhoto, and Emanuel Said

Abstract Extant literature has predominantly viewed value co-creation as a voluntary process of value creation between the customer and the service provider (e.g., Grissemann and Stokburger-Sauer 2012; Sugathan, Ranjan, and Mulky 2017). However, the customer may not always enter into the value co-creation process voluntarily. As chatbots are increasingly replacing traditional customer service options (Belanche et al. 2020), customers may find themselves in situations where they are forced to use automated technologies (Reinders, Frambach, and Kleijnen 2015). Indeed, several service providers have started to offer chatbots as the only customer solution, especially as the first point of contact for customer service queries (Forrester 2017). Such cases, where the customer does not have a choice as to whether to interact with a chatbot or a human representative, represent instances of mandatory customer participation (Dong and Sivakumar 2017; Tsai, Wu, and Huang 2017).

Limiting consumers' perceived freedom of choice in co-creating, may result in severe negative attitudes towards the evaluation of the technology and the service provider (Reinders, Dabholkar, and Frambach 2008). Such attitudes may be further exacerbated when a situation requiring the forced use of a technology leads to service failure. We argue that in cases of service failure, forced co-creation (no choice but to interact with chatbot) will have a distinct impact on customer responsibility attributions of controllability, stability and locus of causality, when compared to voluntary co-creation (choice between chatbot and human representative). We also investigate the role of customer expectations and propose that expectations mediate the relationship between each co-creation setting and the resulting responsibility attributions.

Experimental research is being proposed to test the research framework in a customer service setting, taking into consideration two types of service failure: out-

D. Castillo (✉) · A. Canhoto
Brunel University, London, UK
e-mail: daniela.castillo@brunel.ac.uk; ana.canhoto@brunel.ac.uk

E. Said
University of Malta, Msida, Malta
e-mail: emanuel.said@um.edu.mt

J. Allen et al. (eds.), *Celebrating the Past and Future of Marketing and Discovery with Social Impact*, Developments in Marketing Science: Proceedings of the Academy of Marketing Science, https://doi.org/10.1007/978-3-030-95346-1_56

come and process failure. Participants will be randomly assigned to two different co-creation settings: forced co-creation and co-creation by choice, and will be required to interact with an actual chatbot, which has been programmed using the IBM Watson platform. Participant responses will be recorded through an online questionnaire.

The findings of this experimental research are expected to contribute to a more insightful understanding of the consequences of forcing consumers to use novel technologies. This is an important research area which has been largely overlooked in service literature to date, as the literature has typically examined the introduction of new technologies within a voluntary context. Insights into these behaviours are also important to achieve a more substantive understanding of the implications of AI technologies, and to find ways to reduce negative reactions to such technologies.

Keywords Artificial intelligence · Chatbots · Service failure · Attribution of responsibility · Expectations · Co-creation · Research framework

Undesired Impulse e-Buying Behavior: An Exploratory Study: An Abstract

Carmen Abril and Sandra Tobon

Abstract E-tailers' marketing strategies and new technology developments on the internet frequently increase the likelihood of impulsive e-buying in consumers. Although, in some cases, these strategies may prove profitable and satisfactory for both the consumer and e-tailer, in other cases, the e-impulsivity of the consumer creates undesired business consequences, such as consumer regret and product returns for refund. Therefore, there are some circumstances under which impulse e-buying should be prevented for the mutual benefit of the consumer and e-tailer.

Impulse buying has been explained as a failure in the management of consumer self-control, together with the influence of contextual variables that lead to unplanned or impulsive buying. Therefore, a person with a tendency to impulsivity and faced with certain external and internal stimuli in the internet environment, is more likely to buy impulsively than one without this personality trait.

This research aims to investigate whether, in the face of undesired impulse e-buying, it is possible to manage the consumer impulsivity through gamified strategies reducing the probability of future returns and thus, to avoid the feeling of shame, guilt, and post-purchase remorse at the customer level and the economic cost at the company level.

An experiment was set, in an online shopping context, designed ad-hoc. A purchase scenario was simulated. One hundred-sixteen (116) Americans ages 18-35 years old participated in the study for a financial incentive and were contacted through MTurk.

This project has been funded with support from the European Commission-GAMIFY project KA+. This publication reflects the views only of the author, and the Commission cannot be held responsible for any use which may be made of the information contained therein.

C. Abril (✉)
Complutense University, Madrid, Spain
e-mail: cabrilba@ucm.es

S. Tobon
CEU San Pablo University, Madrid, Spain
e-mail: sandra.tobonperilla@ceu.es

J. Allen et al. (eds.), *Celebrating the Past and Future of Marketing and Discovery with Social Impact*, Developments in Marketing Science: Proceedings of the Academy of Marketing Science, https://doi.org/10.1007/978-3-030-95346-1_57

Our results show that gamification approaches may help consumers reevaluate their decisions and retract them, thus reducing the volume of product returns resulting from impulse e-behavior.

As managerial implications, in industries where impulse e-buying provokes high volumes of product returns, it will be appropriate for e-tailers to help consumers make timely and better decisions, in turn reducing the cost of reverse logistics and promoting consumer satisfaction with their brands.

Keywords Impulse buying · Product returns · Gamification · Nudge theory

Automated Technologies: Do They Co-Create or Co-Destruct Value for the Customer? An Abstract

Tichakunda Rodney Mwenje, Anne Marie Doherty, and Graeme McLean

Abstract As service functions based on automated technologies become more prevalent there is an increased likelihood that the way in which value is co-created and co-destructed is changing (Karteemo and Helkkukla 2018; Paschen et al. 2019; Van Esch et al. 2019). Vargo et al. (2017) assert that there is an imperative need to study fast, technology induced changes in service eco-systems. These technology induced changes along with their impact on customers' experience of value co-creation and value co-destruction are the central phenomenon of this research. Specifically, the research presented in this study explores how (and if) customers' experience value co-creation when interacting with brands' automated technology in service-based value networks. The two proposed research questions are as follows: (1) How do customers perceive the impact of automated technology (chatbots) on value co-creation and value co-destruction? (2) What are the characteristics of chatbots that influence customers experience of value co-creation or value co-destruction? In doing so, this paper reveals a more accurate understanding of how novel automated technologies shape the dynamics of value co-creation and value co-destruction.

A qualitative approach using exploratory interviews for data collection was chosen for this paper. Research on value co-creation and technology has predominantly adopted a quantitative survey-based approach to data collection (Balaji and Roy 2017; Zhang 2016; Khotamaki and Rajala 2016; See-To and Ho 2014). This paper offers an alternative approach seeking rich data about an under researched area. In addition, the findings of this paper provide the platform for a future quantitative study. The overall aim of the interviews was to achieve an in-depth understanding on customers' interactional experiences with brands or service providers' automated technology, while highlighting the characteristics of these automated technologies which co-create or co-destruct value for the customer during the service encounter

T. R. Mwenje (✉) · A. M. Doherty · G. McLean
University of Strathclyde, Glasgow, UK
e-mail: tichakunda.mwenje@strath.ac.uk; annemarie.doherty@strath.ac.uk; graememclean@strath.ac.uk

J. Allen et al. (eds.), *Celebrating the Past and Future of Marketing and Discovery with Social Impact*, Developments in Marketing Science: Proceedings of the Academy of Marketing Science, https://doi.org/10.1007/978-3-030-95346-1_58

A total of six themes were revealed from the exploratory interviews. These included, instantaneous support (i.e., social presence), informational benefits (i.e., information quality), personalisation, perceived control, consistency and understanding (i.e., comprehension of the service -related issue) and irreplaceability of humans (i.e., empathy). The findings of the current study indicate that customers may experience both value co-creation and value co-destruction when interacting with firms' chatbots for service delivery depending on the characteristics of the chatbots. The current study is the first to explore both value co-creating and value co-destructing potentials of automated technology in value-based service networks. In addition, these emergent themes offer a differing perspective from the existing literature, thus, providing the scope to examine the identified themes in a wider quantitative study. Moreover, the study offers practitioners an understanding of the characteristics they need to pay attention to when implementing chatbots for service delivery. Doing so will increase the possibility of value co-creation for the customer during the service encounter, as well as enhance the customer experience which in turn could yield better customer brand engagement.

Keywords Value co-creation · Value co-destruction · Automated technology · Artificial intelligence

Everything Seems Further Away on the Smartphone: The Effect of Mobile Attachment on the Perception of Psychological Distance: An Abstract

Nguyen Hoang Linh and Marie-Helene Fosse-Gomez

Abstract Mobile is emerging as the dominant platform on which consumers spend most of their time. Unlike the PC, many consumers form an emotional attachment relationship with their mobile (Vincent 2006). Consequently, these attached consumers demonstrate unique behaviors with and without their mobile (e.g., Kolsaker et al. 2009; Konok et al. 2016; Melumad and Pham 2020). Research to date has focused mainly on the consequence of separating from mobile while paying little attention to other aspects of mobile attachment. This study aims to uncover the impact of mobile attachment on their perception and the underneath mechanism. The context of our research is based on climate change communication. Through three laboratory experiments based on a combination of Attachment Theory and Construal Level Theory, we highlight the importance of psychological distance, attachment styles, and gender for the perceived credibility of an ad.

Our results suggested that attached to mobile consumers tend to have a more psychological distant perspective on their mobile than when they are on PC. This is achieved by a heightened level of anxiety when attached to mobile consumers are away from their device, which leads to a more proximal psychological distance perception. This change in perception directly impacts the perceived credibility of the ad. This effect is moderated by their personal attachment style and by their gender. However, the actual differences between conditions are marginal, albeit statistically significant. The reported level of anxiety also seems high across our sample, which could be attributed to the ongoing pandemic at the time of data collection. Our findings have important implications for effective communication planning in climate-related subjects and various others within the emerging context of mobile. A

N. H. Linh (✉) · M.-H. Fosse-Gomez
Université de Lille, Lille, France
e-mail: linh.nguyenhoang.etu@univ-lille.fr; marie-helene.fosse-gomez@univ-lille.fr

J. Allen et al. (eds.), *Celebrating the Past and Future of Marketing and Discovery with Social Impact*, Developments in Marketing Science: Proceedings of the Academy of Marketing Science, https://doi.org/10.1007/978-3-030-95346-1_59

dedicated approach should be made for heavy mobile users. And climate change ad should be described abstractly to match the consumers' viewpoint on mobile. Further studies are recommended to address our limitations and validate the results externally.

Keywords Climate change · Mobile attachment · Advertising · Psychological distance

What's in it for Me? Exploring Intrusiveness for Online Ads When Intending to Sell Products versus When Intending to Buy Products: An Abstract

Sphurti Sewak and Kimberly A. Taylor

Abstract A large body of research has explored how online customized ads can drive the perception of intrusiveness and result in customer behavioral intentions when the intention is to purchase a new product. However, little is known about how the perception of intrusiveness differs when the intention is to sell used products and the resultant behavioral intentions, like clickthrough and intent to sell. This is an issue of significant importance as more and more retailers from various product segments are offering customers options for selling their used products along with the options of buying their new products. For example, companies like ThredUp that provided an avenue for selling good quality clothes have partnered with Walmart, Gap, Reebok, and many other brands for providing resale experience to customers (Rosenbaum and Caminiti 2020). Further, it is not only in the apparel segment where reselling used products is prevalent; this trend has shown an upward trajectory in many other segments such as electronics and furniture as well, besides being a well-established business model for cars already. Recently, IKEA launched its first refurbished store in Sweden, taking advantage of this trend. Also, as more and more companies face the pressure of presenting themselves as a "sustainable" brand, and adding the current crisis faced by all due to the pandemic, this issue will only gain momentum.

Our daily lives are replete with examples of times when we are faced with the option of letting go of something that has been sitting idle or not being used for a long time. With the opportunities provided by secondary markets, defined as markets for selling used goods, (Shulman and Coughlan 2007), it is imperative to ask how are the customized ads encouraging consumers to sell are received. What about that crib lying in the garage now that the kid is all grown up? Or that expensive Calvin Klein dress that is hanging in your closet with the hope of someday fitting you like it once did? Apps like Letgo and platforms like eBay provided great oppor-

S. Sewak (✉) · K. A. Taylor
Florida International University, Miami, FL, USA
e-mail: ssewak@fiu.edu; taylork@fiu.edu

J. Allen et al. (eds.), *Celebrating the Past and Future of Marketing and Discovery with Social Impact*, Developments in Marketing Science: Proceedings of the Academy of Marketing Science, https://doi.org/10.1007/978-3-030-95346-1_60

tunities to people wanting to get rid of such stuff, that someone else might be interested in buying. Given the widespread use of the internet by all age groups, how receptive are customers when they are faced with a customized ad for a product they have been deliberating to sell online? Our research takes the first step towards attempting to answer such questions by linking the perception of intrusiveness associated with such customized ads, with a concrete established measure like Clickthrough.

Keywords Intrusiveness · Customized ads · Clickthrough · Secondary markets · Behavioral intentions

Costly Price Adjustment and Automated Pricing: The Case of Airbnb: An Abstract

Qi Pan and Wen Wang

Abstract On many e-commerce platforms such as Airbnb, StubHub and TURO, where each seller sells a fixed inventory over a finite horizon, the pricing problems are intrinsically dynamic. However, many sellers on these platforms do not update prices frequently. In markets where sellers have fixed inventories and limited selling time, optimal prices respond to both the remaining inventory and time (Gallego and van Ryzin 1994). Empirical studies (Williams 2018; Cho et al. 2018) examining pricing problems in these environments also support Gallego and van Ryzin's (1994) theoretical prediction. However, on many e-commerce platforms where small sellers are facing a fixed inventory and limited selling time problem, we commonly observe price rigidity, which seems to contradict Gallego and Ryzin's theory.

Automated pricing, which uses machine learning algorithms to automatically price products, is becoming a standard feature on some of these platforms. One key feature of automated pricing is that it reduces the seller's burden; the seller does not need to carry out a price-optimization problem every day. This paper develops a dynamic pricing model to study the revenue and welfare implication of automated pricing, which allows sellers to update their prices without manual interference. The model focuses on three factors through which automated pricing influences sellers: price adjustment cost, buyer's varying willingness to pay and inventory structure. In the model, we also take into account competition among sellers.

Utilizing a unique data set of detailed Airbnb rental history and price trajectory in New York City, we find that the price rigidity observed in the data can be rationalized by a price adjustment cost ranging from 0:9% to 2:2% of the listed price. Moreover, automated pricing can increase the platform's revenue by 4.8% and the

Q. Pan (✉)
The Chinese University of Hong Kong (Shenzhen), Shenzhen, China
e-mail: panqi@cuhk.edu.cn

W. Wang
The Hong Kong University of Science and Technology, Hong Kong, China
e-mail: wenwangww@ust.hk

J. Allen et al. (eds.), *Celebrating the Past and Future of Marketing and Discovery with Social Impact*, Developments in Marketing Science: Proceedings of the Academy of Marketing Science, https://doi.org/10.1007/978-3-030-95346-1_61

hosts' (sellers') by 3.9%. The renters (buyers) could be either better off or worse off depending on the length of their stays.

Keywords Dynamic pricing · Price-adjustment cost · Platforms · Airbnb

References Available Upon Request

Exploring Metaphors and Metaphorical Reasoning for Developing Marketing Thought and Practice: An Abstract

Oswald A. J. Mascarenhas, Anup Krishnamurthy, and Caren Rodrigues

Abstract Metaphors and metaphorical thinking have enriched business management in general, but have hardly impacted marketing management even though marketing as science, theory, and practice could benefit from metaphors more than other disciplines in management. This paper explores the rich potential of metaphors, root metaphors, and metaphorical thinking and reasoning as an overarching methodology for developing marketing theory.

In this context, we first review the three major theories of metaphor origins – the comparison theory, the semantic interaction-tension theory, and the cognitive theory – for developing metaphoric thinking and reasoning in marketing. The comparison theory focuses on metaphors being a matter of words, as a deviant from normal literal usage, and is based on the similarities between two things. However, it has been argued that this theory ignores the crucial role of differences. This gave rise to the semantic interaction-tension theory, which introduced the notion of tension to describe the literal incompatibility relationship between the subject and that which embellishes it.

While the semantic interaction-tension theory was an improvement over the comparison theory, it did not solve the issue of transition from literal incongruence to metaphorical congruence between two semantic fields. Thus, the cognitive theory argued that metaphor usage is not only emotive, but a cognitively potential vehicle of knowledge possessing special meaning other than the literal meaning and reading of text. In sum, a metaphor should not only encourage a premature analytical closure (and thus knowledge dissemination) by emphasizing similarity, but also work on tension that dissimilarities create for knowledge generation.

Next, in our search for a suitable root metaphor for use in marketing, we formulate several research propositions to illustrate the sub-metaphor *producer-consumer* relationship under the root metaphor of the Free Enterprise Capital System.

O. A. J. Mascarenhas
Xavier School of Management, Jamshedpur, India
e-mail: ozzie@xlri.ac.in

A. Krishnamurthy (✉) · C. Rodrigues
St. Joseph's Institute of Management, Bengaluru, India
e-mail: anup@sjim.edu.in; caren@sjim.edu.in

J. Allen et al. (eds.), *Celebrating the Past and Future of Marketing and Discovery with Social Impact*, Developments in Marketing Science: Proceedings of the Academy of Marketing Science, https://doi.org/10.1007/978-3-030-95346-1_62

Finally, along each of the three theories of metaphor origins we extract layers of metaphorical utterances that we label as zero-order data sentences, first-order theory sentences, and second-order value sentences that indicate higher layers of conceptual and theoretical richness in marketing science. We discuss managerial implications, limitations, and new directions for research.

Keywords Metaphors · Root-metaphors · Metaphorical thinking · Producer-consumer relationships

The Effect of Robot-Human Interactions on Immersion and Store Visit Duration: An Abstract

Gaia Rancati and Isabella Maggioni

Abstract The application of service robots is rapidly spreading across several store types, with robots performing more complex tasks and interacting with customers, welcoming and assisting them (Meyer et al. 2020; van Doorn et al. 2017). Although retailers are striving to identify the right balance between robot and human sales associates, there is still a need for further research assessing how the introduction of service robots can influence the customer experience and affect customer responses (Lu et al. 2020; Larivière et al. 2017).

In this study, we examine the degree of customer immersion in human-human (HHI) vs. human-robot (HRI) in-store interactions across the stages of the selling process and we assess how immersion affects store visit duration. Specifically, we focus on four different stages of the selling process (welcome, store introduction, brand storytelling, and surprise) and apply a neuroscientific approach to measure immersion, which is defined as an experience of deep involvement with an aspect of the environment (Zak and Barraza 2018), in this case the sales associate.

Based on a field experiment conducted in a retail store selling premium leather goods (n = 50 participants), we use a neuroscientific approach to collect customers' biometrics through wearable sensors during the interactions that participants had with a service robot (Condition 1) or a human sales associate (Condition 2). Interactions were timed to obtain visit duration data and were analyzed using the Immersion Neuroscience™ platform, ANOVA and regression analysis through Hayes' PROCESS model 1 with 5000 bootstrapping.

Results show how the presence of a service robot has positive effects on customers during the service encounter. Customers enjoy interacting with service robots and this leads to higher levels of attention and engagement (Shamdasani et al. 2008; Iwamura et al. 2011). The interaction with a service robot increases the level of immersion in the welcome and surprise stages of the service encounter. By offering

G. Rancati
Allegheny College, Meadville, PA, USA
e-mail: grancati@allegheny.edu

I. Maggioni (✉)
ESCP Business School, Turin, Italy
e-mail: imaggioni@escp.eu

J. Allen et al. (eds.), *Celebrating the Past and Future of Marketing and Discovery with Social Impact*, Developments in Marketing Science: Proceedings of the Academy of Marketing Science, https://doi.org/10.1007/978-3-030-95346-1_63

a small gift, the robot engaged in a social-relational task that was unexpected by customers and resulted in a higher degree of engagement. This study also confirms that immersion positively affects visit duration. This provides support from a neuroscientific perspective to past research proposing that the more consumers are engaged in a shopping experience, the more likely they are to spend more time in-store, with this effect being significantly stronger when customers interact with a human sales associate than a service robot. Service robots increase the efficiency of the shopping experience but reduce the level of immersion in the store introduction and the brand storytelling moments, leading customers to spend less time in the store. Thus, the role of human sales associates is critical for developing customer engagement and extending store visit duration.

Keywords Service robots · Service encounter · Personal selling process · Neuroscience · Immersion · Customer experience · Store visit duration

Mexican Idiosyncrasy and Efforts to Reduce Obesity Rates: A Proposed Research Agenda: An Abstract

Monica D. Hernandez

Abstract Obesity and chronic diseases are the leading causes of mortality in Mexico. According to Barquera and Rivera (2020), the latest national survey indicated 36.1% of Mexican adults are considered obese, whereas only 23.5% has a healthy weight. The situation is attributable to a shift of the Mexican diet over the past 40 years, shifting from mainly fresh and organic foods to ultra-processed products high in sugar, salt and fat. The recent pandemic exacerbated the public health problem.

Considered by many as having weak regulations in place, the Mexican government implemented a series of strategies and regulations in order to promote a healthier lifestyle. To date, no studies have been conducted to analyze public attitudes towards the regulations, legislation or any other recent effort. In order to fill this gap, the purpose of the study is to provide a research agenda of the Mexican society's attitudes towards recent government efforts to reduce obesity rates and promotion of healthier lifestyles, such as the imposed soda tax and new labeling system.

The drivers of obesity are varied, including economic, political, social, education, cultural, infrastructural and legal drivers. A model is proposed considering these drivers and their effect on demand and supply of junk food. Understanding the complex interactions between the drivers with supply and demand requires sound research that relies on an understanding of (i) Mexican idiosyncrasy, (ii) the role of supply and demand, as well as the exploration of the interactions from (iii) varied perspectives applying multiple consumer research approaches. Accordingly, a research agenda is presented.

With collaboration across all parties involved, it would be possible to provide a holistic view of the problem. An understanding of Mexican idiosyncrasy can assist marketing managers and policy makers to tailor the appropriate messages to the consumer. Researchers may provide the first step towards building the harmonic effort needed by providing an understanding of the elements that prevent consumers to embrace practices for the society's greater good.

M. D. Hernandez (✉)
St. Edward's University, Austin, TX, USA
e-mail: mherna71@stdwards.edu

J. Allen et al. (eds.), *Celebrating the Past and Future of Marketing and Discovery with Social Impact*, Developments in Marketing Science: Proceedings of the Academy of Marketing Science, https://doi.org/10.1007/978-3-030-95346-1_64

Keywords Mexico · Obesity rates · Obesity drivers · Public attitudes
References Available Upon Request

Disclosure of Brand-Related Information and Firm Value: An Abstract

Qiong Tang, Sascha Raithel, Alexander Mafael, and Ashish S. Galande

Abstract Research on voluntary disclosure highlights the role of informative financial reporting for capital markets. Information asymmetry impedes the efficient allocation of resources in capital markets while credible disclosure between managers and investors plays an important role in mitigating these problems. Existing research provides limited insight into firms' disclosure of information about their market-based assets such as brands, although brand is an important part of firms' value proposition.

This study aims to fill this research gap by investigating brand-related information (BRI) disclosure in US firms' annual reports with three research steps. First, we develop the conceptualization of BRI, based on which, we build a BRI coding dictionary. We then conduct text mining on 10-K reports and construct a BRI disclosure index to capture the BRI disclosure level in firms' 10-K reports. In the third step, we intend to explore the key factors driving BRI disclosure as well as its financial market consequences. We propose to empirically investigate how different levels of BRI disclosure are explained by firm characteristics and actual brand performance. We will also examine how BRI disclosure influences firm value, as well as the role that BRI disclosure plays in explaining the relationship between brand performance and firm value.

This study fills the research gap in the field of information disclosure concerning BRI by conceptualizing a BRI framework and providing evidence on whether firms disclose BRI in financial reporting. This study will also contribute to marketing-finance literature by empirically investigating the informational value of BRI disclosure to firm value. The findings will provide managers and financial market

Q. Tang (✉) · S. Raithel
Freie Universität Berlin, Berlin, Germany
e-mail: qiong.tang@fu-berlin.de; Sascha.Raithel@fu-berlin.de

A. Mafael
Stockholm School of Economics, Stockholm, Sweden
e-mail: alexander.mafael@hhs.se

A. S. Galande
Indian Institute of Management Udaipur, Udaipur, India
e-mail: ashish.galande@iimu.ac.in

J. Allen et al. (eds.), *Celebrating the Past and Future of Marketing and Discovery with Social Impact*, Developments in Marketing Science: Proceedings of the Academy of Marketing Science, https://doi.org/10.1007/978-3-030-95346-1_65

participants (e.g., analysts, investors) who need to communicate and evaluate the performance implications of branding strategies and related activities with enlightenment on the value relevance of BRI disclosures.

Keywords Brand-related information · Information disclosure · Text mining · Firm value · Brand value

Consumer Support for Small Business during COVID-19: An Abstract

Michelle Childs, Sejin Ha, Christopher Sneed, Ann Berry, and Ann Fairhurst

Abstract The coronavirus outbreak (i.e., COVID-19) has swept across a growing number of countries worldwide, including the United States. In response, the U.S Department of Health and Human Services/Centers for Disease Control and Prevention has aggressively responded to the world health crisis to protect individuals from the virus. Official guidelines not only included recommendations such as social distancing and use of personal protective equipment, but also included several mandated business closures, which severely impacted small businesses. This study sought to understand factors that may attract consumers to small businesses during the ongoing COVID-19 to assist with business continuity. Specifically, this study explored whether consumer support for small business (shopping frequency and number of services used) during a pandemic can be explained by consumers' emotional and cognitive experiences and whether there are any differences in consumer support for small business during a pandemic, depending on their demographic characteristics such as gender, generation, education and/or employment status. Using a national survey sample (n = 313), this study found that consumers' support for small business during a pandemic can be explained by emotional and cognitive (resilience and optimism) experiences and demographic characteristics. Specifically, active resilience and negative and positive emotions influences small business shopping frequency and active resilience influences the number of services used at small businesses. Differences were found by generation, education and employment status on shopping frequency and services used. Differences were also found by annual income on shopping frequency. No differences were found by gender on shopping frequency or services used. Theoretically, this study contributes to research on disaster response by incorporating findings from the unprecedented global pandemic. Based on findings, small businesses may seek to trigger active resilience and emotions (negative and positive) in their advertising avenues to attract consumers. Small

M. Childs (✉) · S. Ha · C. Sneed · A. Berry · A. Fairhurst
The University of Tennessee, Knoxville, TN, USA
e-mail: mlchilds@utk.edu; sha5@utk.edu; csneed@utk.edu; aaberry@utk.edu; fairhurs@utk.edu

J. Allen et al. (eds.), *Celebrating the Past and Future of Marketing and Discovery with Social Impact*, Developments in Marketing Science: Proceedings of the Academy of Marketing Science, https://doi.org/10.1007/978-3-030-95346-1_66

businesses may consider pivoting to attract particular consumer segments that are more likely to patronize frequently and use services offered by small business.

Keywords COVID-19 · Small business · Emotional experiences · Cognitive experiences · Demographics

Applying Phrase-Level Text Analysis to Measure Brand-Related Information Disclosure: An Abstract

Qiong Tang, Sascha Raithel, Alexander Mafael, and Ashish S. Galande

Abstract Financial reporting and disclosure are important means for management to communicate firm performance and governance to external stakeholders. Existing research provides limited insight into firms' disclosure of information about their market-based assets such as brands, although brand is an important part of firms' value proposition. Our research intends to address this research gap through (1) a theory-based conceptualization of brand-related information (BRI) and (2) an empirical analysis of BRI disclosure in corporate reports, more specifically, in US firms' annual reports on Form 10-K.

We incorporate automated text analysis to identify and measure BRI disclosure in 10-K reports. Automated text analysis allows us to process massive amounts of text efficiently and reliably. Extant studies using automated text analysis are primarily rely on word-level analysis, yet most concepts entail multiword terms or phrases to convey meaning. We address this limitation of existing methods by applying phrase-level analysis to BRI disclosure. First, we draw on the literature on customer-based brand equity and intellectual capital disclosure to develop the conceptualization of BRI. Building on this conceptualization, we explore the capacity of natural language processing to build a phrase-level BRI coding dictionary. Second, we use automated text analysis to construct a BRI disclosure index that captures the BRI disclosure level in firms' 10-K reports. Unlike prior studies that focus on word-level analysis for construct measurement, our method utilizes proximity search to match phrases in the BRI coding dictionary with texts and incorporate a proximity-weighing mechanism to conduct a phrase-level analysis of BRI disclosures.

Q. Tang (✉) · S. Raithel
Freie Universität Berlin, Berlin, Germany
e-mail: qiong.tang@fu-berlin.de; Sascha.Raithel@fu-berlin.de

A. Mafael
Stockholm School of Economics, Stockholm, Sweden
e-mail: alexander.mafael@hhs.se

A. S. Galande
Indian Institute of Management Udaipur, Udaipur, India
e-mail: ashish.galande@iimu.ac.in

J. Allen et al. (eds.), *Celebrating the Past and Future of Marketing and Discovery with Social Impact*, Developments in Marketing Science: Proceedings of the Academy of Marketing Science, https://doi.org/10.1007/978-3-030-95346-1_67

The contribution of this study is twofold. First, this study fills the research gap in the field of information disclosure concerning BRI by conceptualizing a BRI framework and providing evidence on whether and how firms disclose BRI in financial reporting. Second, our method broadens the possibility of utilizing automated text analysis in constructing research-specific coding dictionaries as well as conducting phrase-level text analysis. While current research has made some efforts to provide a structured process for phrase-level text analysis, there is limited guidance regarding the operationalization of phrase match with proximity search.

Keywords Brand-related information · Information disclosure · Automated text analysis · Phrase-level analysis · Natural language processing

Effects of Government-to-Contractor Revolving Door Appointments on Customer Relationship Performance: An Abstract

Shuai Yan and Ju-Yeon Lee

Abstract Marketing scholars have increased their focus on examining the role of political connections (e.g., a donation to political parties) in enhancing performance. However, most studies have overlooked a unique approach in which business-to-government (B2G) firms proactively forge their relationship with the government—*government-to-contractor revolving door appointments* (*revolving door appointments* hereafter). Revolving door appointments refer to a firm's hiring of former public employees from government agencies as corporate executives and directors. Though revolving door appointment is a prevalent approach to build relational ties with government customers, the implication of revolving door appointments in managing customer relationship remains highly underdeveloped.

Prior studies predominantly examine a firm's financial performance (e.g., abnormal stock returns) as outcome variables, neglecting the role of relational value that revolving door appointments bring in a buyer-seller relationship. We thus evaluate its effect on *customer relationship performance*, which refers to the firm's success in building (*customer acquisition performance*) and enhancing customer relationships (*cross-selling performance*). Therefore, we propose our research question: *what is the effect of revolving door appointments on customer relationship performance?*

Analyzing multisource secondary panel data of 102 publicly-traded U.S. firms in the B2G market over 14 years (2004–2017), we demonstrate that revolving door appointment has a positive effect on customer relationship performance. It implies that a firm can leverage revolving door executive's and director's ties with customers (i.e., government agencies) and gain first-hand information about potential customers and identify the new needs of customers. We also identified two crucial contingent factors critical to the leverage of knowledge from revolving door appointments: *market knowledge* (a firm's experiences and knowledge in serving govern-

S. Yan · J.-Y. Lee (✉)
Iowa State University, Ames, IA, USA
e-mail: shuaiyan@iastate.edu; leejy@iastate.edu

J. Allen et al. (eds.), *Celebrating the Past and Future of Marketing and Discovery with Social Impact*, Developments in Marketing Science: Proceedings of the Academy of Marketing Science, https://doi.org/10.1007/978-3-030-95346-1_68

ment customers) and *product scope* (the narrowness of the firm's product knowledge). Market knowledge strengthens the effects of revolving door appointments on customer relationship performance because market knowledge enables the firm to better leverage the connections with and knowledge of customers from revolving door appointments. Product scope weakens the positive effects of revolving door appointments because revolving door executives and directors have limited opportunities to apply their connections and knowledge when providing offerings. These results offer unique contributions to marketing theories and policymakers.

Keywords Government-to-contractor revolving door appointments · Customer acquisition performance · Cross-selling performance · Business-to-government · Panel data

Consumer Response to Irresponsible Firm Behavior: A Cross-National Study in the United States, Mexico and Thailand: An Abstract

Suwakitti Amornpan and Edith Galy

Abstract This study examines consumer response to firm's irresponsible behavior that is damaging to the environment and infringes upon sustainable development goals. We measure consumer reactions to information provided in six scenarios from respondents in the US, Mexico, and Thailand. The spectrum of emotional reactions that is measured ranges from expressing anger to becoming active in demanding sustainable practices wanting to make the company pay for the irresponsible behavior. We examine the various circumstances that damage the consumer-supplier relationship and the factors that impact this relationship, such as physical proximity to the consumer and the severity of the violation. According to construal theory, a person perceives distance of objects or events in both psychological and physical terms (Trope and Liberman 2010). Drawing from this theory, individuals engage their emotions toward the physical proximity of the violation differently (Strizhakova and Coulter 2019). When individuals perceive the negative effect of such incident from close distance (i.e. local area), they tend to perceive negative consequences more concretely than compared to the distant occurrence. In addition, according to the attribution process framework proposed by Hartmann and Moeller (2014), the severity of incident plays a role in the blame and responsibility of incidents for more severe incidents compared to incidents of low severity (Tennen and Affleck 1990). When people perceive the effects of incidents as severe, they are likely to react to those incidents emotionally with anger. The experimental research design includes six conditions forming a 2 X 2 (Distance of effect: Close vs Distant) X 2 (Severity: High vs Low) possible combinations that test fluctuation in consumer response.

S. Amornpan
University of Texas Rio Grande Valley, Edinburg, TX, USA
e-mail: suwakitti.amornpan01@utrgv.edu

E. Galy (✉)
University of Texas Rio Grande Valley, Brownsville, TX, USA
e-mail: edith.galy@utrgv.edu

J. Allen et al. (eds.), *Celebrating the Past and Future of Marketing and Discovery with Social Impact*, Developments in Marketing Science: Proceedings of the Academy of Marketing Science, https://doi.org/10.1007/978-3-030-95346-1_69

Keywords Corporate social irresponsibility · Sustainability · Greenwashing · Consumer-supplier relationship · Attribution · Anger

The Implications of Short-Term and Long-Term B2B Touchpoints: An Abstract

Jesús Cambra-Fierro, Yolanda Polo-Redondo, and Andreea Trifu

Abstract Marketing literature on customer-firm interactions acknowledges the role of touchpoints on customer-firm relationships, as successful encounters through touchpoints lead to stronger relationships. However, there is little empirical evidence on the long-term impact of touchpoints on important measures of customer perceptions. In this context, the purpose of this study is to compare the short- and long-term impacts of different provider-controlled touchpoints on customer perceptions. Specifically, this study assesses the impact of touchpoints related to sales force, product, consulting, communication, tangibles and standardized contacts.

To test the proposed model, data from a multinational insurance company are used to obtain a random panel dataset of 2175 customers over 5 years. A six-equation seemingly unrelated regression model is developed to assess the effectiveness of provider-controlled touchpoints. The results reveal that some touchpoints have important consequences both in the short and long term. Touchpoints related to sales force and product are vital in maintaining long-term positive customer perceptions. Other touchpoints have significant short-term effects, but no long-term consequences on customer perceptions. The results also indicate that an overuse of some touchpoints may potentially damage the customer-firm relationship in the long term.

The findings of this pioneering research provide empirical evidence of how the impact of some touchpoints on customer perceptions changes over time. The impor-

---

The authors appreciate the financial support received from the projects ECO2017-83993-P (MICINN, FEDER), SS54_17R (Gobierno de Aragón and Fondo Social Europeo), and the grant "Ayuda para contratos predoctorales para la formación de doctores, del Ministerio de Ciencia, Innovación y Universidades" (PRE2018-085652) assigned to Andreea Trifu.

J. Cambra-Fierro
University Pablo de Olavide, Seville, Spain
e-mail: jjcamfie@upo.es

Y. Polo-Redondo · A. Trifu (✉)
University of Zaragoza, Zaragoza, Spain
e-mail: ypolo@unizar.es; atrifu@unizar.es

J. Allen et al. (eds.), *Celebrating the Past and Future of Marketing and Discovery with Social Impact*, Developments in Marketing Science: Proceedings of the Academy of Marketing Science, https://doi.org/10.1007/978-3-030-95346-1_70

tance of identifying short- and long-term implications of touchpoints on customer perceptions is confirmed. As a result, the implications of this study are relevant for academia and best practices alike. By differentiating between these types of effects on customer perceptions, this research adds breadth and depth to the limited academic knowledge about long-term effectiveness of touchpoints. As regards managerial implications, this study is relevant in terms of resource allocation, as it specifically analyzes changes occurring over time and identifies the interactions that will have the most important long-term effect on the customer-firm relationship.

Keywords Touchpoints · Standardized contacts · Sales force · Short-term · Long-term · Customer perceptions

Consumers' Attitudes and Privacy Concerns on Value Co-Creation: A Cross Cultural Study on Big Data Perspective: An Abstract

Melisa Mete, Gozde Erdogan, and Ruya Yuksel

Abstract This study adopts the Communication Privacy Management Theory (CPM), and the Social Exchange Theory (SET) to investigate consumers' trust, commitment, and satisfaction behaviours on companies' value co-creation, and aims to find out how the privacy concerns of consumers affect consumer behaviour on the way of creating value for the organisation.

Prior studies show the negative relationship between trust and privacy concerns (Cases et al. 2010), and privacy concerns and value co-creation (Tajvidi et al. 2018; Wang and Hajli 2014) consumer commitment and satisfaction (Inman and Nikolova 2017; Wang et al. 2019). Hence, we propose that high level of trust in usage of online social sites have a significant negative effect on privacy concerns (H1), high level of privacy concerns have a significant negative effect on creation of value for the organization (H2), and high level of privacy concerns in usage of online social sites have a significant negative effect on consumers' commitment (H3), and satisfaction (H4). Trust can also lead consumers' value co-creation behaviors. According to Dabhholkar and Sheng (2012), the consumers' trust level is related to their participation in online communities. If consumers' trust increases, they will be more eager to provide to the community by sharing knowledge, participating in debates, and creating relationships with others which drives value co-creation by producing data and interaction (Pappas 2016; Toufaily et al. 2013). Hence, we propose that high level of commitment in usage of online social sites, leads to create value for the

M. Mete (✉)
University of Reading, Reading, UK
e-mail: m.mete@henley.ac.uk

G. Erdogan
Universidad de Deusto, San Sebastian, Spain
e-mail: gozdeerdogan@deusto.es

R. Yuksel
The City University of New York, New York, NY, USA
e-mail: zyuksel@gradcenter.cuny.edu

J. Allen et al. (eds.), *Celebrating the Past and Future of Marketing and Discovery with Social Impact*, Developments in Marketing Science: Proceedings of the Academy of Marketing Science, https://doi.org/10.1007/978-3-030-95346-1_71

organization (H5), high level of satisfaction in usage of online social sites, leads to create value for the organization (H6), and high level of trust in usage of online social sites, leads to create value for the organization (H7).

An online survey is distributed to collect the data in two countries (UK and Turkey). The preliminary data is analysed, and the analyses show that the relationship between trust and privacy concerns, and privacy concerns and value co-creation, commitment, and satisfaction are not significant (H1, H2, H3, H4 are rejected). Satisfaction and value co-creation relationship is found to be significant for Turkey, but not significant for the UK (H6), and commitment and value co-creation and trust and value co-creation relationships are both significant (H5 and H7). The multi-group analysis with the overall model does not show any statistically significant differences between the two countries.

As the global competition between organisations are increasing in these days, a better understanding of how big data becomes valuable organisational asset is necessary for developing and obtaining a long-term success for cross-cultural perspective, and this study contributes to literature by investigating the privacy concerns of consumers from value co-creation perspective.

Keywords Privacy concerns · Value co-creation · Trust · Commitment · Satisfaction

Employee or Contractor? On the Employment Status of Drivers and Compensation Design by Ridesharing Platforms: An Abstract

Xiaoyi Sylvia Gao and Sreya Kolay

Abstract Ridesharing platforms like Uber and Lyft have recently comc under public scrutiny regarding the "independent contractor" vs "employee" status of their drivers in the State of California and the Biden-Harris administration. Proponents of employee status argue that it establishes a safety net for the drivers like the protection from federal minimum-wage and overtime laws. Opponents argue that it removes working flexibility in participation valued by many drivers and adds labor costs to the sharing economy.

To address whether or under what circumstances, the platform, the drivers and consumers are better off under the "employee" or under the "independent contractor" status, we derive the optimal compensation design and pricing strategy under each of these two statuses. We show how the profitability and welfare comparisons for the platform, drivers and consumers across the two statuses depend on key market characteristics, such as difference in demand between rush hour and non-rush hour periods, number of total drivers and the degree of heterogeneity in the outside options of drivers.

Our paper provides support for the concerns in the public arena by highlighting potential regions of conflict where the platform's preferred choice of the contractor status can leave drivers worse off. At the same time, we show that there are also scenarios where the drivers and the platform are aligned in their preference for the contractor status, and any regulatory intervention forcing a switch to an employee status may leave drivers worse off. It happens when the degree of heterogeneity in the outside options of drivers is relatively high and surge demand in rush hour period is relatively low. In addition, we highlight areas where such intervention can

X. S. Gao (✉)
University of Auckland, Auckland, New Zealand
e-mail: sylvia.gao@auckland.ac.nz

S. Kolay
University at Albany, Albany, NY, USA
e-mail: skolay@albany.edu

J. Allen et al. (eds.), *Celebrating the Past and Future of Marketing and Discovery with Social Impact*, Developments in Marketing Science: Proceedings of the Academy of Marketing Science, https://doi.org/10.1007/978-3-030-95346-1_72

improve drivers' welfare but hurt consumers in the process, as well as areas where the intervention can benefit both drivers and consumers. Our results have significant managerial implications to ridesharing platforms and other gig economy like food-delivery companies and grocery-delivery companies.

Keywords Theoretical modeling · Platforms · Compensation schemes · Employee · Independent contractor

Examination of Online Bicycle Touring Communities

Michael Basil

Abstract The internet has allowed the development on online communities, or "e-tribes" that are dedicated to narrow interest groups. This research used a qualitative netnographic examination of people's participation in four online Facebook groups dedicated to bicycle touring. These groups appear to be online "leisure communities". The results demonstrate that these groups provide a considerable amount of information and support to these niche communities. In this case a small but devoted following of bikers made use of these Facebook groups as their online community. Participants requested and shared information and opinions on equipment, planning, routes, and experiences on the road. Posters varied in their use of the online community, from frequently active to one-time users. Almost all requesters seem to benefit from basic information on equipment and routes. The groups are generally supportive where more experienced bikers mentor and encourage potential bikers. We did not investigate how long people remained a member of the groups, or what percentage moved from novices to more experienced riders, or what could lead to a lasting commitment to a group. Finally, although this analysis used several groups, our results may not generalize to other e-tribes or social networks in general.

Keywords Online communities · Leisure · Bicycling · Netnography · Facebook

Introduction

The nature of the internet allows connectivity with people anywhere in the world (Palloff and Pratt 1999). Early in growth of the internet, some theorists predicted that virtual communities would develop where participants could share information

---

M. Basil (✉)
University of Lethbridge, Lethbridge, AB, Canada
e-mail: michael.basil@uleth.ca

J. Allen et al. (eds.), *Celebrating the Past and Future of Marketing and Discovery with Social Impact*, Developments in Marketing Science: Proceedings of the Academy of Marketing Science, https://doi.org/10.1007/978-3-030-95346-1_73

on a variety of topics. The evolution of the internet into "Web 2.0", appears to have fulfilled many of these predictions (Kozinets 1999). Specifically, online communities do appear to serve as a resource for participants to communicate and share information regardless of where they are in the world (Etzoni and Etzoni 1997; Grabher and Ibert 2013).

Some evidence suggest there are many online communities or "e-tribes" that are dedicated to specialized or narrow interest groups (Kozinets 1999). These interest groups are relevant to a narrow segment of the population. Some have noted that subcultures are emerging through the internet (Williams 2006). Recent work proposes that people often become aware and even attached to various online groups (Ren et al. 2007). As a result, a "common bond" theory has been proposed (Ren et al. 2007). Previous research, however, has placed more focus on the structure of the online environment than on the nature of the communities themselves.

When do these communities develop? Social psychology research dating back to the 1960s demonstrates that providing a common goal can build community and reduce conflict. Perhaps the most famous study in this area is Sherif et al.'s "Robbers Cave" study (Sherif et al. 1961). Building upon these findings, we expect that groups organized around a superordinate goal will be more likely to assist others in that community (Amichai-Hamburger and McKenna 2006). Here we propose that online communities which are focused around a superordinate goal in which members are interested in a similar hobby are likely to generate this form of support (Butler et al. 2008).

Directionally, the narrower and more specialized the topic, the fewer people would know others with similar interests, and therefore the greater the potential and benefit for online communities (Butler 2001; Wellman et al. 2002). As a result, face-to-face interaction among these people are generally not viable. Because there are "many interest groups, organizations, and associations are available on the Internet that it is exceptionally easy to find the niche web site or specific discussion group that reflects one's particular beliefs and interests" (Norris 2002, pg. 5). In support of this assertion, Anderson and Taylor (2010) examined online "leisure communities" from two seemingly diverse groups – skydivers and gun collectors (Anderson and Taylor 2010). Their study examined ways in which members of these two communities identified themselves, their activities, and their organizations within the broader society. Their findings supported the notion that leisure activities can provide an important source of one's social identity in modern society.

There are a variety of hobbies that are made up of a small but devoted following. One of these is bike touring – long distance bicycling. Bicycle touring has a long history (Dickinson and Lumsdon 2010; Emanuel 2017). The types of tours varies from people who might go out on a one or two-night trip to those who bicycle across a country or even a whole continent. Some evidence suggests that bicycle touring is growing in popularity, and may even be seen as an important contributor to the economy of a region (Ritchie 1998). That said, bicycle touring constitutes a small segment of the population. Further, this hobby is typically done in relative isolation and perhaps even obscurity. Given that, how do people interested in bicycle touring get information on the hobby and share their experiences? Some previous research has proposed that this form of leisure tourism could be understood as a process according to the Theory of Planned Behaviour (Han et al. 2017). In this case online forums would seem especially useful.

This case study examines one form of information seeking from online communities dedicated to bicycle touring. Given goals common to the whole group, what do people how and what to people share with other members?

Methods

This research used a qualitative netnographic examination of people's participation in online groups dedicated to the bicycle touring. A preliminary analysis revealed several Facebook groups – Bicycle Touring & Bikepacking, Bikepacking, Expedition Bike Touring, and Biking Across Canada.. The groups varied in size from fairly large with Bicycle Touring & Bikepacking (52,000 members), Bikepacking (41,212), to smaller groups including Expedition Bike Touring (4300 members) and Biking Across Canada (1700 members).

Here are the group descriptions…

1. Bicycle Touring & Bikepacking. "We don't have many rules, but the few which we do have we take very seriously. They are in place to ensure that our group is an enjoyable environment to spend time in, attracts high-quality, varied content and maintains an atmosphere of politeness and respect. 01. Shared posts must include a synopsis or reason above the post. We're trying to encourage interaction and engagement while eliminating link dumping, empty sharing, and 'like' harvesting. Include a reason, description, question and/or synopsis with each post. 02 All posts, comments and replies to be in English please. Although there is a translator, we get more member engagement when all interactions are in one language. We've chosen English as this common language for the group. 03 Be Kind and Courteous and No Profanity We're all in this together to create a welcoming environment. Let's treat everyone with respect. Healthy debates are natural, but kindness is required…
2. What's bikepacking? The short answer: it's backpacking with a bike. Longer answer: any ride that includes an overnight stay. This could be anything from ultralight singletrack tours to fully loaded dirt road touring (e.g. on the Great Divide Mountain Bike Route). This group focuses on off-road touring, away from cars. But the concepts and gear transfer equally well to all types of rides that stretch overnight. Our aim is to distill the collective knowledge about routes, gear and planning. We have a strong community of bikepackers, and are excited to promote this new and very exciting way to travel.
3. Welcome to Expedition Bike Touring Life (NoMad Forum). This is Part of the Expedition Bicycle Touring Group https://www.facebook.com/groups/Biketouringhobos/ ……" A Rolling Stone Gathers no Moss"……(A Person who does not Settle in one Place will not Accumulate Wealth, Status, Responibilites,

or Commitments). Dedicated to those People who tread off the beaten path. Adventures who enjoy the outdoors, and take every Advantage of Experiencing the World around them: So all is Welcome on the Group on Facebook:

Expedition Bicycle Touring and Bicycle Touring and On/Off Road Bicycle Touring, Stealth Camping and Cyclo-Cross Talk, Stealth Bike Camping and Information on Bicycle Touring Gear and Stealth Camping Gear, Camping Gear and Bicycle Parts Talk for Bicycle Touring is Welcome here……..

4. A group for everyone with thoughts of biking across Canada on their mind – whether they are planning the trip, have completed, it, or just enjoy vicariously doing so while reading the stories of others.

These groups were joined, followed, and postings subjected to analysis. The groups varied in activity ranging from a 40 or 50 posts a day among the larger groups to dozen posts a day for the smaller groups. These online posting provide a foundation in understanding contemporary virtual communities.

Kozinets (1999) explains the value of netnography and (2006) argues that relevant experience with consumer "tribes" improves the depth of understanding of qualitative research. To this end I am uniquely qualified to understand this experience because I have bicycled for many years and complete three cross-country trips – Canada (1980), the United States (1983), and Scotland (2019). With this perspective I reviewed the tens of thousands of postings on these Facebook groups between over the course of more than 2 years – from February 2018 through November 2020. Over this period the netnography analysis involved thousands of posts and at least 20,000 responses.

Results

Postings by New Members and Novices

These Facebook groups are generally not important in helping people first learn about bicycle touring. With hindsight, this should not be surprising. After learning about bike touring, however, is when people turns to online communities. Once people became aware of the possibility, likely when none of their friends were bike tourists, they then turned to these Facebook groups, likely through a search. Evidence of when people made their discovery can be seen by the posting of questions that would be ascribed to "newbies". Several people posted that they were "thinking about touring" in a future year.

Some people announced their addition to a group with comments such as "Thanks for the add. Looking forward to seeing everyone's adventures" (Bikepacking, Sept 14, 2020). A number of postings expressed the poster's happiness at meeting like-minded individuals. For example, "Just a quick post to say: This must be the best bike group on Facebook. In a short few weeks, I've found all the information, ideas, suggestions and opinions I could want. All of you have definitely made my experience in coming back to biking far better than it would be if I hadn't found this group. Thanks and Cheers!" (Bikepacking, Oct 26, 2020). Some asked direct questions such as, "Hey guys, I am new here and I am an absolute beginner when it comes to bikepacking. I do about 25 kms a day around the lake where I live, but that is all. I have been considering the option of bikepacking for a while, but I just I really know where/how to start. I have a few basic ideas, but I thought I'd make it easier on me trying to ask for help here. I'd like to do this with a mate next year in the summer (hopefully the covid madness will be at an acceptable level by then), (Bikepacking, Oct 4, 2020). This generated 16 comments, including welcomes, simple advice, and links to bicycle touring sites on the internet.

Several postings illustrated the importance of the value of the size of the virtual community for this narrow interest. For example, "I've never struggled meeting friends, but can't figure out a way to meet others in the St. Louis area who are also into bikepacking. Any tips? I've been a roadie for a long time, but over the last year started gearing up to do more bikepacking. It sure would be more fun to go on these adventures with others (Bikepacking Nov 1, 2020). This posting generated 55 responses in the next week including a wide variety of responses including suggestions to meet other locals ("Join some STL Facebook groups and ask. I'm sure someone will speak up", "Meetup?", "Talk to the folks in your Local Bike Shop"), commiserating ("In Maryland with same issue", "I have the same problem in Kansas city. It's hard to find folks who know what they are getting into when you do a 300 mile trip. It's not for everyone"), and several folks who were close enough to make a connection).

There is also evidence of people who are seeking support from like-minded others, such as this posting, "Am I the only one who has chosen to just live like this?" (Bicycle Touring & Backpacking, Sep 29, 2020); clearly the posting generated support from others who had chosen the same lifestyle or were at least supportive, with not only 41 likes, but 98 comments including "Hubby and I, 6 months on the road so far (unplanned). Just sold our house so we may never go back 😁", "Been living on and off the bike for the past 4 years or so. Canadian winters make it hard to do full time but let's me live my other passion, skiing!", and "Been a homeless nomad for years! Just recently added a bicycle to the mix. It's better than working 9 to 5 just to sit on the couch and watch tv after!"

Speaking to the international nature of the internet, one posting proclaimed "My first long distance cycling was 275 km From Mombasa to Lunga Lunga and back to Mombasa" (Long Distance Cyclists, Nov 10, 2020). Similarly, one post asking for advice finished with, "I am based in Europe." (Bikepacking, Oct 4, 2020).

There were a good number of postings providing advice or support for solo women travelers. One, for example, posted a link to an inspiring article entitled "50+ Solo Women Cyclists Who Have Epic Bicycle Touring Experience" (Bicycle Touring & Backpacking, Oct 8, 2020).

Another important question that appears frequently is about gear and training. Equipment questions ranged from bikes themselves to panniers, sleeping bags, and stoves. Rookie riders would often ask advice on which products were best, whether a particular product was good, whether the price of a used article was fair and other similar questions. For example a new member's first post was, "I'd love to get into bike packing but as I look around at my bikes I wonder if I have one that will work. I have a road bike, rigid full carbon trail bike, full suspension specialized MTB and then I have this beauty- old stump jumper. Would any of these work? I can't wrap my mind around buying another bike....or maybe I just need to sell a few? (Bikepacking ,Nov 15, 2020). This posting generated 65 comments, mostly suggestions on which bike the poster could ride, or whether they needed a new bike at all, with several asking about what types of routes the poster was hoping to ride. Other bicyclists posted photos on their new gear such as "Check out my new ride" (Bikepacking, Sept 11, 2020). Some people posted slightly less direct but more provocative comments such as "Fatbikes Fad or here to stay?" (Bikepacking, Aug 23, 2020) which also resulted in more than 100 replies ranging from being a fan to not. With regard to specific equipment there were posts such as, "Does anyone in the group have experience with these Tubolito tubes? Pretty expensive, but I stacked some REI discounts and got them for a decent price. Will definitely bring them on my cross-country trip next year. Just wondering about any experience with using them as primary inner tubes or just spares?" (Bikepacking, Nov 13, 2020).

There were a number of posts from people who were communicating appreciation for the group by reporting success on their first bike tour – often this was a short trip. Clearly there is a social aspect to the groups as communicated by the post "Hello! Just wanted to introduce myself to the community, this is my current set up and yes am already working on a new off road bike to travel longer distance! Just came back after little 1 sleep over trip ☺ Any tips are welcome 😀 Thanks ☺" (Bikepacking, Sept 10, 2020). "First test ride with my full camping kit. Really pleased with the setup and how the bike handled. Thought it would be a lot worse than it was." (Bikepacking, Sep 20, 2020) which resulted in 29 supportive comments and 155 likes. Similarly, "First bikepacking overnighter was a roaring success. We rode from Carpinteria, CA to Refugio State Beach. The hike/bike spaces at Refugio are less than 100 yards from the water – having the sound of the ocean lull us to sleep was lovely. So was listening to the bagpiper on the bluffs at sunset." (Bikepacking, Oct 12, 2020). Similarly, "Hi everyone!5 days ago I finished my first long distance bike tour. From Belgium to South France. What an incredible experience! Thanks for all the tips and inspiration!" (Bikepacking, Sep 16, 2020) and also posted links to route details and an Instagram account. This generated a few dozen congratulations and 473 likes.

Postings About Planning

Another very important part of the discussion on groups is trip planning. Because road conditions and weather are critical factors in bike touring, many of the postings are dedicated to questions on places to tour and what time of year is best. For example, "What do you think the safest/least expensive country is to bike pack in?" (Bikepacking, July 8, 2020) which garnered more than 100 replies.

One participant posted a link to a news article, "Turkey opens world's longest uninterrupted bike path" (Bicycle Touring & Bikepacking, Aug 19, 2020) – https://www.trtworld.com/life/turkey-opens-world-s-longest-uninterrupted-bike-path-38786 which resulted in almost 100 replies, some pointing out other routes that were longer and then a discussion of how this claim had some level of validity.

Other posters asked more general questions about routes or tours in general. For example one poster said, "Hi! A Swedish girl here thinking about cycling back home to Sweden from Croatia in about 3 weeks. Been here working as a sports instructor at a hotel in Makarska. It will probably be 2500 km and 18,000 meters elevation gain. Throw Slovenia, Austria, Germany and Denmark then up throw sweden a bit 🙃 Any tips for this adventure? How do you think it will go crossing borders? Anyone how have cycling experience from this country's? Thankful for any answers 🙏 (Bicycle Touring & Bikepacking, Sep 9, 2020). Another poster asked, "How many of you have biked in Poland, how was your experience?" (Bikepacking Nov 11, 2020).

The year 2020 generated a great deal of discussion about the safety and morality of engaging in a bike tour in the face of Covid-19. "Hi, I am leaving tomorrow for my first long distance cycling trip. From Belgium to South France. I am planning to stay on campgrounds and maybe have a room once in a while. I was thinking about where to stay and am in doubt to use warmshowers because of covid and because I did not yet used it before. People used it already during Covid? Do you think people are more cautious right now? (of course they are) but would it be worth it to use it right now? And in general is warmshowers a good way to find places to sleep? Of course I am aware that covid is a serious thing and I am pretty cautious myself during travelling through the country (Bikepacking, Aug. 24, 2020). This generated 21 comments, some along expected lines such as, "I've travelled for almost 3 months this summer and stayed always in campsites and hotels when the weather was really bad. No issue in campsites. I was in Austria, Italy, Germany and Norway", "You have as much of a chance getting COVID at a campground as you do at a hotel or any other place. I just completed a two week bike pack trip that used a combination of camp grounds and hotels/motels and my wife and I are just fine. Wear a mask when necessary, wash your hands, and live your life my friend. I wrestled with this same issue before my trip. We go to stores, gas stations, and other places to get supplies along the way that have far more people handling and using the facilities, and somehow this is ok, but a hotel or hostel is somehow more dangerous? Makes no sense in my opinion." To which the original poster replied' "thanks! Of course I will be wearing a mask a lot and wash my hand! 😁 Another poster offered information on insurance. If you have a plan in the works for a bike packing adventure overseas in 2021, this might be worth a read. We did some research on travel insurance and there are some options that cover covid-19." (Bikepacking, Oct 29, 2020). Other posters shared their personal experiences, for example, "Last September I did the first few hundred miles of TAT. I stopped on the N Carolina/Tennessee border. Riding during covid is ok. I was stressed at first because of covid but after few days I got used to all the rules I need to follow. Overall a good ride. Hopefully I will start in April again and finish it" (Bicycle Touring & Backpacking, Oct 29, 2020).

Another important aspect of planning is budgeting, and there were several posts about budgets. For example, “I once came across a detailed budget breakdown of someone’s cross Canada ride but can’t seem to find it now. Does anyone have theirs available? For reference, I’m planning June 1st to mid-September next year for my niece and I, Victoria to St. John’s. I’m just trying to get some info together for my employer as my potential sponsor. Any help would be greatly appreciated!” (Biking Across Canada, Sep 14, 2020). This generated 8 comments, including a link, likely to the one the paster asked about, but also 5 other rough budget estimates.

Postings by Experienced Riders

Of course there were a good number of posting from experienced riders. In some cases participants were encouraged to learn about a group. For example, in the “Bikepacking” group, “I’ve been bike touring since 1986, so far in California, Oregon, Washington, Idaho, Alaska, Colorado, New Mexico, Utah, Canada, Spain, Ireland, and Italy, and I’m finally switching from panniers to a seat pack. I don’t know what size to get, and I’m wondering what ya’ll use, and recommend. Thanks! P.s. I was thinking about deleting Facebook until I came across this page, and now the photos and discussions here make my day. Every day. Thanks for that…” (Bikepacking, Nov 9, 2020). This generated 16 responses and 22 likes.

Some posters shared their success on an adventure with the group. For example, “On my very first bicycle touring adventure lasting just over 16-months, I had a lot to learn. I aimed to experience as much as I could, in any way I wanted. But most of all, I wanted to have a great time. I covered so much on what I consider a life-adjusting adventure. But now, as I’m just a couple of years from 60, and in just a few weeks a grandad, I’m thinking of much shorter journeys to soak in the cultures, people, and scenery. I want to travel super light with some simple but essential camping gear, and maybe even a new bike. I’m thinking the length of the island of Great Britain. I live in Liverpool England and, like a lot of us, I still haven’t seen all that much of my own country.” (Long Distance Cyclists, Aug 13, 2020). Similarly, another poster offered, “Dear friends! I asked some months ago for suggestions on where to cycle in Hungary. A couple of you suggested Nagykanizsa and surrounds... well I’ve finally got there (via Balaton) and it was wonderful. Thank you! Over four days I rode: Veszprém - Tihany - Badacsony - Hevíz - all around Zala county – Nagykanizsa (Bicycle Touring & Bikepacking, September 20, 2020).”

Some posters shared what they enjoyed about bicycle touring. For example, “We all know bike touring brings adventure, thrill, and the perfect gateway into getting a true feel for the land and its people. But what are some little unique or oft-overlooked things in bike touring that bring you joy? One of mine is packing up my bike. For some reason, I love waking up every morning and methodically taking down my tent and readying my steed for the day. The air is crisp, the day is full of possibilities and everything you own gets packed neatly into its place. It is almost meditative. What are yours?” This generated 162 likes and 87 comments. Some comments were about the simple pleasures of being outdoors such as "I love the smells of the countryside. Fresh grass, first rain on the soil, wild flowers 😄"," Being woken up by owls" "Everything tastes so much better after a few hours cycling, you've got a real appetite and you're usually eating in the fresh air. I recently slept in an alpine meadow. One of life's little pleasures. It smelt incredible." Several comments were about the people they had met. "After recently completing my first bike tour... I really enjoyed my packed bike being an open invite for people to chat to me. It was great feeling like people were interested in what I was doing and where I was going." "Love the off road little town cafes for breakfast. Love the small town folks and their stories. And they love to hear the adventure of our cycling trip. These people are real!" Some posters reflected on the simplicity. "I think for me it the overarching feeling of adventure and the freedom that comes from carrying everything you need with you. Living with less to remind myself that I don't need much, yet being more appreciative when the "more" comes my way", "I like the self-sufficiency. Carrying the home on your back like a snail (today: also with the speed of a snail uphill 😉). Shower or swim at the end of the day and hopefully not being cold." Finally, other posters expressed a sense of accomplishment. "Seeing places I would have never been able to go through on bike. Looking at the map and seeing how far I've traveled… Feeling of accomplishment, solitude and peacefulness", "Cycling over an international border is more fun than it should be."

Other posters offered that their bicycle tours had changed their life or self-identity. "How has bike touring changed your life, or the way you look at life/the everyday life most people have, just living at one single place all the time, just seeing the same things all the time? My first bike tour changed me completely and I have never been able to look at the everyday life the same way again. I can't stand that type of lifestyle anymore and all I want is just jump up in the saddle, cycle away and not look back, but the departure date for my next bike tour is so far away." (Long Distance Cyclists, Aug 10, 2020) which resulted in 34 likes and 28 comments which also supported the notion of self-identity including "Touring, especially solo is a discovery of one's self", "When everything is new every day, I feel better, I think better, and I write better," and "My trek across America made me simplify. Keep life simple." There was a much longer self-disclosure that said, "helped me overcome the some bad childhood stories. It made me reclame my own body, made me feel strong and achy and powerful. It made me realize I am able to make good decision and able to survive, even thrive, when alone and in a unprecedented situation. Also made me proud of my muscles, made me accept the changes in my body with more ease: gain weight, loose weight, gain muscle, loose muscle...? It's just a phase my body is in depending on what I do with it...which is something I struggled with a lot before long biking trips (as a lot of women I think). It's great to get out of this mindset that women have to be frail little thing, shouldn't have muscles because it's judged as disgraceful and « too masculine ». You get the idea. Weirdly enough, it grounds me as well. Now, instead of hopping from one city to another every three months, I need to go on a long bike trip every three years: it resets me. I love the whole cycle of it: a time to resettle at home, a time to implement everything I've learnt in my daily normal life, then comes the glimpse of balance when everything seems at its best...but unsurprisingly comes the time where I want more and need to get moving again! So comes the dreaming, the planing, the saving and organizing, the farewell departure party with friends and hop! Starts the adventure again ♡ It gave me a whole different length of time...now it is a circle of three years, instead of three months."

In other cases experiences cyclists made use of their experience to offer advice for new bicycle tourists. For example one posting offered "Greetings Bicycle Tourers! I'm super stoked to share with you a piece of work I've been preparing for some months. This piece is the distilled learnings of more than a decade in the saddle of heavily laden bicycles…" and then went on to make recommendation for rookie riders (Bicycle Touring & Backpacking, Sep 18, 2020). This only generated 7 responses, but all expressed thanks.

Discussion

This study appears to illustrate the type of "e-tribes" that Kozinets (1999) describes. In this case we examine niche Facebook groups dedicated to a particular interest – bicycle touring (Norris 2002, pg. 5). These groups appear to be one of the online "leisure communities" described by Anderson and Taylor (2010). In this case a small but devoted following of bikers make use of Facebook as their online community. Participants requested and shared information and opinions on equipment, planning, touring in general, and their experiences on the road. Posters varied in their use of the online community, from active almost every day to one-time users.

Ridings and Gefen (2004) suggested that the main reason people join virtual communities is for information exchange but noted that often they also seek friendship and social support. In this case, almost all requesters seem to benefit from the online groups with regard to basic information gathering as guidance and opinions on the best equipment or route advice. The groups are generally supportive and offer a means where more experienced bikers mentor and encourage potential bikers. Further, the interactive nature appears to be generally engaging for some experienced riders. Requestors receive a lot of advice rather quickly, often in a matter of a day. Responders are supported through this advice with generally positive comments. They also often experienced a sense of recognition from the direct "thank yous" that occur. In this case it appears that the "common bond" that participants felt may have been tilted toward the group instead of individual group members (Ren et al. 2007; Ren et al. 2007). The findings support the notion that cooperation does not require strong existing social relationships (Faraj et al. 2011), but instead may have resulted from the superordinate goal of bicycle touring (Amichai-Hamburger and McKenna 2006; Butler et al. 2008).

Although the high level of social support found on these online communities appears to be a result of a superordinate goal, it may be that bikers are simply more supportive of one another regardless of the context. People interested in a niche hobby may be more prone to assist others interested in their small community and hobby. This possibility suggests further research should examine exiting levels of social support across a wider variety of groups and examine if that predicts the level of support and encouragement offered in the associated online communities. Another important study would examine other possible reasons for participants' perceptions and satisfaction with online communities. We did not investigate whether how long people would remain a member of the groups, or what percentage moved from novices and less experiences riders to more experienced riders, and what may have led to a lasting commitment to a group. Finally, although this analysis used several Facebook groups, our results may not generalize to other Facebook groups or social network sites in general. Additional research is necessary to understand how generalizeable these findings are.

References

Amichai-Hamburger, Y., & McKenna, K. Y. (2006). The contact hypothesis reconsidered: Interacting via the Internet. *Journal of Computer-Mediated Communication, 11*(3), 825-843.

Anderson, L., & Taylor, J. D. (2010). Standing out while fitting in: Serious leisure identities and aligning actions among skydivers and gun collectors. *Journal of Contemporary Ethnography, 39*(1), 34-59.

Butler, B. S. (2001). Membership size, communication activity, and sustainability: A resource-based model of online social structures. *Information systems research, 12*(4), 346-362.

Butler, B., Sproull, L., Kiesler, S., & Kraut, R. (2008). Community effort in online groups: Who does the work and why. In S. Weisband (Ed.), *Leadership at a distance: Research in technologically supported work* (pp. 171-194). New York: Erlbaum.

Dickinson, J.E., & Lumsdon, L. (2010). *Slow Travel and Tourism*. Washington, DC: Earthscan.

Emanuel, M. (2017). Seeking adventure and authenticity: Swedish bicycle touring in Europe during the interwar period. *Journal of Tourism History, 9*(1), 44-69.

Etzoni, A. & Etzoni, O. (1997, 18 July). Communities: Virtual vs. real. *Science, 277* (5324), 295.

Faraj, S., Jarvenpaa, S. L., & Majchrzak, A. (2011). Knowledge collaboration in online communities. *Organization Science, 22*(5), 1224-1239.

Grabher, G., & Ibert, O. (2013). Distance as asset? Knowledge collaboration in hybrid virtual communities. *Journal of Economic Geography, 14*(1), 97-123.

Han, H., Meng, B., & Kim, W. (2017). Emerging bicycle tourism and the theory of planned behavior. *Journal of Sustainable Tourism, 25*(2), 292-309.

Kozinets, R. V. (1999). E-tribalized marketing?: The strategic implications of virtual communities of consumption. *European Management Journal, 17*(3), 252-264.

Norris, P. (2002). The bridging and bonding role of online communities. *Press/Politics, 7*(3), 3-13.

Palloff, R. M., & Pratt, K. (1999). *Building learning communities in cyberspace* (Vol. 12). San Francisco: Jossey-Bass.

Ren, Y., Kraut, R., & Kiesler, S. (2007). Applying common identity and bond theory to design of online communities. *Organization Studies, 28*(3), 377-408.

Ridings, C. M., & Gefen, D. (2004). Virtual community attraction: Why people hang out online. *Journal of Computer-Mediated Communication, 10*(1). https://doi.org/10.1111/j.1083-6101.2004.tb00229.x

Ritchie, B. W. (1998). Bicycle tourism in the South Island of New Zealand: planning and management issues. *Tourism management, 19*(6), 567-582.

Sherif, M., Harvey, O.J., White, B.J., Hood, W.R., & Sherif, C.W. (1961) *Intergroup Conflict and Co-operation: The Robbers Cave Experiment*. Norman, OK: University of Oklahoma Book Exchange.

Wellman, B., Boase, J., & Chen, W. (2002). The networked nature of community: Online and offline. *IT & Society, 1*(1), 151-165.

Williams, J. P. (2006). Authentic identities: Straightedge subculture, music, and the internet. *Journal of Contemporary Ethnography, 35*(2), 173-200.

Consumer Responsiveness to Covid-19 Related Cues in Advertising: An Abstract

Bidisha Burman and Sacha Joseph Matthews

Abstract The Covid-19 pandemic has impacted lives globally and caused physical, economic and social havoc across the world. The impact to businesses in some instances has been catastrophic, while other businesses are figuring out how to navigate interactions with customers and modifying business models as the crisis ebbs and flows. Part of the unique challenge associated with the pandemic is navigating messaging to consumers. Now that the pandemic has continued for over a year, advertisers have had to consider the new normal in all of their advertising messaging. This notion of message development and effectiveness during a natural disaster stands at the core of this study.

This study examines the impact of different types of advertising cues on consumer attitude formation and contributes to the literature by understanding how relation of cues to the current pandemic can be used to create effective advertising. We manipulate relationship of the cues to Covid at three levels in the advertisements to examine differences in consumer responsiveness to the ads.

Data was collected from 228 participants. The findings indicated that an ad with high levels of Covid related cues (focus on active social responsiveness) was favorably evaluated by consumers. However, the ad with the lowest level of Covid related cues (focus on product efficiency) was just as effective. This may be due to the high relevance of the product being utilitarian in preventing Covid. It is noteworthy that the ad with moderate level of Covid related cues had the least favorable evaluation of consumers. The findings also suggest that it is important for companies to pay attention to self-referencing as a moderator in their advertising during a natural disaster.

Keywords Pandemic · Cues · Self-referencing · Advertising effectiveness

B. Burman (✉) · S. J. Matthews
University of the Pacific, Stockton, CA, USA
e-mail: bburman@pacific.edu; sjoseph@pacific.edu

J. Allen et al. (eds.), *Celebrating the Past and Future of Marketing and Discovery with Social Impact*, Developments in Marketing Science: Proceedings of the Academy of Marketing Science, https://doi.org/10.1007/978-3-030-95346-1_74

Consumer Responsiveness to Covid-19 Related Cues in Advertising: An Abstract

Should a Luxury Brand's Chatbot Use Emoticons? An Abstract

Yuan Li and Hyunju Shin

Abstract Luxury online sales continue to grow despite the pandemic setback. Luxury brands have increasingly relied on chatbots, an AI-powered computer program to serve as a 24/7 virtual agent for online communications with customers. Even though chatbots have many benefits such as enhancing productivity and giving customers instant feedback, communication with chatbots can be viewed as impersonal and robotic. This drawback is a concern as customers expect a more personalized experience from luxury brands. Previous research has examined ways to humanize chatbots. But little is known about whether a luxury brand chatbot should use emoticons to resemble human interactions in luxury brand communication. This research seeks to address this question. Across three studies using different luxury products and services, we found consistent evidence that using emoticons in a luxury brand's chatbot communications can lower the luxury brand's status perception. In addition, the research has uncovered the underlying process by showing such negative effect was due to the lowered perceived appropriateness. We also found such effect only existed for the traditional luxury brands but not for masstige brands. Masstige brands are priced well below the traditional luxury brands. They are not associated with scarcity and rarity as they give ordinary people access to luxury. This research contributes to the luxury brand communication literature. It aligns with previous research and suggests what works for other industries may not work for the luxury industry. This research also contributes to the understanding of emoticon usage in the human-chatbot interaction while emoticon's senders are chatbots. More importantly, our research contains managerial implications. Luxury brand managers need to be cautious with using emoticons in the chatbot communications. It may be good for traditional luxury brands to stay away from using emoticons in chatbot communication.

Y. Li (✉) · H. Shin
Georgia Southern University, Statesboro, GA, USA
e-mail: yuanli@georgiasouthern.edu; hshin@georgiasouthenr.edu

J. Allen et al. (eds.), *Celebrating the Past and Future of Marketing and Discovery with Social Impact*, Developments in Marketing Science: Proceedings of the Academy of Marketing Science, https://doi.org/10.1007/978-3-030-95346-1_75

Keywords Luxury · Brand communication · Chatbot · Emoticon · Brand status · Artificial intelligence

To Diet or Not to Diet? The Role of Exercise Self-Efficacy in Fitspiration Exposure: A Pretest: An Abstract

Daniela De Luca and Kate Pounders

Abstract The fitspiration trend, which is supposed to help achieve fitness goals, has been found to influence individuals' perception of the ideal body shape and size (Ho et al. 2016), and to increase body dissatisfaction rates (Tiggemann and Zaccardo 2015). This pre-test looked into models that will be used for our main study, which will evaluate the role of other factors that may affect the relationship between fitspiration exposure and body dissatisfaction, such as emotions, exercise self-efficacy, and self-improvement motivation. This study will also compare differences in body dissatisfaction rates between exposure to fitspiration vs the thin-ideal in Instagram posts.

Specifically, fitspiration has also been found to influence maladaptive behaviors including obsessive-compulsive exercising, engagement in excessive and rigid fad diets (Ratwatte and Mattacola 2019), and an increase in body dissatisfaction (Ho et al. 2018), all known precursors of eating disorders. However, Heinberg and colleagues (2016) argue that some degree of body dissatisfaction may motivate engagement in healthy behaviors such as exercising and healthy dieting. Similarly, Moffitt and others (2018) found self-compassion reduces body dissatisfaction and influences self-improvement motivation. In thinking about the role of emotions, appraisal theory (see Roseman 1991) argues emotions are responses to how an individual perceives and interprets any situation corresponding to the relevance it has on their personal goals. However, Pounders and colleagues (2018) found emotions play a significant role in message acceptance, along with self-efficacy.

With this in mind, we propose that by manipulating emotions (hope, guilt, and pride) in the fitspiration messages on Instagram captions, the effects of exposure body dissatisfaction may differ. We also argue these differences may depend on whether the exposure is to the thin-ideal or to the fitness ideal. As such, in this pretest we exposed 94 students to different fitness levels models for a manipulation check, and after performing a between subject analyses, selected the models that will be used to test our hypotheses in the main study.

D. De Luca (✉) · K. Pounders
University of Texas at Austin, Austin, TX, USA
e-mail: danideluca@utexas.edu; kate.pounders@utexas.edu

J. Allen et al. (eds.), *Celebrating the Past and Future of Marketing and Discovery with Social Impact*, Developments in Marketing Science: Proceedings of the Academy of Marketing Science, https://doi.org/10.1007/978-3-030-95346-1_76

Keywords Emotions · Body dissatisfaction · Exercise self-efficacy
Self-improvement motivation

Be Good or Do Good? A Construal Level Theory Perspective on Corporate Ambivalent Behaviors: An Abstract

Gagandeep Choongh, Erika Hernandez-Gonzalez, Karla Corres Luna, and Meng-Hsien Jenny Lin

Abstract During the COVID-19 crisis it is crucial that companies understand that the brand messages they are delivering to their consumers may be perceived differently based on mental distance, hence being mindful of the decisions they make. The goal of this research is to understand how psychological distances can influence the perceptions of consumers toward organization's decisions in ambivalent situations. We examine such responses from the view of consumers and rely on Construal Level Theory (CLT) to inform and predict possible outcomes. Their actions, which can often send mixed messages, indicate ambivalence depending on whether they convey morality or competence efforts more. It is important, through the lenses of CLT, to examine how psychological distance formed from messaging can influence how consumers perceive an organization's level of competence or morality. We investigate the perspectives and evaluations of consumers regarding ambivalence acts of an organization based on spatial distance (near vs. far). A between subject's behavioral experiment design was used and we randomly assigned participants to one of the two different spatial conditions, near or far. Participants read about the ambivalent situation we created regarding the university's decision during COVID-19 and were randomly assigned to either competence ambivalent or morality ambivalent. We demonstrate that this can result in varying customer perceptions toward the organization. Our findings show that customers at a distance (far spatial distance) will value the moral decisions made by the organization more than its

Funded by HSI: #P031C160221
Funded by Koret Foundation: #20-0068

G. Choongh (✉) · E. Hernandez-Gonzalez · M.-H. J. Lin
California State University Monterey Bay, Monterey Bay, CA, USA
e-mail: gchoongh@csumb.edu; ehernandez-gonzalez@csumb.edu; jelin@csumb.edu

K. C. Luna
University of Massachusetts, Boston, MA, USA
e-mail: karla.corres@umb.edu

J. Allen et al. (eds.), *Celebrating the Past and Future of Marketing and Discovery with Social Impact*, Developments in Marketing Science: Proceedings of the Academy of Marketing Science, https://doi.org/10.1007/978-3-030-95346-1_77

level of competency. Whereas there was no significant difference when customers are local (near spatial distance). Our results suggest that in order to be perceived more positively and increase customer satisfaction levels, organizations should take morality based actions over competence based actions.

Keywords Construal level theory · Ambivalence · Corporate association · Corporate social responsibility

A Thematic Exploration of the Development of Investor-Owned Business-Like Entitativity in the Member-Owned Cooperative: An Abstract

Spencer M. Ross

Abstract Marketplace competition is typically associated with firms with corporate ownership and governance structures. However, alternate ownership and governance structures such as cooperatives (and credit unions and mutual insurance companies), offer internal social cohesion, while also allowing firms to compete externally. Typically, co-ops are either producer-, consumer-, worker-, or purchaser-owned, or consist of a combination of these member-owned types. By diffusing ownership, these member-owned businesses (MOB) become more democratized in governance than investor-owned business (IOB), as each member-owner has a single voting share. Democratizing ownership and governance requires increased co-operation among members, as it equally pools individual interests together in the shared interests and objectives of the firm.

In the face of economic uncertainty, democratized ownership and governance leads to a long-term approach to sustainability, which increases the economic stability of cooperatives. While the cooperative structure is commonly found in countries outside the U.S., American co-ops such as Ace Hardware and Ocean Spray are multi-billion-dollar enterprises. Despite the growing popularity of co-ops as a business model in the U.S., there is scant marketing literature that assesses how co-op governance converges with consumer interests. How can co-ops leverage the comparative advantage of MOBs' democratized ownership and governance and turn it into a competitive advantage within the actually existing capitalist marketplace context of corporate social responsibility and IOBs?

The goal of the author's research is to explore the co-op context relative to marketplace competition for consumers. Using qualitative data, the author explores the role of cooperatives, how MOB practices are shaped by the democratic ownership structures, how these firms "reach" consumers, and how consumers respond to the

S. M. Ross (✉)
University of Massachusetts Lowell, Lowell, MA, USA
e-mail: spencer_ross@uml.edu

J. Allen et al. (eds.), *Celebrating the Past and Future of Marketing and Discovery with Social Impact*, Developments in Marketing Science: Proceedings of the Academy of Marketing Science, https://doi.org/10.1007/978-3-030-95346-1_78

cooperative environment. The author develops a thematic analysis of how entitativity is developed in MOBs, by which marketers, particularly in the MOB context, can glean insights to create value for consumers. Observational and interview data highlight how marketing strategy can ensure the internal ownership and governance model of MOBs are leveraged as a sustainable advantage, while presenting externally as similar to investor-owned competitors.

Keywords Sustainability · Cooperatives · Entitativity · Thematic analysis

The "Diversity" in Politics: A Segmentation Criterion?: An Abstract

Emna Bouladi

Abstract The results of the participation in the French elections indicate that citizens with an immigrant background (immigrants and their descendants) participate less in elections (INSEE 2017). To provide elements of understanding of this phenomenon, we examine what meaning voters with an immigrant background give to the exercise of vote and how do they perceive the political marketing implemented for minorities or diversity.

We focused in particular on French nationals of North African (Maghrebi) ethnicity insofar as they represent the largest minority in France (Tribalat 2011). Their vote has therefore a significant impact on certain elections.

In an exploratory approach, we opted for a qualitative methodology. We carried out in-depth semi-structured interviews with 16 French people of North African origin between 27 and 46 years old. They had diversified professional categories and obtained French nationality in all possible ways: by descent (i.e. parents were already French citizens), by naturalization, by marriage, and by juris solis (INSEE 2012).

These in-depth interviews were then analyzed using the content analysis method based mainly on a thematic semantic analysis and on a lexical and syntactic analysis.

After analyzing these preliminary results, we observe multiple meanings assigned to the concept of diversity. The only common demand of this market seems to be accepted as French without further qualification.

This assumes that diversity should not be deployed as a segmentation criterion impacting decision-making paths in terms of types and sources of information, projects or ideas, but rather in terms of discourse that emphasizes blindness to origin among French nationals.

In addition, the people interviewed expressed their feelings of being badly categorized in the politicians' speeches. Therefore, marketers, considered as "cultural agents" (Penaloza and Gilly 1999) should ensure the voters are not incorrectly represented or excluded from the public sphere (Servais 2017). They must be able to

E. Bouladi (✉)
IRG, Paris, France
e-mail: ebouladi@etud.upem.fr

J. Allen et al. (eds.), *Celebrating the Past and Future of Marketing and Discovery with Social Impact*, Developments in Marketing Science: Proceedings of the Academy of Marketing Science, https://doi.org/10.1007/978-3-030-95346-1_79

know the antecedents and consequences of the categorization processes (Durand and Paolella 2013), to study the status and dynamics of categories (Delmestri and Greenwood 2016) and finally to focus on the origin of these categories and their creation process (Blanchet 2018; Durand and Khaire 2017).

On a theoretical level, this exploratory research contributes to the concept of diversity by bringing new registers of meaning. Moreover, this study prompts us to question the identity categorization processes deployed in the political marketing theories. On a practical level, this research questions the relevance of segmenting voters as ethnic targets and offer an attempt at finer segmentation based on the mode of acquisition of French nationality which could provide a better understanding of differences in behavior.

Keywords Consumer behavior · Political marketing · Electoral market segmentation · French of North African descent

Players, Prices, Pixies: Exploring Masculinity across Magazines: An Abstract

Shuang Wu, Nina Krey, and Ryan E. Cruz

Abstract Over the last 50 years, advertising in men's lifestyle magazines continue to act as a medium to portray the evolving concept of masculinity as a reflection of commercial culture (Tan et al. 2013). According to Zayer et al. (2020), marketers and advertisers mirror these developments in their campaigns portraying multiple perspectives on masculinity to reflect gender (Tan et al. 2013; Zayer et al. 2020). This influx in mass media depicting different types of masculinity has led male audiences to re-evaluate and compare their own masculinity to those within media (Tan et al. 2013; Zayer et al. 2020). Therefore, the role of the male actor in an advertisement is of critical importance to image creation, interpretation, and critical analysis.

The current study applies a comparative content analysis. This methodology focuses on how masculine appeals and objectification appear in the content of popular magazine ads. Findings contribute to the existing literature by detailing differences in masculinities and masculine appeals identifying which stable and fluid masculine attributes across magazine genre. According to these data, the 'ideal' masculinity across the sample that is communicated to male readers who construct their own variation of masculine identity and aesthetic through a process of encoding the advertisement content, retaining information, and later retrieving the information and replicating the public messages into their private lives. Findings presents descriptive evidence of masculine representation in the sampled public space. Future studies should investigate the psychological effects of advertisements on the behavior of men when exposed to advertisements over an extended period. Moreover, to gain a more comprehensive perspective of the psychological and social utility consumers derive from consuming advertisements, a

S. Wu (✉) · N. Krey
Rowan University, Glassboro, NJ, USA
e-mail: wus@rowan.edu; krey@rowan.edu

R. E. Cruz
Thomas Jefferson University, Philadelphia, PA, USA
e-mail: ryan.cruz@jefferson.edu

J. Allen et al. (eds.), *Celebrating the Past and Future of Marketing and Discovery with Social Impact*, Developments in Marketing Science: Proceedings of the Academy of Marketing Science, https://doi.org/10.1007/978-3-030-95346-1_80

cognitive processing model should be developed in relation to the masculinity appeals and target audience identity.

Keywords Masculinity · Print advertisements · Content analysis · Magazines

Comparing Shopping Behaviors across Environments: An Abstract

Nina Krey, Karine Picot-Coupey, and Shuang Wu

Abstract Consumers shopping behaviors have transformed and changed with evolving digital elements across channels such as websites and mobile applications. Prior studies have started to substantiate the specific nature of in-store shopping, online shopping and, to a lesser extent, mobile app shopping. Thus, in-store shopping and its distinctive characteristic, namely the ability of consumers to experience an offer on a multisensory level (Childers et al. 2001) contrasts with the limited sensory exploration (e.g., touch and scent) in online and app shopping. Contrary, online shopping is viewed as differing in terms of production information available to consumers, allowing them to compare offers on multi-attributes (e.g., Park and Kim 2003; Scarpi 2011). A few studies have assessed shopping on mobile apps (e.g., Wang et al. 2015) and have identified habitual shopping as the primary reason to utilize apps. Much of the current understanding of the different retail environments draws from research assessing each context individually or comparing consumer behaviors across two contexts (Liu et al. 2019; Newman et al. 2018; Rohm and Swaminathan 2004) rather than multiple environments. The current research contributions hinge on the comparison of shopping behaviors and experiences across store, online, and app environments from a holistic perspective. Previous research primarily assesses each retail environment individually, yet the current research provides a comparison of consumer behavior and shopping experience across three main shopping environments: store, online, and mobile applications.

Study 1 (N = 232) focused on providing initial evidence for the proposed differences in shopping behaviors across store, online, and app environments. Study 2 (N = 594) examined how shopping environments shape overall consumer experi-

N. Krey (✉) · S. Wu
Rowan University, Glassboro, NJ, USA
e-mail: krey@rowan.edu; wus@rowan.edu

K. Picot-Coupey
University of Rennes 1, Rennes, France
e-mail: karine.picot@univ-rennes1.fr

J. Allen et al. (eds.), *Celebrating the Past and Future of Marketing and Discovery with Social Impact*, Developments in Marketing Science: Proceedings of the Academy of Marketing Science, https://doi.org/10.1007/978-3-030-95346-1_81

ences by assessing commonly studied outcome variables in this area: utilitarian and hedonic value, satisfaction, word-of-mouth, repatronage intention, and flow (Babin et al. 1994; Jones et al. 2006; Maxham and Netemeyer 2002; Wang et al. 2007).

Current findings reveal diverging shopping behaviors driven by shopping environments. For example, online and app shopping is mainly done weekly by most consumers, who spend the most amount of money when shopping online. In addition, shopping experiences elicit varying consumer responses such as higher levels of hedonic value in store versus online and app contexts.

Overall, managers need to consider these differences when creating comprehensive shopping experiences as part of a comprehensive customer journey. In creating a seamless omni-channel customer journey, companies need to carefully consider and adjust strategic approaches to offer positive experiences throughout various touchpoints. Clearly, distinctive consumer behavioral trends emerged across shopping environments.

Keywords Shopping experience · Shopping value · Retailing · Omni-channel · App · Online shopping · Store

Too Real or Just Real Enough? Service Adaptation and Authenticity Perception in Cross-Cultural Service Encounters: An Abstract

Ayesha Tariq, Melanie P. Lorenz, and W. Frank Thompson

Abstract With limited travel in a post COVID-19 world, consumers seek cultural experiences closer to home. Services like ethnic dining provide consumers the opportunity to immerse in a culturally authentic experience not a part of their daily lives (Southworth 2018; Yu et al. 2020). However, to date, research has not determined how authentic is authentic enough or if customer need some adaptation of the service encounter to their own culture for full satisfaction. On the one hand, prior research suggest that cross-cultural service encounter adaptation is associated with positive customer outcomes such as rapport, satisfaction, and WOM (Azab and Clark 2017). On the other hand, cultural authenticity is suggested to be a driver of successful service encounters (Wang and Mattila 2015), increasing customers' satisfaction and loyalty (Park et al. 2019). Thus, adaptation and authenticity present conflicting forces in optimizing the cross-cultural service experience and satisfying customers' demand to immerse in a foreign culture. Further complicating the situation, there is a lack of generalization across different customer groups.

In this study, the authors explore the following research questions; (1) Could higher service adaptation lead to lower satisfaction if it is perceived to take away from cultural authenticity? Does too much authenticity lead to discomfort, reducing positive customer outcomes? Is there an optimum level of authenticity-adaptation? (2) Do the same assumptions hold across different generations? Is seeking authentic or more adapted cultural service experiences a generational phenomenon? (3) What role do cultural competences play - can customer cultural competences bridge the perceived authenticity – customer experience gap?

A. Tariq (✉) · W. F. Thompson
Troy University, Troy, AL, USA
e-mail: atariq@troy.edu; wfthompson@troy.edu

M. P. Lorenz
Florida Atlantic University, Boca Raton, FL, USA
e-mail: lorenzm@fau.edu

J. Allen et al. (eds.), *Celebrating the Past and Future of Marketing and Discovery with Social Impact*, Developments in Marketing Science: Proceedings of the Academy of Marketing Science, https://doi.org/10.1007/978-3-030-95346-1_82

The authors explore these research questions using scenario-based experiments set in the context of an Indian restaurant. Results show that too much authenticity may hinder the optimum service experience (Study 1). While younger customers prefer moderate adaptation/ authenticity (rather than low adaptation), older generation seems more adventurous and perceives a better experience (satisfaction, WoM, repatronage) when there is low to no adaptation (full authenticity) (Study 1 and 2). We find that positive outcomes are significantly higher for older generations when adaptation is low (Study 2). The effect of cultural competences is yet to be determined (Study 3).

This study contributes to the literature by revealing that high levels of perceived authenticity do not always ensure positive outcomes, and that outcomes associated with perceived authenticity vary across generations. Managerially, the study helps organizations tailor the optimal level of authenticity by adjusting the level of adaptation of the offering to suit particular clientele.

Keywords Cross-cultural service encounter · Service adaptation · Authenticity perception · Satisfaction · WOM · Repatronage intentions

Virtual Reality and Wine Tourism: An Abstract

Bora Qesja, Susan Bastian, and Svetlana De Vos

Abstract Virtual reality (VR) experiences can be utilized as differentiating promotional tools to increase immersion and illicit emotions for the purpose of impacting the development of wine tourism and wine sales. Wine tourism is a continuously growing industry that plays an important role in the development of rural areas. However, wine regions, such as the Riverland wine region in South Australia, face difficulties in differentiating themselves and motivating tourists to visit. For the purpose of this study, a Riverland wine region VR experience was created to showcase what the region has to offer with the goal of promoting national and international tourism (particularly from China and the USA). This study explores the role of a VR experience on behavioral outcomes such as desire to visit the region as well as desire to purchase products produced in the region (such as wine). Moreover, it explores elements of a VR experience that play a role in influencing perceptions of immersion as well as behavioral outcomes. Focus groups were conducted in both USA (4 focus groups) and China (4 focus groups) in order to explore factors that play a role in the creation of a VR experience that can positively influence behavioral outcomes in a tourism context. A second quantitative stage was also conducted in Australia. Data was analyzed using Leximancer (qualitative data) and SPSS (quantitative data). Sensory engagement, perceived quality of the VR experience, presence of an authority figure (such as a tour guide), perceptions of authenticity of

This research was funded by Australian grape growers and winemakers through their investment body, Wine Australia, with matching funds from the Department of Primary Industries and Regions (PIRSA), Riverland Wine Industry Development Council Inc, the University of Adelaide, and 57 Films. Moreover, we would like to acknowledge key contributors to the project namely: Dr. Lukas Danner, Dr. Wenyu Kang, Natalja Ivanova, Laura Noqué, Edison West as well as our participants for their time and assistance.

B. Qesja (✉) · S. De Vos
Australian Institute of Business, Adelaide, SA, Australia
e-mail: bora.qesja@aib.edu.au; svetlana.devos@aib.edu.au

S. Bastian
University of Adelaide, Adelaide, SA, Australia
e-mail: sue.bastian@adelaide.edu.au

J. Allen et al. (eds.), *Celebrating the Past and Future of Marketing and Discovery with Social Impact*, Developments in Marketing Science: Proceedings of the Academy of Marketing Science, https://doi.org/10.1007/978-3-030-95346-1_83

the experience and perceived control within the experience were all found to play an important role in influencing perceptions of immersion in the VR experience as well as desire to visit and purchase products produced in the region. The outcomes of the study indicate that virtual reality is a successful new approach in influencing tourism.

Keywords Virtual reality · Wine tourism · Immersion · Authenticity perceptions

Consumer's Perception Journey: Examining the Psychophysiological Antecedents and Effects of Multisensory Imagery Strategy: An Abstract

Sasawan Heingraj, Michael S. Minor, and Mario Gil

Abstract This research presents three studies that explore psychophysiological mechanisms regarding implementing a multisensory imagery strategy on consumer's perception. Based on our first study's self-report data, the effectiveness of this strategy will depend on the consumer's masculine-feminine self-concept. Specifically, the multisensory imagery marketing messages tend to provide consumers with a higher degree of femininity a greater level of involvement and engagement than consumers with higher masculinity. This is because this advertisement facilitates the linkage between the consumer's self-concept and their emotional memories. The second study will triangulate the results from the self-report data with brain activation using electroencephalography (EEG) signals, particularly in the prefrontal cortex and temporal lobe areas. The third study will triangulate the results from self-report data (Study 1) and brand activation (Study 2) with the neurological data via the examination of Postsynaptic Density Protein 95 (PSD-95) and Brain-Derived Neurotrophic Factor (BDNF) expressed particularly in the prefrontal cortex and hippocampus areas of the laboratory animal (*Monodelphis domestica*: gray short-tailed opossum). These proteins are also a conserved structure that presents in the human brain.

This study contributes to the sensory imagery stream of research and contributes to the expanding literature on consumer neuroscience. Based on our knowledge, this study is the first marketing research that triangulates and utilizes multiple methods—the use of self-report data, brain activations (i.e., EEG signals), and the neurological indicators (i.e., PSD-95 and BDNF protein) in the laboratory animal to obtain a better understanding of the effect of multisensory imagery marketing strategy on consumer's perception. Additionally, this study also offers new insights to marketing practitioners and public policymakers. When creating an advertisement, marketers should pay attention to the different degrees of consumer's masculine-

S. Heingraj (✉) · M. S. Minor · M. Gil
The University of Texas Rio Grande Valley, Edinburg, TX, USA
e-mail: sasawan.heingraj01@utrgv.edu; michael.minor@utrgv.edu; mario.gil@utrgv.edu

J. Allen et al. (eds.), *Celebrating the Past and Future of Marketing and Discovery with Social Impact*, Developments in Marketing Science: Proceedings of the Academy of Marketing Science, https://doi.org/10.1007/978-3-030-95346-1_84

feminine self-concept. Public policymakers can utilize multisensory imagery cues when introducing a new public policy campaign since multisensory imagery messages offer consumers a greater ability to recall information.

Keywords Multisensory imagery · Consumer neuroscience · Advertisement · Perception

Effective Consumer Journey- Personalizing Touchpoints and Optimizing Conversion for Mature-Age Online MBA Prospective Students: An Abstract

Svetlana De Vos and Bora Qesja

Abstract This study contributes to the stream of literature focused on the business education in the digital age. In particular, this research maps out the critical first stages of consumer journey (service pre-experience and pre-purchase stages) of mature-age online MBA prospective students in Australia and identifying relevant factors that may influence the conversion rates. This research embraced a deep consumer insight approach, enabling to understand why customers do or do not engage with businesses (Price et al. 2015) with student journey mapping steps followed in line with Rains (2017). In–depth interviews were conducted with 30 online MBA prospective students (35–65 years old) that have approached one of the largest online MBA providers in Australia. A traditional thematic analysis conducted by researchers and the text minding analysis (Leximancer) were used to further identify themes.

Two distinctive types of personas emerged. Although each persona seemed to progress along the decision-making timeline in a similar way, they varied substantially in how they engage with each touch point in their journey. In particular, one persona type spent a considerable amount of time following social media posts pertinent to the online provider and approached MBA recruitment team via email, seeking information on the website regarding the subjects' content; while another predominately explored price and payment options preferring to call and speak with the recruitment team directly. For both personas the major motivation for their online MBA study consideration emerged as a career advancement/career grow with the second theme being learning and personal development. Both personas attributed value to online MBA for flexibility and mobility, subjects' contemporary content, support of facilitators, reasonable price for value, and easy access to learning materials. Major reference points were work consultants, colleagues, friends and family members. 'Positive word of mouth' via MBA forum reviews and personal sources were important determinants prompting in–depth search. Touch

S. De Vos (✉) · B. Qesja
Australian Institute of Business, Adelaide, SA, Australia
e-mail: svetlana.devos@aib.edu.au; bora.qesja@aib.edu.au

J. Allen et al. (eds.), *Celebrating the Past and Future of Marketing and Discovery with Social Impact*, Developments in Marketing Science: Proceedings of the Academy of Marketing Science, https://doi.org/10.1007/978-3-030-95346-1_85

points with the recruitment team generated the following themes: personal and professional characteristics of the advisor expected to be prompt, friendly, non-intrusive, offering follow up communication in a timely manner and having in–depth understanding of MBA offering. The emerged 'pain-points' revolved around a very generic and intrusive 'sale pitch' by the recruitment individuals without understanding the 'why' behind each student's motives to engage into online MBA. Overall, this study revealed the importance of consumer journey mapping for mature-age online MBA prospective students in Australia, capturing service pre-experiences and pre-purchase stages that, when executed right, enable a transition of prospects into the next decision- making stage.

Keywords Consumer journey · On-line MBA · Mature-age prospects · Service pre-experiences and pre-purchase stages

Listening to Your Customer's Heart or Head? Uncovering the Trade-Offs between Customer Experience and Lock-In

Xuehui Lily Gao, Evert de Haan, Iguácel Melero Polo, and F. Javier Sese

Abstract Improving the customer experience and building barriers to lock customers are two key strategies employed by firms to enhance customer retention. Although pursuing the same goal, these strategies work differently: the former promotes the affective aspects of the relationship while the latter relies more on a calculative, cost–benefit approach to the exchange. Integrating experiential learning theory, we provide an integrative conceptual understanding of the separate and joint effects of customer experience and lock-in on customer retention. Using a dataset containing perceptual, competitive, and transactional information for a sample of 13,761 customers covering all firms in the telecom market for two different services, we empirically test the proposed framework via multinomial logit modeling. The results offer novel insights into the presence of trade-offs between these two key strategies. We show that with one lock- in, the role of customer experience becomes weaker. However, with multiple lock-in methods where negative interaction is captured, customer experience does matter. Our contribution consists of identifying whether customer experience and lock-in complement or substitute each other and when such effects occur, thereby helping firms optimally allocate marketing resources to retain customers.

Keywords Customer retention · Customer experience · Lock-in · Spillover effect · Multinomial logit models · Telecom industry

---

X. L. Gao (✉) · I. M. Polo · F. J. Sese
University of Zaragoza, Zaragoza, Spain
e-mail: lilygao@unizar.es; imelero@unizar.es; javisese@unizar.es

E. de Haan
University of Groningen, Groningen, The Netherlands
e-mail: evert.de.haan@rug.nl

J. Allen et al. (eds.), *Celebrating the Past and Future of Marketing and Discovery with Social Impact*, Developments in Marketing Science: Proceedings of the Academy of Marketing Science, https://doi.org/10.1007/978-3-030-95346-1_86

Introduction

Successfully designing and providing customers with an optimal experience has become a central priority for marketing theory and practice (Becker and Jaakkola 2020; Homburg et al. 2017; Keiningham et al. 2020). Companies are increasing their investment in customer experience in an exponential manner, with the expectations that these investments will ultimately provide positive financial returns. For example, Gartner's (2019) global survey across a wide range of industries reveal that 75% of organizations increased customer experience investments in 2018 and will continue to be one of the biggest investments in the following years. Previous conceptual studies suggest that this may be the case, as improving customer experiences may lead to better customer attitudes, purchase intentions, and thus, customer profitability (De Keyser et al. 2020). For multi-product firms the economic return may be even larger, as previous studies have indicated that customer attitudes and perceptions toward one product category may spill over to other (related or unrelated) product categories (Keller et al. 2020). While the conceptual basis for investing in customer experience is strong and suggests the need for companies to do that, empirical evidence on the real behavioural and/or economic implications of customer experience investments are lacking (Becker and Jaakkola 2020).

An important aspect to consider is that, together with customer experience investments, companies also invest in other strategies to retain their customers, such as building switching barriers (e.g., charging customers with financial fees for breaking contracts, bundling different products together) (Nitzan and Ein-Gar 2019). These actions, which we label under the term "lock-in strategies" (Mcquilken et al. 2015), focus more on the calculative aspects of developing and maintaining customer-firm relationships (vs. the affective aspects for the customer experience), by which customers make a rational assessment of the benefits vs. costs of continuing doing business with the firm. An important question emerges as to whether locking customers in the relationship through these actions may intensify or weaken the impact of customer experience investments (Nitzan and Ein-Gar 2019). On the one hand, customers who are "trapped" in the relationship with a firm may value positively that the firm is investing in improving the customer experience, leading to positive behavioural outcomes (i.e., complementary effect). On the other hand, if customers perceive a high cost of leaving the relationship, their experiences may be less relevant in their decisions to stay or leave (i.e., substituting effect) (Shamsollahi, Chmielewski-Raimondo, Bell and Kachouie 2020). Given this, the impact of customer experience investments should not be evaluated in an isolated manner, but jointly with other retention strategies to properly understand their effectiveness in driving customer behavioural responses.

This study intends to fill these gaps in the literature. Grounded on experiential learning theory (Kolb 1984), our study provides a conceptual understanding of the main effect of the customer experience on customer retention in the focal product category and in other product categories (i.e., spillover effects) as well as the moderating effect of customer lock-in strategies. Using a panel dataset which combines both transactional and perceptual information for a sample of 13,761 customers, covering the all firms from the telecom industry in one European country for two core service categories (mobile and broadband) and a period of 48 months, we test the framework empirically applying multinomial logit modelling techniques.

In doing so, our work intends to make several important contributions to the marketing literature. First, this research provides early empirical evidence revealing the actual behavioural consequences of the customer experience. Importantly, our study accounts also for the experiences that customers receive at other competing service providers, thus offering novel insights into the competitive effects of the customer experience. Second, the study investigates the impact of the customer experience not only on the focal product category, but also on other related categories (i.e., spillover effects). This is especially relevant for multi-product companies, as the return on customer experience investments critically depend on whether experience effects span to other categories. Third, the study offers novel insights into the degree to which the main and spillover effects of the customer experience are strengthened or weakened in the presence of other mechanisms aimed to retain customers (i.e., lock-in strategies). The findings of this study can be of value to marketing managers to help them better design their mix of strategies to retain customers (i.e., customer experience and lock-in) and improving the financial accountability of these investments.

Conceptual Framework and Research Hypotheses

Building on experiential learning theory (Kolb 1984), we develop a conceptual framework (Fig. 1). The tenet of experiential learning theory is that individuals learn from the transformation of experience. Specifically, customers tend to process and learn from all occurred experiences, which contain a wide range of information about various product service categories and multiple firms, including competitors. In this way, individuals can update their knowledge scheme about an entity (the focal firm), which later may serve as guides for customers to draw actions (customer choice across firms). We thus establish the linkages among customer experience within a product/service category, the spillover effect to other categories, and their competitive effect among multiple firms in the previous period, and their joint impact on customer retention.

Furthermore, drawing from the literature in customer relationship management (Nitzan and Ein-Gar 2019), which recognize that in addition to firm's investment in customer experience, firms tend to retain their customers through lock-in strategies by providing offers to customers with added value and increased switching barriers, thereby preventing the possibility of migration to competitors. In our framework, based on previous studies (Mcquilken et al. 2015), we focus on three frequently implemented lock-in mechanisms in practice: (1) bundling, or offering two or more separate products as a package for a single discounted price or a convenience to customers; (2) binding contract, or a signed contract for a predetermined length of

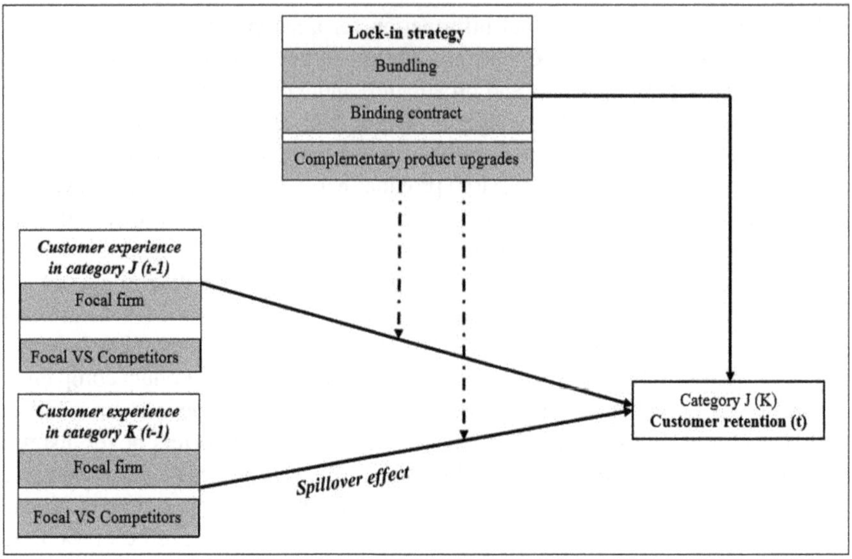

Fig. 1 Conceptual framework

time with economic penalties for customers if they break it; and (3) complementary product upgrades, or upgrading the add-on product to the core category. We propose that each of the lock-in mechanisms will have a direct effect on customer retention. We further suggest a moderating effect of lock-in mechanisms on the established relationships between customer experience (e.g., experience on the focal product category, on other related categories [i.e., spillover effects] and relative experience in comparison to competitors) and customer retention.

Direct Impact of Customer Experience in the Core Category

Delivering favourable customer experience and superior customer experience than competitors have been widely acknowledged as an essential strategic lever for firms to maintain long-term customer relationship (De Haan et al. 2015; Keiningham et al. 2020). As noted by experiential learning theory (Kolb 1984), customers may take a broader perspective and shape their experience with an organization based on the gained experience with the focal firm and competitive alternatives as the reference point, which is referred as "competitive" customer experience in this study. The perceived experiences above the framed reference points are considered as gains, and thus encouraging customers to stay with the focal firm.

H1a: Customer experience with the focal firm in one category will have a positive impact on customer retention in that category.

H1b: Competitive customer experience within one category will have a positive impact on customer retention in that category.

Customer Experience Spillover Effect in another Category

Consistent with the tenet of experiential learning theory (Kolb 1984), customers are at the very core of their own experience in terms of acting as "experience integrator" assembling and coordinating interrelated experiences gained from all product categories (De Keyser et al. 2015). As such, positive customer experience in other categories will strengthen the positive image generated from the central product/service category. Similarly, higher customer experience than competitors in another category will perceived as gains obtained from the focal firm (De Haan et al. 2015).

H2a: Customer experience with the focal firm with one category will have a positive impact on customer retention for another category at the focal firm.

H2b: Competitive customer experience with the focal firm in another category will have a positive impact on customer retention.

Direct Impact of Lock-In Mechanisms

As consistently evidenced by previous studies (Mcquilken et al. 2015; Nitzan and Ein-Gar 2019), enabled by lock-in strategies (i.e., bundling, binding contract, and complementary product upgrades), a strong tie will be established between customers and organizations. Therefore, customers tend to repeat transactions with the focal firms due to the associated value, perceived convenience and/or barriers to switch (Nitzan and Ein-Gar 2019; Polo and Sese 2013).

H3a-c: Bundling, binding contract, and complementary product upgrades will positively affect customer retention.

Moderating Role of Lock-In Mechanisms

Bundling Bundling is expected to play a negative moderating role. On the basis of the literature on bundling (Balachander et al. 2010), customers' major attention is placed on the price as well as the composition the bundled products or services, thereby mitigating customers' focus on customer experience. The underlying reason is that customers are required more efforts to assess a bundled offering in comparison to a single product or service. Moreover, once choosing a bundled offer, customers might overlook the shortcoming of customer experience and tend to stay with the firm due to the increased switching costs (Nitzan and Ein-Gar 2019).

H4a-d: Bundling will weaken the effects of H1a, H1b, H2a, and H2b.

Binding Contract In accordance with Ou et al. (2017), customers who are contractually bound to a specific firm tend to maintain the relationship with the firm during the contractual period due to the highly associated switching costs, which could be monetary or non-monetary (Polo and Sese 2013). Assumed such a barrier to exit, customers have to continue the transaction with the focal firm until the end of the contract, regardless the level of the perceived customer experience. Importantly, according to Ou et al. (2017), binding contract might lead the feeling of powerlessness to customers because of the loss of freedom. In particular, when the customer experience is resulted unsatisfactorily and the choice of migration to competitors is taken away by the competitors through the established contract.

H5a-d: Contractual setting will weaken the effects of H1a, H1b, H2a, and H2b.

Complementary Product Upgrades From one side, upgrading complementary products may deliver a positive feeling to customers toward the main product/service categories due to its complementary characteristic to the core categories. As indicated by Nitzan and Ein-Gar (2019), providing complementary product upgrades related to the core product/service category is usually perceived as added-value from the perspective of customers. However, this mechanism might trigger customers to switch to competitors. Stimulated by the focal firm's offering of complementary product upgrades, customers might search for competitors' alternatives. Indeed, prior research (i.e., Nitzan and Ein-Gar 2019) observes that for the time of encouraging customers to upgrade the complementary product (e.g., better handset device), customers are more likely to churn driven by this event (e.g., changing the handset).

H6a-d: Complementary product upgrades will weaken effects of H1a, H1b, H2a and H2b.

Data and Methodology

Data and Sample

To empirically test the proposed framework and its hypotheses, multiple data sources have been integrated into a unified panel dataset. It includes a total of 13,671 customers, representative for major European telecom market. This database contained monthly customer information for a time window of 48 months (January 2013 to December 2016) related to two major telecommunication service categories (mobile and broadband). All firms operating in the industry at this time period are encompassed, ranging from single service providers to multiple service providers.

The dataset combines perceptual and transactional information. In each of the two service categories, we can observe customers' yearly perceptual measures (customer experience with the focal firm and competitors) and monthly measured objective information (e.g., choices related to bundling, binding contract, complementary product upgrades, and usage). The former information is collected through a survey at the end of each year. For the information about customer choices, enabled by the panel structure, we are able to track customer switching decisions in both service categories. Finally, we have also information about a set of control variables related to firm characteristics (e.g., market shares, advertising expenditures, social media mentions), context characteristics (e.g., acquisitions, new entrants, iPhone release dates), and customer characteristics (e.g., gender, age, working status, and social class).

Methodology

As displayed in Eq. 1, we estimate a pair of utility maximization based multinomial logit models, one for each service category to test the conceptual framework, whereby we are allowed to identify key determinants that affect customer choice possibilities across multiple firms (Elshiewy et al. 2017). Specifically, we examine the impact of customer experience with focal firm and competitive customer experience in mobile service category, customer experience spillover effect in broadband service category, as well as the direct impact and moderating role of the set of lock-in mechanisms on firm choice in mobile service category. Same estimation procedure has been conducted in the broadband service category.

$$
\begin{aligned}
& Ln\left[\Pr\left(Y_{!"\#}\right)/\Pr\left(Y_{!\$\#}\right)\right]_{Mobile/Broadband} = \alpha + \beta_1 \boldsymbol{Mobile\,CX}_{!"\#\%\&} \\
& +\beta_2\left(\boldsymbol{Mobile\,CX}_{!"\#\%\&} - \boldsymbol{Mobile\,CX}_{\#\%\&}\right) + \beta_3 \\
& \boldsymbol{BroadbandCX}_{!"\#\%\&} + \beta_4\left(\boldsymbol{BroadbandCX}_{!"\#\%\&} - \boldsymbol{BroadbandCX}_{\#\%\&}\right) \\
& \quad + \beta_{5,6,7}\boldsymbol{Lockin}_{!\#\%\&} + \mathrm{B}_{8,9,10} \\
& \boldsymbol{Lockin}_{!\#\%\&}{}^{*}\boldsymbol{Mobile\,CX}_{!"\#\%\&} \\
& \quad + \mathrm{B}_{11,12,13}\boldsymbol{Lockin}_{!\#\%\&}{}^{*}\left(\boldsymbol{Mobile\,CX}_{!"\#\%\&} - \boldsymbol{Mobile\,CX}_{\#\%\&}\right) + \mathrm{B}_{14,15,16} \\
& \boldsymbol{Lockin}_{!\#\%\&}{}^{*}\boldsymbol{BroadbandCX}_{!"\#\%\&} \\
& \quad + \mathrm{B}_{17,18,19}\boldsymbol{Lockin}_{!\#\%\&}{}^{*}\left(\boldsymbol{BroadbandCX}_{!"\#\%\&} - \boldsymbol{BroadbandCX}_{\#\%\&}\right) + \mathrm{B}_{20}Control_{!\#} \\
& \quad + \varepsilon_{it}
\end{aligned}
\quad (1)
$$

Note: where i, f, c, M, t, t-1 indexing customer i, focal firm f, competitor c, all available firms M, at current period t, and previous period t-1, respectively.

Findings

The results of the empirical estimations are shown in Table 1. In support of H1a-H1b, the results reveal that gaining favourable customer experience from the focal firm in mobile (broadband) service category and superior customer experience than competitors will decrease the possibility that customers migrate to competitors in the correspondent category. In addition, the results demonstrate the existence of the spillover effect, since positive experience with the focal firm and higher customer

Table 1 Estimation results

Hypothesis	Variable	Estimation results		Tested hypothesis	
		Mobile	Broadband		
Main effect					
H1a	Mobile CX	**.170*****	**.078*****	S	S
H1b	Mobile competitive CX	**.335*****	**1.411*****	S	S
H2a	Broadband CX	**.416*****	**1.059*****	S	S
H2b	Broadband competitive CX	**.953*****	**.379*****	S	S
H3a	Bundling	**1.165*****	**1.662*****	S	S
H3b	Binding contract	**.237*****	**.093*****	S	S
H3c	Complementary product upgrades	**−4.376*****	**−.674*****	N	N
Moderating effect					
H4a	Bundling*Mobile CX	**−.167*****	**−.087*****	S	S
H4b	Bundling*Mobile competitive CX	**.124****	.084	N	N
H4c	Bundling*Broadband CX	.037	**−.422*****	N	S
h4d	Bundling*Broadband competitive CX	**−.531*****	**−.545*****	S	S
H5a	Binding contract*Mobile CX	**−.019*****	**−.005*****	S	S
H5b	Binding contract*Mobile competitive CX	**.009***	0.003	N	N
H5c	Binding contract*Broadband CX	**−.009****	**−.011*****	S	S
H5d	Binding contract*Broadband competitive CX	**−.031****	.001	S	N
H6a	Complementary product upgrades*Mobile CX	**−.022***	**−.054****	S	S
H6b	Complementary product upgrades*Mobile competitive CX	**−.049***	−.036	S	N
H6c	Complementary product upgrades*Broadband CX	−.010	**−.603*****	N	S
H6d	Complementary product upgrades*Broadband competitive CX	**−.164****	**−.502*****	S	S

*Note: Significant parameters highlighted in bold: *** p. <.01; **p < .05; *p < .10;* CX *refers to customer experience;* S *means supported hypothesis;* N *means not supported.*

experience than competitors in broadband (mobile) service category also help firms to retain their customers in mobile (broadband) service category, thereby supporting H2a-b. About the direct impact of lock-in mechanisms, as we expected, bundling and binding contract are useful tools for firms to retain their customers. However, the result suggests that upgrading complementary product might trigger customers to switch to competitors. Thus, H3a-b are supported while H3c cannot be confirmed.

About the moderating role of lock-in mechanisms, consistent to our expectation, we first discover that bundle generally weakens the direct impact of customer experience with the focal firm in the core category and its spillover effect on customer retention (supporting H4a-c in mobile service and H4a-c-d in broadband service).

These patterns suggest that customers who have acquired the two service categories in a bundled manner, they tend to maintain the relationship with the focal firm irrespective to the degree of perceived customer experience. We hypothesized a negative moderating role of binding contract in the joint impacts of customer experience with the focal firm, competitive customer experience within a category and spillover effect from another category on customer retention. They are all confirmed from the analyses in mobile service category, except the relationship between competitive customer experience in the core category and customer retention (supporting H5a-b-d). In broadband service category, we observe that with binding contract, customers tend to pay less attention on competitive customer experience in both mobile and broadband service categories (in support of H5a and H5c).

Finally, we also find support for the expectation that offering complementary product upgrades might trigger customers to search for competitors' offers, thereby decreasing the positive influence of customer experience with the focal firm and competitive customer experience in the core category and its spillover effect from another category. More precisely, H6a-b-d are supported in mobile service category whereas H6a-c-d are confirmed in broadband service category, taking into account that all the associated parameters are significant and pointed in the expected direction. A set of firm, context, and customer related characteristics as control variables are included in the model estimation (e.g., market shares, advertising expenditures, social media mentions, acquisitions, new entrants, iPhone release dates, gender, age, working status, and social class).

Theoretical and Empirical Implications

With this empirical investigation, this study provides important implications for academicians and practitioners. From a theoretical perspective, it contributes to the customer experience literature. By providing an integrative framework, this research shows the critical role of customer experience in terms of preventing customers from switching to competitors from a comprehensive manner: its spillover effect (influence from another product/service category) and competitive effect (influence from firms' competitors), thereby enabling us to address the recent calls on this topic (Lemon and Verhoef 2016). This study also contributes to the literature on customer relationship management. While previous studies consistently find that both customer experience and lock-in mechanism are effective strategies to retain customers, they are mainly studied in a separate manner. This study reveals that the effect of customer experience on customer retention varies depending on the applied lock-in mechanism, thereby shedding light on the understanding of the effectiveness of implemented strategies in customer retention.

This study also provides managers with some guidelines about how to manage marketing investments to promote superior customer experience that at the same time can fit with the lock- in strategy in order to maximally reduce the possibility of customer switching behaviors. Specifically, with the discovery of customer experience spillover effect, firms are suggested to visualize the offered product/service categories from a broader and connected perspective. This is especially relevant for multi-service providers, considering that negative customer experience with one category might spill over to another category and jointly trigger customers to switch to competitors. Most importantly, this research is also helpful for firms to concisely identify the extent to how each of the executed lock-in strategic lever could enhance, weaken neutralize the retention effect of customer experience with the focal firm and competitive customer experience in the core category and the spillover effect from another category on customer choices, and thus prioritize their investments accordingly.

References

Balachander, S., Ghosh, B., & Stock, A. (2010). Why bundle discounts can be a profitable alternative to competing on price promotions. *Marketing Science*, *29*, 624-638.

Becker, L., & Jaakkola, E. (2020). Customer experience: Fundamental premises and implications for research. *Journal of the Academy of Marketing Science*, *48*, 630-648.

De Haan, Verhoef, P. C., & Wiesel, T. (2015). The predictive ability of different customer feedback metrics for retention. *International Journal of Research in Marketing*, *32*(2), 195-206.

De Keyser, A., Lemon, K. N., Klaus, P., & Keiningham, T. L. (2015). A framework for understanding and managing the customer experience. *Marketing Science Institute Working Paper Series*, 85(1), 15-121.

De Keyser, A., Verleye, K., Lemon, K. N., Keiningham, T. L., & Klaus, P. (2020). Moving the Customer Experience Field Forward: Introducing the Touchpoints, Context, Qualities (TCQ) Nomenclature. *Journal of Service Research.* Advance online publication. doi:https://doi.org/10.1177/1094670520928390.

Elshiewy, O., Guhl, D., & Boztug, Y. (2017). Multinomial logit models in marketing-from fundamentals to state-of-the-art. *Marketing ZFP*, 39, 32-49.

Gartner (2019). *Customer Experience Trends at Gartner Customer Experience & Technologies Summit 2019.* Retrieved November 26, 2009 from https://www.gartner.com/en/newsroom/press-releases/2019-06-13-gartner-reveals-75%2D%2Dof- organizations-surveyed-increas

Homburg, C., Jozić, D., & Kuehnl, C. (2017). Customer experience management: Toward implementing an evolving marketing concept. *Journal of the Academy of Marketing Science*, *45*, 377-401.

Keiningham, T., Aksoy, L., Bruce, H. L., Cadet, F., Clennell, N., Hodgkinson, I. R., & Kearney, T. (2020). Customer experience driven business model innovation. *Journal of Business Research*, *116*, 431-440.

Keller, K. O., Geyskens, I., & Dekimpe, M. G. (2020). Opening the umbrella: The effects of rebranding multiple category-specific private-label brands to one umbrella brand. *Journal of Marketing Research*, *57*, 677-694.

Kolb, D. A. (1984). *Experiential learning: experience as the source of learning and development.* New Jersey: Prentice Hall.

Lemon, K. N., & Verhoef, P. C. (2016). Understanding customer experience throughout the customer journey. *Journal of Marketing*, *80*, 69-96.

McQuilken, L., Robertson, N., Polonsky, M., & Harrison, P. (2015). Consumer perceptions of bundles and time-limited promotion deals: Do contracts matter?. *Journal of Consumer Behaviour*, *14*, 145-157.

Nitzan, I., & Ein-Gar, D. (2019). The "commitment projection" effect: when multiple payments for a product affect defection from a service. *Journal of Marketing Research*, *56*, 842-861.

Ou, Y. C., Verhoef, P. C., & Wiesel, T. (2017). The effects of customer equity drivers on loyalty across services industries and firms. *Journal of the Academy of Marketing Science*, *45*, 336- 356.

Polo, Y., & Sese, F. J. (2013). Strengthening customer relationships: what factors influence customers to migrate to contracts?. *Journal of Service Research*, *16*, 138-154.

The Effect of Genetic Predispositions on Salespeople's Canvassing and Closing: An Abstract

Christian Winter, Nicolas Zacharias, Ad de Jong, and Johannes Habel

Abstract The beginning and the end of the sales cycle, canvassing (i.e., approaching new customers) and closing (i.e., the process of trying to sign and finalize a deal), represent key moments of potential rejection. While these moments can induce significant stress and are prone to avoidance and procrastination (Bagozzi and Verbeke 2020; DeCarlo and Lam 2016; Ingram et al. 2017), they are crucial for a salesperson's success (DeCarlo and Lam 2016; Sabnis et al. 2013). Some salespeople react with procrastination while others dive headfirst into these challenges (e.g., Bolander et al. 2020; DeCarlo and Lam 2016).

This study explores whether these different reactions relate to genetic predispositions. Drawing on differential susceptibility theory (DST) (e.g., Belsky and Pluess 2009; Homberg and Jagiellowicz 2021) and stress research (e.g., Nelson and Cooper 2007), our study proposes that carrying the Serotonin Transporter Gene S allele (SERT S) together with the psychological traits of sensation seeking and neuroticism interactively affects a salesperson's propensity to canvass and close. Based on a rich sample of genetic information and survey data from 597 salespeople, the empirical results show that carrying SERT S has a positive relationship with canvassing and closing if sensation seeking is high. In contrast, this relationship is negative if neuroticism is high.

The findings of the study contribute to sales research, DST, and organizational stress research, and provide actionable implications for business practice. First, we contribute to the sparse literature explaining the genetic roots of variation in salesperson behavior (e.g., Verbeke et al. 2017) by showing how genetic variations interact with psychological traits to influence sales behavior. Second, we introduce a

C. Winter (✉) · N. Zacharias
Martin Luther University Halle-Wittenberg, Halle (Saale), Germany
e-mail: christian.winter@wiwi.uni-halle.de; nicolas.zacharias@wiwi.uni-halle.de

A. de Jong
Copenhagen Business School, Frederiksberg, Denmark
e-mail: adj.marktg@cbs.dk

J. Habel
University of Houston, Houston, TX, USA
e-mail: jhabel@bauer.uh.edu

J. Allen et al. (eds.), *Celebrating the Past and Future of Marketing and Discovery with Social Impact*, Developments in Marketing Science: Proceedings of the Academy of Marketing Science, https://doi.org/10.1007/978-3-030-95346-1_87

DST perspective to marketing and sales research, showing that the same genetic variation can have diametrical effects on performance-related behavior. Third, we add to DST and organizational stress research by providing a new angle on the occurrence of eustress and distress at the workplace.

Keywords Genes · Sales · Neuroticism · Sensation seeking · Serotonin transporter gene (SERT) · Differential susceptibility theory · Eustress · Distress

Challenging Vulnerability Perceptions towards Voice Activated Assistants: An Abstract

Valentina Pitardi and Hannah R. Marriott

Abstract Artificial Intelligence (AI) refers to the ability of technology to acquire and apply knowledge and skills to a variety of settings. Intelligence is often likened to emotion, logic, reason, critique, creativity and ability to learn and/or problem-solve. Although these forms of intelligence are usually only perceived to be capable by humans, technology has advanced it applications and usage in being able to replicate these forms of intelligence for different purposes. For example, Amazon Alexa is perceived as being able to problem-solve through creative, logical and, occasionally, emotional, means. As such, AI agents can adopt different types of conversational styles when interact with users resulting in conversations characterised by a more social-oriented or task-oriented approach (Chattaraman et al. 2018). Although these capabilities are far beyond what technology has previously been capable of, AI is inherently limited surrounding its ability to plan, reason, move and empathise, thus leading to an apparent lack of user trust in their capabilities (PwC 2018). Accordingly, users are often reluctant to engage with AI due to negative perceptions surrounding the ability to perform tasks.

Alongside these perceived limitations of AI, users are often concerned over what happens once they have chosen to use it. Users are aware that Alexa is "always listening" and is capable of collecting vast amounts of consumer data, thus resulting in heightened privacy perceptions (PwC 2018). In this sense, vulnerability appears to be prevalent at both the pre-adoption and post-adoption of AI. Previous studies have observed that technology has the capabilities of increasing consumer vulnerability, which in turn hinders usage and adoption (Bucchia et al. 2020; Elms and Tinson 2012; Ratchford and Barnhart 2012). Yet, consumers vulnerability in interactions with AI conversational agents remains underexplored. Most importantly, the factors that can prevent individuals perception of vulnerability and then facilitate continuous usage are unknown.

V. Pitardi (✉)
University of Portsmouth, Portsmouth, UK
e-mail: valentina.pitardi@port.ac.uk

H. R. Marriott
Cardiff Metropolitan University, Cardiff, UK
e-mail: hmarriott@cardiffmet.ac.uk

J. Allen et al. (eds.), *Celebrating the Past and Future of Marketing and Discovery with Social Impact*, Developments in Marketing Science: Proceedings of the Academy of Marketing Science, https://doi.org/10.1007/978-3-030-95346-1_88

By focusing on voice-activated assistants (VAs), this study wants to fill this gap and it aims to investigate how interaction with VAs can foster consumers trust and usage based on the AI conversational style. Specifically, we expect that VAs social-oriented conversations will increase consumers trust and usage. In addition, we suggest that this process will be mediated by the consumers perception of vulnerability such that when the VAs conversational style is social-oriented, consumer will feel less vulnerable and thus more willing to trust and use the AI agent. Finally, we propose that individuals' locus of control will moderate such effect.

The study employs a mixed-method approach. Preliminary findings from the qualitative analysis offer a broad picture of how perceptions of vulnerability and trust are elicited in interactions with VAs. Further, the importance of the social nature of conversation and perceptions of vulnerability is clearly shown in this study.

Keywords Artificial intelligence · Voice based assistants · Consumer vulnerability · Trust

Will Robots Judge Me? Examining Consumer-Service Robots Interactions in Embarrassing Service Encounters: An Abstract

Valentina Pitardi, Jochen Wirtz, Stefanie Paluch, and Werner Kunz

Abstract Service robots are gradually replacing humans service providers in numerous industries and their development is profoundly impacting the way in which service is delivered (Bornet et al. 2021; Wirtz et al. 2018). Accordingly, service robots encounters represent a primary research area in service. To date, researcher and practitioners have applied service robot across various contexts such as medical (Yoon and Lee 2019), hospitality (Tung and Au 2018) and tourism (Murphy et al. 2019), and have focused on the general application and acceptance of the technology (Huang and Rust 2017; van Doorn et al. 2016; Wirtz et al. 2018) and on services that may be executed by or improved by such technologies (Paluch and Blut 2013; Jörling, Bohm, and Paluch 2019). In addition, few studies have analysed service robot interactions in the service and consumer behaviour fields (Longoni et al. 2019), mainly focusing on the consumers' reactions to specific service robot characteristics such as the level of human-likeness (Castelo et al. 2019; Kim et al. 2019; Mende et al. 2019).

These approaches usually try to determine general principles of the service robot delivery, yet not much attention has been given to the particular boundary condition of the service delivery context under which human-robots encounters might be more beneficial than traditional human-to-human encounters. A typical consumption set-

V. Pitardi (✉)
University of Portsmouth, Portsmouth, UK
e-mail: valentina.pitardi@port.ac.uk

J. Wirtz
National University of Singapore, Queenstown, Singapore
e-mail: jochen@nus.edu.sg

S. Paluch
RWTH Aachen University, Aachen, Germany
e-mail: paluch@time.rwth-aachen.de

W. Kunz
University of Massachusetts, Boston, MA, USA
e-mail: werner.kunz@umb.edu

J. Allen et al. (eds.), *Celebrating the Past and Future of Marketing and Discovery with Social Impact*, Developments in Marketing Science: Proceedings of the Academy of Marketing Science, https://doi.org/10.1007/978-3-030-95346-1_89

ting where the presence of other individuals can damage the general consumers' experience is embarrassing service encounters. Consumer embarrassment is a widespread social emotion induced when a transgression is witnessed or perceived to be witnessed by others (Krishna et al. 2019). For embarrassment to be elicited, individuals have to be concerned for what others are perceiving or thinking about them (Dahl et al. 2001), thus embarrassment is dependent on the presence of others.

In this study, we suggest that interactions with a service robots in the context of a potentially embarrassing service encounter may reduce consumer embarrassment. We posit that this occurs because of the global attribution of mind to the robots such that consumers do not ascribe intentionality, cognition, and emotion to a service robot, thus ability to socially evaluate one's purchase or behaviour (Gray et al. 2007). Moreover, we propose to investigate the impact of service robot human-likeness on consumer embarrassment (Mende et al. 2019).

The study employs a mixed-method approach. Preliminary findings from the qualitative analysis identifies perceptions of mind and human-likeness appearance as potential factors influencing feelings of embarrassment. Further, findings from a first experimental study show that, in embarrassment service encounters, interaction with service robots decrease feelings of individuals' consumer embarrassment. Theoretical and managerial contributions are discussed.

Keywords Service robots · Consumer embarrassment · Mind attribution · Artificial intelligence

Analyzing the Powerful Impact of Touchpoints in a B2B Context: An Abstract

Lily Xuehui Gao, Iguácel Melero-Polo, Miguel Á. Ruz-Mendoza, and Andreea Trifu

Abstract The purpose of this study is to shed more light on service touchpoints in a business-to-business environment, a relevant topic in the marketing literature. Since the vast majority of the work in this area has focused on B2C service touchpoints, this study represents a starting point for research in B2B settings. To date, little is known about the topic and the current state of the literature lacks a clear representation of the B2B service touchpoints and their role in determining essential customer perceptions and outcomes over time. Specifically, this paper proposes a chain of effects path, taking into consideration provider touchpoints, customer perceptions and customer outcomes.

A panel dataset is used to test the proposed framework. Data is obtained from B2B insurance services and contains a sample of more than 2,000 companies from 2013 to 2017. The results of the study confirm there are specific touchpoints that positively influence customer's perception with the provider and the service, which in turn have a positive effect on profitability, cross-buy and relationship strength. Study results demonstrate the importance of the sales force in B2B relationships, along with the relevance of firm expertise, service excellence and service reliability as drivers of profitability, cross-buy and relationship strength.

The authors appreciate the financial support received from the projects ECO2017-83993-P (MICINN, FEDER), SS54_17R (Gobierno de Aragón and Fondo Social Europeo), and the grant "Ayuda para contratos predoctorales para la formación de doctores, del Ministerio de Ciencia, Innovación y Universidades" (PRE2018-085652) assigned to Andreea Trifu.

L. X. Gao · I. Melero-Polo · A. Trifu (✉)
University of Zaragoza, Zaragoza, Spain
e-mail: lilygao@unizar.es; imelero@unizar.es; atrifu@unizar.es

M. Á. Ruz-Mendoza
University Pablo de Olavide, Seville, Spain
e-mail: maruzmen@upo.es

J. Allen et al. (eds.), *Celebrating the Past and Future of Marketing and Discovery with Social Impact*, Developments in Marketing Science: Proceedings of the Academy of Marketing Science, https://doi.org/10.1007/978-3-030-95346-1_90

This paper provides empirical evidence on the role of touchpoints and customer perceptions on determining customer outcomes over time. Given its longitudinal approach, this investigation provides strong empirical evidence of the influence of touchpoints and customer perceptions on the outcomes of the interactions from one period of time to another. This is a vital issue for marketers, as firms gain a better understanding of company-customer interactions and the extent to which different factors impact decisive customer outcomes in a B2B context. As a result, these findings help broaden the narrow understanding the literature has about the topic and provide valuable implications for practitioners for a better allocation of resource when designing service touchpoints.

Keywords Service touchpoints · Customer perceptions · Profitability · Cross-buy · Relationship strength · Insurance services

Exercise Behavior in the Context of Covid 19 Pandemic: An Abstract

Asli Elif Aydin

Abstract The Covid-19 related restrictions have severe effects on individuals' ability to perform physical activities. As a result of the isolation measures, people stayed at home and could not sustain an active lifestyle. However, maintaining physical activity is even more critical during the pandemic considering its positive impact on mental well-being and its impact on general health (Dwyer et al. 2020; Matias et al. 2020; Teferi 2020). Given the importance of adherence to physical activity during the pandemic, understanding factors that influence exercise behavior is valuable.

The objective of the study is to test a model of leisure-time exercise behavior that integrates participatory and regulatory motives in the context of Covid-19 pandemic conditions. It is suggested that physical participation motives, which relate to physical goals individuals try to achieve with exercise, influence regulatory motives, which relate to exercise behavior's underlying reasons (Ingledew and Markland 2008). The effects of isolation, positive and negative affect, amount of stress, and ability to handle stress on exercise participation motives and exercise behavior are also examined.

An online survey is employed to gather data from 283 university students. The data is analyzed using structural equation modeling. The study results demonstrate that physical and psychological exercise participation motives are significantly associated with exercise behavior. Concerning the behavioral regulation constructs, it is revealed that intrinsic and introjected regulation predict exercise behavior. Additionally, while isolation and negative affect have a negative impact, coping with stress positively impacts exercise behavior. Moreover, it is shown that the indirect effects of participatory motives on exercise behavior are mediated by amotivation and intrinsic regulation. Finally, significant mediating effects of exercise participation motives are shown linking positive and negative affect, ability to cope with stress, and exercise behavior.

A. E. Aydin (✉)
Istanbul Bilgi University, Istanbul, Turkey
e-mail: aslielif.aydin@bilgi.edu.tr

J. Allen et al. (eds.), *Celebrating the Past and Future of Marketing and Discovery with Social Impact*, Developments in Marketing Science: Proceedings of the Academy of Marketing Science, https://doi.org/10.1007/978-3-030-95346-1_91

The findings of the study provide practical implications for exercise promotion and intervention programs. For instance, since isolation and negative affect reduce exercise behavior, designing in-home physical activity routines, providing counseling for people, and teaching them stress reduction techniques such as meditation and breathing are recommended. Furthermore, it is suggested that emphasizing the fun aspect of exercise and avoidance of guilt may improve the persuasiveness of exercise promotion campaigns.

Keywords Exercise behavior · Motives · Isolation · Covid 19

Toward a Better Understanding of C2C Misbehavior: Typology and Thresholds: An Abstract

Annelie Wustlich, Jana Möller, and Ilias Danatzis

Abstract Fueled by technological advances and the rise of the collaborative economy, service encounters today are increasingly characterized by a high degree of customer-to-customer (C2C) interactions. C2C interactions are crucial to customers' overall perception of service quality as they may positively or negatively influence their satisfaction. However, C2C interactions are oftentimes outside the direct control of the service provider. In such service settings customer misbehaviors targeted at other customers (C2C misbehavior) is particularly problematic, not only because it is contagious, but also because it can potentially damage the service provider, frontline employees, and other bystanding customers.

Prior definitions and typologies primarily focus on general customer misbehavior and do not take sufficient account of the particularities of C2C misbehavior such as customers' perceived severity of the experienced incivility of other customers and their expectations towards the service provider to intervene or prevent such behavior. In contrast to previous customer misbehavior typologies, this study aims at providing a typology specifically geared towards customer misbehavior that is directed at other customers or their property. It represents the first attempt in service literature to define C2C misbehavior from a norm-based perspective while emphasizing the importance of how norm deviances are interpreted by those customers who – directly or indirectly – have become the target of other customers' misbehavior. We further demarcate C2C misbehavior from related concepts and systematically delineate different types of C2C misbehavior in relation to their perceived severity. Drawing on over 25 in-depth interviews, we use the repertory grid technique and employ comparative questioning to derive constructs that underpin customers' complex perceptions of C2C misbehavior severity across various service settings. Based on these constructs, we aim to provide a comprehensive typology of C2C misbehavior according to its perceived severity that is applicable across ser-

A. Wustlich (✉) · J. Möller
Freie Universität Berlin, Berlin, Germany
e-mail: annelie.wustlich@fu-berlin.de; jana.moeller@fu-berlin.de

I. Danatzis
King's College London, London, UK
e-mail: ilias.danatzis@kcl.ac.uk

J. Allen et al. (eds.), *Celebrating the Past and Future of Marketing and Discovery with Social Impact*, Developments in Marketing Science: Proceedings of the Academy of Marketing Science, https://doi.org/10.1007/978-3-030-95346-1_92

vice contexts. Thus, we provide the necessary theoretical scaffolding for further empirical research and theory development in this domain. We further explore what constitutes customers' individual thresholds that mark the line between perceived tolerable vs. intolerable C2C misbehavior or when customers expect the service provider to intervene.

Managerially, our typology will allow service providers to better categorize C2C misbehavior according to its severity. This differentiation is critical as it will support service providers in designing more targeted prevention and intervention measures, thus helping to reduce the occurrence and the spread of C2C misbehavior in service settings.

Keywords Customer-to-customer misbehavior · Customer-to-customer interactions · Service experience · Social norm deviance

The Performance of Digital Ecosystem: The Moderating Effects of Internationalization Stage: An Abstract

Qijing Li, Ye Zheng, and Ge Zhan

Abstract According to Gartner's forecast in January 2020, global IT spending will reach $3.9 trillion in 2020, an increase of 3.4% over 2019. It is estimated that global IT spending will exceed $4 trillion in 2021. This trend signals the tendency of building digital ecosystem globally. An emerging trend among multinational firms is to digitalize global operation and build digital ecosystem. E-commerce platform, as a digital platform for coordination among sellers, online payment providers, logistics providers and customer relations personnel, emerges as an efficient channel to build a digital ecosystem (Senyo et al. 2019). The use of e-commerce platform in the development of an ecosystem can enhance the diversity and innovation of complements in the platform (Gawer and Cusumano 2014; Song et al. 2018).

With the progress of technology, digitization improves the overall effectiveness of resource integration, thus promoting the construction of enterprise ecosystem (Sklyar et al. 2019). The digital platform has become an effective interface to facilitate multilateral transactions and exchanges between users and providers of complementary products and services. The internationalization of a digital platform depends largely on whether the platform can attract ecosystem participants in the local market and align their goals with those of the platform (Ojala et al. 2018).

By investigating digital-platform firms listed in U.S. stock market, we challenge the doctrine thinking in international marketing that firms have a better chance to make good financial performance when expanding to more foreign markets over time. Annual-report data were collected by visiting the corporate websites of Chinese tourism firms listed in U.S. stock market. Firm performance (return on equity) data were drawn from the annual reports. A text-analytics approach was used in data processing and analysis. We collected annual report data which were processed with Python to compile a database with approximately 30,000 sentences. The findings indicate that digital-platform firms gain better performance in early stage internationalization. Managers when building digital ecosystem should be aware the potential challenges in their later stage internationalization

Q. Li · Y. Zheng · G. Zhan (✉)
BNU-HKBU United International College, Zhuhai, China
e-mail: m730006075@mail.uic.edu.cn; m730006223@mail.uic.edu.cn; garygezhan@uic.edu.cn

J. Allen et al. (eds.), *Celebrating the Past and Future of Marketing and Discovery with Social Impact*, Developments in Marketing Science: Proceedings of the Academy of Marketing Science, https://doi.org/10.1007/978-3-030-95346-1_93

Keywords Digital ecosystem · International marketing · Text analysis · Firm performance

Why Do Customers Disengage in a Digital-Mediated Informal Learning Environment? A Motivation Perspective: An Abstract

Chu-Heng Lee, Shu-Yi Chen, and Ming-Huei Hsieh

Abstract Engaged customers positively influence a firm's performance and co-create value with a firm through contributing operant resources. How a firm can effectively prolong customer engagement (CE) for generating operant resources remains challenging. To identify essential drivers for enhancing customers' continuous engagement in digital environment, this study shifts the research focus on understanding motivational mechanism of customer disengagement (CDE). This study leverages self-determination theory to examine the linkage between ineffective customer resource integration and CDE in self-directed informal learning, a highly customer-controlled context.

The definitions of engagement can be divided into psychological and behavioral manifestations towards focal offerings (e.g., a brand, a firm). Although the fact that CE is driven by customer's motivation has been taken for granted, there remain major debates about the antecedents of CE. Customer resource integration of operant and/or operand resources is treated as the required CE antecedent which is necessary during customer knowledge sharing and customer learning. However, Hibbert and her colleagues (2012) broadened the understanding of a customer's proactive role as a self-directed learner that customer learning facilitates resource integration process. To solve the puzzle about CE essential antecedent of continuous engagement, this research tried to answer two research questions: How do customers' initial motivations affect disengaged behavior consequences, given that the CE state is a continuous spectrum ranging from nonengaged to highly engaged? How do we reframe the understanding of customers' motivational states to foster resource integration toward focal offerings?

C.-H. Lee · M.-H. Hsieh
National Taiwan University, Taipei City, Taiwan
e-mail: d00724007@ntu.edu.tw; minghsieh@ntu.edu.tw

S.-Y. Chen (✉)
Ming Chuan University, Taoyuan City, Taiwan
e-mail: maxchen@mail.mcu.edu.tw

J. Allen et al. (eds.), *Celebrating the Past and Future of Marketing and Discovery with Social Impact*, Developments in Marketing Science: Proceedings of the Academy of Marketing Science, https://doi.org/10.1007/978-3-030-95346-1_94

With in-depth interview data collected from ten self-directed informal learners and based on the degree of incompletion in internalizing the value of digital-mediated activity, three motivational forms of disengagement were identified: amotivation, extrinsic regulatory failure, and intrinsic conflict. The research reveals the underlined mechanism of how initial motivation to perform the embedded task determines the intention of learners' operant resource integration toward adapting digital-mediated learning. The disengagement from a focal offering results from insufficient supports of learners' autonomy and competence linking with the task originated in focal offering and with the activity to which the focal offering contributes. This analysis foregrounds to contribute theoretical implications of customer engagement process as well as practical guidance for supporting customer resource integration of continuous engagement.

Keywords Customer disengagement · Resource integration · Self-determination theory · Informal learning

Pandemic Impulse Buying Behavior: Exploring the Antecedents of Impulsive Buying Across Product Categories During COVID-19 in the US

Pei Wang and Sindy Chapa

Abstract In 2020, online purchases have increasingly become a coping mechanism for those affected by the COVID-19 pandemic. This study explores the antecedents of impulsive behavior and investigates the kind of products that are bought in response to the pandemic. First, the study aims at understanding the role retail websites, as online marketing stimuli, play on impulsive buying. Likewise, the relationships that product involvement, perceived usefulness, perceived enjoyment, and hedonic values have on consumers' impulsive behavior are investigated. Finally, the types of product bought are identified. An online survey was conducted using a convenience sample of college students. Overall, the study presents a nested model identifying the direct effect of hedonic values on the urge to purchase a product. Participants indicated personal care, followed by sports equipment, were significantly more likely to be purchased because of the pandemic than any category. Yet, those who believe they engaged in the online purchase because of the pandemic cues were more likely to purchase all kinds of product categories, including products for group and products for individual consumption.

Keywords COVID-19 · Consumer behavior · Impulsive buying · Product categories

Introduction

Epidemics and pandemics are the most pressing public health challenges in the world (Bonneux and Van Damme 2006), especially in the case of COVID-19. Many reports indicate online shopping behaviors has increased all over the world. In South

P. Wang (✉) · S. Chapa
Florida State University, Tallahassee, FL, USA
e-mail: pw19a@my.fsu.edu; sindy.chapa@cci.fsu.edu

J. Allen et al. (eds.), *Celebrating the Past and Future of Marketing and Discovery with Social Impact*, Developments in Marketing Science: Proceedings of the Academy of Marketing Science, https://doi.org/10.1007/978-3-030-95346-1_95

Korea, 60.7 percent of consumers made digital purchases while 39.3 purchased offline in response to COVID-19 (eMarketer 2020). Another report has shown that the share of e-commerce in total US retail increased to 16.4% in Q2 of 2020, from just 12.1% the previous quarter (eMarketer 2020). E-commerce sales in the US rose from 12% in February 2020 to 14.5% in May 2020 (eMarketer 2020). This in mind, it is time to consider the online shopping behaviors of consumers in the context of the pandemic.

Previous research on consumer behavior during crisis moments (i.e., Ebola) investigated psychological factors (i.e., attitudes, norms, abilities, and self-regulation, etc.) that were the essential impacts of emotional arousal among consumer decision-making process (Gamma et al. 2020). Li et al. (2020) examined the severity of a pandemic has a directly positive impact to impulsive consumptions, this during the COVID-19 pandemic. Laato et al. (2020) and Islam et al. (2020) stated the external stimuli, such as information sources, product shortages, and time scarcity, have played major roles in influencing unusual consumer behavior during the COVID-19 pandemic. However, little research has examined the impact of marketing stimuli, such as task relevant cues and product involvement, on consumer behaviors during public health emergencies.

The purpose of this study is to investigate the antecedents of impulsive purchase behavior, while exploring the product categories most likely to be consumed as a result of the COVID-19 pandemic. Previous marketing researchers demonstrated the predictive power of S-O-R in online environments (Adelaar et al. 2003; Eroglu et al. 2001; Floh et al. 2013; Khalifa and Shen 2007; Parboteeah et al. 2009). Based on fundamental stimuli-organism-response (S-O-R) framework, a model is proposed to understand consumers' impulsive shopping behavior. Therefore, this study aims at exploring the impact online marketing stimuli play on website appearance, ease of navigation, and product involvement. The study compares to the extent that these variables affect a consumer's reaction, such as in the factors of perceived usefulness, perceived enjoyment and hedonic values. Furthermore, the study investigates relationships between variables and consumers' urge to buy products online, and finally, by compares the effect of the pandemic on the most purchased product categories of 2020.

Theoretical Framework and Hypotheses Development

Responses to Pandemic Cues

Research on pandemics focus on preventive health behaviors, not consumer behaviors (Laato et al. 2020). Yet, the unique and unexpected situation of the COVID-19 pandemic demands a careful examination on how communication tools affect consumer impulsive behaviors. In the communication context, a cue is a signal or a sign given to the audience or consumers. Laato et al. (2020) documented an unusual purchasing behavior occurring globally in March 2020, concluding it a result of quarantine preparations. These preparations were the pandemic cue sent to consumers. If a consumer engages in an activity because of the pandemic, it can be considered a result of receiving a pandemic cue. According to the S-O-R model (Parboteeah et al. 2016), there are relevant cues (high and low) representing the marketing stimuli. In the context of the global outbreak, the perceived pandemic cue represents an essential predictor that can lead consumers to cognitive and affective reactions. Therefore, the pandemic cues are included in the conceptual model.

The literature on online shopping behaviors identifies key indicators affecting consumer decision, including perceived usefulness, perceived enjoyment and perceived ease of use (Adams et al. 1992; Davis et al.1989; Ramayah and Ignatius 2005). The theory of acceptance model (TAM) has also supported the assertion that these indicators are key predictors of a consumer's intention to behave (Amoako-Gyampah and Salam 2004). Likewise, hedonic valuehas been found to be key a determinant explaining impulsiveness regarding online purchase behavior (Chung et al. 2017; Ramanathan et al. 2006). In the proposed research model (Fig. 1), pandemic cues act as stimuli to test relationships with perceived usefulness, perceived enjoyment, and hedonic shopping value. Therefore, based on the S-O-R model, TAM theory and previous premises, the following hypothesis is proposed:

H1: Pandemic cues (PC) will have a significant effect on (a) perceived usefulness (PU), (b) perceived enjoyment (PE), and (c) hedonic shopping value (HSV).

Online Communication Stimuli: Easy to Use and Website Appearance

According to the Eroglu et al. (2001), the effect of website characteristics on a consumer's impulsive purchase behavior can also serve as elements of stimuli that lead to cognitive and affective reactions. Based on the S-O-R model, the high

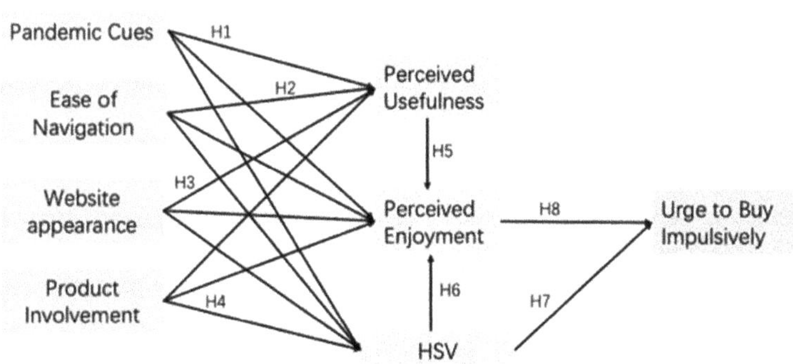

Fig. 1 Conceptual model

task-relevant cues, exist in the utilitarian aspects of the website, including ease of navigation, website security, and download delay (Bauer et al. 2002; Palmer 2002; Zhang and Von Dran 2001–2002). One of the low task relevant cues identified in the literature is website appearance, which includes colors, music, and font (Eroglu et al. 2001; Van der Heijden et al. 2003). This model chose ease of navigation to represent high-task relevant cues and website appearance to represent low-task relevant cues. Both variables have been found to have a positive influence on usefulness and the hedonic aspects of impulse buying (Parboteeah et al. 2016). Thus, the following hypothesis is proposed:

H2: Ease of navigation (EV) will positively affect (a) perceived usefulness (PU), (b) perceived enjoyment (PE) and (c) hedonic shopping value (HSV).

H3: Website appearance (WA) will positively affect (a) perceived usefulness (PU) and (b) perceived enjoyment (PE) (c) hedonic shopping value (HSV).

Product Involvement

Product involvement is typically defined as a consumer's enduring perceptions of a product based on their inherent needs, values, and interests (Mittal 1995; Zaichkowsky 1985). Product involvement had been used as one of several explanatory variables in consumer behavioral studies (Dholakia 1998). In the consumer decision making process, product involvement has been found to be an essential factor leading to both planned and impulsive purchases (Charters and Pettigrew 2006; Cox 2009; Parboteeah et al. 2016; Rahman and Reynolds 2015). The level of product involvement can be cognitive or affective during the consumer choice process (e.g. Chakravarti and Janiszewski 2003; Kleiser and Wagner 1999; Kokkinaki 1999). Thus, in line with the work by Parboteeah et al. (2016), the following hypothesis is proposed:

H4: Product involvement (PI) will positively affect (a) perceived usefulness (PU), (b) perceived enjoyment (PE), and (c) hedonic shopping value (HSV).

Perceived Enjoyment and Perceived Usefulness

Extensive studies have concentrated on the interplay between cognition and affect (Holbrook and Batra 1987; Shiv and Fedorikhin 1999). Holbrook and Batra (1987) stated that cognition influences affect, and then ultimately determines behavior. In integrated marketing, this definition can be used on consumer behavioral studies, such as on impulsive buying behavior. Parboteeah et al. (2009) concluded that there should be an interaction between perceived usefulness and perceived enjoyment to certain stimuli. They propose this relationship should be positive, which will increase the enjoyment factor of online impulse buying. Thus, the following hypothesis is proposed:

H5: Perceived usefulness (PU) will positively affect perceived enjoyment (PE).

Hedonic Shopping Value

Hedonic shopping value (HSV) is an experiential, emotional, and irrational value. Consumers who seek hedonic shopping value see shopping as a positive emotional experience (Babin et al. 1994). Kim and Eastin (2011) stated HSV is more effective than utilitarian shopping value because the former is linked to pleasure and entertainment. Shukla and Babin (2013) discussed consumers who are more likely to purchase in a new system often shop for fun. It is the same in online shopping environments, where there are no time and location limitations, resulting in consumers being more likely to make unplanned purchases, such as impulsive buying (LaRose 2001). Thus, it is proposed HSV will significantly affect perceived enjoyment.

H6: Hedonic shopping values (HSV) will have a significant effect on perceived enjoyment (PE).

Urge to Buy Impulsively

According to S-O-R framework, an individual's emotional response to the environment will determine their behavior (Mehrabian and Russell 1974). In other words, a consumer will change his or her decision when they receive affective reactions. The extant literature on impulse buying indicates hedonic shopping value has a direct effect on consumer impulse buying behaviors (Kukar-Kinney et al. 2015). Affective reactions have been stated to positively affect the urge to buy impulsively; this relationship was replicated in traditional shopping contexts (Beatty and Ferrell 1998), as well as in online impulse buying (Adelaar et al. 2003; Parboteeah et al. 2009; Parboteeah et al. 2016). Thus, based on previous premises, the following hypothesis are proposed:

H7: Hedonic Shopping Values (HSV) will positively affect the urge to buy impulsively.
H8: Perceived enjoyment (PE) will positively affect the urge to buy impulsively.

Product Categories

There literature indicates consumers evaluate product by category (i.e., Bearden and Etzel 1982; Chapa et al. 2006; Fetscherin et al. 2014). There are numerous consumer reports addressing the most popular products purchased during the pandemic, yet a lack of empirical research exists in relation to the products consumed. Therefore, the following research questions are presented:

RQ1: What product categories are purchased in 2020 because of the pandemic?
RQ2: How does the product categories variation differ because of the pandemic cues?

Research Design and Methodology

This was a multi-stage, multimethod study. First, a focus group was conducted to identify the item selection for the "pandemic cues" measure and for the product categories selection. At this stage, group of 10 college students participated in the item identification. Then, an online survey was designed test the conceptual model using a sample of college students in the State of Florida. A total sample of 220 was collected from July to September of 2020. After cleaning the data, a total of 208 comprises the total sample of this study. The sample was 78 percent female; and 66 percent were between 18 and 20 years, 30 percent between 21 and 25 years, and 4 percent older than 25 years.

Measurements

Except for the measure of the pandemic cue, which was created for this study, seven already developed and validated scales were adapted to measure the variables in the model. Taylor et al.'s (2010) task-relevant cues scale was used to measure the perceived ease of navigation and appearance of the website. The hedonic shopping value (HSV) was measured using a 7-item scale adapted from Babin et al. (1994) and Griffin et al. (2000). Product involvement was measured using the Zaichkowsky's (1994) scale. Perceived usefulness was measured by adapting the 4-item scale from Davis, et al. (1989). Perceived enjoyment was measured by using a 3-item scale adapted by Chang and Cheung (2001). A 3-item scale measuring purchase impulsivity was adapted from Rook and Fisher (1995). A scale to measure the presence of the pandemic cue on consumers' purchases was created for this study; a 3-item construct using a 7-point Likert scale (1 for strong agree, 7 for strong disagree) was developed and tested. Finally, the demographics questions were included as well. Items are listed in Table 1.

Validation of the Measures

To validate the measure for the pandemic cue scale, an exploratory factor analysis (EFA) was conducted across measures. The purpose was to identify the items as unidimensional measures, testing for convergence and discriminant validity. The convergent validity of the data was tested using the Fornell and Larcker (1981) criteria. Next, due to low loadings and cross-loadings, items were removed as followings: five items from the scale of product involvement, one item from the scale of website appearance, two items from HSV scale. Last, to test reliability, Cronbach's alphas were used for each construct. The results revealed reliability levels were above the recommended 0.7 (Nunnally and Bernstein 1994). The results in Table 1 show all items meet this criterion. Finally, the average variance extracted (AVE) by each variable was confirmed. All variables satisfied the criteria of 0.50. It demonstrated that a construct shares more variance with its indicators than with error variances (Fornell and Larker 1981) (see Table 2).

Hypotheses Testing

In order to test the conceptual model and hypotheses, structural equation modeling (SEM) was ran in AMOS. Following the suggestions from Hu and Bentler (1999) and Steenkamp and Baumgartner (1998): $\chi2/\text{df} \leq 3.0$, comparative fit indices (CFI), goodness of fit index (GFI) and Tucker-Lewis index (TLI) ≥ 0.90, and root mean square error of approximation (RMSEA) ≤ 0.80. These values indicate a good fit. However, the theoretical model fit indexes did not reach recommended levels: $\chi2/\text{df} = 12.709$, CFI = 0.744, GFI = 0.853, TLI = 0.403, RMR = 0.177 and RMSEA = 0.238. Therefore, an alternative model was explored and tested using the modification index. All of the values meet the recommendation criteria: $\chi2/\text{df} = 1.291$, CFI = 0.992, GFI = 0.977, TLI = 0.985, RMR = 0.082 and RMSEA = 0.037.

The alternative model proposes new relationships between website appearance, ease to navigation, and product involvement. The results indicate ten hypotheses are accepted (H1a, H1c, H2b, H3c, H4a, H4b, H4c, H5, H6, H7). The model rejects six relationships: pandemic cues to perceived enjoyment (H1b), ease of navigation to perceived usefulness (H2a) and HSV (H2c), website appearance to perceived usefulness (H3a) and perceived enjoyment (H3b), and perceived enjoyment to urge to buy impulsively (H8) in which coefficient paths were not significant. The results are shown in Fig. 2.

During the qualitative stage of this investigation thirteen product categories were identified as being purchased during the pandemic: books, electronic, personal care, videogames and consoles, home tools and hard ware, pet related items, CDs and DVDs, phone and tablets accessories, home appliances, kitchen tools, home gardens, clothing, and sports equipment. In order to answer the questions about relationship between product category and the pandemic cue, a correlation was run

Table 1 Standardized loadings and reliability coefficients for each construct

Item	Item loading	Cronbach's α
Factor 1: Pandemia cues (self-developed)	0.93	0.83
I bought the product(s) listed above because of the COVID-19 pandemic	0.93	
I bought the product(s) listed above primarily because of the COVID-19	0.72	
pandemic		
I would not have bought the product(s) listed above if it was not for the		
COVID-19 pandemic		
Factor 2: Ease of navigation (adapted Taylor et al., 2010)	0.83	0.93
Navigating these web pages where I purchased the item mentioned above	0.89	0.92
was easy for me	0.89	
I found that my interaction with the website where I purchased the item	0.89	
was clear and understandable	0.82	
It is easy for me to become skillful at navigating the pages of this	0.83	
website where I purchased the item	0.87	
Overall, I find the pages where I purchased the item easy to navigate	0.88	
It was pleasant to follow the overall flow of the website where I	0.90	
purchased the item	0.76	
It is pleasant to follow and use the menu structure of the site where I	0.83	
purchased the item	0.81	
Factor 3: Website appearance (adapted Taylor et al., 2010)		
The shopping site where I purchased the item was visually pleasing		
The shopping site where I purchased the item displayed visually pleasing		
design		
The shopping site where I purchased the item was visually appealing		
The images and typographies used in the shopping sites where I		
purchased the item were stylish		
The overall atmosphere and screen displays of the shopping sites where I		
purchased the item were well coordinated		
It was pleasant to see the provided information on each screen of the		
shopping site where I purchased the item		
Factor 4: Hedonic shopping value (adapted Babin et al., 1994; Griffin	0.81	0.87
et al., 2000)	0.86	
This online shopping experience was truly a joy during this hard time	0.80	
Compared to other things I could have done, the time spent online	0.87	
shopping was truly enjoyable	0.77	
I enjoyed the online shopping for its own sake, not just for the items I		
may have purchased		
During my online shopping, I felt the excitement of the hunt		
While I was online shopping, I felt a sense of adventure		
Factor 5: Product involvement (adapted Zaichkowsky, 1994)	0.72	0.87
To me, the product(s) I purchased online is interesting	0.85	
To me, the product(s) I purchased online is exciting	0.79	
To me, the product(s) I purchased online means a lot to me	0.87	
To me, the product(s) I purchased online is appealing	0.84	
To me, the product(s) I purchased online is fascinating.		

(continued)

Table 1 (continued)

Item	Item loading	Cronbach's α
Factor 6: Perceived usefulness (adapted Davis et al., 1989) Using the these product(s) I purchased online, I can improve my performance in life during the COVID-19 pandemic. Using the these product(s) I purchased online, I can increase my productivity during the COVID-19 pandemic. Using the these product(s) I purchased online, I can enhance my effectiveness in daily life during the COVID-19 pandemic. I would find product(s) I purchased online useful in my life during the COVID-19 pandemic.	0.88 0.86 0.90 0.85	0.89
Factor 6: Perceived enjoyment (adapted Chang and Cheung, 2001) My interaction with the product(s) purchased online during the COVID-19 pandemic is enjoyable. My interaction with product(s) purchased online during the COVID-19 pandemic is exciting. My interaction with product(s) purchased online during the COVID-19 pandemic is pleasant.	0.90 0.90 0.89	0.87
Factor 7: Urge to buy impulsively (adapted Rook and Fisher, 1995) During the COVID-19 pandemic, I had the urge to purchase items other than or in addition to my specific shopping goal. During the COVID-19 pandemic, I had a desire to buy items that did not pertain to my specific shopping goal. During the COVID-19 pandemic, I had the inclination to purchase items outside my specific shopping goal.	0.90 0.95 0.95	0.93

Note. N = 208

Table 2 Construct correlations and AVEs

	AVE	PC	PI	HSV	WA	EV	PU	PE	IB
PC	**0.673**	**0.820**							
PI	**0.584**	0.153	**0.866**						
HSV	**0.622**	0.229	0.676	**0.789**					
WA	**0.665**	0.061	0.374	0.452	**0.815**				
EV	**0.687**	−0.013	0.312	0.338	0.573	**0.829**			
PU	**0.680**	0.194	0.302	0.115	0.014	0.099	**0.824**		
PE	**0.697**	0.199	0.764	0.670	0.376	0.369	0.418	**0.835**	
IB	**0.813**	0.179	0.224	0.517	0.173	0.175	0.025	0.275	**0.902**

between the product categories and the pandemic cues. Two products were significantly correlated with the pandemic cue, care products ($r = 0.20$, $p = 0.002$) and sports equipment ($r = 0.14$, $p < 0.001$). Participants assert they felt they purchased these particular products because of the pandemic cues.

Then, in order to explore whether the pandemic cues affected consumers' consumption across categories, the overall product consumption of the participants was estimated; a cluster analysis was created to identify product categories by the type of consumption. Three categories were created: products consumed individually

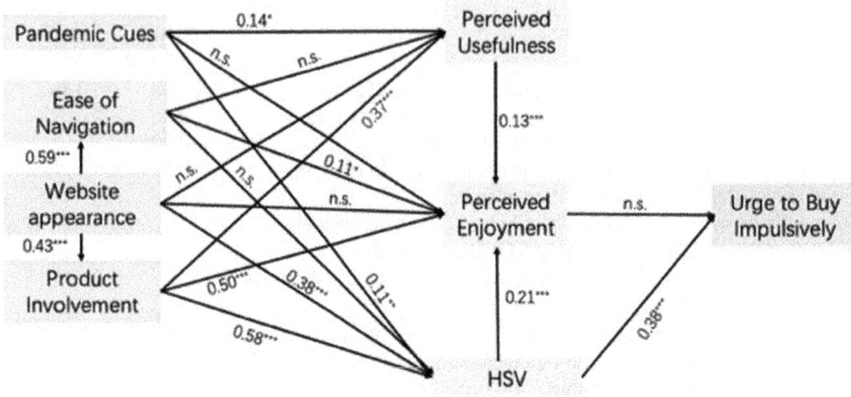

Fig. 2 Proposed model

(book, cloths, personal care, cloths and sports equipment), products consumed by the individual and their family/group (home garden, kitchen tools, home appliances), and electronics, which can be either consumed individually or by a family/group (such as videogames, DVD, CDS, cellphone, tablet, and computers). Then, four variations of consumers were identified: consumers (1) who purchased products for personal used only, (2) who purchased electronic products for personal use only, (3) who purchase products for personal and family/group use, and (4) consumers who purchase all kind of products categories.

Next, a one way ANOVA was tested using a single factor for the pandemic cue across the four consumption patterns. Results shows significant difference among the four groups indicating that the urge to buy the products as a result of pandemic cues were highest across those who reported to have purchased all kinds of product categories, followed by those who purchased items for individual use only and family/group use, those who purchase electronics for individual and family/group and last, by those who purchase products for individual use only (see Tables 3 and 4).

Discussion, Limitations and Direction for Future Research

This study has theoretical and practical implications. Theoretically, the study provides an alternative model that explains the role of website appearance, and ease of use on impulsive buying behavior. This study proposes the latter variables relate to consumers' product involvement, which affect the hedonic value and, in turn, predicts impulsive behavior. Overall, participants indicated the most purchased products in response to COVID-19 pandemic cue in 2020 were personal care items and sports equipment. Yet, compared to those who purchased items for personal use only, those who reported to have purchased all kinds of product categories reported the highest pandemic cue scores.

Table 3 ANOVA results – Pandemic cues

	Sum of squares	df	Mean Square	F	Sig.
Between group	62.54	3	20.84	9.44	.000
Within group	446.32	202	2.21		
Total	508.86	205			

Table 4 Product categories

	Personal use only(1)	Personal and Family use products (3)	Electronic product and other products (2)	All three categories products (4)
M	5.22_a	4.33_b	4.96_a	3.37_c
SD	1.51	1.41	1.61	1.05

$F(3, 202) = 9.44$, $p < .001$, partial $\eta 2 = .12$

Note: Means with no subscript in common differ at $p < .05$ using Bonferroni post hoc comparisons

Practically, this study can serve to guide marketing practitioners about the importance of website design. In addition, the findings can serve to help understand how the participants cope during the pandemic. That is, those who believe they made online purchases because of pandemic cues were more likely to purchase all kind of product categories.These results can be used as consumer insights for creative briefs and the execution of messages.

Despite the strengths of this study, several limitations are identified preventing the generalization of the results. The sample was limited to college students. The sample was collected in an eastern state were the quarantine was not obligatory. The product selection was limited to 13 categories. Future research should expand the sample frame, data collection technique, and product categories. Future research must investigate the role of utilitarian value, not included in this study in the proposed model.

*** p-value is less than 0.001; **p-value is less than 0.01; * p-value is less than 0.05.

References

Adams, D. A., Nelson, R. R., & Todd, P. A. (1992). Perceived usefulness, ease of use, and usage of information technology: A replication. *MIS Quarterly*, *16*(2), 227–247.

Adelaar, T., Chang, S., Lancendorfer, K. M., Lee, B., & Morimoto, M. (2003). Effects of media formats on emotions and impulse buying intent. *Journal of Information Technology*, *18*(4), 247–266.

Amoako-Gyampah, K., & Salam, A. F. (2004). An extension of the technology acceptance model in an ERP implementation environment. *Information & management*, *41*(6), 731–745.

Babin, B.J., Darden, W.R. & Griffin, M. (1994), Work and/or fun: measuring hedonic and utilitarian shopping value, *Journal of Consumer Research*, *20*(4) , 644–656.

Bauer, H. H., Grether, M., & Leach, M. (2002). Building customer relations over the internet. *Industrial Marketing Management*, *31*(2), 155–163.

Beatty, S. E., & Ferrell, M. E. (1998). Impulse buying: modeling its precursors. *Journal of Retailing*, *74*(2), 169–191.

Bearden, W. O., & Etzel, M. J. (1982). Reference group influence on product and brand purchase decisions. *Journal of consumer research*, *9*(2), 183-194.

Bonneux, L., & Van Damme, W. (2006). An iatrogenic pandemic of panic. *Bmj*, *332*(7544), 786–788.

Chakravarti, A., & Janiszewski, C. (2003). The influence of macro-level motives on consideration set composition in novel purchase situations. *Journal of Consumer Research*, *30*(2), 244–258.

Chapa, S., Minor, M. S., & Maldonado, C. (2006). Product category and origin effects on consumer responses to counterfeits: comparing Mexico and the US. *Journal of International Consumer Marketing*, *18*(4), 79–99.

Chang, M. K., & Cheung, W. (2001). Determinants of the intention to use internet/WWW at work: A confirmatory study. *Information & Management*, *39* (1), 1–14.

Charters, S., & Pettigrew, S. (2006). Product involvement and the evaluation of wine quality. *Qualitative Market Research: An International Journal*, *9*(2), 181–193.

Chung, N., Song, H. G., & Lee, H. (2017). Consumers' impulsive buying behavior of restaurant products in social commerce. *International Journal of Contemporary Hospitality Management*, *29*(2), 709–731.

Cox, D. (2009). Predicting consumption, wine involvement and perceived quality of Australian red wine. *Journal of Wine Research*, *20*(3), 209–229.

Davis, F. D., Bagozzi, R. P., & Warshaw, P. R. (1989). User acceptance of computer technology: A comparison of two theoretical models. *Management Science*, *35*(8), 982–1003.

Dholakia, U. M. (1998). Involvement-response models of joint effects: An empirical test and extension. *ACR North American Advances*.

Fetscherin, M., Boulanger, M., Gonçalves Filho, C., & Souki, G. Q. (2014). The effect of product category on consumer brand relationships. *Journal of Product & Brand Management*, *23*(2) 78–89.

Floh, A., & Madlberger, M. (2013). The role of atmospheric cues in online impulse-buying behavior. *Electronic Commerce Research and Applications*, *12*(6), 425–439.

Fornell, C., & Larcker, D. F. (1981). Evaluating structural equation models with unobservable variables and measurement error. *Journal of Marketing Research*, *18*(1), 39–50.

Gamma, A.E., Slekiene, J., & Mosler, H.J. (2020). The impact of various promotional activities on Ebola prevention behaviors and psychosocial factors predicting Ebola prevention behaviors in the Gambia evaluation of Ebola prevention promotions. *International Journal of Environmental Research and Public Health, 16*(11).

Griffin, M., Babin, B. J., & Modianos, D. (2000). Shopping values of Russian consumers: The impact of habituation in a developing economy. *Journal of Retailing*, *76*(1), 33–52.

Holbrook, M. B., & Batra, R. (1987). Assessing the role of emotions as mediators of consumer responses to advertising. *Journal of Consumer Research*, *14*(3), 404–420.

Hu, L. T., & Bentler, P. M. (1999). Cutoff criteria for fit indexes in covariance structure analysis: Conventional criteria versus new alternatives. *Structural Equation Modeling: a Multidisciplinary Journal*, *6*(1), 1–55.

Islam, T., Pitafi, H., Wang, Y., Aryaa, V., Mubarik, S., Akhater, N., & Xiaobei, L. (2020). Panic Buying in the COVID-19 pandemic: A multi-country examination. *Journal of Retailing and Consumer Services*, Article 102357.

Khalifa, M., & Shen, K. (2007). System design effects on online impulse buying. *Internet Research*, *22*(4), 110.

Kim, S., & Eastin, M. S. (2011). Hedonic tendencies and the online consumer: An investigation of the online shopping process. *Journal of Internet Commerce*, *10*(1), 68–90.

Kleiser, S. B., & Wagner, J. A. (1999). Understanding the pioneering advantage from the decision maker's perspective: the case of product involvement and the status quo bias. *ACR North American Advances*.

Kokkinaki, F. (1999). Predicting product purchase and usage: the role of perceived control, past behavior and product involvement. *ACR North American Advances*.

KuKar-Kinney, Monika, Scheinbaum, A. C., & Schaefers, T. (2015). Compulsive buying in online daily deal settings: An investigation of motivations and contextual elements. *Journal of Business Research*, 69(2), 691-699.

Laato, S., Islam, A. N., Farooq, A., & Dhir, A. (2020). Unusual purchasing behavior during the early stages of the COVID-19 pandemic: The stimulus-organism-response approach. *Journal of Retailing and Consumer Services*, *57*, 102224.

LaRose, R. (2001). On the Negative Effects of E-Commerce: A Socio-Cognitive Exploration of Unregulated On-Line Buying. *Journal of Computer-Mediated Communication*, 6(3).

Li, M., Zhao, T., Huang, E., & Li, J. (2020). How does a public health emergency motivate People's impulsive consumption? an empirical study during the COVID-19 outbreak in China. *International Journal of Environmental Research and Public Health*, *17*(14), 5019.

Mehrabian, A., & Russell, J. A. (1974). *An approach to environmental psychology*. MA: MIT.

Mittal, B. (1995). A comparative analysis of four scales of consumer involvement. *Psychology & Marketing*, *12*(7), 663–682.

Nunnally, J. C., & Bernstein, I. H. (1994). *Psychometric theory* (3rd ed.). New York: McGraw-Hill.

Palmer, J. W. (2002). Web usability, design, and performance metrics. *Information Systems Research*, *13*(2), 151–167.

Parboteeah, D. V., Taylor, D. C., & Barber, N. A. (2016). Exploring impulse purchasing of wine in the online environment. *Journal of wine research*, *27*(4), 322–339.

Parboteeah, D. V., Valacich, J. S., & Wells, J. D. (2009). The influence of website characteristics on a consumer's urge to buy impulsively. *Information systems research*, *20*(1), 60–78.

Ramanathan, S., & Menon, G. (2006). Time-varying effects of chronic hedonic goals on impulsive behavior. *Journal of Marketing Research*, *43*(4), 628–641.

Ramayah, T., & Ignatius, J. (2005). Impact of perceived usefulness, perceived ease of use and perceived enjoyment on intention to shop online. *ICFAI Journal of Systems Management (IJSM)*, *3*(3), 36–51.

Rahman, I., & Reynolds, D. (2015). Wine: Intrinsic attributes and consumers' drinking frequency, experience, and involvement. *International Journal of Hospitality Management*, *44*(1), 1–11.

Rook, D. W., & Fisher, R. J. (1995). Normative influences on impulsive buying. *Journal of Consumer Research*, *22*(3), 305–313.

Shiv, B., & Fedorikhin, A. (1999). Heart and mind in conflict: The interplay of affect and cognition in consumer decision making. *Journal of Consumer Research*, *26*(3), 278–292.

Shukla, P. & Babin, B.J. (2013), Effects of consumer psychographics and store characteristics in influencing shopping value and store switching, *Journal of Consumer Behaviour*, *12*(3), pp. 194–203.

Taylor, D. C., Parboteeah, D. V., & Snipes, M. (2010). Winery websites: Effectiveness explored. *Journal of Business Administration Online*, *9*(2), 1–11.

Van der Heijden, H., T. Verhagen, M. Creemers. (2003). Understanding online purchase intentions: Contributions from technology and trust perspectives. European Journal of Information Systems, *12*(1) 41–48.

Zaichkowsky, J. L. (1985). Measuring the involvement construct. *Journal of Consumer Research*, *12*(3), 341–352.

Zaichkowsky, J. L. (1994). The personal involvement inventory: Reduction, revision, and application to advertising. *Journal of Advertising*, *23*(4), 59–70.

Zhang, P., & Von Dran, G. M. (2001–2002). User expectations and rankings of quality factors in different web site domains. *International Journal of Electronic Commerce*, *6*(2), 9–33.

Mindset and Goal Orientation in Sales: Results from a Qualitative Approach

Romain Farellacci and Sandrine Hollet-Haudebert

Abstract This research presents a first exploration in the field of management sciences, on mindset and goal orientation theories with a qualitative approach through semi-structured interviews. We partnered with a company in the telecom sector in France to interview 12 salespeople and 7 store managers. The analysis of results show among others: (1) the mindset is present in the speeches of salespeople and store managers, (2) the mindset is specific to an attribute (selling ability or personality), (3) goal orientation is promoted by the social support and managers' mindset, (4) according to salespeople and store managers, customers can also adopt a goal orientation, especially during a visit to the store, and these goals can alter the exchange with the salesperson, especially in terms of the help requested and according to the predominant goal orientation of the salesperson. The theoretical and managerial implications of these results are discussed.

Keywords Salespeople · Store manager · Mindset · Goal orientation · Store

Introduction

When we look at the way things go today, salespeople have a great chance of being disturbed and challenged by the growing power of the consumer, new patterns of consumption and distribution, and changes in sales methods and techniques. They may be required to adapt their missions in the face of the digital world and technology. In the same way, they are exposed to an ever-increasing level of awareness and to a consumer who has become knowledgeable. The COVID-19 health crisis has also reminded companies of the importance of adaptability to change, as

R. Farellacci (✉) · S. Hollet-Haudebert
University of Toulon, Toulon, France
e-mail: romain.farellacci@univ-tln.fr; sandrine.hollet-haudebert@univ-tln.fr

J. Allen et al. (eds.), *Celebrating the Past and Future of Marketing and Discovery with Social Impact*, Developments in Marketing Science: Proceedings of the Academy of Marketing Science, https://doi.org/10.1007/978-3-030-95346-1_96

salespeople need to be resilient and agile, which are key elements for being successful (Sharmaa et al. 2020). This crisis only increases the changes in consumer behavior and the potential challenges for salespeople and retailers (Donthu and Gustafsson 2020; Roggeveen and Sethuraman 2020). In order to face these challenges, the motivation of the salesperson seems to us to be a determining attitude. In this context, we believe that two motivational theories, the mindset theory and the goal orientation theory, can be an interesting theoretical framework to better understand salesperson motivation and behavior. They appear in the social-cognitive model of motivation by Dweck and Legett (1988), and have shown their application and theoretical and managerial implications for more than 30 years in different fields (education, human resources, sales and marketing). They have significant consequences on the motivation and behaviour of individuals (Murphy and Dweck 2010; Vandewalle et al. 2019), and are especially important in performance environments during challenges or difficult contexts (Dweck 2000). The concept of mindset is used today by companies such as Microsoft or Nokia. The NeuroLeadership Institut (an applied research organization) develops numerous research projects in partnership with companies in order to apply the concept within them. We note that a number of organizations (e.g. the Growth Mindset Institute) are designing mindset training programs for companies. Indeed, an individual's mindset can be transformed (Dweck 2017; Novell et al. 2016). While both theories have been investigated in different fields through quantitative and experimental approaches, we consider it important to apprehend them by means of a qualitative approach. Thus, through interviews conducted with salespeople and managers, the objectives of the research are twofold: (1) is the mindset reflected in the speeches of salespeople and store managers? (2) is the mindset specific to an attribute (personality, selling ability)? (3) understanding the link between the salesperson's goal orientations and that he perceives from the customer during the sales exchange. Let us review the origins of and research on the theory of mindset and its links with goal orientation. Next, in a second part, we will focus on goal orientation theory. We will then develop our research objectives, methodology, and main findings. Finally, we will discuss and conclude by pointing out the limits and avenues for future research.

The Theoretical Framework

This first part will be divided into four subsections. First, we will elaborate on the origins of the mindset theory, then we will focus on developing fundamental research in human resources, sales and marketing. Next, we will outline the origins of goal orientation theory and then focus on the basic research in human resources and sales.

Mindset Theory: Decades of Research

Mindsets are beliefs that individuals may or may not be aware of, which strongly affect what they want and whether or not they succeed in getting it (Dweck 2017). The starting point for Dweck's research has been to understand how people cope with failure, and to study this phenomenon by observing how students tackle difficult problems (Diener and Dweck 1978). According to several authors (Dweck 1986; Dweck et al. 1995), people can refer to two distinct mindsets[1] regarding their abilities and personal attributes (intelligence, social abilities, sales abilities, etc.): the growth mindset,[2] and the fixed mindset.[3] The growth mindset regards ability as a malleable, controllable quality that can be enhanced over time, the second views ability as a fixed, uncontrollable trait (Dweck 2017). It is based on the belief that abilities are characteristics that individuals can cultivate through their efforts. The latter considers that although individuals may differ in their initial talents and abilities, interests or temperament, everyone can change and develop through work and experience. Individuals' belief that their qualities are fixed (fixed mindset) creates a compelling need to demonstrate their qualities over and over again. After the least failure, individuals with this mindset would see what happened as a direct measure of their competence and worth. A great deal of research on mindsets has been undertaken in the field of education. For example, some have determined the relationship between mindset and risk (Hong et al. 1999), challenge, interest, and enjoyment (Mueller and Dweck 1998).

Mindset Theory: An Applied Theory in Human Resources, Sales and Marketing

Wood and Bandura (1989) and Tabernero and Wood (1989) have shown the interest of mindsets in the field of management through experiments. Research has exposed the interest of this theory in the relationship between mindset (intelligence or general capacity) on the one hand, and risk-taking and overconfidence in business on the other (Koebel et al. 2016; Montford et al. 2019). In organizations, mindsets affect how managers evaluate their employees, perceptions of procedural fairness, and the effectiveness of people's leadership (Heslin et al. 2005; Heslin and Vandewalle 2011; Kouzes and Posner 2019). Other research has demonstrated its influence on employee performance (Zingoni and Corey 2017). It is important to note that mindsets are domain-specific (personality, intelligence, etc.) (Dweck 2017). While a person may have a fixed mindset with respect to intelligence, he or she may also have a growth mindset with respect to personality. For example, the

---

[1] The literature also uses the term "*implicit theories*" interchangeably.

[2] The literature also uses the term "*incremental theory*" interchangeably.

[3] The literature also uses the term "*entity theory*" interchangeably.

intelligence mindset comes into play when situations involve mental abilities; and the personality mindset comes into play when situations involve the personal characteristics of individuals, for example, the extent to which they are reliable, cooperative, caring, or socially competent. In other words, beliefs about ability in one area do not affect other areas. Human resource mindset theory has many applications for career development, training, and organizational development (Han and Stieha 2020). At the same time, mindset has also been adapted at the organizational level to show its impact on the cultural norms of the company and the level of employee trust and commitment (Canning et al. 2019). Some research has also expanded the interest of the mindset theory within a sales context. Novell et al. (2016) have highlighted the effect of the salesperson's mindset on learning goals and performance-avoid goals, on the search for feedback and on confidence in his or her selling abilities. The latter authors have demonstrated that the mindset can be changed in salespeople. In a service context, Wentzel et al. (2010) show that the impact of advertisements can be determined not only by factors inherent to advertisements (e.g. excessive promises) but also by the mindset of the staff in contact. Other research explains that when the performance of contact personnel is attributed to effort rather than natural talent, it leads consumers to perceive them as warmer (Leung et al. 2020). In a context of negotiation, Kray and Haselhuhn (2007) have highlighted the influence of the mindset on performance and the moderating role of the perceived capacity for the latter relationship. Haselhuhn et al. (2017) demonstrate that the mindset of customers towards a seller has an impact on the decline in the perceived integrity (trust dimension) of the salesperson as a result of deception about the product sold. Research on mindset has also demonstrated its validity in the field of consumer behaviour. Leung et al. (2020) find that when a company highlights the effort versus the talent of its contact personnel, it is more likely to induce customers to engage in word-of-mouth behaviors, to communicate comments and ideas for the company. Yorkston et al. (2010) indicate that consumers with a growth mindset are more accepting of brand extensions than consumers with a fixed mindset. Marketing research still has interesting new insights into the role of consumer mindset in the consumption process (Jain and Wainten 2020).

The mindset theory is connected to the theory of goal orientation. Indeed, both theories are found in the socio-cognitive model of motivation (Dweck and Legett 1988; Novell et al. 2016). Individuals' mindset is an antecedent to the goals they pursue.

Goal Orientation Theory[4]: Decades of Research

In four decades, goal orientation theory has been studied to explain behaviour and performance in the world of education (Dweck 1986; Nicholls 1984; Elliot and Hulleman 2017). In the early 1980s, Nicholls (1984) and Dweck (1986) laid the

[4] The literature also uses the term *"achievement goals theory"* interchangeably.

foundations for what would become known as goal orientation theory. They introduced the distinction between two types of goals representing two ways of defining and assessing competence:

(a) a learning goal ("*learning goal*" for Dweck and "*task-involvement goal*" for Nicholls) consisting of seeking to develop skills, acquire new skills and master new situations;
(b) a performance goal ("*performance goal*" for Dweck, "*ego-involvement goal*" for Nicholls) seeking to demonstrate, validate one's competence by seeking favorable judgments and avoiding negative judgments about one's competence.

Initially one-dimensional, Heyman and Dweck (1992) explained that individuals can have both a learning goal and a performance goal. Then, considering the potential conceptual distinction between seeking favourable judgements and avoiding negative judgements that could be incorporated into the performance goal, researchers (Elliot and Harackiewicz 1996; Vandewalle 1997) divided the latter goal into two goals:

(a) performance-prove goal ("*performance-approach goal*" for Elliot and Harackiewicz): the desire to prove one's competence and to obtain favourable judgements about it.
(b) performance-avoid goal ("*performance-avoidance goal*" for Elliot and Harackiewicz): the desire to avoid disapproval and negative judgments about one's competence.

Following an explanation of the foundations and origins of this theory, particularly in the field of psychology, we will now focus on demonstrating its importance in the field of human resources and sales.

Goal Orientation Theory: An Applied Theory in Human Resources and Sales

Goal orientations theory has demonstrated a strong interest in human resource and sales research. Van Yperen et al. (2011) demonstrated that, in performance contexts (work, sport and education), individuals with a dominant performance (prove or avoid) goal had stronger intentions to cheat than those with a dominant learning goal. Matzler and Mueller (2011) reported that a learning goal (vs. performance goal) had a positive (negative) relationship on knowledge sharing with colleagues. Coad and Berry (1998) explained that a manager's learning goal had a positive relationship with being classified as a transformational leader by direct reports. In sales, researchers have demonstrated a positive relationship between the salesperson's learning goal and performance (McFarland and Kidwell 2006; Silver et al. 2006). Ahearne et al. (2010) emphasize that for a learning-related change, goal orientations are very important. Several authors (Vandewalle et al. 1999; Sujan et al. 1994) found that a learning goal was positively related to the salesperson's effort. Significantly, a learning goal encourages salespeople to adopt adaptive sales behaviour (Chai et al. 2012; Sujan et al. 1994). Authors have shown that a salesperson's learning goal has a positive relationship with his or her customer-oriented behaviour (Harris et al. 2005).

Research Objectives

As we have developed in our theoretical framework, mindset theory and goal orientation theory have been studied almost exclusively in an experimental or quantitative manner, in the field of management sciences. In all research undertaken in human resources, marketing and sales, no research has undertaken a qualitative methodology with semi-structured interviews for either theory. While quantitative research is necessary to measure linkages, qualitative research is equally necessary to advance research and/or confirm results. Indeed, a qualitative approach would allow us to confirm but also bring unexplored answers. Thus, through interviews with store managers and salespeople, the objectives of the research are threefold: (1) to identify whether the mindset is found in the speeches of salespeople and store managers? (2) to confirm or refute the literature on whether the mindset is specific to an attribute (selling ability and personality)? (3) Do salespeople and store managers identify goal orientations in customers? Do these goals change the exchange relationship between the salesperson and the customer?

Research Methodology

We partnered with a company in the telecom sector in France to interview 12 salespeople and 7 store managers. We were careful to have different types of salespeople and store managers in terms of gender, professional experience, and diplomas. The interviews took place between April and May 2019, they were recorded and have been transcribed in full. The corpus of data totals 218 pages or 132,393 words. To conduct the interviews, we developed two interview guides: one for salespeople, and one for store managers. The analysis of the recorded qualitative data was inspired by grounded theory (Glaser and Strauss 1967) and we performed coding after a floating reading of all the collected material (Huberman and Miles 1991).

The Main Results

Our research led to four main findings: (1) the mindset is well present in the speeches of salespeople and store managers, (2) both mindset are well specific to an attribute (selling ability or personality), (3) goal orientation is promoted by the social support and managers' mindset, (4) customers can also adopt goal orientation especially during a visit to the store and they can alter the exchange with the salesperson especially in terms of the help requested and according to the predominant goal orientation of the salesperson.

The Mindset of Selling Ability and/or Personality Are Present in Salespeople and Store Managers

We find the two types of mindset (fixed or growth) on personality (8/12 salespeople and 5/7 store managers) and/or selling ability (12/12 salespeople and 7/7 store managers). For example, some managers have a fixed mindset about selling ability: "*You either have it or you don't (...) I think it's innate, or at least that's the way I feel*" (manager 5); and some salespeople also have a fixed mindset about sales abilities: "*when you sell, you have to have something. For me, you can't learn how to sell (...), it's either you have it or you don't have it*" (salesperson 9). This last element is very revealing because managers' mindset is a determining factor on employee coaching, evaluation, and organizational citizenship behavior (Heslin et al. 2005, 2006; Ozduran and Tanova 2017). It is important to take action and change managers' mindset in order to create a climate of growth in the company (Dweck 2017). We note that the organizational growth mindset (Canning et al. 2019) is very real, can be found in the speeches of salespeople and store managers, and is very important for them: "*To create it, or to reveal it (the potential). If it is there, it is exploited, and if there is not a potential that stands out, we make sure that it is created from above. In the end, that's the feeling I have in this company*" (salesperson 10).

The Mindset Is Specific to Each Attribute (Personality or Selling Ability)

Our results confirm that the perception of the mindset (fixed or growth) varies according to the attribute or domain (selling ability and personality). For example, we find that a salesperson can have a growth mindset of selling ability and a fixed mindset of personality: "*It will only last for a while, because if you're not a salesperson and you force yourself to be a salesperson, you're not going to be happy. It's going against his nature*" (salesperson 6) (fixed mindset of selling ability); "*So it's something that can be learned and that can develop, because I didn't have it at all.*

I was a person who didn't already speak, basic. I couldn't have a discussion like a normal person. And by dint of learning, pushing myself, working on it, working on it (...) I had it" (salesperson 6) (growth mindset of personality). We also find the same result among store managers. For example, a store manager can have a growth mindset of selling ability and a fixed mindset of personality: *"knowing about knowledge to do, it's difficult to progress on it"* (manager 1) (fixed mindset of personality); *"we can progress and go from an average to an expert salesperson"* (manager 1) (growth mindset of selling ability). This result seems important because two types of mindset are essential in the context of sales: that concerning selling ability and that concerning personality.

Goal Orientation Promoted by the Social Support and Managers' Mindset

First of all, we can point out that the learning goal, for example, provides a better experience and contributes to the development of the salesperson: "*It brought me a lot. Because before I didn't know all that, I didn't even know the customer himself, I didn't even know the job, I didn't know sales techniques, I didn't know all that (...) It brought me a lot of things, a good experience*" (salesperson 5). We note that the store manager plays an important role and must have a growing mindset in order to limit the development of a counter-productive goal (performance-avoid): "*Because since I wasn't necessarily succeeding, instead of being told off or saying 'you're not doing it right' she said 'you're going to make it, you have to progress' finally she really pulled me up instead of putting me down*" (salesperson 8). The salesperson explains the manager's contribution, which appears to be an indispensable pivotal element to avoid adopting a counterproductive goal (performance-avoid) for the company and for customer relations: "*And I'm in total progress, since I started, I'm just increasing (...) And afterwards, what I miss a little is a little bit of confidence, which I've managed to gain thanks to this job precisely, thanks to the fact that I'm well supervised*" (salesperson 8). Relationships with the team seem indispensable to create a learning climate in order to encourage salespeople towards a learning goal: "*in the end, it is through the transmission I give to others that I myself am made more competent by them. And it's really rewarding for me to see them progress and to see them make me progress, because both in sales and in training it helps me progress*" (salesperson 10).

Goal Orientation of Salespeople and Customers: A Decisive Relationship in the Exchange?

Our results demonstrate that (a) according to salespeople and store managers, goal orientation can also be adopted by customers during their visit to the store and modify the assistance requested from the salesperson, (b) the confrontation of the goals of customers and salespeople can considerably disrupt the sales exchange.

Goal Orientation Also Adopted by the Customer at the Sales Outlet that Modifies the Level of Assistance Requested From the Salesperson

Salespeople have pointed out to us the existence of goal orientation in customers during their visit to the store. Indeed, customers may adopt a learning goal: *"when they come to the store they want at least a confirmation ... or an opinion from the salesperson, or an explanation*" (salesperson 7). Customers can also adopt a performance-prove goal whose objective would not be to receive explanations and knowledge but to prove their knowledge and even provoke the salesman on his field of expertise: "*There are people like that, they are at their best, they look at everything on the Internet, they watch videos, they test the phones, what have you, they do tests that make them value to say 'that I knew and the salesman of the store he didn't know'* " (salesperson 9). We also find the same result among store managers. We also point out that customers with a performance-prove goal would look less for help from the salesperson but more for confrontation: *"selling is difficult because you can hardly tell them anything, they always try to counter, yes it's very complicated, very complicated. I think that some people, to a certain extent, they expect an exchange but perhaps a little confrontational"* (salesperson 9).

A Potential Tension in the Exchange With a Different Goal Orientation of Customer and Salesperson

We can also see that the learning goal of the customer and the salesperson can create a certain tension in the sales exchange. A salesperson with a predominant performance (prove) goal seems to have difficulty adapting to a customer who also has the same predominant goal: "*After me it tends to irritate me, when people do things like I know everything, it irritates me, so the exchange becomes more complicated in the sense that I am less open to the exchange*" (salesperson 9). On the other hand, we can say that a salesperson with a learning goal could be more comfortable with a customer who would like to demonstrate his knowledge (performance-prove goal): "*And sometimes the customer will teach me things that I don't know ... that's fine, I say 'you're teaching me something' so I'll take note of what he tells me and I'll set up the next time with the same case. It's good, it enriches me*" (salesperson 5).

Discussion, Theoretical and Managerial Implications

This research focuses on Dweck and Legett's (1988) socio-cognitive model of motivation by studying the theories of mindset and goal orientation in a sales context. Our first contribution is methodological by exploring these theories through a qualitative approach by interviewing store managers and salespeople. Our second contribution is to demonstrate that both mindset (fixed or growth) appear in the speeches of salespeople and store managers, and that many of them have a fixed mindset (personality and/or sales abilities) predominant. This is important because much research has shown that the mindset of teachers, coaches and managers is critical for their teams (Dweck 2017). This result is all the more important in the current health crisis situation, where sales techniques must be adapted in view of customer exchanges and transformed consumption patterns; but also because the mindset is contagious (King 2019). Companies must therefore train managers in the mindset of growth in terms of both personality and sales abilities, but also ensure that they have the right mindset when recruiting. Moreover, we also find in some speeches the perception of an organizational mindset (Canning et al. 2019). As Dweck (2017) explains, a company should not make the mistake of being in a talent culture and advises to create an organization that values capacity development and is able to observe emerging leaders. As McCall (1998) explains, many organizations believe in innate talent and do not look for people with the potential to develop. McCall (1998) points out that these organizations are likely to miss out on potential leaders, and that their belief in innate talent may even end up crushing the very individuals they think are naturally gifted, making them unlearnable, arrogant, and defensive. Next, our third contribution is to confirm the literature on mindset (Chiu et al. 1997; Novell et al. 2016), developing that the latter can be different depending on the attribute, in this case a person may have a fixed personality mindset and a growing mindset for selling ability (and vice versa). This last element can be verified with store managers and salespeople. Therefore, it is important to choose or create a scale to measure the mindset that is not general but relates to the ability and/or attribute being studied (intelligence, leadership, selling ability, personality, ...). Our fourth contribution is to show that goal orientation is promoted by the social support and managers' mindset. Indeed, we demonstrate that relationships with the team seem indispensable to create a learning climate in order to encourage salespeople towards a learning goal. Also, we note that the store manager plays an important role and must have a growth mindset in order to limit the development of a counter-productive goal (performance-avoid). These latter results may allow companies to create a favorable context for the salesperson to develop a learning goal by discarding the adoption of a performance-avoid goal. Much research has shown that the learning goal leads to positive behaviors at work while the performance-avoid goal involves counterproductive behaviors.

Our fifth contribution proposes that customers should be able to adopt goal orientation, especially during a visit to the store, and alter the exchange with the salesperson, as we have seen in the salesperson's speech. These goals adopted by the customer could be decisive in many consumer sectors such as electronics, multimedia, automotive, telecom but could also be extended to the service sector especially in the context of tourism. This result is interesting because, while the marketing literature has focused on the different goals (motivations) (for example task shopping, social shopping, experiential shopping) that a customer may adopt during a store visit (Babin et al. 1994; Baker and Wakefield 2012; Buttner et al. 2013), no marketing research has focused on goal orientation (learning, performance-prove and performance-avoid) among consumers. The study of goal orientation in customers could, among other things, enable companies to understand its influence in exchanges with the salesperson, but also, for example, the level of assistance envisaged by the customer with the salesperson. This would confirm work in psychology in a learning context that has demonstrated that people with a predominant learning goal were more willing to ask for help (Nosaki 2003). Indeed, for example, a customer with a predominant performance goal might be reluctant to ask the salesperson for help or information because it might represent a lack of knowledge and/or ability. This could lead to problems with the cooperation that is often necessary in a sales exchange. We may also question the adoption of a performance goal by the seller and have an effect on the willingness to ask the customer for help from the seller. Butler and Shibaz (2008) have demonstrated that the adoption of a learning goal by teachers leads to a strong demand for help from students. On the other hand, we have reported that the predominant goal orientation adopted by the salesperson and the customer can deteriorate the sales exchange. For example, a salesperson with an overriding performance goal might have a more difficult exchange with a customer with the same overriding goal; the performance goal being a goal for which social comparison is important. As a result, the performance goal may cause the individual to perceive the other as a threat (Darnon et al. 2006). By identifying the goal orientation of customers and salespeople, firms might consider assigning a particular salesperson compatible with the customer's goal. This would also help to understand the different tensions during a sales exchange. Moreover, while two studies have demonstrated the effect of the learning goal of contact personnel on service quality and customer satisfaction (Yee et al. 2013, 2018), we believe that the goal orientation adopted by the customer could have a moderating effect on his or her satisfaction or on the perceived quality of service. Likewise, companies, knowing the predominant goal orientation of the salesperson and the customer, should take it into account in the analysis and understanding of customer satisfaction studies. Furthermore, when certain brands offer store training for customers, does the customer's goal orientation have an impact on the company's willingness and appreciation of this initiative? It would also be interesting to quantitatively test the link between the customer's mindset and his goal orientation (a relationship demonstrated in the literature in psychology and sales), a relationship not shown in marketing. We may wonder about the consequence of a different mindset between the customer and the salesperson, does it modify the exchange relationship? Indeed, adopting a mindset represents a totally different vision of the world that impacts the behavior of individuals. Moreover, Dweck (2017) explains that they have an impact on interpersonal relationships.

Conclusion, Limitations and Prospects for Research

This research is the first to our knowledge in the field of management sciences that focuses on mindset and goal orientation theories with a qualitative approach through semi-structured interviews. Our original position through a qualitative study does not pretend to revolutionize research but to bring a stone to the edifice of this theoretical framework which is more and more studied in sales and marketing. Through this approach, our research has led to three main results and demonstrates, among others: (1) the mindset is present in the speeches of salespeople and store managers, (2) the mindset is specific to an attribute (selling ability or personality), (3) goal orientation is promoted by the social support and managers' mindset, (4) according to salespeople and store managers, customers can also adopt a goal orientation, especially during a visit to the store, and these goals can alter the exchange with the salesperson, especially in terms of the help requested and according to the predominant goal orientation of the salesperson. Our research has certain limitations that can be considered as potential future research avenues. The first limitation of our research is to have interviewed only salespeople and managers of a single company. It would be interesting to continue our research by diversifying the companies and sectors of activity. In addition, we could question salespeople and managers in BtoB. The second limitation is that we have not interviewed customers, however, we would like to continue our research and interview customers in order to understand the direction of their goals during a purchase at the store and the links with the customers' mindset and those of the salespeople. Finally, we encourage research to adapt goal orientation measurement scales for customers and test our proposals quantitatively.

References

Ahearne, M., Lam, S. K., Mathieu, J. E., & Bolander, W. (2010). Why are some salespeople better at adapting to organizational change? *Journal of Marketing, 74*(3), 65–79.

Babin, B. J., Darden, W. R., & Griffin, M. (1994). Work and/or fun: Measuring hedonic and utilitarian shopping value. *Journal of Consumer Research*, 20, 644–654.

Baker, J., & Wakefield, K. (2012). How consumer shopping orientation influences perceived crowding, excitement, and stress at the mall. *Journal of the Academy of Marketing Science*, 40(6), 791-806.

Butler, R., & Shibaz, L. (2008). Achievement Goals for Teaching as Predictors of Students' Perceptions of Instructional Practices and Students' Help Seeking and Cheating. *Learning and Instruction*, 18, 453-467.

Büttner, O., Florack, A., & Göritz, A. (2013). Shopping Orientation and Mindsets: How Motivation Influences Consumer Information Processing During Shopping. *Psychology & Marketing, 30*, 779-793.

Canning, E., Murphy, M., Emerson, K., Chatman, J., Dweck, C., & Kray, L. (2019). Cultures of Genius at Work: Organizational Mindsets Predict Cultural Norms, Trust, and Commitment. *Personality and Social Psychology Bulletin*. 46(4), 626–642.

Chai, J., Zhao, G., & Babin, B. J. (2012). An empirical study on the impact of two types of goal orientation and salesperson perceived obsolescence on adaptive selling. *Journal of Personal Selling and Sales Management*, 32(2), 261-273.

Chiu, C., Dweck, C., Tong, J., & Fu, J. (1997). Implicit theories and conceptions of morality. *Journal of Personality and Social Psychology, 73*(5), 923–940.

Coad, A. F., & Berry, A. J. (1998). Transformational leadership and learning orientation. *Leadership & Organization Development Journal*, 19(3), 164-172.

Darnon, C., Buchs, C., & Butera, F. (2006). Buts de performance et de maîtrise et interactions sociales entre étudiants: la situation particulière du désaccord avec autrui. *Revue française de pédagogie*, 155(2), 35-44.

Diener, C., & Dweck, C. (1978). An analysis of learned helplessness: Continuous changes in performance, strategy and achievement cognitions following failure. *Journal of Personality and Social Psychology*, 36, 451-462.

Donthu, N., & Gustafsson, A. (2020). Effects of COVID-19 on business and research. *Journal of business research*, 117, 284-289.

Dweck, C. (2000). *Self-theories: Their role in motivation, personality, and development.* New York: Psychology Press.

Dweck, C., Chiu, C., & Hong, Y. (1995). Implicit theories and their role in judgments and reactions: A world from two perspectives. *Psychological Inquiry*, 6, 267-285.

Dweck, C. (2017). *Mindset: Changing The Way You think To Fulfil Your Potential.* London: Robinson.

Dweck, C. (1986). Motivational Processes Affecting Learning. *American Psychologist*, 41(10), 1040–1048.

Dweck, C., & Leggett, E. L. (1988). A social-cognitive approach to motivation and personality. *Psychological Review, 95*(2), 256–273.

Elliot, A. J., & Harackiewicz, J. M. (1996). Approach and avoidance achievement goals and intrinsic motivation: A mediational analysis. *Journal of Personality and Social Psychology, 70*(3), 461–475.

Elliot, A. J., & Hulleman, C. S. (2017). Achievement goals. In A. J. Elliot, C. Dweck, & D. S. Yeager (Eds.), *Handbook of competence and motivation. Theory and application* (Second ed., pp. 43–60). New York: The Guildford Press.

Glaser, B. G., & Strauss, A. L. (1967). *The Discovery of Grounded Theory: Strategies for Qualitative Research.* Chicago, IL: Aldine.

Han, S. J., & Stieha, V. (2020). Growth Mindset for Human Resource Development: A Scoping Review of the Literature with Recommended Interventions. *Human Resource Development Review*, 19(3), 309-331.

Harris, E. G., Mowen, J. C., & Brown, T. J. (2005). Re-examining salesperson goal orientations: Personality influencers, customer orientation, and work satisfaction. *Journal of the Academy of Marketing Science*, 33(1), 19-35.

Haselhuhn, M. P., Schweitzer, M. E., Kray, L. J., & Kennedy, J. A. (2017). Perceptions of high integrity can persist after deception: How implicit beliefs moderate trust erosion. *Journal of Business Ethics, 145*(1), 215–225.

Heslin, P. A., & VandeWalle, D. (2011). Performance appraisal procedural justice: The role of a manager's implicit person theory. *Journal of Management*, 37(6), 1694-1718.

Heslin, P. A., Latham, G. P., & VandeWalle, D. (2005). The effect of implicit person theory on performance appraisals. *Journal of Applied Psychology*, 90(5), 842-856.

Heslin, P. A., VandeWalle, D., & Latham, G. P. (2006). Keen to help? Managers' implicit person theories and their subsequent employee coaching. *Personnel Psychology*, 59, 871–902.

Hong, Y., Chiu, C., Dweck, C., Lin, D., & Wan, W. (1999). Implicit theories, attributions, and coping: A meaning system approach. *Journal of Personality and Social Psychology*, 77, 588-599.

Huberman, M., & Miles, M. B. (1991). *Qualitative Data Analysis: A Collection of New Methods.* Bruxelles: De Boeck.

Jain, S. P., Weiten, T. J. (2020). Consumer psychology of implicit theories: A review and agenda. *Consumer Psychology Review*, 3(1), 60-75.

King, R. B. (2019). Mindsets are contagious: The social contagion of implicit theories of intelligence among classmates. *The British journal of educational psychology*. 90(2), 349-363.

Koebel, B., Schmitt, A., & Spaeter, S. (2016). Do Self-theories on Intelligence Explain Overconfidence and Risk Taking? A Field Experiment. *Revue économique*, 67(5), 977-1006.

Kouzes, T., & Posner, B. (2019). Influence of managers' mindset on leadership behavior. *Leadership & Organization Development Journal*, 40, 829-844.

Kray, L., & Haselhuhn, M. (2007). Implicit negotiation beliefs and performance: Longitudinal and experimental evidence. *Journal of Personality and Social Psychology*, 93, 49- 64.

Leung, F., Kim, S., & Tse, C. (2020). Highlighting Effort Versus Talent in Service Employee Performance: Customer Attributions and Responses. *Journal of Marketing*, *84*(3), 106-121.

Matzler, K., & Mueller, J. (2011). Antecedents of knowledge sharing–Examining the influence of learning and performance orientation. *Journal of Economic Psychology*, *32*(3), 317-329.

McCall, M. W. (1998). *High flyers: Developing the next generation of leaders*. Boston: Harvard Business School Press.

McFarland, R. G., & Kidwell, B. (2006). An examination of instrumental and expressive traits on performance: The mediating role of learning, prove, and avoid goal orientations. *Journal of Personal Selling and Sales Management*, 26(2), 143-159.

Montford, W. J., Leary, R. B., & Nagel, D. M. (2019). The impact of implicit self-theories and loss salience on financial risk. *Journal of Business Research*, 99, 1-11.

Mueller, C. M., & Dweck, C. (1998). Intelligence praise can undermine motivation and performance. *Journal of Personality and Social Psychology*, 75, 33-52.

Murphy, M. C., & Dweck, C. (2010). A culture of genius: How an organization's lay theory shapes people's cognition, affect, and behavior. *Personality and Social Psychology Bulletin*, 36, 283-296.

Nicholls, J. G. (1984). Achievement motivation Conceptions of ability, subjective expérience, task choice, and performance. *Psychological Review*, 91, 328-346.

Nosaki, H. (2003). Academic Help-Seeking: Achievement Goal Orientations and Perceptions of Competence. *Japanese Journal of Educational Psychology, 51*(2), 141-153.

Novell, C. A., Machleit, K. A., & Sojka, J. Z. (2016). Are good salespeople born or made? A new perspective on an age-old question: Implicit theories of selling ability. *Journal of Personal Selling & Sales Management, 36*(4), 309–320.

Özduran, A., & Tanova, C. (2017). Manager mindsets and employee organizational citizenship behaviours. *International Journal of Contemporary Hospitality Management*, 29(1), 589-606.

Roggeveen, A. L., & Sethuraman, R. (2020). How the COVID-19 Pandemic May Change the World of Retailing. *Journal of Retailing*, 96(2), 169–171.

Sharma, A., Rangarajan, D., & Paesbrugghe, B. (2020). Increasing resilience by creating an adaptive salesforce. *Industrial Marketing Management*, 88, 238–246.

Silver, L. S., Dwyer, S., & Alford, B. (2006). Learning and performance goal orientation of salespeople revisited: The role of performance-approach and performance-avoidance orientations. *Journal of Personal Selling and Sales Management*, 26(1), 27-38.

Sujan, H., Weitz, B. A., & Kumar, N. (1994). Learning orientation, working smart, and effective selling. *Journal of Marketing, 58*(3), 39–52.

Van Yperen, N., Hamstra, M., & van der Klauw, M. (2011). To win, or not to lose, at any cost: The impact of achievement goals on cheating. *British Journal of Management, 22*, 5–15.

VandeWalle D., Brown, S. P., Cron, W. L., & Slocum, J. W. (1999). The influence of goal orientation and self-regulation tactics on sales performance: A longitudinal field test. *Journal of Applied Psychology*, 84(2), 249-259.

Vandewalle, D. (1997). Development and Validation of a Work Domain Goal Orientation Instrument. *Educational and Psychological Measurement*, *57*(6), 995–1015.

Wentzel, D., Henkel, S., & Tomczak, T. (2010). Can I Live Up to That Ad? Impact of Implicit Theories of Ability on Service Employees' Responses to Advertising, *Journal of Service Research*, *13*(2), 137–152.
Wood, R., & Bandura, A., (1989). Social cognitive theory of organizational management. *Academy of management Review*, 14, 361-384.
Yee, R., Lee, P., Yeung, A., & Cheng, T. (2013). The relationships among leadership, goal orientation, and service quality in high-contact service industries: An empirical study. *International Journal of Production Economics, 141*, 452-464.
Yee, R., Lee, P., Yeung, A., & Cheng, T. (2018). Employee learning in high-contact service industries. *Management Decision*, 56(4), 793-807.
Yorkston, E. A., Nunes, J. C., & Matta, S. (2010). The malleable brand: The role of implicit theories in evaluating brand extensions. *Journal of Marketing*, *74*(1), 80–93.
Zingoni, M., & Corey, C. (2017). How Mindset Matters: The Direct and Indirect Effects of Employees? Mindsets on Job Performance. *Journal of Personnel Psychology*, 16(1), 36–45.

[illegible]

An Artificial Intelligence Method for the Analysis of Marketing Scientific Literature: An Abstract

Antonio Hyder and Ronjon Nag

Abstract We suggest a machine-based research literature reading method specific to the academic discipline of marketing, adopting artificial intelligence (AI) developments from the field of materials science.

Keeping up with research publications is untenable due to exponential growth. Researchers have become much better at the generation of information than at its deployment. AI can help to simplify the use of such knowledge. In materials science, Tshitoyan et al. (2019) have made steps in trying to achieve 'a generalized approach to the mining of scientific literature' using text mining and natural language processing. Using AI, research can be extracted from documents, classified, tokenised in individual words, and encoded as information-dense word embeddings, which are vector representations of words, without human supervision (Tshitoyan et al. 2019). Building on these developments we suggest a methodology specific to marketing science.

The first step is to compile consolidated bodies of offline marketing research on topics such as branding, retail or advertising following Tshitoyan et al. (2019) method of knowledge extraction and relationships for the handling of large bodies of scientific literature. For this we shall use CrossRef Application Programming Interface (API) for the retrieval of large lists of article Digital Object Identifiers (DOIs). This is used by a number of publisher APIs, such as Elsevier https://dev.elsevier.com and Springer Nature https://dev.springernature.com to download full-text journal articles. Secondly, the embeddings will be trained with the scientific abstracts from each of the topics. For this we shall use article abstracts from 1975 to 2021 from more than a thousand journals and also articles likely to contain marketing-related research directly retrieved from the aforementioned databases (i.e. Elsevier and Science Direct) combined with web scraping. The performance of the algorithm is deemed to improve when irrelevant abstracts are removed. The

A. Hyder (✉)
Hackers and Founders Research, San Jose, CA, USA
e-mail: ah@hf.cx

R. Nag
Stanford University & R42 Institute, Stanford, CA, USA
e-mail: ronjon@dci.stanford.edu

J. Allen et al. (eds.), *Celebrating the Past and Future of Marketing and Discovery with Social Impact*, Developments in Marketing Science: Proceedings of the Academy of Marketing Science, https://doi.org/10.1007/978-3-030-95346-1_97

remaining abstracts will then be classified as relevant and tokenised using ChemDataExtractor (Swain and Cole 2016). Correct pre-processing, especially the choice of phrases to be included as individual tokens should improve the results. In the third and final step, we shall repeat the first two steps integrating offline topics with the equivalent online topics, e.g. online branding.

As AI is also capable of predictive writing using bidirectional encoders BERT and ELMo used to produce contextual word embeddings (Devlin et al. 2018), our work in progress will consider developing automated hypotheses formulation in marketing science (Spangler et al. 2014). Simplification of knowledge could also facilitate its transfer to practice.

Keywords Artificial intelligence · Machine learning · Text mining · Natural language processing · Marketing science

Retail Employee Technology: Focused on Job Demand-Resource Model: An Abstract

Claire Whang and Chitra Dabas

Abstract Retail employee technology such as mobile POS, advanced analytics software, inventory management systems, and other in-store equipment is converging to strengthen retailer-customer relationships. Despite the increasing adoption of new retail employee technology in-store, there is little empirical evidence identifying job demands imposed by retail employee-specific technologies and how they affect frontline employees' well-being. Thus, the purpose of this study is to understand the effect of new retail employee technology on retail frontline employees' well-being. Using the job demand-resource model (Demerouti et al. 2001), this study focuses on the impact of retail technology-specific job demands (cognitive load, fear of public failure, information distrust) and job resources (employee training) on employees' burnout and work engagement.

This study uses multi-level modeling to test hypotheses. An online survey was conducted using previously validated measures, and a total of 487 US retail employees (42.1% female, 25-29 years old 33.9%, Caucasian 65.8%) with experience of using retail employee technology as part of their job were collected through Amazon MTurk.

A structural equation modeling with partial least square analysis in SmartPLS3.0 was used to test the proposed model. Results show that job demands (cognitive load, fear of public failure, information distrust) led to increased burnout while job resources (employee training) led to enhanced work engagement. Further, job resources buffered the impact of cognitive load on burnout. However, unexpectedly, job demands were not negatively associated with work engagement. Specifically, cognitive overload positively predicted work engagement. The positive effect of cognitive overload may be because certain stressors can positively foster personal growth and achieve mastery as a result of the effort involved in learning (Cavanaugh et al. 2000). The moderating effect of employee training to buffer the impact of cognitive overload on burnout may support this notion because employee training can assist in achieving personal growth. The study

C. Whang (✉) · C. Dabas
California State Polytechnic University, Pomona, CA, USA
e-mail: cwhang@cpp.edu; cdabas@cpp.edu

J. Allen et al. (eds.), *Celebrating the Past and Future of Marketing and Discovery with Social Impact*, Developments in Marketing Science: Proceedings of the Academy of Marketing Science, https://doi.org/10.1007/978-3-030-95346-1_98

findings extend the prior job demand-resource model and provide comprehensive insights for retail managers.

Keywords Job demands-resource (JD-R) model · Burnout · Employee engagement · Frontline employees · Retail employee technology

Investigating the Variables Affecting Brand Performance in the S-O-R Framework

Neda Sharifi Asadi Malafe, Salman Kimiagari, and Ensieh Kazemi Balef

Abstract This research assesses brand performance on the social network by adopting the stimulus-organism-response framework to understand service branding in the insurance industry. We used an applied research method, collected data through an online survey, and used structural equation modeling under partial least squares to analyze the data. The results showed that brand community engagement influences cognitive and affective attitudes. Also, community relationship investment positively affected brand community engagement and affective attitude but did not predict cognitive attitude. Also, cognitive and affective attitudes affected brand loyalty and brand recommendation. The results confirm the significance of all mediating relationships except the relationship between community relationship investment relationship and brand performance through cognitive attitude. This research may help firms in the insurance industry enhance their brand performance by involving customers by controlling appropriate stimuli.

Keywords Brand community engagement · Community relationship investment · Cognitive attitude · Affective attitude

Introduction

Companies constantly try to interact and keep long-term relationships with customers and discover the factors affecting brand performance (Flores and Parraga 2015). Companies use various tools to interact with customers (Xue et al. 2020). Information and communication technology have played a significant role in forming these interactions (Barbars 2016). To this day, social networking is seen

N. S. A. Malafe (✉) · E. K. Balef
Islamic Azad University, Sari, Iran
e-mail: bpj.nedasharifii@iausari.ac.ir; bpj.ensiehkazemibalf@iausari.ac.ir

S. Kimiagari
Thompson Rivers University, Kamloops, BC, Canada
e-mail: skimiagari@tru.ca

J. Allen et al. (eds.), *Celebrating the Past and Future of Marketing and Discovery with Social Impact*, Developments in Marketing Science: Proceedings of the Academy of Marketing Science, https://doi.org/10.1007/978-3-030-95346-1_99

as an interactive environment for many companies (Szabla and Blommaert 2020), and customer engagement is considered an essential phenomenon in these networks (Li and Wang 2020). In this globalized and unsure market, the insurance industry faces enormous competitive pressure (Biener et al. 2019). Insurance trading on social networks has become increasingly popular today due to reducing negative environmental impacts like a paper waste (Luo et al. 2019). Recent studies show that the insurance business through social networks can expand and improve the brand image and customer engagement and expansion (Castriotta et al. 2013; Delafrooz et al. 2017; Verma and Gangul 2019). Improving brand performance depends on increasing customer satisfaction and loyalty to the brand, which will be possible by providing superior value to customers (Delafrooz et al. 2017; Minta 2018; Nugraheni and Fauziah 2019; Ogbechi et al. 2018; Nguyen et al. 2018). So the survival of insurance companies depends on their customers (Delafrooz et al. 2017). Many researchers in brand management studies (Al-Zyoud 2018; Ali 2018; Dias et al. 2017; Rufaidah 2016) stated that branding had been a company strategy for many years. Keller (2003) stated that "branding involves the process of endowing products and services with the advantages that accrue to building a strong brand (p. 595)." Using brand attitudes as an organism in the marketing process can affect brand performance (Foroudi 2019). This attitude is formed following many stimuli, including customer engagement in the marketing process (Raajpoot and Ghilni-Wage 2019; Yang et al. 2017). The brand's attitude towards engaging the customer in the marketing process leads to collecting and evaluating brand information (Liu et al. 2020). Some studies have examined attitudes from both affective and cognitive perspectives (Liu et al. 2020; Verplanken et al. 1998), which result from customers' judgments about brand messages. Brand performance is measured from both financial and non-financial perspectives. From a non-financial perspective, brand performance consists of brand loyalty (Foroudi 2019; Liu et al. 2020) and brand recommendation (Foroudi 2019). In recent years, companies have paid particular attention to creating online brand communities (OBCs) for customer management; perhaps one of the reasons for this is the high level of influence and power in the acceptance of corporate brands, which expands business relationships (Carlson et al. 2019; Johnston and Taylor 2018). In this regard, as an essential member of marketing literature (Kumar and Nayak 2018), brand community relationships consider the desired attitude and behaviors of customers towards the community and the brand (Mcalexander et al. 2002). Brand community engagement (BCE), as a powerful and effective communication variable in the community as well as an essential factor in the success of the brand community by encouraging members to perform appropriate voluntary behaviors towards OBC and reducing the normative pressure of community, is defined as the recognition and participation in the brand communities (Loureiro and Kaufmann 2018; Kumar and Kumar 2020; Wirtz et al. 2013). This variable is mentioned as a strong predictor of brand performance (Kumar and Kumar 2020). Community relationship investment (CRI) by strengthening the customer's behavioral goals toward the brand affects business relationship quality (Shi et al. 2011).

Community relationship investment is also one of the variables of brand community that can influence brand performance through BCE (Kumar and Kumar 2020). In general, BCE and CRI are suggested as brand community stimuli in this study. While the link between the brand community and brand performance has been identified in the general marketing literature, several essential research gaps have been evident: First, fewer experimental studies focusing on brand attitudes in terms of cognitive and emotional dimensions were conducted in the insurance industry in Iran. Second, the insurance industry's brand community may affect brand attitudes from both cognitive and emotional dimensions and non-financial brand performance from two dimensions: loyalty and recommendation. Third, it is unknown whether the insurance industry's brand attitude plays a role in the relationship between the brand community and non-financial performance.

To address the research gaps mentioned above, this study investigates (1) the direct and indirect effect of brand community stimuli on brand performance, (2) the effect of cognitive and affective attitude in customer's evaluation process, and each on brand performance. This research seeks to answer the question: What is the brand community's role in the insurance industry's brand performance by considering the mediating role of brand attitude?

Theoretical Background

The model presented in this study is designed on the S-O-R framework and has the following literature review.

Insurance Industry

Protecting the body and soul against unpredictable dangers and harms is a principle for life (Syamsiar 2015). These concerns have led people to the nature of insurance and insurance companies (Minta 2018). Various insurance companies operate publicly and privately (Kunreuther and Lyster 2016). Based on this, customers face many choices (Asthana 2020). Insurance companies are trying to increase their performance through various stimuli (Purnami and Mujiati 2019). With the advent of information and communication technology, competition boundaries between these companies have expanded (Delafrooz et al. 2017). Numerous studies have shown that today insurance companies use social networks for their activities, advertising, and marketing; they also invite their customers to participate and engage in these networks (Castriotta et al. 2013; Delafrooz et al. 2017; Grant 2016; Shrestha et al. 2019; van den Broek-Altenburg and Atherly 2019).

Brand Community and Brand Attitude

Algesheimer, Dholakia, & Herrmann (2005) defined brand community engagement, as one of the components of the brand community, as "the intrinsic motivation of the customer to interact and cooperate with the members of the community" (p. 21). On the other hand, Kumar and Nayak (2018) described brand community engagement as "reflecting customer altruistic behaviors toward other members, dynamic participation in joint activities, and voluntary actions in support of the initiatives endorsed by the community to strengthen community value for oneself and others."(p. 66). The active participation of members in the OBCs creates and shares content regularly and helps people interact with other community members and the brand (Zheng et al. 2015). Baldus, Voorhees, & Calantone (2015) also see BCE as an inherent motivation to continue interacting with OBC. Because the engagement of the brand community, with the integration of the community and more robust business relationships, is vital for the sustainability of the community and the improvement of strategic value for customers (Ray et al. 2014; Reza et al. 2014; Zheng et al. 2015). Various studies have examined online brand community (Islam and Rahman 2017; Mosavi and Kenarehfard 2013) and the relationship between BCE and brand attitude (Jung et al. 2014; Yang et al. 2017; Wang et al. 2019) and brand performance (Coelho et al. 2018; Kuo and Feng 2013; Laroche et al. 2012; Lee et al. 2011; Reza et al. 2014; Zheng et al. 2015). Another factor that researchers in the brand community have considered is community relationship investment. Investing in relationships is a resource offered by retailers to maintain and strengthen customer relationships (Cho and Auger 2017; Popp et al. 2016). Understanding relationship investment is widely discussed in the customer marketing literature (Kumar and Kumar 2020). Community relationship investment leads to customer management and social communication among brand fans (Muñiz and Jensen Schau 2005). It is perhaps not unreasonable to say that increasing investment in the community can increase brand engagement. Customers who join OBCs may be loyal to the brand or have an initial relationship with the brand (Coulter et al. 2012). When they achieve a positive assessment of their target community's investment resources (time, money, etc.), they will be more willing and eager to join that community and participate in its activities. Also, investing in a perceived relationship can strengthen members' identities (Shi et al. 2011). Various studies have examined the relationship between investment and engagement (Kumar and Kumar 2020) and brand attitude and brand performance (Popp et al. 2016; Recuero Virto et al. 2019), which supports our proposition in this study. Therefore, the following hypotheses are proposed:

H1. Brand community engagement has a positive effect on cognitive attitude in the insurance industry.

H2. Brand community engagement has a positive effect on affective attitude in the insurance industry.

H3. Community relationship investment has a positive effect on brand community engagement in the insurance industry.

H4. Community relationship investment has a positive effect on cognitive attitude in the insurance industry.
H5. Community relationship investment has a positive effect on affective attitude in the insurance industry.

Brand Attitude and Brand Performance

Attitude to the brand is vital because it helps customer choices (Keller 1993). Zeithaml (1988) emphasizes the brand's attitude through customer beliefs towards the tangible and intangible (symbolic) features of the product that led to a brand stand out or not. Perhaps the attitude can be considered the overall customer evaluation of the brand to meet the needs. These needs can be motivational, participatory, and so on (Rositter and Percy 1987). Brand attitude also plays a vital role in marketing research. Researchers believe that attitudes consist of different dimensions (affective, cognitive, and conative) (Liu et al. 2020). Attitudes include cognitive and emotional actions. Cognitive attitude refers to behavioral logic (involvement or perceived risk of purchasing choice), and affective attitude refers to behavioral emotion (dominant motivation for brand choice) (Percy and Rossiter 1992). Cognitive attitudes express a product or other marketing stimulus to attract customers (Bettman and Park 1980; Lutz 1975). Moreover, the affective attitude is derived from marketing and advertising stimuli that affect customers' final attitude (Fazio et al. 1989; MacKenzie and Lutz 1989). These two types of attitudes affect a customer's behavioral intent (Liu et al. 2020). Because brand attitude, as a general brand assessment, brand attitude affects customer choice options and may also affect brand performance (Liu et al. 2020). Cognitive attitudes can be derived from actual knowledge or perceived knowledge of a product (Bettman and Park 1980; Lutz 1975). The customer's understanding of insurance can affect loyalty to that insurance and its advice to others (Ansari and Riasi 2016; Purnami and Mujiati 2019). Various studies have examined the relationship between brand attitude and brand performance (Dolbec and Chebat 2013; Liu et al. 2020). On the other hand, brand performance is examined from financial and non-financial perspectives (Eneizan et al. 2016; Nguyen et al. 2020). In this research, brand performance means the non-financial performance of the brand. In various studies, brand performance has referred to brand loyalty (Foroudi 2019; Kumar and Kumar 2020; Liu et al. 2020), brand satisfaction (Liu et al. 2020), the brand recommendation to others (Foroudi 2019; Jiménez-Castillo and Sánchez-Fernández 2019; Raajpoot and Ghilni-Wage 2019), brand re-purchase (Foroudi 2019), brand love (Zhou et al. 2020), and brand equity (Augusto and Torres 2018). In general, in the insurance industry (especially online), it is essential to pay attention to brand loyalty and brand recommendation (Alok and Srivastava 2013; Lesage et al. 2019). As the goal of branding in the insurance industry and any other industry is to provide benefits to customers and insurance companies, how branding makes this possible requires the formation of a model within the S-O-R framework that is based on effective stimuli on customers attitude organism

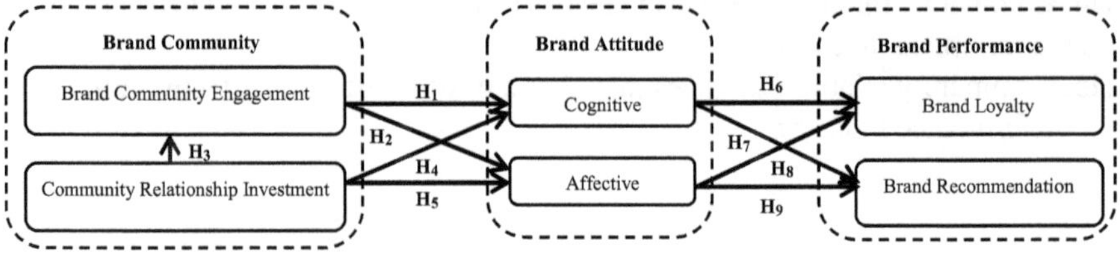

Fig. 1 The conceptual model of the research

that led to their responses (Liu et al. 2020). Therefore, the following hypotheses are proposed:

H6. Cognitive attitude has a positive effect on brand loyalty in the insurance industry.
H7. Cognitive attitude has a positive effect on brand recommendation in the insurance industry.
H8. Affective attitude has a positive effect on brand loyalty in the insurance industry.
H9. Affective attitude has a positive effect on brand recommendation in the insurance industry.

Accordingly, Fig. 1 illustrates the conceptual model of this research.

Methodology

Sample and Data Collection

The research method is descriptive as it describes the values. The purpose of this research, a survey in nature, is practical since the findings are applied in electronic commerce. The most important advantage of a survey is its generalizability. Data collection is done through library studies and supported by questionnaires, and it can be field research. The statistical population of the current study was the customers of the Pasargad insurance in Iran. According to the "rule of thumb" of Barclay et al. (1995) and the G*Power software, at least 85 people should be selected as a sample. Based on this, we selected 298 Pasargad insurance customers in groups on the Telegram social network by random sampling. The research model of this study was examined using the component-based Partial Least Squares Structural Equation Modelling (PLS-SEM) method. We have collected 435 questionnaires over two weeks. Of these, (26% = 104) of the questionnaires were incomplete and (74% = 298) were correct. Our criteria for selecting respondents (1) were insured persons active in the social network, (2) insured persons familiar with Pasargad Insurance and its products. Hence, the results of the respondents' survey based on demographic characteristics such as gender, age, education, and community visiting frequency showed: 66% of respondents were female, and 34% were male, 2% were below 18, 24% 19–30, 27% 31–40, 29% were 41–50, 17% 51–60, and 1% upper than 61 years old, 8% had diploma/Less, 20% below graduate, 33% graduate, and 39% postgraduate and higher, 43% visited the company's channel on daily, 42% weekly, 9% monthly, 4% quarterly (three months), and 2% more than three months.

Measurement Instrument

The data collection tool of the current study is the standard questionnaire. The five-point Likert, with the following items: completely disagree (1), disagree (2), neutral (3), agree (4), completely agree (5), the scale used to measure the questions, which is one of the most common measurements. The measurement tools have shown in Table 1.

There were 25 items in the measurement of the research variables. Data collected through an online questionnaire. The participants were invited to the survey by linking the online questionnaire at the Pasargad insurance Telegram channel.

Evaluation of Measurement Model

In the current research, the Cronbach alpha, a kind of intrinsic homology, was used to assess questionnaires' reliability. Typically, the Cronbach alpha coefficient ranges from zero, which means no positive relation to one, which means a complete relationship. If the outcome number is closer to one, the questionnaire will be more reliable. As shown in Table 1, the alpha level above 0.7 for each questionnaire indicates the proper reliability of all six questionnaires used in this research. Also, the overall reliability of the questionnaire was 0.92. Divergent validity, convergent validity, and indicator reliability are used to measure the measuring model's fitting. For evaluating the validity of constructs, Fornell and Larcker (1981) introduced three criteria: divergent validity, composite reliability of each construct, and the average variance extracted (convergent validity). The results of these indices in Table 1 verify the convergent validity and composite reliability of the constructs and indicate the fitting of this criterion and the appropriate reliability of measurement models.

On the other hand, the divergent validity is measured in three ways: (1) cross-loading method, and (2) the Fornell and Larcker criterion, (3) Heterotrait-Monotrait (HTMT). Based on the cross-loading assessment, each construct's value loading should at least be 0.1 higher than that of the other items in the model with the same construct. The Fornell-Larcker criterion is the value of the correlation between a construct and its indices compared with that construct's correlation with other constructs. Using the Fornell-Larcker method, our model was reliable, and the validity of the numbers in the primary diameter exceeded their lower values. Moreover, in this research, HTMT (Heterotrait-Monotrait) is investigated as the new approach to analyze the discriminant validity in variance-based SEM, which Henseler et al. (2015) recommended. HTMT calculates by run the bootstrapping routine, and it is

Table 1 Measurement tools

Variables	Scales	Loadings	Mean	SD	α	rho_A	CR	AVE
Brand Community								
Brand community engagement (Modified from Kumar & Kumar, 2020)	I profit from following the community's rules.	0.749	3.771	0.732	0.766	0.766	0.850	0.587
	I am motivated to participate in the activities because I feel good afterward or like them.	0.778						
	I am motivated to participate in the community's activities because I can support other members.	0.763						
	I am motivated to participate in the community's activities because I can reach personal goals.	0.775						
Community relationship investment (Modified from Kumar & Kumar, 2020)	This community makes efforts to maintain members associated and loyal.	0.790	3.746	0.731	0.822	0.831	0.874	.580
	This community constantly tries to improve its relationships with its members.	0.767						
	This community provides trusty benefit programs and services.	0.783						
	This community is not worried about its members.	0.744						
	I am confident that this community provides the best deals.	0.723						
Brand Attitude								
Cognitive (Modified from Liu et al., 2020)	This company's products are useful.	0.753	3.761	0.789	0.761	0.762	0.847	0.580
	I think that designing this company has a positive environmental attitude.	0.738						
	This company provides modern plans and gives me free consultations to get to know them.	0.764						
	Compared to similar companies, I think this company is more reliable.	0.790						

Variables	Scales	Loadings	Mean	SD	α	rho_A	CR	AVE
Brand Community								
Affective (Modified from Liu et al., 2020)	This company motivates a feeling of increased self-identity.	0.799	3.577	0.658	0.746	0.750	0.840	0.568
	This company makes me feel that it meets my needs.	0.771						
	The discipline and design of the company are pretty in line with my personality.	0.724						
	I like to activity in this company.	0.717						
Brand Performance								
Brand Loyalty (Modified from Foroudi, 2019)	I consider myself to be loyal to this company.	0.737	3.735	0.686	0.843	0.846	0.888	0.615
	I will not buy products from other companies when this company exists.	0.730						
	Compared to other companies with similar features, I am willing to pay a higher price for this company.	0.828						
	I believe this company has credibility.	0.815						
	I enjoy selecting this company.	0.807						
Brand Recommendation (Modified from Foroudi, 2019)	I would say positive things about this company to other people.	0.802	3.810	0.859	0.748	0.748	0.856	0.665
	I would recommend that everyone use the products of this company.	0.813						
	I would encourage friends and relatives to use the products of this company.	0.831						

Table 2 HTMT results

Variable	1	2	3	4	5	6
Affective attitude						
Brand Community engagement	0.775					
Brand loyalty	0.850	0.805				
Brand recommendation	0.715	0.852	0.841			
Cognitive attitude	0.862	0.798	0.821	0.826		
Community relationship investment	0.363	0.308	0.316	0.286	0.260	

Table 3 Value of determinant coefficient (R^2) and prediction power coefficient (Q^2)

	Affective attitude	Brand community	Brand loyalty	Brand recommendation	Cognitive attitude
R^2	0.363	0.061	0.544	0.425	0.385
Q^2	0.194	0.034	0.314	0.268	0.204

based on the average of the heterotrait-heteromethod correlations relative to the average of the Heterotrait-Monotrait correlations (Henseler et al. 2015). HTMT value range should be below 0.90 (Gold et al. 2001; Teo et al. 2008) or 0.85 (Clark and Watson 1995; Kline 2015) to confirm the discriminant validity between constructs. As shown in Table 2, no constructs had a higher value than 0.90. Therefore, there is not a lack of discriminant validity.

Overall, according to the convergent validity and discriminant validity results, there is no concern about the measurement model's convergent validity and discriminant validity.

Assessment of Construct Model

After evaluating the measurement's reliability and validity, a constructed model was assessed through the relationship among latent variables. In the current research, two criteria were used: the determination coefficient (R2) and the prediction power coefficient (Q2) (Stone-Geisser criterion). R2 is a criterion showing the influence of an independent variable on a dependent variable, and three values of 0.19, 0.33, and 0.67 are the number of indicators for the low, moderate, or high level of R2. Meanwhile, Q2 evaluated the model's prediction power (Stone-Geisser criterion). The three values of 0.02, 0.15, and 0.35 are the number of indicators for the low, moderate, or high level of Q2. Table 3 shows the results of these two indicators.

Finally, the standardized root mean square residual value (SRMR) is defined as a "comparison of the constant root of the difference between the observed correlation and the predicted correlation matrix." Acceptable values of this index should be less than 0.08 (Henseler et al. 2015). Since the SRMR value of this model is 0.069, the model has a good fit.

Results

After evaluating the fitting of measurement models and constructing models, and enjoying the proper fitting of models, the research hypotheses were examined and tested. Then, the results of significant coefficients for each hypothesis, standardized coefficients for each hypothesis's paths, and the outcomes of examination of hypothesis at 95% confidence level are presented in Table 4.

Table 5 indicates the role of mediating variables (indirect effects).

Discussions and Implications

Summary of Finding

Considering customer responses to the questionnaire about service branding and the statistical analysis, the result showed that brand community engagement influences the insurance industry's cognitive and affective attitude. Community relationship investment positively affected brand community engagement and affective attitude but did not predict cognitive attitude. Cognitive and affective attitudes also affected brand loyalty and brand recommendation. The results confirm the significance of all

Table 4 Test of the hypotheses of the research

	Path	Path Coefficient (β)	(T-Value)	P-Value	Test Result
H_1	Brand Community Engagement -> Cognitive	0.605	16.665	0.000****	Confirmed
H_2	Brand Community Engagement -> Affective	0.545	13.966	0.000****	Confirmed
H_3	Community Relationship Investment -> Brand Community Engagement	0.254	4.179	0.000****	Confirmed
H_4	Community Relationship Investment -> Cognitive	0.064	1.195	0.233 n.s.	Rejected
H_5	Community Relationship Investment -> Affective	0.161	3.541	0.000****	Confirmed
H_6	Cognitive Attitude -> Brand Loyalty	0.392	6.663	0.000****	Confirmed
H_7	Cognitive Attitude -> Brand Recommendation	0.493	8.219	0.000****	Confirmed
H_8	Affective Attitude -> Brand Loyalty	0.423	7.614	0.000****	Confirmed
H_9	Affective Attitude -> Brand Recommendation	0.217	3.345	0.001***	Confirmed

Note: *$p < 0.1$; ** $p < 0.05$; *** $p < 0.01$; **** $p < 0.001$, n.s. not significant.

Table 5 Test of mediator effects

	Standardized Coefficients				
Structural Path	Direct	Indirect [95%CI]	Total effect [95%CI]	P-Value	Decision
CRI -> BCE -> AA	0.162	0.138 (0.069; 0.0199)	0.300 (0.167; 0.389)	0.000****	Supported
BCE -> AA -> BL	0.238	0.230 (0.158; 0.301)	0.468 (0.395; 0.525)	0.000****	Supported
CRI -> BCE -> AA -> BL	0.153	0.059 (0.027; 0.093)	0.212 (0.118; 0.297)	0.001***	Supported
CRI -> AA -> BL	0.144	0.068 (0.027; 0.114)	0.212 (0.118; 0.297)	0.003***	Supported
BCE -> CA -> BL	0.231	0.237 (0.162; 0.323)	0.468 (0.395; 0.525)	0.000****	Supported
CRI -> BCE -> CA -> BL	0.152	0.060 (0.030; 0.102)	0.212 (0.118; 0.297)	0.001***	Supported
CRI -> CA -> BL	0.187	0.025 (−0.013; 0.073)	0.212 (0.118; 0.297)	0.244 n.s.	Rejected
BCE -> AA -> BR	0.299	0.118 (0.048; 0.201)	0.417 (0.342; 0.479)	0.002***	Supported
CRI -> BCE -> AA -> BR	0.142	0.030 (0.010; 0.061)	0.172 (0.085; 0.245)	0.020**	Supported
CRI -> AA -> BR	0.137	0.035 (0.013; 0.068)	0.172 (0.085; 0.245)	0.020**	Supported
BCE -> CA -> BR	0.119	0.298 (0.208; 0.380)	0.417 (0.342; 0.479)	0.000****	Supported
CRI -> BCE -> CA -> BR	0.096	0.076 (0.037; 0.117)	0.172 (0.085; 0.245)	0.000****	Supported
CRI -> CA -> BR	0.141	0.031 (-0.018; 0.085)	0.172 (0.085; 0.245)	0.247 n.s.	Rejected
CRI -> BCE -> CA	0.063	0.154 (0.077; 0.224)	0.217 (0.098; 0.336)	0.000****	Supported

CRI Community Relationship Investment, *BCE* Brand Community Engagement, *AA* Affective Attitude, *BL* Brand Loyalty, *CA* Cognitive Attitude, *BR* Brand Recommendation.
Note: *p < 0.1; ** p < 0.05; *** p < 0.01; **** p < 0.001, n.s. not significant.

mediating relationships except the relationship between community relationship investment relationship and brand performance through cognitive attitude. These results align with those of prior studies, some of which are discussed in the next section.

Discussions

This study aimed to explain the role of brand community in the insurance industry's brand performance by mediating brand attitude. The following compares our results with those of previous studies. Islam and Rahman (2017), Jiménez-Castillo and Sánchez-Fernández (2019), Jung et al. (2014), Kaur et al. (2020), Kumar and Kumar (2020), Kumar and Nayak (2018), Raajpoot and Ghilni-Wage (2019), Ray et al. (2014), Reza et al. (2014), Wirtz et al. (2013), and Zheng et al. (2015), studied brand community engagement in service branding. They believed that community engagement in the online community has a significant impact on brand performance. This can happen through various intermediary variables, such as brand attitude (Raajpoot and Ghilni-Wage 2019). They as well as Lee et al. (2011), Pedeliento et al. (2020), and Xue et al. (2020), studied various factors like community engagement stimuli in the process of branding. Based on current research and previous studies, engagement in the online community considerably affected branding. The growth of information and communication technology has created many incentives to encourage customers to participate in online activities. Participating in online networks has become an involuntary activity for some customers. On the other hand, the results of Kumar and Kumar (2020) research have been consistent with the results of this study on the relationship between community relationship investment and brand community engagement. Also, Recuero Virto et al. (2019), in line with the present study, showed that community relationship investment has also affected brand performance in their research. However, this study examined the relationship between community relationship investment and brand performance through brand attitudes. This study indicated that the cognitive attitude did not play a significant mediating role in this regard, while the affective attitude has a significant mediating role. Perhaps one of the reasons for this is the insurance company's investment in sales and marketing promotions to build relationships with customers. These incentives are designed to evoke excitement in customers, and customers become involuntarily and irrationally loyal to the brand, recommending it to others and marketing it. Today, due to the fierce competition between insurance companies, we are witnessing many of these incentives, which cause the customer to be involved in the brand and affect the brand's performance affectively. Another achievement of this research was the alignment of its results with the results of researches of Augusto and Torres (2018), Foroudi (2019), Gómez and Rubio (2010), Hwang et al. (2011), Lee et al. (2011), Lee et al. (2017), Lee and Cho (2019), Liu et al. (2010), Park et al. (2015), Raajpoot and Ghilni-Wage (2019), on the relationship between brand attitude and brand performance. According to Liu et al. (2020), brand performance may be affected by brand attitudes. Brand attitude has also played a role in this research as a mediating variable. This suggests that if the insurer has a positive attitude towards the insurance brand, it can be loyal to it and recommend it to others. However, cognitive (through the involvement it creates in the customer) and affective attitudes cause insurance branding. Therefore, theoretical and managerial implications are provided as follows.

References

Al-Zyoud, M. F. (2018). Social media marketing, functional branding strategy, and intentional branding. *Problems and Perspectives in Management, 16*(3), 102–116.

Alok, K. R., & Srivastava, M. (2013). The Antecedents of Customer Loyalty: An Empirical Investigation in Life Insurance Context. *Journal of Competitiveness, 5*(2), 139–163.

Baldus, B. J., Voorhees, C., & Calantone, R. (2015). Online brand community engagement: Scale development and validation. *Journal of Business Research, 68*(5), 978-985.

Bettman, J. R., & Park, C. W. (1980). Effects of Prior Knowledge and Experience and Phase of the Choice Process on Consumer Decision Processes: A Protocol Analysis. *Journal of Consumer Research, 7*(3), 234.

Cho, M., & Auger, G. A. (2017). Extrovert and engaged? Exploring the connection between personality and involvement of stakeholders and the perceived relationship investment of nonprofit organizations. *Public Relations Review, 43*(4), 729–737.

Coelho, P. S., Rita, P., & Santos, Z. R. (2018). On the relationship between consumer-brand identification, brand community, and brand loyalty. *Journal of Retailing and Consumer Services, 43*(February), 101–110.

Delafrooz, N., Zendehdel, M., & Fathipoor, M. (2017). The Effect of Social Media on Customer Loyalty and Company Performance of Insurance Industry. *International Journal of Economics and Financial Issues, 7*(3), 254–264.

Dolbec, P. Y., & Chebat, J. C. (2013). The Impact of a Flagship vs. a Brand Store on Brand Attitude, Brand Attachment and Brand Equity. *Journal of Retailing, 89*(4), 460–466.

Fazio, R. H., Powell, M. C., & Williams, C. J. (1989). Attitude to behavior. *The Journal of Consumer Research, 16*(3), 280–288.

Henseler, J., Ringle, C. M., & Sarstedt, M. (2015). A new criterion for assessing discriminant validity in variance-based structural equation modeling. *Journal of the Academy of Marketing Science, 43*(1), 115-135.

Islam, J., & Rahman, Z. (2017). The impact of online brand community characteristics on customer engagement: An application of Stimulus-Organism-Response paradigm. *Telematics and Informatics, 34*(4), 96–109.

Jung, N. Y., Kim, S., & Kim, S. (2014). Influence of consumer attitude toward online brand community on revisit intention and brand trust. *Journal of Retailing and Consumer Services, 21*(4), 581–589.

Kaur, H., Paruthi, M., Islam, J. U., & Hollebeek, L. D. (2020). The role of brand community identification and reward on consumer brand engagement and brand loyalty in virtual brand communities. *Telematics and Informatics, 46*(October 2019), 101321.

Kuo, Y. F., & Feng, L.H. (2013). Relationships among community interaction characteristics, perceived benefits, community commitment, and oppositional brand loyalty in online brand communities. *International Journal of Information Management, 33*(6), 948–962.

Lee, H., & Cho, C. H. (2019). An empirical investigation on the antecedents of consumers' cognitions of and attitudes towards digital signage advertising. *International Journal of Advertising, 38*(1), 97–115.

Loureiro, S. M. C., & Kaufmann, H. R. (2018). The role of online brand community engagement on positive or negative self-expression word-of-mouth. *Cogent Business & Management, 5*(1), 1508543.

MacKenzie, S. B., & Lutz, R. J. (1989). An Empirical Examination of the Structural Antecedents of Attitude toward the Ad in an Advertising Pretesting Context. *Journal of Marketing, 53*(2), 48-65.

Nguyen, H.T., Nguyen, H., Nguyen, N.D., & Phan, A.C. (2018). Determinants of customer satisfaction and loyalty in Vietnamese life-insurance setting. *Sustainability (Switzerland), 10*(4), 1–16.

Ogbechi, A. D., Okafor, L. I., & Onifade, T. A. (2018). Determinants of customer satisfaction and loyalty in relation to corporate performance of insurance industry in Nigeria. *International Journal of Economics, Commerce and Management, 6*(4), 256-268.

Park, H.H., Jeon, J.O., & Sullivan, P. (2015). How does visual merchandising in fashion retail stores affect consumers' brand attitude and purchase intention? *International Review of Retail, Distribution and Consumer Research, 25*(1), 87–104.

Purnami, N.M., & Mujiati, N.W. (2019). Customer Brand Engagement and Brand Loyalty Insurance Users in Bali Province. *Journal of Business Management and Economic Research, 3*(4), 18.

Reza, M., Laroche, M., & Richard, M. (2014). Computers in Human Behavior The roles of brand community and community engagement in building brand trust on social media. *Computers in Human Behavior, 37*, 152–161.
Wang, X. W., Cao, Y. M., & Park, C. (2019). The relationships among community experience, community commitment, brand attitude, and purchase intention in social media. International *Journal of Information Management, 49*, 475-488.
Xue, J., Liang, X., Xie, T., & Wang, H. (2020). See now, act now: How to interact with customers to enhance social commerce engagement? *Information & Management*, 103324.
Yang, Y., Asaad, Y., & Dwivedi, Y. (2017). Examining the impact of gamification on intention of engagement and brand attitude in the marketing context. *Computers in Human Behavior, 73*, 459–469.
Zhou, F., Mou, J., Su, Q., & Jim Wu, Y. C. (2020). How does consumers' Perception of Sports Stars' Personal Brand Promote Consumers' brand love? A mediation model of global brand equity. *Journal of Retailing and Consumer Services, 54*, 102012.

Systematic Literature Review of the Female Stereotypes in Advertising Within the Different Periods of Feminism: An Abstract

Claudia Lizzette Gomez Borquez, Anna Török, Edgar Centeno, and Erzsébet Malota

Abstract With the rise of feminist and social movements, new sorts of advertisements have emerged, signaling a change toward a more gender-neutral portrayal. Femvertising is a new type of advertising that aims to show women in an equal and diverse way. It strives to empower women while avoiding depictions of traditional gender stereotypes and sexuality. The aim of this study is to analyze all the research on female stereotypes in advertising conducted between January 2000 and March 2021 during the various stages of feminism: pre-feminism, feminism, and post-feminism. The systematic literature review method is used in this study, and it discusses the key research methods, the context (country, sector), and the main research topics related to female stereotypes in advertising. In addition to identifying future research directions, the current study seeks to determine the place and role of femvertising in relation to the different feminist periods.

The findings reveal that the vast majority of the studies rely on data from a single nation, with research in the United States and the United Kingdom dominating the field. About half of the studies in the current article gathered data from only one sector, with the apparel industry receiving the most attention. The other most prominent sectors in the research were beauty, personal care, and advertising. Except for the studies related to femvertising, qualitative studies predominated in all periods of feminism. The reviewed articles identify the major research trends related to consumer attitudes, the evolution of female portrayal in advertising, the objectification of women, and the social movement of women empowerment. The number of arti-

C. L. G. Borquez (✉) · E. Centeno
Tecnolgico de Monterrey – EGADE Business School, Monterrey, Mexico
e-mail: a00937922@itesm.mx; ecenteno@tec.mx

A. Török · E. Malota
Corvinus University of Budapest, Budapest, Hungary
e-mail: anna.torok@uni-corvinus.hu; erzsebet.malota@uni-corvinus.hu

J. Allen et al. (eds.), *Celebrating the Past and Future of Marketing and Discovery with Social Impact*, Developments in Marketing Science: Proceedings of the Academy of Marketing Science, https://doi.org/10.1007/978-3-030-95346-1_100

cles on the latter topic has been rapidly increasing in recent years, owing to the femvertising trend.

Keywords Female stereotypes · Feminism · Women empowerment · Femvertising · Advertising

Study of the Factors Affecting the Intention to Adopt and Recommend Technology to Others: Based on the Unified Theory of Acceptance and Use of Technology (UTAUT)

Salman Kimiagari, Ensieh Kazemi Balef, and Neda Sharifi Asadi Malafe

Abstract The present study investigates the factors affecting the intention to adopt and recommend technology to others: based on the Unified Theory of Acceptance and Use of Technology. This applied research is descriptive-analytical in terms of data collection. According to the analytical model presented in this research, the environmental characteristics of websites are more important in the early stages of the online shopping process. The information on a website is critical to examine a product with customers' criteria or needs. An attractive website creates a more positive feeling in the audience, keeps users on the website for a more extended period, and attracts new customers. Also, as part of both the emotional and logical aspects of using technology, individual factors influence the intention to adopt and recommend Internet banking by customers. In the realm of e-commerce, how environmental and individual characteristics affect user intent is still challenging. After data collecting and hypotheses tested, it was concluded that also in this research, these factors affect the acceptance and recommendation of internet banking to others.

Keywords Intention to adopt · Use recommendation · UTAUT · Internet banking

---

S. Kimiagari (✉)
Thompson Rivers University, Kamloops, BC, Canada
e-mail: skimiagari@tru.ca

E. K. Balef · N. S. A. Malafe
Islamic Azad University, Sari, Iran
e-mail: bpj.ensiehkazemibalf@iausari.ac.ir; bpj.nedasharifii@iausari.ac.ir

J. Allen et al. (eds.), *Celebrating the Past and Future of Marketing and Discovery with Social Impact*, Developments in Marketing Science: Proceedings of the Academy of Marketing Science, https://doi.org/10.1007/978-3-030-95346-1_101

Introduction

The acceptance and use of information technology (IT) have been among the major issues and research priorities of the late 1980s (Miltgen et al. 2013). Research in this area is constantly evolving (Jin et al. 2015). The evolution of new technologies provides organizations with the opportunity to retain and deliver new services and products to customers (Martins et al. 2014). The Internet is ideal for banking affairs because of its capacity for cost savings and data transfer speed. It is technological and economically logical to perform banking affairs online (Floh and Treiblmaier 2006). Banks use technology not only to improve their internal performance but also to provide better customer services. The emergence of internet banking first began in the 1980s, but its growth occurred in the 1990s, and Europe was recognized as the pioneer of using internet banking as one of the most profitable e-commerce software globally (Raza and Hanif 2011). Internet banking refers to "a banking channel that enables customers to perform a wide range of financial and informal services through a banking website." Internet banking provides customers with an opportunity to manage and control their financial and transaction accounts through a banking website. Banks are trying to find new ways to cut the customer relationship with the physical banking system (Rahi and Ghani 2016). The banks are also differentiated by providing innovative services and active Internet strategies (Rahi et al. 2019). It is essential in internet banking to frequently ensure that customers frequently visit their business applications because it indicates increased loyalty and reduced offline transactions. With increased customer engagement and loyalty, banks receive more money.

For this reason, accepting Internet banking services is beneficial for banks and provides an opportunity for banks to respond to the needs of their remote customers (Martins et al. 2014). Despite the potential benefits of internet banking, such as faster transaction, time-saving, and lower costs, acceptance of internet banking is limited and, in many cases, less than expected (Rahi and Abd. Ghani 2018). There are still many customers who refuse Internet banking because of uncertainty and security concerns. Despite the growth of e-banking services and products, there are social (culture, tradition, and education), economic (information, profitability, and security), and personal (ease of use, learning, enjoyment, and utility) factors that harm customers (Rodrigues et al. 2016). Therefore, it is necessary to understand the factors affecting the intention to use Internet banking. Recent studies have provided various theories to understand the characteristics of internet banking acceptance. One of them is the Unified Theory of Acceptance and Use of Technology (UTAUT). This model was developed by Venkatesh et al. (2003), which outlines the conditions for people to adopt the technology. This model examines people's perception of technology's usefulness and its intended use in social impacts and perceptual processes. Previous studies have also shown that consumers with higher technology intentions are more likely to recommend it to others (Kuo and Yen 2009; Lee et al. 2011). The present study investigates the factors affecting the intention to adopt and recommend the technology to others: based on the Unified Theory of Acceptance and Use of Technology.

Theoretical Framework and Development of Hypotheses

Unified Theory of Acceptance and Use of Technology (UTAUT)

The acceptance of new technology by users is a complex phenomenon that requires more than a single model (Shen et al. 2010). In 1985, Davis introduced the Technology Acceptance Model (TAM) to improve the understanding of information system users' acceptance processes and evaluate new systems (Ramírez-Correa et al. 2019). Technology Acceptance Model explains the technology acceptance behavior and analyzes the behavior and intention of using technology, like other technology acceptance models (Rahi and Ghani 2018) and noting that the two main elements of perceived usefulness (PU) and perceived ease of use (PEOU) are considered as the main factors influencing the intention to adopt the technology (Venkatesh and Davis 1996). PU refers to the degree to which the performance of a task is improved by the use of technology, while PEOU refers to the degree to which a technology is effortless (Van Der Heijden 2003, p. 176).

For decades, the TAM model has been the dominant model for understanding the user's acceptance of information systems. Venkatesh et al. (2003) presented the UTAUT model, an extension of the technology acceptance model. Based on the meta-analysis of technology acceptance, the existing models can only explain 40% of the variance in accepting technology. In response to this criticism, the unified theory of acceptance and use of technology is presented, with the ability to explain 70% of the variance of the intention to adopt Technology. Hence, this is the reason for using this theory in the conceptual model of the present study.

The UTAUT model is based on eight models: logical act theory, programmed behavior theory, technology acceptance model, social cognition theory, innovation promotion theory, the motivational model for personal computer use, and a composite model of technology acceptance models programmed behavior theory. It also consists of four constructs: performance expectancy, effort expectancy, social impact, and facilitation conditions that affect the intention to use technology. Gender, age, experience, and desire to use technology were introduced as moderator variables to understand better the complexity of technology acceptance in this model (Bùi and Bùi 2018).

Performance Expectancy and Effort Expectancy

About our purposes, we focused on two main factors of the UTAUT model, namely the performance expectancy and the effort expectancy. Performance expectancy is the degree to which people believe that using technology increases their performance (Venkatesh et al. 2012, p. 159). This dimension of UTAUT consists of five structures in different models, i.e., perceived utility, job fit, extrinsic motivation, relative advantage, and expectations. Recent studies (Alwahaishi and Snásel 2013; Brown et al. 2010) showed that when using technology is low and its benefit is high, its value is using technology will increase. According to Martins et al. (2014), internet banking's performance expectancy is the degree to which a person believes that using internet banking will earn money. Research by Wang and Yang (2005) showed that performance expectancy significantly and positively impacts accepting technology. The second structure of the UTAUT model is the effort expectancy, which is the degree of ease of use of the system (Venkatesh et al. 2003). Easy access to technology raises users' motivation and increases their desire to use Technology (Baabdullah et al. 2019). According to research literature, the research hypotheses are as follows:

H1. Performance expectancy has a positive impact on the intention to adopt internet banking.
H2. Effort expectancy has a positive impact on the intention to adopt internet banking.

Personal Innovativeness

Thakur and Srivastava (2015) define innovativeness as a risk. Having desires in specific individuals and not in all. These people desire to try new things and be able to cope with high levels of uncertainty. Innovativeness in information technology has been introduced based on diffusion theory. Innovation has a significant impact on the user's intention to use innovative Technology (Mun et al. 2006). Theoretically and empirically, innovativeness is a critical variable in accepting innovation (Hartman and Samra 2008). The model presented by Rogers has been widely used in various studies on technology acceptance and innovation dissemination (Chedrawi et al. 2019). Kombe and Wafula (2015) define innovation as a multistage process whereby organizations transform ideas into new products, services, or processes to differentiate themselves from their competitors in the market. The Rogers model assumes that certain factors such as perception, characteristics of innovation, decision making, communication channels, and social systems affect the speed at which people accept innovation (Chedrawi et al. 2019). Innovation not only has a direct impact on user behavior for technology use, but it also has a positive and significant impact on performance expectancy, effort expectancy, and adaptability (Oliveira et al. 2016; Rahi and Abd. Ghani 2018). Thus, according to the mentioned points, the following hypotheses is explained:

H3. Personal innovativeness has a positive impact on the intention to adopt internet banking.

Anxiety

Anxiety has been introduced as an emotional and individual aspect of using Technology (Rana et al. 2016). Agarwal (2000) perceive anxiety as a person's fear while using a computer. Some research shows that consumers' concerns about online shopping, such as identity theft, credit card fraud, privacy violation, access to unauthorized accounts, misleading advertisements increase the level of anxiety about dealing with virtual sellers (Celik 2016). Anxiety is an inhibiting factor in technology acceptance. Park et al. (2019) concluded in their research that the social effects and anxiety of using technology affect the multiple benefits of mobile payment services. Another study by Demoulin and Djelassi (2016) showed that technology anxiety hurts self-service technology acceptance. Therefore, according to the mentioned points, the following hypotheses is explained:

H4. Anxiety has a negative impact on the intention to adopt internet banking.

Website Design and Characteristics

Research on website usability has shown that website design and web page layout affect consumers' thoughts about the website content. Therefore, website owners should do their utmost to design and create a website environment to support website content (Walker 2011). Holloway and Beatty (2008) believe those website characteristics are crucial in the early stages of the online shopping process. An influential website should display key and functional features in its appearance and content (Rahi and Abd. Ghani 2018). When the websites with the best content are rendered incorrectly, users' evaluation of this content is affected (Walker 2011). In addition to website design, web page characteristics and content are also essential factors in the online consumer shopping process. An attractive website generates more powerful positive emotions, forces users to spend more time on the website, and attracts new customers. Research conducted by Al-Qeisi et al. (2014) shows that the technical, general, and visual dimensions are critical to users. These dimensions directly and indirectly positively affect the behavioral intent of individuals. Also, research has been conducted by Rahi et al. (2019), Holloway and Beatty (2008), and Udo et al. (2010). In this research, the relationship between website design and characteristics with effort and performance expectancy was examined. The results showed that the design and characteristics of the website, customer service, and effort expectancy have a positive effect on the performance expectancy and acceptance of Internet banking. As a result, the hypotheses are proposed:

H5. Website characteristic has a positive impact on the performance expectancy.
H6. Website characteristic has a positive impact on the effort expectancy.
H7. Website design has a positive impact on performance expectancy.
H8. Website design has a positive impact on the effort expectancy.

Intention to Recommend Internet Banking to Others

Consumers with higher intentions to adopt technology are more likely to recommend it to others (Rahi and Abd. Ghani 2018). Leong et al. (2013) showed that users with high technology acceptance could influence the intention to recommend the technology to others in social networks. Ghani showed that the intention to adopt technology positively impacted the intention to recommend it to others. Social networks present challenges and opportunities for users to express their views and experiences on new products or technologies (Oliveira et al. 2016; Rahi et al. 2019). Oliveira et al. (2016) believe that intention to adopt technology positively affects its recommendation to others. Therefore, the following hypotheses are proposed:

H9. User intent to adopt internet banking has an impact on user intent to recommend internet banking.

According to the research literature, the conceptual model of this research is as shown in (Fig. 1):

Research Methodology

This applied research is descriptive-analytical in terms of data collection. Data collection was carried out using library and field studies. A questionnaire was used in the field study. The statistical population of this study consisted of Tejarat Bank of Iran in Mazandaran province. A total of 384 samples were selected using a non-random sampling method (the non-random sampling method was chosen because

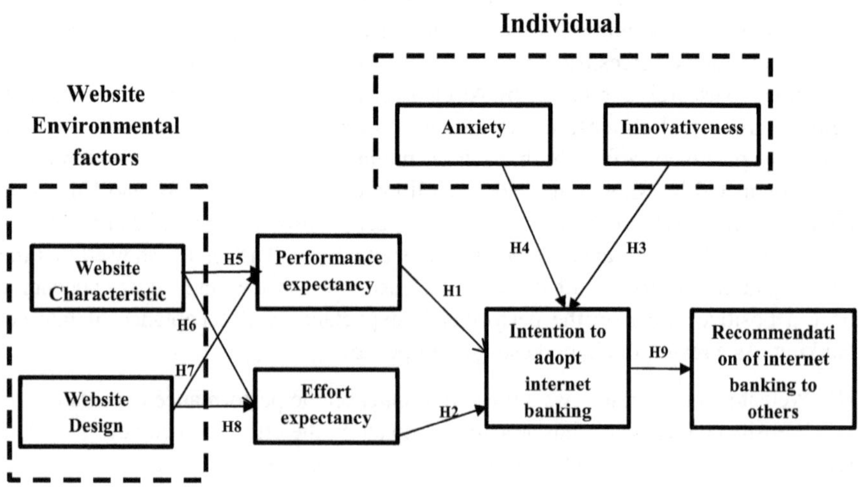

Fig. 1 Conceptual model of research

the list of customers was not available. With this in mind, the sample size was selected through the available sampling method) at a 95% confidence level based on Cochran's sampling formula. The data collection tool is a standard questionnaire. The 5-point Likert scale was used as one of the most common measures. The specifications of the measurement tool are set out in Table 1.

In general, the research variables were measured in 28 items. We collected the data through an online questionnaire. Participants shared their comments in an online questionnaire link.

Evaluation of Measurement Model

In the present study, Cronbach's alpha method, internal consistency, was used to evaluate the questionnaires' reliability. Typically, the Cronbach's alpha coefficient ranges from zero (i.e., no positive relationship) to 1 (complete relationship); the closer is the number to 1, the questionnaire's reliability increases. As shown in Table 2, the alpha coefficient above 0.7 for each questionnaire indicates the appropriate reliability of the nine questionnaires used in this study.

Table 1 Measurement tool specifications

Variables	Number of items	Source
Website characteristics	3	Rahi et al. (2019)
Website design	4	Rahi and Ghani (2018)
Performance expectancy	4	Celik (2016) and Rahi and Ghani (2018)
Effort expectancy	4	Celik (2016) and Rahi and Ghani (2018)
Anxiety	4	
Innovativeness	3	Rahi and Ghani (2018)
Intention to adopt	3	Celik (2016) and Rahi and Ghani (2018)
Intention to recommend	3	

Table 2 Results of convergent validity and composite reliability

Latent variable	Cronbach's alpha coefficient ($\alpha > 0.7$)	AVE > 0.5	CR > 0.7
Website characteristics	0.77	0.67	0.86
Website design	0.73	0.54	0.82
Performance expectancy	0.75	0.57	0.84
Effort expectancy	0.82	0.65	0.88
Anxiety	0.79	0.53	0.81
Innovativeness	0.76	0.67	0.86
Intention to adopt	0.78	0.69	0.87
Intention to recommend	0.76	0.68	0.86

Index reliability, convergent, and divergent validity were used to measure the model fit. Fornell and Larcker (1981) introduced three criteria to examine the validity of constructs, including divergent validity, composite reliability of each construct, and average variance extracted (convergent validity). Values greater than 0.5 for average variance extracted and more significant than 0.7 for composite reliability indicate the appropriate fit of measurement models and their convergent reliability and validity. The results of these indices in Table 2 confirm the convergent validity and composite reliability of the constructs, indicating that this criterion is suitable and the reliability of the measurement models is appropriate.

On the other hand, the construct's validity is measured in two ways: (1) cross-loading method; (2) The Fornell-Larcker Criterion, which is the relationship between a construct and its indicators compared with the relationship between that construct and other constructs. In the present study, the Fornell-Larcker Criterion was used to measure divergent validity. This model has acceptable divergent validity when the numbers in the original diameter exceed their lower values. According to Table 3, all numbers on the original diameter are more significant than the other numbers in the column, so its divergent validity is confirmed.

Evaluation of Structural Model

After measuring the model's validity and reliability, the structural model was evaluated through the latent variables' relationships. In the present study, two criteria of the coefficient of determination (R^2) and Stone-Geisser criterion (Q^2) were used.

R^2 is a criterion indicating the effect of an exogenous variable on an endogenous variable. This criterion takes three values of 0.19, 0.33, and 0.67 as weak, moderate, and strong. According to Table 4, the R^2 value is calculated for the endogenous constructs of the study. The goodness of the structural model fit can be confirmed by considering the three criteria values. Also, a criterion called Q^2 was used to investigate the predictive power of the model. Three values of 0.02, 0.15, and 0.35 are

Table 3 Divergent validity matrix by Fresnel and Larker method

Variables	1	2	3	4	5	6	7	8
Anxiety	**0.73**							
Effort expectancy	0.11	**0.80**						
Innovativeness	0.06	0.78	**0.82**					
Intention to adopt	0.03	0.66	0.62	**0.83**				
Intention to recommend	0.1	0.67	0.66	0.53	**0.82**			
Performance expectancy	0.07	0.72	0.65	0.55	0.68	**0.76**		
Website characteristics	0.08	0.64	0.63	0.51	0.61	0.70	**0.82**	
Website design	0.1	0.65	0.65	0.50	0.65	0.67	0.70	**0.73**

Table 4 Coefficient of Determination (R^2) and Prediction Power (Q^2)

	Effort expectancy	Performance expectancy	Intent to adopt	Intent to recommend
R^2	0.49	0.56	0.47	0.28
Q^2	0.30	0.30	0.29	0.18

considered small, medium, and large Q^2 values. Based on the results for this criterion (at the medium level for the four criteria variables) in Table 4, it can be concluded that the model has "medium" predictive power.

Research Findings

In this study, to test the hypotheses and investigate the research model fit, structural equation modeling and partial least squares method (PLS software) have been applied to the two properties of insensitivity to sample size and data normality. Structural equation modeling with partial least squares (PLS) approach has been used to analyze the data. The software that uses structural equation modeling based on this statistical approach is compatible with conditions such as the co-linearity of independent variables, data normality, and sample shrinkage. Structural equation models typically combine the measurement model (representing sub-components of latent variables) and the structural model (representing relationships between independent and dependent variables). The two sections of the measurement model test and the structural model test are presented above.

After evaluating the fit of the measurement and structural models and having an appropriate fit, the research hypotheses were investigated and tested. Then, the results of the significant coefficients for each hypothesis, the standardized coefficients of each hypothesis's paths, and the hypothesis test results at a 95% confidence level are presented in Table 5.

The significant coefficients of the variables are shown in Table 5. Since the significant coefficients of the research hypotheses' variables are more remarkable than absolute value 1.96, these hypotheses are subsequently confirmed. Only the seventh hypothesis is rejected because of being contrary to this assumption. Also, the relationship between all variables was positive; only the variable "anxiety" had a negative relationship with the variable "intention to adopt," which was not significant despite the negative relationship.

According to Table 5, it was found that the effort expectancy ($ß = 0.362$; $t = 5.026$), and the performance expectancy ($ß = 0.123$; $t = 2.098$) affected the intention to adopt internet banking. In the research analysis model, the individual factors of technology acceptance were examined. The results showed that innovativeness affected ($ß = 0.263$; $t = 3.766$) intends to adopt internet banking, but anxiety has not affected ($ß = -0.028$; $t = 0.532$). Other results indicate the effect of website environmental factors on the performance and effort expectancy. Website

Table 5 Research hypotheses test

Hypothesis	Path coefficient (ß)	Significance coefficient (T-Value)	Test result
First: Performance expectancy-> Intention to adopt internet banking	0.123	2.098	Confirmed
Second: Effort expectancy-> Intention to adopt internet banking	0.362	5.026	Confirmed
Third: Innovativeness-> Intention to adopt internet banking	0.263	3.766	Confirmed
Fourth: Anxiety-> Intention to adopt internet banking	−0.028	0.532	**Rejected**
Fifth: Website characteristics-> Performance expectancy	0.456	9.738	Confirmed
Sixth: Website characteristics-> Effort expectancy	0.360	6.349	Confirmed
Seventh: Website design-> Performance expectancy	0.359	8.372	Confirmed
Eighth: Website design-> Effort expectancy	0.396	7.888	Confirmed
Ninth: Intention to adopt internet banking-> Recommendation of internet banking to others	0.530	13.370	Confirmed

characteristics and website design effectively affected performance expectancy (ß = 0.456; t = 9.738, ß = 0.359; t = 8.372) and effort expectancy by (ß = 0.360; t = 6.349) and (ß = 0.396; t = 7.888), respectively. Moreover, finally, the intention to adopt internet banking effectively affected the recommendation of internet banking to others (ß = 0.530; t = 13.370). Since the T-value of the relationship between anxiety and the intention to adopt internet banking was less than 1.96, it can be stated that anxiety does not affect the intention to adopt internet banking.

Conclusion and Suggestions

In this study, website individual and environmental factors on internet banking adoption and recommendation to others have been investigated. The results of inferential statistics showed that the performance and effort expectancy has a significant positive effect on the acceptance of internet banking, which is in line with the results of He and Lu (2007).

This research also has theoretical and practical implications. This study and its results help managers and researchers in the field of Internet banking. Research shows that e-banking customers are the most profitable and valuable customers in the banking services market. Banks play a crucial role in business by establishing close and almost permanent relationships with people, and for this reason, they are always trying to expand their services in quantitative and qualitative dimensions to surpass their competitors (Celik 2016). This study helps to accept Internet banking and recommend it to others by examining the two dimensions of cognitive (innovativeness) and affective (anxiety) individual technology acceptance model as a starting point for future research. Also, considering the adequate environmental dimensions in attracting and retaining customers helps increase the efficiency of the service model provided. Since UTAUT is one of the most essential and complete theoretical models in information systems research, it is always essential to identify the factors that spread it. Understanding this model's critical and key structures is very important for designing, modifying, and implementing Internet banking services that interest many customers.

In this study, only the anxiety and innovativeness were considered individual factors to accept internet banking, so it is suggested to investigate the effect of other personal characteristics in future research. It is suggested that the websites be designed more accessible and more attractive for users to use at the minimum time and with the minimum mental involvement. It is also suggested to increase advertising and communication and reduce anxiety during new banking systems. On the other, in this research, the moderator variable has not been used to avoid the complexity of the model. In future research, it is suggested that instead of using environmental characteristics, researchers examine the role of moderating variables (such as age, gender, experience, volunteering, etc.) along with individual characteristics in accepting Internet banking in the output model. Also, in this research, the available non-random sampling method has been used. It is suggested that in future research, researchers use other sampling methods to increase the generalizability of the results.

Based on the research results, the following suggestions are provided:

- Improving awareness of technology benefits customers through training and information programs.
- Developing policies regarding integrated law of adoption and use of technology such as data protection, security, and marketing standards.
- Providing infrastructure, financial support for the development of technology deployment.
- Developing effective programs to learn about and use services through advanced training courses in which cultural studies, educational planning, and nurturing of experts in internet implementation and maintenance should be considered in addition to specialized and technical aspects.
- Taking the effort to introduce users to the fundamental concepts of integrated adoption and use of technology by promoting collaboration to implement e-commerce programs successfully.

References

Agarwal, R. (2000). Individual acceptance of information technologies. *Framing the domains of IT management: Projecting the future through the past*, 85-104.

Al-Qeisi, K., Dennis, C., Alamanos, E., & Jayawardhena, C. (2014). Website design quality and usage behavior: Unified Theory of Acceptance and Use of Technology. *Journal of Business Research*, *67*(11), 2282–2290.

Alwahaishi, S., & Snásel, V. (2013). Acceptance and use of information and communications technology: a UTAUT and flow-based theoretical model. *Journal of Technology Management & Innovation*, *8*(2), 61–73.

Baabdullah, A. M., Alalwan, A. A., Rana, N. P., Kizgin, H., & Patil, P. (2019). Consumer use of mobile banking (M-Banking) in Saudi Arabia: Towards an integrated model. *International Journal of Information Management*, *44*, 38–52.

Brown, S. A., Dennis, A. R., & Venkatesh, V. (2010). Predicting collaboration technology use: Integrating technology adoption and collaboration research. *Journal of Management Information Systems*, *27*(2), 9–54.

Bùi, T. T. H., & Bùi, H. T. (2018). Gamification impact on the acceptance of mobile payment in Ho Chi Minh City, Vietnam. *International Journal of Social Science and Economic Research*, *3*(9), 4822–4837.

Celik, H. (2016). Customer online shopping anxiety within the Unified Theory of Acceptance and Use Technology (UTAUT) framework. *Asia Pacific Journal of Marketing and Logistics*, *28*(2), 278–307.

Chedrawi, C., Harb, B., & Saleh, M. (2019). The E-banking and the adoption of innovations from the perspective of the transactions cost theory: Case of the largest commercial banks in Lebanon. In ICT for a Better Life and a Better World (pp. 149–164). Springer, Cham.

Demoulin, N. T., & Djelassi, S. (2016). An integrated model of self-service technology (SST) usage in a retail context. *International Journal of Retail & Distribution Management, 44*(5), 540–559.

Floh, A., & Treiblmaier, H. (2006). What keeps the e-banking customer loyal? A multigroup analysis of the moderating role of consumer characteristics on e-loyalty in the financial service industry. *A Multigroup Analysis of the Moderating Role of Consumer Characteristics on E-Loyalty in the Financial Service Industry. (March 26, 2006).*

Fornell, C., & Larcker, D. F. (1981). Evaluating structural equation models with unobservable variables and measurement error. *Journal of marketing research 18.1*, 39–50.

Hartman, J. B., & Samra, Y. M. (2008). Impact of personal values and innovativeness on hedonic and utilitarian aspects of web use: An empirical study among United States teenagers. *International Journal of Management 25.1*, 77.

He, D., & Lu, Y. (2007, September). Consumers perceptions and acceptances towards mobile advertising: an empirical study in China. In *2007 International Conference on Wireless Communications, Networking and Mobile Computing* (pp. 3775–3778). IEEE.

Holloway, B. B., & Beatty, S. E. (2008). Satisfiers and dissatisfiers in the online environment: A critical incident assessment. *Journal of Service Research*, *10*(4), 347–364.

Jin, L. Y., Osman, A., Romle, A. R., & Haji-Othman, Y. (2015). Attitude towards online shopping activities in Malaysia public university. *Mediterranean Journal of Social Sciences*, *6*(2 S1), 456.

Kombe, S. K., & Wafula, M. K. (2015). Effects of internet banking on the financial performance of commercial banks in Kenya a case of Kenya Commercial Bank. *International Journal of Scientific and Research Publications 5.5*, 1–10.

Kuo, Y. F. & Yen, S. N. (2009). Towards an understanding of the behavioral intention to use 3G mobile value-added services. *Computers in Human Behavior*, *25*(1), 103–110.

Lee, K., Yan, A., & Joshi, K. (2011). Understanding the dynamics of users' belief in software application adoption. *International Journal of Information Management*, *31*(2), 160–170.

Leong, L. Y., Hew, T. S., Tan, G. W. H., & Ooi, K. B. (2013). Predicting the determinants of the NFC-enabled mobile credit card acceptance: A neural networks approach. *Expert Systems with Applications, 40*(14), 5604–5620.

Martins, C., Oliveira, T., & Popovič, A. (2014). Understanding Internet banking adoption: A unified theory of acceptance and use of technology and perceived risk application. *International Journal of Information Management, 34*(1), 1–13.

Miltgen, C. L., Popovič, A., & Oliveira, T. (2013). Determinants of end-user acceptance of biometrics: Integrating the "Big 3" of technology acceptance with privacy context. *Decision support systems, 56*, 103–114.

Mun, Y. Y., Jackson, J. D., Park, J. S., & Probst, J. C. (2006). Understanding information technology acceptance by individual professionals: Toward an integrative view. *Information & Management, 43*(3), 350–363.

Oliveira, T., Thomas, M., Baptista, G., & Campos, F. (2016). Mobile payment: Understanding the determinants of customer adoption and intention to recommend the technology. *Computers in Human Behavior, 61*, 404–414.

Park, J., Ahn, J., Thavisay, T., & Ren, T. (2019). Examining the role of anxiety and social influence in multi-benefits of mobile payment service. *Journal of Retailing and Consumer Services, 47*, 140–149.

Rahi, S., & Ghani, M. (2016). Internet banking, customer perceived value and loyalty: The role of switching costs. *J Account Mark, 5.4*, 188.

Rahi, S., & Ghani, M. A. (2018). A structural equation modeling (SEM-AMOS) for investigating brand loyalty and customer's intention towards adoption of internet banking. *Economic and Social Development: Book of Proceedings*, 206–220.

Rahi, S., & Ghani, M. A. (2018). Investigating the role of e-service quality and brand image in internet banking acceptance context with structural equation modeling (SEM-PLS). *Economic and Social Development: Book of Proceedings*, 427–442.

Rahi, S., Ghani, M. A., & Ngah, A. H. (2019). Integration of unified theory of acceptance and use of technology in internet banking adoption setting: Evidence from Pakistan. *Technology in Society*.

Rana, A., Kalla, P., Verma, H., & Mohnot, J. (2016). Recycling of dimensional stone waste in concrete: A review. *Journal of Cleaner Production, 135*, 312–331.

Ramírez-Correa, P., Rondán-Cataluña, F. J., Arenas-Gaitán, J., & Martín-Velicia, F. (2019). Analyzing the acceptation of online games in mobile devices: An application of UTAUT2. *Journal of Retailing and Consumer Services, 50*, 85–93.

Raza, S. A., & Hanif, N. (2011). Factors affecting internet banking adoption among internal and external customers: a case of Pakistan.

Rodrigues, L. F., Oliveira, A., & Costa, C. J. (2016). Playing seriously–How gamification and social cues influence bank customers to use gamified e-business applications. *Computers in Human Behavior, 63*, 392-407.

Shen, Y. C., Huang, C. Y., Chu, C. H., & Hsu, C. T. (2010). A benefit-cost perspective of the consumer adoption of the mobile banking system. *Behaviour & Information Technology, 29*(5), 497–511.

Thakur, R., & Srivastava, M. (2015). A study on the impact of consumer risk perception and innovativeness on online shopping in India. *International Journal of Retail & Distribution Management, 43*(2), 148–166.

Udo, G. J., Bagchi, K. K., & Kirs, P. J. (2010). An assessment of customers'e-service quality perception, satisfaction and intention. *International Journal of Information Management, 30*(6), 481–492.

Van Der Heijden, H. (2003). Factors influencing the usage of websites: the case of a generic portal in The Netherlands. *Information and Management, 40*(6), 541–549.

Venkatesh, V., & Davis, F. D. (1996). A model of the antecedents of perceived ease of use: Development and test. *Decision sciences 27.3*, 451–481.

Venkatesh, V., Morris, M. G., Davis, G. B., & Davis, F. D. (2003). User acceptance of information technology: Toward a unified view. *MIS Quarterly, 27*, 425–478.

Venkatesh, V., Thong, J. Y., & Xu, X. (2012). Consumer acceptance and use of information technology: extending the unified theory of acceptance and use of technology. *MIS Quarterly*, 157–178.

Walker, P. R. (2011). *How does website design in the e-banking sector affect customer attitudes and behavior?* (Doctoral dissertation, University of Northumbria).

Wang, H. I., & Yang, H. L. (2005). The role of personality traits in UTAUT model under online stocking. *Contemporary Management Research, 1*(1), 69–82.

Special Session: Data Analytics Methods for Marketing Strategy Researchers: An Abstract

Stephen L. France, Daniel Ringel, and Wenjun Zhou

Abstract Methods research has been a core part of the marketing discipline for over 50 years. Methods researchers provide tools both for academic researchers to explore marketing phenomenon and for marketing practitioners to better analyze commercial data. There are several reasons for the continuing relevance of methods research in marketing. First, in both the commercial world and in academia, there is an increasing focus on methodology for dealing with the increasingly large and complex data generated by modern business. These data include, but are not limited to, data from internet search, smartphone app/location tracking, customer systems, social media, online reviews, biometric systems, and data-enabled appliances. Work on such data, often comes under the banner of big data analytics and academic researchers require knowledge of new methods to work with these data. Second, methodological courses for business doctoral students increasingly incorporate advanced data analytics methods, with students being trained in widely used programming languages for analytics, such as R and Python. These reasons give a great deal of potential for methods researchers in marketing to "meet in the middle" with applied marketing strategy researchers.

This session is designed to introduce marketing strategy researchers to recent marketing methods and analytics work and to facilitate collaboration between methods researchers and strategy researchers in marketing. This will be done by introducing three different methods. For each method, there will be a non-technical discussion of the method and its assumptions. A short hands-on application of the method will be given, along with references to more detailed resources (e.g., docu-

S. L. France (✉)
Mississippi State University, Mississippi State, MS, USA
e-mail: sfrance@business.msstate.edu

D. Ringel
University of North Carolina, Chapel Hill, NC, USA
e-mail: dmr@kenan-flagler.unc.edu

W. Zhou
University of Tennessee, Knoxville, TN, USA
e-mail: wzhou4@utk.edu

J. Allen et al. (eds.), *Celebrating the Past and Future of Marketing and Discovery with Social Impact*, Developments in Marketing Science: Proceedings of the Academy of Marketing Science, https://doi.org/10.1007/978-3-030-95346-1_102

mentation, publications, and tutorials), and a discussion of how best the technique can be employed by strategy researchers.

The three chosen methods cover important areas of marketing modeling and data analytic research, with commonalities in the analysis of consumer brand behavior and brand positioning. The first method allows researchers to build and validate a range of brand equity indices from web-search data. The second method provides an innovative method of brand mapping and positioning analysis, where researchers can analyze the trajectories of brands and how brand competition changes over time. The third method utilizes online reviews and automatic language feature selection to perform a dynamic segmentation of reviewers, which helps characterize different opinions in different segments.

Keywords Analytics · Methodology · Visualization · Segmentation · Branding · Google trends

International Expansion Alternatives: A Modeling Approach

Marina Kyriakou and Markos Tsogas

Abstract The aim of this study is to explore strategic alternatives of exporting firms when considering international market expansion. These alternatives are – for the first time – being considered as a set of four mutually exclusive options which guide decisions about the number of foreign markets and the timing of entry in these markets. A sample of exporting companies is investigated and a complex multivariate model is proposed and tested. The results reveal that managers perceive these strategic alternatives in one unified conceptual domain and thus they concurrently analyze and evaluate them, while confirming the strong relationship of the degree of company's export involvement to company's export success. To a satisfying extent, the adopted strategies are explained by idiosyncrasies of the product, the adopted approach to international markets and the acts of international players and competitors, whereas factors of the market environment and the internal characteristics of the exporting firm act as moderators to the aforementioned relationship.

Keywords Expansion strategies · Diversification · Concentration · Market spreading · Non-linear modeling

Introduction

The selection of a suitable expansion strategy is the most crucial decision a company takes during the process of internationalization (Cavusgil and Zou 1994). Two critical questions have to be answered in order for an expansion strategy to be designed: (a) Will entry be concentrated or diversified across international markets? and (b) Will entry be incremental or simultaneously to various markets? (Hollensen 2011). Although these strategies have been studied in pairs in the past, no evidence has been found supporting their strategic consideration as a set.

M. Kyriakou (✉) · M. Tsogas
University of Piraeus, Piraeus, Greece
e-mail: mkyriakou@unipi.gr; mtsogas@unipi.gr

J. Allen et al. (eds.), *Celebrating the Past and Future of Marketing and Discovery with Social Impact*, Developments in Marketing Science: Proceedings of the Academy of Marketing Science, https://doi.org/10.1007/978-3-030-95346-1_103

The main objective thus of this study is to investigate the concurrent consideration of these strategies by marketing managers, during their strategic evaluation of international markets. We examine whether marketing managers make concurrent decisions about the number of countries and the speed of international expansion, i.e. selecting between one of the four targeting strategies which emerge by this combination.

An extensive list of items, grounded in literature and related to company, product, technology, market and competition characteristics act as antecedents of such options, and can be used in order to explain and predict successfully the reported adopted strategy. To that effect, country evaluation dimensions as identified in the literature are brought to bear (Katsikeas and Leonidou 1996; Kalish et al. 1995). But these factors have been previously examined as antecedents of each strategic dilemma (Katsikeas and Leonidou 1996; Katsikea et al. 2005; Kalish et al. 1995) whereas we investigate their exploratory power for the totality of presented options.

In the past, a number of studies have investigated the relationship between the market expansion strategy and the company's international performance (Cieślik et al. 2012), but with emphasis on the number of markets entered, partially ignoring the speed of internationalization. In this paper, we study for the first time, the relationship between the many facets of the adopted international expansion strategy and company's exports success, controlling for company's international experience and attitude to exports. Finally, company's success is connected to the degree of company's export involvement, as suggested in the literature.

The paper starts with a brief review of the literature in order for a solid conceptual framework to be developed and the accompanying hypothesis to be formed. The findings of the survey of exporting companies is then reported, with discussion on the accepted and rejected hypothesis. Managerial and theoretical implications are presented thereafter.

Theoretical Background

During a company's internalization process, the market selection stage is followed by the selection of the expansion strategy (Hollensen 2011). In particular, it is supported that a company has to take two major decisions in order to design its expansion strategy to international markets. The first one is related to the number of international markets the company targets, whereas the second is associated with the time frame of internationalization.

The first dimension, which is related to the number of international markets, identifies two alternatives along a concentration – diversification continuum (Ayal and Zif 1979; Katsikeas and Leonidou 1996; Katsikea et al. 2003). Companies following a strategy closely to the one end, focus their efforts and resources on few, carefully chosen, foreign markets. In contrast, companies which adopt the strategy at the other end of the spectrum, disperse efforts and resources in as many as possible foreign markets.

At the same time, companies have to decide along a timing dimension from incremental to simultaneous entry. These strategies have been named "waterfall" and "sprinkler/shower" respectively (Kalish et al. 1995). In the first option the company chooses to enter in all foreign markets gradually, while in the second case the company chooses to enter the same number of market, simultaneously (Keegan et al. 2000).

Expansion Strategy Based on the Number of New Markets

The selection between a wider diversification or a concentration on core foreign markets has been the object of study in numerous empirical paper (for a recent review see Cieślik et al. 2012). The aforementioned deliberation is referred in the literature as "the concentration versus spreading debate" (Crick and Jones 2000; Katsikea et al. 2003; Cieślik et al. 2012). Trying to conclude upon normative guidelines, researchers investigated the relationship between the expansion strategy and a company's performance but evidence is still broadly inconclusive (Ayal and Zif 1979; Cooper and Kleinschmidt 1985; Fenwick and Amine 1979; Piercy 1981; Tessler 1977; Leonidou et al. 2010).

More specifically, several studies propose the adoption of a market concentration strategy, arguing that the fewer the markets that an export company focuses, the higher the gained market share (Tessler 1977; Tookey 1975). Evidently, this strategy seems to enhance the company's profitability in the long term, as it is positively correlated to sales increases (Leonidou et al. 2002). In contrast, the implementation of the market spreading strategy, whereas a less risky alternative with lower overall sales volume, achieves a similar performance result through claiming a relatively lower market share, but on a much larger number of disparate foreign markets (Hammermesh et al. 1978; Hirsch and Lev 1973; Lee and Yang 1990; Katsikea et al. 2003; Lages et al. 2006; Lu and Beamish 2006; Pangarkar 2008).

Although it is not possible to conclude on the superiority of one strategy over the other, there are specific and well defined reasons why companies follow a particular approach to their expansion in foreign markets (Piercy 1982). Mostly market and company specific characteristics determine to a large extent the mature of the focal strategy (Ayal and Zif 1979; Fenwick and Amine 1979; Piercy 1982). These characteristics are clear antecedents of the strategic dilemma and in no case performance or success criteria.

However, large multinational companies have adopted a dual strategy using both expansion paths simultaneously (Aspelund et al. 2007; Crick and Jones 2000; Morgan-Thomas and Jones 2009), developing thus ambidextrous capabilities. Ambidexterity provides the global firm with the opportunity to deploy an exploratory and innovative new market strategy, milking at the same time its presence in a variety of international markets (March 1991; Barkema and Drogendijk 2007; Cellard and Prange 2008).

Expansion Strategy Based on Time Frame of Internationalization

The traditional internationalization models place emphasis to an incremental learning process which favors gradual expansion into international markets, initiating firms entry into psychic close and usually neighboring markets (Eriksson et al. 1997; Johanson and Vahlne 1977). At a later stage, the development of the strategic paradigm and approach brought about the competitive environment of a firm and the totality of its resources as the main ressons explaining the adoption of a waterfall or sprinkler approach (Sleuwaegen and Onkelinx 2014). The former is associated with a small initial investment and the gradual penetration into new international markets, allowing thus the firm to reap the benefits from the lead and spillover effects. The later entails the simultaneous entrance to a considerable number of foreign markets with a systematic way, conquering thus a prominent competitive position in the global market (Kalish et al. 1995; Keegan et al. 2000).

The traditional approach has been challenged by new models of international businesses, like the born–global firms and the globally savvy ones (Chetty and Campbell-Hunt 2004; Knight and Cavusgil 2004; Preece et al. 1999). In addition, a company's desire to have a large dispersion of international markets stems from the need to ensure the further development and exploitation of critical resources, like patents or brand names (Knight et al. 2004; Madsen and Servais 1997; Oviatt and McDougall 1994, 1995).

According to Kalish et al. (1995) theoretical framework about the introduction of a new product into global markets, an effort is made to (a) investigate the optimal timing and scope (number of countries) of new product introduction and (b) identify alternative strategies to maximize profits. In such an occasion companies are able to select the most suitable expansion strategy, taking into consideration environmental factors of the industrial sector they operate in, the domestic and foreign markets' conditions and of course the cost of entry to foreign markets.

After taking into account the trade of nature of international expansion strategic decision making, between the maximization of internationalization revenues and the minimization of expansion risks (Stremersch and Tellis 2004), the current study adopts as a suitable research framework and adapts the work of Kalish et al. (1995) .

Conceptual Model and Hypothesis

The literature provides seminal efforts in developing typologies of internationalization strategies, which thought focus either on the time dimension of expansion (eg. Kuivalainen et al. 2012; Vissak and Masso 2015; Oviatt and McDougall 1994) or at the number of markets penetrated or targeted (Rugman and Verbeke 2004). The authors have failed to pinpoint published research that investigates concurrent decision making along the dimensions of time and number of markets entered, which in this paper are studied.

Following the stream of previous research which identifies two separate strategies for the number of foreign markets (concentration vs diversification) and two similarly separate strategies for the timing of entry (waterfall vs sprinkler), it is evident that the combination of these produces for distinctive strategic options among which companies can select. Therefore, companies can either focus resources on few international markets, in which they expand gradually or diversify efforts and resources among many markets in which again choose to expand incrementally. In addition, firms can either expand in many global markets simultaneously, a strategy that requires the deployment of the greatest amount of resources, or to expand at the same time but to a limited number of carefully chosen markets.

The strategic expansion options in this paper are conceptualized, for the first time, along a continuum of varying degree of involvement. That is achieved through the measurement approach of the firms' adopted strategy and by the construction of a latent formative variable which is comprised by the two distinct options of expansion (Hollensen 2011; Katsikea et al. 2005; Kalish et al. 1995). Bell et al. (1998) have argued that the nature and pace of internationalization is conditioned by product, industry, and other external environmental variables, as well as by firm-specific factors (Crick and Jones 2000). The use of a more complex construct which depicts the adopted strategy, necessitates the reshuffling of the proposed in the literature antecedent variables. The resulting constructs are thus formed by items which have previously been used for the modeling of either the degree of diversification or the speed of expansion, but never before concurrently in one model.

Thus, we develop the following hypothesis:

H1: market expansion strategy is determined by (a) Product factors, (b) Company's dynamism and innovativeness, (c) Company's approach to markets, (d) Company's strength of dominance and (e) Level of foreign market development.

In accordance to previous studies (Aspelund et al. 2007; Crick and Jones 2000; Cooper and Kleinschmidt 1985; Fenwick and Amine 1979; Cunningham and Spiegel 1971) measures of internationalization success have been included in the model, in order to provide further validation, forming our second hypothesis:

H2: The adopted strategy is positively associated with company's export success

Furthermore, the model has been enriched with additional involvement variables, (1) attitude to exports, (2) experience in global markets and (3) export commitment (Crick and Jones 2000; Cooper and Kleinschmidt 1985; Fenwick and Amine 1979) and Company's descriptive characteristics and resources (Aspelund et al. 2007; Crick and Jones 2000). These are depicted in Hypotheses 3 and 4.

H3: Company's (1) attitude to exports, (2) experience in global markets and (3) export commitment are positively associated with company's export success

H4: Company's descriptive characteristics and resources is positively associated with company's export success

Research Methodology

Scope of Research

The main aim of this study is to investigate whether firms examine their international market expansion options as a function of two major variables: (a) the total number of foreign markets to be penetrated and (b) the number of markets selected for simultaneous entry. Concurrent examination of these two variables creates a continuum of strategic options from a very limited number of markets entered sequentially at the one end, to a broad number of markets entered simultaneously to the other end. It is suspected that the examination of these two variables in parallel by marketing managers, creates a considerably different dynamic of decision making patterns than those studied in the existing literature.

In order to achieve this main objective, international market expansion decision is modeled as a consequence of a mix of previously researched antecedents (Hollensen 2011; Katsikea et al. 2005; Katsikeas and Leonidou 1996; Kalish et al. 1995). But never before have all these variables been combined in order to predict international expansion decisions of place and time, in one conceptual domain.

Sampling Frame and Sample Description

In order to investigate the perceived deployment of the four targeting strategies, a mail survey took place among export companies in a single southern European country. The sample, which was provided by a Gallup subsidiary, consisted of 1000 export companies, from various sectors, including pharmaceuticals and cosmetics, electronics, plastic materials, chemicals, timber furniture and cement, providing thus a cross-sectional sample of high and low technology sectors of varying dynamism (mature vs emerging markets).

After a second reminder, the collection yielded a final usable sample of 139 completed questionnaires resulting to a 13.9% response rate. The firms in the sample are representative to a good extent to the majority of exporters in the area, i.e. small and very small family firms with small to medium exporting experience. More specifically, 53.2% of the firms employ less than 25 employees, whereas only 4.3% employ more than 500. In addition, for more than half of the responding firms (53.3%), the ratio of foreign to domestic sales does not exceed 20% of total sales. Only 7.2% of the firms report sales from foreign markets which exceed 75% of total revenue.

In contrast, 43.2% of managers who answered the questionnaire reported greater than 11 years international experience, indicating a strong antithesis in the sample which is comprised by relatively experienced managers – respondents, employed by relatively inexperienced firms.

Research Instrument

For the purposes of the research a structured questionnaire has been developed, being comprised of four parts. The first part of the questionnaire consisted of questions about the company's internationalization experience. In the second part, respondents were asked to position the followed expansion strategy along two distinct dimensions (axes). Firstly, they had to indicate on the Y axis, their adopted strategy regarding the number of new international markets they were targeting and then to indicate on the X axis the adopted strategy regarding the speed of entrance to these markets, using in both cases a 20-point scale.

In the third part of the questionnaire the variables reflected the antecedents of the adopted strategies wcrc included. These items were reflecting all relevant factors as suggested in the literature, i.e. product and technology factors, competition & international market factors and company factors. Most of these items were derived from Hollensen (2011) and were enriched from Katsikea et al. (2005) regarding the number of foreign markets decisions and Kalish et al. (1995) for decisions about the time frame of internationalization and measured by 7-point Likert scales.

Data Analysis

The structural equation modeling (SEM) using the WarpPLS 5.0 software was used for data analysis. The WarpPLS 5.0 applies the partial least squares (PLS) based SEM technique (PLS-SEM). The PLS-SEM was favorably selected in this study because it is better suited for complex models with large number of constructs and links (Pavlou and Fygenson 2006; Ahuja et al. 2007; Au et al. 2008) and equally important PLS-SEM is more suitable than other statistical tools for testing the effects of moderators (Pavlou and Sawy 2006; Limayem et al. 2007), as in the case of the current study. Further, WarpPLS 5.0 is equipped with measures related to the quality of the model, such as the ten powerful goodness-of-fit indices, p-values and multi collinearity estimates (Kock 2015).

Findings

In accordance with the nature of the firms which participated in the survey, i.e. relatively small firms of limited international experience, it is of no surprise that the majority of the companies (56.1%) has been found to focus efforts and resources on a few new foreign markets. At the same time and for the same reasons, almost 80% of the sample enters into new international markets gradually, reporting thus a slow pace of internationalization.

In order to obtain a clearer picture and following the expansion strategies' classification described above, the responding companies have been allocated accordingly. Thus, it can be said that 55.4% of the firms opt for a concentration strategy to a limited number of international markets in which they enter incrementally, whereas 29.2% of the sample keeping their gradual pace in time, chooses to diversify into a large number of markets. On the contrary, 12.3% of the firms follow a diversification strategy but deploying it on a rapid time frame, while the remaining 3.1% of the sample opts for a concentration strategy in the number of markets, but entering them at a very fast pace.

The amalgamation of the alternative expansion strategies into one continuum of options has been tested in the proposed model, which includes 24 items describing five latent constructs: Approach to market, Company's dynamism and innovativeness, Product factors, Company's dominance, Level of foreign market development. The structural equation modeling (SEM) using the WarpPLS 5.0 software was used to provide the necessary analysis to serve the objectives of this study. The measurement model test resulted in statistically accepted goodness of fit between the data and the proposed measurement model. The various goodness-of-fit statistics are shown in Table 1. Consequently, in accordance to Kock (2015), the model has a good fit to the data.

Figure 1 presents the significant structural relationships among the research variables and the standardized path coefficients with their respective significance levels. Three out of the five paths composing H1 have been found significant. The remaining two constructs (Company's dynamism and level of foreign market development), as discussed in the following paragraph, are acting only as moderators and more precisely as boosters of (a) the reported significant direct effect of the "approach to market" variable and (b) the effect of variable "company' dominance" respectively. The model explains substantial variance of the adopted strategy ($R2 = 0.54$), which in terns explains 50% of the variance in company's self-reported internationalization success. Company's attitude to exporting, experience in global

Table 1 Model evaluation overall fit measurement

Measure	Value	P-values
Average path coefficient (APC) (<0.05)	0.209	$P = 0.003$
Average R-squared (ARS) (<0.05)	0.374	$P < 0.001$
Average adjusted R-squared (AARS)	0.358	$P < 0.001$
Average block VIF (AVIF)	1.342	Good if ≤5, ideally ≤3.3
Average full collinearity VIF (AFVIF)	1.633	Acceptable if ≤5, ideally ≤3.3
Tenenhaus GoF (GoF)	0.413	Small ≥0.1, medium ≥0.25, large ≥0.36
Sympson's paradox ratio (SPR)	1.000	Acceptable if ≥0.7, ideally = 1
R-squared contribution ratio (RSCR)	1.000	Acceptable if ≥0.9, ideally = 1
Statistical suppression ratio (SSR)	1.000	Acceptable if ≥0.7
Nonlinear bivariate causality direction ratio (NLBCDR)	1.000	Acceptable if ≥0.7

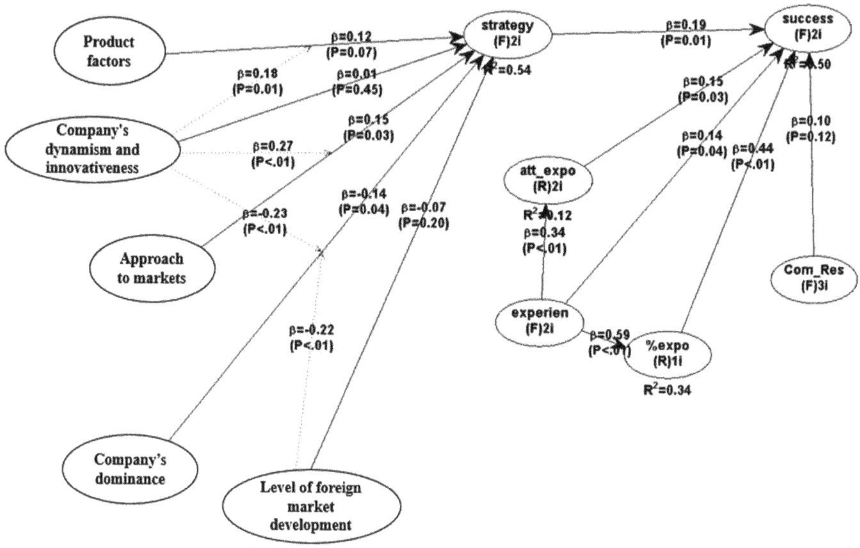

Fig. 1 Measurement model

markets and export commitment and descriptive characteristics and resources play a significant role in predicting internationalization success (explaining 50% of the variance), providing support for H2 to H4 as explained earlier.

Discussion

This current study has revealed that exporting firms during international market expansion, take decisions by judging the number of foreign markets and the time horizon of further internationalization, simultaneously. Such decisions are finally reflected in the adopted expansion strategy. This strategy is determined by a number of factors related to the product, the characteristics of the exporting firm, the international market environment, etc., as has already been well documented in the existing literature.

More specifically, it has been deduced that Product factors, Company's approach to market and Company's Dominance to foreign markets are significant determinants of the followed strategy. The study also identified the moderating role of *Company's dynamism & innovativeness* and the *Level of foreign market development* for the selection of foreign market expansion strategy. In reality, this type of analysis is absent from the relevant literature. Therefore, this study can be considered as a first attempt to hypothesize the relationships among constructs in the expansion model to be moderated by company's and market's dynamic development.

Taking a closer look at the derived results, product and marketing organization's level of adaptation to the various market differences, favors the rapid expansion to a larger number of foreign markets. Such an expansion is further stipulated by the innovativeness of new products, which require careful adaptation. Equally rapid and diverse expansion, is favored by firms which adopt a proactive approach to internationalization, have set international expansion issues at a priority to domestic ones and the global markets they wish to operate are characterized by high sales volume and high potential.

On the other hand, companies which exhibit high degree of dominance over their competitors in their foreign markets, tend to prefer a more conservative strategy of gradual concentration. Dominance is achieved when firms are confronted with ample and easily accessible market data and with a relatively stable environment, characterized by the lack of significant opportunities. Such dominance creates the equivalent of an international comfort zone and leads to some complacency effects because firms stick to their successful "formula". This strategy is further supported by high costs of entry into new markets in which few, weak competitors are prone to cooperate with a new international entrant.

References

Ahuja, M. K., Chudoba, K., Kacmar, C. J., McKnight, H., George, J. F. (2007). IT road warriors: Balancing work-family conflict, job autonomy, and work overload to mitigate turnover intentions. *Mis Quarterly, 30*, 1–17.

Aspelund, A., Madsen, T.K. & Moen, O., (2007). A review of the foundation, international marketing strategies, and performance of international new ventures. *European Journal of Marketing*, 41(11/12), 1423–1448.

Au, N., Ngai, E. W., & Cheng, T. E. (2008). Extending the understanding of end user information systems satisfaction formation: An equitable needs fulfillment model approach. *MIS Quarterly, 32*(1), 43–66.

Ayal, I. & Zif, J., (1979). Market expansion strategies in multinational marketing. *Journal of Marketing*, 43 (Spring), 84–94.

Barkema, H.G. and Drogendijk, R., (2007). Internationalising in small, incremental or larger steps?. *Journal of International Business Studies*, 38(7), pp. 1132–1148.

Bell, J., Crick, D., & Young, S. (1998). A holistic perspective on small firm growth and internationalisation. In Academy of International Business Conference, City University Business School. *Academy of Management Journal, 41*(1), 7–26.

Cavusgil, S.T. & Zou, S., (1994). Marketing strategy-performance relationship: an investigation of the empirical link in export market ventures. *The Journal of Marketing*, 1–21.

Cellard, S., & Prange, C. (2008). How do age and speed of internationalization affect foreign growth. *In Academy of Management Conference*, Anaheim.

Chetty, S. & Campbell-Hunt, C., (2004). A strategic approach to internationalization: a traditional versus a "born-global" approach. *Journal of International Marketing*, 12(1), 57–81.

Cieślik, J., Kaciak, E. & Welsh, D. H. B., (2012). The impact of geographic diversification on export entrepreneurship. Online First, 11 February 2012, 1–24.

Cooper, R. G. & Kleinschmidt, E. J., (1985). The impact of export strategy on export sales performance. *Journal of International Business Studies*, 37–55.

Crick, D. & Jones, M.V., (2000). Small high-technology firms and international high-technology markets. *Journal of International Marketing*, 8(2), 63–85.

Cunningham, M. T., & Spiegel, R. I. (1971). A study in successful exporting. *European Journal of Marketing, 5*(1), 2–12.

Eriksson, K., Johanson, J., Majkgard, A. & Sharma, D. D., (1997). Experiential knowledge and cost in the internationalization process. *Journal of International Business Studies*, 337–360.

Fenwick, I. & Amine, L., (1979). Export Performance and Export Policy: Evidence from the UK Clothing Industry. *Journal of the Operational Research Society*, 30 (8), 747–54.

Hammermesh, R.G., Anderson, M.J. & Harris, J.E. (1978). Strategies for Low Market Share Business. *Harvard Business Review*, 56 (May–June), 95–102.

Hirsch, S., Lev, B., (1973). Foreign marketing strategies. Management International Review, 13, 81–90.

Hollensen, S., (2011). Global marketing: A decision-oriented approach (5th Edition), Prentice Hall.

Johanson, J. & Vahlne, J.E., (1977). The internationalization process of the firm: a model of knowledge development and increasing foreign market commitment. *Journal of International Business Studies*, 8(1).

Kalish, S., Mahajan, V. & Muller, E., (1995). Waterfall and sprinkler new-product strategies in competitive global markets. *International Journal of Research in Marketing*, 12(2), 105–119.

Katsikea, E. S., Papavassiliou, N., Theodosiou, M. & Morgan, R. E., (2005). Export market expansion strategies of direct-selling small and medium-sized firms: implications for export sales management activities. *Journal of International Marketing*, 13(2), 57–92.

Katsikeas, C. S., & Leonidou, L. C., (1996). Export market expansion strategy: differences between market concentration and market spreading. *Journal of Marketing Management*, 12(1–3), 113–134.

Keegan, Warren J.; Green, Mark, Global Marketing, 2nd, (2000). Electronically reproduced by permission of Pearson Education, Inc., Upper Saddle River, New Jersey.

Knight, G. A. & Cavusgil, S. T., (2004). Innovation, organizational capabilities, and the born-global firm. *Journal of International Business Studies*, 35(2), 124–141.

Knight, G., Madsen, T.K. & Servais, P., (2004). An inquiry into born-global firms in Europe and the USA. *International Marketing Review*, 21 (6), 645–665.

Kock, N. (2015). Common method bias in PLS-SEM: A full collinearity assessment approach. *International Journal of e-Collaboration (ijec), 11*(4), 1–10.

Kuivalainen, O., Saarenketo, S. and Puumalainen, K., (2012). Start-up patterns of internationalization: A framework and its application in the context of knowledge-intensive SMEs. *European Management Journal*, 30(4), pp. 372–385.

Lages, L.F., Lages, C. & Lages, C.R., (2006). Main consequences of prior export performance results: an exploratory study of European exporters. *Journal of Euromarketing*, 15(4), 57–75.

Lee, Chong S. & Yoo S. Yang, (1990). Impact of Export Market Expansion Strategy on Export Performance. *International Marketing Review*, 7 (4), 41–51.

Leonidou, L.C., Katsikeas, C.S. & Samiee, S., (2002). Marketing strategy determinants of export performance: a meta-analysis. *Journal of Business Research*, 55(1), 51–67.

Leonidou, L. C., Katsikeas, C. S., & Coudounaris, D. N., (2010). Five decades of business research into exporting: a bibliographic analysis. *Journal of International Management*, 16(1), 78–91.

Limayem, M., Hirt, S. G., & Cheung, C. M. K. (2007). How habit limits the predictive power of intention: The case of information systems continuance. *MIS quarterly, 31*(4), 705–737.

Lu, J.W.& Beamish, P.W., (2006). SME internationalization and performance: growth vs. profitability. *Journal of International Enterprise*, 4(1), 27–48.

Madsen, T.K. & Servais, P., (1997). The internationalization of born globals: an evolutionary process. *International Business Review*, 6, 561–583.

March, J.G., (1991). Exploration and exploitation in organizational learning. Organization science, 2(1), pp. 71–87.

Morgan-Thomas, A. and Jones, M.V., (2009). Post-entry Internationalization Dynamics Differences between SMEs in the Development Speed of their International Sales. *International Small Business Journal*, 27(1), pp. 71–97.

Oviatt, B.M. & McDougall, P.P., (1994). Toward a theory of international new ventures. *Journal of International Business Studies*, 25(1), 45–62.

Oviatt, B.M. & McDougall, P.P., (1995). Global start-ups: entrepreneurs on a worldwide stage. *Academy of Management Executive*, 9 (2), 30–43.

Pangarkar, N., (2008). Internationalization and performance of small- and medium-sized enterprises. *Journal of World Business*, 43(4), 475–485.

Pavlou, P. A., & Fygenson, M. (2006). Understanding and predicting electronic commerce adoption: An extension of the theory of planned behavior. *MIS quarterly, 30*, 115–143.

Pavlou, P. A., & El Sawy, O. A. (2006). From IT leveraging competence to competitive advantage in turbulent environments: The case of new product development. *Information Systems Research, 17*, 198–227.

Piercy, N.F., (1981). Export strategy: concentration on key markets vs market spreading. *Journal of International Marketing*, 1(1):56– 67.

Piercy, N.F., (1982). Export strategy: markets and competition. George Allen and Irwin, London.

Preece, S. B., Miles, G., & Baetz, M. C., (1999). Explaining the international intensity and global diversity of early-stage technology-based firms. *Journal of Business Venturing*, 14(3), 259–281.

Rugman, A.M. and Verbeke, A., (2004). A perspective on regional and global strategies of multinational enterprises. *Journal of International Business Studies*, 35(1), pp. 3–18.

Sleuwaegen, L. and Onkelinx, J., (2014). International commitment, post-entry growth and survival of international new ventures. *Journal of Business Venturing*, 29(1), pp. 106–120.

Stremersch, S., Tellis, G.J., (2004). Understanding and managing international growth of new products. *International Journal of Research in Marketing* 21, 421–438 (Marketing Science, 22(2): 188–208).

Tessler, A., (1977). Alternative Strategies and the Key Market Principle. Paper presented at a conference sponsored by the London Chamber of Commerce and the Institute of Export, Graham and Trotman Ltd.

Tookey, D., (1975). Export Marketing Decisions. London: Penguin Venturing, 28 (2), 316–334.

Vissak, T. and Masso, J., (2015). Export patterns: Typology development and application to Estonian data. *International Business Review*, 24(4), pp. 652–664.

Direction-Setting in Stakeholder Management: A Marketing Strategy Approach: An Abstract

David Duncombe

Abstract This paper explores how the application of standard marketing processes and tools could create clearer strategic direction for stakeholder management. While this approach has been encouraged by many ever since Philip Kotler and Sidney Levy proposed "broadening marketing" to "publics" other than customers (Kotler and Levy 1969), it has never been explored systematically. This lack of response comes despite repeated requests by leading marketing academics for more conceptual studies that provide guidance as to how to coordinate marketing plans across business functions (Kumar 2015). It also comes despite the relative prominence among academics and practitioners of the stakeholder concept, which counts the customer as just one of many potential stakeholder categories. Despite stakeholder theory's success, it also suffers from some fundamental weaknesses that leave it a challenged concept (Miles 2017) and in need of additional insights that it seems the marketing discipline could provide.

The article begins with a critical review of the stakeholder theory and stakeholder marketing literature as it applies to the direction-setting stage of the strategic planning process. The direction-setting phase involves stakeholder identification, values analysis, and salience determination. The literature within stakeholder theory in each of these areas is extensive, but, as this and other reviews have noted, there remains considerable debate over the definitions and prescriptions in each step.

Subsequently, the article describes how common, "generic" marketing planning steps (Kotler 1972; Kotler and Keller 2012) that involve targeting customers and positioning offerings affect the prioritization of and promises to one particular stakeholder, the customer. It then shows how these customer-oriented decisions indirectly determine who the non-customer stakeholders are, which of their values are met, and their relative salience. Furthermore, it explains how the processes and analytic tools commonly used in marketing for customer management can and are used directly by other business functions to manage the stakeholders for which they are primarily responsible (e.g., human resources for employee acquisition and

D. Duncombe (✉)
University of Wisconsin-Oshkosh, Oshkosh, WI, USA
e-mail: duncombd@uwosh.edu

J. Allen et al. (eds.), *Celebrating the Past and Future of Marketing and Discovery with Social Impact*, Developments in Marketing Science: Proceedings of the Academy of Marketing Science, https://doi.org/10.1007/978-3-030-95346-1_104

retention). Lastly, it argues that the marketing planning process provides a natural mechanism for cross-stakeholder management.

The article concludes that tighter integration of stakeholder theory with common marketing planning concepts, processes, and tools would strengthen both stakeholder theory and the marketing discipline. For stakeholder theory and management, the marketing planning process offers a means to better define and prioritize promises, offerings, and communications across all stakeholders. For the marketing discipline, embracing the stakeholder paradigm more fully provides a framework to move beyond its customer-obsessed myopia (Smith et al. 2010) to a more holistic, stakeholder marketing approach.

Keywords Stakeholder theory · Stakeholder marketing · Stakeholder saliency · Targeting

Examining Users' Emotions, Expectations and Engagement with Nutritional Apps Using Affordances Theory: An Abstract

Maureen Bourassa, Cindy Caldara, Agnès Helme-Guizon, and Monica LaBarge

Abstract Food is one of the cornerstones of well-being. But food and food-related decisions are sometimes experienced as difficult or stressful (Mennell et al. 1992) due to a lack of appropriate food knowledge (Colatruglio and Slater 2014). In this context, mobile apps are flourishing in order to help people make healthier food choices (Flaherty et al. 2019). While the literature on mobile food applications is rich in the health field for their potential to change dietary behaviors (Covolo et al. 2017; Gilliland et al. 2015; Mateo et al. 2015; McKay et al. 2018; Mendiola et al. 2015; Michie et al. 2017; Palacios et al. 2018), there is limited research on how consumers engage with them (Bezançon et al. 2019; Doub et al. 2015; Flaherty et al. 2018, 2019; Gilliland et al. 2015; Samoggia and Riedel 2020).

In this paper, we ask: how can we better understand the consumer engagement process for nutritional apps? Using data from 15 semi-structured interviews with users of the French nutritional app Yuka, we conducted thematic analysis, applying a lens of affordance theory (Gibson 1977).

Proposed by Gibson (1977), the concept of affordances designates the potentialities of action perceived by the individual, resulting from an interaction between the latter and their environment. Affordances are an analytical tool to explore the complex relationship between the individual and technology (Hutchby 2001). Our data

This research was funded in part by the 2020/2021 AMS-AFM Joint Research Initiative Committee. The authors are grateful for this support. Authors are listed in alphabetical order.

M. Bourassa (✉)
University of Saskatchewan, Saskatoon, SK, Canada
e-mail: bourassa@edwards.usask.ca

C. Caldara · A. Helme-Guizon
Université Grenoble Alpes, Grenoble, France
e-mail: cindy.caldara@univ-grenoble-alpes.fr; agnes.helme-guizon@univ-grenoble-alpes.fr

M. LaBarge
Queen's University, Kingston, ON, Canada
e-mail: monica.labarge@queensu.ca

J. Allen et al. (eds.), *Celebrating the Past and Future of Marketing and Discovery with Social Impact*, Developments in Marketing Science: Proceedings of the Academy of Marketing Science, https://doi.org/10.1007/978-3-030-95346-1_105

and analysis helped us to arrive at a model of engagement based on affordances, in which we examine the impact that emotions experienced during the affordance actualization stage has on user engagement at various points of app usage.

Through our research, we highlight the dynamic nature of engagement. As users attempt to actualize affordances offered by nutrition apps, emotional mechanisms influence (re)adjustments in usage, which in turn influence modes of engagement.

Keywords Nutrition · Apps · Qualitative research · Technology · Food well-being

The Impact of Service Failures on Brand Perceptions: The Context of Sharing Economy: An Abstract

Alexis Moore and Shuqin Wei

Abstract The sharing economy, also known as the collaborative consumption or the technology-facilitated peer-to-peer business model (such as Uber and Airbnb services), is on the rise (Hamari et al. 2016). As more and more consumers participate in sharing economy, service failures are inevitable. Despite the prevalence of service failures in the context of sharing economy, scant academic research exists on what companies should do to recover the failures. Some interesting yet underexplored research questions include: First, in the context of sharing economy, how do different types of service failures affect consumers' perceptions and behaviors toward the brand? Second, what companies can do as a method of recourse when a service failure occurs?

This research is designed to examine the ramification posed by sharing economy businesses when one of their independent contractors commits a service failure and uses different methods of recovery. By manipulating both the type of service failure and the method of recovery using scenarios, we hoped to unveil the factors most important to customer loyalty and trust in the context of a sharing economy. Specifically, a 2 × 2 experimental design scenario-based survey was conducted to determine what methods of recovery generated the best response for each type of service failure. A total of 210 participants were recruited through Amazon Mechanical Turk for the study. The participants were randomly assigned a scenario in which either an outcome-based or process-based service failure occurs and then presented with either a recovery performed by the independent service provider or a recovery performed by the company. We then asked the participants how satisfied they were and how this recovery made them view the brand in terms of trustworthiness, forgiveness, ethicality, and justice.

The results showed that if there is an outcome-based failure customers prefer a recovery performed by the service provider, but if there is a process-based failure customers prefer a recovery performed by the company. Our findings contribute to the service failure and recovery literature by showing that independent service pro-

A. Moore · S. Wei (✉)
Marshall University, Huntington, WV, USA
e-mail: moore787@marshall.edu; weish@marshall.edu

J. Allen et al. (eds.), *Celebrating the Past and Future of Marketing and Discovery with Social Impact*, Developments in Marketing Science: Proceedings of the Academy of Marketing Science, https://doi.org/10.1007/978-3-030-95346-1_106

vider's failures can affect customers' perception and action toward the company/brand and that different recovery methods are preferred depending on the type of failure. Implications of this study show that different types of failures that occur in the context of the sharing economy require different forms of recovery to maintain a positive brand image in the minds of consumers.

Keywords Sharing economy · Service failure · Service recovery · Brand perceptions

Stopping the Spread: The Role of Blame Attributions and Service Provider Measures in Curbing C2C Misbehavior Contagion: An Abstract

Ilias Danatzis and Jana Möller

Abstract Customer misbehavior is part of the daily business of service firms. Generally understood as acts that disrupt service encounters and violate generally accepted codes of conduct, customer misbehavior occurs regularly and with varying degrees of severity across service sectors. Traditionally, research on customer misbehavior has focused on misbehavior that is either targeted at the service provider, the frontline service staff, or the service provider's property. However, service encounters today are increasingly characterized by customer-to-customer (C2C) interactions in which customers regularly become targets of other customers' misbehavior. Despite its increasing prevalence, research on C2C misbehavior remains very limited today. This spareness is even more concerning given that previous research provides initial evidence of the contagiousness of customer misbehavior in access-based settings. Yet it remains unclear whether this contagiousness likewise translates to other contexts and forms of misbehavior, and what service providers can do to effectively curb its spread and attenuate potential negative firm evaluations. Three online experiments in the context of Airbnb, gym and transportation services reveal that provider-directed blame attributions mediate the contagiousness of C2C misbehavior. That is, C2C misbehavior spreads because customers blame the service provider for the wrongdoings of other customers; regardless of whether this misbehavior is targeted towards another customer's personal belongings or at other customers directly. Moreover, our results indicate that preventative and interventive service provider measures can effectively reduce blame attributions which, in turn, attenuate negative customer attitudes towards the firm while simultaneously curbing subsequent C2C misbehavior. By explicating the central role blame attribu-

I. Danatzis (✉)
King's College London, London, UK
e-mail: ilias.danatzis@kcl.ac.uk

J. Möller
Freie Universität Berlin, Berlin, Germany
e-mail: jana.moeller@fu-berlin.de

J. Allen et al. (eds.), *Celebrating the Past and Future of Marketing and Discovery with Social Impact*, Developments in Marketing Science: Proceedings of the Academy of Marketing Science, https://doi.org/10.1007/978-3-030-95346-1_107

tions play in the spread of C2C misbehavior, this study extends previous research on customer misbehavior and misbehavior contagiousness. Managerially, this research provides firms with explicit guidance on how to tackle the spread of C2C misbehavior and reduce negative firm evaluations with targeted measures. Overall, our findings provide first experimental evidence that tackling the spread of C2C misbehavior is both possible and advisable with targeted provider measures.

Keywords Customer misbehavior · C2C interactions · Blame attributions · Services marketing

Do the Powerful Conserve? Understanding the Role of Power in Sustainable Consumption Intentions: An Abstract

Khaled Aboulnasr and Amro Maher

Abstract According to the United Nations, as the world population approaches 10 billion people by the year 2050, triple the amount of natural resources that are available today would be required to sustain existing lifestyles (https://www.un.org/sustainabledevelopment/sustainable-consumption-production/). Despite the importance of power in the context of consumption behavior, its impact has not been explored in the context of socially responsible consumption. Furthermore, the literature on the effect of power on self-serving vs. pro-social behaviors have been mixed (Righetti et al. 2015). As such, the objective of the present research is to explore the multifaceted role that power may play in the context of sustainable consumption behavior. Additionally, this study aims to examine the role of moral identity; a critical construct known to interact with power in shaping self-serving vs. pro-social behavior. Moral identity is defined as the degree to which an individual's morality is a central component of his/her self-concept (DeCelles et al. 2012).

Respondents were recruited through Amazon Mechanical Turk to complete an experiment. They were first asked to complete a power manipulation (Galinsky et al. 2003), followed by a power manipulation check. Half of the respondents were randomly assigned to a high power condition, while half of the respondents were exposed to a low power condition. Next, they were exposed to a scenario that describing a hypothetical scenario in which they were planning to buy a water bottle and were told that they came across an environmentally friendly bottle. This was followed by a 4 item measure of purchase intention (Edinger-Schons et al. 2018), a measure of sustainable consumption attitude (Webb et al. 2008) and finally a measure of moral identity (Aquino and Reed 2002). 109 responses were received. 3 respondents were excluded resulting in 106 usable responses.

The results support that moral identity has a positive impact on purchase intention and that power had a marginally significant and negative impact on purchase intention. The results also support a three-way interaction between power, moral identity and attitude toward sustainable consumption. The effect of attitude toward

K. Aboulnasr · A. Maher (✉)
Florida Gulf Coast University, Fort Myers, FL, USA
e-mail: Kaboulna@fgcu.edu; Amaher@fgcu.edu

J. Allen et al. (eds.), *Celebrating the Past and Future of Marketing and Discovery with Social Impact*, Developments in Marketing Science: Proceedings of the Academy of Marketing Science, https://doi.org/10.1007/978-3-030-95346-1_108

sustainable consumption on purchase intention, for low moral identity consumers is the same regardless of the level of power. However, the results, show that for high moral identity consumers, the positive effect of attitude on purchase intention exists only when power is high.

Keywords Power · Sustainable consumptions · Moral identity · Social responsibility

The Influence of Self-Disclosure on User-Generated Content (UGC) Communication Effects: An Abstract

Yeon Jae Choi and Sanghak Lee

Abstract Consumers nowadays are transforming from passive information recipients to active information producers. User-generated content (UGC) has become a significant factor affecting their purchase decision-making. Considering that little attention has been given to an individual's tendency that shapes the assessment of UGC, this study focuses on self-disclosure in UGC settings. The overarching purpose of this research is to assess the consequences of voluntary self-disclosure in social media functioning as a consumer's personality trait by examining UGC perception – drawn from source credibility and attractiveness – and UGC behavior – drawn from consumer online brand-related activities (COBRAs). This study examines the extent to which self-disclosure favorably impacts perceived UGC trustworthiness and familiarity, and how this, in turn, affects subsequent brand attitude and purchase intention. This study further looks into how UGC behavior affects purchase intention. Using 301 valid responses, a confirmatory factor analysis (CFA) and structural equation modeling (SEM) are employed to comprehensively evaluate and develop a hypothesized research model. The hypothesized research model fit turns out to be good in general. The results indicate that consumers with a high level of self-disclosure not only generate trust and familiarity toward UGC but are also active in engaging in UGC behavior. The findings suggest that the more consumers create, consume, or contribute to UGC, the more they want to purchase the products and/or brands shown in UGC. Perceived UGC trustworthiness and familiarity, in turn, lead to positive brand attitudes and purchase intentions. Coincidently, this study confirms that self-disclosure begets positive UGC behavior using UGC perception as a mediator. This research provides several practical insights into the mechanisms underlying UGC perception and UGC behavior, and it ultimately helps facilitate consumers' self-disclosure to improve brand attitude and purchase intention. This study provides a further understanding of the important role of consum-

Data collection of the present study was supported by the Korea Advertising Society in 2020.

Y. J. Choi (✉) · S. Lee
Korea Aerospace University, Goyang-si, South Korea
e-mail: yeonjae4647@kau.kr; sanghak.lee@kau.ac.kr

J. Allen et al. (eds.), *Celebrating the Past and Future of Marketing and Discovery with Social Impact*, Developments in Marketing Science: Proceedings of the Academy of Marketing Science, https://doi.org/10.1007/978-3-030-95346-1_109

ers' voluntary self-disclosure in UGC marketing campaigns. The results analysis suggests that it is advisable for marketing firms to understand their target consumers' self-disclosure tendency when using UGC in their marketing strategies.

Keywords User-generated content · Self-disclosure · Source trustworthiness · Source familiarity · Brand attitude · Purchase intention · Structural equation modeling

What a Trip! How Patients Evaluate Centers of Excellence in the Medical Tourism Industry: An Abstract

Shawn Thelen, Boonghee Yoo, and Kristina Harrison

Abstract Employers and insurance companies are increasingly offering patients various options for having surgical procedures performed and have been turning to "centers of excellence" that are renown for specific procedures resulting in better quality treatment than found at local hospitals. Medical tourism is also an option that has become more popular among employers and patients. Breadth and depth of healthcare marketing research is growing as the importance of marketing to healthcare organizations continues to increase (Crié and Chebat 2013) and research efforts in the area of healthcare marketing have been very informative investigating the fields of medical tourism, health marketing communication, strategic management and marketing in healthcare, pharmaceutical marketing, service quality, dietary habits, and the growing field of digital healthcare (Butt et al. 2019). However, research into the healthcare field requires industry-specific insight and knowledge (Stremersch and Van Dyck 2009). Thus, a greater understanding is needed regarding how perspective patients generally perceive the risks associated with each of these options with respect to the type of surgery being performed. This research seeks to make theoretical contributions about the nature and determinants of customer expectations of service in the healthcare context via Zeithaml et al. (1993) conceptual framework. We employed a mixed methods design collecting both qualitative and quantitative data, which seeks to contribute to a deeper understanding of patient evaluation and expectations of service in the medical tourism industry. Within-subjects 2 × 3 experimental design format was employed altering the type of surgery performed and the location of the surgery along with financial responsibilities/incentives. The findings can better communicate the benefits of healthcare tourism while minimizing perceived risks. Service providers can work to re-define country of origin effects related to their specific healthcare service by showcasing awards, credentials, and advertising where their doctors received their degrees. To mitigate

S. Thelen · B. Yoo
Hofstra University, Hempstead, NY, USA
e-mail: Shawn.T.Thelen@hofstra.edu; Boonghee.Ypp@hostra.edu

K. Harrison (✉)
University of Southern Mississippi, Hattiesburg, MS, USA
e-mail: kristina.m.harrison@usm.edu

J. Allen et al. (eds.), *Celebrating the Past and Future of Marketing and Discovery with Social Impact*, Developments in Marketing Science: Proceedings of the Academy of Marketing Science, https://doi.org/10.1007/978-3-030-95346-1_110

fearful emotions, service providers can also increase communications between the healthcare service providers and the patients to put them at ease through calming "bed-side manner".

Keywords Medical tourism · Patient satisfaction · Patient service evaluation · Healthcare marketing

The Robot Won't Judge Me: How AI Healthcare Benefits the Stigmatized: An Abstract

Lam An and Laura Boman

Abstract The rise of AI healthcare applications is changing the way consumers receive treatment, diagnosis, and health advice. Despite the rapid growth of AI in healthcare contexts, prior literature suggests that consumers experience reservations about AI in healthcare due to the concerns that automation reduces providers' ability to take into consideration the uniqueness of consumers' health-related characteristics in comparison to human providers (Longoni et al. 2019) and privacy concerns (Brooks 2019). However, might there be times when consumers might prefer an AI provider over a human healthcare provider?

Consumers who suffer stigmatized health issues often experience self-conscious emotions such as fear, shame, and embarrassment. Negative emotions can create barriers for communication between patients and doctors and negative health outcomes. Thus, by developing solutions which reduce consumers' negative emotions related to stigmatized health issues, consumer well-being may be enhanced. In the current research, we suggest consumers with stigmatized (versus non-stigmatized) health issues will prefer AI to human health care providers.

In Study 1, two hundred and forty-two undergraduates were randomly assigned to a 2 (disease type: contagious or non-contagious) × 2 (healthcare provider type: human or AI) between-subjects design. In the heart disease scenario, participants were significantly more likely to schedule a screening appointment if the healthcare provider was a human physician. However, in the seasonal flu scenario, which was perceived as a more stigmatized disease, participants were significantly more likely to schedule a screening appointment if the healthcare provider was a computer.

In Study 2, one hundred and fifty four undergraduates were randomly assigned to either a human or AI healthcare provider conditions. All participants were asked to imagine that they had a close friend who was overweight/obese and experienced health issues as a result. Participants were then shown a brochure of a workout pro-

L. An (✉)
University of Central Florida, Orlando, FL, USA
e-mail: lam.an@ucf.edu

L. Boman
Mercer University, Macon, GA, USA
e-mail: boman_lk@mercer.edu

J. Allen et al. (eds.), *Celebrating the Past and Future of Marketing and Discovery with Social Impact*, Developments in Marketing Science: Proceedings of the Academy of Marketing Science, https://doi.org/10.1007/978-3-030-95346-1_111

gram with either a virtual workout program or an in-person one. Results showed that participants expected their obese friend would feel more shame and negative judgement if he/she enrolled in the in-person program compared to the virtual workout program.

In summary, findings from two studies provided support for our hypotheses that consumers dealing with stigmatized health conditions prefer artificial intelligence healthcare providers to human ones. These findings have important implications for early diagnosis and potential recovery of these health conditions, as well as to prevent spreading of contagious diseases.

Keywords Stigma · Health care · Artificial intelligence · Social judgement

AI Companionship or Loneliness: How AI-Based Chatbots Impact Consumer's (Digital) Well-Being: An Abstract

Kerry T. Manis and John Matis

Abstract With the recent proliferation of "smart" technologies, consumers increasingly interact with these technologies the same way they would interact with their fellow humans (e.g., having a conversation with Siri or Alexa) (Novak and Hoffman 2019). Indeed, some consumers are turning to technology to fulfill desires for friendship and/or romance (Olson 2020). While technology can be successfully designed to positively influence consumer well-being (Dekker et al. 2020; Peters et al. 2018), scant research exists examining this phenomenon beyond a conceptual level. Recently, however, scholars show that the detrimental impact of technology on consumer well-being (i.e., consisting of overall life satisfaction and positive and negative affective states; Burroughs and Rindfleisch 2002) may be less harmful than previously thought (Orben and Pryzbylski 2018; Pryzbylski and Weinstein 2016). In contrast, other research shows that the detrimental effect of technology may exist under certain conditions, such as long-term isolation (e.g., Lastovicka and Sirianni 2011). Therefore, technology can have beneficial and/or detrimental impacts on consumer well-being (Hefner and Vorderer 2017; Mick and Fournier 1998; Pryzbylski et al. 2012). Understanding the relationship between technology and consumer well-being is further marred by data collection issues such as research participants being unable to accurately estimate their own technology usage (Scharkow 2016). As such, the purpose of this research was to develop a deeper understanding of how technology and the interaction with technology can impact consumer well-being. Specifically, we develop theory regarding how consumer's interact with technology via two qualitative studies following a grounded theory approach (Corbin and Strauss 1990). Because our data are cross-sectional, future research would benefit from a longitudinal perspective to assess when technology might improve (digital) well-being (e.g., potentially initially) and where technology might worsen (digital) well-being overtime due to increased isolation (e.g., if used for a long period) (Lastovicka and Sirianni 2011).

K. T. Manis (✉) · J. Matis
Texas Tech University, Lubbock, TX, USA
e-mail: kt.manis@ttu.edu; john.matis@ttu.edu

J. Allen et al. (eds.), *Celebrating the Past and Future of Marketing and Discovery with Social Impact*, Developments in Marketing Science: Proceedings of the Academy of Marketing Science, https://doi.org/10.1007/978-3-030-95346-1_112

Keywords Artificial intelligence · Consumer well-being · Human computer interaction · Mental health · Technology · Thematic analysis · Topic modeling · AI-based chatbot · Emotional attachment

The Impact of Purchase Types on Consumer's Polarized Product Opinions: An Abstract

Meichen Dong, Yunmei Kuang, and Wei Chen

Abstract This research examines the impact of purchase types on consumer's purchasing decision while the product exhibits polarizing reviews. The authors propose when facing a higher level of polarized review, consumers are less likely to make an experiential purchase (vs. material purchase). This effect is driven by the higher perceived risk that is associated with experiential purchase. Our study will contribute to the word-of-mouth research and extend the research in the field of purchase type. Moreover, our work will provide practical implications for marketing managers to help them improve their product quality and manage the mixed feedback from consumers.

In the past, consumers were more likely to be exposed to traditional word of mouth, where information came from friends or family members (Arndt 1967; Brown and Reingen 1987). However, the development of information technology has given consumers more resources to get external information before they make purchase decisions. Online platforms, such as Yelp, TripAdvisor, or Amazon's consumer review section have offered valuable feedback from other consumers to give potential buyers more references. Because of the proliferation of information sources, consumers are more likely to encounter a mix review about a product than ever. Previous research has suggested that consumers mixed opinions are common across all kinds of products (Hu et al. 2009). On one hand, the availability of product reviews has facilitated the consumer's decision-making process, providing them more references from others' experiences. On the other hand, the existence of polarized opinions may also bring an even more difficult decision for them to make.

M. Dong (✉)
Valparaiso University, Valparaiso, IN, USA
e-mail: meichen.dong@valpo.edu

Y. Kuang
Saint Louis University, Saint Louis, MO, USA
e-mail: yunmei.kuang@slu.edu

W. Chen
University of Texas at Arlington, Arlington, TX, USA
e-mail: wei.chen2@mavs.uta.edu

J. Allen et al. (eds.), *Celebrating the Past and Future of Marketing and Discovery with Social Impact*, Developments in Marketing Science: Proceedings of the Academy of Marketing Science, https://doi.org/10.1007/978-3-030-95346-1_113

Admittedly, word of mouth is a critical element to impact consumer's purchase decision. A growing body of research regarding word of mouth has examined the effect of word-of-mouth volume, valence and central tendency on consumer's behavior (Chevalier and Mayzlin 2006; Mudambi and Schuff 2010), however, little work has looked into the influence of product review dispersion on consumer's purchase behaviors, more specifically, the effect of polarized opinions on consumer's purchase intention. For marketing practitioners, it is also important for them to understand how they could deal with their product review polarization situations and how to better communicate with consumers when polarizing reviews happen.

Keywords Experiential purchase · Material purchase · Opinion polarization · Word of mouth

Google, Google on the Wall: Which One Is the Most Successful New Product Demonstration of Them All? An Abstract

Amir Javadinia and Melanie Lorenz

Abstract Firms aim to constantly develop new products and selectively reveal information about those activities to influence different parties, i.e., consumers, investors, and competitors. An important medium for this purpose is new product demonstration, which is defined as the disclosure of a new product at any stage of development and commercialization to the public. While new product demonstrations mainly aim to familiarize consumers with the new product characteristics and make sales efforts more efficient, they may also increase consumers' interest in a brand, and hence, brand purchase.

In this paper, we investigate (by means of secondary data modeling) how the demonstration of new products may impact consumers' online search behavior for the brand, and subsequently firms' market performance. We believe that consumers' search behavior reveals consumers' mindset about brands and is an important predictor of future brand purchases. We also explore how the relationship between new product demonstrations and the online brand search could vary with the product's development stage at the time of the demonstration.

Using automobile industry as our empirical context, we collected new car demonstrations in 10 different world-renowned international trade shows from 2005 to 2018. Our unbalanced, pooled, time-series dataset comprises 3447 observations of 22 brands from 10 major automakers and 108 trade shows. We also collected online search data for brands from the Google Trends database. The amount of "Googling" for a brand, demonstrated by the Google search volume index in near real-time, can serve as a proxy for the number of consumers seeking information about the brand. Our findings reveal that while new product demonstrations, on average, improve market performance through a boost in consumers' online brand search, this relationship is stronger for new products at early and advanced stages of development, compared to the new products at the middle stage of development.

Our research has important implications for academicians as well as managers. From an academic perspective, responds to research calls for studies on investigat-

A. Javadinia · M. Lorenz (✉)
Florida Atlantic University, Boca Raton, FL, USA
e-mail: sjavadinia@fau.edu; lorenzm@fau.edu

J. Allen et al. (eds.), *Celebrating the Past and Future of Marketing and Discovery with Social Impact*, Developments in Marketing Science: Proceedings of the Academy of Marketing Science, https://doi.org/10.1007/978-3-030-95346-1_114

ing consumers' behavioral responses to a firm's new product efforts in novel ways (e.g. Google Trends Data). From a managerial perspective, being aware of the consumers' online search helps managers to align their new product decisions with other marketing strategies such as advertising and promotions.

Keywords New product demonstration · Online search · Market performance · Development stage

Consumer Engagement in Online Product Reviews: A Win-Win for Firms and Micro-Influencers: An Abstract

Tai Anh Kieu

Abstract The advances of the Internet and social media allow consumers to access more channels and sources of information to inform their purchase decisions. This has also given rise to micro-influencers, who generate content and gradually form a community following and interacting with their social accounts. Micro-influencers differ with traditional celebrities in that the latter become renown through sporting, art or the like (De Veirman et al. 2017). Micro-influencers are perceived as more reflective of their followers (Jin et al. 2019), and are argued to wield powerful influence over consumer choice, despite their much less popularity and followings than traditional celebrities (Boerman 2020). This study examines the relationships among social communication variables relating to micro-influencers on social platforms: online opinion leadership (OOL) and parasocial interaction (PSI) as personal and interpersonal source characteristics, respectively (Sweeney et al. 2008); message quality as a message characteristic (Le et al. 2020); online interaction propensity (OIP) as a receiver characteristic (Labrecque 2014); and consumer engagement behaviours (CEBs) as responses with respect to product review elements including the content, the micro-influencer, and the product/ brand embedded in the post (Casaló et al. 2020). An online survey was conducted with a convenience sample of Vietnamese consumers who have previously purchased or planned to buy a mobile phone within 6 months and have viewed online reviews about mobile phones as part of their information search. A valid data of 371 responses was analysed using smart-PLS 3.3.3. Findings reveal that OOL and PSI have significant impact on message quality ($p < 0.05$), which in turn affects significantly CEBs ($p < 0.05$): Intention to interact with the post; intention to follow advice of the micro-influencer; and intention to recommend the micro-influencer to others. While the result only finds OIP elevates the impact of message quality on consumers' intention to interact with the post at $p < 0.10$; findings show significant direct impact of OIP on CEBs, though not hypothesised. This research contributes to communication literature concerning consumers' processing of persuasive cues and information exposed to them through

T. A. Kieu (✉)
Ho Chi Minh City Open University, Ho Chi Minh City, Vietnam
e-mail: tai.ka@ou.edu.vn

J. Allen et al. (eds.), *Celebrating the Past and Future of Marketing and Discovery with Social Impact*, Developments in Marketing Science: Proceedings of the Academy of Marketing Science, https://doi.org/10.1007/978-3-030-95346-1_115

the online environment. The research highlights the importance of essential factors requiring attention in micro-influencer marketing: OOL, PSI, message quality and OIP. The study also contributes to consumer engagement literature with evidence concerning the focal object as micro-influencers' online product reviews. Practically, insights from this research suggest marketers need to detect micro-influencers, target them with appropriate communication strategies so as to influence their generated and disseminated content. Marketers can take the findings of effects on intention with the post and intention to recommend the micro-influencers in approaching micro-influencers for a win-win collaboration. The study also demonstrates OIP as an important individual trait in segmenting consumers for effective consumer engagement.

Keywords Micro-influencer · Opinion leadership · Parasocial interaction · Consumer engagement · Online product reviews · Online interaction propensity

The Drivers of the Dissolution of Interfirm Partnerships by Emerging Market Multinationals: An Abstract

Billur Akdeniz and Berk Talay

Abstract An international interfirm partnership is a formalized arrangement between two or more firms from different countries focusing on various value chain activities including but not limited to product development, manufacturing, and technology (Pedada et al. 2019). In terms of its organizational structure, it can either take the form of a distinct corporate entity or an interorganizational entity (Varadarajan and Cunningham 1995). International interfirm partnerships have become ubiquitous as they help firms reach economies of scale, hedge risks, learn new skills and technologies, and facilitate effective resource sharing (e.g., Beamish and Berdrow 2003; Beamish and Inkpen 1995; Julian and O'Cass 2004).

Despite their popularity and benefits, international interfirm partnerships are inherently risky, and most of them dissolve shortly after their inception (Cui 2013; Tower et al. 2019). Previous studies have investigated a variety of factors that affect the dissolution of these partnerships in various environmental and organizational contexts such as equity structure (Dhanaraj and Beamish 2004), resource dependence (Xia 2011), cultural differences (Talay and Akdeniz 2009), and lack of cooperation (Luo and Park 2004) between partners. While extant literature provides valuable insights, our knowledge of the drivers of the dissolution of interfirm partnerships by emerging-market multinational enterprises (EMNEs) is rather limited. Yet, one of the most significant developments in international business has been understanding the role of emerging markets in international business as well as the rise of EMNEs and their contributions to globalization (Buckley and Tian 2017; Griffith et al. 2008). This study is based on the premise that EMNEs in general, and their international partnerships in particular, deserve scholarly attention because EMNEs are different from multinational enterprises from developed countries (DMNEs) with respect to the amount and type of resources they afford in an international partnership (Pedada et al. 2019).

B. Akdeniz (✉)
University of New Hampshire, Durham, NH, USA
e-mail: billur.akdeniz@unh.edu

B. Talay
University of Massachusetts Lowell, Lowell, MA, USA
e-mail: berk_talay@uml.edu

J. Allen et al. (eds.), *Celebrating the Past and Future of Marketing and Discovery with Social Impact*, Developments in Marketing Science: Proceedings of the Academy of Marketing Science, https://doi.org/10.1007/978-3-030-95346-1_116

With a focus on international joint ventures (IJVs) as a type of interfirm partnerships, this study develops a typology based on home- and host-countries as either a developed or emerging market, and hence, examines how the country-of-origin of the IJV partners' home countries and the IJV host country affect the likelihood of dissolution. In addition, we compare how the effects of these drivers vary compared to IJVs founded with DMNEs. Using a large dataset of IJVs spanning almost 20 years and more than 100 countries, our analyses reveal that along with some partner-firm and host-country related factors, IJV partners' home countries and the IJV host country affect IJV dissolution likelihood.

Keywords International joint venture · Dissolution · Emerging market · Developed market

How Artificially Intelligent (AI) Leadership Impacts Trust and Recommendation Quality among Consumers: An Abstract

Devdeep Maity, Juha Munnukka, Ashwini Gangadharan, and Daeryong Kim

Abstract There has been a renewed discussion of the role of leadership in current times in several media outlets that span from political and corporate leadership to leadership in the context of activism, consumerism, and public life. Partly, this demonstrates the urge of a huge mass of population wanting to be led by a leader, even if such leadership may land up in an epic failure or may encompass undertakings comprising of huge risks or at times outright against the law. Take, for example, the role of "the professor" in the recent worldwide popular series by Netflix which broke several records regarding its viewership in the entertainment industry (Pearce 2019). The character of the professor and his charismatic leadership in guiding his accomplices through complicated and detailed oriented heists, which despite being unlawful, have drawn tremendous fan following from the audience, thereby displaying an ardent desire of humans to be led and coached by another towards a purposeful goal. Such an idea of leadership has, however, not been studied in the context of Virtual Service Assistants (VSAs) or Artificially Intelligent (AI) chatbots such as Amazon's Alexa, Apple's Siri, Microsoft's Cortana, or Google home to name a few. Presently, the VSAs have been looked primarily at providing services to answer consumer questions or helping them with product selections, ordering, and pur-

This research project has received funding as a part of Dean's Summer Research Grant from the College of Business at Delaware State University, Dover, DE, USA.

D. Maity (✉) · D. Kim
Delaware State University, Dover, DE, USA
e-mail: dmaity@desu.edu; dkim@desu.edu

J. Munnukka
Jyväskylä University School of Business and Economics, Jyväskylä, Finland
e-mail: juha.t.munnukka@jyu.fi

A. Gangadharan
Kutztown University of Pennsylvania, Kutztown, PA, USA
e-mail: gangadharan@kutztown.edu

J. Allen et al. (eds.), *Celebrating the Past and Future of Marketing and Discovery with Social Impact*, Developments in Marketing Science: Proceedings of the Academy of Marketing Science, https://doi.org/10.1007/978-3-030-95346-1_117

chases. However, the notion that such AIs and VSAs can grow beyond their traditional role of being assistants is not distant, though unexplored at this point. With the development of the prototype of Alexa prize chatbots (Amazon 2019) that engage consumers in near organic conversations, (without even using the wake word "Alexa" repeatedly) such as jokes, riddle, opinion on a subject, news and movie reviews insinuates the possibility of VSAs to play a more significant role such as that of a friend, a guide, and an impactful leader. The current study explores the role of artificially intelligent leaders, in the context of VSA enabled smart speakers such as Amazon Alexa in instilling a trusting relationship with its consumers and its influence on the consumers' perception of the quality of their product recommendation. Although the idea of brand anthropomorphism (displaying human-like traits and qualities) in the context of AI has been recently introduced in the field of Marketing, existing scholarship has not looked at the specific leadership influences, such as leading, guiding, that these AIs have on its consumers.

Keywords AI leadership · Artificial intelligent leadership · Virtual service assistants (VSAs) · Artificially intelligent (AI) chatbots · Trust · Recommendation quality · Amazon Alexa

Using Website Builders as a Tool for Teaching the Website Development Process: An Abstract

Janna M. Parker, Kevin W. James, and Cassandra Ditt

Abstract Within marketing, a new sub-discipline of digital marketing has emerged, and, in this field, there has been a call to recognize "a new marketing DNA" for marketing education (Harrigan and Hulbert 2011). This new approach requires that marketing educators create a curriculum that integrates theory and practice with the technology and digital tools used in the industry. This research discusses a digital marketing-oriented, semester-length project in which students create personal branding websites; the assignment is referred to as *Website Builders*. Utilizing Website Builders allows professors to teach digital marketing technical skills such as search engine optimization (SEO), content creation, and the website development process while incorporating marketing strategy and theory. Website Builders incorporates key SEO strategy components and takes students through the website development process (Zahay and Roberts 2017).

We propose that the Website Builders Method is an optimal means for teaching SEO strategy and website design and assessing student learning outcomes. The assignment is aligned with Krathwohl's (2002) Taxonomy Table, which is based upon Bloom's (Remember, Understand, Apply, Analyze, Evaluate, and Create) and incorporates the Knowledge and Cognitive Process dimensions (Factual, Conceptual, Procedural, and Metacognitive. The assignment maps out activities for the semester on the Taxonomy Table.

Throughout the semester, the marketing educator will deliver lectures on the website development process, including essential marketing concepts related to websites and digital marketing. To use this assignment effectively, the marketing educator must create a website of his/her own. Students create and publish a website

J. M. Parker (✉)
James Madison University, Harrisonburg, VA, USA
e-mail: parke4jm@jmu.edu

K. W. James
The University of Texas at Tyler, Tyler, TX, USA
e-mail: kjames@uttyler.edu

C. Ditt
McNeese State University, Lake Charles, LA, USA
e-mail: cditt@mcneese.edu

J. Allen et al. (eds.), *Celebrating the Past and Future of Marketing and Discovery with Social Impact*, Developments in Marketing Science: Proceedings of the Academy of Marketing Science, https://doi.org/10.1007/978-3-030-95346-1_118

by mid-semester and then promote their websites using social media and email campaigns to solicit feedback. Website traffic is analyzed using Google Analytics. Students refine based on feedback and traffic analysis. Peer review is conducted, which allows the students to evaluate other students' websites and their implementation of the concepts taught. After completing all these steps, students submit their website for a final grade.

This learning process facilitates higher learning by having students develop knowledge of the terminology and abstract concepts. By creating a website, students utilize their critical thinking skills and demonstrate that they can apply, analyze, and evaluate information. After completing the website assignment, the students write a reflection paper that brings each student to Bloom's final stage of Create based on Metacognitive Knowledge. An analysis of papers (n = 37) revealed that all but 3 students identified key learning objectives in their reflection.

Keywords Website development · Krathwohl's Taxonomy Table · SEO · Bloom's Taxonomy · Personal branding website

Escapism Motive on a Virtual Platform during the Pandemic: An Abstract

Christine Eunyoung Sung

Abstract Currently, the world is experiencing considerable unpredictability due to the COVID-19 pandemic, and retailers have been struggling to adjust to the new consumption environment, which embodies online/virtual platforms. During this global upheaval, many activities that used to occur primarily in the physical environment (e.g., shopping; attending movies, musicals, and concerts; taking classes; participating in meetings; working) have already shifted to the virtual environment throughout the world.

The current study investigates (a) the use intention of a virtual platform (virtual reality fitness) as a form of disease prevention behavior, and (b) consumers' applied technology ad experience on a virtual platform during the pandemic among young people who are described as being tech-savvy (Lee et al. 2020; Smith 2017) during the pandemic.

In the study, data came from 46 undergraduate students at a U.S. university who were majoring in business. For the U.S. sample, among the elements of experience economy, only esthetics, entertainment, and escapism were measured based on the context of the current study (VR fitness). Among these elements, esthetic influences escapism; escapism positively influences VR fitness advertising satisfaction during the pandemic. Stress during the pandemic influences escapism experience. Perceived virtual platform benefit also influences VR fitness advertising satisfaction during the pandemic. In addition, VR fitness advertising satisfaction influences the use intention of virtual platforms during the pandemic and after the pandemic.

The findings reveal that managers should improve users' online experiences by implementing applied technology marketing strategies to impress consumers in the consumption environment, in line with the escapism motive. Therefore, in the main study, the effectiveness of applied technology marketing on the online/virtual format with a chosen VR stimulus will be conducted and compared across cultures

C. E. Sung (✉)
Montana State University, Bozeman, MT, USA
e-mail: christinesung@montana.edu

J. Allen et al. (eds.), *Celebrating the Past and Future of Marketing and Discovery with Social Impact*, Developments in Marketing Science: Proceedings of the Academy of Marketing Science, https://doi.org/10.1007/978-3-030-95346-1_119

(individualism vs. collectivism), in line with the escapism motive during the pandemic.

Keywords Virtual reality · VR fitness · Advertising · Virtual platform during the pandemic

Inclusive Integrated Marketing Framework for Relationship Quality and Value Co-creation for Higher Education: An Abstract

Varsha Jain, Emmanuel Mogaji, Himani Sharma, and Anantha Babbili

Abstract One of the defining characteristics of higher education is creating relationships with the stakeholders who define the ecosystem. The associations have become increasingly important for higher education marketing and developing strategies of co-creation. Being a highly knowledge-intensive industry driven by human capital, higher education universities need to improve their relationship with the stakeholders including the learners, faculty, administrators and industry professionals. Though different dimensions of relationship quality have received great academic attention across disciplines, there is still a need to explore the role of various intrinsic and extrinsic cues influencing relationship quality from the lens of value co-creation in higher education marketing. Accordingly, this study focuses on discussing the antecedents (intrinsic and outside) of relationship quality between the universities and the stakeholders in the digital era. It proposes an integrated higher education marketing framework using the Cue-Utilization approach with perceived situational appropriateness as the frame of reference. A multi-stakeholder perspective is explored using semi-structured in-depth interviews with participants from India, UK, Nigeria, and Dubai. The study's findings suggest that the discussed intrinsic and extrinsic cues are the surrogate indicators of high relationship quality with the stakeholders. A high level of relationship quality enhances stakeholder engagement in higher education marketing and leads to value co-creation with the universities. Also, digital interactions can influence the quality of the relationship between the universities and the stakeholders. This adds yet another layer of com-

V. Jain · H. Sharma (✉)
MICA, Ahmedabad, India
e-mail: varsha.jain@micamail.in; himani_fpm18@micamail.in

E. Mogaji
University of Greenwich, London, UK
e-mail: e.o.mogaji@greenwich.ac.uk

A. Babbili
Texas A&M University-Corpus Christi, Corpus Christi, TX, USA
e-mail: anantha.babbili@tamucc.edu

J. Allen et al. (eds.), *Celebrating the Past and Future of Marketing and Discovery with Social Impact*, Developments in Marketing Science: Proceedings of the Academy of Marketing Science, https://doi.org/10.1007/978-3-030-95346-1_120

plexity in redesigning the startegies for higher education. Therefore, nurturing the relationships and increasing digital scalability can constitute to be the most relevant factors for the growth of higher education marketing. The implications of the findings are discussed to understand the scope for an inclusive framework and policies needed for higher education marketing both in the context of the ongoing pandemic and the post-pandemic era.

Keywords Relationship quality · Higher education marketing · Stakeholders · Value co-creation

Customer-Perceived Reputation and Sustainable Satisfaction in the German Banking Sector: An Abstract

Svenja Damberg

Abstract The reputation of companies is an important and well-researched topic in the marketing discipline. Positive reputation is known for having a positive influence on customer satisfaction and loyalty, which can lead to competitive advantage as well as an increase in a firm's performance (Otto et al. 2020). This study looks at the drivers of reputation in the German banking sector as well as its influence on sustainable satisfaction from a customer perspective. The German banking sector is three-fold by tradition, in that it divides by commercial banks, savings banks, and cooperative banks. More recently, additional types of banks have evolved, such as online banks or sustainable banks. This study focuses on developing an overarching model, and builds on the reputation model by Schwaiger (2004). Accordingly, reputation is modeled as a two-dimensional construct, consisting of competence and likeability. The model is extended by sustainable satisfaction, which is a combination of the satisfaction and loyalty scales combined into a single target construct (cf. Höck et al. 2010).

An online survey was conducted and sent out to a sample of the German population consisting of bank customers above the age of 18 having at least one bank account. A variance-based statistical analysis method, partial least squares structural equation modeling (PLS-SEM), that allows to analyze the strength of the influence of the predictive constructs on the target construct in a path model, is applied. For evaluation, the SmartPLS 3 software (Ringle et al. 2015) is used. The findings show that, for the German banking sector, perceived attractiveness is the most important driver of both dimensions of corporate reputation, namely competence and likeability. Perceived quality is the second most important driver of likeability, whereas perceived performance is the second influential driver of competence.

The author thanks the Förderverein Industrielles Management (FIM) e.V. for funding the data collection.

S. Damberg (✉)
Hamburg University of Technology, Hamburg, Germany
e-mail: svenja.damberg@tuhh.de

J. Allen et al. (eds.), *Celebrating the Past and Future of Marketing and Discovery with Social Impact*, Developments in Marketing Science: Proceedings of the Academy of Marketing Science, https://doi.org/10.1007/978-3-030-95346-1_121

Furthermore, the affective dimension, likeability, is more important in explaining sustainable satisfaction, than competence.

The main theoretical contribution of this study is the adaptation of an established corporate reputation model to the German banking context and its extension with the concept of sustainable satisfaction. The results further have practical implications for the marketing departments of banks and their strategic positioning in the market. Future research might build on this extended model and use data from multiple countries in order to create a potential index for various types of banks and/or various customer segments. Moreover, the model should be controlled for demographic variables, such as age, gender, and income, as well as be tested with potential mediators, such as trust in banks, in future studies.

Keywords Customer-perceived reputation · Sustainable satisfaction · Bank marketing · PLS-SEM

The Role of VR in Influencing Tourism Consumers' Attitudes Towards a Tourist Destination: An Abstract

Graeme McLean and Mansour Alyahya

Abstract Virtual reality (VR) has been outlined as one of the most important technological developments to influence the tourism industry due to its ability to engage consumers and to market tourism destinations. The use of VR has spread across the entire tourism industry with the presence of VR in hotel previews, destination branding, tourism experiences including museums, theme parks, and cultural heritage sites (see: Bogicevic et al. 2019; Griffin et al. 2017; Wei et al. 2019). The application of VR in each of these sectors is based on the premise that the technology can transform experiences and positively influence behaviour (Zeng et al. 2020).

Despite the growing interest in VR by both tourism consumers and tourism marketers, both largely rely on the presentation of destinations through a computer-mediated website displaying basic non-dynamic images of the destination or venue (Israel et al. 2019). While basic non-dynamic images can present vivid non-verbal information to tourism consumers, VR has the capability to provide numerous verbal and non-verbal sensory information including visual, haptic, gustatory, auditory or olfactory cues (Miller and Stoica 2004). The depth of immersion and presence experienced within VR distinguish it from any other technology (Wei et al. 2019). Thus, VR provides a fundamentally different experience to consuming destination information in comparison to basic non-verbal images due to the sensory and media rich content (Wei et al. 2019). The purpose of this research is to understand the role of VR in influencing tourism consumers' attitudes towards a tourist destination.

Through a lab-based experiment with 204 tourism consumers this research found that following a VR preview experience of a tourist destination consumers will have more positive attitudes towards the tourist destination than prior to the VR experience. Interestingly, in comparison, a website preview has no significant effect on influencing tourism consumers' previously held attitudes towards the destination. More so, the results indicate that tourism consumers have more positive attitudes

G. McLean (✉)
University of Strathclyde, Glasgow, UK
e-mail: graeme.mclean@strath.ac.uk

M. Alyahya
King Faisal University, Al-Ahsa, Saudi Arabia
e-mail: malyahya@kfu.edu.sa

J. Allen et al. (eds.), *Celebrating the Past and Future of Marketing and Discovery with Social Impact*, Developments in Marketing Science: Proceedings of the Academy of Marketing Science, https://doi.org/10.1007/978-3-030-95346-1_122

towards a tourist destination in a VR preview in comparison to a less immersive website preview. Thus, the inherent interactive, immersive, and sensory rich attributes of VR have a positive effect on tourism consumers' attitudes towards a destination.

Hence, for managers, the use of pop-up VR stations in shopping malls or other entertainment venues would be an advantageous marketing strategy, while also providing VR previews to download from relevant stores such as the Oculus store for consumers to use on their own devices within the comfort of their own home.

Keywords Virtual reality · Consumer attitude change · Tourism · Tourism virtual reality

The Effects of Conversational Agents' Emotion Cues on Their Perceived Responsiveness and Consumers' Intention to Act: An Abstract

Justina Sidlauskiene

Abstract Conversational agents allow products and services to be sold through real-time one-on-one conversations. However, consumers tend to engage with humans and resist conversational agents. Further, conversation abandonment without leaving personal information (e.g., email) leaves marketers without the ability to re-engage with potential customers.

Drawing on the Social Information Processing theory and Affect-as-Information model, this study investigates how emotion cues: a higher positive tone from the conversational agent and emojis influence (1) the agent's responsiveness perception, and (2) consumers' intention to disclose personally-identifying information (email) to the agent retailer. The research uses a computerized text analysis of the chat scenarios and a 2 (low vs higher emotional tone) × 2 (emoji use vs. no emoji use) between-subjects experimental design.

This research focuses on the effect of emotional tone and emoji use on the conversational agent's perceived responsiveness and consumers' intention to disclose their personal information to the agent in a text-based conversational commerce context. When the conversational agent's emotional tone was higher, it was perceived as being more responsive. However, the effect of emoji use on the perception of agents' responsiveness was not significant. Finally, the present research found that the effect of higher emotional tone, emoji use, and the interaction term was significant for consumers' intention to disclose their email to the agent retailer.

This study provides several managerial implications; although emoji use did not result in higher perceived responsiveness, emojis and higher emotional tone can be used to promote email disclosure to the agent retailers and thus enable marketers to collect valuable consumer data. Further, an emotional tone can benefit a conversational website, particularly one in need of incorporating customers' personal information to provide personalized products. The findings contribute to the growing

J. Sidlauskiene (✉)
ISM University of Management and Economics, Vilnius, Lithuania
e-mail: 017624@stud.ism.lt

J. Allen et al. (eds.), *Celebrating the Past and Future of Marketing and Discovery with Social Impact*, Developments in Marketing Science: Proceedings of the Academy of Marketing Science, https://doi.org/10.1007/978-3-030-95346-1_123

research stream on integrating emotion cues into conversational agents and their impact on consumers' perceptions and personal information disclosure.

Keywords Conversational agents · Emotional tone · Non-verbal cues · Emojis · Perceived responsiveness · Information disclosure · Conversational selling · Personalization

How Do Online Customer Reviews Impact Online Purchases? The Role of Online Review Examination as a Guilt/Shame Reduction Strategy: An Abstract

Raika Sadeghein, Paula Fitzgerald, and Stephen He

Abstract Consumers often face situations where they have to choose between emotional gratification and functionality. For example, they have to decide between buying a sports car or a minivan; they have to choose a healthy snack or a tempting dessert. One of the factors that influence consumer choice in this context, is the anticipation of emotions that will be experienced as a result of this choice. Researchers have established the impact of shopping motive (i.e., utilitarian vs. hedonic) on choice and the aversive state of guilt (e.g., Choi et al. 2014; Okada 2005). Okada (2005) found that given a choice between a hedonic and a utilitarian item, consumers have a higher preference for the utilitarian item and that hedonic purchases lead to feelings of guilt unless the shopper can formulate a justification (e.g., I have gone to the gym today, so it is okay if I choose a high-calorie dessert). However, this stream of research commonly ignores the significance of shoppers' personal values and belief system. In this study, we argue that feelings of guilt are not a consequence of hedonic shopping, but rather a byproduct of the value violation occurring in association with the hedonic shopping motive and purchase behavior. We explore and demonstrate that when a purchase decision does not involve a value violation, consumer purchase intention is similar regardless of shopping motive (i.e., hedonic or utilitarian). However, when a value violation is involved, it leads to anticipation of aversive states such as shame and guilt which in turn reduce purchase intention. In addition, we suggest that online customer reviews provide an ideal context for justification of a value-violating purchase. Our results indicate that as a result of the negative emotional states evoked by the value-violating purchase, customers' online information search behavior change.

R. Sadeghein (✉)
University of Richmond, Richmond, VA, USA
e-mail: rsadeghe@richmond.edu

P. Fitzgerald · S. He
West Virginia University, Morgantown, WV, USA
e-mail: paula.fitzgerald@mail.wvu.edu; stephen.he@mail.wvu.edu

J. Allen et al. (eds.), *Celebrating the Past and Future of Marketing and Discovery with Social Impact*, Developments in Marketing Science: Proceedings of the Academy of Marketing Science, https://doi.org/10.1007/978-3-030-95346-1_124

Keywords Shopping motive · Value congruence · Shame · Guilt · Utilitarian · Hedonic

Gifts Are Sacred Until the Deal Strikes: An Abstract

Bidisha Burman, Pia A. Albinsson, and Robert M. Schindler

Abstract Gifts are commonly used to represent and reinforce personal relationships that are important and often sacred (Belk et al. 1989). To support the sacredness of a gift, it should represent some considerable monetary sacrifice (Branco-Illodo and Heath 2020), but also should be removed from profane considerations of money by, for example, the removal of price tags (Belk et al. 1989). Given these aspects of a gift, it is interesting that some deal-prone consumers justify their urges to purchase bargain items that they don't need by noting the usefulness of these items as potential gifts (Thomsen and Zaichkowsky 2015).

In this research, we tested how purchasing an item at a discount affects the item's suitability as a gift. Participants were asked to assume that they were looking for a gift for a friend's birthday celebration. They were told that they found the perfect gift item online, and the online retailer gave them two alternatives. The first alternative was to buy the item for the regular price of $29.99; the second alternative was to buy the same item in good condition but with a damaged box (i.e., tainted packaging) for a discounted price. The three discount conditions had the sale price set at $21.99 (25% discount), $14.99 (50% discount) and $7.99 (75% discount). We then measured the participants' willingness to buy the tainted gift item.

We collected data from 92 participants in three age groups: younger (ages 24 and below), middle (ages 25–44), and older (ages 45 and above). Consumers in the younger age group were generally favorable toward purchasing the package-damaged and discounted item as a gift and were not affected by the size of the discount. Consumers in the older age group were less favorable toward buying the

B. Burman
University of the Pacific, Stockton, CA, USA
e-mail: bburman@pacific.edu

P. A. Albinsson (✉)
Appalachian State University, Boone, NC, USA
e-mail: albinssonpa@appstate.edu

R. M. Schindler
Rutgers University – Camden, Camden, NJ, USA
e-mail: robert.schindler@rutgers.edu

J. Allen et al. (eds.), *Celebrating the Past and Future of Marketing and Discovery with Social Impact*, Developments in Marketing Science: Proceedings of the Academy of Marketing Science, https://doi.org/10.1007/978-3-030-95346-1_125

package-damaged and discounted item (although not significantly so) and were also not affected by the size of the discount.

What is noteworthy is that our middle age group, the millennial participants, showed a statistically significant effect of discount size on their likelihood of purchasing the package-damaged discounted item. When the package-damaged item was discounted by only 25% or 50%, these respondents showed a level of interest comparable to that of the other age groups. However, when the item was discounted by 75%, the 25–44 year-old respondents reported being less likely to make the purchase. This result offers some preliminary evidence in support of the possibility that a discount can reduce the attractiveness of an item as an imaginable gift.

Keywords Gift-giving · Price promotions · Consumer sacredness · Deal proneness

Analysis of Gen Z Marketing Student Preference for Different Instructional Methods: An Abstract

Michael Garver, Richard Divine, and Steven Dahlquist

Abstract Today's higher education students are part of a generational cohort now commonly referred to as Generation Z (Gen Z), and it is not known the extent to which Gen Z's will demonstrate similar preferences and decision-making behavior as those of previous generations. The purpose of this research study is to examine undergraduate marketing student preferences for various instructional methods. Gen Zs are perceived as pragmatic in nature, motivated to maximize the utility of their spending, burdened with student debt, and are the first generation to regard the physical and digital world as borderless. Our primary question is "how do Gen Z college students prefer to learn?"

Faculty today have available to them an almost overwhelming number of options when it comes to instructional methods and how to design their courses. Advances in technology and events such as the Covid-19 pandemic has made distance learning not only viable and necessary, but for some learners even superior to traditional face-to-face delivery. Innovations in pedagogy have produced a variety of alternatives to traditional lecture-based teaching formats such as flipped classrooms, problem-based learning, the case method, and team based-learning. Indeed, the calls within marketing academia (e.g., Crittenden et al. 2019; Rohm et al. 2019) for faculty to innovate and embrace the digital world in order to properly prepare marketing students for the demands of the marketplace are compelling. Instructors also have numerous decisions to make on how to structure their courses, such as rigor, workload, and supplemental materials.

College marketing student preference to six different instructional methods was determined using a choice-based conjoint analysis. Each instructional method was a significant determinant of students' choice of a given class, but the six methods varied significantly in terms of their importance weights. Results of conjoint analysis indicate that the three most preferred drivers of student choice for a marketing

M. Garver · R. Divine
Central Michigan University, Mt. Pleasant, MI, USA
e-mail: garv1ms@cmich.edu; divin1rl@cmich.edu

S. Dahlquist (✉)
Grand Valley State University, Grand Rapids, MI, USA
e-mail: dahlquis@gvsu.edu

J. Allen et al. (eds.), *Celebrating the Past and Future of Marketing and Discovery with Social Impact*, Developments in Marketing Science: Proceedings of the Academy of Marketing Science, https://doi.org/10.1007/978-3-030-95346-1_126

class are (1) it employs a flipped classroom, (2) its class sessions are interactive and hands-on, rather than lecture-based and (3) it has a moderate, rather than a heavy workload.

Keywords Student preference · Delivery methods · Gen Z · Generation Z

The Four Faces of Electronic Health Record Adopters: A Patients' Typology Based on Perceived Benefits and Concerns: An Abstract

Emna Cherif and Manel Mzoughi

Abstract Patients' adoption of Electronic Health Records (EHRs) varies substantially. Governments need to deal with the patients' disparities to reach the expected high performance for healthcare systems, grasp efficiency, and improve the quality of diagnoses and care delivery. This study investigates patients' perceived benefits and concerns of EHR in order to develop a typology of patients, identify characteristics of different clusters, and propose practical measures for public policy makers.

Cluster analyses identified four patient clusters: *the worried*, qualified by the highest means of privacy concerns and perceived risk, are the most concerned by health data disclosure. Conversely, *the ready adopters,* showing an absolute lack of privacy concerns and risks, are the most motivated by EHR benefits. Yet, compared to *the worried*, *concerned adopters* express far less privacy concerns about their health data and perceive more favourably EHR benefits. Finally, *the balanced adopters*, relatively close to *the ready adopters* for EHR motives, are still concerned about their health data, suggesting a segment easier to convince of EHR adoption. ANOVA analyses on intentions to create EHR and willingness to disclose health data across clusters confirm that *ready adopters*, followed by *balanced adopters*, are more likely to create an EHR and disclose health data. *The concerned adopters* and lastly *the worried* exhibit the lowest intentions for EHR creation and data disclosure.

Results provide meaningful insights of patients' profiles and expectations regarding EHR adoption. Findings underscore the need to (1) implement particular targeting policies for each cluster and (2) design concrete solutions for improving EHR performance.

E. Cherif (✉)
Université Clermont Auvergne, Clermont-Ferrand, France
e-mail: emna.cherif@uca.fr

M. Mzoughi
ICD International Business School, Paris, France
e-mail: mmzoughi@groupe-igs.fr

J. Allen et al. (eds.), *Celebrating the Past and Future of Marketing and Discovery with Social Impact*, Developments in Marketing Science: Proceedings of the Academy of Marketing Science, https://doi.org/10.1007/978-3-030-95346-1_127

Keywords Electronic health record · Patient typology · Privacy concerns · Trust · Ease of use · Usefulness · Control · Intention to adopt · Willingness to disclose personal health data

Humanizing the Terminator: Artificial Intelligence Trends in the Customer Journey: An Abstract

Melanie B. Richards and Dana E. Harrison

Abstract Current use of artificial intelligence (AI) in marketing is to assist and empower consumers or a human workforce. While AI is not yet replacing humans (Chen et al. 2019; Davenport et al. 2020), it is transforming many industries (Huang and Rust 2018; Rust 2020; Wirth 2018). Whether consumers recognize it or not, AI is already embedded into many aspects of today's customer journey. In this process, tradeoffs between data privacy, AI driven technology, and resulting benefits have blurred and at times, been accepted by consumers via social complacency. There is evidence that this tradeoff can create a feeling of cognitive dissonance within some users of AI.

The theory of cognitive dissonance proposes that when a person has two inconsistent thoughts, beliefs, attitudes, or actions, dissonance (mental distress) will occur (Festinger 1957). Dissonance is uncomfortable, and thus people will seek to resolve that discomfort through various strategies, such as creating an explanation that allows the inconsistency to exist or rejecting new information that is in conflict with existing beliefs (Festinger 1964). Research by Levin et al. (2010) supports that cognitive dissonance is increased in human-robot interactions as compared to human-human interactions for similar purposes.

Much of the existing research has examined perceptions and behaviors of those aware of an AI-based interaction, not those who may be interacting with AI unknowingly. The purpose of this research is to explore the differences in attitudes and behaviors of consumers when they are and are not aware of the existence of AI and how cognitive dissonance may play a role in their AI interactions. This study will employ a mixed-methods approach consisting of a consumer survey and interviews to better understand this phenomena.

M. B. Richards (✉) · D. E. Harrison
East Tennessee State University, Johnson City, TN, USA
e-mail: richardsmb@etsu.edu; harrisondl@etsu.edu

J. Allen et al. (eds.), *Celebrating the Past and Future of Marketing and Discovery with Social Impact*, Developments in Marketing Science: Proceedings of the Academy of Marketing Science, https://doi.org/10.1007/978-3-030-95346-1_128

Keywords Artificial intelligence · Automation · Cognitive dissonance · Customer journey · Marketing

An Affective Route to Product Evaluation Under Ordered Presentation of Product Information: An Abstract

Priya Narayanan and Arvind Sahay

Abstract We demonstrate a mechanism for product evaluation under ordered presentation based on feelings (Schwarz 2012) through the affect-eliciting nature of a strong brand (Yeung and Wyer 2005). Our model differs from prior models of product evaluation under ordered presentation by relying on affect rather than on cognitive mechanisms. Four experiments using existing brands, including a mall intercept, demonstrate higher willingness to pay (WTP) under brand-first presentation compared to attribute-first presentation. Following this, we intend to investigate whether two different kinds of processing are triggered by high and low positive affect engendered by the two forms of presentation.

Research on attribute order (Schrift et al. 2017), order of product and price (Karmarkar et al. 2015), and composite brand alliances (Park et al. 1996) shows that information presented first typically forms an anchor for product evaluation (Hogarth and Einhorn 1992), setting the context for subsequent processing (Karmarkar et al. 2015; Yeung and Wyer 2004). Our work builds on this research to determine the impact on evaluation if the first piece of information, such as a brand, were to generate strong positive affect.

When product information elicits affect, as information about a strong brand does (Keller 2003; McClure et al. 2004; Yeung and Wyer 2005), this affect leads to heuristic processing and more favourable product evaluation due to the higher level of positive affect. When attribute information is presented first, we expect systematic processing and less favourable evaluation due to relatively low level of initial positive affect. Such a difference in evaluation is not expected for weak brands as they do not elicit sufficient positive affect. We also expect to observe the effect of ordered presentation on WTP under promotion focus due to greater reliance on affect compared to prevention focus. Finally, we posit that brand-first (attribute-first) presentation leads to heuristic (systematic) processing due to higher positive

P. Narayanan (✉)
Indian Institute of Management Kozhikode, Kozhikode, India
e-mail: npriya@iimk.ac.in

A. Sahay
Indian Institute of Management Ahmedabad, Ahmedabad, India
e-mail: asahay@iima.ac.in

J. Allen et al. (eds.), *Celebrating the Past and Future of Marketing and Discovery with Social Impact*, Developments in Marketing Science: Proceedings of the Academy of Marketing Science, https://doi.org/10.1007/978-3-030-95346-1_129

affect. The current research uses experimental methods, both lab studies and a mall intercept, to validate the hypotheses, in order to arrive at causes inferences.

This research contributes to extant research on ordered presentation and on branding. Findings of our research hold managerial implications in the domain of product communication, advertising, and packaging. Further research could examine the impact of affect and determine boundary conditions for the observed effect, which could include consumer goals or mindsets, or contextual factors. Our findings also hold implications for quick heuristic processing arising from time pressure or low category familiarity.

Keywords Brand · Attribute · Affect · Order of presentation · Information processing

Internal Brand Management and the Effects on International Firm Performance: An Abstract

Katharina Maria Hofer

Abstract While extant branding literature has focused on external communication, internal branding has received much less research attention. Internal brand management can be characterized as a subset of internal marketing and it requires a mid-term to long-term effort to change structures and processes (Piehler et al. 2015). Drawing upon contingency theory, stakeholder theory and other conceptual foundations, this study investigates the antecedents and consequences of internal branding in internationally operating firms.

A conceptual model is developed, and the study employs a quantitative, survey-based approach. The hypotheses are tested through structural equation modelling, i.e. Partial Least Squares – Structural Equation Modelling using SmartPLS 3 (Ringle et al. 2015) based on data collected from managers of firms with international business activities in Central and Eastern Europe. Data analysis includes the assessment of common method bias, the evaluation of the reflective measurement model (Hair et al. 2014), i.e. internal consistency, indicator reliability, convergent validity, discriminant validity using HTMT ratio (Henseler et al. 2015), and the evaluation of the structural model based on the bootstrapping procedure using 5000 subsamples (Hair et al. 2014).

The results of the structural model show the positive outcomes of both standardized employee behavior and leadership. Various antecedents contribute to enhancing performance in internationally operating firms. Thus, a standardized strategy of internal branding measures is feasible for internationally operating firms. Moreover, the importance of leadership has to be highlighted in terms of managerial implications. The limitations are discussed from a conceptual and empirical point of view. Future research could investigate alternative variables and conceptual models including moderating variables, as well as different empirical settings. The results contribute to the branding literature where international studies are scant.

K. M. Hofer (✉)
Johannes Kepler University Linz, Linz, Austria
e-mail: katharina.hofer@jku.at

J. Allen et al. (eds.), *Celebrating the Past and Future of Marketing and Discovery with Social Impact*, Developments in Marketing Science: Proceedings of the Academy of Marketing Science, https://doi.org/10.1007/978-3-030-95346-1_130

Keywords Internal branding · Performance · Brand management · International business

Do Black Lives Matter More to Companies Represented by Women? An Examination of Gender Differences in Corporate Responses to Racial Reckoning: An Abstract

Pamela Richardson-Greenfield, Monique Bell, Alyssa J. Reynolds-Pearson, and Ryan E. Cruz

Abstract Conventional stakeholder theory suggests that corporations and their agents should avoid engaging in potentially controversial social and political debates, which may alienate existing and potential customers. However, as Bhagwat et al. (2020) note, this wisdom has been challenged as customer and other firm stakeholders have increased pressure on firms to embrace activism promoting societal well-being on myriad topics (e.g. immigration, environmentalism, LGBTQ rights, gender equity, economic inequities, and antiracism) and increase their role in benefiting society globally.

2020 was a historic year marked by tragedy surrounding a global pandemic and notably, in the United States, an increased presence of public protests in response to ongoing national social injustice and racism faced by African Americans. In particular, the publically documented deaths of Ahmaud Arbery, Breonna Taylor, and George Floyd at the hands of police made national and international headlines and became a clarion call for increased sociopolitical activism in support of the Black Lives Matter (BLM) Movement and support against systemic racism of African

P. Richardson-Greenfield
Radford University, Radford, VA, USA
e-mail: prichardson5@radford.edu

M. Bell
California State University at Fresno, Fresno, CA, USA
e-mail: mbell@csufresno.edu

A. J. Reynolds-Pearson
Winston-Salem State University, Winston-Salem, NC, USA
e-mail: reynoldsa@wssu.edu

R. E. Cruz (✉)
Thomas Jefferson University, Philadelphia, PA, USA
e-mail: ryan.cruz@jefferson.edu

J. Allen et al. (eds.), *Celebrating the Past and Future of Marketing and Discovery with Social Impact*, Developments in Marketing Science: Proceedings of the Academy of Marketing Science, https://doi.org/10.1007/978-3-030-95346-1_131

Americans. A rise in and visibility of sociopolitical activism increased pressure on firms to evaluate corporate mores and embrace *corporate sociopolitical activism* involving taking public demonstrations against racism, in the form of official statements, internal corporate actions to ameliorate internal systemic bias, and/or explicit support for external partisan causes intended to influence public policy and social structures.

Drawing on literature from Sociopolitical Activism (CSA), Situational Crisis Communication Theory (SCCT), and the Theory of Universal Human Values, we examine the linguistic features of public corporate responses to the death of George Floyd and the Black Lives Matter (BLM) movements. Our research investigates the compositional features of corporate sociopolitical activism, paying particular attention to functional language related to allyship, activism, authenticity, affect, causal language, harm acknowledgement, and psychological stress. Additionally, we report findings suggesting that corporate responses vis-à-vis these language variables differ based on the statement issuer's sex. We note these contextual differences and close with managerial recommendations.

Keywords Brand activism · Crisis communication · Corporate sociopolitical activism · Language · Values

The Impact of Marginalization on Online Marketing

Nicole R. Fuller, McDowell Porter III, and Elyria A. Kemp

Abstract Despite the opportunities and benefits associated with establishing a web presence, there is a significant subset of entrepreneurial ventures that are offline. Given the proliferation of internet use across the United States, exploring the factors contributing to this counterintuitive decision unearths new insights on entrepreneurial behavior. Through a survey of 260 small business owners and managers in the United States and additional interviews with 18 leaders at small entrepreneurial firms, we examine how marginalization, an external challenge that creates barriers to success, can influence an entrepreneur's perceptions about digital marketing, and ultimately contribute to performance issues within the firm. We find that marginalization heightens the level of risk entrepreneurs assign to internet use. This risk perception limits the extent to which an entrepreneur responds to online customer feedback, which has implications for the venture's relationship and reputation management efforts with buyers, ultimately impacting the firm's performance.

Keywords Entrepreneurship · Marginalization · Entrepreneurial risk · Webcare · Customer engagement · Firm performance

Contributors and Funding Sources
The University of New Orleans provided funding for this research through a professorship which the authors used to pay for interview and survey participant incentives.

N. R. Fuller (✉) · E. A. Kemp
University of New Orleans, New Orleans, LA, USA
e-mail: nrfuller@uno.edu; ekemp@uno.edu

M. PorterIII
California State University-Fresno, Fresno, CA, USA
e-mail: mporter@csufresno.edu

J. Allen et al. (eds.), *Celebrating the Past and Future of Marketing and Discovery with Social Impact*, Developments in Marketing Science: Proceedings of the Academy of Marketing Science, https://doi.org/10.1007/978-3-030-95346-1_132

Introduction

Despite its pervasion through society, the internet remains an under-utilized resource among entrepreneurs. Today, roughly 86% of the U.S. population accesses the web. Between 2015 and 2020, the number of internet users in the United States grew from approximately 264 million people to 284 million people. Researchers project that another 12 million users will come online within the next five years (Clement 2020). In conjunction with these shifts in the general environment, media articles and academic research in the last several decades have explored the opportunities the internet presents for small businesses. A Forbes survey highlighted the revenue enhancement benefits entrepreneurs realize through engaging with customers online (Fertik 2019). Entrepreneurship scholarship identified that the internet allows entrepreneurs to develop new markets and bring venture ideas to fruition with fewer resources (Davis and Harveston 2000; Cumming and Johan 2010). Yet, a CNBC survey of small businesses reveals that 45% of entrepreneurs do not have a web presence, citing fears associated with technology. Only 40% of the surveyed firms report using social media to communicate with current and potential customers (Reuber and Fischer 2011; Rosenbaum 2017; Ngoasong 2018). Although almost half of all ventures fail to capitalize on the advantages of web-based marketing, scholars extend less consideration to this segment of entrepreneurs.

This study builds upon the counterintuitive phenomenon of internet avoidance within entrepreneurial firms by considering the influence of operating as a marginalized entrepreneur. Marginalized people are detached from peers and relegated to the periphery within a social setting due to their identities, associations, environment or practices (Hall et al. 1994). This disconnection from important ties with majority groups yields access challenges for the entrepreneur in terms of garnering resources, support and even customers (Kaplan 1998; Bates and Robb 2016; Malmström et al. 2017). Accordingly, entrepreneurs experiencing marginalization must work to overcome barriers above and beyond those of their self-employed, in group (nonmarginalized) counterparts.

In the research that follows, we relied on interviews and surveys with owners and managers of small business ventures to gauge marginalization's impact on the individual's web engagement and firm performance. We first conducted exploratory interviews with eighteen small businesses with some form of an online presence with respect to their marketing and sales related activities. Participants responded to questions about their perceptions of consumers overlooking or undervaluing their venture, their online interactions with customers, and the extent to which they use the internet to manage the firm's reputations. Based on the theses we identified across these conversations, we developed a survey that we distributed to 260 small businesses.

This paper makes important contributions to the marketing literature. Namely, we explore the way marginalization informs business owners' risk perceptions and marketing efforts. The marginalized entrepreneur not only contends with being under-resourced and isolated from majority networks, but she may unintentionally perpetuate additional challenges within the firm as she avoids opportunities to expand sales channels and strengthen relational ties with customers. Our results suggest that marginalized entrepreneurs are more likely to perceive digital marketing as risky and are therefore less likely to interact with customers online, although engagement with customers online is associated with increased firm performance.

Marginalization and Risk Perceptions

The homophily principle asserts that entities are attracted to seemingly similar others (Kandel 1978). Accordingly, membership within majority groups results from shared or familiar characteristics among the affiliates within the group. Non-members of these groups face barriers in integrating with the in-group and realizing any benefits therein, as majority group members eschew ties with non-members, choosing to emphasize in group similarities and out group differences to undergird in-group distinction (Mehra et al. 1998). Unique, or minority, identities, associations, practices, or environments relegate entities to the periphery of the majority group (Hall et al. 1994). In our interview a Black, female entrepreneur discussed feeling overlooked at times:

> *At times I do [feel like my business is undervalued] but I think it's the nature of what I do. Diversity and inclusion work has always rubbed some folks the wrong way so I do have to remind myself of that if ever I feel unseen. -Andrea, Founder, Educational Services*

Specific threats stemming from the entrepreneur's minority characteristics along with the separate challenge of detachment from key networks may create stigma and isolation, respectively. Such stigmatized disconnection from peer businesses, certain consumer groups, and supplier organizations may render the venture marginalized. Marginalization describes isolation, exclusion, a dearth of proximal peers and relational ties, and disadvantage based on an individual's characteristics (Salenius 2016). For an entrepreneur, this social separation means disconnection from mentors and models, trade associations, suppliers, or industry peers. Unlike their marginalized counterparts, formal and informal ties are customary among members belonging to the in group (Bendick and Egan 1993; Alcácer and Chung 2014).

An outcast existence presents a unique set of challenges. Disconnection may render the entrepreneur without a business model exhibiting the route to success in a field (Magretta 2002), which requires the business owner to contrive a new, unprecedented path to success. Extant research indicates that membership within networks yields important resources paramount for a venture's survival (Hernández-Carrión et al. 2017). It is no surprise, then, that marginalized entities tend to underperform (Boje 1995). Ties between organizations within a business environment help fortify the community, leading to greater economic development (Hoyman et al. 2016). Accordingly, marginalized entrepreneurs may be more likely to operate ventures in disinvested communities (Wacquant and Wilson 1989). In group members cocreate institutions, or agreed upon rules of doing business, in ways that benefit the majority group and reinforce barriers obstructing the minority outgroup (Gaudreault et al. 2017). Thus, business environments in which marginalized groups are relegated to adhering to the self-serving rules that majority group members create engenders a power imbalance between the groups (Ragins and Sundstrom 1989). In sum, marginalized entrepreneurs experience a vast array of opposition above and beyond the obstacles already inherent in entrepreneurship.

The enhanced threat that marginalized entrepreneurs experience influences their perceptions of risk. The experience of previous or current challenges fosters fearful perceptions of the future (Braaf et al. 2019). Even neutral factors in the environment can appear threatening for business owners expending significant resources to combat disadvantage. Ascribing risk to otherwise risk-neutral elements informs the extent to which individuals approach and engage with those factors (Grupe and Nitschke 2013). Accordingly, an entrepreneur who is biased towards perceiving risk may underutilize tools that her non-marginalized counterparts regularly employ in their ventures. More specifically, the challenges stemming from working to overcome social or physical exclusion may embed a sensitivity toward potential threats in the environment. Further, the uncontrollable nature of marginalization, and the challenges therein, can predispose the entrepreneur to viewing other business hazards as potentially unmanageable (Braaf et al. 2019). In considering the risks associated with marketing and selling on the web, the marginalized entrepreneur may feel compelled to limit or avoid internet use to mitigate additional economic injury. As such, we advance the following:

Hypothesis 1. Organizational marginalization is positively related to an entrepreneur's risk perceptions about the web.

Digital Marketing and Consumer Behavior

The perceived threat of receiving negative reviews online from customers may differ across entrepreneurs. While some business owners view the impact of cautionary feedback as redeemable, others may experience a sense of foreboding at the prospect of receiving negative reviews, imagining detrimental outcomes for the business. In associating customer reviews with irreparable harm to the venture, entrepreneurs may limit the extent to which they engage with customer feedback or opt to avoid it completely (Lipsey and Shepperd 2019). An African American entrepreneur shared her thoughts about the arbitrary nature of buyer criticisms.

> *It is very effective in swaying potential customers. Yes, I think that many times people make negative comments without telling the full story or knowing the background, and it is purely off of emotion. – Joy, Franchisee, Accommodation and Food Services*

Firms addressing customer feedback online engage in webcare. Webcare describes organizational electronic replies to online reviews and engagement in virtual conversations with customers (Van Noort and Willemsen 2012). While any webcare response is better than none (Weitzl and Einwiller 2020), researchers have found that webcare providing a clear, polite and timely explanation for the product or service deficit is most effective at appeasing customers and shifting their failure perceptions. Further, customers view webcare efforts directly from the business owner or manager as more compelling than that from lower level employees (Ghosh 2017). In other words, webcare from the entrepreneur is useful in restoring and strengthening customer relationships after a product or business falls short of customer expectations. One business manager commented the following in our interview:

> *My company values the feedback of all of our clients, whether it is positive or negative. Once I complete a service, I encourage all clients to write a review about their experience. I use what they give to me as an opportunity to learn and grow. -Gina, Manager, Finance*

Entrepreneurs viewing the web as risky may miss out on the benefits of webcare. To them, the potential threats of the internet may overshadow prospective gain. As a result, we assert the following inverse relationship.

Hypothesis 2. Risk perceptions of the web are negatively related participation in webcare.

Webcare is a conduit through which business owners can receive valuable feedback from customers and explain or redeem a service or product failure. The venture's webcare influences buyers' perceptions and most tangibly, their purchase decisions (Sreejesh and Anusree 2016). Webcare after a service or product failure can engender buyer forgiveness and loyalty (Ghosh 2017). These online conversations with customers provide a way to mitigate potentially harmful consequences of public complaints about the business (Weitzl and Hutzinger 2017). In other words, webcare helps business owners potentially reshape and repair negative assessments about the brand. Intentional communication with customers online, beyond the purchasing process, engenders greater attachment and allegiance between customers and the business (Ajiboye et al. 2019). An African American entrepreneur shared that he recognized the importance of interacting with customers online, even if he failed to take full advantage of the opportunities therein.

> *I would say Google reviews are pretty helpful. I haven't gotten too deep into many other forms of social media, but everything counts. The more interaction the better. – Paul, Entrepreneur, Real Estate Rental and Leasing*

It behooves firms to proactively attempt to shape the narrative around their corporate reputations, as external parties can potentially and meaningfully impact public perception in negative ways (Philippe and Durand 2011; Fauchart and Cowan 2014). The business owner's avoidance of web-based interactions nonetheless serves as a form of communication to customers. Without webcare, entrepreneurs leave customers to draw their own conclusions about the venture without any input from the firm, itself. Placing sole responsibility on customers to make their own assessments of the venture rarely behooves the firm. Research has found that buyers respond less favorably to organizational silence than they do to organizational responses, even when those responses have a defensive or combative tone (Weitzl 2019; Casado-Díaz et al. 2020). Accordingly, a lack of webcare results in a consequential disconnection between the business and its customers. Thus, we assert that attempts to connect with consumers online behooves a business's reputation.

Hypothesis 3: Webcare is positively associated with reputation management.

Beyond using the internet to respond to customer reviews and enhance the company's reputation, ventures can also use online platforms to build community with current and prospective buyers. As the use of social media increases globally, some businesses are intentionally pursuing online interactions across platforms to engender emotional or psychological ties with customers (Brodie et al. 2013; Kumar and Pansari 2016; Gill et al. 2017). Firms create communities on social network platforms that become spaces for learning, interaction between consumers and the firm, and collaboration (Chiang et al. 2017). Such customer engagement initiatives center on information exchange between businesses and their pool of current and potential buyers.

These customer engagement initiatives behoove the company in practical ways. Online interactions between firms and buyers yield greater loyalty, satisfaction, and trust (So et al. 2016; Chiang et al. 2017). Fostering these relationships also produces measurable benefits for ventures. A 2016 study found that engagement initiatives contribute to 22% growth in cross-selling, a 38% rise in up-selling, and a five percent to 85% increase, on average, in customers' order size (Fertik 2019). Ultimately, these efforts can prompt stronger firm performance. A White, female retailer expressed the key role customer engagement and personal connection with her customers play in the success of her firm.

> *There is significant online participation as my primary platform for community building and sales on Facebook. Likes, reactions, comments, shares, etc. are strongly encouraged and my community knows that these are helpful to me and my business. Because I make my business extremely personal, many of my followers are invested in helping me succeed. -Lula, Fashion Retailer, Retail Trade*

While the potential benefits from investing in customer engagement are clear, there exists a segment of businesses choosing not to interact with customers online (Rosenbaum 2017). One reason for this decision may be the salient barriers stemming from an entrepreneur's membership within a marginalized group and related risk perceptions. Entrepreneurs experiencing the consequences of marginalization may be compelled to limit their exposure to additional challenges the internet poses. In contrast, entrepreneurs actively responding to customer feedback through webcare may also be open to other forms of internet-based interactions with buyers. Generally, ventures adopting positive perspectives of potential business opportunities are likely to pursue high reward prospects that enhance firm performance (Matthews et al. 2018). Accordingly, participation in webcare may predispose an entrepreneur to pursue deeper ties with consumers through customer engagement initiatives. Such entrepreneurs have a higher risk tolerance and can leverage this in profitable ways. Figure 1 displays our full model.

Hypothesis 4: Webcare is positively associated with customer engagement initiatives.

Hypothesis 5: Customer engagement initiatives are positively associated with firm performance.

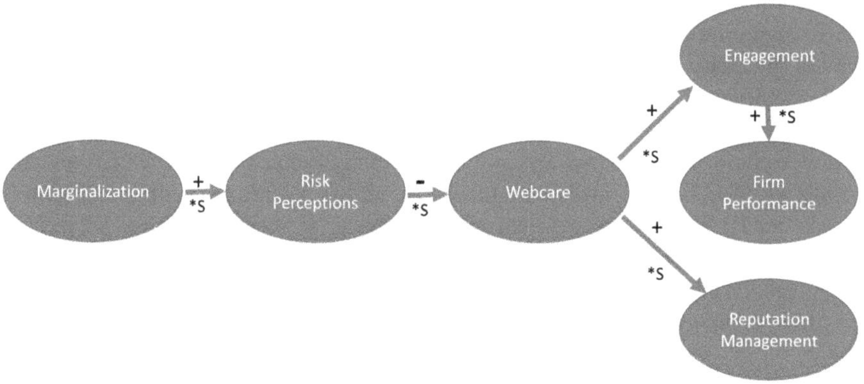

Fig. 1 Displays the full model

Methods

The sample consisted of a cross-section of small businesses. Small business is defined as fewer than 1000 employees. However, nearly 95% of our sample included small businesses with fewer than 50 employees (94%). The survey participants were recruited using Qualtrics panel services. The number of participants (i.e., small business owners, executives, and managers) totaled 260; 32% of the sample was male, 68% of the sample was female. Twenty-seven percent of the sample were in the age range of 33–44 while the next largest age range were 55–64 (21%) followed by the 45–54 age group (20%). Nearly half of the sample (47%) had been in business 5 years or fewer: 23% were fewer than 3 years, 24% of the companies had been in operation from 3 to 5 years, and 22% had been in business between 6 and 10 years. A wide variety of industries were represented from agriculture and hospitality to manufacturing and technology.

Marginalization refers to the perception of detachment from others within a business social setting (Hall et al. 1994). The four-item measure for Marginalization (e.g., "Our business receives less recognition than other businesses in our line of work across the city" on a 7-point Likert scale) had a Cronbach's Alpha of .877. Risk perceptions describe the expectation of loss when encountering or contemplating a stimulus (Stone and Gronhaug 1993). The six-item measure (e.g., "Using the web will cause personal, financial losses" on a 7-point Likert scale) had a Cronbach's Alpha of .927. Webcare is defined as proactive organizational replies to online consumer opinion and interactivity (Van Noort and Willemsen 2012). Webcare's reliability was accessed by four items on a 7-point Likert scale (Cronbach's Alpha = .867, e.g., "Our company actively searches the web (outside of our own sites) so that we are aware of any comments customers have written about our company"). Reputation management, concerns the consumer sentiment regarding the entrepreneurial venture, was accessed using three items on a 5-point semantic differential scale (1 = Never, 5 = Always). The Cronbach's Alpha = .764 (e.g., "To what extent do you think your company works to manage its reputation online by encouraging customers to review its product(s)/organization"). Customer engagement denotes the intensity of interaction with the entrepreneur's' products or services (Vivek et al. 2014). The seven-item measure (e.g., To what extent has your company seen a reduction/decrease or growth/increase the amount of time viewers spend looking at content on our web platforms," anchored by 1 = much less and 5 = much more) had a Cronbach's Alpha of .931. Finally, firm performance refers the business's commercial returns (Yadav et al. 2013). The two-item measure (using a 7-point semantic differential scale, e.g., not actively participating/very actively participating) to the following question: "What do you think about your business's market share growth over the past year compared to your competitors". The scale had a Cronbach's Alpha of .853.

Results

Structural equation modeling (SEM; AMOS 26) two-step process was use to analysis the predicted relationships. The first step is to perform a confirmatory factor analysis to test the convergent and discriminant validity of the measurement model (Hair et al. 2010). The second step is to test the structural model fit and the predicted paths for significance (Hair et al. 2010). The results of the confirmatory factor analysis indicates a good fitting measurement model: $\chi^2 = 518.996$, p = .000, CFI = .951, IFI = .952, TLI = .944, and RMSEA = .057. Acceptable convergent validity is indicated by the standardized factor loading exceeds the established recommended 0.6 threshold (Hair et al. 2010). Further evidence of convergent validity shows the variance explained by the construct is greater than the variance due to measurement error by each constructs' average variance extracted exceeding 0.5, which is the established rule of thumb threshold (see Table 1). Discriminant validity is tested using the Fornell and Larcker (1981) method. The constructs pass this strict test by having each construct's average variance extracted exceeding the squared correlation between constructs.

Discussion

While research addresses the advantages entrepreneurs realize from web-based marketing, scholars extend less consideration to the segment of business owners choosing to remain offline. To address this gap, our paper sheds light on the experience of entrepreneurs experiencing marginalization. Isolation from the majority group breeds disadvantaged circumstances for marginalized entities. Entrepreneurs experiencing isolation from peer networks must grapple with restricted access to resources and disregard (Zhao and Wry 2016). These external challenges color the business owner's approach to other decisions within the business. Specifically, we find that marginalized entrepreneurs are more likely to perceive web use as risky.

Table 1 displays means, standard deviation, reliability, average variance extracted, and Pearson correlations. The predicted structural paths were tested using SEM (AMOS 26). The overall structural model was a good fit: $\chi 2 = 583.908$, $p = .000$; CFI = .940, IFI = .940, TLI = .933, and RMSEA = .062 as recommended by Hair et al. (2010). H1is supported in which marginalization is positively related to risk perceptions ($\beta = .203$, S.E. = .076, $p = .008$). Conversely, H2, which predicts that risk perceptions is *negatively* related to webcare, is also supported ($\beta = -.351$, S.E. = .084, $p < .001$). The results of H3 show that there is a significant positive relationship between webcare and reputation management ($\beta = .441$, S.E. = .050, $p < .001$). The fourth hypotheses (H4) predicts that webcare is positively associated with customer engagement, which was supported ($\beta = .260$, S.E. = .031, $p < .001$). Finally, the path between customer engagement to firm performance was significant ($\beta = .963$, S.E. = .071, $p < .001$), supporting H5 (see Table 2)

Construct	Means	SD	Composite Reliability	Cronbach's Alpha	AVE	MAR	RP	WC	RM	EN	EP
Marginalization (MAR)	3.98	1.40	.73	.88	.64	1.00					
Risk Perceptions (RP)	2.61	1.34	.86	.93	.69	.184*	1.00				
Webcare (WC)	4.45	1.53	.72	.87	.62	.096	−.251**	1.00			
Reputation Management (RM)	3.38	1.26	.83	.76	.76	.01	−.279**	.569**	1.00		
Engagement (EN)	3.50	.76	.94	.93	.66	−.068	−.281**	.537**	.539**	1.00	
Firm Performance (FP)	3.66	.84	.88	.85	.75	−.127	−.355**	−.451**	.596**	.851**	1.00

Notes: *significant at the 0.05 level; **significant at the 0.01 level

Table 2 Shows structural equation modeling results

Hypothesis	Standardized Coefficient	Standard Error	Critical Ratio	Test Result
H1 MAR → RP	.203	.076	2.669	$p = .008$
H2 RP → WC	−.351	.084	−4.185	$p < .001$
H3 WC → RM	.441	.050	8.822	$p < .001$
H4 WC→ EN	.260	.031	8.427	$p < .001$
H5 EN → FP	.963	.071	13.615	$p < .001$

The threat level they attribute to the internet is associated with less engagement in webcare. However, the decision to respond to customer feedback online is associated with efforts to manage the firm's reputation on the internet and foster customer engagement on the venture's social media platforms. Practically, we find that engagement initiatives with buyers online are associated with increased firm performance.

There are limitations within our study. First, the inferences are cross-sectional, rendering us with a snapshot of the phenomenon. Future research may issue several rounds of surveys over multiple time periods to better understand the relationship between the marginalized entrepreneur and the internet, and the extent to which the association may change over time. Our model explores the relationship between marginalization and risk perceptions of the web across a sample composed of marginalized and non-marginalized (in group) small business owners and managers. A direct comparison between the two groups' perceptions and web presence may provide more granularity with respect to differences in business decisions and performance outcomes for these firms.

This paper makes important contributions to existing marketing literature. Our study presents a path by which external disadvantage can perpetuate additional challenges internally through influencing the entrepreneur's marketing decisions, which may also unintentionally contribute to lower firm performance. This paper specifically considers how marginalization limits an entrepreneur's use of the sales and customer relationship building channels available to her.

References

Ajiboye, T., Harvey, J., & Resnick, S. (2019). Customer engagement behaviour on social media platforms: A systematic literature review. *Journal of Customer Behaviour, 18*(3), 239-256.

Alcácer, J., & Chung, W. (2014). Location strategies for agglomeration economies. *Strategic Management Journal, 35*(12), 1749-1761.

Bates, T., & Robb, A. (2016). Impacts of owner race and geographic context on access to small-business financing. *Economic Development Quarterly, 30*(2), 159-170.

Bendick, M., & Egan, M.L. (1993). Linking business development and community development in inner cities. *Journal of Planning Literature, 8*(1), 3-19.

Boje, D. M. (1995). Stories of the storytelling organization: A postmodern analysis of Disney as "Tamara-Land". *Academy of Management journal, 38*(4), 997–1035.

Braaf, S., Ameratunga, S., Ponsford, J., Cameron, P., Collie, A., Harrison, J., Ekegren, C., Christie, N., Nunn, A., & Gabbe, B. (2019). Traumatic injury survivors' perceptions of their future: a longitudinal qualitative study. *Disability and Rehabilitation*42(19), 2707-2717.

Brodie, R.J., Ilic, A., Juric, B., & Hollebeek, L. (2013). Consumer engagement in a virtual brand community: An exploratory analysis. *Journal of Business Research, 66*(1), 105-114.

Casado-Díaz, A.B., Andreu, L., Beckmann, S.C., & Miller, C. (2020). Negative online reviews and webcare strategies in social media: effects on hotel attitude and booking intentions. *Current Issues in Tourism, 23*(4), 418-422.

Clement, J. (2020). *Number of internet users in the United States from 2015 to 2025.* Accessed from https://www.statista.com/statistics/325645/usa-number-of-internet-users/

Chiang, C.-T., Wie, C.-F., Parker, K.R., & Davey, B. (2017). Exploring the drivers of customer engagement behaviors in social network brand communities: Towards a customer-learning model. *Journal of Marketing Management, 33*(17-18), 1443-1464.

Cumming, D., & Johan, S. (2010). The differential impact of the internet on spurring regional entrepreneurship. *Entrepreneurship Theory and Practice, 34*(5), 857-884.

Davis, P.S., & Harveston, P.D. (2000). Internationalization and organizational growth: The impact of internet usage and technology involvement among entrepreneur-led family businesses. *Family Business Review, 13*(2), 107-120.

Fauchart, E., & Cowan, R. (2014). Weak links and the management of reputational interdependencies. *Strategic Management Journal, 35*(4), 532-549.

Fertik, M. (2019). *Why customer engagement should be every business's top priority in 2020.* Accessed from https://www.forbes.com/sites/michaelfertik/2019/12/16/why-customer-engagement-should-be-every-businesss-top-priority-in-2020/#3f6ad45f6214

Fornell, C., & Larcker, D. F. (1981). Evaluating structural equation models with unobservable variables and measurement error. *Journal of Marketing Research, 18*(1), 39-50.

Gaudreault, K.L., Richards, K.A.R., & Mays Woods, A. (2017). Initial validation of the physical education marginalization and isolation survey (PE-MAIS). *Measurement in Physical Education and Exercise Science, 21*(2), 69-82.

Gill, M., Sridhar, S., & Grewal, R. (2017). Return on engagement initiatives: A study of a business-to-business mobile app. *Journal of Marketing, 81*(4), 45-66.

Ghosh, T. (2017). Managing negative reviews: the persuasive role of webcare characteristics. *Journal of Internet Commerce, 16*(2), 148-173.

Grupe, D.W., & Nitschke, J.B. (2013). Uncertainty and anticipation in anxiety: an integrated neurobiological and psychological perspective. *Nature Reviews Neuroscience, 14*(7), 488-501.

Hall, J.M., Stevens, P.E., & Meleis, A.I. (1994). Marginalization: A guiding concept for valuing diversity in nursing knowledge development. *Advances in Nursing Science, 16*(4), 23-41.

Hair, J. F., Black, W., Babin, B., & Anderson, R. (2010). *Multivariate Data Analysis*, 7.

Hernández-Carrión, C., Camarero-Izquierdo, C., & Gutiérrez-Cillán, J. (2017). Entrepreneurs' social capital and the economic performance of small businesses: The moderating role of competitive intensity and entrepreneurs' experience. *Strategic Entrepreneurship Journal, 11*(1), 61-89.

Hoyman, M., McCall, J., Paarlberg, L., & Brennan, J. (2016). Considering the role of social capital for economic development outcomes in US counties. *Economic Development Quarterly, 30*(4), 342-357.

Kandel, D.B. (1978). Homophily, selection, and socialization in adolescent friendships. *American Journal of Sociology, 84*(2), 427-436.

Kaplan, D.H. (1998). The spatial structure of urban ethnic economies. *Urban Geography, 19*(6), 489-501.

Kumar, V., & Pansari, A. (2016). Competitive advantage through engagement. *Journal of Marketing Research, 53*(4), 497-514.

Lipsey, N.P., & Shepperd, J.A. (2019). The role of powerful audiences in health information avoidance. *Social Science & Medicine, 225*(2019), 51-59.

Magretta, J. (2002). Why business models matter. *Harvard Business Review, 80*(May), 86-92.

Malmström, M., Johansson, J., & Wincent, J. (2017). Gender stereotypes and venture support decisions: how governmental venture capitalists socially construct entrepreneurs' potential. *Entrepreneurship Theory and Practice, 41*(5), 833-860.

Matthews, R.S., Chalmers, D.M., & Fraser, S.S. (2018). The intersection of entrepreneurship and selling: An interdisciplinary review, framework, and future research agenda. *Journal of Business Venturing, 33*(2018), 691-719.

Mehra, A., Kilduff, M., & Brass, D.J. (1998). At the margins: A distinctiveness approach to the social identity and social networks of underrepresented groups. *Academy of Management Journal, 41*(4), 441-452.

Ngoasong, M.Z. (2018). Digital entrepreneurship in a resource-scarce context. *Journal of Small Business and Enterprise Development, 25*(3), 483-500.

Philippe, D., & Durand, R. (2011). The impact of norm-conforming behaviors on firm reputation. *Strategic Management Journal, 32*(9), 969-993.

Ragins, B.R., & Sundstrom, E. (1989). Gender and power in organizations: A longitudinal perspective. *Psychological Bulletin, 105*(1), 51-88.

Reuber, A.R., & Fischer, E. (2011). International entrepreneurship in internet-enabled markets. *Journal of Business Venturing, 26*(6), 660-679.

Rosenbaum, E. (2017). *You'll be shocked to learn how many small businesses still don't have a website.* Accessed from https://www.cnbc.com/2017/06/14/tech-help-wanted-about-half-of-small-businesses-dont-have-a-website.html#:~:text=Almost%20half%20(45%20percent)%20say,to%20customers%20and%20potential%20customers

Salenius, S. (2016). Marginalized Identities and Spaces: James Baldwin's Harlem, New York. *Journal of Black Studies, 47*(8), 883-902.

So, K.K.F., King, C., Sparks, B.A., & Wang, Y., 2016. The role of customer engagement in building consumer loyalty to tourism brands. *Journal of Travel Research, 55*(1), 64-78.

Sreejesh, S., & Anusree, M.R. (2016). The impacts of customers' observed severity and agreement on hotel booking intentions: moderating role of webcare and mediating role of trust in negative online reviews. *Tourism Review, 28*(6), 711-742.

Stone, R.N., & Gronhaug, K. (1993). Perceived risk: Further considerations for the marketing discipline. *European Journal of Marketing, 27*(3), 39-50.

Van Noort, G., & Willemsen, L.M. (2012). Online damage control: The effects of proactive versus reactive webcare interventions in consumer-generated and brand-generated platforms. *Journal of Interactive Marketing, 26*(3), 131-140.

Vivek, S.D., Beatty, S.E., Dalela, V., & Morgan, R.M. (2014). A generalized multidimensional scale for measuring customer engagement. *Journal of Marketing Theory and Practice, 22*(4), 401-420.

Wacquant, L.J., & Wilson, W.J. (1989). The cost of racial and class exclusion in the inner city. *The Annals of the American Academy of Political and Social Science, 501*(1), 8-25.

Weitzl, W.J., 2019. Webcare's effect on constructive and vindictive complainants. *Journal of Product and Brand Management, 28*(3), 330-347.

Weitzl, W.J., & Einwiller, S.A. (2020). Profilinf (un-)committed online complainants: Their characteristics and post-webcare reactions. *Journal of Business Research* 117:740-53.

Weitzl, W.J., & Hutzinger, C. (2017). The effects of marketer-and advocate-initiated online service recovery responses on silent bystanders. *Journal of Business Research, 80*(2017), 164-175.

Yadav, M. S., De Valck, K., Hennig-Thurau, T., Hoffman, D. L., & Spann, M. (2013). Social commerce: a contingency framework for assessing marketing potential. *Journal of interactive marketing, 27*(4), 311-323.

Zhao, E.Y., & Wry, T. (2016). Not all inequality is equal: Deconstructing the societal logic of patriarchy to understand microfinance lending to women. *Academy of Management Journal, 59*(6), 1994-2020.

COVID-19 and Social Injustice Messages Impact on Stress: An Abstract

Kelly O. Cowart and Aberdeen Leila Borders

Abstract This project probes the impact of COVID-19 and social injustice message framing on employee stress. Diversity in the workforce is a competitive advantage. Many organizations develop statements to signal their diversity appreciation (Jayne and Dipboye 2004). These messages receive favor from some stakeholders, but ridicule from others (Avery and McKay 2010). The appropriate message framing (self vs. other) can have consequences on employee behavior (Hung and Wyer 2011) and judgment (Chang and Hung 2018). It increases message elaboration and persuasion (Burnkrant and Unnava 1995).

Ongoing messages and images about social injustice have had significant, negative effects on the physical and mental health of Black employees (Smith et al. 2011; Williams 2018). For Black people, the ability to regulate emotions during crisis is imperative. Non-Black people who experience stress from these sources may be less adept at emotion regulation in these instances. It is important to expose the effect of these messages as they may add stress communities experience during a crisis.

A non-student sample of 174 subjects were randomly assigned to one of the three experimental conditions in which they read and considered a COVID-19 message and a social injustice message. The message content was manipulated through the use of other-focus language ("We"), self-focus language ("You") or the absence of personal pronouns (Cober et al. 2001). Pre- and post-stress measures were completed for each message. The average stress level before the experiment was neutral ($x = 4.11$) with no significant group differences. Exposure to a COVID-19 message did not significantly change the stress level ($t(169) = 1.46$, $p = .15$, $x = 4.35$). However, exposure to the social injustice message following the COVID-19 message produced significant changes ($t(171) = 2.94$, $p < .001$, $x = 3.22$). The stress level of non-White subjects ($x = 2.82$) was reduced while the stress level of White

K. O. Cowart (✉)
University of South Florida, Sarasota, FL, USA
e-mail: cowartk@usf.edu

A. L. Borders
Kennesaw State, Kennesaw, GA, USA
e-mail: aborder4@kennesaw.edu

J. Allen et al. (eds.), *Celebrating the Past and Future of Marketing and Discovery with Social Impact*, Developments in Marketing Science: Proceedings of the Academy of Marketing Science, https://doi.org/10.1007/978-3-030-95346-1_133

subjects (x = 4.99) increased. Self-focus message framing (x = 4.47) received significantly higher evaluations than other-focus message framing (x = 3.69) and the control condition (x = 3.31) ($F(2,167) = 5.08$, $p < .001$).

COVID-19 messages had no impact on stress levels. When the COVID-19 message was followed by a social injustice message, stress levels were lowered significantly for non-White subjects while they increased for White subjects. Self-focus message framing was most effective in communicating these messages versus other-focus messaging or non-specific messages.

Culture influences how people perceive and respond to the world (Smith et al. 2009) whether at work or at home. An organization attempting to engage its cultural competence by supporting one demographic group may confront feelings of marginalization by another group. This is an important avenue of inquiry due to the gravity of events that preceded and followed COVID-19. It offers insight into how different groups evaluate corporate responses to social issues. Employees and consumers are watching.

Keywords COVID-19 · Social injustice · Emotion regulation · Message framing · Corporate communication

From Print to Protest: Examining How Advertisements May Spur Social Activism: An Abstract

Jazmin Henry, Kevin D. Bradford, and Tonya Williams Bradford

Abstract Race is at the forefront of marketers and consumers' minds as the need for social justice and a focus on anti-racism enter daily conversations. Race strongly influences consumer behavior (Pitts et al. 1989; Sexton 1972), and consumers are increasingly engaging in various forms of protest which attempt to shape markets and organizations within them (Bradford 2020; Kates and Belk 2001; Klein et al. 2004; Kozinets et al. 2012; Kozinets and Handelman 2004; Scaraboto and Fischer 2013; Sen et al. 2001). Though research has established strong links between race and consumer behavior, there remains an opportunity to examine how race influences consumer behaviors that seek to contest the marketplace. This study seeks to examine how perceptions of racially stereotyped advertisements may affect consumer willingness to participate in forms of activism.

Primarily, race is viewed as a demographic variable upon which to assess differences among consumers (Akers 1968; Barban and Cundiff 1964). Recent research challenges prior notions of race in the marketplace and orients race as more than a demographic variable to consider the many ways in which race is culturally constructed (Grier et al. 2019). Such an expanded view creates additional opportunities to examine how race influences consumer responses in marketplaces.

Alternatively, literature provides examples of how consumers may respond to market messages through boycotts and protests in attempts to alter markets or society (Kates and Belk 2001; Klein et al. 2004; Kozinets et al. 2012; Sen et al. 2001). Generally, these responses to markets are viewed as consumer movements which are meant to mobilize consumers against business in efforts to transform both business behaviors and consumer culture (Kozinets and Handelman 2004). These movements have the potential to change interactions between consumers and businesses where consumers intend to alter marketplace demand until desired changes are obtained (Weber et al. 2008).

This study utilizes a framework to examine the extent to which an individual's perception of racially stereotyped advertisements may lead to forms of activism. In

J. Henry (✉) · K. D. Bradford · T. W. Bradford
University of California Irvine, Irvine, CA, USA
e-mail: jhenry3@uci.edu; kdbradfo@uci.edu; twbrad@uci.edu

J. Allen et al. (eds.), *Celebrating the Past and Future of Marketing and Discovery with Social Impact*, Developments in Marketing Science: Proceedings of the Academy of Marketing Science, https://doi.org/10.1007/978-3-030-95346-1_134

a 2 (message characteristics: stereotypical vs. non-stereotypical) × 2 (model characteristics: Black vs. White) between-subjects designed study, the findings reveal that individuals who view racially stereotyped advertisements are likely to participate in monetary activism (e.g., raising money to support a cause) and protest activism (e.g., attend a protest).

Keywords Racism · Advertisements · Consumer movements · Activism

Leveraging Diversity as a Tacit Resource: An Exploration into an Organization's Antecedent and Succedent Factors for a Model of Successful Multicultural Marketing: An Abstract

J. P. James

Abstract Given the level of diversity in the United States, companies are implementing multicultural marketing to be competitive in the marketplace. Multicultural marketing, the practice of integrated marketing strategies and tactics for products and services that are race- and ethnic-neutral and agnostic to sexual orientation, has become a conventional marketing strategy. However, both for-and non-profit organizations are challenged when it comes to execution. The mainstreaming of multicultural marketing has presented marketers with challenges in executing an optimal strategy to target diverse consumers, giving rise to what is known as the Total Market Approach to Multicultural Marketing. Unfortunately, marketers rely on the objective attributes of culture in multicultural consumer segmentation. Thus, multicultural consumers are more predisposed to being unfairly represented in advertising due to stereotyping. As a result, there has been an ongoing marketing practitioner debate on multicultural marketing strategy (e.g., what exactly is the Total Market Approach to multicultural marketing, the necessity of hiring a multicultural advertising agency, and the important role of diversity within the marketing organization).

This manuscript answers the following marketing-relevant research question: What are the important measurable organizational factors necessary for successful U.S. multicultural marketing? The marketing literature is scant relative to multicultural marketing strategies and tactics. What has not been discussed in previous marketing literature is how an organization's visible human resource diversity—and its commitment to diversity—can be leveraged as a tacit resource when marketing to multicultural consumers. This paper proposes that an organization's Diversity Avouchment can be a sustainable, tacit, competitive advantage to a company as it relates to multicultural marketing. Leveraging the theory of the Resourced-Based

J. P. James (✉)
Salem State University, Salem, MA, USA
e-mail: jjames@salemstate.edu

J. Allen et al. (eds.), *Celebrating the Past and Future of Marketing and Discovery with Social Impact*, Developments in Marketing Science: Proceedings of the Academy of Marketing Science, https://doi.org/10.1007/978-3-030-95346-1_135

View of the Firm and practitioner multicultural marketing research, a sample of marketing practitioners was queried on their multicultural marketing practices. An empirical model identifying the meaningful and measurable constructs within an organization that can predict multicultural marketing success was developed. Findings demonstrate that through greater Diversity Avouchment and the implementation of a Total Market strategy, organizations have higher financial and strategic performance, more effective advertising, and creative latitude to develop culturally relevant marketing communications. The empirical model of multicultural marketing in this paper, sampled from marketing practitioners across various U.S. companies, will make a unique contribution to the area of marketplace diversity, contributing to what is already known about the theory of the Resourced-Based View (RBV) of the Firm.

This paper can make management teams within various organizations aware that multicultural marketing is a legitimate and profitable strategy to be competitive in the marketplace. Trade organizations such as the American Marketing Association (AMA) and the Association of National Advertisers (ANA) will have a prescription for successful multicultural marketing. As a result, stereotypes can be mitigated, resulting in better, more effective, and more inclusive marketing communications.

Keywords Multicultural marketing · Diversity · Ethnic marketing · Advertising

Mobile Financial Services at the Base of the Pyramid: A Systematic Literature Review: An Abstract

Charlene A. Dadzie, Marcia Kwaramba, and Esi Elliot

Abstract With an estimated 1.1 billion unbanked adults in the world, mobile financial services, including mobile money services are being used to increase access to low-cost financial services (Demirguc-Kunt et al. 2018). Although mobile financial services are growing at a dynamic and rapid pace, the share of adults (44%) in developing countries reported to using digital payments with mobile phones or the internet is still low (Demirguc-Kunt et al. 2018). There still remains a large percent of the population in BoP (base of the pyramid) markets with limited access to sustainable formal financial services like credit, savings, payment systems, insurance and pension (Ouma et al. 2017).

The growth and potential of mobile financial services in BOP markets is well documented in practitioner reports (e.g. GSMA- Mobile for Development report, World Bank- Global Findex reports, Deloitte- Leveraging digital to unlock the base of the pyramid market in Africa report). Mobile phones and the internet have given rise to a new generation of financial services, sparking a digital revolution. Although BOP market literature has mention that the mobile financial services process is becoming increasingly dynamic with benefits to many stakeholders, there has been little light thrown on mobile financial inclusion processes and outcomes. Hence, the main aim of this study is to conduct a systematic literature review and synthesize the literature on strategies to upscale utilitarian and hedonic benefits to all consumers at the micro, meso and macro levels – all stakeholders - to get a comprehensive understanding of mobile financial inclusion.

C. A. Dadzie (✉)
University of South Alabama, Mobile, AL, USA
e-mail: cdadzie@southalabama.edu

M. Kwaramba
University of Colorado-Boulder, Boulder, CO, USA
e-mail: marcia.kwaramba@colorado.edu

E. Elliot
University of Texas – Rio Grande Valley, Edinburg, TX, USA
e-mail: esi.elliot@utrgv.edu

J. Allen et al. (eds.), *Celebrating the Past and Future of Marketing and Discovery with Social Impact*, Developments in Marketing Science: Proceedings of the Academy of Marketing Science, https://doi.org/10.1007/978-3-030-95346-1_136

We employed a systematic literature review approach for this study as our data collection method. Systematic literature review (SLR) is a distinct and organized method to analyze and assess literature (Briner and Walshe 2014).

We have proposed a conceptual model to delineate mobile financial services usage in BOP markets. The model shows the factors that take place prior to mobile financial services usage among BOP consumers, as well as the usage experience and outcomes associated with MFS at the BOP. As such, this model serves as a visual representation of the previously discussed antecedents, usage experience, outcomes, and strategy. Additionally, we specify that the mobile financial services environment includes micro level household strategies, meso level firm strategies, and macro level national strategies. These micro, meso and macro level relationships require continuous re-adaptations amongst stakeholders for increasing dynamism in MFS.

Mobile financial services present an opportunity for financial inclusion and poverty alleviation. Consequently, understanding the antecedents, process and outcomes associated with their use and provision is key. Our conceptualization of the mobile financial services process and environment suggest that precursors impact mobile financial services usage which in turn impacts outcomes additionally elements of the micro, meso, and macro environment impact each of these elements.

Keywords Base of the pyramid · Mobile money · Financial services · Poverty alleviation

If I Tap It, Will They Come? An Introductory Analysis of Fairness in a Large-Scale Ride Hailing Dataset: An Abstract

Aylin Caliskan and Begum Kaplan

Abstract Ride hailing service market is by far the fastest growing industry. Increased consumer demand resulted in a significant shift from traditional taxis to ride hailing services (Pyzyk 2019). According to a 2017 report of Goldman Sachs, this industry is expected to reach a market size of $285 billion by 2030 (Huston 2017). Uber is the largest ride hailing company in the market, followed by Lyft and few other relatively small companies such as Via, Gett and Juno (Lam and Liu 2017). There are limited regulations on these ride hailing services which are black-box algorithmic decision makers. Consequently, there are growing concerns about algorithmic fairness in ride hailing.

To investigate fairness in ride hailing services, we analyzed data provided by the City of Chicago on 73,247,231 ride hailing Uber, Lyft, and Via trips combined between November 2018 and June 2019 for 5,459,609 drivers. City of Chicago has been first to publish city level data on ride hailing trips in 2019. Our findings indicate that there are some concerns in terms of fairness in their practices. As our findings suggest, low-income neighborhoods pay higher prices for their trips than high income neighborhoods. Additionally, consumers from minority and low-income neighborhoods have less ride hailing service usage as opposed to consumers from white dominant, high-income neighborhoods. Our findings also show that popular pick-up and drop-off neighborhoods have higher ride hailing prices which explains the demand-based surge pricing practices of these ride hailing companies. Finally, we found that young and active consumers that use ride hailing services in their communities pay higher prices in comparison to other populations of different ages.

A. Caliskan
George Washington University, NW, Washington, DC, USA
e-mail: aylin@gwu.edu

B. Kaplan (✉)
Florida International University, Miami, FL, USA
e-mail: beoz@fiu.edu

J. Allen et al. (eds.), *Celebrating the Past and Future of Marketing and Discovery with Social Impact*, Developments in Marketing Science: Proceedings of the Academy of Marketing Science, https://doi.org/10.1007/978-3-030-95346-1_137

This paper contributes to an increased understanding of fairness in ride hailing services by analyzing the detailed large-scale ride hailing dataset obtained from Chicago Data portal. The results provide a preliminary understanding about the demographic patterns of consumers' ride hailing usage. This is one of the first city level datasets on ride hailing services that is publicly available and provides insights about the practices of these services. This research contributes to the literature of ride hailing services as well as practices of these services in terms of fairness. Managerially, by better understanding the factors that create unfair practices in the ride hailing market, marketers, researchers and policy makers can offer solutions or work together to set regulations aiming to prevent disparate impact in the ride hailing industry. Finally, our findings suggest that further exploration of ride hailing services with sophisticated machine learning techniques can provide insights as to how fair ride hailing services are, how they affect consumers and to what extent these services contribute to the growth of communities.

Keywords Fairness · Ride-hailing · Machine-learning · Consumer well-being

Augmented Reality Brand Experiences: Exploring Psychological, Cognitive, and Sensory Aspects: An Abstract

Jennifer B. Barhorst, Graeme McLean, Nina Krey, Heiner Evanschitzky, and Ana Javornik

Abstract Augmented reality (AR), which overlays a virtual world onto the real world (Javornik 2016), provides tremendous opportunities for brands to engage consumers through psychological, cognitive, and sensory processes as they interact with the technology. Due to the rapid development of AR, however, there is a dearth of research to understand how individual psychological, cognitive, and sensory aspects associated with AR brand experiences influence commonly studied outcome behaviors. With company investments in AR technology set to increase to $195 billion by 2025 and consumer downloads of mobile AR applications expected to reach 5.5 billion by 2022 (Statista 2020), the need to deepen the understanding of this burgeoning technology's impact on consumption experiences is of importance to both firms and scholars. We seek to address this gap by examining the psychological, cognitive, and sensory aspects of AR experiences that foster positive brand outcomes through the elicitation of episodic memories.

A concept that was initially introduced by Tulving (1972) over 40 years ago, episodic memory is a memory system that facilitates the remembrance of personally

J. B. Barhorst (✉)
College of Charleston, Charleston, SC, USA
e-mail: barhorstj@cofc.edu

G. McLean
University of Strathclyde, Glasgow, UK
e-mail: graeme.mclean@strath.ac.uk

N. Krey
Rowan University, Glassboro, NJ, USA
e-mail: krey@rowan.edu

H. Evanschitzky
University of Manchester, Manchester, UK
e-mail: heiner.evanschitzky@manchester.ac.uk

A. Javornik
University of Bristol, Bristol, UK
e-mail: ana.javornik@bristol.ac.uk

J. Allen et al. (eds.), *Celebrating the Past and Future of Marketing and Discovery with Social Impact*, Developments in Marketing Science: Proceedings of the Academy of Marketing Science, https://doi.org/10.1007/978-3-030-95346-1_138

experienced events associated with particular times or places that are triggered by a retrieval cue. Episodic retrieval involves an interaction between a 'retrieval cue' (self-generated or by the environment) and a memory trace leading to some or all aspects of the episode in the trace (Rugg and Wilding 2000). It does so by inducing Chronethesia, a conscious awareness of being present while remembering the past (Tulving 1985). Further, and of interest to marketers, priming of episodic memory not only induces memories of the past, but also triggers the ability to re-experience one's own previous experiences through mental time travel. During this particular experience, one not only remembers the past but feels like being in and re-living a specific past moment. This feeling of re-living the experience is a state that includes characteristics such as seeing, hearing, and feeling what occurred in the past event (Tulving 2002).

In this between-subjects study with over 800 participants, we compare AR to a range of digital brand stimuli from one seasonal campaign. The campaign stimuli included an AR experience, a branded website 360-experience, a video advertisement, and a static image. The results suggest that sensory and atmospheric aspects of AR not only have the capability of triggering episodic memories, but when compared to other conditions, they enhance episodic memory's effect on behavioral intentions through the elicitation of mental time travel. Therefore, findings from this study add to the extant literature on AR's ability to foster positive brand outcomes through the elicitation of episodic memory and mental time travel.

Keywords Augmented reality · Episodic memory · Mental time travel · Branding

Understanding Customer Spending Behavior during COVID-19 Using Real-time Anonymized Data from Private Companies: An Abstract

Dana E. Harrison, Haya Ajjan, Lucy Matthews, Astrid Keel, and Prachi Gala

Abstract The COVID-19 pandemic has significantly disrupted the global economy at an unprecedented scale since its start in early 2020. Furthermore, it is estimated that a third of the workforce in the U.S. changed to work from home (Brynjolfsson et al. 2020). As consumers are spending more time at home, data shows that panic buying changed demand for items such as hand sanitizer and toilet paper. The increase for certain categories in consumer spending during the pandemic has been accompanied by a spike in the utilization of e-commerce channels. COVID-19 accelerated consumers move to purchasing goods online versus traditional physical stores by five years (Perez 2020). According to the U.S. Census Bureau, consumers increased their e-commerce spending to $211.5 billion during the second quarter, an increase of 31.8% quarter over quarter (Palmer 2020). The sudden nature of the changes related to COVID-19 purchase behavior makes it harder for marketers to respond effectively.

As research on the topic of COVID-19 is starting to appear in the literature, there is not enough work in the area of consumer purchase behavior. In this paper, we

D. E. Harrison
East Tennessee State University, Johnson City, TN, USA
e-mail: harrisondl@etsu.edu

H. Ajjan (✉)
Elon University, Elon, NC, USA
e-mail: hajjan@elon.edu

L. Matthews
Middle Tennessee State University, Murfreesboro, TN, USA
e-mail: lucy.matthews@mtsu.edu

A. Keel
La Verne University, La Verne, CA, USA
e-mail: akeel@laverne.edu

P. Gala
Kennesaw State University, Kennesaw, GA, USA
e-mail: pgala4@kennesaw.edu

J. Allen et al. (eds.), *Celebrating the Past and Future of Marketing and Discovery with Social Impact*, Developments in Marketing Science: Proceedings of the Academy of Marketing Science, https://doi.org/10.1007/978-3-030-95346-1_139

utilize three real-time datasets to understand customer dynamics from March 2020 to December 2020 during the pandemic. Combining these data sources allows us to enhance our understanding of the general purchasing behavior at city level during the pandemic. We identify product categories that were the primary drivers of a sharp increase (decrease) in spending and the extent to which this increase (decrease) was maintained over time. We also shed light on stressors such as the number of COVID-19 cases and death by city and their impact on time spent at home and retail stores. By doing so, we contribute to the literature on panic buying which is still not well understood in the literature (Barnes et al. 2020).

Keywords COVID-19 · Consumer spending · Purchase behavior · Panic buying

Cyborgs and the Interactive Self: An Abstract

Vitor M. Lima

Abstract In what ways do individuals exercise their morphological freedom to become cyborgs? Does becoming more machine-like enrich or diminish their identities as humans? In pursuing answers to these research questions, I relied on an existential-phenomenological framework (Sartre 1976) and a three-year qualitative study of near-field communication (NFC) microchip consumers that resulted in a new conceptualization: The Interactive Self. Differently from the extended self (Belk 1988) that is composed of everything humans can call theirs (James 1890), the interactive self is nurtured by cyborgs' experiential and embodied sense of ownership and a sense of agency for their actions (Gallagher 2013).

Drawing on Transhumanism (Sorgner 2020), cyborg anthropology (Hables-Gray et al. 2020), and theories of the self (Gallagher 2013), the concept has three conceptual dimensions: Firstly, the Identity-Enabler Object is an object (e.g., an NFC microchip) that has the power to change the human ontological status to that of fledgling cyborgs. Secondly, the iMine Boundarylessness comprises the physical, symbolic, and digital boundaries that are crossed or blurred, allowing for the simultaneous process of extension & incorporation into the self. Finally, the third conceptual dimension is the Data Meshwork, which is a bundle of data that flows through the cyborgs' internal (e.g., an NFC microchip) and external digital organs (e.g., a smartphone).

This study contributes, firstly, to the understanding of work on identity projects in the transhumanist era. Since Belk's (1988) seminal contribution, consumer researchers directly or indirectly draw on the notion that "knowingly or unknowingly, intentionally or unintentionally, we regard our possessions as parts of ourselves" (Belk 1988, 139). However, from the Interactive Self perspective, this premise does not fully encompass the cyborg ontology since there is no point in having an implanted microchip and not doing anything with it (i.e., interacting to exchange data). Still further, from the identity project perspective, I also introduce the simultaneous processes of extension & incorporation into the self, as recently

V. M. Lima (✉)
York University, Toronto, ON, Canada
e-mail: lmv2607@yorku.ca

J. Allen et al. (eds.), *Celebrating the Past and Future of Marketing and Discovery with Social Impact*, Developments in Marketing Science: Proceedings of the Academy of Marketing Science, https://doi.org/10.1007/978-3-030-95346-1_140

suggested (e.g., Connell and Schau 2013). The third theoretical implication of this research relates to technology consumption studies, which thus far are essentially about what consumers can or cannot do with technology. However, when technology changes our ontological framing of ourselves as human beings, we must change our view of technology as well (Belk 2020; Schmitt 2020). Cyborgs do not use technology; they are technology. In this sense, my findings challenge prior consumer and marketing theories and research in which technology is portrayed as a purely instrumental means to an end.

Keywords Transhumanism · Cyborgs · Self · Human enhancement technologies

Process Analysis for Marketing Research: An Abstract

Constant Pieters

Abstract Process analysis is indispensable to contemporary marketing research. It is the theorization and testing of moderation and/or mediation hypotheses to obtain theoretically and managerially relevant insights into marketing processes. This dissertation presents three essays that apply, compare and extend such process analysis methodologies.

Essay 1 applies mediation in an investigation of the referral reinforcement effect: referred customers are more inclined to make referrals than non-referred customers are. Study 1 is an analysis of a field-experiment among ridesharing customers. Study 2a re-analyzes a published combination of archival and survey data of a bank's referral reward program. Study 2b is a new survey among moviegoers. Study 3 is a controlled lab-experiment. All find support for the referral reinforcement effect. Study 4 investigates customer lay beliefs and finds that other-directed rather than self-directed or product-directed motives drive the referral reinforcement effect. Overall, these studies find support for the referral reinforcement effect and provide insights in its processes. The referral reinforcement has useful implications for managers who aim to grow a customer base.

Essay 2 compares six existing moderation methods in the face of measurement error. A quantitative literature review shows that taking a product of unweighted means is predominantly used for moderation analysis, in 94% of investigated articles. The remaining methods, multi-group, factor scores, corrected means, product indicators and the latent product method are barely used. A comparison of the assumptions of the methods and follow-up Monte Carlo simulations conclude that the accessible factor scores method performs much better than the dominant means method, and equally good or better than the remaining more sophisticated methods. We recommend the use of the factor scores method for moderation analysis and advise using samples that are 60% larger than that are currently common.

Essay 3 focuses on discriminant validity as a precondition for meaningful process analysis. It extends bivariate discriminant validation criteria by taking a multi-

C. Pieters (✉)
Tilburg University, Tilburg, The Netherlands
e-mail: c.pieters@tilburguniversity.edu

J. Allen et al. (eds.), *Celebrating the Past and Future of Marketing and Discovery with Social Impact*, Developments in Marketing Science: Proceedings of the Academy of Marketing Science, https://doi.org/10.1007/978-3-030-95346-1_141

variate perspective. The proposed implementation is applicable to both raw and summary statistics data, accounts for measurement error in the variables and uses statistical tests of discriminant validity rather than heuristics. Case studies and an online web-based application apply the proposed methods in important multivariate theory-testing domains, multiple mediation and multidimensional measurement. Usage of the proposed methods contributes to construct validation and meaningful substantive theory tests.

In sum, we hope that this dissertation demonstrates the strengths of process analysis methodologies, fosters valid applications, and inspires future research.

Keywords Process analysis · Customer referrals · Mediation · Moderation · Discriminant validity · Research methods

Organizational Frontline Marketing and a High-Tech World: Dissertation Proposal: An Abstract

Riley T. Krotz

Abstract This three-essay dissertation explores the intersection of organizational frontline marketing and a high-tech world, utilizing mixed-method approaches. The traditional retail and service environment is swiftly and drastically changing, and this fundamental shift in the retail and service landscape provides marketers with both great challenges and opportunities for great success. Some have attributed this retail apocalypse to the inability of traditional retailers to evolve quickly enough to handle the drastically-changing retail landscape. This fundamental change in retailing has been associated with increasing in-store technology and digital touchpoints which have changed how retailers and service organizations communicate with their customers along their purchase journey. One way retailers can stay competitive in this swiftly-changing environment is the development of their frontline management practices. Using field, manager-provided, experimental, attitudinal, and behavioral data, *Essay I* explores (1) What effect does providing free food have on FLEs' customer responsiveness and sales; (2) Through what mechanisms does free food affect key outcome variables; and (3) Are there boundary conditions to the free food effect? Adopting a longitudinal field experimental approach with behavioral data, *Essay II* examines (1) How frontline technology can influence five dimensions of the consumer experience and retail sales; (2) Through what mechanism does frontline technology affect key outcome variables; (3) How the frontline consumer experience develops longitudinally over time through three developmental variables; and (4) How the consumer experience changes when multiple products are experienced at one touchpoint. Utilizing field, archival, experimental, attitudinal, and behavioral data, *Essay III* investigates (1) Whether online social media use affects offline blood donations; (2) Through which mechanisms does social media affect blood donations; (3) Whether there are boundary conditions for these effects; and (4) how blood donations can be increased in the field. Across all three essays,

R. T. Krotz (✉)
Texas Tech University, Lubbock, TX, USA

University of Tennessee, Knoxville, TN, USA
e-mail: riley.krotz@ttu.edu

J. Allen et al. (eds.), *Celebrating the Past and Future of Marketing and Discovery with Social Impact*, Developments in Marketing Science: Proceedings of the Academy of Marketing Science, https://doi.org/10.1007/978-3-030-95346-1_142

implications and discussion are provided for academics, marketing managers, retailers, and service providers.

Keywords Organizational frontlines · Technology · Frontline employees · Retailing · Services · Blood donations · Prosocial behavior

Impact of Big Data Analytics in Marketing on Firm Bottom Line: An Abstract

Myriam Ertz and Imen Latrous

Abstract Big Data is defined as high-volume, high-velocity, high-variety (and more recently, high-veracity) information assets that demand cost-effective, innovative forms of capturing, storing, distributing, managing and analyzing that information (Gartner IT Glossary, n.d.; TechAmerica Foundation's Federal Big Data Commission 2012). Big Data Analytics (BDA) refers therefore to the "application of statistical processing, and analytics techniques to big data for advancing business" (Grover et al. 2018, p. 360). In marketing, despite much interest to the concept of Big Data and analytics, there is a lack of empirical evidence of the benefits associated with BDA. More surprisingly, little attention has been paid to the empirical investigation of the impact of BDA for market purposes on financial performance, despite the critical importance of such a relationship to reach strategic objectives.

Using the resource-based theory (RBT) framework (Barney 1991; Lee and Grewal 2014), this study fills that void in the literature by adopting an interdisciplinary perspective to assess the impacts of BDA for marketing purposes on firm financial performance. More specifically, the research involves a large-scale study of organizations that are part of the S&P 500 (Standard & Poors 500) in the USA, and of the S&P/TSX 60 (Standard & Poors/Toronto Stock Exchange 60), in Canada, to identify to what extent the implementation of BDA, in the marketing function, forms a competitive advantage that materializes through financial performance.

Overall, the findings suggest that BDA has a significant and extensive impact on corporate performance. Second, while descriptive analytics contribute positively to profit-related performance indicators (i.e., share price), prescriptive analysis load more significantly on revenue and profit-related performance indicators. Furthermore, the contribution of BDA to the revenue performance of the manufacturing industry is greater than in other industries.

M. Ertz (✉)
University of Quebec in Chicoutimi, Saguenay, QC, Canada
e-mail: myriam_ertz@uqac.ca

I. Latrous
University of Quebec in Chicoutimi, Saguenay, QC, Canada
e-mail: imen_latrous@uqac.ca

J. Allen et al. (eds.), *Celebrating the Past and Future of Marketing and Discovery with Social Impact*, Developments in Marketing Science: Proceedings of the Academy of Marketing Science, https://doi.org/10.1007/978-3-030-95346-1_143

This study contributes uniquely to past research and professional practice by providing an exploratory research on the impact of particular big data analytics (i.e., descriptive, predictive, and prescriptive) on the financial performance of 560 large capitalization companies (i.e., S&P500 and S&P/TSX60 stock indices).

Keywords Big data · Marketing · Financial performance · Big data analytics

Tackling Online Gaming Addiction among Adolescents: The Role of Parental Resilience and Parenting Styles: An Abstract

Sangeeta Trott, Paurav Shukla, and Veronica Rosendo-Rios

Abstract Online gaming addiction is a globally pervasive challenge and a major health problem that is affecting the societal fabric (Basol and Kaya 2018). The prevalent rate of internet addiction varies from 12.6% to 67.5% globally (Kuss et al. 2021). Hence, Interventions to tackle the problem of online gaming addiction is of utmost importance (Kuss et al. 2021). Therefore, the proposed study seeks to address the problem of online gaming addiction among adolescents (age 12–19 years) by adopting a novel resilience-based approach.

This research study grapples with two important research objectives. Firstly, the research will examine the role of parental resilience in avoiding/reducing online gaming addiction and identify the types of resilience tactics that can control and/or reduce gaming addiction among adolescents. Secondly, using secondary data sources, we wish to examine the pervasiveness of online gaming addiction among the adolescents to demonstrate the acuteness of the problem and the challenge it poses for the present and the future of the society.

The study will be divided into three phases (Secondary data-based review, qualitative exploration, and quantitative examination) followed by dissemination activities. So far, we have covered up phase 1 and Phase 2 of the study. *Phase 1 – Secondary data-based review*: The aim of this phase was to examine the current literature

---

Funding: Proposal accepted under AMS-AFM Action Grant, 2020

S. Trott (✉)
ITM University, Navi Mumbai, Maharashtra, India
e-mail: sangeetat@itm.edu

P. Shukla
University of Southampton, Hampshire, UK
e-mail: p.v.shukla@soton.ac.uk

V. Rosendo-Rios
CUNEF, Madrid, Spain
e-mail: vrosendo@cunef.edu

J. Allen et al. (eds.), *Celebrating the Past and Future of Marketing and Discovery with Social Impact*, Developments in Marketing Science: Proceedings of the Academy of Marketing Science, https://doi.org/10.1007/978-3-030-95346-1_144

around online gaming addiction globally and identify the nature and pervasiveness of the problem. The review involved a study of 50 most cited papers in online gaming addiction domain within the last decade. *Phase 2 – Qualitative exploration*: The second phase of the study involved in-depth dyadic interviews with parents (n = 10) of adolescents in India. The interviews focused on the online gaming habits of children, parental interaction with their kids (parenting styles) and varying resilient behaviour observed among parents.

We believe that our qualitative study makes an important contribution both theoretically and practically. Theoretically, it addresses a vast gap in the literature of online gaming addiction by showcasing parenting styles play an important role in controlling/reducing online gaming addiction among adolescents. Practically, the study has substantial implications for policy makers as well. Based on the findings of the study, policy makers can design interventions and training programmes that address the challenge of online gaming addiction through the aspects of resilience and parenting styles.

Keywords Pervasive challenge · Interventions · Parental interaction · Health problem

Overly Attached? When Brand Flattery Generates Jealousy in Social Media: An Abstract

Andria Andriuzzi, Géraldine Michel, and Claudiu Dimofte

Abstract Given the context of the rising use and importance of social media for brand management, this research examines how brand attachment influences the effect of consumer-brand online interaction strategies on consumer attitude. In particular, using Goffman's 'face-work' (1955) and social comparison theory (Schmitt 1988) as theoretical lenses, we investigate how brand flatteries towards consumers in social media impact the perception of brand humanization and the feeling of jealousy.

According to face-work theory, individual interactions involve avoiding face-threatening acts and producing face-flattering acts in order to maintain one's own face as well as the other participants' (Brown and Levinson 1987; Kerbrat-Orecchioni 1997). Thus, appreciation and politeness should positively impact brand interaction perception in social media. However, the positive impact of brand flattery does not take into account the existing brand-consumer relationship and the consumer profile. Still, managers address various types of consumers on social media, for example those who have already experienced a relation with the brand and those who have not (i.e., consumers with high or low brand attachment). According to our conceptual development, we assume that brand comments flattering individuals (appreciation by the brand) have a higher positive effect on brand anthropomorphism when consumers have a low attachment to the brand than when

Acknowledgement: This project was encouraged by the AMS-AFM Call for Common Research Proposals

A. Andriuzzi (✉)
Université Jean Monnet, Saint-Etienne, France
e-mail: andria.andriuzzi@univ-st-etienne.fr

G. Michel
IAE Paris-Sorbonne, Paris, France
e-mail: michel.iae@univ-paris1.fr

C. Dimofte
San Diego State University, San Diego, CA, USA
e-mail: cdimofte@sdsu.edu

J. Allen et al. (eds.), *Celebrating the Past and Future of Marketing and Discovery with Social Impact*, Developments in Marketing Science: Proceedings of the Academy of Marketing Science, https://doi.org/10.1007/978-3-030-95346-1_145

they have a high attachment to it. Moreover, we assume that when a brand flatters others this generates jealousy for observing consumers.

Based on two between-subject experiments, our results reveal the negative moderating effect of brand attachment, showing that the impact of brand appreciation on brand anthropomorphism is higher for consumers with low brand attachment versus those with high attachment. We also demonstrate that brand appreciation generates higher jealousy when addressed to others, compared to the self.

On the one hand, this research contributes to the face-work, brand-consumer interaction and brand anthropomorphism literature. Indeed, our results depict brand attachment as a moderating variable of the effect of flattering expressions on anthropomorphism perceptions. Moreover, we demonstrate that brand appreciation has a detrimental effect on lurking consumers when the brand addresses other consumers. On the other hand, this research has managerial implications in the fields of branding and community management by proposing that managers could segment their online conversation platforms depending on the kind of brand relationships experienced by consumers. We also suggest that appreciation should be used with parsimony in order to avoid negative reactions from consumers who are not the targets of the brand's appreciation.

Keywords Anthropomorphism · Attachment · Brand jealousy · Social media

Using Analytics to Segment American, French, and French-Canadian Consumers' Choice: An Abstract

Aidin Namin, Maria Petrescu, and Marie-Odile Richard

Abstract This study entails a state-of-the-art quantitative modeling approach to latent class analysis (i.e., marketing segmentation and targeting analysis) of American, French, and French-Canadian consumers' perception of American and French products based on their demographics and individual level cultural values. It identifies 'hidden' segments of consumers in the American/French/French-Canadian cultures and subcultures using their perception on US and France's level of competitiveness, similarities between the French, American, and French-Canadian cultures, and understanding of these consumers towards France and US. We unveil these segments for three major French and American product categories. For the former, we study car, wine, and perfume, where car represents durable, wine represents shopping, and perfume covers luxury products; and for the latter we include large electronics (durables), apparel (shopping), and designer sunglasses (luxury).

To the best of our knowledge, this is the first study investigating such a segmentation research question for French and American products by marrying analytics/modeling with individual level cultural values and the international business field. Results of this analysis have implications for marketing French and American products in the US, France, and French-Canadian markets and have applications for managers in improving the effectiveness of their segmentation/targeting processes, helping them get better responses as they target different segments, hence, reaching higher sales levels.

This analysis contributes to academics and practitioners in at least three major levels: (1) it extends the marketing and international business literature by empirically unveiling hidden segments of American/French/French-Canadian consumers

A. Namin (✉)
Loyola Marymount University, Los Angeles, CA, USA
e-mail: aidin.namin@lmu.edu

M. Petrescu
International University of Monaco, Monaco, Monaco
e-mail: mpetrescu@inseec.com

M.-O. Richard
State University of New York Polytechnic Institute, Utica, NY, USA
e-mail: richarm3@sunypoly.edu

J. Allen et al. (eds.), *Celebrating the Past and Future of Marketing and Discovery with Social Impact*, Developments in Marketing Science: Proceedings of the Academy of Marketing Science, https://doi.org/10.1007/978-3-030-95346-1_146

based on their demographics towards American and French products, (2) it offers managerial implications to those managers selling American and French products in the US/French/French-Canadian markets helping them better choose their target markets, and (3) by lowering targeting/advertising costs, it sets the ground for higher profits. The paper also further develops and updates the globalization and cultural change theory in additional markets and provides insights into the evolution of globalization and cosmopolitanism in consumer behavior.

Keywords Analytics · Cultural differences · Segmentation · Latent class analysis

A Framework to Understand Local Food Shopping: Towards a New Definition of the Multichannel Shopper Journey: An Abstract

Aurélia Michaud-Trévinal, Catherine Hérault-Fournier, and Patricia Harris

Abstract 82% of French people buy local food products and 59% of them at least once a week (Hérault-Fournier et al. 2020). While supermarkets remain the main place to buy local products, markets, convenience stores and specialty stores are very popular. More shoppers of local products are turning to digital channels, which were previously neglected. With the introduction of periods of containment (in France as in most countries), local food shopping journeys were disrupted with a strong adoption of pickup stores and home delivery (Chabault 2020).

Existing theoretical frameworks have difficulties in understanding the complexity of food shopping journeys, focusing on a particular angle of approach, motivations or shopping orientations (Michaud-Trévinal and Héralt-Fournier 2018). Cervellon et al. (2015) called for the use of Theory of Practice (TP) developed by (Reckwitz 2002; Schatzki 1996) in order to extend the understanding of the multichannel shopping journey.

We answer this call by using TP to propose a new framework for the shopper journey and we make an additional contribution to the literature by combining TP with situation theory. Following Schatzki et al (2001) and Warde (2005), the analysis of food shopping journeys focuses on the practical activity and its representations. We examine the ways in which local food shopping practice, shaped by bodies, minds, things, knowledges, discourses, and structures (Reckwitz 2002). Our resulting framework focuses not on consumers but on activities, competences, literacy and tools, that are embedded in a particular situation.

Funding by "Dyal Connect" Regional Research Project

A. Michaud-Trévinal (✉) · C. Hérault-Fournier
La Rochelle University, La Rochelle, France
e-mail: amichaud@univ-lr.fr; catherine.herault-fournier@univ-lr.fr

P. Harris
Kingston University, Kingston upon Thames, UK
e-mail: harris@kingston.ac.uk

J. Allen et al. (eds.), *Celebrating the Past and Future of Marketing and Discovery with Social Impact*, Developments in Marketing Science: Proceedings of the Academy of Marketing Science, https://doi.org/10.1007/978-3-030-95346-1_147

Our research questions are: (1) To develop a new framework for local food shopping; (2) To propose a practice-based typology of local food shopping journeys.

The methodology implemented meets the requirements of theory of practice by focusing data collection on acting and saying: a convenience sampling of 21 French shoppers was employed. The use of the narrative technique allows shopping stories to be collected.

Full results and discussion will be presented at the conference.

Keywords Multichannel shopping journey · Theory of practice · Local food · Situation

An Empirical Experiment to Measure Perceived Brand Literacy: An Abstract

Ananya Rajagopal

Abstract Brand literacy is the capacity of the consumers to understand the strategic pathway implemented by the organizations to promote their products and services in the marketplace. Acculturing consumers in order to position the brand as top of the mind is part of the process of generating brand literacy. Through the effective implementation of this process, consumers gain the ability not only to understand the brand etymologically but also their value proposition and relate it with consumer satisfaction propositions. The co-designing and co-evolution strategies also include co-branding, which is based on the degree of consumer literacy developed by the brands. The study proposes a new concept 'consumer perceived brand literacy' and presents a measurement scale development process. The scale presented here will help in understanding the perceived brand literacy by the consumers across the two selected brands and validate various dimensions explained in this study. The principal purpose is to explain the brand literacy perceived by consumers via five proposed dimensions.

The data collection process involved application of the research instrument among 100 respondents, using a homogeneous and convenience sampling method. The process of developing the scale was based on two stages, taking into account two different brands for this study. The study revealed that among the various dimensions considered for the construct, brand personality and brand image perceived by the consumers were among the most prominent. This means that the brands would need to co-design marketing strategies with the consumers in order to inculcate the brand literacy among consumers since the initial stage of the firm. Hence, the marketing strategies would also need to be directed towards developing a strong brand personality and brand image among the consumers to assure the consumer perception is similar to the brand communication.

A. Rajagopal (✉)
Universidad Anahuac Mexico, Mexico City, Mexico
e-mail: ananya.rajagopal@anahuac.mx

J. Allen et al. (eds.), *Celebrating the Past and Future of Marketing and Discovery with Social Impact*, Developments in Marketing Science: Proceedings of the Academy of Marketing Science, https://doi.org/10.1007/978-3-030-95346-1_148

Keywords Consumer perception · Brand literacy · Brand image · Scale development

When Descriptive Social Norm Interventions Malfunction: First Evidence on Reversed Effects in Anonymous Donation Calls: An Abstract

Vita E. M. Zimmermann-Janssen

Abstract For most nonprofit organizations (NPOs) the procurement of donations is the core function of nonprofit marketing efforts (Bennett 2019). As NPOs are facing increasing competition (i.e. McKeever 2018) and a decline in number of donors in several OECD countries (i.e. Giving USA 2019), NPOs have begun to engage in online fundraising to approach especially younger donors (Aldridge and Fowles 2013).

Research has shown that social information about others' donation behavior can positively affect donation rates in public solicitation settings. To date, similar experiments in online environments are lacking but are particularly worth studying as theories suggest a malfunction of descriptive normative information (DNI) in anonymous donation calls (Van Teunenbroek et al. 2019). Based on the assumptions that (1) anonymity weakens social pressure and that (2) anonymity gives relatively more explanatory power to altruistic considerations, it is hypothesized that the positive effect of DNI should be at least weakened in anonymous settings.

This hypothesis was tested in an online experiment (n = 392) covered as a price-draw to incentivize survey participation. At first, subjects were informed that they can win 100 Euro when finishing the survey and have the choice to donate a freely selectable share to an NPO. On the next page, subjects then decided whether they want to donate and were randomly assigned to the treatment or control condition. In the treatment condition the DNI that "87% of participants donate a portion" was shown. No information was given in the control condition. The comparison of donor proportions between control (68%) and treatment group (60%) reveals a marginally significant decline of 12 percent when DNI was shown, X^2 $(2,N = 392) = 12.746$, $p = .09$. The finding's robustness on individual level was tested using multiple logistic regression with sociodemographic variables, *trust in charities,* and *charitable giving behavior of friends and family* as covariates. Under control for these covari-

V. E. M. Zimmermann-Janssen (✉)
Heinrich Heine University Düsseldorf, Düsseldorf, Germany
e-mail: vita.zimmermann@hhu.de

J. Allen et al. (eds.), *Celebrating the Past and Future of Marketing and Discovery with Social Impact*, Developments in Marketing Science: Proceedings of the Academy of Marketing Science, https://doi.org/10.1007/978-3-030-95346-1_149

ates, 12.3 percent of the variance in donation decision can be explained ($R^2_{Nagelkerke}$ = .123, x^2 = 36.701, p < .001). The effect of DNI stays marginally significant and negative (*Exp(B)* = .667, *B* = −.405, *p* = .07).

Results indicate not only a weakened but even reversed effect of DNI on the overall decision to donate on both group (donation rate) and individual level (donation likelihood). This preliminary finding raises exciting tasks and questions that should be addressed in subsequent experiments. E.g., alterations in the communicated donor rate and different anonymity levels should be included in more sophisticated setups to (1) gain process evidence and (2) test alternative explanations and interactions.

Keywords Nonprofit marketing · Online fundraising · Donation · Social norms · Descriptive information · Reversed effects · Anonymity

Do You Trust that Brand Selfie? A New Scale to Measure Brand Selfie Credibility: An Abstract

Thusyanthy Lavan, Udo Gottlieb, Sven Tuzovic, and Rory Mulcahy

Abstract There were 300 million selfies posted on Instagram in 2018 (Smith 2019), and many people are taking selfies with brands (Sung et al. 2018). Although brand selfies of average consumers are generally perceived as credible, some consumers generate fake brand selfie pictures. Furthermore, viewers evaluate credibility of a brand selfie based on its composition, as well as its components such as brand, person and context. Even though marketers need to choose reasonably credible brand selfies to use for their promotions, little is known about how viewers assess the credibility of a brand selfie. Hence, this research aims to develop a scale to empirically measure brand selfie credibility from the viewer's perspective, and to identify the antecedents and outcomes of brand selfie credibility. The scale development followed established scale development methods (e.g., Churchill 1979; Gerbing and Anderson 1988). Based on exploratory qualitative and quantitative studies, this research project developed a 9-item scale to measure brand selfie credibility. Three dimensions identified through an exploratory qualitative study and confirmed by two expert panels are: brand selfie image trustworthiness, brand selfie congruence, and brand selfie meaning. This research also finds that brand selfie credibility is influenced by brand-related (consistency of the brand and clarity of the brand), person-related (altruistic motivation), and image-related (positive affect) antecedents. Additionally, brand selfie credibility impacts on purchase intention and positive word-of-mouth. This study provides a tool for marketers to understand consumers' perception of brand selfies and consumers' reactions. Marketers can identify how the brand selfie and its credibility can be leveraged for marketing purposes, and to choose credible brand selfie pictures for their marketing communication strategies. This is the first study to develop and validate the measures for brand

T. Lavan (✉) · U. Gottlieb · S. Tuzovic
Queensland University of Technology, Brisbane, QLD, Australia
e-mail: thusyanthy.vadivelu@hdr.qut.edu.au; udo.gottlieb@qut.edu.au; sven.tuzovic@qut.edu.au

R. Mulcahy
University of the Sunshine Coast, Maroochydore, QLD, Australia
e-mail: rmulcahy@usc.edu.au

J. Allen et al. (eds.), *Celebrating the Past and Future of Marketing and Discovery with Social Impact*, Developments in Marketing Science: Proceedings of the Academy of Marketing Science, https://doi.org/10.1007/978-3-030-95346-1_150

selfie credibility on social media which contributes to user-generated content, influencer-generated content, photographic credibility and branding literature.

Keywords Brand selfie · Credibility · User-generated content · Influencer-generated content

Cultural Accommodation: Does Online Sensory Marketing Count? Examining the Effects of Fashion Brands' Cultural Accommodation through Multisensory Website Design: An Abstract

Zhiying Ben, Hongfei Liu, Victoria-Sophie Osburg, and Vignesh Yoganathan

Abstract We study how foreign brands' cultural accommodation delivered through multisensory website design influences local consumers' perceptions and purchase decisions. We place particular emphasis on the Chinese fashion industry, where many non-Chinese brands suffer because they confront with a dilemma, between adapting to the local culture and retaining their western originality. Drawing upon theories of cultural accommodation and homophily bias, our experimental results indicate that foreign brands' use of cultural accommodating multisensory cues (both visual and auditory) in website design positively influence consumers' purchase intention, while the congruence of culturally accommodating multisensory cues also enhances of consumers' purchase intention to some extent. We also demonstrate the psychological mechanism in transmitting multisensory cues of cultural accommodation into purchase intention and identify the mediating roles of consumer-brand identification and brand image in this mechanism.

Our study takes a novel perspective to contribute to the emerging research stream of online multisensory marketing and contextualizes the application of multisensory cues in the increasingly digitized and international marketplace. Specifically, we identified the significant impact of the application of online multisensory cues on signaling brands' cultural accommodation effort and facilitating consumer purchase. Besides, we added new empirical evidence to effects of multisensory integra-

Z. Ben (✉) · H. Liu
University of Southampton, Southampton, UK
e-mail: z.ben@soton.ac.uk; hongfei.liu@soton.ac.uk

V.-S. Osburg
University of Montpellier, Montpellier, France
e-mail: vs.osburg@montpellier-bs.com

V. Yoganathan
University of Sheffield, Sheffield, UK
e-mail: v.yoganathan@sheffield.ac.uk

J. Allen et al. (eds.), *Celebrating the Past and Future of Marketing and Discovery with Social Impact*, Developments in Marketing Science: Proceedings of the Academy of Marketing Science, https://doi.org/10.1007/978-3-030-95346-1_151

tion and congruence on audiences' perceptions and identified the cultural accommodation through sensory cues attracting consumers' attention on the congruence between different senses. Finally, we advanced the understanding of homophily bias effects and demonstrate the mechanism of translating multisensory cues that carry messages of cultural accommodation into consumers' purchase intention. This highlights the significance of shared identity between consumers and a brand (i.e. consumer-brand identification) in developing consumers' evaluation and behavioral intention towards the brand. From a managerial perspective, we shed a new light on foreign brands' cultural accommodation strategies in local markets and suggest multisensory website design as a cost-effective avenue for delivering the brands' cultural accommodation effort.

Keywords Online sensory marketing · Cross-cultural marketing · Online retailing · Cultural accommodation · Homophily bias effects · Consumer-brand identification

Customer Engagement in Online Brand Communities, Value Co-creation and Co-destruction Directly and Indirectly Effects: An Abstract

Yi Bu, Park Thaichon, and Joy Parkinson

Abstract At present, customer engagement in brand communities and value co-creation have increasingly grown into two focal areas in marketing research (Merrilees 2016). This study aims to examines, in online brand communities, the direct and indirect relationship between customer engagement and value co-creation and value co-destruction. The purpose of this study is twofold: firstly, to examine the direct effects from customer engagement in online brand communities to value co-creation and co-destruction; and second, to explore the indirect mediating effects from brand resonance and attitudinal brand loyalty as well as the moderating effect from brand satisfaction in the online brand communities.

The quantitative method will be used to test the proposed model. An online questionnaire survey will be applied for gather data in online brand communities. Structure equation modelling with partial least squares (PLS-SEM) will be performed to examine both the measurement model and the structural model. Expected results are that the positive relationship between customer engagement in online brand communities and brand resonance, attitudinal brand loyalty, value co-creation and co-destruction (Hollebeek et al. 2019; Pansari and Kumar 2017; Ranjan and Read 2014). Brand resonance has a positive relationship with value co-creation and a negative relationship with value co-destruction. Attitudinal brand loyalty has positive relationship with value co-creation and a negative relationship with value co-destruction. In the proposed model, both brand resonance and attitudinal brand loyalty take the mediating roles, and brand satisfaction plays a moderating role.

This study provides a theoretical significance for further investigation of customer engagement in online brand communities, adds to the literature on brand

Y. Bu (✉) · P. Thaichon
Griffith University, Gold Coast, QLD, Australia
e-mail: yi.bu@griffithuni.edu.au; p.thaichon@griffith.edu.au

J. Parkinson
Griffith University, Brisbane, QLD, Australia
e-mail: j.parkinson@griffith.edu.au

J. Allen et al. (eds.), *Celebrating the Past and Future of Marketing and Discovery with Social Impact*, Developments in Marketing Science: Proceedings of the Academy of Marketing Science, https://doi.org/10.1007/978-3-030-95346-1_152

satisfaction, brand resonance and attitudinal brand loyalty, and will likely drive further research into value co-creation and co-destruction in the context of online brand communities. In particular, brand satisfaction, as a moderating variable, is introduced into the discussion of customer brand engagement in online community. It expands the theoretical research on customer brand engagement marketing and clarifies the important role of value co-creation and co-destruction (Quach and Thaichon 2017). The expected results would suggest brand marketers should focus more on customers' affective, cognitive, behaviour reflections, subtly using customer experience resource that leads to brand resonance and increases attitudinal brand loyalty, thereby inspiring value co-creation and avoiding value co-destruction (Thaichon et al. 2019).

Keywords Customer engagement · Online Brand Communities (OBC) · Brand resonance · Attitudinal brand loyalty · Value co-creation · Value co-destruction

Traditional Celebrity or Instafamous Starlet? The Role of Origin of Fame in Social Media Influencer Marketing: An Abstract

Rico Piehler, Michael Schade, Julia Sinnig, and Christoph Burmann

Abstract Marketers have started to recognize the potential of social media influencers (SMIs) and engage in SMI marketing, which is a strategy that uses the influence of SMIs as opinion leaders to drive consumers' brand awareness, brand image and brand-related behavior. In addition to SMI selection criteria such as number of followers, costs per post, engagement rate or audience characteristics, practitioners are also confronted with the decision problem of choosing the type of SMI based on their origin of fame, which refers to the way SMIs became known to their audience. Two types of SMIs can be distinguished based on their origin of fame. The first type is celebrities who became famous outside of social media (e.g., by being singers, actors or athletes). Because these SMIs have a non-social media origin of fame, they are referred to as "non-original SMIs". The second type is celebrities who became famous in social media (e.g., by presenting their lifestyle). Because these SMIs have a social media origin of fame (e.g., "instafamous"), they are referred to as "original SMIs".

To explain the effects of SMIs' origin of fame on social media users' purchase behavior, this study draws on the concept of identification. In this context, identification is defined as the adoption of attitudes and behaviors of media personae through the process of social influence. With similarity and wishful identification, two distinct types of identification have been discussed in the literature. While the object of similarity identification are media personae that are similar to actual self of the media user, the object of wishful identification are media personae that are similar to the ideal self of the media user. In which type of identification media users engage depends on their level of self-esteem. While the favorite media persona of

R. Piehler (✉)
Macquarie University, Sydney, NSW, Australia
e-mail: rico.piehler@mq.edu.au

M. Schade · J. Sinnig · C. Burmann
University of Bremen, Bremen, Germany
e-mail: mschade@uni-bremen.de; jsinnig@uni-bremen.de; burmann@uni-bremen.de

J. Allen et al. (eds.), *Celebrating the Past and Future of Marketing and Discovery with Social Impact*, Developments in Marketing Science: Proceedings of the Academy of Marketing Science, https://doi.org/10.1007/978-3-030-95346-1_153

media users with low self-esteem is closer to their ideal self (i.e., wishful identification), the favorite media persona of media users with high self-esteem is closer to their actual self (i.e., similarity identification).

This study investigates if social media users' self-esteem moderates the effect of SMIs' origin of fame on social media users' purchase behavior. It thus aims to examine the effectiveness of the type of SMI based on social media users' self-esteem. The results of an online experiment with 129 social media users in Russia reveal that non-original SMIs affect social media users' purchase intentions stronger than original SMIs if social media users have low self-esteem. In contrast, original SMIs affect social media users' purchase intentions stronger than non-original SMIs if social media users have high self-esteem.

Keywords Social media · Social media influencer · Influencer marketing · Origin of fame · Self-esteem

RTE Versus RTC Food Products: A Practice Theory Perspective of 'Meaning' in Food Consumption: An Abstract

Meenal Rai

Abstract Changing socio-economic environment in India has altered food consumption. Despite a promising market for packaged foods, understanding of consumers' behaviour for ready-to-eat (RTE) and ready-to-cook (RTC) food products is limited. Greater understanding of food consumption practices and socio-cultural dispositions in specific geographies will inform markets about food product design and development. The current study adopts a Practice theory lens to explore changes in routine food consumption in a select group of Indian middle-class households. 32 semi-structured interviews along with projective technique exercises were conducted with food provisioners. Observations were made during the home visit, and in shop along situations. Food and pantries were photographed.

The study finds that within the elements; meaning, materials and competence constituting a practice, the meaning usually governs the way the practice is engaged in. lifestyle changes have constrained the routinised performance of food provisioning. Food practitioners therefore use products that enable them to maintain their practices. Participants were found to accept and reject RTEs based on the meaning they attached to a specific context of food provisioning. While ready-to-cook type of food products are accepted in time and skill constrained situations, the same is not true for ready-to-eat packaged meals. Despite their ability to ease and expedite food provisioning, the RTE food products were rejected by both employed as well as at-home food provisioners. Apart from questioning the quality of ingredients provisioners' rejection for these also stemmed from relinquished care and control over food provisioning processes. Having incorporated part of herself into the end-product that embodies her emotions, the food provisioner derives pleasure and satisfaction from preparing the meal.

The performance of food provisioning is in accordance with the different goals and meanings attached to the contexts of food. Such a Practice theory perspective

M. Rai (✉)
Auckland University of Technology, Auckland, New Zealand
e-mail: meenal.rai@aut.ac.nz

J. Allen et al. (eds.), *Celebrating the Past and Future of Marketing and Discovery with Social Impact*, Developments in Marketing Science: Proceedings of the Academy of Marketing Science, https://doi.org/10.1007/978-3-030-95346-1_154

explains why participants in the current study were found using ready-to-eat food products like herb extracts and powders for use in performance of morning food related rituals but not for provisioning household meals. Thus, when the goal of a food provisioner is to engage in a food related health routine, the availability of ready food product (material) from the market, enables competence for engaging in the practice, whereas with regards food provisioning for the family, the goal involves, along with providing food, the provisioner's greater involvement in the production and serving of that meal, hence ready-to-eat food products are rejected in the performance of those practices. Lifestyle based constraints on meeting embodied meanings of food provisioning and food consumption are being managed by consumers with market offerings like RTC and RTE food products. However, by opting for and against RTE food products in different contexts of food provisioning, the food provisioners illustrate the importance of meaning in practice.

Keywords Ready-to-eat · Ready-to-cook · Practice theory · Consumer behaviour · Food-provisioning · Food-consumption

A Self-expansion Theory for Driving Tourist's Attitudes and Behavioral Intentions: An Abstract

Lan-Lung Luke Chiang, Chung-Ping Wu, Huang-Chu Chen, and Sonic Wu

Abstract With continuous changes in tourists' needs, destination marketers keep attempting to facilitate creative and satisfactory strategies in destinations which support their goals (e.g., create long-term successful pop-culture tourism). This suggests that a better understanding of the holistic perspective and the factors relevant for determining the complex relationship with regard to pop-culture tourism is needed. However, studies on the effects on psychological concepts from fans' perspective in pop culture phenomena are limited (Lee et al. 2008). Their importance has not been comprehensively investigated in the context of travel and tourism. In this study, the authors further extend self-expansion theory in the pop-culture tourism setting.

The self-expansion model mainly introduced a concept in which human motive for the desire to expand the self through the acquisition of resources, perspectives, and identities that help one's ability to achieve goals in conscious and unconscious processes (Aron and Aron 1986). The self-expansion model has two key dimensions: (1) self-expansion motivation, and (2) inclusion of close others in the self (Aron et al. 2005). Along with a concept, it is suggested that the self-expansion theory be applied into broader areas in which there are significant person-object relationships, such as environmental psychology, political psychology, and social psychology (Reimann and Aron 2009). By adopting self-expansion theory, this study argues that fans who are attached to the pop-star and involved in his and her activities are not just recipients of the pop-star's creative resources (e.g., music, films, and TV); they also actively invest their own resources in the pop-star so as to maintain their close relationship with the pop-star. As for pop-culture tourism, tourists driven by pop-culture mostly consist of zealous fans who seek some sort of experience associated with a particular pop-culture or media themes. Particularly, pop-star fans are a unique group of individuals as many are highly involved with and have an emotional attachment to their pop-star (Fiske 1992)

L.-L. L. Chiang (✉) · C.-P. Wu · H.-C. Chen · S. Wu
Yuan Ze University, Taoyuan City, Taiwan
e-mail: lukech@saturn.yzu.edu.tw; s1059412@mail.yzu.edu.tw; s1049411@mail.yzu.edu.tw; s1049411@mail.yzu.edu.tw

J. Allen et al. (eds.), *Celebrating the Past and Future of Marketing and Discovery with Social Impact*, Developments in Marketing Science: Proceedings of the Academy of Marketing Science, https://doi.org/10.1007/978-3-030-95346-1_155

Accordingly, the authors in this study successfully applied self-expansion theory as a theoretical foundation to bridge the relationship between fans and destinations - pop-stars' homelands. Thus, findings of this study provide a more in-depth understanding of international fans and tourists' emotional and behavioral responses.

Keywords Pop-culture tourism · Self-expansion theory · Attitudes · Behavioral intentions

What Causes Users' Unwillingness to Spend Money for In-App Purchases in Mobile Games?: An Abstract

Imam Salehudin and Frank Alpert

Abstract Worldwide In-app Purchase (IAP) revenues reached almost US$37 billion in 2017 and are expected to double in 2020. Yet, only 5% of total app users make any IAPs and 70% of those in-app purchases come from big spenders or 'Whales' who account for only the top 10% of the paying users. *What causes mobile game players to be unwilling to spend money on in-app purchases (IAP)?* We attempt to answer this question with a multi-stage mixed-method study combining qualitative and quantitative approaches. First, we developed and validated a new construct of perceived aggressive monetisation which combined psychological reactance with fairness theory to describe users' inherent aversion to excessive effort to monetise through the in-app purchase business model. Second, *we tested the research model using a survey of 527 US and 526 Australian mobile gamers. Third, we conducted a scenario-based experiment with 264 US mobile gamers to test the replicability of the survey findings in a more specific context, as well as test additional hypotheses on the effects of marketing tactics to user's willingness to spend money on IAPs.* The findings supported our conceptualisation of the IAP spending decision as *a separate decision mechanism between conversion (i.e., to spend money or not) and the size of spending (i.e., how much money to spend). User* self-control and perceived aggressive monetisation act as hurdles preventing the initial spending. However, once the user makes the initial spending, the actual size of IAP spending is an impulsive mechanism explained by users' time-spent playing and exposure to marketing tactics. A follow up field experiment of 264 US mobile gamers showed how the marketing tactics of app publisher can influence IAP spending for loot boxes -an infamous type of IAP- by manipulating the size of the offers, mode of currency, and informed probability for the loot box.

I. Salehudin (✉)
University of Indonesia, West Java, Indonesia
e-mail: imams@ui.ac.id

F. Alpert
University of Queensland, Brisbane, QLD, Australia
e-mail: f.alpert@business.qu.edu.au

J. Allen et al. (eds.), *Celebrating the Past and Future of Marketing and Discovery with Social Impact*, Developments in Marketing Science: Proceedings of the Academy of Marketing Science, https://doi.org/10.1007/978-3-030-95346-1_156

Keywords In-app purchase · Perceived aggressive monetization · Willingness to pay · Mobile games · Hurdle model

How to Choose the Fitting Partner in Sustainability Sponsorship? A Decision Model Integrating Multiple Fit Dimensions

Guido Grunwald, Jürgen Schwill, and Anne-Marie Sassenberg

Abstract Numerous studies and practical examples point to the high relevance of sustainability as a communication message in sponsoring. The core of such a sustainability sponsorship concept is the involvement of sustainable partners to promote common but also individualized goals. For example, a company can improve its image through social or eco-sponsoring, while at the same time providing publicity to its sponsoring activities. In this article a model for the selection of suitable sponsoring partners is developed taking into account multiple fit dimensions. For each fit dimension specific questions are formulated in order to obtain information about the degree of fit. The model can be used to select suitable sponsoring partners and also to derive communication strategies and measures to position sponsoring partners sustainably.

Keywords Sustainability sponsorship · Sponsoring · Sustainability marketing · Fit construct · Fit measurement · Decision model

Introduction

The topic of sustainability has a growing influence on almost all sectors of the economy and thus also on the sponsoring industry. Studies show that sustainability is becoming increasingly important for those interested in sports and that sustainability measures are becoming increasingly relevant for sports clubs such as football

G. Grunwald (✉)
Osnabrück University of Applied Sciences, Lingen (Ems), Germany

J. Schwill
Brandenburg Technical University of Applied Sciences, Brandenburg an der Havel, Germany
e-mail: juergen.schwill@th-brandenburg.de

A.-M. Sassenberg
University of Southern Queensland, Springfield, QLD, Australia
e-mail: anne-marie.sassenberg@usq.edu.au

J. Allen et al. (eds.), *Celebrating the Past and Future of Marketing and Discovery with Social Impact*, Developments in Marketing Science: Proceedings of the Academy of Marketing Science, https://doi.org/10.1007/978-3-030-95346-1_157

clubs (AdvantPlanning 2013). At the same time, the increasing ineffectiveness of traditional forms of communication, (e.g., media advertising) as well as the growing interest in various target groups, are arousing more and more interest of companies in sponsoring. Since sponsoring enables companies to target specific groups for the promotion of their products and services, combining sponsorship with sustainability marketing is a promising approach for companies (Putzing and Menn 2014, p. 340).

In this context, sustainability sponsorship can be understood as the (financial) promotion of projects and initiatives for the balanced pursuit of ecological, social and economic goals. This is either aimed at reducing the impact of human activity on the natural environment and/or contributing to solving societal problems while generating economic added value for both the sponsor and the endorsed sponsee in the medium to long term (Putzing and Menn 2014, p. 341). The sponsee in this study refers to the sponsoring objects, such as the sports club, sport organization, sports event and sport celebrity. For example, a company can improve its image through social or eco-sponsoring, while at the same time providing publicity to its sponsoring activities.

In spite of the potential to target consumers and reach sustainability goals, sponsoring activities can only be found in a small number of sustainability reports (AdvantPlanning 2013). This indicates that many sponsors have not yet adequately coordinated their sustainability and sponsoring activities. In addition, in many cases the sponsoring activities of the individual sponsors lose their selectivity. The distinction between the individual sponsors is becoming increasingly difficult for the target group and the image gain for the sponsors remains marginal (Putzing and Menn 2014, p. 340). It is thus vital for sponsor managers to rely on specific critieria to ensure building sustainability sponsorship. This development requires criteria that simplify selecting the appropriate partner and projects in sustainability for both the sponsor and the sponsee; the criteria also need to assist in choosing sponsoring and to evaluate sustainability sponsoring activities. On this basis, targeted communication and a desired effect of sponsoring can be achieved (MEC 2009).

Against this background, the aim of this paper is to develop a decision model that integrates criteria for the comprehensive assessment of sponsoring partners and measures for sustainability activities. By applying these criteria, the fit between characteristics of the sponsor and sponsee for given sustainability marketing goals of the respective party needs to be recorded multi-dimensionally. The model can be used both for the selection of partners and for designing communication strategies and measures to position sponsoring partners sustainably.

The next section explains the fundamentals and mechanisms of sponsorship, drawing on theories that can be used to explain the various effects of sponsoring. From these theoretical considerations, relevant fit dimensions for sustainability sponsorship are derived. For the purpose of capturing a comprehensive understanding of the relationships between the various sponsoring partners, several fit dimensions are considered drawing on the relevant sponsoring and sustainability marketing literature. Each fit dimension is deconstructed into multiple fit criteria in order to fully reflect all relevant factors that can contribute to the relationships between sustainability sponsoring partners. Finally, the decision model for sustainability sponsorship is conceptualized. A conclusion and avenues for future reasearch are provided in the final chapter.

Fundamentals and Mechanisms of Sponsorship

The mechanisms responsible for attitude change during sponsorship include: the brand image transfer model, balance theory and social identity theory (Fink et al. 2009). Since sustainability partnerships involve relationships in which the quality of each partner prior to entering into the relationship is uncertain, further explanatory approaches such as the information economy approach and the principal agent theory are of relevance (Grunwald and Schwill 2017a, pp. 52–57).

Brand image transfer literature is dominated by discussions on the transfer of positive brand images between the endorsed sponsee and the sponsor (Gwinner et al. 2009; McCracken 1989; Miller and Laczniak 2011; Pope et al. 2009). The aim of the brand image transfer process, as described in these theories, is to transfer positive images between the sponsee, such as a sport celebrity or an event, to the sponsored brand image (Gwinner et al. 2009; McCracken 1989). Consistent with the brand association theory (Keller 1993), the connectivity between the sponsee and the sponsor means that the specific attributes of the sponsee and the sponsor affect each other (Henseler et al. 2009; Rossiter and Bellman 2005). McCracken's (1989) work focuses on the sport celebrity as a sponsee and offers a foundation to investigate the transfer effect of the brand image of the sport celebrity. Studies investigating the event as a sponsee indicate the transfer of the event brand image to the sponsored brand image (Gwinner 1997; Kim and Kim 2009). In line with this reasoning it is thus possible that when a sponsee aligns with a sustainable project the positive image may transfer to the associated sponsoring partners.

Balance theory can be valuable in sustainability sponsorship, since it considers ways to construct positive associations in consumers' minds about sustainability. The theory states that consumers perceive elements in their environment as appearing in groups of three, and desire the relationship between the elements in the triad to be in balance (Basil and Herr 2006; Cornwell and Coote 2005; Crimmins and Horn 1996; Pracejus et al. 2004; Rifon et al. 2004). Balance theory in sponsorship is used to describe the incentive of an individual to develop a positive attitude towards the sponsor (Basil and Herr 2006; Crimmins and Horn 1996; Dean 2002; Pracejus et al. 2004; Rifon et al. 2004;). Furthermore, when the pre-existing attitudes towards the two entities were positive, the attitudes in the triad will be further enhanced toward the triad (Basil and Herr 2006). The perceived fit between the elements in the triad also enhance perceptions regarding the strength of the relationship. Therefore, by aligning with a sponsee that associates with a sustainable project, the sponsoring can generate a "halo effect". The consumer may thus seek balance, by re-examining their pre-exiting attitudes towards the sponsor in a positive direction, in order to strive for consistency and resolve incongruent thoughts (Cornwell and Coote 2005), resulting in the creation of goodwill towards associated sponsoring partners (Dean 2002).

Social identity develops primarily from important group membership (Hogg and Terry 2000). A group based on a particular system of values, to which the consumer is susceptible, and is likely to be a group of enduring importance to the individual (Ashforth and Mael 1989; Brewer 2001; Turner 1999). Scholars further group members in terms of in-groups and out-groups (Hogg et al. 1990). In-groups refer to people who are members of a specific group, while out-groups represent people who are not considered members of that group. As a positive self-esteem is derived from group membership, people compare others on the basis of group membership (Hogg et al. 1990). Often, people classify members of an out-group as lesser than members of an in-group (Hogg and Terry 2000). These findings may implicate how consumers perceive sustainability sponsorship. For example, when the consumer perceived himself/herself and the sponsee that aligns with a sustainable project as part of a team, (i.e. an in-group member) and the sponsor aligns with that specific sponsee, the consumer reconciles the positive feelings about the sponsee with the sponsor, thus contributing to sustainability sponsorship.

Information economics refer to the performance characteristics between potential partners in a sustainability sponsorship relationship/agreement and deals with partners in different situations, such as providers and consumers. This resulted in an increasing challenge to evaluate the relevant relationship qualities of a sponsoring partner fit (Bruhn 2016, pp. 24–30). Information economics distinguishes between search, experience and credence attributes (Weiber and Adler 1995; Wirtz and Lovelock 2016, pp. 56–60). Search attributes represent the previous activities of companies or organizations in the field of sustainability. Experience attributes refer to the personal experience of sponsor partners, and can thus only be assessed from third parties. Credence attributes show the ability of the sponsor to fulfill the promised support that can not be estimated perfectly either before or after entering into the relationship. For example, funding a promotion of an environental event cannot be assessed at reasonable cost before or even after entering the sponsorship agreement. It is thus evident that partners involved in sustainability sponsorship should screen and signal brand agents. Screening and signaling can be used to reduce uncertainty in partner selection (Bruhn 2016, pp. 26–28). Above all, the risk of potential incompatibilities in the fit dimensions can be counteracted in this way. Signaling implies providing information from the better to the less informed partner. Screening is the search for information emanating from the less informed partner.

The principal agent theory examines the cooperative relationships between principal (e.g., the sponsoring partner) and agent (e.g., the sponsee) with regard to potential conflicts and solutions. It is assumed that the sponsee possesses knowledge advantages over the sponsoring partner (information asymmetry), which they can exploit selfishly at the expense of the other party – also referred to as partner costs (Weber and Schäffer 2016, p. 28). Both signaling and screening measures can be applied by all associated partners in sustainability sponsorship. For example, a company may, as part of its signaling activities, offer itself as a suitable sponsor, or it can conduct market research as part of screening measures to find suitable partners for sustainability sponsorship.

Derivation of Fit-Dimensions

As can be deduced from the theories outlined above, successful sustainability sponsoring depends on the suitability of the partners involved. The partners typically involved in sustainability sponsorship are shown in Fig. 1. Herein, the arrows designate the respective relationships between the partners, which can be used as a basis to derive fit dimensions.

As part of a sponsorship engagement, the sponsor (e.g., a brand manufacturer or a retail company) provides financial and, or human resource support to existing projects or develops new projects in collaboration with the sponsee. The sponsee, in turn, collaborates with a non-profit organization (e.g. an environmental protection organization), and creates publicity for the project and supports it through staff and existing know-how (Putzing and Menn 2014, p. 342). Thus, the sponsor can enhance the brand image, gain the image of a socio-ecological sponsorship together with the publicity of sport sponsoring and the sponsee, at the same time increase its sponsoring revenues (Heine 2009, pp. 69–72; Putzing and Menn 2014, p. 342). This project may involve several sponsors; for instance, several brand manufacturers can provide support for the implementation of the sustainability project. The target groups of the sponsor(s), the sponsee and/or the nonprofit organization (such as consumers and sports fans) are all associated with the project.

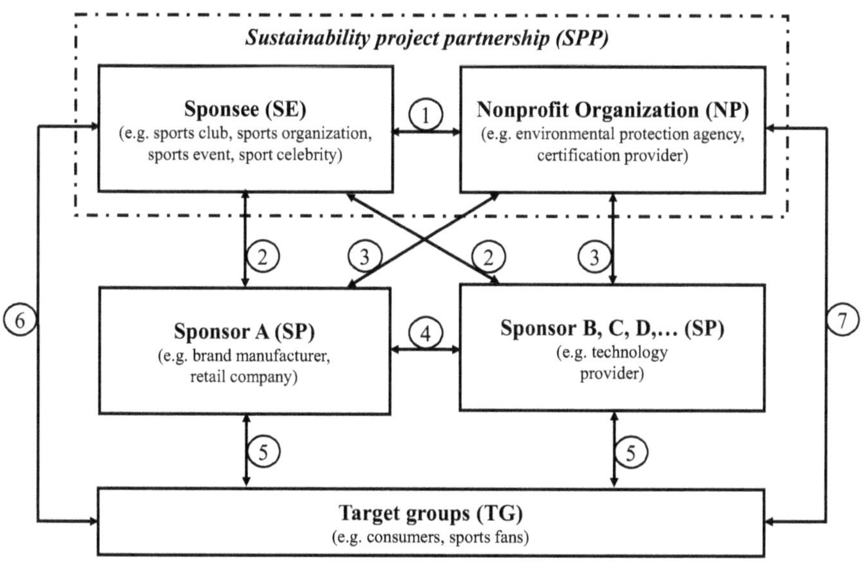

Fig. 1 Parnters and partner-relations in sustainability sponsoring

The Fit Principle

Fit relates to the subjective assessment of the relationship between sponsorship partners (Baumgarth 2000, p. 48), and is used to select relationship partners in sustainability sponsoring (Nitschke 2006, pp. 28–31). The term fit is interchangeably used in previous research to refer to congruence, relatedness, match-up or compatibility. The evaluation of the relationship refers to the fit perceived by the sponsorship partner with respect to certain characteristics. The fit reflects the similarity or the degree of agreement between the characteristics of the relationship partners (Cornwell 1995; Olson and Thjømøe 2011; Rifon et al. 2004; Speed and Thompson 2000; Walzel and Schubert 2018, pp. 124–125).

A high fit has a positive, reinforcing influence on the sponsoring effects, such as: improved image transfer (e.g., Becker-Olsen and Hill 2006; Gwinner and Eaton 1999; Meenaghan 2001; Menon and Kahn 2003); higher recall effect (Johar and Pham 1999); positive consumer attitudes (e.g., Ellen et al. 2000; McDaniel 1999; Speed and Thompson 2000); and sympathy towards the sponsor (Haley 1996). Lastly, competitive partnerships that are perceived as congruent can also result in competitive advantages and higher market shares (Amis et al. 1999; Chandon et al. 2000).

Dimensions of the Fit Principle

Sustainability sponsorship involves several relationship partners interacting on several relationship levels (see Fig. 1). A multi-dimensional modeling of the fit construct therefore seems appropriate (Bruhn 2018, pp. 373–380; Olson and Thjømøe 2011; Sturm 2011, pp. 15–18). The literature on the fit principle can be grouped into two dimensions, including overall fit and specific fit. In this study overall fit refers to the congruence between all or the various levels of a relationship between all sponsoring partners. Specific fit dimensions relate to attributes that affect a specific individual relationship between partners; for example, the fit between a sponsor and a sport celebrity.

Overall fit dimensions include: responsibility fit; attitude fit and regional fit. *Responsibility fit* seems particularly important in sustainability sponsorship. Partner selection should take into account the ethical obligation of partners to assume responsibility for ecological and social issues and to contribute to solving issues beyond merely pursuing their own economic interests. If recipients have a similar attitude towards the relationship partners actively involved in sustainability sponsorship, then there is an *attitude fit*. A positive attitude towards the sponsor can also transfer to the sponsee (brand image transfer and spill-over effect). If relationship partners share the same regional origin, they may perceive a *regional fit*. For example, if a company with a regional identity supports a geographically located social project (e.g., a local cultural event), then there is a strong regional or local anchoring that the target group may find appropriate.

Specific fit dimensions can include: target group fit; identity fit; image fit; knowledge fit; strategy fit and cultural fit. A *target group fit* exists when relationship partners have similar areas of interest and preferences (Cotting 2000, p. 33). The more pronounced the overlap of the target groups, the more likely the brand and the transfer between partners (Sturm 2011, p. 18). There is an *identity fit* when the characteristics of the brands are judged equally by the relationship partners (Ringle 2006, pp. 32–33). If, for example, different stakeholders evaluate a product as ecologically compatible, it can be assumed that there is a high level of product identity with regard to the fulfillment of ecological standards. An *image fit* occurs when the set of brand associations of the partners coincide. This is the case, for example, when relationship partners are characterized by congruent representations (Gwinner 1997, pp. 152–153). In addition, a brand image transfer can occur if the relationship partners communicate their images to third parties (e.g., customers). If companies use their resources to solve certain environmental or social problems, this knowledge can justify a *knowledge fit*. For example, companies can communicate knowledge regarding their environmentally friendly brands. The longer a partnership between sponsor and sponsee exists the more the two relationship partners are perceived as matching each other (Walzel and Schubert 2018, p. 126). The *strategy fit* is characterized by the consistent implementation of an offensive strategy orientation or a proactive approach regard sustainable action (Grunwald and Schwill 2017b, p. 1369). Strategy fit is based on *cultural fit*, which is characterized by the fact that relationship partners share a common cultural foundation consisting of matching norms (Grunwald and Schwill 2017a, p. 322).

Conceptualizing a Decision Model for Sustainability Sponsorship

The fit dimensions can be analyzed based on the information received via signaling and screening. Where appropriate, further information (e.g., from associations, consumer organizations or individual companies) should be obtained in order to clarify specific aspects relating to individual fit dimensions. The analysis can be supported by answering fit-specific questions reflecting various fit criteria as shown in Table 1. Answers to these questions provide information that can be used as a basis for further steps in the decision-making process of partner selection.

Selection criteria for determining a fit relationship between partners are: existing goals, power, legitimacy, commitment, urgency of claims and relationship quality (Grunwald and Schwill 2017a, pp. 22–29 and pp. 74–78). Potential *goals* of relationship partners in the context of sustainability sponsorship can include financial support, image and reputation. *Power* includes a social influence that enables relationship partners to successfully prevail against others in conflicts of interest. Power

Table 1 Analysis of overall and specific fit dimensions

Overall fit dimensions	
Responsibility fit (relevant for all relationship levels 1–7)	What values does the potential relationship partner have? Does the possible relationship partner show a fundamental interest in sustainability? How does that express itself? Is the potential relationship partner committed to pursuing sustainable principles?
Attitude fit (relevant for all relationship levels 1–7)	What attitude does the potential partner have regarding sustainability? What is the attitude of the potential relationship partner in relation to other actors involved in sustainability sponsoring?
Regional fit (relevant for all relationship levels 1–7)	Is the potential partner regionally located? What is the regional identity of the potential relationship partner?
Specific fit dimensions	
Target group fit (especially relationship levels 5, 6, 7)	Does the potential relationship partner have similar target groups? Will sustainability sponsorship contribute to the joint solution of social or environmental problems? Can a target group-related connection to a funding area be established?
Identity fit (especially relationship levels 2–7)	Are characteristic features of a product, a brand, a person or other reference objects judged the same by the potential relationship partners? Do the potential partners identify themselves with sustainability principles?
Image fit (especially relationship levels 5, 6, 7)	Does the potential relationship partner have similar affective associations with regard to products, brands or organizations? Does the image in relation to subjects or objects match from the point of view of the relationship partners?
Knowledge fit (especially relationship levels 2, 3, 4)	Does the potential relationship partner have the know-how to solve environmental and/or social problems? Does the potential partner have sufficient resources to solve ecological and/or social problems?
Strategy fit (especially relationship levels 3, 4)	What strategy does the potential relationship partner pursue? Are sustainability principles anchored in the strategy? Is the strategy offensive or is it possible to identify long-term proactive behavior?
Cultural fit (especially relationship levels 3, 4)	Which cultural foundation (values) does the possible relationship partner have? Is "sustainable thinking", "sustainable willingness" and "sustainable action" perceivable and how is it expressed?

can be based on various sources, such as access to scarce material resources or information, and can take various forms such as reward or punishment (French and Raven 1959). *Legitimacy* refers to the perceived degree of appropriateness and correctness of actions; for example, the conformity of action with existing values and norms or legal provisions (Theuvsen 2001, p. 8). *Commitment* refers to the relationship partners' amount of resources that is risked for achieving the goals. *Urgency* describes how quickly the company has to deal with the claims of its relationship partners, i.e. how time-critical the claims are (Theuvsen 2001, p. 9). *Relationship quality* can be defined as the degree of suitability of a relationship to fulfill the specific needs of the relationship partners (Hennig-Thurau and Klee 1997, p. 751).

Evaluating relationship quality seems less difficult between existing partners (ex-post analysis), than new and unknown partners (Hadwich 2003, p. 21). In this respect, when selecting the relationship partners in sustainability sponsorship, the future expected quality of the relationship also plays a role as a relationship fit criteria (anticipated relationship quality). Relationship marketing research suggests satisfaction, trust and commitment as independent but interrelated constructs forming the key components of relationship quality (Backhaus 2009, pp. 50–55; Hadwich 2003, pp. 22–25).

In the context of sponsoring relationships, first of all the relationship *satisfaction* should be considered. It is cross-transactional and represents a rather stable, non-performance-related judgment that can compensate or outlast individual negative experiences. In this respect, satisfaction with relationships must be distinguished from satisfaction with transactions, which refers to individual, completed transactions or – as in the context of interest here – to sponsor experiences (von Stenglin 2008, p. 53). If experience with relationship partners is lacking, the selection process is carried by a mental anticipation of desired results to be achieved by the sponsoring activity. For this, the anticipated satisfaction could be used as a decision criterion. Studies have shown that anticipated satisfaction with the achievement of goals (e.g., achieving image advantages through sustainability sponsorship) can act as an incentive for further action (Schmitz 2002, p. 115). Anticipation can also be derived from the definition of *trust* as outlined above. Trust can be used as a selection criterion before engaging in a relationship in order to be able to make judgments about the future performance and motivation of the relationship partners. As a relationship-relevant construct, *commitment* can generally be understood as a behavioral intention to make every effort to establish or maintain a relationship (Morgan and Hunt 1994, p. 23). In the context of sustainability sponsorship, commitment can be expressed, for example, by the psychological strong attachment of a sponsee to a sponsor.

The evaluation of the criteria can now be carried out individually by each relationship partner in their selection process. In order to achieve consensus-building in the selection process and to reduce complexity of the decision problem, especially in the case of multicriteria decision problems, the Analytic Hierarchy Process (AHP) can be applied to select the suitable relationship partner in sustainability sponsorship (Grunwald and Hempelmann 2017, pp. 74–86; Saaty 1980).

Figure 2 indicates the proposed decision funnel model to select the fitting partners for sustainability sponsorship.

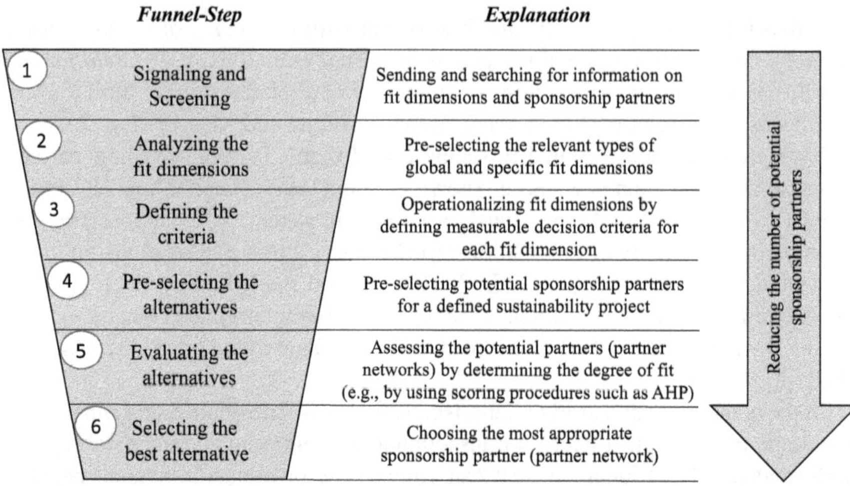

Funnel-Step
Explanation
1
Signaling and Screening
Sending and searching for information on fit dimensions and sponsorship partners
2
Analyzing the fit dimensions
Pre-selecting the relevant types of global and specific fit dimensions
3
Defining the criteria
Operationalizing fit dimensions by defining measurable decision criteria for each fit dimension
4
Pre-selecting the alternatives
Pre-selecting potential sponsorship partners for a defined sustainability project
5
Evaluating the alternatives
Assessing the potential partners (partner networks) by determining the degree of fit (e.g., by using scoring procedures such as AHP)
6
Selecting the best alternative
Choosing the most appropriate sponsorship partner (partner network)
Reducing the number of potential sponsorship partners

Fig. 2 Decision funnel for selecting partners in sustainability sponsorship

Conclusion

This paper review contributes to understanding the selection of suitable partners to ensure sustainability sponsorship. In particular, this study proposes a model that includes multiple fit dimensions, including: overall fit and specific fit. Three overall fit dimensions are identified as: responsibility fit, attitude fit and regional fit while specific fit dimensions incorporate: target group fit; identity fit; image fit; knowledge fit; strategy fit and cultural fit. Signaling and screening appear to be vital in the analysis of these fit dimensions. Further, specific selection criteria for the selection of a fit relationship between partners are identified as existing goals, power, legitimacy, commitment, urgency of claims and the existing relationship quality. The selection of suitable partners for sustainability sponsorship may be explained following a decision funnel. Sustainability sponsorship is a rapidly evolving area of marketing communication, with changing community values continuing to challenge marketers and consumers alike. Ongoing research into the selection of suitable sponsoring partners will prove highly beneficial in establishing a model for sponsor and brand managers to optimize sponsorship spending by applying various fit dimensions amongst all sponsor partner relationships. Future research can apply the model to select suitable sponsoring partners and also to derive communication strategies and measures to position sponsoring partners sustainably.

References

AdvantPlanning (2013). Nachhaltiges Sportsponsoring wird immer bedeutender! Retrieved from http://www.faspo.de/de/insights/d/uid-4dfbdb3b-c6c1-90c3-19a7-de12c2028f3d.html

Amis, J. M., Slack, T. & Berrett, T. (1999). Sport sponsorship as distinctive competence. *European Journal of Marketing, 33*(3/4), 250-272.

Ashforth, B. E., & Mael, F. (1989). Social identity theory and the organisation. *The Academy of Management Review, 14*(1), 20-39.

Backhaus, C. (2009). Beziehungsqualität in dienstleistungsnetzwerken. Theoretische fundierung und empirische analyse. Wiesbaden: Gabler.

Basil, D. Z., & Herr, P. M. (2006). Attitudinal balance and cause-related marketing: An empirical application of balance theory. *Journal of Consumer Psychology, 16*(4), 391-403.

Baumgarth, C. (2000). Methoden zur markenfitanalyse. *Planung & Analyse*, 5, 48-51.

Becker-Olsen, K. L., & Hill, R. P. (2006). The impact of sponsor fit on brand equity. The case of nonprofit service providers. *Journal of Service Research, 9*(1), 73-83.

Brewer, M. B. (2001). The many faces of social identity: Implications for political psychology, *Political Psychology, 22*(1), 115-125.

Bruhn, M. (2016). Relationship marketing. Das management von kundenbeziehungen, 5th ed., München: Vahlen.

Bruhn, M. (2018). Sponsoring: Systematische planung und integrativer einsatz, 6th ed., Wiesbaden: Gabler.

Chandon, P., Wansink, B., & Laurent, G. (2000). A benefit congruency framework of sales promotion effectiveness. *Journal of Marketing, 64*(4), 65-81.

Cornwell, T. B. (1995). Sponsorship-linked marketing development. *Sport Marketing Quarterly, 4*(4), 13-24.

Cornwell, B. T., & Coote, L. (2005). Corporate sponsorship of a cause: The role of identification in purchase identification in purchase intent. *Journal of Business Research, 58*(3), 268-276.

Cotting, P. (2000). Der sponsoring- und eventmarkting-ansatz (S&E): Dimensionen, wirkung, erfolgsfaktoren, planung und controlling. Linz: Rudolf Trauner.

Crimmins, J., & Horn, M. (1996). Sponsorship: From management ego trip to marketing success. *Journal of Advertising Research, 36*(4), 11-21.

Dean, D. H. (2002). Associating the corporation with a charitable event through sponsorship. *Journal of Advertising, 31*(4), 77-87.

Ellen, P. S., Mohr, L. A., & Webb, D. J. (2000). Charitable programs and the retailer: Do they mix? *Journal of Retailing, 76*(3), 393-406.

Fink, J. S., Parker, H. M., Brett, M., & Higgins, J. (2009). Off-field behavior of athletes and team identification: Using social identity theory and balance theory to explain fan reactions. *Journal of Sport Management, 23*, 142-155.

French, J. R. P., & Raven, B. (1959). The bases of social power. In: D. Cartwright (Ed.): *Studies in social power* (pp. 150-167). Ann Arbor: Institute for Social Research.

Grunwald, G., & Hempelmann, B. (2017). Angewandte marketinganalyse – Praxisbezogene konzepte und methoden zur betrieblichen entscheidungsunterstützung. Berlin: De Gruyter

Grunwald, G., & Schwill, J. (2017a). Beziehungsmarketing. Gestaltung nachhaltiger Geschäftsbeziehungen – Grundlagen und Praxis. Stuttgart: Schäffer-Poeschel.

Grunwald, G., & Schwill, J. (2017b). Nachhaltigkeitsmarketing: Ziele, strategien, instrumente, *Das Wirtschaftsstudium (wisu), 46*(12), 1364-1373.

Gwinner, K. P. (1997). A model of image creation and image transfer in event sponsorship. *International Marketing Review, 14*(3), 145-158.

Gwinner, K. P., & Eaton, J. (1999). Building brand image through event sponsorship. The role of image transfer. *Journal of Advertising, 28*(4), 47-57.

Gwinner, K. P., Larson, B. V., & Swanson, S. R. (2009). Image transfer in coporate event sponsorship: Assessing the impact of team identification and event-sponsor fit. *International Journal of Management & Marketing Research, 2*(1), 1-15.

Hadwich, K. (2003). Beziehungsqualität im relationship marketing. Konzeption und empirische analyse eines wirkungsmodells. Wiesbaden: Gabler.

Haley, E. (1996). Exploring the construct of organization as source. Consumers' understandings of organizational sponsorship of advocacy advertising. *Journal of Advertising, 25*(2), 19-35.

Heine, C. (2009). Gesellschaftliches engagement im Fußball. Berlin: Erich Schmidt.

Hennig-Thurau, T., & Klee, A. (1997). The impact of customer satisfaction and relationship quality on customer retention: A critical reassessment and model development. *Psychology & Marketing, 14*(8), 737-764.

Henseler, J., Wilson, B., & de Vreede, D. (2009). Can sponsorships be harmful for events? Investigating the transfer of associations from sponsors to events. *International Journal of Sports Marketing and Sponsorship, 10*(3), 47-54.

Hogg, M. A., & Terry, D. J. (2000). Social identity and self-categorisation processes in organisational contexts. *The Academy of Management Review, 25*(1), 121-140.

Hogg, M. A., Turner, J. C., & Davidson, B. (1990). Polarized norms and social frames of references: A test of the self-categorization theory of group polarization. *Basic and Applied Social Psychology, 11*(1), 77-100.

Johar, G. V., & Pham, M. T. (1999). Relatedness, prominence, and constructive sponsor identification. *Journal of Marketing Research, 36*(3), 299-312.

Keller, K. L. (1993). Conceptualizing, measuring, and managing customer-based brand equity. *Journal of Marketing, 57*(1), 1-22.

Kim, Y., & Kim, S. (2009). The relationships between team attributes, team identification and sponsor image. *International Journal of Sports Marketing & Sponsorship, 10*(3), 215-229.

McCracken, G. (1989). Who is the celebrity endorser? Cultural foundations of the endorsement process. *Journal of Consumer Research, 16*(3), 310-321.

McDaniel, S. R. (1999). An investigation of match-up effects in sport sponsorship advertising. The implications of consumer advertising schemas. *Psychology & Marketing, 16*(2), 163-184.

MEC (2009). Sensor Fußball & Bundesliga 2009. Retrieved from https://www.esb-online.com/fileadmin/dokumente/News/2009-11_Fussball-Sensor_2-pager.pdf

Meenaghan, T. (2001). Sponsorship and advertising: A comparison of consumer perceptions. *Psychology & Marketing, 18*(2), 191-215.

Menon, S., & Kahn, B. E. (2003). Corporate sponsorships of philanthropic activities. When do they impact perception of sponsor brand? *Journal of Consumer Psychology, 13*(3), 316-327.

Miller, F. M., & Laczniak, G. R. (2011). The ethics of celebrity-athlete endorsement: What happens when a star steps out of bounds? *Journal of Advertising Research, 51*(3), 499-510.

Morgan, R. M., & Hunt, S. D. (1994). The commitment-trust theory of relationship marketing. *Journal of Marketing, 58*(3), 20-38.

Nitschke, A. (2006). Event-marken-Fit und kommunikationswirkung. Eine längsschnittbetrachtung am beispiel der sponsoren der FIFA-Fußballweltmeisterschaft 2006™. Wiesbaden: Deutscher Universitäts-Verlag.

Olson, E. L., & Thjømøe, H. M. (2011). Explaining and articulating the fit construct in sponsorship. *Journal of Advertising, 40*(1), 57-70.

Pope, N., Voges, K. E., & Brown, M. (2009). Winning ways. *Journal of Advertising, 38*(2), 5-20.

Pracejus, J. W., Olsen, G. D., & Brown, N. (2004). On the prevalence and impact of vague quantifiers in the advertising of cause-related marketing (CRM). *Journal of Advertising, 32*(4), 19-28.

Putzing, F., & Menn, A. (2014). Nachhaltigkeitssponsoring im sport: Chancen, risiken und nutzen für akteure und stakeholder. In: A. Hildebrandt (Ed.): *CSR und sportmanagement* (pp. 337-352). Berlin, Heidelberg: Springer.

Rifon, N. J., Choi, S. M., Trimble, C. S., & Li, H. (2004). Congruence effects in sponsorship: The mediating role of sponsor credibility and consumer attributions of sponsor motive. *Journal of Advertising, 33*(1), 29-42.

Ringle, T. (2006). Strategische identitätsorientierte markenführung. Mit fallstudien aus der automobilindustrie. Wiesbaden: Deutscher Universitäts-Verlag.

Rossiter, J. R., & Bellman, S. (2005). Marketing communications: Theory and applications. *Australasian Marketing Journal, 13*, 77-80.
Saaty, T. L. (1980). The analytic hierarchy process. New York: McGraw-Hill.
Schmitz, G. (2002). Die Zufriedenheit von Versicherungsvertretern als unternehmerische Zielgröße. Stellenwert, Erfassungskonzept und empirische Befunde. Wiesbaden: Deutscher Universitäts-Verlag.
Speed, R., & Thompson, P. (2000). Determinants of sports sponsorship response. *Journal of the Academy of Marketing Science, 28*(2), 226-238.
von Stenglin, A. (2008). Commitment in der Dienstleistungsbeziehung. Entwicklung eines integrierten Erklärungs- und Wirkungsmodells. Wiesbaden: Gabler
Sturm, H.-J. (2011). Markenfit und Markenwirkung. Theoretische modellierung, methodische Validierung und empirische befunde. Wiesbaden: Gabler.
Theuvsen, L. (2001). Stakeholder-management – Möglichkeiten des Umgangs mit Anspruchsgruppen. Münsteraner Arbeitspapiere zum Nonprofit-Sektor, No. 16. Wiesbaden: Leske+Budrich.
Turner, J. C. (1999). Some current issues in research on social identity and self-categorization theories. In: N. Ellemers, R. Spears, & B. Doosje (Eds.): *Social identity* (pp. 6-34). Oxford: Blackwell.
Walzel, S., & Schubert, M. (2018). Sportsponsoring. Grundlagen, Konzeption und wirkungen. Berlin: Springer Gabler.
Weber, J., & Schäffer, U. (2016). Einführung in das controlling. 15th ed., Stuttgart: Schäffer-Poeschel.
Weiber, R., & Adler, J. (1995). Informationsökonomisch begründete Typologisierung von Kaufprozessen. *Zeitschrift für Betriebswirtschaftliche Forschung, 47*(1), 43-65.
Wirtz, J., & Lovelock, C. H. (2016). Services marketing. People, technology, strategy, 8th ed., New Jersey: World Scientific.

When Calorie Counters Influence Food Choices: An Abstract

Ben Lowe, Diogo Souza-Monteiro, and Iain Fraser

Abstract Nutrition labels are displayed on an individual product-by-product basis and are designed to simplify the decision making process by making such labels easier to understand. Despite being intuitively simple, the evidence for the effectiveness of such labels in reducing obesity and other food related health conditions is mixed. Digital technologies that present information in simpler, more accessible ways are increasingly demanded by consumers, yet we know little about how they impact decision making. One way to assist consumer processing of the available nutritional information is to present it in a more aggregated format (e.g., by basket) to overcome numeracy biases. To see how such aggregated nutritional information impacted food choices we designed an online shopping experiment which presented consumers with aggregated calorie information and compared the choices made to those with individual product nutritional information (and a control group with no nutritional information). We also looked at the impact of time pressure (no time pressure versus time pressure) and shop type (3-day fill-in shop versus 5-day full shop). The experiment was run on two groups of people, including a general sample of the UK population and a subset of this population who had an existing health condition. The results show the calorie counter leads to a reduction in the amount of calories chosen by about 9%. This is comparable to some estimates of the effectiveness of the UK's 20% sugar tax (5%). Results were moderated by whether or not the respondent had an existing health condition, shopping duration and time pressure (which nullified the effect of any nutritional information). The findings illustrate that such technologies hold a great deal of promise in affecting food choice but further research is needed in the field to observe what happens in more realistic settings. There is also a need to study what is being *consumed* rather than what is being *bought*.

B. Lowe (✉) · I. Fraser
University of Kent, Canterbury, UK
e-mail: b.lowe@kent.ac.uk; i.m.fraser@kent.ac.uk

D. Souza-Monteiro
Newcastle University, Newcastle, UK
e-mail: diogo.souza-monteiro@newcastle.ac.uk

J. Allen et al. (eds.), *Celebrating the Past and Future of Marketing and Discovery with Social Impact*, Developments in Marketing Science: Proceedings of the Academy of Marketing Science, https://doi.org/10.1007/978-3-030-95346-1_158

Keywords Digital health technologies · Calorie counter · Numeracy bias · Food choice

Innovation and Adoption in Emerging Industrial Markets: The Role of Trust and Commitment in Interfirm Relationships: An Abstract

Mayoor Mohan, Munyaradzi Nyadzayo, and Riza Casidy

Abstract While business-to-business (B2B) firms proactively pursue global opportunities, doing business in emerging markets (EMs) obligates B2B managers to strategize specifically around the conditions prevalent in such settings (Mohan et al. 2018; Simões et al. 2015).

B2B marketing research has made significant inroads into examining emerging market (EM) phenomenon, which as the theoretical and empirical evidence shows, operates differently than developed markets. This is especially true of interfirm relationship dynamics, where social contracts, local culture, unique institutions, and special forms of relationships (e.g., Guanxi in China) that are unique to EMs require distinct relationship management protocols. However, our understanding of how interfirm relationships in EM settings influence one firm's (i.e., supplier) decision to be innovative and another firm's (i.e., customer) decision to adopt innovations is lacking. This is a significant concern as innovation decision making among suppliers and customers is important for both multinationals and domestic firms doing business in EMs because of its influence on firms' innovation, relational, and performance prospects (Wu et al. 2016).

The purpose of this research, therefore, is to addresses how interfirm relationship dynamics among suppliers and customers in EMs influences key innovation-related decisions. Specifically, relying on commitment-trust theory (Morgan and Hunt 1994), the current research examines the relationship between supplier innovativeness and a customer's innovation adoption behaviors among Chinese B2B firms.

M. Mohan (✉)
Virginia Commonwealth University, Richmond, VA, USA
e-mail: mmohan@vcu.edu

M. Nyadzayo
University of Wollongong in Dubai, Dubai, UAE
e-mail: munyarnyadzayo@uowdubai.ac.ae

R. Casidy
Macquarie University, Sydney, NSW, Australia
e-mail: riza.casidy@mq.edu.au

J. Allen et al. (eds.), *Celebrating the Past and Future of Marketing and Discovery with Social Impact*, Developments in Marketing Science: Proceedings of the Academy of Marketing Science, https://doi.org/10.1007/978-3-030-95346-1_159

This social exchange perspective suggests that implied social contracts between B2B partners in EMs can establish a powerful mechanism that establishes norms and expectations in a relationship (Lee et al. 2015; Morgan and Hunt 1994). This regulating force or social capital includes relational resources like trust and commitment (Ireland et al. 2002), which can influence a customer's ad hoc innovation adoption decisions (Asare et al. 2016).

Specifically, data collected from a large sample of top-level Chinese B2B executives shows that when interfirm communications are weak, supplier innovativeness can serve as a basis on which customers build trust in a supplier. This is due to the voluntary, innovative investments that a supplier commits that can benefit a customer. This, in turn, forges a reciprocal obligation or commitment on the part of customers which manifests in favorable adoption decisions. Overall, the findings present a unique picture of how the relationship management in EMs has a bearing on firms' innovation-related decisions.

Keywords Innovativeness · Innovation adoption · Relationship marketing · Emerging markets

Pretension of Morality: Stakeholders, Shared Values, and Perceived Corporate Hypocrisy: An Abstract

Saheli Goswami and Gargi Bhaduri

Abstract Corporations, as moral agents, are responsible to choose ethical ends beyond legal compliances. Corporate moral responsibilities (CMR) focus on stakeholder relationships and explain corporations' core obligations towards stakeholders (Hormio 2017). However, often, such CMR are pledged by corporations as mere window-dressings and are followed with contradictory actions (Ha-Brookshire 2017). Corporations, being inconsistent between their moral responsibility assertions and actions, create perceptions of corporate hypocrisy (PCH: Goswami et al. 2018) amongst stakeholders. Accordingly, PCH undermines their attitudes and beliefs, and in turn threatens corporations' reputation, social standing, economic performance, and stakeholder relationships. Given the importance and critical consequences of PCH (Goswami and Bhaduri 2021), this research analyzes how PCH might be variably evoked in different types of stakeholders, i.e., corporations' consumers, and employees, based on their shared moral values when experiencing an inconsistency between CMR pledges and actual doings. A 2 (stakeholder types: retail consumers/retail employees) × 2 (corporation name variance: ABD/XYZ) × 4 (text variance: version 1/version 2/version 3/version 4) between-subjects experiment was designed and 321 stakeholders participated in this study. The results indicate that retail employees (more than consumers) perceive higher shared value with the corporation's moral responsibility pledges. However, when corporations fail to follow up to their pledges, these retail employees are more negatively influenced than consumers, leading to higher PCH. The study findings make theoretical contributions to expand PCH literature and draw the industry's attention to the importance of internal marketing initiatives to communicate with moral responsibility initiatives employees and meet their needs to reduce PCH. With the growing trend of value-based consumers and employees seeking employers with high moral values,

---

S. Goswami (✉)
University of Rhode Island, Kingston, RI, USA
e-mail: sgoswami@uri.edu

G. Bhaduri
Kent State University, Kent, OH, USA
e-mail: gbhaduri@kent.edu

J. Allen et al. (eds.), *Celebrating the Past and Future of Marketing and Discovery with Social Impact*, Developments in Marketing Science: Proceedings of the Academy of Marketing Science, https://doi.org/10.1007/978-3-030-95346-1_160

the findings not only establish the need for value-based marketing but also indicate the negative implications of a lack thereof.

Keywords Stakeholders · Corporate hypocrisy · Shared values · Moral responsibility

Social Responsibility of Apparel: A Study of Gen Z: An Abstract

Lauren Copeland and Sphoorthy Masa

Abstract Since their expectations are consistent with the evolution of the market, it is essential to explore Gen Z's expectations for the future of online shopping because Gen Z is more capable than any previous generation to redefine production and consumption (Steiner et al. 2016). To bridge the gap between sustainable fashion and customer purchase intentions, the purpose of this study is carried out to analyze the current trends and offer techniques to increase sustainable fashion awareness among gen z and millennial consumers.

Online surveys were conducted with a sample size of 29 questions targeting participants between the ages of 18–25 from a large Midwestern University. Additionally, three focus groups of approximately 23 students was also conducted. Questions pertaining to sustainable traits of apparel that include product quality, environmental effects, product pricing, purchase intentions and green awareness of apparel were of focus.

Surveys found that this age group was willing to pay up to 25% more for a sustainable apparel item and that uniqueness of the item was of utmost importance as well as being able to shop second hand. Most of this age group learn about a brands sustainability through a simple google search (n = 267, 59.6%) followed by a brands marketing/advertising (n = 132, 29.5%) and only 5 indicating they learn from celebrity endorsements (1.1%) leading to the conclusion that brands need to be marketing from their own influence not an endorser when sustainability and responsibility is in question. Uniqueness of product was of utmost importance as well as being able to shop second. Moving from wearing items once, this generation is trying to find creative ways to wear clothes as much as possible and consider quality and uniqueness when shopping for apparel over price. Recycling and upcycling are also areas of interest that not just industry marketers and retailers need to consider but also educators in how they approach a new era of design and merchandising to these new consumers. Companies should invest in campaigns and social events to advertise their sustainable practices. There also should be a push for understanding among

L. Copeland (✉) · S. Masa
Kent State University, Kent, OH, USA
e-mail: lcopela6@kent.edu; smasa@kent.edu

J. Allen et al. (eds.), *Celebrating the Past and Future of Marketing and Discovery with Social Impact*, Developments in Marketing Science: Proceedings of the Academy of Marketing Science, https://doi.org/10.1007/978-3-030-95346-1_161

this age group that is highly concerned with sustainability what their purchase gets them, i.e. price per wear rather than just highlighting the price itself among the garments. This study leads to the understanding that Gen Z and even millennials are operating under a deeper understanding of the role apparel plays in environmental and social responsibility.

Keywords Social responsibility · Gen Z · Consumer behavior · Millennials

Will Consumers Risk Privacy for Incentives in Mobile Advertising? A Cross-Cultural Examination of the U.S. and South Korea: An Abstract

Ying Wang and Ebru Genç

Abstract Mobile advertising has become an important digital marketing tool for marketers to reach targeted consumers worldwide. Much research has been done on identifying factors influencing consumers' adoption and usage of mobile advertising based on established theoretical frameworks such as Theory of Reasoned Action and Technology Acceptance Model. However, prior researches largely failed to give specific considerations of the unique characteristics of mobile communication such as being highly personal, interactive, and location sensitive. To address this issue, this study focuses on two most relevant but under-examined factors affecting mobile advertising effectiveness including incentives and privacy concerns in a cross-cultural setting of the U.S. and South Korea. South Korea and the U.S. are selected because both countries are leading players in the mobile advertising market and they represent two largely different cultures, which warrant meaningful cross-cultural comparisons. Our results show that incentive was a positive and significant influencing factor in both South Korea and the U.S and the effect is stronger in the South Korean sample than that of in the U.S. sample. Similarly, privacy concerns was a significant negative factor of consumers' intention to use mobile advertising in both countries. However, as an unexpected result, the impact of privacy concerns on consumers' attitude towards mobile advertising is stronger in South Korea than in the U.S. Moreover, in both markets, we found that beliefs about mobile advertising significantly influence consumers' attitude towards mobile advertising (ATMA), which in turn influences intention to use mobile advertising and purchase intention. Specifically, perceived informational usefulness, perceived entertainment usefulness and perceived ease of use emerged as significant benefits influencing consum-

---

Y. Wang
Youngstown State University, Youngstown, OH, USA
e-mail: ywang01@ysu.edu

E. Genç (✉)
Hiram College, Hiram, OH, USA
e-mail: gence@hiram.edu

J. Allen et al. (eds.), *Celebrating the Past and Future of Marketing and Discovery with Social Impact*, Developments in Marketing Science: Proceedings of the Academy of Marketing Science, https://doi.org/10.1007/978-3-030-95346-1_162

ers' attitude toward mobile advertising. Perceived entertainment usefulness emerged as the strongest influencing factor on ATMA in both countries. Therefore, increasing the entertainment value for users is key to increase the effectiveness of mobile advertising. Perceived social usefulness is a significant predictor among Korean consumers but not among Americans. This can be attributed to the individualistic culture orientation in the U.S. South Korea is a typical collective culture in which social relations are important and emphasized in people's everyday life.

Keywords Mobile advertising · Incentive · Privacy concerns · Cross-cultural

Do Scents Evoke Emotion?: An Abstract

Usha Pappu

Abstract This paper encompasses two research areas, odor (the translation of a chemical stimulus into the smell sensation) (Wolfe et al. 2015), and emotion (a set of physiological changes, and evaluative, subject-related experiences as evoked by external events and the significance of such events) (Frijda 1986). In marketing, the terms *odor*, *scent*, and *smell* have been used interchangeably to represent both positive and negative scents.

The most immediate response we have to a scent is not analytical but hedonic (Herz 2010). Marketers often use scents that have distinctive chemical properties so consumers could recognize and differentiate each scent by its distinctive smell (e.g. lemon, vanilla). Distinctive smell thus is a critical factor in the experience of pleasure—a liking response to the hedonic impact of a stimulus (Berridge and Kringelbach 2008). Odor hedonic perception (an affective evaluation that centres on liking) is, therefore, central to sensory pleasure and subsequent behavior (Herz 2010).

Prior research demonstrates a link between odor and emotion (Lin et al. 2018). This is attributed to the close connection between olfaction and the limbic system of the brain, which governs the processing of emotions (Cahill et al. 1995; Eichenbaum 1996). Hence, scents often trigger powerful emotional responses (Herz 2010). Moreover, as emotion and olfaction are functionally analogous, they effectively convey the same binary responses (e.g. like/dislike, approach/avoid) (Bosmans 2006; Herz 2010).

Although humans can extract emotional information from scents, just as they can from facial expressions and music (Herz 2009), the critical question remains, however, which scent affects which type of emotion. The literature on consumer olfaction does not satisfactorily answer this important question. Assessing the differential role of odor-elicited emotional information can contribute to a better understanding of consumer behavior across a broad range of areas. The aim of this paper is to develop a scent-emotion wheel for 19 scents that have been used in prior consumer research and are familiar to most consumers. The wheel could serve as a practical guide and as a road map for both researchers and practitioners in identifying which scent affects which specific emotion. With the aid of the

U. Pappu (✉)
University of Queensland, Brisbane, QLD, Australia
e-mail: u.pappu@business.uq.edu.au

J. Allen et al. (eds.), *Celebrating the Past and Future of Marketing and Discovery with Social Impact*, Developments in Marketing Science: Proceedings of the Academy of Marketing Science, https://doi.org/10.1007/978-3-030-95346-1_163

scent-emotion wheel, marketers could effectively evaluate and determine appropriate scents in the marketplace.

Keywords Emotion · Odor · Olfaction · Scent · Scent wheel · Smell

How Fair Rewards Motivate Customers to Engage On-Line: An Abstract

Tetsuya Aoki

Abstract This study demonstrates that customers change their motivation to engage in on-line settings depending on the interaction between the company and other customers. When customers can observe how others are treated, they compare their own treatment with that of others (Adams 1965). In on-line settings, where customers can observe how the company rewards other customers, customers compare own treatment with that of others, and consequently change their motivation to engage.

Previous studies clarify the effect of rewards on customer motivation by studying customer referral programs or conducting classroom experiments (Kumar et al. 2010; Verlegh et al. 2013). However, they do not consider the effect of rewards on other customers who just observe the rewarding activity. This research provides theoretical and managerial implications on how companies can manage customer motivation when companies' behavior to the individual customer is visible to all customers.

In order to understand how a company's attitude toward an individual influences other members' motivation, this study introduces organization citizenship behavior's theoretical framework. It researches how companies treat employees who in engage in citizenship behavior is visible to other employees in the firm. This situation is similar to the interaction between the company and customers in on-line. Therefore, knowledge about motivating employees in the organization can apply to customer engagement management in on-line.

Organization citizenship behavior research points out the importance of expectancy and fairness. The member who sees that other members are rewarded by the firm is motivated to engage with the firm, because of the expectancy. In addition, the member who observes a firm's consistent attitude to all members who engage is more motivated to engage with the firm, because of the fairness.

The analysis presented in this paper is based on a unique data set of company and customer interactions drawn from YouTube, consisting of 1.2 million comments.

T. Aoki (✉)
Hitotsubashi University, Tokyo, Japan
e-mail: bd191001@g.hit-u.ac.jp

J. Allen et al. (eds.), *Celebrating the Past and Future of Marketing and Discovery with Social Impact*, Developments in Marketing Science: Proceedings of the Academy of Marketing Science, https://doi.org/10.1007/978-3-030-95346-1_164

This study defines a user comment as a customer engagement and a video maker (i.e. YouTuber) replay as a reward. In order to determine whether the customer changes motivation by viewing the company attitude toward other customers, this study analyzes whether the reply ratio, which is the firm's pattern of rewarding other customers at time t (*reply* $ratio_t$), affects the likelihood of user comment in the next time period ($comment_{t+1}$).

This research suggests that firms can maximize engagement from customers through providing rewards to all customers in a way that is perceived as fair. In an on-line context, when a firm cannot reward all customers, not providing any rewards may be the best strategy.

Keywords Customer engagement · Customer engagement marketing · Organization citizenship behavior · YouTube

Are Ethical Boycotts Merely Signaling Value? The Financial Effect of Ethical Boycotts

P. Sergius Koku

Abstract Using 'economic pressure', the first of Garret's (1987) three benchmarks for measuring the success of a boycott, this study analyzes the financial effect of ethical boycotts, a form of anti-consumption behavior that has gained popularity during the past two decades. The results show that, on average, these boycotts have not been able to inflict a statistically significant financial damage on their targets. The average cumulative abnormal returns were −0.90% with a z-value of −1.071 which is not statistically significant. Specifically, only four out of the twenty targets experienced negative financial effect, and three of the four returns were only marginally significant. It is, however, possible that these boycotts may have succeeded it portraying the targeted organizations in a negative light.

Keywords Boycotts · Ethical consumption · Ethical boycotts · Event study technique

Introduction

Using economic pressure', the first of Garret's (1987) three benchmarks for measuring the success of a boycott, this paper analyzes the financial effect of ethical boycotts, a form of anti-consumption behavior, on targeted firms. According to Koku (2011), the Internet has contributed greatly to the proliferation of boycott calls. With the increasing number of boycotts comes an increasing number of anti-consumption research and studies on boycotts (Lee et al. 2009). However, to the best of our knowledge, none of the studies on boycotts and anti-consumption behaviors has explicitly examined the effectiveness of ethical boycotts, a category of boycotts that is motivated by ethical considerations, fairness and/or moral issues. This research gap has allowed questions such as whether those who call for, or organize ethical

P. S. Koku (✉)
Florida Atlantic University, Boca Raton, FL, USA
e-mail: koku@fau.edu

J. Allen et al. (eds.), *Celebrating the Past and Future of Marketing and Discovery with Social Impact*, Developments in Marketing Science: Proceedings of the Academy of Marketing Science, https://doi.org/10.1007/978-3-030-95346-1_165

boycotts are merely engaged in value signaling (see Hambin 2019). The current study contributes to closing the existing research gap and evaluates the effectiveness of ethical boycotts in inflicting economic damage on their targets.

The boycott literature has amply demonstrated that not all boycotts are similarly motivated; in other words, not all boycotts are organized for the same reasons. Some boycotts are motivated and organized to punish a perceived greedy corporation for relocating a plant or for offshoring production activities (Hoffman 2011; Hoffman and Muller 2009); some are organized to protect the environment (Garrett 1987), while others are organized to support a labor union or simply to exert pressure on management to change certain practices (Davidson III et al. 1995; Pruitt et al. 1988).

While the exact statistics are not available anywhere, a cursory search through the archives of the news media reveals that a particular class of boycotts which we herein call ethical boycotts seems to be more prevalent these days (Plante 2019). Even though oblique references have been made to "ethical boycott" in previous studies (see Friedman 2001), to the best of our knowledge, no previous study in the boycott literature has explicitly defined the terminology. Thus, we proceed first by defining what we mean by "ethical boycott".

By ethical boycott we mean a boycott action that has been called in order to cure an injustice or (put) right a perceived wrong. These boycotts are generally third-party boycotts in the sense that those who call for the boycott do not stand to benefit directly from the success of the boycott. By this definition, we consider Stevie Wonder's call for artistes to boycott Florida in the wake of Trayvon Martin's murder which implicated Florida's "stand your ground law" an example of an ethical boycott (see Reliable Source July 2013). Note that Stevie Wonder does not live in Florida, and does not even have a house in Florida, hence it would seem that his action is motivated purely to "right" a perceived injustice. Similarly, actor George Clooney's call for the boycott of Beverly Hills Bel Air Hotel because of the hotel owner's (Sultan of Brunei's) stance against gays, lesbians and transgender individuals (see Mozingo et al. 2019) is also an ethical boycott. Here again, we note that George Clooney is neither gay nor lives in Brunei and therefore does not stand to benefit directly from the success of this boycott, hence is actions are arguably motivated to right what he perceives as an injustice.

Theoretical Background

Boycotts

The term boycott has been defined slightly differently by different authors, however, the common thread that underlies all the different definitions is that a boycott is a voluntary refusal of a group or groups of consumers to patronize the services or products of a company or a country (Friedman 1985; Koku et al. 1997; Kozinets and Handelman 1998; Sen et al. 2001).

Even though boycotts are now common, and the word is used as a *verb* or *noun* in the literature and in the media depending on the context, they are not new. The practice dates as far back to the 1800s in Ireland (Friedman 1971). Boycotts have often been used, as a last resort, by different organizations such as labor unions to force management or a company to accept their demands. They are used by political movements such as the Civil Rights Movement in the United States to cause unjust laws to be changed for equal treatment for minority group members. They are also used by groups that stand for protecting the environment and animals to force companies to adopt environmentally and/or animal friendly policies (see Friedman 1985; Koku et al. 1997).

A search of the word "boycott" and "anti-consumption" using a common search engine such as Google Scholar yields an extensive record that spans a wide range of activities that are motivated by several different triggers. In reviewing the different strands of boycott activities, Friedman (1999) developed a taxonomy of five main groups along which boycotts could be classified; these are: (1) labor boycotts, (2) consumer boycotts, (3) minority boycotts, (4) ecological boycotts, and (5) religious boycotts.

Labor boycotts are boycotts that are organized by labor unions and labor organizations against management or companies to negotiate better conditions or pay and have been extensively studied by scholars such as (Pruitt et al. 1988; Koku et al. 1997). Consumer boycotts are boycotts that are organized by consumer groups such as housewives and other consumer groups. Consumer boycotts are often directed at companies or countries to address perceived unfair practices (Friedman 1985). Minority boycotts are boycotts that are organized by minority groups such as the National Association of Advancement of Colored People in United States to demand equal treatment for minority group members. The Montgomery bus boycott of 1965 in which African-Americans demanded equal treatment on public transportation is one of the more famous Civil Rights boycotts (Friedman 1995). Boycotts organized in the United States and elsewhere these days to demand equal treatment by gay, lesbian and transgender persons would also fall under contemporary civil rights boycotts.

A large number of consumers are now more aware of the environmental impact of their consumption habits (Plante 2019). Similarly, because of a new era of transparency and consumer vigilance more consumers are now aware of company practices that have negative impact on the environment. Ecological boycotts therefore are boycotts that are organized to persuade companies whose actions/activities are perceived to be harming flora and fauna to change their practices. Religious boycotts, as suggested by its name, are motivated by religious beliefs and are directed at companies or brands that some religious organizations perceive to be anti-religious in their practices. The boycott organized against Disney for having the first gay characters in its remake of the film Beauty and the Beast (Merrit 2017) or against Heinz for having two men in their ads kissing (Clout 2008) are examples of a religious boycott.

Even though Friedman's (1999) boycott taxonomy is useful, we believe it is incomplete, in view of current developments. For example, the taxonomy does not include such categories as ethical boycotts, that is a boycott that is motivated by ethical consideration such as those organized by PETA (People for Ethical Treat of Animals). It also, does not include political boycotts that are motivated by political ideologies. Furthermore, the Friedman (1999) did address the effectiveness of the different boycott categories in accomplishing their goals. Garrett (1987) outlined three goals that could serve as the benchmarks for measuring the effectiveness of a boycott. These are: (1) to exert economic pressure on targeted entity (a firm or country), (2) to create a public relations problem for the targeted entity by portraying it in a negative light, and (3) to attack the targeted entity's policy commitment and persuade it to change.

Garrett (1987) outlined three goals that could serve as the benchmarks for measuring the effectiveness of a boycott. These are: (1) to exert economic pressure on targeted entity (a firm or country), (2) to create a public relations problem for the targeted entity by portraying it in a negative light, and (3) to attack the targeted entity's policy commitment and persuade it to change. Garrett (1987) however did not offer any guidance on how these benchmarks ought to be used.

As indicated earlier ethical boycotts have received significant media coverage during the past two decades, yet to the best of our knowledge no study has specifically evaluated the effectiveness of these boycotts. The current study corrects this research deficiency by focusing on ethical boycotts and by using the first of the three benchmarks suggested by Garrett (1987) to evaluate their effectiveness, i.e., in inflicting economic damages on their target.

Ethical Consumerism and Ethical Consumer

Ethical consumerism is a form anti-consumption movement that argues that when consumers purchase a product or a service, their purchase is not limited to the consumption of the product or service alone, but also constitutes an endorsement of the company's production process. Hence, consumers whose personal values are not consistent with the values of companies (or countries) that run sweatshops, embark on destructive environmental practices or disregard human rights should refrain from patronizing the products or services produced by such companies (or countries) (Kirchoff 2007).

The *Ethical Consumer* movement was started in 1989 in Manchester, U.K. by Rob Harrison and Jane Turner (EthicalConsumer.org). The movement describes itself as "an independent, not-for-profit, multi-stakeholder co-operative with open membership" (EthicalConsumer.org). The movement publishes a bi-monthly magazine and maintains a website (EthicalConsumer.org) that publishes a list of all ethical boycotts. The magazine was the first to publish "ratings tables that awarded negative ethical scores to companies based on a wide range of ethical considerations including, but not limited to animal rights, concerns about the environment, and human rights." Today, the rating criteria have expanded to 19 and the movement openly calls for boycott of companies that are perceived to be cruel to animals and/or violate human rights (EthicalConsumer.org).

Data and Methodology

Because the current study's focus is on the effectiveness of ethical boycotts, our data consisted of only boycotts have been endorsed by *Ethical Consumer* and listed at the movement's website. Ethical consumer's boycott list explains why the targeted companies, persons or countries must be boycotted. In other words, it provides rationale for consumers to withhold their financial support from the targets. It also lists the primary organization that is organizing the boycott, and the date on which the boycott started.

There were 38 targets listed in the organization's boycott list as of August 30, 2019. It should be noted that this list changes periodically. More names are added when the organization endorses more boycotts, and names are deleted when a boycott is successfully settled. Out of these 38 targets, 28 are publicly traded firms. Five are non- publicly traded firms, four are countries, and one is a person. The "oldest" boycott still on the list was against L'Oreal; it started on June 1, 2000. The latest is against Ecover; it started on April 24, 2018. We extracted the daily market returns data from CRSP tapes (Center for Research in Security Prices, University of Chicago) and analyzed the effect of boycott of boycott announcements on the stock prices of the targeted companies.

Consistent with the event study techniques, we treated each boycott call as an event that potentially has negative financial repercussions for the company. Thus, we used the event study methodology (Fama et al. 1969) which has been widely used in the field of finance and management to analyze the financial effects of unanticipated news/events in the market and by Koku (2011) and Koku et al. (1997) to analyze the financial effects of boycotts.

The event study technique (Fama et al. 1969) is based on the market model and holds that expected returns on any asset in the market is linearly related to the contemporaneous return on the market portfolio as such asset prices in equilibrium adjust to news and events that were not already internalized. It is important to note that we chose to use the traditional Fama et al. (1969) instead of Fama and French (1992), the three-factor which controlled for differences in size of the targeted companies, and Fama and French (2012), the five-factor model which controlled for profitability and investment because of the small sample of the lack of variability within the sample in terms of size.

Because it is assumed that the market is equilibrium when all the publicly available information is internalized, in which case the average abnormal residuals are not significantly different from zero, accumulation of positive abnormal returns is an indication of the arrival of a significant positive unanticipated or unexpected news in the market. The arrival of a significant unanticipated or unexpected news in the market will have the opposite effect. Because boycotts urge for the withdrawal or withholding of financial support from the targeted companies, they are negative news, as such we expect accumulation of negative abnormal returns, if they are unexpected or unanticipated.

Results

We analyzed the data for cumulation of abnormal returns using three different event windows (t-30, −1) that is approximately a month before the event day (t0), t-1, t0, that is the event day, and t0, t30 that is a month after the event day. Using different event windows before the event day allows us to investigate possible leakage of the news, and examining the residuals a month after the event day allows us to look for the lasting effects of the event.

The results show that on average, the boycotts did not inflict any significant financial damage on the targets. The average cumulative abnormal returns on the day of the announcement which is event date t0 is −0.90% with a z-value of −1.071%. While the negative sign is in the expected direction, it is statistically insignificant. Analysis of the individual boycott target shows that only four of the twenty corporations experienced statistically significant negative returns. British Petroleum, PLC experienced abnormal returns of −8.78% with standardized cumulative abnormal returns of −5.377 on the day of the boycott. This is statistically significant with 0.001 significance level. However, it should be noted that BP was already a target of several other sanctions because of its oil well explosion in the Gulf of Mexico which occurred on April 20th 2010, hence we cannot be sure that BP's loss was solely caused by the boycott.

Kellogg, Co. also experienced negative cumulative abnormal returns on the announcement day. Its abnormal returns were at −2.13% with standardized cumulative returns of −1.316 on the event day (t0). This was marginally significant at 0.10% level. Similarly, Starbucks experienced cumulative abnormal returns of −2.13%, standardized cumulative abnormal returns of −1.335 with a significance level of 0.10%. Wendy's, the fourth company, experienced a slightly higher negative cumulative abnormal returns of −4.86%, with standardized cumulative abnormal returns of −2.161. This has a significance level of 0.05. It should be noted that Wendy's boycott was organized by a coalition of Immokalee workers because Wendy's refused to join the Fair Food Program which addresses abuse of farm laborers. All of Wendy's competitors such as McDonald's and Burger King signed on to the program. Therefore, Wendy's boycott is a little more complex since it has the involvement of farm laborers who stood to gain from the success of the boycott, hence it cannot be classified entirely as an ethical boycott, given out definition of ethical boycott at the beginning of this study.

Several reasons could account for the inability of the boycotts listed by Ethical Consumer to cause the financial damage that the organizers sought. Boycotts are by themselves effective in causing financial pain as evidenced in several studies (Koku et al. 1997; Pruitt et al. 1988). However, it important to note that the vast majority of the (primary) organizers of the boycotts endorsed by *Ethical Consumer* are mostly unknown. For example, *Nature Watch* which was responsible for organizing boycotts against S.C. Johnson, and L'Oreal for "animal testing" is virtually unknown, and their only boycott activity was to issue a boycott call online. A boycott against well-known and established companies/brands must take more than a "passive" website as the boycott targets are not going to sit unconcerned. Besides engaging massive advertising to either make their case or "crowd out" boycott calls, recent studies have shown that boycott targets also enlist their supporter to organize "buycotts" which are intended to neutralize the effect of the boycotts (Endres and Panagopolous 2017; Kelm and Dohle 2018).

The results of this study, though a disheartening news to ethical boycott organizers, are nonetheless interesting and consistent with Koku (2011) which found that boycotts that are solely organized through the Internet have a slim chance of being successful in inflicting economic damage on their targets. Koku (2011) argued that consumers who participate in boycotts pay a price for their participation, for instance, they are giving up their first or best choice of product or services for the second best, as such they need to know the people behind the boycotts in order to ascertain their credibility or seriousness of their purpose. They must know not only what they are sacrificing for, but who they are in solidarity with. In fact, camaraderie is a reason behind some consumers' participation boycott activities (Kozinets and Handelman 1998; Puttnam and Muck 1991).

Furthermore, several means communicating (social media, radio and TV announcements, demonstrations, leaflets, etc.) need to be used simultaneously for a boycott to be successful. Enough people or enough purchasing power must be withheld from the target in order to inflict an economic damage. This is clear from the successful boycotts that have been organized by labor unions, for example who used multiple means to attract attention and to win the support of consumers (Koku et al. 1997; Pruitt and Friedman 1986).

General Discussion

Boycotts are now more pervasive today than they were three to four decades ago. Popular among contemporary boycotts are ethical boycotts that are organized by third parties, and motivated by ethical considerations. However, these boycotts currently do not seem to have much traction or inflict financial damage of the targets because their organizers either rely solely on one-time news conference as in the case of Stevie Wonder, or a one-time editorial piece written for a newspaper (as in the case of George Clooney), or on a "passive" website with no other supporting efforts or activities.

The results of our analysis show these boycotts are not able to inflict a statistically significant economic damage on their targets. For these boycotts to be successful, recommend they "borrow" strategies used by labor unions and adopt multi-prong efforts. They should constantly remind the public about why the boycott must be supported. Finally, the issue or the activity that is necessitating the boycott movement must be framed in a way that the rightness of the cause is clear and it appeals to the conscience of significant number of consumers.

As an anti-consumption activity, boycotts cannot be overlooked by marketers. To the extent that they are successful or not in inflicting economic damages, they can bring negative attention to the target, as such all boycotts must be taken seriously by marketers who must work to avert them through pro-active measures. While the results of our study revealed no significant financial injury was experienced by the targets, it is possible that other objectives beyond the scope of this study may have been accomplished. For example, the boycotts may have created public relations nightmare for the targets or they may have succeeded in dislodging the target from its commitment. However, the fact that a company such as L'Oreal has been on Ethical Consumers boycott list since 2000 makes us doubt the effectiveness of the boycotts in other ways also.

References

Clout, L. (2008). Gay rights group boycotts Heinz after 'men kissing' row. *The Daily Telegraph*. Retrieved on August 17, 2019.

Davidson, III, W. N., Worrell, D. N., & El-Jelly, A. (1995). Influencing Managers to Change Unpopular Corporate Behavior through Boycotts and Divestiture: A Stock Market Test. *Business & Society*, 34(2), 171-197.

Endres, K., & Panagopolous, C. (2017), Boycotts, Buycotts, and Political Consumerism in America. Research and Politics (November), 1-9

Fama, E. F., Fisher, L., Jensen, M. C., & Rolle, R. (1969). *International Economic Review*, 10(1), 1-21.

Fama, E. F. & French, K. R. (1992). The Cross-Section of Expected Stock Returns. *The Journal of Finance,* 47 (2), 427-466.

Fama, E. F. & French, K. R. (2012). Size, value, and momentum in international stock returns. *Journal of Financial Economics*, 105 (3), 457-472.

Friedman, M. (1971). The 1966 Consumer Protest as Seen by its leaders. *Journal of Consumer Affairs,* 5(1), 1-23.

Friedman, M. (1985). Consumer Boycotts in the United Sates, 1970-1980: Contemporary Events in Historical Perspective. *Journal of Consumer Affairs*, 19(1), 96-117.

Friedman, M. (1995). American Consumer Boycotts in Response to Rising Food Prices: Housewives' Protest at the Grassroots Level. *Journal of Consumer Policy*, 18 (1), 55-72.

Friedman, M. (1999). *Consumer Boycotts: Effecting Change Through the Marketplace and the Media*, London, U.K., Routledge.

Friedman, M. (2001). Ethical Dilemmas Associated with Consumer Boycotts. *Journal of Social Policy*, 32(2), 232-240.

Garrett, D. E. (1987). The Effectiveness of Marketing Policy Boycotts: Environmental Opposition to Marketing. *Journal of Marketing*, 51 (2), 46-5.

Hambin, J. (2019). People Actually Quit SoulCycle at https://www.theatlantic.com/healtharchive/2019/09/soulcycle-boycott/597478/. Retrieved on December 29, 2019.

Hoffman, S. & Muller, S. (2009). Consumer boycotts due to factory relocation. *Journal of Business Research*, 62(20, 239-247.

Hoffman, S. (2011). Anti-consumption as a Means of saving jobs. *European Journal of Marketing*, 45 (11/12), 1702-1714.

Kelm, O., & Dohle, M. (2018). Information, Communication and Political Consumerism: How (online) Information and (online) Communication Influence Boycotts and Buycotts. *New Media & Society*, 20(4), 1523-1542.
Kirchoff, C. (2007). Ethical consumerism. In M. Bevir (Ed.), *Encyclopedia of Governance*. Vol. 2. 285-285. Thousand Oaks, CA: SAGE Publications Ltd. https://doi.org/10.4135/9781412952613.n169
Koku, P. S., Akhigbe, A., & Springer, T. (1997). The Financial Impact of Boycotts and Threats of Boycotts. *Journal of Business Research*, 40 (1), 15-20.
Koku, P. S. (2011). On the Effectiveness of Consumer Boycotts Organized through the Internet. *Journal of Marketing Development and Competitiveness*, 26(1), 20-26.
Kozinets, R. V., & Handelman, J. (1998). Ensouling Consumption: A Netographic Exploration of the Meaning of Boycotting Behavior in *Advances in Consumer Research eds.* Alba J. W., & Hutchinson, J. W. Association for Consumer Research, Provo, UT: 25, 475-480.
Lee, S. W. M., Fernandez, K. V. & Hyman, M. (2009). Anti-consumption: An Overview and research agenda. *Journal of Business Research,* 62(2), 145-147.
Merrit, J. (2017). https://www.usatoday.com/story/opinion/2017/03/07/Christian-evangelical-disney-beauty-beast-gay-column/98812856/. Retrieved on September 1, 2019.
Mozingo, B., Bengali, S., & Oston, B., (2019). Can George Clooney Persuade Hollywood to Boycott Hotels over Brunei's Antigay Laws? In https://www.latimes.com/local/lanow/la-me-ln-clooney-boycott-sultan-brunei-20190402-story.html. Retrieved on June 1, 2019.
Plante, S. G. (2019). https://vox.com/the-goods/2019/10/7/20894134/consumer-actvism-concious-consumerism-explained. Retrieved on September 1, 2019.
Pruitt, S. W. & Friedman, M. (1986). Determining the Effectiveness of Consumer Boycotts: A Stock Price Analysis of Their Impact on Corporate Targets. *Journal of Consumer Policy*, 9(4), 375-387
Pruitt, S. W., Wei, J. K. C., & White, R. E. (1988). The impact of union-sponsored boycotts on the stock prices of target firms. *Journal of Labor Research*, 9(3), 285-289.
Puttnam, T. & Muck, T.(1991). Wielding the boycott weapon for social change. *Business and Society Review*, 78 (2), 5-8.
Reliable source (July 2013). What does Stevie Wonder's boycott at Florida really mean? At https://www.washingtonpost.com/news/reliable-source/wp/2013/07/16/what-does-stevie-wonders-boycott-of-florida-really-mean/ Retrieved on July, 10, 2019
Sen, S., Gurhan-Canli, Z., & Morwitz, V. (2001). Withholding Consumption: A Social Dilemma Perspective on Consumer Boycotts. Journal of Consumer Research, 38(3), 399-417.

From Hybridization to Modularity: The Affordance of Variable-Geometry Innovations Design: An Abstract

Dhouha El Amri

Abstract In the high tech field, we are witnessing the proliferation of variable-geometry innovations with shape-shifting structures and architectures, combining different categories of products into a single one called New Hybrid Products (NHP). The design of these products informs the user about their affordance. This ability of design to suggest the potential uses of new hybrid products can be considered by companies to emphasize the distinctiveness and to facilitate the understanding, categorization, evaluation and adoption of new hybrid products.

Our article poses some fundamental questions to designers about the place of affordance in the design of communicating new hybrid products and how to anticipate this affordance precisely in the case of variable-geometry innovations design (e.g. monolithic (made of a single block), protean (able to change shape) or modular (formed of various removable parts) designs).

A qualitative study, which involved Hi-Tech design experts, explores the importance of variable-geometry innovations affordance and its implications on their willingness to conceive them. Our findings confirm the divergence in the literature on communicating new hybrid products affordance. The result of the study with the Hi-Tech design experts reveals the non-existence of a consensus on this issue. This divergence is visible as much for existing monolithic communicating NHPs such as smartphones and tablets as for the polymorphic communicating NHP studied in our research, namely, the « Flip phone ».

Depending on whether the communicating new hybrid product has a monolithic or polymorphic form, it may or may not be perceived as affordant. Therefore, designers of communicating new hybrid products are reluctant to design these variable-geometry hybrid products. They prefer simple monolithic products to hybrid shape-shifting products, considered as difficult to understand, not at all intuitive and not very affordant.

In addition to this multitude of issues raised, the theoretical and managerial implications of the study are finally addressed.

D. El Amri (✉)
University Paris-Est Creteil, IRG, Creteil, France
e-mail: dhouha.el-amri@u-pec.fr

J. Allen et al. (eds.), *Celebrating the Past and Future of Marketing and Discovery with Social Impact*, Developments in Marketing Science: Proceedings of the Academy of Marketing Science, https://doi.org/10.1007/978-3-030-95346-1_166

Keywords Affordance · Design · Innovation · New product development
References Available Upon Request

On the Legal Liabilities of Food Tampering in the U.S.: A Review & Marketing Implications

P. Sergius Koku

Abstract This paper reviews the legal, jurisdictional, public policy and the marketing issues implicated in food tampering cases in the United States. It offers some insights to inform marketing strategy development. Furthermore, because food tampering endangers the health of the nation as a whole, the paper argues that the government must play a major role in designing anti-tampering devices instead of leaving such developments to the private sector.

Keywords Food tampering · Food safety · Legal liabilities · Marketing implications

Introduction

This paper reviews the various jurisdictional issues involved in food tampering cases, examines legal theories under which liability could ensue, and offers suggestions on strategy formulations. The paper adds to Morgan's (1988) contribution in which he discussed negligence and strict liability issues by discussing such other legal theories as breach of warranty, the role of the FDA (Food and Drug Administration), and the role of FBI (Federal Bureau of Investigation) in food tampering cases. Food tampering occurs all over the world, however, it seems to occur more frequently in the United States, hence this review.

Food tampering (a specific class of product tampering) is said to have occurred when a third party without permission or authority of the manufacturer or seller introduces or attempts to introduce a foreign object into that which is being sold (Food and Drug Administration 2006). Often, the foreign substance is harmful, but it need not always be harmful for tampering to have taken place. The mere act of

P. S. Koku (✉)
Florida Atlantic University, Boca Raton, FL, USA
e-mail: koku@fau.edu

J. Allen et al. (eds.), *Celebrating the Past and Future of Marketing and Discovery with Social Impact*, Developments in Marketing Science: Proceedings of the Academy of Marketing Science, https://doi.org/10.1007/978-3-030-95346-1_167

introducing or attempting to introduce, without authority, an object into that which is being sold constitutes food tampering.

Food adulteration which is defined as the presence of poisonous, insanitary or deleterious ingredients which may render food injurious (U.S.F.D. Regulatory Information 2007) is a specific case of product tampering. However, in many instances, food adulteration is carried out by the producers/sellers who intentionally add the foreign substance in an effort to maximize profit. An example of food adulteration is the reported case of milk being mixed with melamine by some Chinese farmers in order to make the milk appear "richer" and thereby attract higher prices (see New York Times, September 29, 2008). The practice of food tampering is not new, and could be seen in the study of history where some ancient leaders met their untimely death by ingesting water or food that was poisoned (see Logan 1993). However, consumers in the U.S. have become more aware of the practice because of several reasons: (1) advancement in news producing technology that has allowed individual non-professionals to post and contribute news item (e.g. "youtubing" and "blogging"), (2) the Tylenol tampering incidents of 1982 in which several people lost their lives, and (3) the more frequent occurrence of tampering incidents, during the last three to four decades, or hoaxes of finding foreign substance in a product that is being sold (see for example, Gonzales 2005).

Theoretical Background

Food Tampering

Even though food tampering could have major implications not only for the company whose product/produce has been tampered with, but also for the confidence of the nation in the safety of its food supply, only a few scattered studies have examined the issue. Morgan (1988) one of the first studies on food tampering suggests that tampering incidents have become more common because of the change in retailing format that now allows the so-called "self-service" in which the consumer now has a direct access to that which is being sold. In his study Morgan (1988) reviews the legal implications of packaging decisions that lead to tampering and offers guidelines to help marketers make improved packaging and channels decisions. However, more still needs to be done in this area. For example, who are the law enforcement actors that a seller/manufacturer is likely to deal with? What are the jurisdictional issues, and what could the seller/manufacturer expect? And what are the public policy issues?

In a subsequent study, Mitchell (1989) focused on the economic effects of product tampering, specifically, on the economic effects of the 1982 and 1986 Tylenol tampering cases. Mitchell (1989) found that Johnson and Johnson suffered significant losses when Tylenol capsules were poisoned, however other drug companies did not suffer significant losses when their capsules were similarly poisoned. The difference in the market reaction, the author said, lies in the fact that Tylenol was the market leader.

Jackson et al. (1992) taking a consumer behavior approach studied consumers' reaction to and perception of food tampering situations. The authors concluded that significant differences exist between the different demographic segments in their perception and reaction to food tampering incidents. The more elderly consumers think that producers of food and over-the-counter drugs are doing all that they can do to protect consumers. Furthermore, older consumers more than younger consumers feel that money spent on developing tamper resistant packaging is a waste of resources, and that the media often exaggerate product tampering-related news.

Food Tampering and Social Policy

Logan (1993) studied food/product tampering from a social policy viewpoint. He reviewed the major product tampering cases which occurred between 1980 and 1990 a developed a list of motives behind product tampering crimes. They include acts such as terrorism, sabotage, homicide, insurance fraud, malicious mischief and attention seeking. Because news that a product has been tampered with could easily cause mass hysteria, Logan (1993) urges the public to be vigilant. He also recommends education which provides information to the public on what it must be on the "look out for" as far as food tampering is concerned. For deterrence, the author encouraged the relevant authorities to make the public aware of the penalties available under the law for threats of product tampering, and for actual acts of product tampering. In actuality, food tampering is a relatively simple act that has an enormous effect as well as implications. Even though it occurs in a local environment and may have violated a local statute (in a small number of states), food tampering is a federal offense in the United States, and therefore requires a close cooperation between local and federal authorities to successfully prosecute.

Because reported cases of product tampering were thought to be isolated before the 1982 Tylenol associated deaths, prosecuting product tampering incidents were pretty much left to the jurisdictional authority of the local authorities (see Logan 1993). However, realizing that threats of food tampering, the actual acts of tampering, and deaths/injuries that are associated with tampering incidents could deal a serious blow to the confidence that the American public has in its supply of food and drugs, the US Congress in 1983 enacted the Federal Anti-Tampering Act (FATA) which amongst other things defined tampering as "The crime of intentionally altering a product in order to cause harm, threatening to do so, or communicating false information" (Food and Drug Administration 2006).

The 1983 FATA established penalties for the crime and assigned investigative responsibilities. The penalty for violating the FATA is a fine of up to $250,000 per offence and/or imprisonment of up to 3 years. Even though the FATA has assigned joint investigative responsibilities to the Food and Drug Administration (FDA), United States Department of Agriculture (USDA) and to the Federal Bureau of

Investigations (FBI), clear lines of responsibilities exist for the different agencies. For example, the FDA is primarily responsible for investigating all consumer complaints of tampering, tainting, or adulterating of products, and under its regulatory control refers matters to the FBI, local law enforcement, and the affected companies.

The USDA is responsible for investigating all consumer complaints regarding meat, poultry, and egg products. It too refers matters to FBI and other agencies as it deems appropriate. The FBI serves as a critical link between the two agencies and local authorities. It is responsible for investigating cases that involve serious threats to human life, threatened or actual acts of tampering, or threatened tampering coupled with extortion demands. It is also responsible for matters referred by the USDA and FDA, and responsible for investigating cases that involve consumer products that are not regulated by the FDA and USDA, or when a death occurs. The FBI's laboratory plays a crucial role in tampering cases. It provides forensic analysis and whatever assistance that is required by law enforcement agencies to process evidence in product tampering cases.

The 1983 FATA has had a series of amendments which were intended tighten its grip. The original Anti-Tampering Act was expanded in scope in 1994 to include product labels as well. This expansion was necessary because another insidious side of product tampering which even though does not involve product poisoning is nonetheless highly undesirable is the use of products as a vehicle to propagate hateful message. This act is often perpetrated by hate groups or individuals pretending to represent such groups. It involves inserting in packages leaflets that "attack African Americans, praise the holocaust, and encourage the killing of immigrants." "One leaflet shows an illustration of man being shot at point blank range with an automatic weapon with the following caption: 'if it ain't white, waste it!'" (see http://www.senate.gov/ – U.S. Senate hearings on "Product Packaging Protection Act of 2001). Other activities involve the insertion of pornographic materials or pornographic information in product packages. The Product Packaging Protection Act of 2001 was enacted as an enhancement of the 1994 Act to close existing loopholes. As indicated above, even though the manufacturer whose product has been tampered with is generally the victim, the manufacturer could nonetheless be liable to the individuals who consumed products that actually been tampered with under the theory product liability, negligence, or breach of warranty (American Law Institute 1966, 1998; Epstein 2000).

Methodology

As a qualitatively study, we undertook and extensive review of the literature on product liability and food tampering in law, marketing, and economics. The review suggests that such issues as manufacturing defects, design defects, strictly liability, negligence, breach of warranty, advertising and the theory of public good are relevant to analyzing issues related food tampering.

Results

There are possibly two theories under which the consumer could bring a civil suit against the manufacturer under product liability. First, the individual who is injured or who has consumed a tainted product could sue on the grounds of manufacturing defects (see *Pouncy v. Ford Motor Co.* 1972, *Halloran v. Virginia* 1977). On this ground, the injured could accuse the manufacturer of putting out a shoddy product that has made it possible for the tamperer to tamper the product. Here, the injured (the person who consumed the tampered food) would have to show that had the product been properly manufactured, the tampering would not have been possible.

Design defect is the second theory under product liability (see *Larsen v. General Motors Corporation* 1968). The individual who consumed the tainted or tampered food could accuse the manufacturer of using a defective design to package the food item. In other words, a better design package which is feasible, but ignored by the manufacturer could have either prevented the tampering or would have made the tampering evident. The theory of strict liability is also available to the injured consumer.

An injured consumer could also seek redress under the theory of strict liability. Here, the injured will alleged that the manufacturer owes a strict duty to the injured, and that the defect brought about as a result of tampering makes the product unreasonably dangerous. Strict liability is effective for products that are inherently dangerous.

A consumer who has been injured by tampered food could bring a civil suit in negligence against the manufacturer (see MacPherson v. Buick Motor Co. 1916, the seminal case in the U.S. legal history on negligence theory). Under negligence theory, the injured consumer must show that the manufacturer owes a duty to any foreseeable consumer to exercise care that a reasonable person would to ensure that the product cannot be tampered with. The injured would also have to allege that the manufacturer has breached the duty owed and that the breach is both the approximate and actual cause of the consumer's injury.

The injured consumer and his/her family could also sue the manufacturer and or seller under the theory of breach of warranty. There are two main kinds of warranties, an explicit warranty from the manufacturer, and an implied warranty. However, two kinds of implied warranties also exist. One, under the implied warranty of merchantability, the manufacturer guarantees that the goods are of acceptable quality and are fit for the ordinary purpose for which they are intended. Two, under fitness for a particular purpose, the seller is presumed to have known that the buyer is relying on the seller's judgment and ability to select or furnish goods that are suitable for a particular purpose. Privity is required under implied warranties, therefore only the buyer, his family, household, and guests can sue for personal injury. Hence, hypothetically, someone who steals a tampered food from a buyer, consumes it and gets injured cannot sue the manufacturer under this theory.

The costs associated with food tampering fall on many individual entities. The general public incurs costs associated with food tampering in several ways. Some individuals who consumed only the brand of food that was tampered with (not the product itself) may develop acute levels of anxiety that may need medical intervention (see Logan 1993). While there is no direct means of quantifying these costs, it is conceivable that the medical costs and time lost from work could in the aggregate be significant. There is also an unquantifiable cost that is associated with the fact that the public's confidence in the nation's food production system will be shaken when news of food tampering is made public; this is particularly true when the tampering leads to death of a consumer. The hysteria or panic that comes with the news of death dues to food tampering could lead to loss in productivity either in the local communities where the death occurs or in the state where the tampering incident occurs.

By far, however, the heaviest costs associated with food tampering comes to individuals who consumed or ingested that which has been poisoned. Take for instance the 1982 poisoned Tylenol capsules. These costs come by way of lost life and lost earning potential. The medical expenses incurred in taking care of the sick, the dying, funeral expenses, and in some cases the loss of companionship could also be significant. Similarly, the cost incurred by the public in terms of man-hours in investigating food tampering cases could, in the aggregate, be large.

Since a manufacturer could be sued for making an unreasonably dangerous product because of inadequate packaging that could prevent tampering, the dilemma confronting manufacturers is to decide when a packaging design is sufficiently safe, or when a product packaging could be deemed tamper resistant. This problem could be vexing, and opens the door to a wide array of considerations given the fact that tampering is not limited to self-serviced food items alone, but in fact spreads to every manufactured product that could be ingested. While packaging technologists have argued that designing a truly tamper-proof packaging is either impossible or prohibitively costly, the Food and Drug Administration, the federal agency that oversees over-the-counter drugs that have often been the target of tamperers, has provided some guidance in terms of what it considers a tamper- resistant packaging. The FDA's definition of a tamper-resistant package is rather pragmatic; it considers as tamper-resistant packaging to be that which "has one or more indicators or barrier to entry which, if breached or missing, can reasonably be expected to provide visible evidence to consumers that tampering has occurred" (Greenberg 2000). What the FDA refers to as tamper-resistant is referred to by many researchers in the field as tamper-evident.

The other practical issue that confronts the manufacturer or seller whose food/product has been tampered with and the law enforcement/investigative authorities is deciding on the most appropriate time to make public news of the tampering. Contrary to public belief, complaints from consumers about suspected food/product tampering are not isolated, neither are threats from unknown individuals to tamper with food/products. For example, the FDA reportedly received, during the 1986 fiscal year alone about 1700 product tampering complaints, and was made aware of 350 threats to tamper with food products within a period of 13 months, from January 1986 to July 1987 (Crow and Erickson 2000). Furthermore, General Mills alone said it receives 20 to 25 complaints of unauthorized messages in packages each year (MacLeod 2001).

With this fairly high frequency of product tampering-related incidents that are hoax, the possibility that making such news public could wreak havoc both on the company and public has to be carefully considered. Thus, extreme care must be exercised by the investigative authorities and the targeted company in making public information/news on product tampering. Making public a false complaint or threat about a tampered product could needlessly hurt the company financially, damage a healthy brand, and may also cause undue public anxiety. On the hand, withholding information from the public on a product that has been actually tampered with exposes the public to unnecessary danger.

The dilemma posed above coupled with the current environmental uncertainties make it imperative for companies to have carefully thought out plans on how to deal with product tampering incidents. Here marketing could play a vital role. To mitigate the negative effects of food tampering, it is important for the targeted firm to move quickly without equivocation when a determination is made that a tampering threat or information is credible. Sometimes, it may be necessary to withdraw item from the market to ensure public safety. If such a step must be taken, the items must be withdrawn in a forthright manner. In other words, the items must not be withdrawn grudgingly. It is important for the targeted company to show the public that it is truly concerned about the public's safety rather than its bottom line (money). This can be done through immediate removal of the targeted item from the market, and through advertisements. It is also important for the company to maintain an open and frank communication with the public. The company must through its communications reassure the public that the company has confidence in its production process, and will do everything in its power to protect the public.

The role of marketing outlined above is necessary to mitigate the effects of tampering when the incident has occurred. However, marketing can also be used proactively to either prevent tampering or to make it difficult for the crime to be committed. This could be done with proper labeling, and a statement on the product packing that reminds consumers not to consume a product if it appears tampered with. Reminding consumers periodically, through advertisements and public service announcements to remain vigilant and be on the "look out" for tampering or those who tamper with food items could also be useful.

The packaging industry has, since the outbreak of the1982 Tylenol incident, been busy researching and designing better ways of packaging to protect the over-the-counter drugs. These research efforts have resulted in innovations such as "mouth-seal covers, shrink-wrap bottle covers, taping over the ends of a folded box, caps that contain a band that must be broken upon first use, and blister packaging, in which individual pills or capsules are encased in a foil-backed plastic sheet" (Greenberg 2002). However, nothing that can be ingested is immune to tampering, as such the scope of research efforts into safer packaging needs to expand beyond the over-the-counter drugs into such other areas as food. The vulnerability of the nation's food supply to tampering by terrorists as highlighted in public comments by Mr. Tommy Thompson (a former secretary of health) should be taken seriously (see Braningin et al. 2004). The fact that Mr. Thompson talked about the need for increased protection for the nation's food supply in terms of national defense suggests, in part, that the debate over the funding of research for packaging could be framed in terms of national defense. Viewed in light of national defense, expenses on packaging research could be considered a public good and therefore paid for by the tax payer. This is not inconsistent with the practice in which the Pentagon funds public research projects that may have defense implications.

General Discussion

The findings of this study have at least two major policy implications. Firstly, even though the object of a criminal sentence is (in most instances) to rehabilitate and punish the guilty person, it appears the penalty for violating the FATA (Federal Anti-Tampering Act) which is a fine of up $250,000 per offence and/or imprisonment of up to 3 years seems a mere slap on the wrist when the gravity of the offense and its potential effects are taken into consideration. The penalty for tampering is strikingly small when it is compared to the sentence of 20 years to life imprisonment provided for violating the RICO (Racketeer Influenced and Corrupt Organizations Act) statute (see Chap. 96 of Title 18 of The United Sates Code, 18 U.S.C. 1961). Thus, there is a pressing need for the legislators, at the federal level, to increase the severity of the penalty for violating the FATA. An enhancement in the severity of the penalty will make the punishment will make the punishment serve as a deterrent as well as make it fit the crime.

Secondly, ingestible products such as food, fruits, and the over-the-counter drugs seem to be more susceptible to tampering; given the easy access to these items, the health of the entire country is at risk, and the supply of the food source is vulnerable to tampering. In this case, the tampering need not be done by extortionists, but rather by a terrorist. Because the health of the country is at the stake, research costs into ways of preventing or making tampering difficult should not be left to the companies that sell packaged goods and agricultural produce, but must be shared by the government. The government should treat the research and development costs as a public good.

The marketing implications in this study are twofold. First, while companies continue to do their part in developing better packaging, they must also seek to limit their liability due to tampering by properly labeling their packages. These labels must seek to educate the public by telling the potential consumers what signs or evidence of tampering to look for. Secondly, it seems one of the major reasons for tampering is that the perpetrators do not appreciate the seriousness of their offence and the magnitude of the financial wreckage that they cause. Hence, advertisements or public service announcements that discourage the act, educate people on the effects of such acts, and inform them about the price that the entire population pays because of their act should be engaged both by private companies and government agencies such as the FDA. Advertisements that also let individuals who intend to tamper know that the punishment for committing such a crime is severe may have a deterrence effect.

References

American Law Institute (1966), *Restatement (Second) of Torts.*

American Law Institute (1998), *Restatement (Third) of Torts.*

Braningin, W., Allen, M., & Mintz, J. (2004). Tommy Thompson Resigns from HHS, in *Washington Post*, December 3, p. 1.

Crow, B., & Erickson, R. J. (2000). *Product Tampering, Guidelines for Employers and Law Enforcemen*t International Association of Chiefs of Police, Alexandra, VA.

Epstein, R. A. (2000). *Cases and Materials on Torts.* 7th Edition, Aspen Law and Busienss, Gaithersburg, N. Y.

Food & Drug Administration (2006). *Regulatory Procedures Manual.* United States Government, Washington, D.C.

Gonzales, S. (2005). Woman Claims to Find Finger in Eatery's Chili. *San Jose Mercury* News, March 2, B3.

Greenberg, E. (2000). *Product Tampering* at www.facsnet.org. First Posted on April 23, 1999. Revised on February 14, 200. Retrieved on December 28, 2018.

Greenberg, E. (2002). Tampering Threats Inspire Packaging Innovations. Packaging Digest, 39(4), 22-23.

Halloran v. Virginia Chemicals Inc. (1977), 361 NE. 2d 991 New York Court of Appeals.

Jackson, G. B., Jackson, R. W., & Newmiller, C. E. (1992). Consumer Demographics and Reaction to Product Tampering. *Psychology and Marketing*, 9(1), 45-57.

Larsen v. General Motors. (1968), 391. 2nd 495, United States Court of Appeals 8th Circuit.

Logan, B. (1993). Product Tampering Crime: A Review. *Journal of Forensic Science,* 38(4), 18-27.

MacLeod, W. C. (2001). GMA, Anti-Tampering Legislation. Committee *Testimony of Grocery Manufacturers' Association*: Washington, D.C.

MacPherson V. Buick Motor Co. (1916)111, NE. 1050 New York Court of Appeals.

Mitchell, M. L. (1989). The Impact of External Parties on Brand-name Capital: The 1982 Tylenol Poisoning and Subsequent Cases. *Economic Inquiry*, 27(4), 601-618.

Morgan, F. W. (1988). Tampered Goods: Legal Developments and Marketing Guidelines. *Journal of Marketing*, 52(2), 86-96.

Pouncey v. Ford Motor Co. (1972) 464 F. 2nd 957 United States Court of Appeals 5th Circuit.

The United States Food and Drug Administration (2007). Section 402 [21 USC Section 342]. Regulatory Information. Washington, D.C.

www.Senate.gov. (2001). The Product Packaging Protection Act of 2001. United States Government, Washington, D.C.

The Impact of Role Conflict on Frontline Employees' Adaptive Service Behavior: The Moderation Effect of Role Ambiguity: An Abstract

Yi-Chun Liao, Huiping Helena Liao, and Hsiuju Rebecca Yen

Abstract Adapting service behavior is one crucial ability for frontline service employees. Since frontline employees inevitably experience role stress due to demands or ambiguous expectations, studies have revealed influence of role stressor (i.e., role conflict, role ambiguity) on adaptive behavior (e.g., Hartline and Ferrell 1996; Miao and Evans 2013; Rapp et al. 2005). These studies in general viewed both role conflict and role ambiguity as role stressors that negatively affect employees' adaptive behavior. However, a review of the literature indicates inconsistent findings regarding the relationship between employees' role stress and job performance; in particular, role conflicts at times also contribute to job outcomes (e.g., Babin and Boles 1996; Knight et al. 2007).

To clarify the relationship between role stressors and adaptive service behavior (ASB), this study redefine role conflict and role ambiguity in terms of the sources causing the stress. First, we argue that frontline employees as organizational boundary spanners typically experience conflict for satisfying demands from their supervisors and customers. Therefore, we characterize role conflicts into either supervisor-related or customer-related. We hypothesize a negative relationship between both types of role conflicts on adaptive behaviors. Sccond, we postulate that task-related role ambiguity, as external cues provided by the organization, could mitigate the negative effects of role conflict on ASB. Lens situational strengthen theory, we infer task-related role ambiguity constitutes a weak situation. Under this working situation, employees have more freedom to interpret their job and decide how to respond to the requirements from work. In addition, we also examine the relationship between employees' ASB and their service performance.

The study surveyed 229 customer service representatives working in a call center. Analyses indicate that supervisor-related and customer-related role conflict negatively relate to employees' ASB that positively relates to service performance.

Y.-C. Liao (✉) · H. H. Liao · H. R. Yen
National Tsing Hua University, Hsinchu City, Taiwan
e-mail: s101073804@m101.nthu.edu.tw; helena.liao@iss.nthu.edu.tw; hjyen@iss.nthu.edu.tw

J. Allen et al. (eds.), *Celebrating the Past and Future of Marketing and Discovery with Social Impact*, Developments in Marketing Science: Proceedings of the Academy of Marketing Science, https://doi.org/10.1007/978-3-030-95346-1_168

As predicted, the negative effect of customer-related role conflict on ASB is weakened when employees perceive high task-related role ambiguity. However, the effects of supervisor-related role conflict on ASB remain the same, regardless of the level of task-related job ambiguity. Further plots on the moderation effects suggest that role conflicts with the customer could increase the degree of ASB when employees receive high ambiguity regarding task-related instruction, which has significant implications for managing frontline service employees.

Keywords Interpersonal role conflict · Task-related role ambiguity · Situational strength theory · Adaptive service behavior · Call center

Hotel Customer Experience: Mediating the Service Quality-Satisfaction Relationship: An Abstract

Maria Dharmesti

Abstract The current study positions guest experience as the focal variable in understanding guest satisfaction. Two sets of hotel studies are reviewed. In the first set, the term experience is used interchangeably with overall satisfaction. For example, Manhas and Tukamushaba (2015) defines the experience quality as the overall level of customer satisfaction with service. In the second set, Ren, Qiu, Wang, and Lin (2016) demonstrates a link between experience and customer satisfaction in the budget hotel context. The Ren et al. (2016) is perhaps the most relevant to the current paper and uses three dimensions of experience: tangible-sensory experience (e.g. cleanliness, quietness); staff interactional experience; and aesthetic experience (visual appeal). However, service quality is not included in their model. Hence, the missing gap in the literature is a comprehensive study that specifies service quality and experience as separate constructs, demonstrates that they are separate discriminate constructs, and examines the differential effect of each on guest satisfaction.

Data was gathered via survey targeting hotels guests who had stayed at 3-star to 5-star hotels in Indonesia, in the past 12 months (n = 324). Ro (2012) three-steps regression was applied to analyse mediating role of experience in service quality-satisfaction relationship.

The results show that both service quality and experience influence customer satisfaction. A major finding of the study is that experience mediates the relationship between service quality and customer satisfaction. The mediation is partial, with a smaller direct role still played by the service quality attribute of ambience. Nonetheless, service quality per se is not as strategically important for its own sake; rather only if it is leveraged to provide a better hotel guest experience. The new vital emphasis must now be on the overall guest experience, not simply on the more operational variables of service quality. Service quality must still be managed by necessity, but managers must give at least equal attention to the overall guest experience. If the hotel management's Key Performance Indicators (KPIs) do not include experience aspects, then they are missing attention to half of their strategic assets.

M. Dharmesti (✉)
Griffith University, Brisbane, QLD, Australia
e-mail: m.dharmesti@griffith.edu.au

J. Allen et al. (eds.), *Celebrating the Past and Future of Marketing and Discovery with Social Impact*, Developments in Marketing Science: Proceedings of the Academy of Marketing Science, https://doi.org/10.1007/978-3-030-95346-1_169

The first contribution of this paper is to evaluate the differential role of service quality and experience in directly influencing guest satisfaction. Secondly, this study reveals that experience mediates the relationship between service quality and guest satisfaction. It can also provide hotel managers with more understandings about hotel guest's experience to improve guest's satisfaction level.

Keywords Experience · Service quality · Satisfaction · Hotel guest

Experiential Marketing in Traditional Industries: The Case of Kyoto Incense Producer Shoyeido

Tadashi Matsuoka, Yoko Aoyama, and Takako Yamashita

Abstract The purpose of this study is to show how firms in traditional craftsmanship-oriented industries can apply experiential marketing to compete in a changing environment in which service-dominant logic is ascendant. The products of traditional industries in Kyoto are made by craftsmanship honed by history. Kyoto's traditional industries therefore tend to be craftsmanship thisted, with the craftsmen at their center maintaining a strong sense of mission and responsibility to preserve tradition. Traditional marketing views consumers as rational decision-makers who care most about the functional features and benefits of what they buy. In contrast to this approach is experiential marketing, as proposed by Schmitt (*Journal of Marketing Management 15*:53–67, 1999). Experiential marketers view consumers as rational and emotional human beings who are concerned with achieving pleasurable experiences. Experiential marketing focuses on getting customers to sense, feel, think, act, and relate, and it has enabled customers to increasingly participate together with companies in creating value. This research examines the shift of traditional industries of Kyoto from a "craftsmanship" orientation toward a "shared value creation" by analyzing the case of Shoyeido, a long-established incense business, from the viewpoint of value co-creation and context value, concepts which underlie experiential marketing. We also discuss the commercialization at tourist sites of traditional exquisite Japanese incense presentation.

Keywords Traditional industries · Experiential marketing · Service-dominant logic · Value co-creation · Value in context · Incense · Japan

---

T. Matsuoka
Shoyeido Incense Co., Kyoto, Japan
e-mail: td-matsuoka@shoyeido.co.jp

Y. Aoyama
Shimadzu International Inc., Kyoto, Japan
e-mail: aoyama@int.shimadzu.co.jp

T. Yamashita (✉)
Doshisha University, Kyoto, Japan
e-mail: tayamash@mail.doshisha.ac.jp

J. Allen et al. (eds.), *Celebrating the Past and Future of Marketing and Discovery with Social Impact*, Developments in Marketing Science: Proceedings of the Academy of Marketing Science, https://doi.org/10.1007/978-3-030-95346-1_170

Introduction

Kyoto is a city with a long history, and home to 1485 enterprises are more than 100 years old. The capital of Japan for over 1000 years, Kyoto has continued to develop its own unique Japanese culture. At the same time, however, it has become increasingly difficult for Kyoto's traditional industries to thrive in a modern society characterized by changes in values, changes in lifestyles, and the influx of inexpensive foreign products. Managers of the city's traditional businesses continue to struggle with difficult issues such as business succession and shrinking markets.

Craftsmen in traditional industries have absolute confidence in their skills, which are honed by history. Many craftsmen have a strong sense of responsibility and mission, which can be summed up as "We are the ones who create value." This clashes with the principles underlying experiential marketing and service-dominant logic, according to which value is created not only by firms but also through co-creation with customers. Co-creation of value requires consumer participation in the value creation process, and redefines the relationship between consumers and enterprises. Enterprises are required to propose or provide the context in which consumers experience value, not simply to provide their products. This paper examines three cases of incense presentation business systems at tourist sites by Shoyeido, a traditional Kyoto incense maker, which illustrate how traditional industries can not only sell incense products as goods but also create value with consumers. The process by which firms in traditional industries can shift from a craftsmanship orientation to a shared-value-creation orientation, which maintaining their management philosophy, is discussed in detail.

Characteristics of Kyoto's Traditional Industries and Shoyeido

Craftsmanship in Kyoto

Producing high-quality products is the most important thing to people working in traditional industries in Kyoto. For many generations, they have had customers who repeatedly and regularly use their products and services, and the quality of those products and services has allowed them to develop relationships of loyalty with their customers. If the quality of their products or services were to decline, loyalty would decline as well, and customers would be lost. A craftsmanship orientation is essential in order to maintain high quality in these traditional industries. As long as quality remains high, even salespeople who do not directly produce a product can confidently recommend it to customers.

Shoyeido Incense Co., a Long-Established Incense Business

Shoyeido was founded in the neighborhood of Nijo-Karasuma in Kyoto in 1705. The head office and main store are still in this location, and management has been kept in the founding family, being passed down from generation to generation. The current president, Masataka Hata, is the 12th family head of the company. Shoyeido's business is the production and sale of a wide variety of unique, hand-blended incense in the form of incense sticks, pastilles, and sachets. The Shoyeido motto is "Life with fragrance," and the company is continually making efforts to develop and promote Japanese incense culture. The main clients for corporate sales are temples, department stores, Buddhist altar paraphernalia specialty stores, general stores, and overseas wholesalers; the company has more than 3000 corporate customers worldwide. The company has 12 directly-managed stores, and energetically carries out activities to directly deliver their products through mail-order and exhibitions of Kyoto products in department stores all over Japan. Shoyeido ranks second in sales in Japan's incense industry; while overall sales in the industry are shrinking, Shoyeido sales have continued to slowly increase, and its market share is also increasing.

Literature Review

Experiential Marketing and Sensory Marketing

Companies in the incense industry must create customer value in order to survive in today's changing society. Experiential marketing, advocated by Schmitt (1999), focuses not just on the product but on the experience of consuming and using the product. From the experiential marketing perspective, customers are emotionally as well as rationally driven. That is, while customers may frequently engage in rational choice, they are just as frequently driven by emotions, as consumption experiences are often "directed toward the pursuit of fantasies, feelings, and fun" (Holbrook and Hirschman 1982). Nagasawa (2006) described the experience provided by Shoyeido incense as an aggregate of experiential values: sense, feel, think, act, and relate. Krishna (2013), writing about sensory marketing, states that incense is very strongly connected with the memory, and produces various semantic associations with the five senses of sight, touch, taste, smell, and hearing. Schmitt (1999) regards sensory sensations as a basic element of experiential marketing. The consumption of incense appeals highly to customers' senses.

Value Co-Creation as a Core Concept of Service-Dominant Logic

Company activities to build relationships with customers are based on the 4Ps of marketing: product, price, place, and promotion. In traditional 4Ps-based marketing management, a distinction is made between physical products (tangible goods) and services (intangible goods). But in recent years, all products and services have come to be regarded as "services." Vargo and Lusch (2004) argue that providing broadly-defined "services" appeals to and builds long-term relationships with customers. They define all economic activities as "service," including both goods and services as the basis of exchange. They call marketing centered on tangible goods "goods-dominant logic." Goods-dominant logic separates producers and consumers; value is seen as embedded into purchased raw materials, and destroyed by the consumption of goods through exchange. Viewed through the lens of goods-dominant logic, craftsmen in traditional industries with a "craftsmanship orientation" are producers.

Service-dominant logic, by contrast, holds that the context value continues even after the customer uses and experiences goods and services obtained through exchange. Customers participate actively in the value creation process, using their knowledge and skills ("operant resources") and proposing ways that additional value can be created by the context in which the goods or services are consumed.

Muramatsu (2015) advocates the "4Cs" of (1) Contact with customers, (2) Communication, (3) Co-creation between companies and customers, and (4) Contextual value, as a guide to realizing value co-creation in accordance with service-dominant logic. Harada (2005) expresses the relationship of Context and Contents to the value proposition to the customer as follows:

$$\begin{aligned} &\boldsymbol{Business\ model}\left(\textit{sightseeing with fragrance}\right) = \\ &\boldsymbol{Contents}\left(\textit{details of the goods or services}\right) \\ &\times\boldsymbol{Context}\left(\textit{method of providing goods or services}\right) \end{aligned}$$

In this relationship, Context performs a catalytic function to realize the latent value held by Contents. A business model that places importance on the context is called *a Context-driven business model.* The focus on the context makes such a business model difficult to imitate. Harada gives Disneyland's business model as an example: in contrast to traditional Japanese amusement parks, which place amusement rides at random, rides at Disneyland are located in the spatial context of Disney characters and stories.

The emergence of service-dominant logic as a concept that emphasizes the co-creation of value by a companies and customers based on service clearly shows that the relationship between companies and customers is shifting to an era that goods-centric marketing cannot sufficiently cope with. Incense is valued by the sensory experience of smell. Therefore, we believe that the incense business is suitable for service-dominant logic which places importance on context value. Next, we analyze

Shoyeido's current marketing activities from the viewpoint of value co-creation under service-dominant logic.

Case Analysis of Value Co-Creation by Shoyeido

Case Selection and Research Method

We analyzed three cases in Kyoto of Shoyeido's experiential marketing of incense: at the Buddhist Tendai sect's Shoren-in temple, the MICE (Meeting, Incentives, Conferences, Exhibitions) promotion office of the Kyoto City Tourism Bureau, and JR Kyoto Isetan Department Store. All three cases have been able to get on the road to commercialization. The outline of each case and the context value created by the presentation of incense are described. Semi-structured interviews were conducted with Shoyeido planning staff and clients to investigate the planning intentions. The interviews were conceptualized based on the theoretical frame of experiential marketing and service-dominant logic, and were transcribed.

The Tendai Sect Shoren-in Temple

Shoren-in is a prestigious Buddhist temple built 1000 years ago. Visitors to the temple in the daytime tend to be older persons, while at night there are more visitors from the younger generation. Special night visits, which were started in 1995, have become popular among people of all ages. Shoren-in Temple began to burn incense at night from around 2000. This has both the role of hospitality and welcoming visitors and the role of a religious offering, and is an important element of constructing the context. The presentation of incense scent in Shoren-in Temple is shown in Fig. 1, using the concepts of the context-driven business model. Content includes not only Buddhist statues, buildings, and gardens but also tea ceremony while viewing gardens and sutra copying experiences. The presentation of incense is involved in all the content. The content is crossed with the context of Shoren-in Temple, and visitors can experience deep impressions as they walk in the temple precincts. The scent of incense pervades the whole area and is a part of the experience.

The MICE Promotion Office of Kyoto City's Tourism Bureau

Kyoto City has established a sightseeing MICE promotion office in the city's Tourism Bureau which in charge of protection and improvement of resources for tourism. One of the events that this office helps put on is the Kyoto Tanabata Star

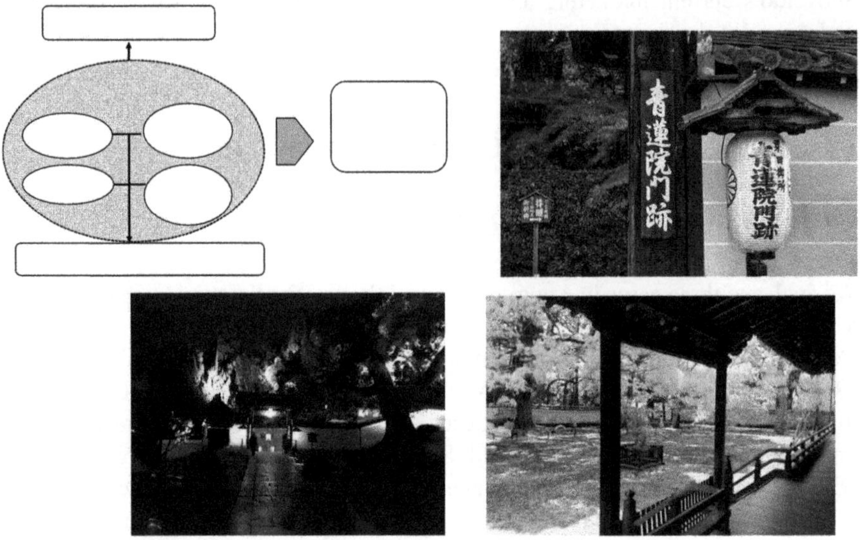

Fig. 1 The presentation of the scent in Shoren-in Temple

Festival. Tanabata is a traditional festival celebrated throughout Japan during which people make wishes on the stars of two star-crossed lovers: Hikoboshi (the star Altair) and Orihime (the star Vega). Kyoto's Tanabata Festival is held at several locations in the city and Kyoto Prefecture.

Aware that visitors to the festival did not come with clear expectation in advance, organizers desired to make the experience something that allowed visitors to "feel 'Kyoto' without any time or economic burden." Starting in 2009, Shoyeido became involved in producing scent at the festival. At the venue, visitors are invited to enjoy an "Aroma Tunnel" at dusk, when the sun begins to set. This was one answer to the MICE office's aim of "responding to faint expectations without burdening visitors." Without being aware of it, visitors participate in and experience the value co-creation process was they enjoy the aroma of incense while strolling in the twilight from the entrance to the exit of the exhibit.

The presentation of scent in Kyoto's Tanabata Festival is shown in Fig. 2 using the concepts of the context-driven business model. Content are places of scenic beauty in Kyoto where Festival events are held. The visitors gathered at nostalgic dusk generate a unique context. Two of the sites where incense scent is presented are Horikawa Tunnel and Nijo Castle. These two venues offer a special context (place), and together with incense provide an extraordinary experience unique to Kyoto. Visitor feedback collected by the MICE office revealed that it was the "scent of incense" that left the strongest impression. It was also found that scent is especially effective in a dark place with little visual information.

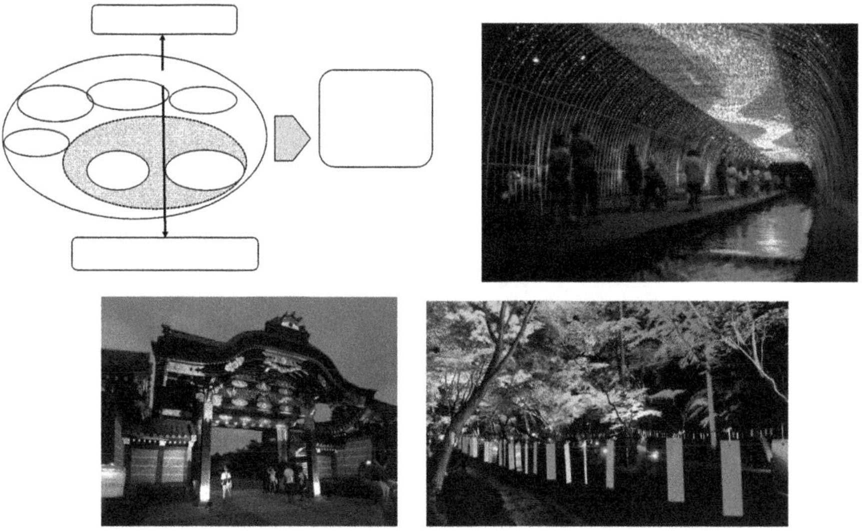

Fig. 2 The presentation of the scent in Kyoto Tanabata Festival

JR Kyoto Isetan Department Store

Kyoto Isetan is a department store established in 1997 as a joint venture between the railway company JR West and Isetan department stores. On September 11, 2017, Mr. Tomoya Sera, President of Kyoto Isetan, declared: "Celebrating Kyoto Isetan's 20-year anniversary, we would like to aim to be a 'glocal' [global + local] store that continues to be rooted in Kyoto and spreads throughout the world." As part of this goal, the department store developed several plans centering on relations with Kyoto. One of these involved the presentation of incense scent by Shoyeido. Named "Shoyeido x Kyoto Isetan Kyoto-scented department store," this started in August 2017. A press release was distributed, and a store representative stated, "The scent is a moderate stimulus for customers and increases the value of their shopping at Kyoto Isetan." In today's environment, online shopping continues to take business away from traditional physical stores, and so Kyoto Isetan has intentionally incorporated scent as "one of the pleasures" of shopping in person at "real stores." This sensory experience obviously cannot be experienced in online shopping. The presentation of the scent not differentiates Kyoto Isetan from other department stores, it is particularly suited for Kyoto. There is a Shoyeido store in Kyoto Isetan where customers can buy the scents they experience on each floor.

The presentation of scent in Kyoto Isetan department store is shown in Fig. 3 using the concepts of the context-driven business model. As in the previous two cases, the context (products and services) can be strengthened by the content. This is an example of an experience (shopping) being made more impressive and enjoyable thanks to being surrounded by a traditional scent.

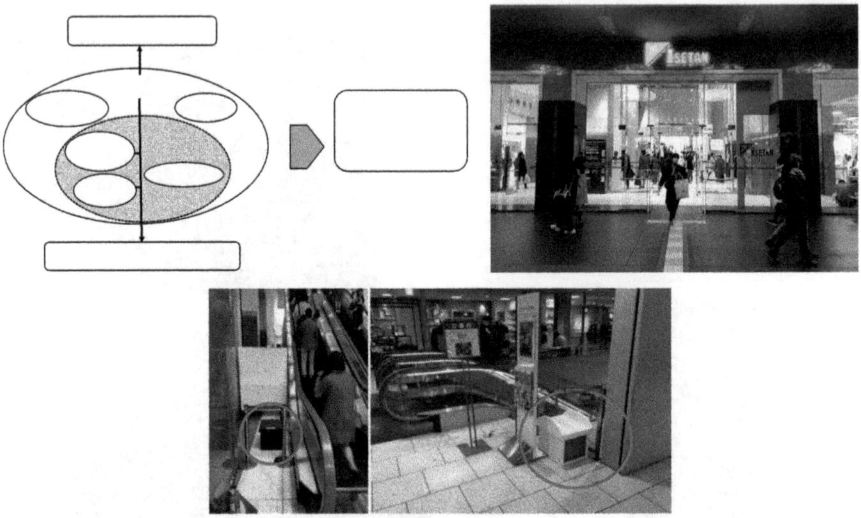

Fig. 3 The presentation of scent in Kyoto Isetan department store

In this section, the importance of context value has been illustrated by value co-creation cases involving the incense of Shoyeido, with special experiences being created by providing contextual value. In these cases, success was achieved thanks to not only cooperative partners but also the results of customer surveys. In the next section, the process of value co-creation and its business possibilities are discussed based on the common points from the three cases.

Discussion

The 4C Approach to Value Creation

The production of incense scent by Shoyeido creates context value that strengthens the original value of content. By analyzing the scent presentation of Shoyeido based on the 4C approach of value co-creation, it is shown that contact with customers is actively at work "in the field." By utilizing customers' knowledge and skills, original context value for the customer is created. In other words, a new business model is established, which leads to continuing transactions with the customer. Table 1 lists 4C items—examples of Contact with customers, Communication, Co-creation, and Context value—and indicates whether or not they were found in the three cases. The implications of these findings for commercialization of the presentation of scent is discussed below.

Table 1 4C items found in the cases

Items	Shoren-in	MICE	Kyoto Isetan
No burden on visitors (contact)	Found	Found	Found
Sales to visitors (contact)	Found	Not found	Found
Get the voices of visitors (contact)	Found	Found	Not found
Machine-burned (not flame-burned) incense (contact)	Not found	Partly found	Found
Long-term relationship with Shoyeido (communication)	Found	Found	Found
Presentation system fully developed (communication)	Found	Found	Not found
Personnel in charge of coordinating with partner companies changed (communication)	Not found	Found	Found
Services that reward business partners (communication)	Not found	Partly found	Found
Sufficient publicity by business partners (communication)	Partly found	Partly found	Partly found
Fragrance-generating equipment maintained mainly by Shoyeido (communication)	Partly found	Not found	Partly found
Solutions are special (co-creation)	Found	Found	Found
Limited original products (scent and packaging) (value-in-context)	Found	Found	Found
Exceeding expectations (value-in-context)	Found	Found	Found

Creation of Commercialization Opportunities for Scent Presentation

The purpose of this paper is to explore ways that traditional industries can shift from a craftsmanship orientation to shared value creation. The presentation of scent is a service which provides context value to sightseers and shoppers through incense. Shoyeido customers include not only general consumers but also business-to-business customers. From examination of the items listed in Table 1, the following commercialization opportunities were identified.

Business Opportunity #1: To Extract a Promising Customer

The organization relationships that Shoyeido has with its existing customers hold the potential for new business opportunities. Shoyeido has more than 3000 corporate customers, but some of them are more suitable for new scent presentation projects than others. Small business partners such as shops which only sell goods are not especially suitable for scent presentation, but customers which stress "hospitality" are. Such customers could be selected, and ways to create context value in the field proposed to them which would have a favorable effect on their customers. This would both strengthen their relationship with Shoyeido and contribute to Shoyeido's sales and profits.

Business Opportunity #2: Examination of Presentation Contents

The content of the scent presentation must be adjusted according to whether or not flame can be used to light the incense. In cases where flame cannot be used (due to the risk of fire), the fragrance is generated by machine, and this requires a testing period to determine the strength of the scent, which varies depending on the space. "In the field" settings where the five senses can be stimulated are best for presentation of the scent. Original fragrances and customized packaging can be also created to match the setting.

Business Opportunity #3: A System for Scent Presentation

Personnel at partner companies are important because they are the ones responsible for actually carrying out scent presentation schemes. Ideally, there would be few or no personnel changes in partner companies; this would facilitate the accumulation of know-how. However, personnel changes do occur, so it is necessary for Shoyeido to establish a format for its scent presentation system to reduce dependence on the knowledge of specific personnel. The system should also incorporate feedback from visitors to current scent presentation projects such as the three cases described in this paper.

Conclusion

In this paper, we have analyzed three cases of scent presentation by traditional Kyoto incense maker Shoyeido based on the concepts of experiential marketing, service-dominant logic, and shared value creation. The cases of Kyoto Isetan department store and Nijo Castle involved presentations that did not use lit incense.

There are many opportunities in tourist-rich Kyoto for traditional craftsmanship-oriented companies like Shoyeido to innovate and practice experiential marketing in order to survive and thrive in a changing world. What this requires above all else is for such companies to change the way they view their relationship with customers. Most traditional Japanese companies, having practiced "product features and benefits" marketing for many years, initially generate weak efforts when they try to employ experiential marketing strategies. To succeed in establishing and managing separate experience-oriented businesses requires making a strong commitment to an experiential approach to marketing.

References

Holbrook, M. & Hirschman, E. (1982). The experiential aspects of consumption: Consumer fantasies, feelings, and fun. *Journal of Consumer Research, 9*, 132-140.

Harada, T. (2005). Kontekusuto doribun bijinesu moderu no kihon gainen: gurōbaru jidai no jizoku-teki kyōsō yūi-sei [Basic concept of context-driven business model: Sustainable competitive advantage in the global era]. *Office Automation 26*(2), 39–48. [published in Japanese]

Krishna, A. (2013). *Customer sense: How the 5 senses influence buying behavior*. New York: Palgrave Macmillan.

Nagasawa, S. (2006). *Shinise burando kigyō no keiken kachi sōzō* [Experiential value creation in a long-established brand company]. Tokyo: Dōyūkan. [published in Japanese]

Muramatsu, J. (2015). *Kachi-kyōsō to māketingu-ron* [Value co-creation and marketing theory]. Tokyo: Dōbunkan Shuppan. [published in Japanese]

Schmitt, B. (1999). Experiential marketing. *Journal of Marketing Management, 15*, 53-67.

Vargo, S.L. & Lusch, R.F. (2004). Evolving to a new dominant logic for marketing. *Journal of Marketing, 68*(1), 1-17.

The Dilemma of Current Business Models in the Japanese Film Market: Causes and Solutions: An Abstract

Dongju Kim and Takako Yamashita

Abstract This paper describes the merits and demerits of the production committee system widely used in the Japanese film industry, examines various financing alternatives, and considers content development challenges. Semi-structured interviews were conducted with producers, distributors, and experts on fund-raising methods in order to conceptualize these structural problems. The data collected were analyzed using the modified grounded theory approach and extracted 14 findings regarding all stages of the Japanese film industry. As a Case study, the author produced the film"Kasagi Rock!", is presented the hardships, experienced in the process from the structure of the Japanese film industry.

The production committee system has a number of limitations, including barriers to utilize intellectual property and difficulties fostering a business mindset in producers. In Japan, where production committees are organized, domestic producers only concentrate on creative work rather than fundraising. The alternative model shown in "Kasagi Rock!" also has its own limitations, including a "lack of motivation" and "burned out" staff stemming from a lack of human resources and insufficient funding. In the case of many small and medium-sized film productions in Japan, the financing, securing of distribution and sales are important challenges. This experience, however, expanded the producer's awareness of the fundraising and promotion aspects of filmmaking, leading to a greater sense of responsibility to see the project through to its completion. By thinking about various ways to raise funds, producers were able to nurture human resources and develop business acumen.

Will the Japanese film industry continue to survive in today's competitive global market? Our findings indicate the importance of changes to the existing business model to meet the challenges of globalization. While publicity is effective, putting too much emphasis on marketing can limit a story and eliminate opportunities for

D. Kim (✉)
Kyoto University, Kyoto, Japan
e-mail: kim.dongju.84n@st.kyoto-u.ac.jp

T. Yamashita
University of Doshisha, Kyoto, Japan
e-mail: tayamash@mail.doshisha.ac.jp

J. Allen et al. (eds.), *Celebrating the Past and Future of Marketing and Discovery with Social Impact*, Developments in Marketing Science: Proceedings of the Academy of Marketing Science, https://doi.org/10.1007/978-3-030-95346-1_171

natural growth. In order to revitalize the Japanese film industry, it is imperative to adopt new strategies for financing, staffing, and casting.

Keywords Film industry · Production committee · Producers · Funding · Globalization

Reconstructing Parental Role Identity through Sensemaking Human-Robot Interaction: An Abstract

Chu-Heng Lee and Ming-Huei Hsieh

Abstract The emerging phenomenon of robot-mediated parenthood is dramatically shifting family life from parent-child dyadic relationship into parent-robot-child triadic interactions. The effort to make sense of parental role identity is thus processed in a new relational context of human-robot interactions. This research leverages sensemaking and sensegiving perspectives of this novel context into identity theory to examine the mechanism of parental role identity reconstruction.

Identity theory explains that persons recognize one another and themselves by self-categorization with naming one's identity as an occupant of a role in a structured society. The naming is critical to activate a set of meanings and expectations associated with self-role for guiding one's own behaviors. A robot, in this sense serving as a new social actor, sustains a relationship with parents to assist childcare and home education. The first research question is: What are the emerged meanings of parental role identity to be recategorized and renamed by parents?

As for dealing with meaning construction and reconstruction, sensemaking is central to inform and constrain a person's identity and action. From the viewpoint of parents, sensemaking and sensegiving about human-robot interactions relies on the share of parental responsibilities and incorporates entrenched needs (e.g., lack of time, educational knowledge demands). Therefore, the second research question is: What underling mechanisms that shape the meanings of parental role are emerged with parents' sensemaking and sensegiving toward parent-robot-child triadic interactions?

Based on in-depth interviews with seven families who live with educational robots, the research outlines three between roles' identities of parent-robot: gateopener-robotic alloparent, learner-robotic teacher, and enabler-future agent. The underlined mechanism of the reconstruction of parental role identity emerged during a linear evolving process which corresponds to attempts at revision, reinforcement, and revitalization. The analysis foregrounds how parents make sense of an intelligent actor and reconstruct their role identity. Marketers can capture the new

---

C.-H. Lee (✉) · M.-H. Hsieh
National Taiwan University, Taipei City, Taiwan
e-mail: d00724007@ntu.edu.tw; minghsieh@ntu.edu.tw

J. Allen et al. (eds.), *Celebrating the Past and Future of Marketing and Discovery with Social Impact*, Developments in Marketing Science: Proceedings of the Academy of Marketing Science, https://doi.org/10.1007/978-3-030-95346-1_172

implications to develop proper facilitators of family-based offerings in an age of human-robot interactions. In addition to explicit value of adopting intelligent technology at home, implicit value of adaptation to challenges between parent and children as well as from dynamically environmental conditions for children is more important for effort in enhancing value.

Keywords Role identity · Sensemaking · Human-robot interaction · Robot-mediated parenthood

Combining the VBN Model and the TPB Model to Explore Consumer's Consumption Intention of Local Organic Foods: An Abstract

Mei-Fang Chen

Abstract The global food system nowadays, whether it is agricultural or livestock activities, as well as mainstream markets, has been considered unsustainable. If the conventional agricultural trend continues, the emissions of food production sector are supposed to surpass the global warming limit of 2 °C by 2050. "Sustainable food consumption" can be a key mitigation strategy to cope with the climate change crisis. Due to the reduction of greenhouse gas emissions in production, organic and locally produced products have a positive impact on the environment. A large number of empirical studies argued environmental issues as the main motivation for consumers to purchase organic and local foods. Production and consumption of locally available OFs will ensure more sustainable, more delicious, and healthier foods for local residences without sacrificing the economic benefits of local communities. The theory of planned behavior (TPB) and the value-belief-norm (VBN) theory of environmentalism are the most commonly used environmental psychology theories with good prediction power. However, both theoretical models have their own drawbacks. This study combines the VBN model and the TPB model to make up the drawbacks of each model to examine the validity of this combined model applied to consumption intention of local organic foods by structural equation modeling analysis. Self-reported questionnaires were collected in Taiwan to examine the environmental psychology theories. The results revealed that the combined model can explain about 47% of the variation in people's consumption intention of local organic foods. In addition, the results indicated that people's attitude and perceived behavioral control determine the consumption intention of local organic foods. This result can be further explained through a causal chain: from an

Acknowledgments and funding: This work was supported by a grant from the Ministry of Science and Technology, R.O.C. (MOST 108-2410-H-036-009).

M.-F. Chen (✉)
Tatung University, Taipei, Taiwan
e-mail: mfchen@ttu.edu.tw

J. Allen et al. (eds.), *Celebrating the Past and Future of Marketing and Discovery with Social Impact*, Developments in Marketing Science: Proceedings of the Academy of Marketing Science, https://doi.org/10.1007/978-3-030-95346-1_173

individual's stable value orientations and environment general beliefs to the beliefs that their actions may affect the environment and beliefs that the individual has responsibility to reduce this threat. People's biospheric value and altruism value are also important.

Keyword Local organic foods · Theory of planned behavior model · Value-belief-norm model · Combined model

Self-Transcendence, Social Mindfulness and Choice of Exchange Offer Incentive: An Abstract

Preetha Menon

Abstract An exchange offer is a consumer sales promotion program in which the seller offers to a prospective buyer an incentive in exchange for an old, used product while purchasing a new one (Menon and Vijayaraghavan 2014). Although a sales promotion incentive, an exchange offer qualifies as one type of collaborative consumption, moving products from the 'haves' to the 'have nots' (Benoit et al. 2017). Researchers have pegged the concept of collaborative consumption to be the next big move in social marketing, leading to sustainable practices within organizations and in communities (Scaraboto 2015). This research is in answer to this growing community of consumers, who support and consume products that lead to a circular economy and collaborative consumption. In a first attempt of its kind, personal values and traits such as self-transcendence and social mindfulness are also studied as two key variables that interact with the type of offer.

This research frames exchange offers as either economic or social transactions. An exchange offer that offers monetary benefits as incentives (exchange for 20% discount) is framed as an economic offer, while exchange offer that provides additional social benefits as incentive (exchange for the 'have nots') is framed as a social offer. These exchange offers framed as either economic or social offers are studied against the light of personal values of self-transcendence and social mindfulness. The consumers' willingness to accept the exchange offer is studied through two cascading laboratory experiments.

The results reveal that there is significant effect of offer type on willingness to accept the exchange offer. Social offers are preferred over pure economic offers. The value of self-transcendence also has a main effect on willingness to accept the exchange offer. Furthermore, the interaction effect between self-transcendence and offer type is also significant. Subjects with high social mindfulness scores also have a high score on self-transcendence, indicated in a high correlation score of $r_s = 0.86$.

This research adds new knowledge to the field of collaborative consumption through the framing of exchange offers. Consumers' value of self-transcendence

P. Menon (✉)
FLAME University, Pune, India
e-mail: preetha.menon@flame.edu.in

J. Allen et al. (eds.), *Celebrating the Past and Future of Marketing and Discovery with Social Impact*, Developments in Marketing Science: Proceedings of the Academy of Marketing Science, https://doi.org/10.1007/978-3-030-95346-1_174

coupled with social mindfulness has provided a strong explanation for the choice of social exchange offers. This study will be pivotal in paving the way for sustainable consumption, providing policy makers and marketers with a solution for their sustainable goals.

Keywords Exchange offers · Self-transcendence · Social mindfulness · Sustainable consumption

The Effect of Time Pressure on Shoppers' Behavior: An Abstract

Ana Maria Soares and Maher Georges Elmashhara

Abstract Time scarcity is a widespread phenomenon with multi-dimensional consequences which has implications for marketing and consumer behavior (Godinho et al. 2016; Nilsson et al. 2017). Consumers' choices are influenced by available resources, and time is increasingly seen as a valuable resource. Hence, time pressure and time management impact how, where and when consumers buy, as well as how much time they spend in shopping venues. Despite several studies looking at the impact of time related variables in consumer behaviour (e.g., Godinho et al. 2016; Lloyd et al. 2014; Mitomi 2018), there is a dearth of studies focusing on how time dimensions impact on the desire to stay in shopping venues.

Hence, we look at the impact of time pressure in utilitarian versus the hedonic shopping motivations to understand how consumers' feelings of time scarcity affect time spent in stores (Lloyd et al. 2014). We propose a conceptual framework of how time pressure affects shopping motivations and how these impact the desire to stay. In addition, we test whether time management moderates these relationships.

Results of a survey show support for the impact of time pressure in hedonic shopping motivations but not in utilitarian motivations. Hedonic motivations impact significantly on desire to stay. Finally, time pressure has a negative significant impact in desire to stay.

The negative impact of time pressure in desire to stay is in line with what would be expected. However, this impact becomes positive when considering the mediating role of hedonic shopping motivations. Finally, the moderating effect of time management in the proposed relationships was not supported.

From the managerial point of view, the results of this paper encourage shopping venues management to increase the recreational component of their tenant mix. This may lead shoppers to stay for a longer time regardless of the time pressure.

A. M. Soares (✉)
University of Minho, CICS.NOVA.UMinho, Braga, Portugal
e-mail: amsoares@eeg.uminho.pt

M. G. Elmashhara
University of Minho, NIPE, Braga, Portugal
e-mail: maher@eeg.uminho.pt

J. Allen et al. (eds.), *Celebrating the Past and Future of Marketing and Discovery with Social Impact*, Developments in Marketing Science: Proceedings of the Academy of Marketing Science, https://doi.org/10.1007/978-3-030-95346-1_175

Desire to stay at the shopping is expected to lead to other outcomes like patronage intentions (Martin and Turley 2004).

Keywords Time pressure · Time management · Desire to stay · Hedonic shopping motivations · Utilitarian shopping motivations

An Exploration of Effects of Launching Empowerment Strategies by Brands for Participating Customers: An Abstract

Hajer Bachouche and Ouidade Sabri

Abstract In the past decade, numerous international brands as Lay's (Frito-Lay), Dop (L'oréal), Danette (Danone) have all embraced consumer empowerment strategies relying on consumers for new product development in consumer goods sector in France. Consumer empowerment, through managerial strategies, is defined as « *a strategy that firms use to give customers a sense of control over a company's product selection process, allowing them to collectively select final products the company will later sell to the broader market* » (Fuchs et al. 2010, p. 65). These authors have distinguished two types of strategies: empowerment-to-create which enable customers to submit ideas for new products and empowerment-to-select which rely on consumers votes to choose products that will ultimately be marketed. On the one hand, with the advent of Internet technologies, brands are increasingly deploying empowerment campaigns through dedicated platforms or facebook pages taking advantage of communicational and innovation opportunities enabled by these practices implementation. On the other hand, marketing scholars studying consumer empowerment theme (Dahl et al. 2015; Fuchs et al. 2010) have addressed several positive effects for companies launching empowerment strategies on various performance indicators (brand attitude, word-of-mouth, purchase intention). However, it appears when reviewing the actual literature that while both empowerment strategies effects on various companies' brand equity metrics have been documented, comparison between empowerment to create and empowerment to select effectiveness didn't get attention while it has a significant importance for managers when deploying marketing actions in a context of pressure on return on investment. Our research is building on avenues of research gaps introduced by Fuchs et Schreier (2011; p.29). More specifically, this research aims at empirically examine (1) benefits retrieved by participants to empowerment campaigns (2) comparison between empowerment to create and to select effects as perceived by both participating and

H. Bachouche (✉)
IPAG Business School, Paris, France
e-mail: h.bachouche@ipag.fr

O. Sabri
IAE de Paris, Paris, France
e-mail: ouidade.sabri@univ-paris1.fr

J. Allen et al. (eds.), *Celebrating the Past and Future of Marketing and Discovery with Social Impact*, Developments in Marketing Science: Proceedings of the Academy of Marketing Science, https://doi.org/10.1007/978-3-030-95346-1_176

non-participating consumers (3) behavioral attitudes arising from participation to these campaigns and changes induced in terms of the perception of brands launching such initiatives. To answer to these questions, we've adopted a qualitative approach aiming at answering to research objectives and combining three series of in-depth interviews (see Annex 1 for profile description of respondents). This research combines a total of 24 interviews conducted with participating consumers (N = 9) that were involved in empowerment campaigns, projective interviews (N = 7) and interviews with non-participant consumers (N = 8). Results show that both participating and non-participating consumers prefer empowerment to create strategies as they are more opened and they enable consumers' freedom of speech letting consumers themselves more than empowerment to select. Consumers discourse analysis also shows that they prefer empowerment to select comparing to create when they feel they don't have the sufficient skills or expertise.

Keywords Empowerment · Relative efficacy · Brands · Participating consumers

Attributing Blame in Customer-to-Customer Interactions in Online and Face-to-Face Environments: An Abstract

Linda W. Lee, Ian P. McCarthy, and Yunzhijun Yu

Abstract Customer-to-customer (C2C) interactions can be pivotal to business performance because they can influence customer satisfaction and other outcomes. While previous studies have largely studied non-group contexts in which C2C interactions are incidental to the service experience, this study examines a group context in which face-to-face and online C2C interactions are deliberate and core to the service being provided: graduate business education. This study compares C2C interactions between face-to-face and online graduate business education where students (whether enrolled in a face-to-face or online program) are expected to interact, engage in discussion, debate, and work with other students within the student cohort.

We seek insights on how C2C interactions may affect customers' perceptions of a group service, and how differences in their experiences of C2C interactions may make them attribute service success or failure to different parties involved in this group service (e.g. the school, the program, students in the same cohort, or themselves). Forty-one semi-structured interviews were conducted with recent alumni of graduate business programmes (MBA, MSc) using the critical incident technique. The data was collected prior to the pandemic and the shift to online teaching.

Preliminary findings indicate that, in positive incidents, other students were most frequently attributed, followed by self attribution, then the professor/university. Also, self attribution was higher in online programmes than in face-to-face programmes. For both online and face-to-face programmes, the value of teamwork and value of diversity were the most frequent themes in the positive incidents. Face-to-face programmes provide opportunities for more emotional relationships vs. online programmes (e.g. bonding and friendships vs. forming professional networks). In

L. W. Lee (✉)
Nottingham Trent University, Nottingham, UK
e-mail: linda.lee@ntu.ac.uk

I. P. McCarthy · Y. Yu
Simon Fraser University, Vancouver, BC, Canada
e-mail: ian_mccarthy@sfu.ca; yunzhijun_yu@sfu.ca

J. Allen et al. (eds.), *Celebrating the Past and Future of Marketing and Discovery with Social Impact*, Developments in Marketing Science: Proceedings of the Academy of Marketing Science, https://doi.org/10.1007/978-3-030-95346-1_177

negative incidents, other students were almost exclusively attributed, with very low self attribution.

These results suggest that the interactions with other graduate business students are important and valuable, not only for their learning of teamwork but for professional networks and friendships beyond the completion of their programmes.

Keywords Customer-to-customer interaction · Attribution theory · Group services · Graduate business education

The Effectiveness of Donation Promises in Charity Auctions as a Cause-Related Marketing Strategy: An Abstract

Ann Wallin, Claudia Gonzalez-Arcos, Wen Mao, Peter T. L. Popkowski Leszczyc, and Leo Wong

Abstract Retailers increasingly use cause-related marketing (CRM) strategies to try to increase sales. It is therefore of great importance to retailers to determine the effectiveness of such strategies, as well as, consumers' perceptions and responses to such CRM activities. This study examines a CRM strategy where the sale of a product is bundled with a donation to charity. We first conducted a field experiment (Study 1), using auctions, augmented with a laboratory study (Study 2), to determine the impact of donation promise (the amount the retailer will donate in a CRM transaction) on consumer willingness to pay (WTP) and retailer revenue.

The controlled field experiment (Study 1) ran auctions with different percentages of the selling price donated to charity. Results indicate that higher donation promises lead to increased selling prices, although at a diminishing rate. Low levels of donation promises incur significant overpayments, suggesting that retailers can profit from their associations with charities.

A laboratory study (Study 2) extended these findings to low and high value products, and explores the influence of motivation for giving (warm glow vs. persuasion) on the relationship between donation promise and WTP. This study shows that both warm glow and persuasion positively influence the relationship between donation promise and WTP, where warm glow mediates and persuasion moderates this relationship. At small donation promises, we find support for warm glow motives over efficacy effects or the legitimizing of paltry donations, whereas for larger donation promises we find that consumers trade off between warm glow and the sacrifice from giving. Interestingly, consumers receive a warm glow from the mere act of

---

A. Wallin (✉) · C. Gonzalez-Arcos · W. Mao · P. T. L. Popkowski Leszczyc
University of Queensland, Brisbane, QLD, Australia
e-mail: a.wallin@business.uq.edu.au; c.gonzalez@business.uq.edu.au; w.mao@business.uq.edu.au; p.popowski@business.uq.edu.au

L. Wong
University of Alberta, Edmonton, AB, Canada
e-mail: ltwong@ualberta.ca

J. Allen et al. (eds.), *Celebrating the Past and Future of Marketing and Discovery with Social Impact*, Developments in Marketing Science: Proceedings of the Academy of Marketing Science, https://doi.org/10.1007/978-3-030-95346-1_178

giving, regardless of the amount of money. However, consumers are more persuaded by higher levels of donation promise.

This study provides guidance when designing cause-related marketing strategies. The findings are valuable in outlining the optimal donation amount that should be connected to a product sale – as more is not necessarily better. The study also contributes to the recent research examining how consumer motivation and perceptions impact the performance of cause-related marketing initiatives. Overall results have important implications for the appeal of CRM offerings in fixed-price retail settings and suggest that charity auctions can be a cost-effective part of a retailer's corporate social responsibility strategy.

Keywords Donation · Cause-related marketing · Charitable motives · Charity auction · Field experiments

Quality Signals in the Cannabis Market: An Abstract

Selena Chavez, Taylan Yalcin, and Ekin Pehlivan

Abstract Emphasizing product attributes that signal quality through commonly accepted standards have been at the core of marketing messages in a variety of different industries. Establishing quality signals for an offering previously considered illicit has become the challenge for marketers upon the legalization of adult cannabis consumption in a growing number of US states, and several other countries such as Canada and Mexico. The existence of a cannabis consumption culture during its prohibition and medicinal use periods provide the opportunity for marketers to use freely available customer input, while these quality signals are established in the marketplace. As this co-creation process unfolds, we seek to explore how the customers contribute to the co-creation of quality signals through online discourse in our future research. In other words, we aim to understand how quality signals can be (and are being) established in the cannabis market, by exploring consumer-generated content (Berthon et al. 2008) on web platforms.

We explore how a 3×2 typology of quality signals is distributed in product descriptions in this newly emerging market. Search (verifiable before purchase), experience (verifiable after use) and trust (hardly verifiable, if ever) signals of both intrinsic (stemming from endogenous traits of the offering) and extrinsic (stemming from the augmentations to the offering) qualities were identified in our preliminary study of company created content. Our initial findings reveal that current product descriptions utilize experience signals, especially extrinsic ones heavily. Whereas extrinsic search signals such as awards and recognitions are not yet established in the market place, trust signals are vague in their promise. We speculate that copywriters are trying to convey experience related quality to provide an idea of what to expect and cannot yet depend on extrinsic search signals as the market is still in the process of institutionalization. In the next stages of this study consumer created content will be analyzed, coded, and compared to company created content to determine how well the marketing copy created fit the consumers' reviews of the same products.

S. Chavez · T. Yalcin · E. Pehlivan (✉)
California State University Channel Islands, Camarillo, CA, USA
e-mail: selena.chavez246@myci.csuci.edu; taylan.yalcin@csuci.edu; ekin.pehlivan@csuci.edu

J. Allen et al. (eds.), *Celebrating the Past and Future of Marketing and Discovery with Social Impact*, Developments in Marketing Science: Proceedings of the Academy of Marketing Science, https://doi.org/10.1007/978-3-030-95346-1_179

Keywords Quality signals · Content analysis · Cannabis market · Typology
References Available Upon Request

Investigating Brandscapes, Retail Ideology, and Experiential Marketing: An Organisational Perspective: An Abstract

Maedbh Donaldson and Aileen Kennedy

Abstract In the clutter of today's saturated marketing landscape, connecting with consumers on an intimate level through immersive and interactive brand experiences can be managed by companies within a constructed and controlled brand environment such as a brand museum. A brand museum combines brand education in a museum atmosphere with the excitement of extraordinary and entertaining visitor experiences and allows marketers to connect with consumers on an emotional, social, and cultural level. Practitioners have embraced the brand museum format as a new and innovative form of interactive retail and brand management, evidenced in the growing number of brand museums globally. However, the brand museum as a contemporary topic in marketing theory remains underexplored resulting in theory lagging industry practice. Although brand museums are recognised as complex environments, housing both cognitively and emotionally stimulating experiences, guidance for practitioners on devising and delivering effective brand museum experiences has been rare. To address this gap in research, this study investigates the key dimensions of the brand museum experience that are most impactful in the structuration of visitor's brand experiences, as identified from an industry and practitioners' perspective. A case study methodology generates empirical evidence from the experience providers of an internationally renowned tourist attraction and brand museum, the Jameson Distillery Bow Street brand museum or 'brand home'. Industry experts share their professional insights and views on what they perceive as the most influential dimensions of the curated Jameson brand museum experience for engaging customers. This practitioner perspective identifies brand heritage, the human connection and storytelling as core dimensions of the curated museum

M. Donaldson
BBDO Dublin, Dublin, Ireland
e-mail: maedbhdonaldson@bbdo.ie

A. Kennedy (✉)
TU Dublin, Dublin, Ireland
e-mail: aileen.kennedy@tudublin.ie

J. Allen et al. (eds.), *Celebrating the Past and Future of Marketing and Discovery with Social Impact*, Developments in Marketing Science: Proceedings of the Academy of Marketing Science, https://doi.org/10.1007/978-3-030-95346-1_180

experience which visitors engage with to co-create their own unique brand experiences. We explore the managerial implications of these marketing assets for the firm. Faced with high costs, growing competition, and increasing levels of sophistication and technology being employed within brand museums a practitioner perspective from a globally successful brand home makes a valuable contribution to this evolving research area and highlight opportunities for further research.

Keywords Brand museum · Experiential marketing · Brand experiences · Storytelling

Rewarding Female Inclusive New Product Teams

Jessica Felix, Felix Flores, and Gary L. Frankwick

Abstract As more women make up the professional management workforce in marketing and engineering, they are becoming a larger percentage of many new product development teams. With the generally acknowledged inequality in compensation between males and females, a question then arises as to the best way to reward teams for their efforts. This study surveyed 150 marketing and new product managers to examine the effect of various rewards on team creativity (originality and usefulness), number of ideas, and new product performance with different levels of female participation. Results of the SEM analysis suggest that greater female participation increases the number of ideas, which increases originality, usefulness, and new product performance. Teams with greater female participation perform better with greater focus on financial rewards.

Keywords Product development · Innovation · Female · Creativity

Introduction

Patents awarded to women went from 2.6% in 1977 to 10.3% in 1998 with 20% of inventions currently attributed to women growing to a projected 50% over the next generation (Bellis 2017).

In the past, the innovation and technology sector has lacked the female perspective, limiting new product development, especially for female-specific products (Chau and Quire 2018). The presence of women, though a consistent minority in businesses, positively influences organization wide innovation (Torchia et al. 2011). Hernández Girón et al. (2004) found that a group composed exclusively of women

J. Felix (✉) · G. L. Frankwick
University of Texas, El Paso, TX, USA
e-mail: jfelix@miners.utep.edu; glfrankwick@utep.edu

F. Flores
Metropolitan State University, Denver, CO, USA
e-mail: fflore11@msudenver.edu

J. Allen et al. (eds.), *Celebrating the Past and Future of Marketing and Discovery with Social Impact*, Developments in Marketing Science: Proceedings of the Academy of Marketing Science, https://doi.org/10.1007/978-3-030-95346-1_181

was able to innovate a sustainable product development process that included the commercialization of a diverse set of products. The increasing presence of women in the workforce brings the benefit of diversity to business but it can also represent a challenge in attempting to motivate these employees.

Extant research on new product development (NPD) teams focuses mostly on functional diversity and the use of instrumental information which have positive effects on new product performance (Haon et al. 2009). Similarly, a study of cross-functional teams found a positive effect of the proportion of multi-knowledge individuals (knowledge of marketing and technology) on new product innovativeness through the management of information (Park et al. 2009). A meta-analytic review of 38 studies on NPD team performance, however, found that functional diversity is not significantly related to NPD market success, efficiency, and time-to-market (Sivasubramaniam et al. 2012). All of this research has yet to explore the influence that women have on new product performance.

Literature has long focused on motivating creativity, but as the business environment changes, there is an increasing need to focus on what motivates women. This study focuses on how women inclusive NPD teams perform with respect to creativity, number of ideas, product usefulness, and new product performance. Additionally, the study measures the relationship between different reward options and teams' creative performance.

Study results suggest that the percentage of women present in NPD teams positively influences the number of ideas generated by the team, which increases the originality of ideas, and consequently product usefulness. Product usefulness, then positively affects new product performance. Finally, financial rewards increase the effect of female participation on number of new product ideas.

Theory and Hypotheses

New Product Performance

New product success has been defined as conformance quality, product cost, time-to-market, market share, and overall profitability (Jayaram and Narasimhan 2007). Im and Workman (2004) measured new product success based on a product's market share, sales, return-on-investment, profitability and meeting of objectives. Osteras et al. (2006) developed three levels of performance objectives; meeting technical and design specifications, business performance such as market share and return on investment, and finally meeting cost and time constraints. Time-to-market, conformance, and product cost along with market share and profitability are also used (Sanongpong 2009). Return on investment, sales, profit margin, and market share were also used by Yang et al. (2017). Based on these studies and other existing literature, our study defines new product performance as the product's technical performance to specifications, projected unit cost, projected R&D budget, time-to-market objective, market share objective, return on investment, and overall commercial success.

Team Diversity

Research in business diversity has typically focused on team performance. For example, Hoisl et al. (2017) found an inverse u-shaped relationship between diversity in experience and performance. Other research has focused on demographics such as, racial, and national diversity (Joshi and Roh 2009), or gender (Hoogendoorn et al. 2013), but results regarding specific effects are still mixed. Apesteguia et al. (2012) concluded from their field study in business schools that two men and one woman was the ideal level of diversity in teams focusing on decision making in innovation, brand management, and corporate social responsibility. However, the study limited teams to a maximum of 50% female participation. In a military study, Hirschfeld et al. (2005) found that team problem solving improved with greater female participation. In engineering, second year majority female teams outperformed majority male teams (Laeser et al. 2003).

In new product development the desired result is a product that performs well in the market, which can be achieved through a path of creativity. A creative thinking study of sixth graders and high school seniors found that the number of ideas generated by an individual is positively related to the quality (measured as originality and appropriateness) of the ideas (Milgram et al. 1978). Measuring novelty and meaningfulness (usefulness) separately rather than as a single concept of creativity seems to have a better effect on new product performance (Im and Workman 2004).

In general, gender diversity in business teams shows an inverted u-shaped relationship between the percentage of women in a team and its performance (Hoogendoorn et al. 2013), while diversity in R&D teams is positively related to both radical and incremental innovation (Garcia Martinez et al. 2017). Indeed, a study on the generation of innovative new software ideas found that, in the absence of any kind of support, all-female teams generated more innovative ideas than mixed and all-male teams (Klein and Dologite 2000). This evidence suggests that female presence in NPD teams can positively influence the number of ideas generated.

H1: The percentage of females in NPD teams is positively related to number of ideas.

Number of Ideas

The number of ideas generated is one of the most important aspects of innovation for a firm (Toubia 2006). Toubia (2006) suggests that incentives affect the number of ideas and the creativity of each idea with a tradeoff between the impact (creativity) of ideas and the number of ideas. This study suggest that a high number of ideas is not conducive to highly creative ideas. Milgram et al. (1978) found that quantity of ideas was necessary to generate high quality, creative ideas. Indeed, in a study rating the originality, quality, and elaboration of ideas generated by college students, participants that were asked to generate multiple ideas (as opposed to a single idea) contributed the highest rated ideas in originality (Reiter-Palmon and Arreola 2015).

H2: Number of ideas generated is positively related to originality of ideas.

H3: Number of ideas generated is positively related to new product performance.

Originality

Creativity is one of the factors that will help market oriented firms reach new product success, measured in market performance (Im and Workman 2004). In a study examining creative behavior, usefulness and novelty/originality were identified as measures of product creativity (Yu-Shan et al. 2018). Zeng et al. (2011) measured creativity in terms of the new product's ease of use, usefulness, and novelty and found that perceived product creativity was positively correlated with product attractiveness and consequently with customer satisfaction. Chang et al. (2014) found that novelty/originality (as a measure of creativity) is positively related to new product performance.

H4: Originality is positively related to new product performance.

Women have historically been considered to be less creative than men, however, women's higher involvement in innovation might mean that these beliefs are not accurate. Mierdel and Bogner (2019) found that, in a study involving ninth graders, girls outperform boys in several aspects of creative model construction. Stephens et al. (2001) found that girls obtained higher originality and creativity scores than boys in all tests administered.

H5: The percentage of females in NPD teams is positively related to the originality of ideas.

Originality is considered a part of creativity but whether original ideas lead to useful products is a separate issue. A proposed construct of creativity is one that ties originality to the usefulness of the product idea along with aesthetics and authenticity (Kharkhurin 2014). This construct suggests that novelty and usefulness are connected and are necessary for new product success. A study of creativity in high technology firms found a significant correlation between novelty (or originality) and meaningfulness (usefulness) (Im and Workman 2004).

H6: Originality is positively related to new product usefulness.

Product Usefulness

Knowledge management not only deals with existing knowledge but also with the creation of knowledge and the SECI model suggests "knowledge is created by the creative tension between tacit and explicit know-how, leading to a dynamic flow of activities that facilitates the generation, transfer and application of knowledge" (Bandera et al. 2017, p. 165). In their study of new product performance, Chang et al. (2014) establish the assumption knowledge creation influences the importance of product usefulness and consequently, new product success.

H7: Product usefulness is positively related to new product performance.

Women throughout history have invented highly creative products that have turned out to be useful to our everyday lives. A few examples are Mary Anderson, who invented windshield wipers, Josephine Cochrane, who invented the dishwasher, Dr. Shirley Ann Jackson, who invented caller ID, and Marie Van Brittan Brown, who invented the home security system (Vyas 2019).

H8: The percentage of women in NPD teams positively affects the usefulness of new products.

Reward Systems

Managers can motivate higher performance through either intrinsic or extrinsic rewards. Several kinds of intrinsic motivation exist and so the best way to motivate creative behavior might depend on the individual (Auger and Woodman 2016). According to Burroughs et al. (2011), rewards along with training are the best ways to enhance creative performance by increasing intrinsic motivation. The focus of this study is on the effect that recognition, promotion and financial rewards have on new product development teams.

Recognition Rewards

Extrinsic and intrinsic motivation and the effect of extrinsic rewards have been studied in depth and a generally accepted belief is that extrinsic rewards have a detrimental effect on motivation (Deci et al. 2017). Acknowledgement, however, tends to increase intrinsic motivation (Deci et al. 2017). Recognition rewards are those that acknowledge an employee's exceptional performance. In a study of reward influence on motivation, Khan et al. (2011) found that supervisor recognition positively influences employee motivation and performance. A survey with employees and managers in the public sector provided evidence that 92% of respondents believe that recognition rewards increase commitment and employee satisfaction (Saunderson 2004). Zhuang et al. (1999) found that employees indicate that recognition is important in rewarding creative individuals.

H9: Recognition rewards positively influence (a) originality, (b) usefulness, (c) number of ideas, and (d) new product performance.

Different rewards can have different effects on creativity, however, it is important to realize that gender might affect the effectiveness of these rewards. An Employee Recognition Survey showed that men and women view recognition as important; 54% of men and 46% of women reported being satisfied with their firm's recognition practices (APA 2014). Recognition rewards are appropriate when the desired behaviors are related to innovation and creativity, inventiveness, commitment, and initiative (Hansen et al. 2002).

H10: Recognition rewards increase the positive effect of female participation on (a) originality, (b) usefulness, (c) number of ideas, and (d) new product performance.

Promotion Rewards

Cognitive Evaluation Theory (CET) states that verbal rewards, including positive feedback, tend to enhance intrinsic motivation (Deci et al. 2001). Promotion rewards include those involving career advancement, prestige among peers and supervisors, and prestige across the organization. Rajendran et al. (2017) found that 43.6% of employees and managers surveyed believe that performance based promotions have a high effect in employee performance and only 4.5% believe it has no effect. In an exploratory study of non-monetary rewards, Sonawane (2008) found that career advancement opportunities represented one of the most important parts of non-monetary rewards.

H11: Promotion rewards positively influence (a) originality, (b) usefulness, (c) number of ideas, and (d) new product performance in NPD teams.

In a study of differences in work values according to gender, Beutell and Brenner (1986) found that men rank career advancement (promotion) higher than women, who in turn rank accomplishment and respect higher. The Employee Recognition Survey reported that women care about 1% more than men about promotion rewards but care much less about these compared to financial rewards (APA 2014).

H12: Promotion rewards positively affect the relationship between female participation and (a) originality, (b) usefulness, (c) number of ideas, and (d) product performance in NPD teams.

Financial Rewards

CET states that tangible rewards will generally decrease intrinsic motivation (Deci et al. 2001). Economists, however, believe in the principle that financial incentives result in performance. Financial rewards refer to any type of monetary incentive given to employees for desirable behavior and results. Literature is divided on whether the effect of financial rewards is positive or negative. Leuven et al. (2010) found that financial rewards have no significant effects in performance. Alternatively, the implementation of financial rewards increased the number of people contributing new ideas and the quality of ideas (Gibbs et al. 2017). Alexy and Leitner (2011) found that financial rewards attract creative individuals as long as the rewards are perceived as a bonus and not part of a regular payment. McClurg (2001) found that human resource managers in the study report to be more satisfied with team performance when using financial rewards (bonuses, cash incentives) than when using recognition rewards.

H13: Financial rewards positively influence (a) originality, (b) usefulness, (c) number of ideas, and (d) new product performance.

According to the Employee Recognition Survey by the American Psychological Association (2014), women are more likely than man to care about salary increases, performance-based bonuses, and gift cards or gift certificates.

H14 Financial rewards increase the positive relationship between female participation and (a) originality, (b) usefulness, (c) number of ideas, and (d) new product performance in NPD teams.

Methods

All scales to measure the constructs were adapted from previously used scales. Initially, marketing and new product managers were interviewed to gain insight to the practicality of the study to industry and to see if the questionnaire was understandable. This was followed by a pretest of 30 marketing and new product managers using the on-line Qualtrics system. After removing a few items because of low loadings, 150 marketing and new product managers responded to our survey through the Qualtrics system. Performance consisted of six items from Mallick and Schroeder (2005) with an alpha of .873. Financial, promotion, and recognition rewards came from Yoon and Choi (2010), and had alphas of .832, .831, and .868 respectively. Number of ideas, originality, and usefulness were all single item indicators from Moreau and Dahl (2005). The model was analyzed using AMOS 25 in the SPSS package.

Results

Results of the analysis are shown in Fig. 1. There is a significant positive relationship between the percentage of females on NPD teams and number of ideas ($ß = 40.965$, $p < .01$), supporting H1. The analysis showed a positive relationship between number of ideas and originality ($ß = .20$, $p < .05$) in support of H2. However, there was no relationship between number of ideas and NPD performance, H3. No relationship was found between originality and NPD performance (H4) and between percentage of females in NPD teams and originality (H5). In support of H6, a significant relationship was found between usefulness and originality ($ß = .166$, $p < .01$). The results also suggest a significant positive relationship between usefulness and new product performance, supporting H7. The results showed no support

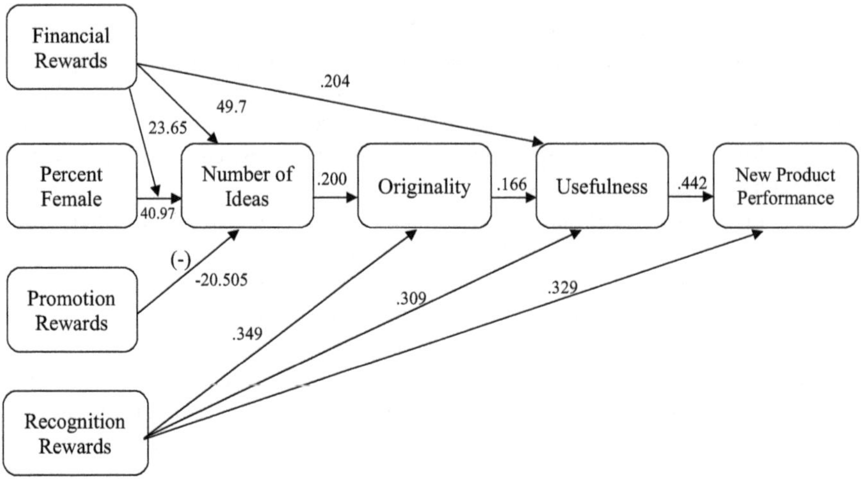

Fig. 1 Supported model results

for a significant relationship between the percentage of women in NPD teams and usefulness, H8.

Results showed a significant positive direct effect between recognition rewards and originality (ß = .349, $p < .05$), recognition rewards and usefulness (ß = .309, $p < .01$), and recognition rewards and NPD performance (ß = .329, $p < .01$). These results show support for H9a, H9b, and H9d. No support was found for a relationship between recognition rewards and number of ideas, H9c. There was no evidence of recognition rewards having any moderating effects so the results fail to support H10a, H10b, H10c, and H10d.

Results suggest a significant negative direct effect of promotion rewards on number of ideas (ß = -20.505, $p < .01$), failing to support H11c. No evidence supporting H11a, H11b, or H11d was found. The results suggest no moderating effects of promotion rewards, failing to support H12a, H12b, H12c, and H12d.

Finally, results show a significant positive direct effect of financial rewards on number of ideas (ß = 49.699, $p < .01$) and on usefulness (ß = .204, $p < .01$), supporting H13b and H13c. Additionally, in support of H14c, results also suggest a moderating effect of financial rewards on the relationship between percentage of females in NPD teams and number of ideas (ß = 23.653, $p < .01$). There were no significant relationships for H13a, H13d, H14a, H14b, and H14d.

Implications, Limitations, and Future Research

Our study makes several main contributions. First, we found that greater participation by females in NPD teams leads to more ideas, more original ideas, more useful ideas, and eventually to better NPD performance. This is important to managers since only 19.9% of engineering students are female (Yoder 2015), and only 11% of practicing engineers are female (Bryce 2018). Second, the relationships found form a causal chain with number of ideas, originality of ideas, and usefulness of ideas mediating the relationship between team composition and NPD performance. Finally, financial rewards was the only reward method that significantly affected team composition and NPD. Future research might examine if this is caused by compensation differences between men and women engineers.

One thing that limits our results is the fact that no NPD team had more than 50% female participation. Our results suggest linear relationships among the variables, but diversity theories would suggest that greater female participation beyond 50% might decrease creativity. Future research could also examine this.

References

Alexy, O. & Leitner, M. (2011). A fistful of dollars: Are financial rewards a suitable management practice for distributed models of innovation?. *European Management Review*, *8*(3), 165-185.

American Psychological Association. (2014). *Employee recognition survey*. Retrieved June 20, 2019 from https://www.apaexcellence.org/assets/general/employee-recognition-survey-results.pdf.

Apesteguia, J., Azmat, G. & Iriberri, N. (2012). The impact of gender composition on team performance and decision making: Evidence from the field. *Management Science, 58*(1), 78-93.

Auger, P., & Woodman, R. W. (2016). Creativity and intrinsic motivation: Exploring a complex relationship. *The Journal of Applied Behavioral Science*, *52*(3), 342–366.

Bandera, C., Keshtkar, F., Bartolacci, M., Neerudu, S., & Passerini, K. (2017). Knowledge management and the entrepreneur: Insights from Ikujiro Nonaka's dynamic knowledge creation model (SECI). *International Journal of Innovation Studies*, *1*(3), 163-174.

Bellis M. (2017). *How many women inventors are there?* Retrieved August 5, 2019 from https://www.thoughtco.com/how-many-women-inventors-are-there-1992649.

Beutell, N. J., & Brenner, O. C. (1986). Sex differences in work values. *Journal of Vocational Behavior, 28*(1), 29-41.

Bryce, M. (2018). Women in engineering: Taking a step to bridge the gap. Retrieved on May 23, 2021 from https://www.cati.com/blog/2018/07/women-engineering-taking-step-bridge-gap/.

Burroughs, J. E., Dahl, D. W., Moreau, C. P., Chattopadhyay, A., & Gorn, G. J. (2011). Facilitating and rewarding creativity during new product development. *Journal of Marketing, 75*(4), 53-67.

Chang, J., Hung, K. and Lin, M. J. (2014). Knowledge creation and new product performance. *R&D Management*, *44*(2), 107-123.

Chau, V.S. & Quire, C. (2018). Back to the future of women in technology: insights from understanding the shortage of women in innovation sectors for managing corporate foresight. *Technology Analysis & Strategic Management*, *30*(6), 747-764.

Deci, E., Koestner, R., & Ryan, R. (2001). Extrinsic rewards and intrinsic motivation in education: Reconsidered once again. *Review of Educational Research*, *71*(1), 1-27.

Deci, E. L., Olafsen, A. H., & Ryan, R. M. (2017). Self-determination theory in work organizations: The state of a science. *Annual Review of Organizational Psychology and Organizational Behavior, 4*, 19-43.

Garcia Martinez, M., Zouaghi, F. and Garcia Marco, T. (2017). Diversity is strategy: The effect of R&D team diversity on innovative performance. *R&D Management*, *47*(2), 311-329.

Gibbs, M., Neckermann, S., & Siemroth, C. (2017). A field experiment in motivating employee ideas. *Review of Economics and Statistics, 99*(4), 577-590.

Hansen, F., Smith, M., & Hansen, R.B. (2002). Rewards and recognition in employee motivation. *Compensation and Benefits Review, 34*(5), 64-72.

Haon, C., Gotteland, D., & Fornerino, M. (2009). Familiarity and competence diversity in new product development teams: Effects on new product performance. *Marketing Letters, 20*(1), 75-89.

Hernández Girón, J.P., Domínguez Hernández, M.L. & Jiménez Castañeda, J.L. (2004). Participatory methodologies and the product development process: The experience of mixtec craftswomen in Mexico. *Development in Practice, 14*(3), 396-406.

Hirschfeld, R. R., Jordan, M. H., Feild, H. S., Giles, W. F., & Armenakis, A. A. (2005). Teams' female representation and perceived potency as inputs to team outcomes in a predominantly male field setting. *Personnel Psychology, 58*(4), 893-924.

Hoisl, K., Gruber, M. and Conti, A. (2017). R&D team diversity and performance in hypercompetitive environments. *Strategic Management Journal, 38*(7), 1455-1477.

Hoogendoorn, S., Oosterbeek, H., & van Praag, M. (2013). The impact of gender diversity on the performance of business teams: Evidence from a field experiment. *Management Science, 59*(7), 1514-1528.

Im, S. & Workman, J. (2004). Market orientation, creativity, and new product performance in high-technology firms. *Journal of Marketing, 68*(2), 114-132.

Jayaram, J., & Narasimhan, R. (2007). The influence of new product development competitive capabilities on project performance. *IEEE Transactions on Engineering Management, 54*(2), 241-256.

Joshi, A., & Roh, H. (2009). The role of context in work team diversity research: A meta-analytic review. *Academy of Management Journal, 52*(3), 599-627.

Khan, S., Zarif, T., Khan, B. (2011). Effects of recognition-based rewards on employees' efficiency and effectiveness. *Journal of Management and Social Sciences, 7*(2), 1-7.

Kharkhurin, A. V. (2014). Creativity. 4in1: Four-criterion construct of creativity. *Creativity research journal, 26*(3), 338-352.

Klein, E. E., & Dologite, D. G. (2000). The role of computer support tools and gender composition in innovative information system idea generation by small groups. *Computers in Human Behavior, 16*(2), 111-139.

Laeser, M., Moskal, B. M., Knecht, R. and Lasich, D. (2003). Engineering design: Examining the impact of gender and the team's gender composition. *Journal of Engineering Education, 92*(1), 49-56.

Leuven, E., Oosterbeek, H., & Van der Klaauw, B. (2010). The effect of financial rewards on students' achievement: Evidence from a randomized experiment. *Journal of the European Economic Association, 8*(6), 1243-1265.

Mallick, D. N. & Schroeder, R.G. (2005). An integrated framework for measuring product development performance in high technology industries. *Production and Operations Management*, 14 (2), 142-158.

Mcclurg, L. (2001). Team rewards: How far have we come?. *Human Resource Management, 40*(1), 73 - 86.

Mierdel, J., & Bogner, F. X. (2019). Is creativity, hands-on modeling and cognitive learning gender-dependent?. *Thinking Skills and Creativity, 31*, 91-102.

Milgram, R. M., Milgram, N. A., Rosenbloom, G., & Rabkin, L. (1978). Quantity and quality of creative thinking in children and adolescents. *Child Development, 49*(2), 385-388.

Moreau, C. P., & Dahl, D. W. (2005). Designing the solution: The impact of constraints on consumers' creativity. *Journal of Consumer Research, 32*(1), 13-22.

Osteras,T., Murthy, D.N.P., & Rausand, M. (2006) Product performance and specification in new product development. *Journal of Engineering Design, 17*(2), 177-192.

Park, M. H., Lim, W. J., & Birnbaum More, P. H. (2009). The effect of multi-knowledge individuals on performance in cross-functional new product development teams. *Journal of Product Innovation Management, 26*(1), 86-96.

Rajendran, M.M.A., Mosisa, K.M., & Nedelea, A. (2017). Effects of non-monetary benefits on employees performance (A case of Bako Agricultural Research Center, Western Shoa, Ethiopia). *Ecoforum,* 6(21).

Reiter-Palmon, R., & Arreola, N.J. (2015). Does generating multiple ideas lead to increased creativity? A comparison of generating one idea vs. many. *Creativity Research Journal*, 27(4), 369-374.

Sanongpong, K. (2009). Automotive process-based new product development: A review of key performance metrics. In *Proceedings of the World Congress on Engineering* (Vol. 1, pp. 1-3).

Saunderson, R. (2004). Survey findings of the effectiveness of employee recognition in the public sector. *Public Personnel Management, 33*(3), 255-275.

Sivasubramaniam, N., Liebowitz, S. J., & Lackman, C. L. (2012). Determinants of new product development team performance: A meta-analytic review. *Journal of Product Innovation Management, 29*(5), 803-820.

Sonawane, P. (2008). Non-monetary rewards: Employee choices & organizational practices. *Indian Journal of Industrial Relations, 44*(2), 256-271.

Stephens, K., Karnes, F., & Whorton, J. (2001). Gender differences in creativity among American Indian third and fourth grade students. *Journal of American Indian Education, 40*(1), 57-65.

Torchia, M., Calabrò, A., & Huse, M. (2011). Women directors on corporate boards: From Tokenism to Critical Mass. *Journal of Business Ethics, 102*(2), 299-317.

Toubia, O. (2006). Idea Generation, Creativity, and Incentives. *Marketing Science, 25*(5), 411-425.

Vyas, K. (2019). *24 inventions by women you might not be aware of.* Retrieved on August 5, 2019 from https://interestingengineering.com/24-inventions-by-women-you-might-not-be-aware-of.

Yang, D., Jin, L., Sheng, S. (2017). The effect of knowledge breadth and depth on new product performance. *International Journal of Market Research*, 59(4), 517-536.

Yoder, B. L. (2015). Engineering by the numbers. In *American Society for Engineering Education* (Vol. 37).

Yoon, H. J., & Choi, J. N. (2010). Extrinsic and intrinsic rewards and creativity in the workplace: Reward importance as a moderator. In *Academy of Management Annual Meeting.*

Yu-Shan, C., Hung-Chang, L.,Yu-Hung, C., & Wan-Hsuan, Y. (2018). Effects of creative components and creative behavior on design creativity. *Thinking Skills and Creativity*, *29*, 23-31.

Zeng, L., Proctor, R. W., & Salvendy, G. (2011). Can traditional divergent thinking tests be trusted in measuring and predicting real-world creativity? *Creativity Research Journal, 23*(1), 24-37.

Zhuang, L., Williamson, D. and Carter, M. (1999). Innovate or liquidate – are all organisations convinced? A two-phased study into the innovation process. *Management Decision*, 37 (1), 57-71.

Deconstructing Self Goal-Related Antecedents of Brand Love: An Abstract

Tai Anh Kieu

Abstract Brand love has ignited renewed attention of researchers and practitioners, with recent development of the first pragmatically useful brand love scales (Bagozzi et al. 2017). As such, further testing of this concept could strengthen its theoretical and practical relevance, given that 'love' is culturally grounded (Albert et al. 2008). Besides, consumers are argued to engage in relationships with brands that serve their self-goals (Ashworth et al. 2009), which are: to express own self (value expressive); to maintain self-esteem (social adjustive); and to bolster self-esteem (affiliation) (Katz 1960; Shavitt 1990). Prior research mostly tested the impact on brand identification and sense of brand community, which are respectively similar conceptually to value expressive and affiliation, on brand relationship constructs that may, but not always, comprise a love dimension. Scant research has been done to examine the roles of all self-related goals that also include social adjustive in construing brand love construct of emotional nature. This research aims to examine the relative impact of self-related goals on brand love, and subsequently behavioural intentions that consist of brand loyalty and positive word-of-mouth. Data collected from a mall-intercept survey with 216 fashion clothing consumers and 198 smartphone consumers were analysed to test hypotheses using SmartPLS 3.3.3. Fashion clothing and smartphone products are selected as the purchases of these products are usually non-routine decision-making situations. The result reveals that brand identification and social adjustive moderately influence brand love (all $p < 0.05$), which in turn affects brand loyalty and positive word-of-mouth (all $p < 0.05$). Mediational analyses show brand love mediates fully the effect of brand identification but only partially the effect of social adjustive on brand loyalty and positive word-of-mouth. The finding also shows that sense of brand community, while not significantly influencing brand love ($p > 0.05$), drives consumers' brand loyalty and positive word-of-mouth (all $p < 0.05$). This study contributes to the brand relationship literature with respect to the formation of brand love and behavioural intentions. Brand love appears to be the main mechanism serving the con-

T. A. Kieu (✉)
Ho Chi Minh City Open University, Ho Chi Minh City, Vietnam
e-mail: tai.ka@ou.edu.vn

J. Allen et al. (eds.), *Celebrating the Past and Future of Marketing and Discovery with Social Impact*, Developments in Marketing Science: Proceedings of the Academy of Marketing Science, https://doi.org/10.1007/978-3-030-95346-1_182

sumer's own-self goal captured by brand identification; evidence concerning the roles of social goal-related constructs on brand love is mixed. While the consumer's perceived brand's ability to deliver social adjustive utility may make them love the brands, their sense of belonging to a community does not guarantee their brand love of the brands. Practically, the findings provide marketers with insights about the meaningful distinction of lower-order self-related goals. For consumers who look to brands for expressing their own self or maintaining their self-esteem, marketers may focus on transformational communication tactics that drive brand love and consequently behavioural intentions. Meanwhile, for those who aim to bolster their self-esteem, marketers may invest in the creation and maintenance of a brand community.

Keywords Brand love · Brand identification · Social adjustive · Sense of brand community · Brand loyalty · World-of-mouth

Empowering Investors: Sustainable Consumption through Micro-Investment Platforms: An Abstract

Claudia Gonzalez-Arcos, Cristyn Meath, Peter T. L. Popkowski Leszczyc, Ernan Haruvy, Jake Ann, and Alexandria Gain

Abstract Younger generations present significant disadvantages compared with their older counterparts due to job instability, cost of living and economic stagnation amongst others, creating significant wealth inequalities across generations (IMF 2018). In light of catastrophic environmental change, economic inequality is contributing to feelings of powerlessness among consumers (Wilkinson and Pickett 2010) as it hinders their ability to reallocate capital towards sustainable businesses to drive social progress. Emerging digital micro-investment platforms provide consumers with limited capital the ability to invest in sustainable firms. This research investigates empowerment in the context of sustainable investments through micro-investment platforms. We focus on the underlying mechanisms of sustainable investing through micro-investment platforms and the role of consumers' perceived empowerment on willingness to invest (WTI).

We provide results of two different studies. The first is a qualitative study aimed at exploring consumers' thoughts, feelings, and behaviors associated with micro-investments and the extent to which micro-investments empower consumers from a financial and sustainability perspective. We conducted 35 in-depth Zoom interviews of customers from a large micro-investment platform. Interviews lasted between 30 and 45 minutes and most participants were 25–31 years old. Findings indicate the importance of perceived empowerment for engaging in sustainable consumption through micro-investment platforms and the effects of voice, tangibility, control and

C. Gonzalez-Arcos · C. Meath · P. T. L. Popkowski Leszczyc (✉) · A. Gain
University of Queensland, Brisbane, QLD, Australia
e-mail: c.gonzalez@business.uq.edu.au; c.meath@business.uq.edu.au; p.popkowski@business.uq.edu.au; a.gain@business.uq.edu.au

E. Haruvy
McGill University, Montreal, QC, Canada
e-mail: ernan.haruvy@mcgill.ca

J. Ann
Raiz Invest Australia Ltd, Brisbane, QLD, Australia
e-mail: jake@raizinvest.com.au

J. Allen et al. (eds.), *Celebrating the Past and Future of Marketing and Discovery with Social Impact*, Developments in Marketing Science: Proceedings of the Academy of Marketing Science, https://doi.org/10.1007/978-3-030-95346-1_183

accessibility on perceived empowerment. We also found that engaging in sustainable investments can result in "warm glow" feelings.

In addition, a choice-based conjoint experiment was conducted to examine consumer preferences for sustainable portfolios and trade-offs between percentage of sustainable assets, screening of companies, rate of return and risk. Data was obtained from a sample of over 200 customers of a micro-investment platform. Results show customers prefer environmental sustainability over social sustainability when making investment decisions. Furthermore, there is a large difference in customers' trade-off preferences between the proportion of investment in social causes and the rate of return. We also compared results for different customer segments and find that investors with greater levels of alignment to sustainability-related outcomes (i.e., those with high levels of biospheric and altruistic values) and customers with high levels of reported feelings of warm glow demonstrate a greater preference for portfolios with a higher percentage of sustainable investments.

Results provide a better understanding of the importance of sustainable investments on willingness to invest in the context of micro-investing platforms. Marketing managers can use results for product development within the investment and banking industry that maximises feelings of empowerment of young investors, and to leverage these emerging platforms to appeal to young consumers.

Keywords Sustainable investments · Consumer empowerment · Micro-investing platform · Sustainable consumption

Location-Based Advertising: The Role of App Design: An Abstract

Hamid Shirdastian, Boris Bartikowski, Michel Laroche, and Marie-Odile Richard

Abstract Recently, with the widespread of mobile devices, mobile marketing, which can be conducted anytime and anywhere, has received increased attention and is strengthened by academics and practitioners. This ever-increasing popularity, besides the actual and potential marketing advantages, has led to optimistic forecasts regarding the adoption of location-based advertising (LBA) (Lin 2016). For example, in the US alone, it is projected that location-based mobile ad spending would grow from 17.1 billion USD in 2017 to 38.7 billion USD in 2022 (Statista 2019). Taking into account the vast potential market for LBA as a novel advertising medium, and also the currently limited literature about it, the aim of this research is to examine how consumers react toward the culture-laden design of mobile applications focusing on the role of application atmospherics in the context of location-based advertising (LBA) and ridesharing apps. Drawing from previous research on culture-laden website design, our experimental study with consumers from Canada confirms that LBA displayed on locally (vs. internationally) designed ridesharing apps elicits less perceived ad intrusiveness and higher intention to purchase. Regarding mobile app atmospherics, we find that consumers perceive a local (vs. international) app design as more informative, more entertaining, and more effective. Furthermore, higher levels of app atmospherics lead consumers to perceive LBA as less intrusive as well as enhance consumers' purchase intentions, thereby emphasizing the important role of app atmospherics to predict and mobile consumer behavior. Our empirical results confirm that two atmospherics (entertainment and effectiveness, but not informativeness) mediate the effects of culture-laden app design on consumer reactions. We discuss the theoretical implications of our find-

H. Shirdastian (✉) · M. Laroche
Concordia University, Montréal, QC, Canada
e-mail: hamid.shirdastian@concordia.ca; michel.laroche@concordia.ca

B. Bartikowski
Kedge Business School, Marseille, France
e-mail: boris.bartikowski@kedgebs.com

M.-O. Richard
SUNY Polytechnic Institute, Utica, NY, USA
e-mail: richarm3@sunyit.edu

J. Allen et al. (eds.), *Celebrating the Past and Future of Marketing and Discovery with Social Impact*, Developments in Marketing Science: Proceedings of the Academy of Marketing Science, https://doi.org/10.1007/978-3-030-95346-1_184

ings as well as managerial implications for mobile application design and LBA effectiveness. Future research could look into the role of destination congruency (spatial distance). Also, for cases where people use both desktops and touch screen devices (booking on Airbnb), the role of touch vs. regular devices is also worthy of research.

Keywords Location-based advertising (LBA) · Atmospheric cues · Cultural congruity · Sharing economy

A Study of Incentives in Charitable Fundraising: Monetary Incentives Crowd out Future Volunteering: An Abstract

Ernan Haruvy and Peter T. L. Popkowski Leszczyc

Abstract To incentivize volunteers, charities award prizes to fundraisers in order to stimulate fundraising efforts. However, it is unclear how effective such incentives are because volunteers may be driven by non-pecuniary incentives. That is, monetary incentives may crowd out intrinsic motivators (charitability), resulting in a negative effect.

The purpose of this study is to determine how intrinsic motivators and monetary incentives (extrinsic motivators) are mediated by effort to affect fundraising outcomes. This integration sheds light on crowding out between the two types of incentives as well the drivers of fundraising outcomes, specifically effort, donations and intent to volunteer in the future.

A field experiment is conducted over a 2-month period, involving an online fundraising campaign with over 300 volunteers assigned to different incentive conditions. A low and a high commission-based incentive, a low and a high tournament incentive and a control group without an incentive. A special website was designed for the fundraiser, where fundraiser created a web page for fundraising purposes, sending e-mail solicitations and receive donations. As a result we were able to observe effort over time, different from previous research in which effort is a latent variable.

We find that commission-based incentives increase current effort and funds raised, while tournament incentives do not. Commission-based incentives had a positive effect on encouraging fundraisers to solicit for donations (effort quality), but were not effective in causing more creative output (effort quality). While commission-based incentives had a positive effect on fundraised they also resulted in a reduced intentions to volunteer in the future. Hence, they may have a detrimental effect in the long-run. In addition, commission-based incentives are predomi-

E. Haruvy
McGill University, Montreal, QC, Canada
e-mail: ernan.haruvy@mcgill.ca

P. T. L. Popkowski Leszczyc (✉)
University of Queensland, Brisbane, QLD, Australia
e-mail: p.popowski@business.uq.edu.au

J. Allen et al. (eds.), *Celebrating the Past and Future of Marketing and Discovery with Social Impact*, Developments in Marketing Science: Proceedings of the Academy of Marketing Science, https://doi.org/10.1007/978-3-030-95346-1_185

nately successful in motivating less charitable fundraisers. Intrinsic (charitable) motives on the other hand both have an effect on donations and intent to volunteer.

An implication of these results is that fundraising managers need to act cautiously when using monetary incentives for recruiting purposes. Commission-based incentives, should be predominately used in the short-run, in particular to attract low charitability fundraisers to participate in fundraising.

We find that effort mediates the impact of both intrinsic and extrinsic motivators on amount of funds raised. Furthermore, effort has an important positive effect on intent to volunteer. As a result, charities may want to design fundraising events that require fundraisers to induce more effort.

Keywords Fundraising · Incentives · Nonprofit marketing · Field experiment

Vinyl Strikes (Not Once But Twice): The Non-Digital Future of Listening to Music?: An Abstract

Markus Wohlfeil

Abstract Deemed to be an obsolete recorded music format over 30 years ago, vinyl records enjoy since 2011 a major comeback with an average year-on-year sales growth of 40% (Jones 2018). And with nearly 48% of today's vinyl consumers being under the age of 35, the return of vinyl records might change the way we listen to recorded music again. But its unexpected resurgence also contradicts the dominant discourse among marketing scholars and the media, who have for over 20 years championed the digitalisation of music as a disruptive technology that is revolutionising and 'democratising' the music industry (Giesler 2008) and the way consumers nowadays and in the future would access and listen to recorded music with the promise of convenience, freedom of choice and unrestricted mobility (Elberse 2010). Hence, every newly-emerging digital format from CDs (Daniel 2019) over MP3s and digital downloads (Denegri-Knott 2015) to streaming (Wlömert and Papies 2016) has been hailed as the future of how consumers access and enjoy listening to recorded music whenever, wherever and however they want – only for it soon to be replaced by the next emerging digital format. Therefore, it comes to no surprise that marketing scholars have studied vinyl consumers only as the 'other' in digital society (Goulding and Derbaix 2019).

This ethnographic study, however, explores how vinyl consumers perceive, experience and negotiate their personal preferences for vinyl records within today's digital age. The data were collected at record stores and the World Record Store Day over a period of 6 months and analysed hermeneutically.

Contrary to previous studies, the findings reveal that today's vinyl consumers, regardless of whether they are not-born digital or born digital, are very savvy when it comes to digital technology and music formats. It is because they have bought into the promised possibilities and hype surrounding the digitalisation of music and embraced the emerging digital music formats, providers and technology wholeheartedly for many years that they now feel being betrayed by those same digital music providers, who instead of democratising the music marketplace have become

M. Wohlfeil (✉)
De Montfort University, Leicester, UK
e-mail: markus.wohlfeil@dmu.ac.uk

J. Allen et al. (eds.), *Celebrating the Past and Future of Marketing and Discovery with Social Impact*, Developments in Marketing Science: Proceedings of the Academy of Marketing Science, https://doi.org/10.1007/978-3-030-95346-1_186

a powerful oligarchy that controls and dictates at will not just the available content but also the means of accessing it. The resurgence and popularity of analogue technologies like vinyl with today's consumers can therefore be understood as a post-digital consumer-driven backlash to the digital technology providers' perceived abuse of their dominant market position and their apparent contempt for the consumer's personal interests – as an unintended result of the digital companies' own actions. By contrast, analogue technologies like vinyl offer an alternative that has already proven itself in the past to be reliable, trustworthy and often a genuinely social medium that can be enjoyed alone or together with others.

Keywords Vinyl records · Resurgence · Digital music · Consumer backlash · Marketplace evolution

Relationship Impact of Pressure on Suppliers to Improve Quality: An Abstract

R. Mohan Pisharodi and Ravi Parameswaran

Abstract Superior Product Quality is generally considered a competitive advantage. Yet literature on quality improvement and new product development have recognized the existence of impediments in the successful practice and implementation of Quality Improvement. In an uncertain and highly competitive business environment, it is not uncommon for organizations to pass on Quality Improvement tasks to supply chain partners. This is often the case in the manufacturing supply chain with powerful OEMs (Original Equipment Manufacturers). We seek to determine whether such "Quality Improvement Pressure" is conducive to good Supplier-OEM Relationships and how this compares with price pressure exerted similarly by OEMs. Overall supplier-OEM relationship is specified as the final dependent variable. Recognizing the role of a set of relationship constructs in influencing overall supplier-manufacturer interactions, *communication and information sharing* is posited as a crucial variable in enabling good supplier-(OEM) relationship. Commitment by the OEM reflected in the *help and assistance* provided to the supplier in meeting price targets and willingness to work together are essential for the success of the relationship. *Successful profit partnership*, a logical outcome of inter-organizational trust is considered a reflection of a high degree of sophistication in cooperation. The specified model has two exogenous variables – one representing price pressure and the other representing pressure to improve quality. After following a multi-stage scale development procedure, data were collected from suppliers in the automotive light vehicles industry and the electronics industry and were analyzed using structural equation modeling. The results of this research advance the understanding of B2B relationship management by demonstrating that OEM pressure to improve quality can coexist with good supplier-OEM relationship. The influence of pressure to improve quality on supplier-OEM relationship takes place through a set of moderating variables which are within the control of management. Unlike price pressure which may be treated by some suppliers as adversarial, pressure to improve quality is likely to be viewed by suppliers more favorably. Analysis shows differences in the

R. M. Pisharodi (✉) · R. Parameswaran
Oakland University, Rochester, MI, USA
e-mail: pisharod@oakland.edu; paramesw@oakland.edu

J. Allen et al. (eds.), *Celebrating the Past and Future of Marketing and Discovery with Social Impact*, Developments in Marketing Science: Proceedings of the Academy of Marketing Science, https://doi.org/10.1007/978-3-030-95346-1_187

impacts of the two initial variables on the outcome variable. Quality Improvement pressure has substantially more positive links with the intermediate relational variables as well as the dependent variable than has price pressure.

Keywords B2B · Quality · Suppliers · Supplier quality improvement · Price · Price-pressure · OEM · Quality-pressure

Personality, Risk Tolerance, and Religiosity on Consumer Credit Card Use: Implications for Sustainability and Social Impact: An Abstract

Heejung Park and Matthew Lunde

Abstract In the past, credit purchases were available only to some consumers at few locations, but nowadays, many consumers use credit purchases through various credit purchase methods. Credit cards have a significant impact on consumer credit (Basnet and Donou-Adonsou 2016) but also why consumers use their credit cards. This study suggests a direction for future value-driven consumer research related to consumers' credit card usage influencing sustainable mindfulness and social impact.

In this study, a dual processing model is used to explain consumer behavior with credit card usage (Cline and Kellaris 2007). Further research has linked the dual process with conservatism or liberalism attitudes (e.g., Yilmaz and Saribay 2016). Because of these attitudes, conservatism is significantly related to the cognitive system, while liberalism is associated with the emotional system. In our study, we examine the impact on consumer credit card usage by dividing individual personality into conservatism and liberalism.

The dual processing model may be useful in understanding consumer attitudes and behaviors, but researchers differ in the content and composition of the model (Stone 2011). It is also not to be overlooked that external factors may control the impact of personality on financial behavior (Perry and Morris 2005). That is, consumers can increase their mindfulness by performing internal value search. Finally, existing research has emphasized the importance of religion for these intrinsic values (Park and Zehra 2018) and behaviors (Minton et al. 2015). Religious consumers will pay more attention to intrinsic value.

Based on our results, we found that there are three significant main effects. First, our ANOVA model indicates a near to statistical significance effect of personality.

H. Park (✉)
Northern Michigan University, Marquette, MI, USA
e-mail: hepark@nmu.edu

M. Lunde
Pittsburg State University, Pittsburg, KS, USA
e-mail: mlunde@pittstate.edu

J. Allen et al. (eds.), *Celebrating the Past and Future of Marketing and Discovery with Social Impact*, Developments in Marketing Science: Proceedings of the Academy of Marketing Science, https://doi.org/10.1007/978-3-030-95346-1_188

Our results also show significant effect of risk tolerance and religion. Second, we conclude that there is a nearly acceptable level of significance of personality risk tolerance interaction, indicating that conservative consumers with high-risk tolerance tend to use their credit cards more than conservative consumers with low-risk tolerance. Third, the last hypothesis in our study is the most important. According to our results, there was statistically significant three-way interaction between personality, risk tolerance, and religion.

Keywords Personality · Risk tolerance · Religiosity · Credit card

New Product Preannouncement Effects on Brand Innovativeness: Examining the Mediating Role of Perceived Risk and Moderating Role of Brand Credibility: An Abstract

Mahmud Hassan, Ravi Pappu, and Sarah Kelly

Abstract This research aims to examine the impact of new product preannouncement (NPP) on brand innovativeness. This study contributes to the NPP and innovation literature by explaining how NPPs affect brand innovativeness. Specifically, the present research deepens our understanding of the relationship between degree of innovation and brand innovativeness by clarifying the role of perceived risk. Moreover, the present study fills an important knowledge gap in the brand innovativeness literature by providing boundary conditions for this new relationship and examines the moderating role of brand credibility. We predict that (a) degree of innovation of the proposed new product positively affects brand innovativeness (H1) and (b) brand credibility moderates the positive impact of degree of innovation on brand innovativeness (H2) and (c) functional risk and financial risk mediate the positive impact of degree of innovation on brand innovativeness (H3 and H4). This study applies signalling theory to understand these relationships. Several variables that were expected to influence brand innovativeness (e.g., brand familiarity, brand attitude and perceived quality) are included as covariates in the analysis.

Two experiments were conducted to test the proposed hypotheses. Both studies employed a 2 (degree of innovation: incremental vs. radical) × 2 (brand credibility: low vs. high) between-subjects design, with brand innovativeness as the dependent variable. The fictitious press releases featured different manipulations, which were determined through several pre-tests. All key variables were measured on a seven-point Likert scales adopted/adapted from the literature. Participants [study 1 ($N = 276$) and study 2 ($N = 246$)] were recruited through an online consumer panel. Participants (51% women) were in the 18–70 years age group.

We tested for the moderating role of brand credibility and the mediating roles of functional and financial risk in the degree of innovation – brand innovativeness rela-

M. Hassan (✉) · R. Pappu · S. Kelly
University of Queensland, St. Lucia, QLD, Australia
e-mail: mahmud.hassan@uq.net.au; r.pappu@business.uq.edu.au; s.kelly@business.uq.edu.au

J. Allen et al. (eds.), *Celebrating the Past and Future of Marketing and Discovery with Social Impact*, Developments in Marketing Science: Proceedings of the Academy of Marketing Science, https://doi.org/10.1007/978-3-030-95346-1_189

tionship using PROCESS Model 5 (Hayes 2018) with brand familiarity, brand attitude and perceived quality as covariates. The independent variables used in this model, degree of innovation (0 = incremental product; 1 = radical product) and brand credibility (0 = low credible; 1 = high credible) are dummy coded while the mediators (functional risk and financial risk) are mean-centered.

Findings suggest that degree of innovation of the proposed new product is positively related to brand innovativeness. Additionally, brand credibility moderates the relationship between degree of innovation and brand innovativeness, and the relationship holds good only for low credible brands. Finally, results do not support the mediating role of functional risk or financial risk.

Keywords New product preannouncement · Brand innovativeness · Degree of innovation · Perceived risk · Brand credibility

Planning for Disaster: Managing a Values-Based Brand Crisis: An Abstract

Stuart Caulton, Cassandra France, and Ravi Pappu

Abstract Brand crises can cause significant financial and reputational damage to a company. The most effective means for a company to mitigate potential damage to its brand during a crisis is with its crisis response. Yet research into the most effective response (corrective action vs reduction of offensiveness vs denial) to a values-based brand crisis is unclear. The present research seeks to clarify the issue of crisis response and expands understanding of this type of crisis by investigating whether brand attitude dilution occurs as a result of values-based brand crises and if the brand attitude dilution effects vary by crisis severity and locus of control.

The hypotheses were tested in three experiments using consumer samples. The results of the first ($N = 283$, Australian consumers) showed brand attitude dilution upon exposure to a value-based brand crisis. However, the brand attitude dilution did not vary by the either crisis response strategy or the severity of the crisis. The results of the second study ($N = 229$) revealed brand attitude dilution upon exposure to a value-based brand crisis. Importantly, corrective action was found to be more effective than the other two response strategies in reducing brand attitude dilution. The brand attitude dilution did not vary by the locus of control. The results of the third study ($N = 218$) further confirmed brand attitude dilution post exposure to a real value-based brand crisis, but the effect did not vary by the type of crisis response.

The present research contributes to the brand crisis literature. It also provides guidance to managers of companies going through values-based brand crises, and allows for the creation of evidence-based crisis management strategies.

The work was supported by the University of Queensland.

S. Caulton (✉) · C. France · R. Pappu
University of Queensland, Brisbane, QLD, Australia
e-mail: stuart.caulton@uq.net.au; c.france@business.uq.edu.au; r.pappu@business.uq.edu.au

J. Allen et al. (eds.), *Celebrating the Past and Future of Marketing and Discovery with Social Impact*, Developments in Marketing Science: Proceedings of the Academy of Marketing Science, https://doi.org/10.1007/978-3-030-95346-1_190

Keywords Values-based brand crisis · Crisis response · Corrective action · Reduction of offensiveness · Locus of control · Crisis severity · Brand attitude

The Role of Consumers' Consciousness in Building Brand Perceptions: A Cross-Cultural Perspective: An Abstract

Lilly Ye and Mousumi Bose

Abstract In today's global marketplace, young consumers' self-expression is manifested through the consumption of branded goods and services (Fam et al. 2008; Liao and Wang 2009). The goal of this article is to explore the impact of the self-concepts among global young consumers to develop a conceptual framework that assists brand managers to leverage these psychological factors in developing brand loyalty. Based on Abe et al. (1996), the study draws on self-consciousness as a key aspect of self-concept and uses gender-consciousness (Gould 1996) to represent the gender aspect of self-concept. Given that brand and self connections might play be a portentous variable in consumers' self-expression and related brand decisions (Escalas and Bettman 2005), the study accommodates brand connections to support the congruity effects between self/gender consciousness and brand perceptions, and further examine how brand connections lead to brand knowledge and then further enhance brand attitudes and brand loyalty.

This study specifically investigates the role of consumer self- and gender consciousness on product knowledge, attitude and purchase intention in a cross-cultural setting. Efforts were made to explore whether consumer brand consciousness played a mediating role between consumer self- and gender consciousness and product knowledge. Using structural equation model to test the hypothesized relationship, the results study demonstrates that consumer gender and self-consciousness impact consumer brand consciousness and the latter is important driver of consumer product knowledge, which in turn, influence consumer brand attitude and purchase intention. The study also demonstrates that culture impacts the role of consumer brand consciousness as it mediates between self- and gender consciousness and product knowledge. While past literature has highlighted the impact of both gender

L. Ye (✉)
Frostburg State University, Frostburg, MD, USA
e-mail: lye@frostburg.edu

M. Bose
Fairfield University, Fairfield, CT, USA
e-mail: mbosegodbole@fairfield.edu

J. Allen et al. (eds.), *Celebrating the Past and Future of Marketing and Discovery with Social Impact*, Developments in Marketing Science: Proceedings of the Academy of Marketing Science, https://doi.org/10.1007/978-3-030-95346-1_191

and self-consciousness on brand consciousness, our study suggests that the results change based on cultural contexts. For US consumers, both self- and gender consciousness impact brand consciousness and product knowledge; however, for Chinese consumers, only gender consciousness and not self-consciousness impact brand consciousness, which impacts product knowledge. Thus, there is complete mediation for Chinese consumers for gender consciousness. This may be contrary to past research that suggests the importance of self-consciousness on brand consciousness for these consumers. However, when one considers the impact of both self- and gender consciousness, it appears that the latter plays a greater role in impacting brand consciousness.

Keywords Gender identity · Self-expression · Brand perceptions · Cross-cultural study

The Impact of Tourist Misbehavior on Ingroup Tourist Responses: An Abstract

Wanting Sun, P. Monica Chien, Brent W. Ritchie, and Ravi Pappu

Abstract The present research examines individuals' responses toward a misbehavior committed by their compatriot tourists in the international travel context. Specifically, it tests the impact of group identification, the mediating role of emotions and moderating effect of misbehavior severity on individuals' evaluations of the misbehaving tourist and the destination involved. The present research employs social identity theory as the overarching theoretical framework to understand the dynamics among tourists and between tourists and destination residents. The hypotheses were tested in a one-factor (misbehavior severity: low vs. high) between-subjects experiment with a control group, with identification with the ingroup (i.e., USA) measured as an independent variable and emotions measured as mediators. 448 Americans with international travel experience were recruited via MTurk. The data were analyzed using PROCESS Models.

Findings revealed a positive effect of ingroup identification on attitudes toward the ingroup perpetrators and a negative effect on intention to punish, providing evidence of ingroup bias. Guilt and shame have been found as two key emotions mediating the relationship between ingroup identification and individuals' responses toward the ingroup perpetrators and the destination involved. Interestingly, the impact of ingroup identification on attitude toward the ingroup perpetrators became negative when shame was activated, suggesting the black sheep effect. Findings also showed a positive effect of ingroup identification both directly and indirectly through guilt. The direct effect was found only when misbehavior severity was low.

The present research contributes to the knowledge of ingroup deviance in the tourism context. It expands the tourism impact literature by examining the psychological mechanism underlying individuals' responses to a misbehavior committed by compatriot tourists, and identifying boundary conditions for their reactions.

The work was supported by the University of Queensland.

W. Sun (✉) · P. M. Chien · B. W. Ritchie · R. Pappu
The University of Queensland, Brisbane, QLD, Australia
e-mail: w.sun@business.uq.edu.au; m.chien@uq.edu.au; b.ritchie@uq.edu.au; r.pappu@business.uq.edu.au

J. Allen et al. (eds.), *Celebrating the Past and Future of Marketing and Discovery with Social Impact*, Developments in Marketing Science: Proceedings of the Academy of Marketing Science, https://doi.org/10.1007/978-3-030-95346-1_192

Practically, this research highlights that the occurrence of tourist misbehavior can be a good opportunity to facilitate desirable tourist behaviors. It informs policy development and destination marketing strategies on mitigating the negative impact of tourist misbehavior, and helps tourist-originating countries educate outbound tourists.

Keywords Social identity theory · Ingroup deviance · Tourist misbehavior · Emotions · Prosocial behaviors · Tourist-host relationship

Promoting Brand Involvement through User Generated Content: An Abstract

Nomita Gupta

Abstract Within the Service-Dominant-Logic – SDL framework (Vargo and Lusch 2004, 2008, 2016), and the Self-Determination Theory – SDT (Ryan and Deci 2000) premise, this study aims to investigate how user generated content (UGC) influences their brand involvement. The intrinsic motivations – need for competence, need for autonomy and need for relatedness underpinned by SDT influence UGC production. Moreover, SDL propounds that firms' reputation and brand involvement is enhanced through customer's active role utilizing their resources (Harmeling et al. 2017), like, their social network and brand knowledge. Overall, the effect of customers' UGC creation is explored on their brand involvement which in turn will enhance loyalty and purchase intentions for the focal brand. This study is an extension of the research published in IEEE conference (Gupta and Gupta 2019) by including an upgraded model with an outcome of 'brand involvement' and creativity as control variable, thus, taking the study to the next level.

This research utilizes a quantitative approach with web-based survey based on a 7-point Likert scale, of 265 Australian customers of various brands, and who have produced UGC for their focal brands on social networking websites (SNSs) in the past. The data is analyzed employing partial least square – structural equation modeling – Smart PLS-SEM. Results demonstrate that 'brand involvement' is positively affected by customers' 'brand UGC participation'. In turn, UGC participation is positively dependent on customers' intrinsic need for relatedness, their 'social network' of online contact and 'brand knowledge', where 'creativity' acts as a control variable.

This research also adds to the vast literature of consumer engagement, online digital-brand management and co creation of value by customers. Moreover, online service providers can enhance brand involvement by developing strategies to fulfil different customers' needs in the service eco-system to increase customers' participation in brand UGC on social media and brand involvement, hence, co-creating value for their brands and services. This study builds on the combination of SDT

N. Gupta (✉)
La Trobe University, Melbourne, VIC, Australia
e-mail: nomita.gupta@latrobe.edu.au

J. Allen et al. (eds.), *Celebrating the Past and Future of Marketing and Discovery with Social Impact*, Developments in Marketing Science: Proceedings of the Academy of Marketing Science, https://doi.org/10.1007/978-3-030-95346-1_193

and SDL combining the customers-owned resources and makes a significant contribution in the fields of customer needs and experiences in service ecosystem in general.

Keywords Brand involvement · Customers' needs · Customer-owned resources · User generated content · Social media · Value co-creation

The Impact of Taste on Credence Services: An Abstract

Sabrina Wong, Nicole Hartley, and Ann Wallin

Abstract Past research shows that strong brands can affect consumers' taste perceptions of food products. For example, Allison and Uhl (1964) found that consumers' identification of a familiar beer brand significantly increased taste perceptions compared with the unbranded beer. Similarly, young consumers preferred the taste of foods and drinks that were associated with a well-known business compared to a blinded evaluation condition (Robinson et al. 2007). A number of service sector organisations with credence attributes are increasingly integrating taste into their physical environments. Examples of food and beverage add-ons to businesses' main service offering include banks, healthcare clinics, car repair shops, investment companies, and management consulting firms. The integration of these taste atmospherics within personalised service settings are aimed at elevating positive associations with the service environment and enhancing customer experiences. Despite this widespread integration of food and beverage in many service settings, there is a lack of empirical understanding as to the benefits and impact of taste on both customer behaviours and emotions within service settings (Segovis et al. 2007). This research seeks to explore whether food and beverage integrations play a role within environments that are high in credence attributes. Credence services are a focus in this research as these environments have witnessed an increased adoption of food within the service interaction. Further, the reliance on tangible and intangible subtle cues, such as complimentary food and beverages, within credence services is higher when it is difficult for consumers to evaluate or obtain objective information.

This research consists of a 2 × 2 between-subjects factorial design to evaluate the impacts of taste on customers in the credence service setting of financial services, focused on home lending. Using hypothetical scenario testing we evaluate the impacts of taste perceptions on customer behaviours and emotions in credence service settings. Findings indicate that taste influences customers' emotions, information retention, and perceived level of interpersonal relationships. Additionally, taste does not influence stress, which contradicts existing sensory research and frame-

S. Wong (✉) · N. Hartley · A. Wallin
University of Queensland, Brisbane, QLD, Australia
e-mail: s.wong@business.uq.edu.au; n.hartley@business.uq.edu.au; a.wallin@business.uq.edu.au

J. Allen et al. (eds.), *Celebrating the Past and Future of Marketing and Discovery with Social Impact*, Developments in Marketing Science: Proceedings of the Academy of Marketing Science, https://doi.org/10.1007/978-3-030-95346-1_194

works. Hence, further research is required to highlight certain exceptions in our existing sensory marketing frameworks. Findings from this research address a literature gap in store atmospherics and provide strategic implications for services management on the importance of environmental cues influencing customers' emotions and behaviours. This research is timely and relevant as the role of personalising attributes and service experiences is a current research priority in cultivating the customer asset and characterising the customer journey. Overall, this research explores the impact of taste atmospherics on customers' evaluations of services high in credence attributes.

Keywords Taste · Taste marketing · Credence services · Sensory marketing

Demythologising Envy in Interdependent Culture: A Pseudo Luxury Consumption Perspective: An Abstract

Tanvir Ahmed, Gillian Sullivan Mort, and Clare D'Souza

Abstract Consumer desire for luxury is driving consumption of luxury branded products in developed and developing markets. Chinese consumers' spending patterns have resulted in China becoming the most significant growth market for luxury in the world. However, Chinese consumers also make use of mimic branded items in their repertoire of luxury or pseudo-luxury goods. To explore the motivating forces of these consumers' aspirations toward pseudo-luxury brands, this research was conducted in Beijing, China and among Chinese consumers. It incorporated in-depth interviews, projective methods, and non-participant observation. The data were analyzed using an iterative approach. The interpretation of data proceeded through a series of part-to-whole iterations that helped us to define concepts and draw out their theoretical implications. The findings reveal how envy as a tacit motive and the desire for identity reflects a change in the dynamics of Chinese consumer culture. As informants in this research, the Chinese consumer sees the elite's lifestyles as vastly better than their own and seek the social prestige that luxury product purchase signifies. According to the findings, most Chinese customers have had unpleasant feelings, and it has been a continual emotion that they have been unable to escape or eliminate: a continuity process. They were unable to come out or employ any form of envy avoidance method. Envy is experienced in three stages: before using pseudo luxury things, while using or considering using pseudo luxury things, and after using pseudo luxury products, according to our research. The informants were unconcerned about how China's elites have risen to such heights of wealth and luxury spending so swiftly. They also showed little hesitation about using pseudo luxury brands to obtain their desired identity of themselves as members of the affluent, contemporary, sophisticated elite. This contrasts with our theoretical understanding of Chinese values and motivations being a reflection of self-construal of interdependence and directed towards social harmony. More broadly, pseudo luxury consumption provides a vehicle for renegotiation of Chinese cultural values in a period of increasing abundance.

T. Ahmed (✉) · G. S. Mort · C. D'Souza
La Trobe University, Melbourne, VIC, Australia
e-mail: a.tanvir@latrobe.edu.au; g.sullivan-mort@latrobe.edu.au; c.dsouza@latrobe.edu.au

J. Allen et al. (eds.), *Celebrating the Past and Future of Marketing and Discovery with Social Impact*, Developments in Marketing Science: Proceedings of the Academy of Marketing Science, https://doi.org/10.1007/978-3-030-95346-1_195

Keywords Consumer desire · Envy · Interdependent culture · Pseudo luxury
References: Available Upon Request

Cultural Intelligence Matters: Its Effects on Tourist Post-Travel Evaluation and Behavioural Intention: An Abstract

Yunen Zhang and Wei Shao

Abstract The prosperity of the international tourism industry implies the need to take a closer look at tourists' cross-cultural adaptability as which is highly correlated with their overseas travel experiences. Earley and Ang (2003) proposed a concept, cultural intelligence (CQ), to measure one's cross-cultural adaptability. CQ refers to one's capabilities to effectively adjust to different cultures (Earley and Ang 2003). Individuals with higher cultural intelligence might alter their ways of thinking and behaving as they understand there are differences between distinct cultures, possess greater cross-cultural knowledge, have a stronger intrinsic motivation to make adjustment, and are able to conduct favourable behaviours based on the host cultural requirement (Ang et al. 2007; Van der Horst and Albertyn 2018). Therefore, this study aims to understand the effect of tourists' cultural intelligence on their post-travel evaluations and behavioural intentions. The purpose of this study is two-fold: first, to explore the relationships between tourist cultural intelligence and satisfaction; and second, to identify the relationships between tourist satisfaction, revisit intention, and electronic word-of-mouth (eWOM) communication.

This study uses an online survey to collect respondents' information. The sampling units in this research are those Chinese tourists who have overseas travel experiences, given their large population and undeniable influences on the development of the global tourism industry (UNWTO 2019). Statistics package for the social sciences (SPSS) and Analysis of Moment Structures (AMOS) are employed as data analysis methods.

The data analysis results suggest that with higher CQ, Chinese tourists are more likely to be satisfied with, revisit, and say positive things about their overseas destinations. Tourist satisfaction leads to positive eWOM but has no significant impact on revisit intention. Tourist satisfaction also mediates the relationship between CQ and eWOM.

This research contributes to the existing literature on cultural intelligence by extending its research context to tourism research. To add, this study is the first to

Y. Zhang (✉) · W. Shao
Griffith University, Gold Coast, QLD, Australia
e-mail: yunen.zhang@griffithuni.edu.au; w.shao@griffith.edu.au

J. Allen et al. (eds.), *Celebrating the Past and Future of Marketing and Discovery with Social Impact*, Developments in Marketing Science: Proceedings of the Academy of Marketing Science, https://doi.org/10.1007/978-3-030-95346-1_196

identify that tourist cultural intelligence is an important antecedent of tourist post-travel evaluations and behaviours, which are the two most important tourism research topics. This study suggests outbound tourists to acquire more knowledge about the host cultures of their destinations for gaining a more satisfying travel experience. Moreover, Local travel agents and government are suggested to strengthen visitors' cultural attachment and enhance cultural influence power, which is an essential index for measuring national soft power (Ning 2018).

Keywords International tourism · Cultural intelligence · Tourist satisfaction · Revisit intention · Electronic word-of-mouth

Necessity Breeds Ingenuity: Exploring the Sustainable Food Practices of Members of a Community Supported Agriculture (CSA): An Abstract

Chris Moran, Mary McCarthy, Claire O'Neill, Shadi Hashem, and Oliver Moore

Abstract Our food practices have been identified as one of the cornerstones of the urgently required transition to more sustainable food consumption (Springman et al. 2016). The aim of this qualitative study is to explore the influence of food supply channels on household food practices. This study sought to explore the household food practices of the members of a Community Supported Agriculture (CSA), which is an example of an Alternative Food Network (AFN) in Ireland.

A practice theory lens was adopted in the current study and a mixed-method approach of ethnographic-style in-depth interviews, non-participant observation and photo food-diaries was used. The case CSA has been operating since 2008 and grew from an 'ecovillage' established in the small rural town in Ireland. Thematic analysis distinguished the food practices of acquiring, storing, cooking, eating, disposing which were analysed in relation to meanings, materials and skills associated with them (Shove et al. 2012).

The findings of this study suggest that the food practices of CSA members are significantly influenced by the varying availability of seasonal produce throughout different seasons of the year. Interviewees evidently adjust some of their food practices to ensure that they have a balanced and nutritious diet throughout the year and minimise and prevent food waste. Examples include cooking practices such as making pesto's and soups along with preservation practices such as pickling vegetables,

This paper is part of the PLATEFORMS project, part of the European transnational ERA-NET SUSFOOD2 initiative, funded in Ireland by the Department of Agriculture, Food, and the Marine (DAFM).

C. Moran (✉) · M. McCarthy · C. O'Neill · S. Hashem · O. Moore
University College Cork, Cork, Ireland
e-mail: chrismoran@ucc.ie; m.mccarthy@ucc.ie; claireoneill@ucc.ie; shadi.hashem@ucc.ie; oliver.moore@ucc.ie

J. Allen et al. (eds.), *Celebrating the Past and Future of Marketing and Discovery with Social Impact*, Developments in Marketing Science: Proceedings of the Academy of Marketing Science, https://doi.org/10.1007/978-3-030-95346-1_197

drying herbs, and freezing fruits in order to extend their lifespan and make them last longer.

Across the 10 CSA interviews it was evident that the CSA, as a food supply channel, has a positive impact on the sustainability of its members' food practices. This can be explained by some of the social and cultural characteristics of eco-village and the CSA: empowerment; community; cooking skills; social connections; physical proximity. Seasonally adjusted food practices appear to necessary for CSA members as they have chosen the CSA as a core food supply channel. This is evidently not the case for the majority of consumers in Ireland. The CSA members can therefore provide inspiration to mainstream consumers on a practical level in relation to how they learn to adjust their day to day food practices in a social way and on a higher level in how they adopt sustainability meanings into their lifestyles such as the culture of community spirit and togetherness and social norms that they build around sustainable food practices.

On a policy and industry level, examples of mainstream interventions that may foster more sustainable consumption practices include promoting and encouraging:

- Greater awareness and understanding of local and seasonal foods.
- Mechanisms to foster social learning and connections.
- Cultivating households' culinary competencies in repurposing leftovers.
- Use of household equipment such as food processers, freezers, and reusable containers.

Keywords Food consumption · Sustainability · Practice theory · Community

Perceived Risk and Private Label Purchasing Behavior: An Abstract

Dan Petrovici, Liuchen Guo, and Andrew Fearne

Abstract Private labels have received much less attention in developing and emerging nations. The aim of this study is to investigate the impact of four types of perceived risk (functional, financial, time and social), familiarity with private labels and perceived quality differences between private labels and national brands on the propensity of supermarket shoppers to purchase Private Labels. The paper is informed by a survey of shoppers in Tesco, the world's third largest grocery retailer, carried out in China and the UK with an overall sample size of 1062 respondents.

In line with the mere exposure effect, familiarity with private labels reduces all four types of perceived risk. This familiarity reduces perceived quality differences between private labels and national brands only in the UK, whilst it has an opposite effect in China. Perceived financial risk lowers the propensity to purchase private labels in the UK. In contrast, only social risk predicts this propensity in China.

The study indicates that risk associated with private labels is significant in the purchase propensity of PL (Erdem et al. 2004; Mitchell 1998; Richardson et al. 1996). The study also confirms hypotheses regarding country differences. Namely, perceived social risk has a greater impact on the propensity to purchase private labels in China compared to the UK. The level of familiarity has a stronger positive impact on the propensity to purchase private labels in China (emerging market with significant growth potential) compared to more saturated market of UK.

In the mature UK grocery market high levels of consumer familiarity with PL may increase the perceived quality differences between PL and national brands. As the effect in China is in complete contrast, retail managers and international marketers may aim to stimulate awareness of and familiarity with PL in an effort to improve

D. Petrovici (✉)
University of Kent, Canterbury, UK
e-mail: d.a.petrovici@kent.ac.uk

L. Guo
Dalian Maritime University, Dalian, China

A. Fearne
University of East Anglia, Norwich, UK
e-mail: a.fearne@uea.ac.uk

J. Allen et al. (eds.), *Celebrating the Past and Future of Marketing and Discovery with Social Impact*, Developments in Marketing Science: Proceedings of the Academy of Marketing Science, https://doi.org/10.1007/978-3-030-95346-1_198

quality perceptions vis-à-vis branded competitors. Retailers in China should develop their brand image rather than focusing on a low-price strategy. Since price and quality are not the only two factors which influence the propensity to buy private labels, retailers should consider reinforcing their brand image and corporate identity which may increase familiarity and prevent them from being considered lesser alternatives. Koschate-Fischer, Cramer and Hoyer (2014) found that when retailers have a large, priced-oriented customer group, private labels can be used as a crucial strategy in order to enhance store loyalty.

The results of the study are confined to one geographic region in each observed nation.

Keywords Private labels · Perceived risk · Familiarity · Perceived quality · Grocery market · China

Special Session: Issues and Answers: Panel Discussion on Data Quality in Present-Day Marketing Research: An Abstract

David J. Ortinau, Barry J. Babin, and John B. Ford

Abstract Fact or fiction: The controversy behind the importance of data quality and external validity of research findings in academic marketing journals is justifiable.

In recent years, there has been a growing concern regarding the roles that data quality and external validity of research findings play in the publishing process of academic based marketing journals. This special session uses a broader research/publication integrity framework in an effort to address the concerns with data quality and external validity issues. A panel of expert researchers breaks down research/publication integrity into different categorical types (or sources) of integrity among the player groups (researcher, respondent/ subjects, authors, reviewers, editors, and publishers) involved in researching and publishing academic marketing journal articles. The session uses a novel approach of discussing whether specific player groups' activities can be interpreted as being "fact" or "fiction" with the audience. The ensuing discussions should provide clearer insight and understanding of the impact that maintaining integrity throughout the researching and publishing processes has on enhancing data quality and external validity of reported results, findings, implications, and added value to body of marketing knowledge.

The session encourages audience questions as a means of driving the discussion centered on important modern-day data validity issues.

Some examples of "fact" or "fiction" activities are:

- The defined target population of a contextual research project has little influence in assessing the generalizability of the research results.
- Convenience sampling is the preferred approach to secure research participants.

D. J. Ortinau (✉)
University of South Florida, Tampa, FL, USA
e-mail: dortinau@usf.edu

B. J. Babin
University of Mississippi, University, MS, USA
e-mail: bbabin@bus.olemiss.edu

J. B. Ford
Old Dominion University, Norfolk, VA, USA
e-mail: jbford@odu.edu

J. Allen et al. (eds.), *Celebrating the Past and Future of Marketing and Discovery with Social Impact*, Developments in Marketing Science: Proceedings of the Academy of Marketing Science, https://doi.org/10.1007/978-3-030-95346-1_199

- College marketing/business students provide some of the best data quality results.
- Reporting screening criteria for qualifying experimental design subjects is not relevant in academic research projects.
- Relationships between populations, sampling plans, research subjects, and data quality have little influence on results and findings.
- The role of "statistically significant" results in generalizability.
- Researcher integrity, respondent/subject integrity, reviewer integrity, and editorial integrity play roles in determining the external validity of academic research.

Keywords Marketing research · Data quality · Probability sampling · Generalizability · Mturk

Ingram Content Group UK Ltd.
Milton Keynes UK
UKHW020728030723
424465UK00003B/17

9 783030 953485